ILLINI LEGENDS, LISTS, & LORE

ILLINI

Greatest Moments of

LEGENDS, LISTS, & LORE

University of Illinois Athletics

Third Edition

Mike Pearson

Foreword by Josh Whitman

UNIVERSITY OF ILLINOIS PRESS
Urbana, Chicago, and Springfield

The University of Illinois Press gratefully acknowledges the support of the University of Illinois Division of Intercollegiate Athletics.

Library of Congress Cataloging-in-Publication Data
Names: Pearson, Mike, 1951– author.
Title: Illini legends, lists, and lore : greatest moments of University
    of Illinois athletics / Mike Pearson; foreword by Josh Whitman.
Description: Third Edition. | Urbana, Illinois: University of Illinois
    Press, [2017] | Includes bibliographical references and index.
Identifiers: LCCN 2017007293 | ISBN 9780252041044 (cloth :
    acid-free paper)
Subjects: LCSH: University of Illinois at Urbana-Champaign—
    Sports—History. | University of Illinois at Urbana-Champaign—
    History.
Classification: LCC GV691.U538 P43 2017 | DDC
    796.04/30977366—dc23 LC record available at https://lccn
    .loc.gov/2017007293

To my wife, Laura;
our children, Parker, Paige, Tom, and Tony;
our daughter-in-law, Stephanie;
and our grandchildren, Nola, Alexa, and Colin.
Thank you for your love and support.

CONTENTS

Foreword by Josh Whitman,
Director of Athletics, University of Illinois. ix

Acknowledgments xi

Inaugural Athletics Hall of Fame Class xiii

The Early Days (1860–95) 1

1895–1904 5

1905–1914 27

1915–1924 49

1925–1934 71

Red Grange: An Original Superstar 74

1935–1944 95

1945–1954 117

1955–1964 139

1965–1974 161

1975–1984 185

1985–1994 227

1995–2004 269

2005–2014 311

2015–2016 353

The Division of Disability Resources and
Educational Services (DRES) 358

Division of Intercollegiate Athletics Awards 363

    Fighting Illini Athletes of the Year 363

    Big Ten Conference Medal of Honor Winners 364

    Illinois Newcomers of the Year 366

    Illinois Spirit Award Winners 367

    Varsity "I" Achievement Award Winners 368

    All-Time Fighting Illini Letter-Winner List 370

Year-by-Year Summaries 434

Men and Women Who Have Portrayed Chief Illiniwek 456

Personnel History of the University of Illinois Division
of Intercollegiate Athletics (Athletic Association) 457

Photo Credits 463

Color illustrations follow page 138.

FOREWORD

On March 5, 2016, I had the privilege, as a proud alumnus, of becoming the fourteenth Director of Athletics at my alma mater, the University of Illinois. Filling this important role was something I had dreamed about since almost the first time I stepped foot on the Urbana-Champaign campus as a freshman football player in 1997. In the nearly two decades since, including my four years as a Fighting Illini football player and business student, continuing with my three years as a law student, and now, early in my tenure as the athletics director, I have gained great appreciation for the UI's many traditions and proud history, some of which date back more than 125 years. The impact this institution has had on me, and thousands of others, is immeasurable. The lessons I have learned here continue to influence every corner of my life.

Former UI Sports Information Director Mike Pearson wrote the first edition of *Illini Legends, Lists, and Lore* in the mid-1990s, updated the second edition in 2001, and has produced this third edition to coincide with the Sesquicentennial Celebration of the University of Illinois in 2017. Every chapter from 1974–75 through 2015–16 has two extra pages, two for the men and two for the women, to highlight memorable moments, a significant list, and several stories about Illini legends from that year.

Another addition is a two-page historical spread about the cutting-edge Illinois program for athletes with disabilities. Mike has included many rarely seen photographs from *Illio* yearbooks, and, again, the book will include the names of every Illini letter winner, coach, and administrator.

You will find information and stories about all the legendary athletes who have worn the Orange and Blue. Illini fans know the names of Huff, Grange, Eddleman, Caroline, Boudreau, Virgin, Felicien, Stricker,

Eggers, Battle, Brown, Williams, and Rice. Now, you can learn more of their stories.

In the twenty years since I arrived on campus, the legends have continued to grow. Added to the annals of Illinois Athletics are notable figures like Robert Holcombe, Kurt Kittner, J Leman, Rashard Mendenhall, Juice Williams, and Whitney Mercilus, all of whom roamed Zuppke Field with great passion and skill. Jason Anderson, Ashley Berggren, Amer Delic, Perdita Felicien, Angela Bizzarri, Scott Langley, and Kevin Anderson are others who have established themselves as all-time Fighting Illini greats. Who are our future stars whose names will become synonymous with Illinois excellence? Lovie Smith, Mike Small, Janet Rayfield, and Justin Spring are among the current coaches who are leading our student-athletes to championship levels. There is nothing more rewarding than watching our student-athletes work tirelessly each season to assume their respective positions in the Illini record books.

I will never forget the sight of majestic Memorial Stadium the first time my parents and I drove down Kirby Avenue. I knew immediately that this was "home" for me. The memories and history contained in this edition of *Illini Legends, Lists, and Lore* will surely remind you of the great times you spent on campus. We owe Mike Pearson a huge thank you for documenting the Illini Legends, Lists, and Lore in a book that can be referenced forever.

I could not be more proud to serve the University of Illinois as its director of athletics. As we prepare for a bright future and the start of our next 150 years as a world-class institution, I hope you enjoy learning about the incredible history that forms the foundation of our future success. I look forward to seeing all of you at the next Fighting Illini game!

Go Illini,

Josh Whitman
Director of Athletics

ACKNOWLEDGMENTS

For me, the acknowledgments might be the most important element of my book, for here's where I express my heartfelt gratitude to the individuals who've answered simple questions or worked hand in hand with me throughout the process.

First, thanks to the tremendous staff at the University of Illinois Division of Intercollegiate Athletics, admirably directed by Josh Whitman. I look forward to the future Big Ten and NCAA championships.

Associate Director of Athletics Kent Brown has provided especially enthusiastic support, and I'm very fortunate to be able to count him as a trusted friend. Other athletic staffers who provided valuable assistance during the last several months include Chad Beyler, Derrick Burson, Jenny Dewar, Jen Fisher, Libby Knight, Jessica Leifheit, Dan Longo, Brett Moore, Derek Neal, and their talented student staff.

Thanks also to Deputy Director of Athletics Warren Hood and Senior Associate Athletics Director Marty Kaufmann, who cleared the way for this third edition of *Illini Legends, Lists, and Lore*, produced in concert with the university's sesquicentennial celebration.

A tip of the hat also to Varsity I Director Chris Tuttle and his assistant Moneesha Sibley. These folks are just a small portion of the DIA's all-star administration.

Next, my appreciation goes out to the fabulous Fighting Illini coaching staff and student-athletes who have produced such consistent success. All those who wear Orange and Blue are very proud of your efforts.

The staff at University Archives went well beyond the call of duty in helping me. Thanks to former director Maynard Brichford for his assistance years ago and, for this third edition, to William Maher, Chris Prom, and Anna Trammell for helping me gather photos and various other nuggets.

To my friends at University of Illinois Press, thank you for your direction and expertise. Former director Willis Regier, current director Laurie Matheson, acquisitions editor Danny Nasset, assistant acquisitions editor Marika Christofides, assistant managing editor Jennifer Clark, copyeditor Julie Gay, marketing and sales manager Michael Roux, catalog and copywriting coordinator Kevin Cunningham, and art director Dustin Hubbart all have played vital roles.

For photographs, we salute the talented Mark and Beth Jones for their fantastic help and friendship. Their photos on the dust jacket, in the color insert, and scattered throughout the inner pages help tell the story about Fighting Illini history. Artist Jack Davis, Executive Editor Jim Rossow and his photo staff of the Champaign *News-Gazette*, and the UI News Bureau also provided the magical images that are included inside these pages.

Special thanks to Jim and Joan Sheppard, who time after time have opened their doors to me and provided fresh linen and delicious meals at the Sheppard Suites. True friends.

Finally, hugs to my wife, Laura, son Tony and his wife Stephanie, son Tom, daughter Paige, son Parker, grandson Colin, and granddaughters Alexa and Nola for their love and support.

GO ILLINI!

INAUGURAL ATHLETICS HALL OF FAME CLASS

On February 23, 2017, the University of Illinois celebrated its legacy in intercollegiate athletes by announcing the inaugural class of its Hall of Fame. A total of twenty-eight individuals were honored including Olympians, national Hall of Famers, NCAA champions, and All-Americans.

The Class of 2017 was introduced at the Fighting Illini Athletics Hall of Fame Gala in Chicago on June 23, then officially inducted at a ceremony on campus the weekend of September 29–30.

Nelison "Nick" Anderson

Basketball (1988–89)

Chicago, Illinois (Simeon High School)

A member of the Illinois men's basketball All-Century Team, Nick Anderson was the Illini Co-MVP in 1988 and MVP in 1989. A first-round selection in the 1989 NBA Draft, he played thirteen seasons in the NBA. His thirty-five-foot buzzer-beating shot at Indiana in 1989 is one of Illinois' most iconic plays.

Louis "Lou" Boudreau

Basketball (1937–38)
Baseball (1937)

Harvey, Illinois (Thornton Township High School)

One of just three Illini athletes to have his jersey number retired (#5), Lou Boudreau is the only Illinois athlete in the National Baseball Hall of Fame. The American League's Most Valuable Player in 1948, he also managed the Cleveland Indians to the 1948 World Series title.

Daniel "Dee" Brown

Basketball (2003–04–05–06)

Maywood, Illinois (Proviso East High School)

The two-time consensus All-American was the 2005 Big Ten MVP, helping lead the Illini to a 37–2 record and a berth in the NCAA Finals. Nicknamed "The One-Man Fastbreak," Dee Brown is one of the most popular players in Illini history. A four-time All-Big Ten selection.

Richard "Dick" Butkus

Football (1962–63–64)

Chicago, Illinois (Vocational High School)

The namesake of college football's annual award for the premier linebacker is Dick Butkus, a member of both the College and Pro Football Halls of Fame. He won the Silver Football Award as Big Ten football's Most Valuable Player in 1963, leading the Fighting Illini to the conference title and a Rose Bowl victory.

Tonja Buford-Bailey

Track and Field (1990–91–92–93)

Dayton, Ohio (Meadowdale High School)

Tonja Buford-Bailey won a total of twenty-five Big Ten titles, more than any other men's or women's athlete. The all-star hurdler won UI's Female Athlete of the Year award in both 1992 and 1993. An Olympic competitor in 1992, 1996, and 2000, she later served as Illinois' women's track and field head coach from 2008–13.

ILLINOIS
HALL of FAME
ATHLETICS

Gerald "Jerry" Colangelo

Basketball (1960–61–62)
Baseball (1960)

Chicago Heights, Illinois (Bloom Township High School)

Though Jerry Colangelo was a fine athlete during his days at Illinois, his greatest impact has come as an administrator in professional sports. He has directed USA Basketball since 2005 and has helped lead Team USA to Olympic gold medals in 2008, 2012, and 2016.

Dwight "Dike" Eddleman

Football (1946–47–48)
Basketball (1947–48–49)
Track and Field (1943–46–47–48–49)

Centralia, Illinois (Centralia High School)

Widely acknowledged as the University of Illinois' finest all-around athlete, Dike Eddleman earned a combined eleven letters in track and field, football, and basketball. UI's annual awards for top male and female athletes are named in his honor. He later served the Illini as a successful fundraiser.

Perdita Felicien

Track and Field (2000–01–02–03)

Pickering, Ontario (Pine Ridge Secondary School)

Perdita Felicien was a three-time NCAA hurdles champion and was named the NCAA's Track and Field Athlete of the Year in both 2001 and 2003. A member of Canada's 2000 and 2004 Olympic Team, she was inducted into her country's Athletics Hall of Fame in 2016.

Harry Gill

Track and Field Coach (1904–29 and 1931–33)

Harry Gill led the Fighting Illini to a pair of NCAA team titles, including the 1921 outdoor track and field championship, the first-ever team title awarded by the NCAA. He was the founder of Gill Athletics in 1918, a company that continues to be a world leader in track and field equipment.

Harold "Red" Grange

Football (1923–24–25)

Wheaton, Illinois (Wheaton High School)

Named the No. 1 icon in Big Ten history by the Big Ten Network in 2010, Red Grange was the sport of football's original superstar. No. 77 is a consensus member of football's all-time greatest teams and a charter inductee in both the College and Pro Football Halls of Fame.

Abraham "Abie" Grossfeld

Gymnastics (1957–58–59–60)

New York, New York (Gompers Technical High School)

From 1957–59, Abie Grossfeld was gymnastics most decorated athlete, winning four gold, three silver, and three bronze medals at the NCAA Championships. He competed in both the 1956 and 1960 Olympics, and later coached American gymnasts at the 1964, 1972, 1984, and 1988 Games.

George Halas

Football (1917)
Basketball (1917–18)
Baseball (1916–17)

Chicago, Illinois (Crane High School)

George Halas was a three-sport star at Illinois, then played both professional baseball and football. One of the original founders of the National Football League, he won six titles as a coach and two more as an owner. He was a charter member of the Pro Football Hall of Fame.

George Huff

Baseball (1889–90–91–92)
Football (1890 and 1992)
Administrator (1901–36)
Baseball Coach (1896–1919)
Football Coach (1895–96)

Champaign, Illinois (Champaign High School)

A player, coach, and athletic director during the first forty-six years of the University of Illinois' Athletic Association, George Huff is considered to be the "Father of Illini Athletics." In 1896, he was instrumental in establishing the Western Conference, forerunner of the Big Ten Conference.

ILLINOIS

HALL of **FAME**

ATHLETICS

Mannie Jackson
Basketball (1958–59–60)

Illmo, Missouri (Edwardsville High School)

Mannie Jackson and former Edwardsville High School teammate Govoner Vaughn became the first African-Americans to start and letter with the Illini basketball team. Jackson purchased the Harlem Globetrotters in 1993. He won the 2015 Theodore Roosevelt Award, the NCAA's top honor.

Karol Kahrs
Administrator (1974–99)

Karol Kahrs created and developed the University of Illinois women's athletics program and was instrumental in its addition to the Big Ten Conference. She was recognized in 2014 by winning the Legacy Award from the National Association of Collegiate Women Athletics Administrators.

Nancy Thies Marshall
Gymnastics (1976–77)

Urbana, Illinois (Urbana High School)

The only Illinois women's gymnast to compete in the Olympics, Nancy Thies Marshall made the 1972 team as a 15-year-old out of Urbana High School. She was a two-time Big Ten Gymnast of the Year and was inducted into the World Acrobatic Society Hall of Fame in 2010.

Herbert "Herb" McKenley
Track and Field (1946–47)

Clarendon, Jamaica (Calabar High School)

Herb McKenley is the only person to have had the world's best times in the 100 meters (10.3), 200 meters (20.4), and 400 meters (46.2). He won a gold and three silver medals as a Jamaican sprinter at the 1948 and 1952 Olympic Games, then later served as coach of Jamaica's national team.

ILLINOIS
HALL of FAME
ATHLETICS

Roy "Allie" Morrison

Wrestling (1929–30)

Marshalltown, Iowa (Marshalltown High School)

Allie Morrison was Coach "Hek" Kenney's most talented wrestler, going undefeated as an Illini. The 1928 Big Ten champion went on to win the freestyle featherweight gold medal that same year at the Olympics. He is a member of the National Wrestling Hall of Fame.

Harold Osborn

Track and Field (1920–21–22)

Butler, Illinois (Hillsboro High School)

A six-time world record holder, Harold Osborn is a charter member of the National Track and Field Hall of Fame. At the 1924 Olympic Games, he won gold in both the decathlon and high jump and, to this day, remains as the only individual to have accomplished such a feat.

Andrew "Andy" Phillip

Basketball (1942–43–47)
Baseball (1942–43–47)

Granite City, Illinois (Granite City High School)

The most decorated member of Illinois' "Whiz Kids" teams of the 1940s, Andy Phillip is the only Illini elected to the National Basketball Hall of Fame as a player. He was a consensus first-team All-America selection in both 1942 and 1943. He also achieved All-America honors in baseball for Illinois.

Renee Heiken Slone

Golf (1990–91–92–93)

Metamora, Illinois (Metamora Township High School)

The most dominant Illini female golfer ever, Renee Heiken Slone was the National College Player of the Year in 1993. She was a two-time medalist at the Big Ten Championship and twice was honored as the conference sport's top athlete. She currently serves as the program's head coach.

Steven "Steve" Stricker
Golf (1986–87–88–89)

Edgerton, Wisconsin (Edgerton High School)

Medalist of the Big Ten Championship tournament in 1986, 1988, and 1989, Steve Stricker earned All-America honors as both a junior and senior. He went on to a glorious professional career, posting five Top 10 finishes at major tournaments. He was ranked No. 2 in the Official World Golf Rankings at one point in his career.

Mary Eggers Tendler
Volleyball (1985–86–87–88)

Aurora, Illinois (West Aurora High School)

Mary Eggers Tendler was the nation's top collegiate volleyball player in 1988 and was a three-time Big Ten Player of the Year. She helped lead Illinois to NCAA Final Four berths in both 1987 and 1988. She has served as head coach at Elon University since 2003.

Craig Tiley
Tennis Coach (1992–2005)

Craig Tiley directed the Illinois men's tennis team to the NCAA championship in 2003, posting a perfect 32–0 record. Altogether, he led the Illini to nine Big Ten regular-season titles and six Big Ten Tournament championships. He has served as Chief Executive Officer of Tennis Australia since 2013.

Craig Virgin
Cross Country (1973–74–75–76)
Track & Field (1974–75–76)

Lebanon, Illinois (Lebanon High School)

Craig Virgin is the Big Ten's first and only four-time cross-country champion, and won the NCAA title as a junior. He was a three-time Olympic qualifier in distance events. A National Track and Field Hall of Famer, he is the only American man to win the IAAF World Cross Country Championships, which he did twice.

Deron Williams

Basketball (2003–04–05)

The Colony, Texas (The Colony High School)

Deron Williams is the most internationally decorated Fighting Illini basketball player ever, helping lead the U.S. Olympic team to gold medals in both 2008 and 2012. Since his 2005 success in leading Illinois to the national championship game, he has played in the NBA.

Claude "Buddy" Young

Football (1944 and 1946)
Track and Field (1944)

Chicago, Illinois (Wendell Phillips High School)

Despite standing just 5-feet-4-inches tall, Buddy Young mesmerized football and track fans with his acceleration and quickness. The world record holder won a pair of NCAA sprinting titles. As an All-America running back, he sparked the Illini to a 1947 Rose Bowl victory, then played 10 years in the NFL.

Robert "Bob" Zuppke

Football Coach (1913–41)

A charter member of the College Football Hall of Fame, Bob Zuppke directed the Fighting Illini to four national championships (1914, 1919, 1923, and 1927) and seven Big Ten titles. The innovative coach was honored in 1966 when Memorial Stadium's playing field was named after him.

ILLINI LEGENDS, LISTS, & LORE

THE EARLY DAYS

The chapters within the third edition of *Illini Legends, Lists, and Lore* specifically cover the history of the University of Illinois athletic program since it became a charter member of the Big Ten Conference in 1896. But many historic events—athletic and otherwise—took place between the initial steps to establish the university and the nearly four ensuing decades. Following is a thumbnail sketch of the UI's historical highlights.

Rev. Jonathan Stoughton

July 2, 1860: Six Champaign County land speculators agreed to a contract with Jonathan C. Stoughton, a Methodist minister who had moved to Urbana from Freeport, Illinois, and his two partners, to purchase 194 acres for the purpose of establishing an eight-acre seminary and to use the balance of the land as adjacent housing lots. In Winton Solberg's book *The University of Illinois 1867–1894: An Intellectual and Cultural History*, he explained that Stoughton's plan was to erect a seminary building and leave that as a gift to the twin cities when he and his partners finished selling the adjacent home sites. The land, which cost about $19,000, was bordered by what are now Wright Street and Lincoln Avenue on the west and east, and Springfield and University Avenues on the south and north. The six local parties to the contract agreed to secure a subscription list of at least $40,000. In return, the individual purchasers would receive tracts of land equal in value to their investments. Stoughton's group promised to turn over the seminary building and its eight acres to the stockholders when the subscriptions were completely paid. Solberg wrote that while "the scheme had educational potential, the promoters had no intention of teaching anything. They offered merely to construct a building designed for educational purposes."

January 1861: Sixty local citizens from Champaign-Urbana petitioned the Illinois legislature to establish a state agricultural school and promised that the aforementioned "Urbana-Champaign Institute" stockholders would donate their building and its grounds to the state for that purpose.

February 1861: The Illinois General Assembly chartered the institute as "a seminary of learning, comprehending an agricultural department, or others departments, as the public may demand."

August 6, 1861: The cornerstone for the proposed seminary building was laid, but the Civil War delayed completion of the structure.

July 2, 1862: President Abraham Lincoln signed the Morrill Act, also known as the Land Grant College Act. Introduced by Vermont congressman Justin Smith Morrill, the grant was set up to establish institutions to educate people in agriculture, home economics, mechanical arts, and other professions that were practical at the time.

President Abraham Lincoln

February 14, 1863: The Illinois General Assembly took steps to secure the advantages of the Morrill Land Grand Act, approving to accept the donation of public lands from Congress for the purpose of establishing a state university.

1864: Politicians introduced a bill into the Illinois House of Representatives for "an act to provide for the organization, endowment and maintenance of the Illinois Industrial University." Section 11 of the bill provided for a commission, made up of legislators from each Illinois congressional district, to appoint one member of the body to identify the location of the institution.

February 10, 1865: A Cook County representative introduced a substitute for Section 11, charging the board of trustees of the university with locating the institution in Urbana. In exchange, the proposing group from Champaign County agreed to turn over a 140-acre property, assessed at the time to have a value of $160,000.

February 25, 1867: A bill proposed by a state legislator, who was a wealthy farmer and former mayor of Urbana, provided for the establishment of an educational institution in Urbana-Champaign. The Griggs Bill was approved and signed by Governor Richard Oglesby three days later.

Governor Richard Oglesby

April 1, 1867: John Milton Gregory was appointed regent of the university.

John Milton Gregory

First known aerial of UI campus

March 2, 1868: The Illinois Industrial University opened for classes with two faculty members and seventy-seven students. University Hall served as the campus's only building.
March 11, 1868: The board of trustees

made "Learning and Labor" the university's motto.
March 9, 1870: The board

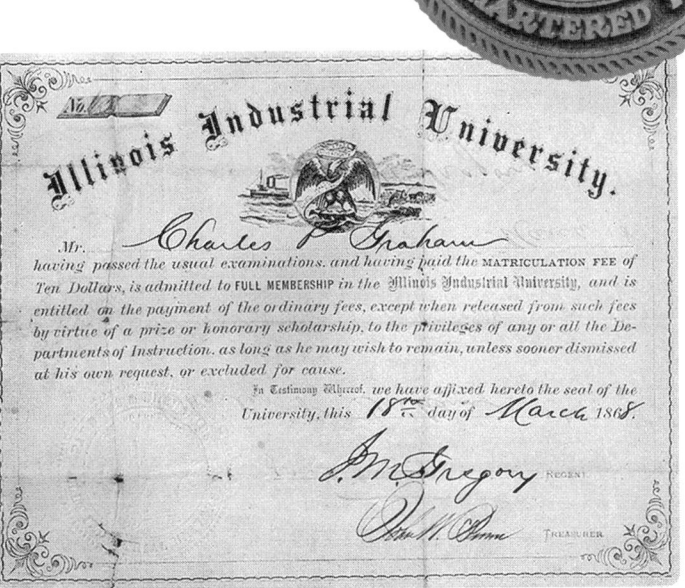

Charles Graham's receipt for his matriculation fee to the Illinois Industrial University

voted to admit women as students. The following fall semester, twenty-four females availed themselves of the privilege.

May 8, 1872: The first athletic contest at the university occurred when a student team defeated the Eagle Baseball Club of Champaign by a score of 2–1.

December 10, 1873: New Main Building, the University of Illinois's new $148,000 structure, was dedicated. The building hosted the library, classrooms, lecture halls, laboratories, and the university's museum.

Dedication program to ceremony for UI's New Main Building

1876: Ethan Philbrick and other students engaged in the first-ever football game played at the University of Illinois.

October 2, 1879: The university initiated intercollegiate athletics in a baseball game versus Illinois College.

1880: Recurring clashes with trustees and students led to the resignation of John Milton Gregory as the university's regent.

April 20, 1883: The university's Athletic Association was approved by the faculty. It was incorporated on February 21, 1890, as a nonprofit organization under the laws of Illinois.

May 1883: The university hosted its first athletic Field Day at the Champaign County Fairgrounds. This event, originally established as a collegiate custom in eastern states, involved baseball and track and field.

June 19, 1885: Illinois Industrial University became the University of Illinois.

UI's first football team

October 2, 1890: Led by coach, captain, and quarterback Scott Williams, the university played in its first intercollegiate football game, losing at Illinois Wesleyan, 16–0.
November 27, 1890: Nearly three hundred people watched Illinois defeat Illinois Wesleyan, 12–6, in the university's first home football game. It also marked the school's first football victory.
December 1890: Mauritz Schmidt, a graduate of the Nor-

The football from Illinois's first victory on November 27, 1890

mal Turner Gymnasium in Milwaukee who was employed in the Chicago public schools, was hired as the first athletic instructor.

April 20, 1891: Regent Selim H. Peabody appointed a faculty committee on athletics, consisting of three professors.

May 15, 1891: The Athletic

Regent Selim Peabody

Park, later named Illinois Field (1896), was inaugurated and opened for Field Day.

A bicycle race highlight from the 1896 Field Day

December 14, 1891: The university approved Sigma Chi as the campus's first Greek fraternity.

April 20, 1892: Illinois's varsity baseball team played Michigan for the first time, losing 18–0.

May 13, 1892: Illinois hosted the Western Intercollegiate Field Day for the first time.

June 1892: At a salary of $1,200, the university hired its first full-time coach and athletic director, Edward Hall, from Dartmouth.

November 6, 1894: The faculty approved orange and navy blue to be the university's official colors.

January 11, 1895: Led by President James Smart of Purdue, the presidents of six other universities—Illinois, Chicago, Minnesota, Northwestern, Purdue, and Wisconsin—met in Chicago and adopted a set of rules for the regulation of athletics. UI's faculty adopted these new rules on February 4, 1895.

Purdue University President James Smart

George Huff became UI athletics' first coach in 1895

June 11, 1895: Illinois president Andrew Sloan Draper named George Huff assistant director of the gymnasium and coach of the athletic teams at a salary of $1,000, half to be paid by the university and half by the Athletic Association.

January 6, 1896: Illinois faculty created an Athletic Advisory Board. The board elected its own officers, supervised all UI athletic events, and controlled all funds entrusted to it for athletic purposes. In 1898 the president of the Athletic Association became a member of the Athletic Advisory Board, and it was renamed the Board of Control.

February 3, 1896: The university adopted its own athletic rules. Although similar to the president's rules that were established in 1895, Illinois's athletic rules set a higher standard. One rule limited participation in intercollegiate contests to four years.

1895–1904

George Huff

"No other individual had the esteem and affection of so many alumni, students, and friends. . . . He stood for everything that was right and honorable not only in his administration and direction of athletics but all of his activities. His personal code of honor and of sportsmanship was based upon a philosophy of life that should inspire any man or woman. The influence of his career on all who knew him and the ideals he has left us will be a cherished heritage."

—A. C. Willard, President, University of Illinois, on the death of George Huff

1895–96

AMERICA'S TIME CAPSULE

October 4, 1895   Newport (Rhode Island) Golf Club hosted the first U.S. Open golf tournament
January 4, 1896   Utah became the forty-fifth state in the Union.
April 6, 1896   The first modern Olympic Games opened in Athens, Greece.
April 23, 1896   The first public showing of a moving picture was presented in New York City.
June 4, 1896   Henry Ford completed the assembly of the first Ford automobile in Detroit.

ILLINI
MOMENT

Formation of the Big Ten Conference

On February 8, 1896, at the Palmer House in Chicago, Illinois, seven men were meeting to establish standards and regulations for the administration of intercollegiate athletics. These faculty representatives from seven of the Midwest's finest universities designated themselves as the "Intercollegiate Conference of Faculty Representatives." Professor Henry H. Everett represented the University of Illinois. Today, the organization is known as the "Big Ten Conference." The seven charter members of the conference included the Universities of Illinois, Chicago, Michigan, Minnesota, Wisconsin, plus Northwestern University and Purdue University. Indiana and Iowa were admitted in 1899, and Ohio State gained entrance in 1912. Three years after Chicago withdrew from the conference in 1946, Michigan State was admitted. It wasn't until 1989 that Penn State accepted the offer to join and began conference play in 1990. The University of Nebraska joined the Big Ten in 2010 and, most recently, in 2014, the University of Maryland and Rutgers University became members.

Chicago's Palmer House

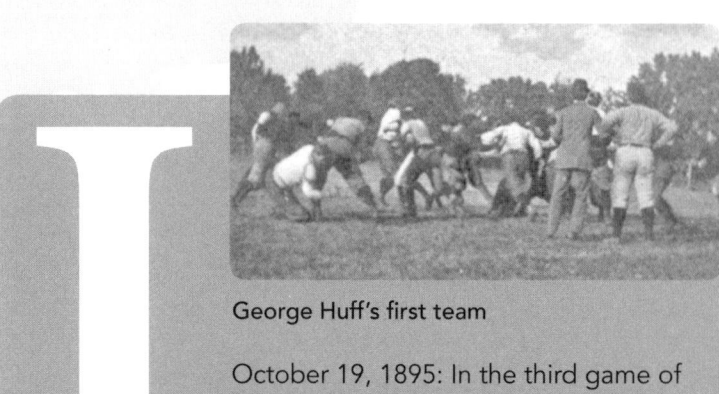

George Huff's first team

I on 1895–96

October 19, 1895: In the third game of twenty-three-year-old George Huff's first season as Illini football coach, Illinois piled up a school-record seventy-nine points in a whitewash versus Illinois College. Over the 123-year history of Illini football, that total has been exceeded only two other times.

ILLINI ITEM

A total of forty men won varsity letters for the University of Illinois's three athletic teams (football, baseball, and track) during the 1895–96 season. Three men—Harry Hadsall, Paul Cooper, and Harvey Sconce—earned letters in both football and baseball. It should be noted that the "I" letters weren't officially awarded to those men until November 3, 1923.

Paul Cooper (left) and Harvey Sconce

ILLINI LISTS

ILLINI FOOTBALL SUCCESS (decade by decade)

Decade	W	L	T	PCT
1890–1899	45	26	8	.620
1900–1909	61	27	6	.681
1910–1919	49	15	7	.739
1920–1929	55	19	3	.734
1930–1939	38	39	5	.494
1940–1949	38	49	5	.440
1950–1959	48	37	6	.560
1960–1969	36	59	1	.424
1970–1979	38	67	4	.367
1980–1989	63	48	4	.565

Illinois football's 1914 backfield

Decade	W	L	T	PCT
1990–1999	50	63	2	.443
2000–2009	45	73	0	.381
2010–2016	34	53	0	.391
Total	600	626	51	.510

ILLINI LEGEND

George Huff

George Huff

When George Huff entered the University of Illinois as a student in 1887, he had no idea how great an impact he would have on his hometown of Champaign over the next half-century. Not only was "G" a member of the school's first football team in 1890, he also molded the lives of hundreds of other young men through his roles as Fighting Illini coach and director of athletics. The rotund Huff lettered twice in football as the team's center and three times as a multiposition player in baseball. As head coach of the Fighting Illini football team from 1895 through 1899, he was only mildly successful (21-16-3). However, as skipper of the Illini baseball squad, Huff dominated his opponents, winning nearly 70 percent of the 544 games he coached from 1896 through 1919. Huff directed the Illini nine to a record eleven Big Ten championships. As UI's athletic director from 1901 to 1936, Huff's contributions were monumental. He had a knack for hiring outstanding coaches (Bob Zuppke, Carl Lundgren, Craig Ruby, and Harry Gill). He helped build a phenomenal athletic plant (Memorial Stadium and Huff Gymnasium). But George Huff will be best known as a man who devoted his life to the honor and glory of the University of Illinois with honesty and fair play. On October l, 1936, uremic poisoning claimed the life of "The Father of Fighting Illini Athletics" at age sixty-four.

ILLINI LORE

During the 1895–96 school year, the University of Illinois had nine instructional buildings and eighty-four faculty members. Of President Andrew Draper's 855 total students, nearly 80 percent were males, and nearly a third of the student body majored in either English or Electrical Engineering.

UI President
Andrew Draper

1896–97

AMERICA'S TIME CAPSULE

July 7, 1896 — The city of Chicago hosted the Democratic National Convention, which nominated William Jennings Bryan as its candidate.

October 1, 1896 — The Federal Post Office established free rural delivery.

November 3, 1896 — William McKinley won the U.S. presidency in a landslide.

January 11, 1897 — Margaret Cannon of Utah officially became the first woman to serve in the United States Senate.

July 18, 1897 — Cap Anson became the first Major League Baseball player to get three thousand hits.

ILLINI
MOMENT

Illinois's First Conference Football Game— October 31, 1896

"It not infrequently happens," reported the University of Illinois student newspaper, *The Illini*, "that a team which is manifestly superior to that lined up against it, comes out the loser. . . . If there ever was a game in which the weaker of the two elevens gained the victory, it was in the contest between Chicago and Illinois on Marshall Field . . . when Stagg's aggregation of hirelings managed to win 12 to 0. . . . The rotten state of athletics at Chicago is well known and her name has become synonymous for corruption in that branch of college life." What made this game particularly momentous was that it was the Fighting Illini football team's very first conference game. Coach Amos Alonzo Stagg's Maroons defeated Illinois that afternoon with an alleged "professional," Frederick Nichols, directing the Maroons to two touchdowns (worth four points each) and two goals after touchdown (two points each).

The 1896 Illini football team

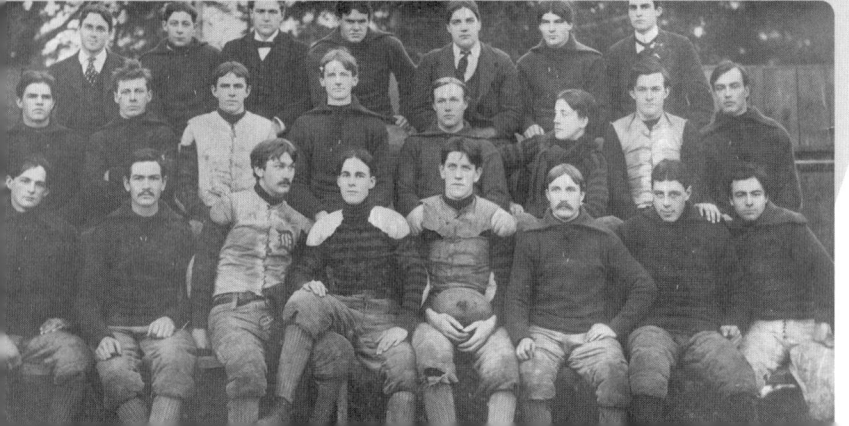

I on 1896–97

George Huff's official job description was "Assistant Director of the Gymnasium and Coach of the Athletic Teams." His salary that year was $1,200.

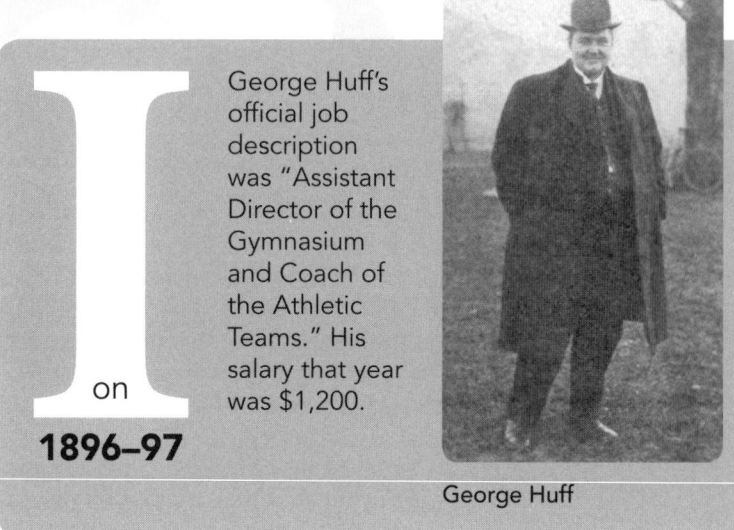

George Huff

ILLINI ITEM

Three Fighting Illini baseball players—second baseman William Fulton, shortstop Hugh Shuler, and center fielder Harry Hadsall—were selected to the 1897 All-Western team by *Harper's Weekly*. Fulton (.302) and Shuler (.304) both hit well, but Hadsall batted just .160 for the year.

ILLINI LISTS

ILLINI ATHLETIC DIRECTORS

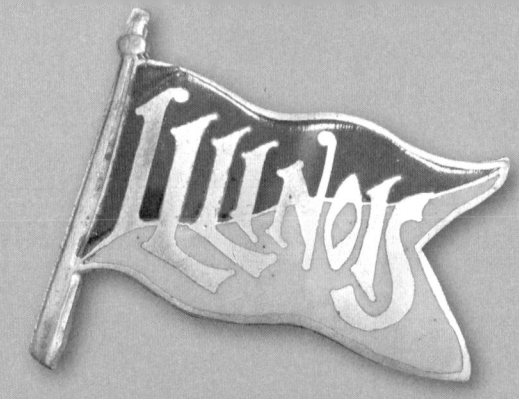

1892–1894	Edward K. Hall
1894–1895	Fred H. Dodge
1895–1898	Henry H. Everett
1898–1901	Jacob K. Shell
1901–1936	George A. Huff
1936–1941	Wendell S. Wilson
1942–1966	Douglas Mills
1967–1972	E. E. (Gene) Vance
1972–1979	Cecil N. Coleman
1979	Ray Eliot (interim)
1980–1988	Neale R. Stoner

1988	Ronald E. Guenther (interim)
1988	Dr. Karol A. Kahrs (interim)
1988–1991	John Mackovic
1991–1992	Robert Todd (interim)
1992–2011	Ronald E. Guenther
2011–2016	Mike Thomas
2016–present	Josh Whitman

ILLINI LEGEND

Henry Everett became UI's third athletics director

Henry Everett

The University of Illinois's third athletic director and first faculty representative was Henry Houghton Everett. A native of Chicago, Everett was an all-star athlete for the University of Chicago Maroons, participating in football, track, and wrestling. He left UC to become assistant superintendent of the Chicago YMCA, but after only a year he quit to enroll at Northwestern University's medical school. Medicine soon took a back seat to Everett's intense interest in athletics, however, and he was on the move again, this time to the University of Wisconsin as an instructor in UW's gymnasium. In 1895 the University of Illinois hired the thirty-one-year-old Everett as its director of athletics, faculty representative, and track coach. Perhaps his greatest contribution was as UI's representative at the January 11, 1895, meeting in Chicago, which formed the Big Ten Conference. Everett gave way to George Huff after one year as AD, but he coached Illini track for three seasons, from 1896 to 1898. He returned to his career in medicine, serving at both Rush Medical College and Chicago's Presbyterian Hospital. Henry Everett died in 1928 at age sixty-one.

ILLINI LORE

Dedicated June 8, 1897, the University of Illinois library—renamed Altgeld Hall in 1940—served students for nearly thirty years as the campus's main resource center. The original structure cost $380,000 and featured a distinctive 132-foot tower, from which a daily chimes concert emanates. Additions to the building were made in 1914, 1919, 1926, and 1956. After its service as the home of the library, it was the headquarters for the College of Law for twenty-eight years and in 1955 was assigned to the Department of Mathematics.

The interior of Altgeld Hall

Altgeld Hall was dedicated in 1897

1897-98

AMERICA'S TIME CAPSULE

September 21, 1897   In response to a letter from young Virginia O'Hanlon, a *New York Sun* editorial declared, "Yes, Virginia, there is a Santa Claus."

July 2, 1897   A coal miners' strike put seventy-five thousand men out of work in Pennsylvania, Ohio, and West Virginia.

February 15, 1898   An explosion destroyed the battleship *Maine*; 260 crew members perished.

March 17, 1898   John Philip Holland achieved a successful test run of the first modern submarine off Staten Island.

April 25, 1898   The United States declared war on Spain, and the Spanish-American War began.

ILLINI
MOMENT

Illinois's First Indoor Football Game—November 20, 1897

The University of Illinois's first night game and its first game played indoors came against the Carlisle Indians at the old Chicago Coliseum. About ten thousand are said to have attended the event, for which the Illini and Indians each received $4,000. The contest, called by one journalist "hair raising in its recklessness," pitted East (Carlisle) against West (Illinois) on a gridiron of sand and sawdust. Though the great Jim Thorpe had already graduated, Carlisle remained a powerhouse team. The Fighting Illini began like a prairie whirlwind, scoring the first touchdown after a series of rushes down the field. Halftime's intermission saw Illinois ahead, 6–5, but that lead evaporated in the second half as the Indians tallied three unanswered touchdowns. After the game, the two teams traveled together by train to Champaign-Urbana, where the Carlisle squad stayed until the following Wednesday as guests of the university.

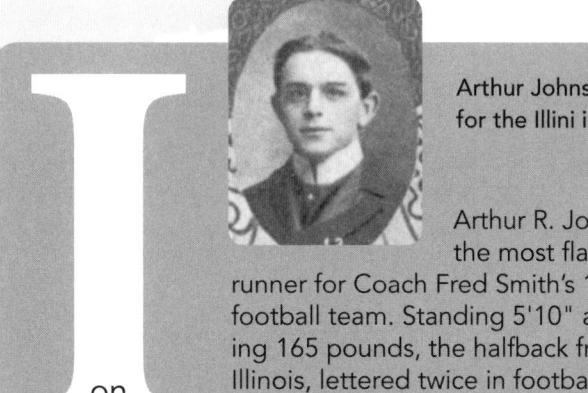

Arthur Johnston starred for the Illini in 1897

Arthur R. Johnston was the most flamboyant runner for Coach Fred Smith's 1897 Illini football team. Standing 5'10" and weighing 165 pounds, the halfback from Joliet, Illinois, lettered twice in football and four times in baseball.

I on 1897–98

ILLINI ITEM

Illinois Track and Field placed fifth among five teams at the first Indoor Western Intercollegiate meet, held in Chicago. J. K. Hoagland of Illinois won the 880-yard walk to become the school's first individual conference track champion.

The 1897 Illini played UI's first indoor game

UI's 1898 track and field team

ILLINI LISTS

ILLINI SINGLE-SEASON FOOTBALL SHUTOUTS

1900: 8 (in 12 games)
1902: 8 (in 13 games)
1910: 7 (in 7 games)
1901: 7 (in 10 games)
1904: 7 (in 12 games)
1917: 6 (in 8 games)
1903: 6 (in 14 games)

ILLINI LEGEND

Fred Smith

Coach Fred
Smith

During the infancy of college athletics in the late 1800s, it was quite common for one individual to hold more than one position within the athletic department. Such was the case with athletic director/baseball coach/football coach George Huff. "G" decided that the multiple responsibilities were diluting his efficiency and affecting his health, so in 1900 he submitted his resignation as the Illini grid mentor. Huff chose former Illini assistant coach Fred Smith as his successor in 1900, a man who had performed the bulk of the head coaching duties for Huff in 1897 and 1998. Smith starred as a quarterback at Princeton, directing the Tigers to a 10-0-1 record and the mythical national championship. During his lone season as Illinois's official head coach, Smith guided the Illini to a very respectable 7-3-2 record, including a victory over Purdue. Altogether, Illinois registered eight defensive shutouts in twelve games, a mark that equals the most in Illinois football history during a single season. Smith eventually settled in New York City, where he doubled as an engineer with the Department of Public Works and as head football coach at Fordham College. He died in 1923 at age fifty.

ILLINI LORE

In April 1897 Charles W. Spalding, treasurer for the University of Illinois, was charged with embezzling $460,000 in university funds. Spalding had secretly invested about 95 percent of that total in land deals in Idaho. Two months after Spalding was caught, the Illinois state legislature appropriated money to cover the deficit caused by his actions. On December l, 1897, Spalding was sent to the state penitentiary to begin a four-year sentence.

UI's campus in 1898

1898-99

AMERICA'S TIME CAPSULE

August 1, 1898	The United States estimated that forty-two hundred servicemen fighting in Cuba suffered from yellow fever or typhoid.
November 8, 1898	Rough Rider Teddy Roosevelt was elected governor of New York.
December 10, 1898	The United States and Spain signed a peace treaty in Paris, ending the Spanish-American War.
February 14, 1899	Congress approved the use of voting machines for federal elections.
July 17, 1899	America's first juvenile court was established in Chicago.

ILLINI MOMENT

The Illini's 11–10 Football Win at Minnesota, November 24, 1898

Coach George Huff's Illini limped into Minnesota with a three-game losing streak, so no one gave the visitors much of a chance that cold and snowy Thanksgiving Day. Only a day after being shut out by the Carlisle Indians, the Illinois party set off on its exceedingly long and tedious trip to the Land of 10,000 Lakes. The first ever matchup between the two schools began predictably, as Minnesota jumped off to a 10–0 first-quarter lead. Illinois battled back, scoring a five-point touch-down just before the whistle sounded to trail 10–5 at inter-mission. In the final twenty-five minutes, the Illini successfully navigated the treacherous field by rushing the ball. All-star full-back A. R. Johnston, the Illini captain, scored the game-tying TD, then kicked the point after for the eventual 11–10 victory.

The Illini topped Minnesota in 1898

I on 1898–99

College football rules in 1898:

- Field marked with transverse lines every five yards; this distance to be gained in three downs to maintain possession.
- Point values: five points for a touch-down, one point for goal after TD.
- Only one man in motion forward be-fore the snap. No more than three players behind the line. One player permitted in motion toward his own goal line.
- Substitutes may enter the game at any time at the discretion of the captains.
- No forward passes (not permitted until 1906).

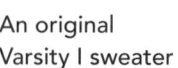

November 19, 1898:
Illinois vs. Carlisle

ILLINI ITEM

In December of 1898 the UI's Athletic Association began is-suing blue sweaters with the orange block "I" to members of the Illini football, baseball, and track teams who won either a contest or an individual event against teams represent-ing the Universities of Chicago, Michigan, Wisconsin, or Minne-sota, or to Illini who won a point in the annual field meet of the Western Intercollegiate Athletic Association.

An original
Varsity I sweater

ILLINI LISTS

JUSTA LINDGREN'S ALL-TIME ILLINI
FOOTBALL TEAM (chosen in 1943)

Ends:	Chuck Carney and Claude Rothgeb
Tackles:	Walter Crawford and Butch Nowack
Guards:	Ralph Chapman and Jim McMillin
Center:	Bob Reitsch
Quarterback:	Potsy Clark
Halfbacks:	Red Grange and Harold Pogue
Fullback:	Jack Crangle

ILLINI LEGEND

Justa Lindgren

For forty consecutive years plus a few more, the name Justa Lindgren was synonymous with Fighting Illini football. "Lindy," as he was known to the legion of players he coached and his many friends, first joined the University of Illinois as a freshman lineman from Moline in 1898. Four letter-winning seasons later, he graduated from the UI and was contacted by Cornell College in Mt. Vernon, Iowa, to become the school's head football coach. After only two seasons in Iowa, Lindgren returned to Urbana-Champaign as one of four graduates in George Huff's alumni coaching system. He served for one season as the Illini's head coach, 1906, but the conservative, detail-minded Lindgren felt more comfortable as an assistant, serving as line coach under Arthur Hall, Bob Zuppke, and Ray Eliot through 1943. Lindgren developed seven All-American players at Illinois during that span and was an integral member of eight Big Ten championship teams. He died in 1951 at age seventy-two.

Justa Lindgren

ILLINI LORE

On May 5, 1899, the University of Illinois Board of Trustees decided to erect a $150,000 agriculture building. The facility, which opened for use on September 10, 1900, eventually came to be known as Davenport Hall, in honor of the College of Agriculture's dean, Eugene Davenport.

Agriculture Hall

1899–1900

AMERICA'S TIME CAPSULE

October 14, 1899	William McKinley became the first president to ride in an automobile.
November 21, 1899	Vice President Garret Hobart died. New York Governor Theodore Roosevelt was nominated as Hobart's replacement. Roosevelt first declined the nomination but later relented at the Republican National Convention.
March 14, 1900	Congress standardized the gold dollar as the unit of monetary value in the United States.
May 14, 1900	Carrie Nation began her anti-liquor campaign.
July 4, 1900	The Democratic Party nominated William Jennings Bryan of Nebraska as its presidential candidate.

ILLINI
MOMENT

Illinois's First Western Conference Title

The beginning of the twentieth century trumpeted the arrival of the University of Illinois's first Western Conference title. Coach George Huff's 1900 baseball squad returned most of its members from the 1899 Big Ten runner-up team and began its preseason with a series of exhibition games against the Chicago White Sox. After winning three and tying one of the nine games, Huff knew he had the makings of a championship club. His standout players included pitchers Carl Lundgren and Harvey McCollum, second baseman Billy Fulton, third baseman Carl Steinwedell, and center fielder Jimmy Cook, all members of Huff's all-time Illinois baseball team. The Illini won seven of their first eight conference games, winding up with an 11-2 record.

The 1900 Illini baseball team

I on 1899–00

December 1, 1899: The Western Conference grew to nine schools when Indiana University and the State University of Iowa were admitted for membership. At that time, Indiana's enrollment was 1,050, Iowa's 1,502.

Iowa joined the Big Ten in 1899

ILLINI ITEM

The simple act of scoring points was the difference between victory and defeat for Illinois's 1899 football team. In the three games the Illini scored—Illinois Wesleyan (6–0), Knox (5–0), and St. Louis (29–0)—they won games. In the six times Illinois didn't score—all shutouts—the Illini were a miserable 0-5-1. It remains the only season in which every Illinois football game ended in a shutout for one team or the other.

1899 football team

ILLINI LISTS

ALL-TIME BIG TEN BASEBALL VICTORIES (through 2016 season)

1.	1,095	Illinois (1896)
	1,095	Michigan (1896)
3.	1,012	Minnesota (1906)
4.	942	Ohio State (1913)
5.	782	Iowa (1906)
6.	745	Indiana (1906)
7.	704	Purdue (1906)
8.	665	Northwestern (1898)
9.	624	Michigan State (1951)
10.	565	Wisconsin (1896*)
11.	311	Penn State (1992)

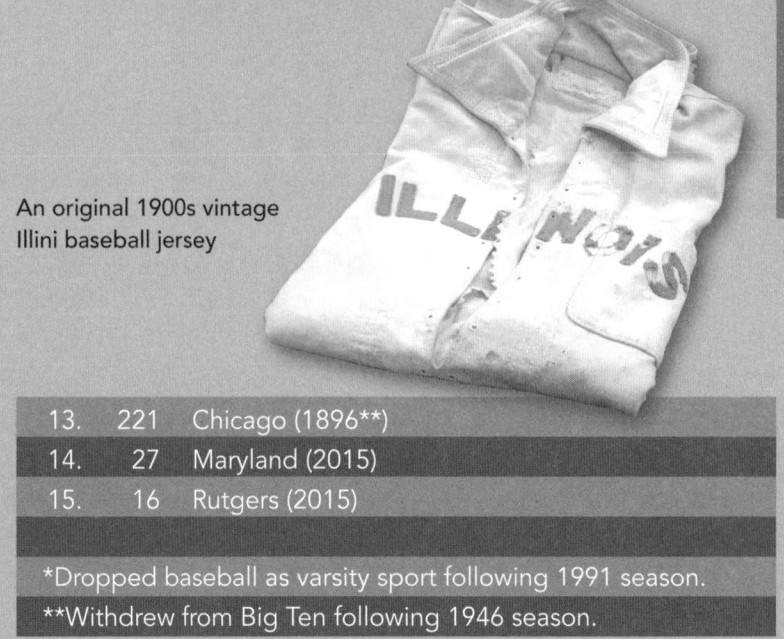

An original 1900s vintage
Illini baseball jersey

13.	221	Chicago (1896**)
14.	27	Maryland (2015)
15.	16	Rutgers (2015)

*Dropped baseball as varsity sport following 1991 season.

**Withdrew from Big Ten following 1946 season.

ILLINI LEGEND

Coach Carl Lundgren

Carl Lundgren

The immortal George Huff called him "the greatest of all college baseball coaches." An early sports magazine, *Athletic World*, praised him as "the peer of all college baseball instructors." In any case, the name Carl Leonard Lundgren is permanently linked with University of Illinois success on the baseball diamond. As a pitcher on the Fighting Illini nines of 1899–1902, "Lundy" led Illinois to Big Ten championships his sophomore and senior seasons. His election not only as the baseball team's captain but also as president of UI's senior class reflected the esteem his fellow students had for him. Lundgren went directly from Illinois into professional baseball, pitching for the Chicago Cubs for seven seasons. Twice the Cubbies were world champs, due in great part to his spectacular pitching, which accounted for ninety-two career victories. After leaving the Cubs, Lundgren began his brilliant coaching career at Princeton as freshman coach, then went to Michigan as varsity coach, where he coached future hall of famer George Sisler. Huff lured Lundgren back to Champaign to coach the Illini in 1921, where he directed Illinois to five conference titles in twelve seasons. Lundgren died on August 24, 1934, of a heart attack at age fifty-four.

ILLINI LORE

Editor-in-Chief
William Walter
Smith

On September 20, 1899, the University of Illinois's student-operated newspaper, *The Illini*, began publishing on a thrice-weekly basis. But did you know that the first editor-in-chief of the newspaper was the school's first African American graduate? William Walter Smith, a native of Broadlands, Illinois, also served as president of the Republican Club, played class football, participated with the rifle team, studied German and Romanic languages, and majored in civil engineering. Smith was eventually employed by Armour & Company, overseeing the company's building of elevators, warehouses, and refrigerating plants in Argentina. Eleven years later, Smith changed his name to Walter Smith Oglesby.

1900–1901

AMERICA'S TIME CAPSULE

September 8, 1900	A hurricane ravaged Galveston, Texas, killing six thousand people and causing property damages of $20 million.
November 6, 1900	William McKinley won the presidency for a second term.
January 10, 1901	A well near Beaumont, Texas, brought in oil, the first evidence of oil from that region.
March 3, 1901	The United States Steel Corporation was incorporated in New Jersey.
June 15, 1901	Willie Anderson won the U.S. Open golf tournament.

ILLINI
MOMENT

Illinois vs. the Cubs— April 13–16, 1901

Before the days of spring training sites in warm climates, Major League Baseball teams frequently would hook up for a series of practice games against teams from the local universities. Such was the case in 1901, when manager Tom Loftus brought his Chicago Cubs to Champaign-Urbana for a nine-game series. The Cubbies featured future hall of famer Frank Chance, he of the famous baseball triumvirate "Tinker-to-Evers-to-Chance." Coach George Huff's Illini surprisingly won four games against the National League club, paced by the hitting of second baseman Jimmy Cook and catcher Jake Stahl. Illinois used the exhibition series as a springboard to a second-place finish in the Big Ten, but the Cubs ultimately finished thirty-seven games behind the Pittsburgh Pirates in the NL race.

1901 Illini baseball team

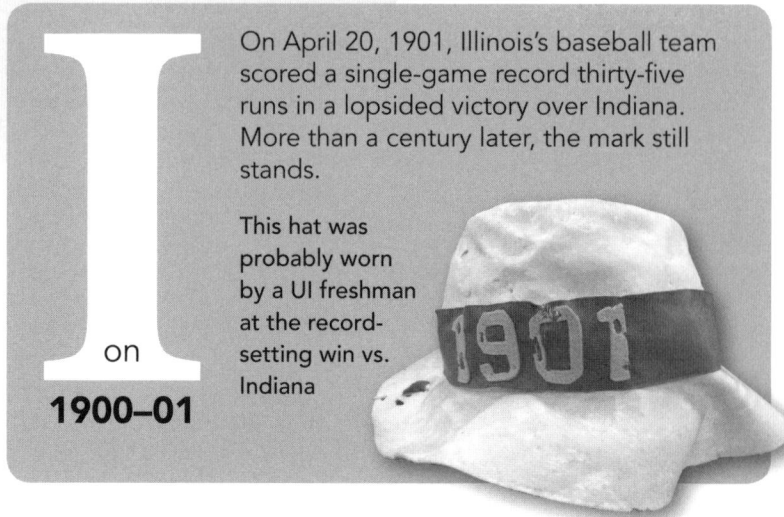

I on **1900–01**

On April 20, 1901, Illinois's baseball team scored a single-game record thirty-five runs in a lopsided victory over Indiana. More than a century later, the mark still stands.

This hat was probably worn by a UI freshman at the record-setting win vs. Indiana

ILLINI ITEM

"Red" Matthews (right) was Illinois's first cheerleader

Robert "Red" Matthews, the nation's first acrobatic cheerleader, served as the University of Illinois's first cheerleader from 1899 to 1900. Said Matthews later, "I just busted out on the sidelines like the measles, and started hollering with my head up, my arms waving, and my legs jumping." Matthews was an institution at the University of Tennessee from 1907 to 1949, serving on the engineering faculty and initiating UT's first cheerleading program. At age ninety-five, he attended Illinois's 1973 Homecoming game and joined the Illini cheerleading squad on the sidelines. Matthews died in 1978 at age ninety-nine.

ILLINI LISTS

ALL-TIME BIG TEN CHAMPIONSHIPS (through 2015–16 season)

(Men's and Women's Sports)					
1.	Michigan	381 (279m, 102w)	11.	Chicago	73 (73m)
2.	Illinois	242 (224m, 18w)	12.	Purdue	71 (53m, 18w)
3.	Ohio State	219 (156m, 63w)	13.	Nebraska	10 (3m, 7w)
4.	Wisconsin	196 (155m, 41w)	14.	Maryland	9 (3m, 6w)
5.	Indiana	171 (135m, 36w)	15.	Rutgers	0
	Minnesota	171 (141m, 30w)			
7.	Iowa	107 (81m, 26w)			
8.	Michigan State	100 (73m, 27w)			
9.	Penn State	80 (18m, 62w)			
10.	Northwestern	76 (44m, 32w)			

ILLINI LEGEND

Dr. Jacob Shell

Dr. Jacob Shell

Dr. Jacob Kinzer Shell's tenure as the University of Illinois's athletic director from 1898 to 1901 was generally accented by achievement. Though football and track successes were minimal, the baseball team won a Western Conference (Big Ten) championship in 1900, the school's first ever. Shell also had a hand in welcoming Indiana and Iowa into the conference, and he helped establish the Urbana-Champaign campus as the training quarters for the Chicago Cubs. During his undergraduate days at the University of Pennsylvania in the early 1880s and during his graduate career at Swarthmore College, Shell was a fantastic athlete. "Doc" starred in football, baseball, gymnastics, track, lacrosse, boxing, and won America's middleweight wrestling championship. Shell resigned his post as UI's director of athletics on May 29, 1901, opening the door for his successor, George Huff. He was one of the founders of the American Athletic Union, serving thirty-four years for the AAU in numerous capacities. Shell died on December 10, 1940, at age seventy-eight.

ILLINI LORE

University of Illinois seniors first wore caps and gowns at commencement exercises on June 12, 1901. The procession of students marched up Burrill Avenue to the old Armory. After they received diplomas, the seniors marched back to the lawn south of Green Street, where they sang "Auld Lang Syne." A total of 174 degrees were issued at the Urbana-Champaign campus in 1900–01, the most in the history of the university at the time.

1911 Commencement exercises

1901–02

AMERICA'S TIME CAPSULE

September 6, 1901   President McKinley was shot as he attended a reception in Buffalo. He died of his wounds eight days later.

September 14, 1901   Forty-two-year-old Theodore Roosevelt took the presidential oath of office.

January l, 1902   Michigan defeated Stanford in the first Rose Bowl game at Pasadena, California.

May 12, 1902   Nearly 140,000 United Mine Workers went on strike.

May 20, 1902   Four years after the end of the Spanish-American War, Cuba achieved independence.

ILLINI MOMENT

1901 Illinois-Chicago Football Game—October 19, 1901

Coach Edgar Holt's Illini were unstoppable through the first four games of the season, rolling up 135 points. Their defensive play was particularly impressive, allowing nary a single opponent to penetrate their end zone. But now came the real test, against Coach Amos Alonzo Stagg's University of Chicago club, on the Maroons' home field. Nearly half of the crowd of seven thousand cheered on the Illini from the east bleachers. Though the first half was scoreless, the Orange and Blue controlled play with a steady ground game that ultimately accounted for 560 total yards by game's end. Illinois continued its dominance in the second half, with Jake Stahl following the blocks of lineman Justa Lindgren for UI's first two scores. The Illini won the game, 24–0, chalking up their fifth consecutive shutout. On the following Monday evening, the team was honored with a parade and a twenty-four-gun salute and was presented with a key to the city of Urbana.

UI's 1901 football team

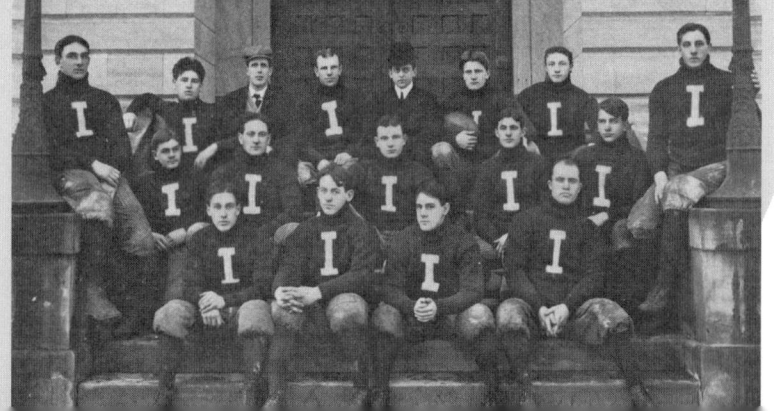

I on **1901–02**

Fred Falkenberg, an Illini baseball letter winner from 1900 to 1902, went on to become a successful Major League pitcher. As a member of the 1913 Cleveland Indians, the 6' 5" right-hander developed his trick pitch, the "emory ball." Falkenberg had a 23-10 record and 2.22 earned run average that season, and completed twenty-six of the thirty-six games in which he pitched.

Fred Falkenberg

ILLINI ITEM

Illinois's 1901 football team posted seven shutouts in ten games, allowing an average of fewer than four points per game. Against Western Conference competition, Coach Edgar Holt's squad won four of six league games, allowing just thirty-nine total points. Guard Jake Stahl and center Fred Lowenthal won All-Western honors for the Fighting Illini.

Fred Lowenthal

ILLINI LISTS

ILLINOIS'S ALL-TIME SINGLE-SEASON BATTING AVERAGES

Darrin Fletcher, 1987	.497
Ben Lewis, 1933	.473
Boyd Bartley, 1943	.460
John Toncoff, 1933	.460
Jerry Jordan, 1926	.447
Jake Stahl, 1903	.444
Jake Stahl, 1901	.443
Fred Major, 1926	.441
Larry Sutton, 1991	.434
Ruck Steger, 1950	.429

Garland "Jake" Stahl

ILLINI LEGEND

Garland "Jake" Stahl

During his era, Garland "Jake" Stahl was a man among boys at the University of Illinois. He was an All-American tackle in football, leading the Illini to twenty-five victories in his last three seasons on the gridiron. As a catcher on the baseball team, Stahl played a level above his teammates, averaging well over .400 from the plate the last three years. His four-hundred-foot, bases-loaded home run against Michigan, May 9, 1903, off the tree in deep right center field at Illinois Field remains one of the most legendary single plays in Illini baseball history. Stahl's senior-year batting average of .444 stood as a school record for twenty-three seasons. But as it turned out, that was only the beginning. Stahl took his act into Major League Baseball, enjoying a magnificent eight-year career. Among the highlights: two World Series championships with the Boston Red Sox (1903 [player] and 1912 [manager]) and an American League–leading ten home runs in 1910. Stahl died on September 18, 1922, at age forty-three.

Boston Red Sox star Jake Stahl

ILLINI LORE

On April 6, 1902, University of Illinois President Andrew Sloan Draper was seriously injured when he was thrown from his horse-drawn carriage. Three days later, doctors amputated his leg. President Draper didn't return to the university until October 1.

President Andrew Draper
in his carriage

1902–03

AMERICA'S TIME CAPSULE

November 4, 1902	In congressional elections, the Republicans maintained their Senate majority over the Democrats, 57–33.
January 22, 1903	The United States and Columbia signed a ninety-nine-year lease that granted America sovereignty over a canal zone in Panama.
June 10, 1903	Crayola crayons debuted. The box of six colors sold for five cents.
July 4, 1903	President Roosevelt sent a message around the world and back in twelve minutes via the first Pacific communications cable.
August 8, 1903	Great Britain defeated the United States in tennis to capture the Davis Cup.

ILLINI
MOMENT

Illinois–Ohio State Football Game, November 15, 1902

Tying a game, it has been said, is like kissing your sister. But Illinois's 0–0 stalemate with Ohio State in the first-ever engagement between the sister institutions was more like a spat. The Buckeyes had not yet become a member of the Big Ten, though they regularly played against conference schools. The Illinois contingent traveled to Columbus expecting an easy victory, since OSU had been pummeled by Michigan earlier in the year by an 86–0 count. Several times during the game, Illinois threatened the Buckeye end zone, but fumbles and two failed field-goal attempts did in the Illini. Coach Edgar Holt's Illini squad wound up the season with a 10-2-1 record, placing fourth in the conference behind Michigan's famous point-a-minute team.

UI's 1902 football team

I on 1902–03

The Fighting Illini baseball team enjoyed its greatest season ever, losing only once in eighteen games. Opening the season with back-to-back shutouts against Northwestern (10–0) and Wisconsin (9–0), Illinois then traveled to Ann Arbor for game 3. Michigan prevailed in a slugfest, 14–10, but the Illini got right back on track and won their remaining fifteen games in a row. Illinois captured the Big Ten title with an 11-1 record, its second championship in four years.

1903 Illini baseball team

ILLINI ITEM

On a seasonably mild day—June 13, 1903—at their home in Forksville, Pennsylvania, Sadie Grange gave birth to a bouncing baby boy named Harold Edward Grange. Little did she know that the youngster would grow up to revolutionize the sport of football.

Young Harold Grange

ILLINI LISTS

MOST BIG TEN CHAMPIONSHIPS BY A SCHOOL IN A
SINGLE SPORT (through the 2015–16 season)

1.	Wisconsin (men's cross-country)	48
2.	Michigan (football)	42
3.	Michigan (men's swimming)	40
4.	Michigan (men's tennis)	36
5.	Ohio State (football)	35
6.	Michigan (baseball)	35
7.	Iowa (wrestling)	35
8.	Michigan (men's track)	31
9.	Illinois (men's fencing)	30

ILLINI LEGEND

Edgar Holt

Before the turn of the century, Harvard and Princeton were two of the kingpins of college football. So, thought Illini athletic director George Huff, why not hire an Eastern coach to turn the sluggish Illinois football program into a winner? Huff's choice was Edgar Garrison Holt, a product of both the Harvard and Princeton systems. Holt had toiled as a lineman during his playing days, so he spent the bulk of his time tutoring UI front-line players such as "Jake" Stahl, Fred Lowenthal, and Justa Lindgren. In two seasons, 1901 and 1902, Holt guided Illinois to its first two winning records in Big Ten play and a cumulative record of 18-4-1. He died April 19, 1924, at age forty-nine.

Coach Edgar Holt

ILLINI LORE

The University of Illinois's new $289,000 Chemical Building opened to students September 28, 1902. At that time, the 165,000-square-foot facility was said to be the largest building in the country devoted exclusively to chemistry. An addition was made to the structure in 1916, and on May 13, 1939, the laboratory was named in honor of longtime department head William Noyes.

UI's Chemistry Building

1903–04

AMERICA'S TIME CAPSULE

October 13, 1903   The Boston Red Stockings defeated the Pittsburgh Pirates in baseball's first World Series.

December 17, 1903   Orville and Wilbur Wright made their first successful flight in a crude flying machine at Kitty Hawk, North Carolina.

March 2, 1903   Milton Hershey, who had introduced his chocolate bar three years earlier, began construction on the world's largest chocolate manufacturing factory in Derry Church, Pennsylvania.

June 1, 1904   At their national convention in Chicago, Republicans nominated President Theodore Roosevelt as their candidate.

July 6, 1904   The Democrats convened in St. Louis to nominate Alton Parker for president.

ILLINI
MOMENT

Illini "9" Captures Conference Title

Nobody gave Coach George Huff's 1904 Fighting Illini baseball team much of a chance to defend the Big Ten title it had won the season before. After all, how would Illinois ever replace such stalwarts as Jake Stahl and Jimmy Cook, both .400 hitters in 1903? Huff's club played a very ambitious nonconference schedule yet lost just one of thirteen games. In conference play, the Illini battled Wisconsin for the top spot, ultimately outdistancing the Badgers with an impressive 11-3 record. The title clincher came on May 28, when Illinois defeated the University of Chicago, 11–0, behind the two-hit pitching of Frank Pfeffer and two home runs by Captain Roy Parker. The leading Illini hitters in 1904 were left fielder Claude Rothgeb at .351 and third baseman R. L. Pitts at .350.

Claude Rothgeb, R. L. Pitts, and Roy Parker

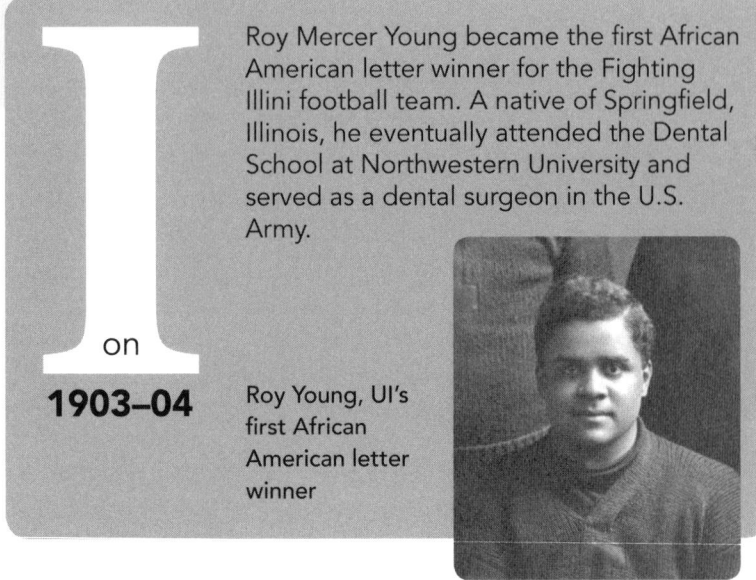

I on 1903–04

Roy Mercer Young became the first African American letter winner for the Fighting Illini football team. A native of Springfield, Illinois, he eventually attended the Dental School at Northwestern University and served as a dental surgeon in the U.S. Army.

Roy Young, UI's first African American letter winner

ILLINI ITEM

Harry Gill, who debuted as the Fighting Illini track and field coach in 1904, was America's premier decathlon performer in 1900. A native Canadian, Gill defeated three-time United States champion Ellery Clark in a one-on-one contest in New York to earn that distinction.

Harry Gill, the athlete

ILLINI LISTS

MULTIPLE LETTER WINNERS (1878–1925)

Claude Rothgeb	10 letters (football, baseball, and track)
Burt Ingwersen	9 letters (football, basketball, and baseball)
A. W. Merrifield	8 letters (baseball and track)
James Cook	8 letters (football and baseball)
Don Sweney	8 letters (football and track)
Walt Kersulis	8 letters (football and basketball)
Charles Carney	7 letters (football and basketball)
Ira Carrithers	7 letters (football, baseball, and track)

George Huff	7 letters (football and baseball)
Arthur Johnston	7 letters (football and baseball)
Garland "Jake" Stahl	7 letters (football and baseball)
Lawrence Walquist	7 letters (football and basketball)

ILLINI LEGEND

Claude Rothgeb

One way to gauge the accomplishments of an athlete is to measure the success of his teams. During the 1903–04 season, the most successful Fighting Illini teams were found over at Illinois Field. The Illinois football teams, though they never were champions, racked up a cumulative record of forty-four victories, fifteen losses, and four ties from 1900 through 1904. In baseball, the 1904 and 1905 clubs were 37–9. The sparkplug of those teams was a talented young man named Claude Rothgeb. As an end for the football squad, Rothgeb lettered four times and served as captain of the 1903 team. So outstanding was he that during his senior year he became only the third Illini gridder to earn All-American honors. As the left fielder for George Huff's baseball team, Rothgeb was the leading hitter (.351) for the 1904 Big Ten champs and the captain of the 1905 conference runnerup. Rothgeb also lettered four times for the Illini track team as a sprinter and shot-putter, winning a Big Ten individual title in the latter event.

Claude Rothgeb

ILLINI LORE

On August 23, 1904, Dr. Edmund James, president of Northwestern University, was elected to the University of Illinois presidency. James replaced President Andrew Draper, who resigned in January to accept a position as commissioner of education for the state of New York. By 1909 James had become a national figure, and by 1916 he was being discussed as a candidate for the presidency of the United States.

President Edmund James

Commemorative pin distributed at President James' inauguration

1904–05

AMERICA'S TIME CAPSULE

October 8, 1904	Automobile racing as an organized sport began with the Vanderbilt Cup race on Long Island, New York.
October 27, 1904	The first section of New York City's subway system was opened to the public.
November 8, 1904	Theodore Roosevelt was reelected president of the United States, defeating Alton Parker by nearly two million votes.
May 5, 1905	Boston's Cy Young threw baseball's first-ever perfect game, retiring twenty-seven consecutive Philadelphia Athletic batters.
June 19, 1905	Nearly five hundred patrons attend opening day of the world's first nickelodeon in Pittsburgh, Pennsylvania.

ILLINI
MOMENT

Illini Tie the Stagg's Maroons

Illinois's 1904 football team was coached by Justa Lindgren, Arthur Hall, Fred Lowenthal, and Clyde Mathews, who led the Illini to a perfect record through their first seven games. On October 29, hundreds of Illini fans filled UC's Marshall Field to witness the Illini versus Coach Amos Alonzo Stagg's Chicago Maroons. The Illini dearly outplayed their hosts in the first half, but neither team was able to score. In the third quarter, Illinois made its only mistake of the game as quarterback William Taylor fumbled the ball on his own twenty-seven-yard line. Chicago's left tackle, Glenn Parry, gathered up the loose pigskin and, with an extra-point kick, gave the Maroons a 6–0 lead. On the ensuing kickoff, Illinois's Claude Rothgeb ran the ball back to Chicago's twenty-yard line. Charles Fairweather then scored a five-point touchdown, and Charles Moynihan kicked the point for a 6–6 final score. Illinois continued its aggressive play against the highly favored Maroons, but time ran out and the game ended in a tie. Back in Champaign, Illini fans frolicked in the streets until midnight.

Chicago's Stagg Field

I on 1904–05

Returning from holiday time at his home in Keokuk, Iowa, Ralph Ousley "Red" Roberts, captain of Illinois's baseball team, was killed in a train wreck on January 10, 1905. The twenty-four-year-old was said to be headed for a career in Major League Baseball.

Ralph "Red" Roberts

ILLINI ITEM

Coach George Huff's Fighting Illini baseball team got only one hit against Wisconsin on May 27, 1905, but they made the most of it and defeated the Badgers, 1-0, at Illinois Field. In the second inning, cleanup hitter Claude Rothgeb smacked a curve ball far into right field. By the time the Badger fielders retrieved it from the bleachers and relayed it home, Rothgeb had rounded the bases, crossed the plate, and was sitting on the bench.

Illinois Field

ILLINI LISTS

POINTS SCORED BY HARRY GILL'S ILLINI TRACK TEAMS
IN BIG TEN OUTDOOR MEETS (1904–29)

Illinois	914
Michigan	587⅓
Chicago	541½
Wisconsin	514½
Iowa	328s
Ohio State	211
Minnesota	186⅓
Northwestern	151½
Purdue	136½
Indiana	101½

Illini track and field action from 1909

ILLINI LEGEND

Coach Harry Gill

Harry Gill

It was a Canadian who brought the University of Illinois to prominence as an American collegiate track power. During a twenty-nine-year coaching career at Urbana-Champaign from 1904 to 1929, then again from 1931 to 1933, Harry Gill's Fighting Illini churned out an amazing nineteen Big Ten championships—eleven titles outdoors and eight indoors. On the national scene, Gill's teams won NCAA titles in 1921 and 1927, plus three Spalding Cups at an annual invitational meet that attracted the nation's top colleges. The height of Gill's coaching career came in 1924, when his Illinois athletes—Harold Osborn, Dan Kinsey, and Horatio Fitch—scored more track and field points in the 1924 Summer Olympic Games than any other nation. In addition to those stars, Gill developed all-time greats Avery Brundage, longtime president of the International Olympic Federation, and "Tug" Wilson, former Olympic performer and Big Ten commissioner. Gill died in 1956 at age eighty. The Harry Gill Company, a sporting goods manufacturer specializing in track equipment, remains in Urbana.

ILLINI LORE

Around 1894, University of Illinois students began displaying their individual class colors by wearing ribbons on their shirts around campus. There was great disdain for the lowly freshmen, especially from the sophomores. Consequently, the two classes engaged in an annual physical battle called the "class rush." The reigning champions defended a greased flagpole from which a flag of their class colors flew. As many as three hundred to four hundred students locked arms and encircled the pole while the challengers used any means to remove their opponent's flag. University officials eventually channeled the students' energy toward a game called push-ball, which only resulted in more injuries than the color rush. Another contest, called the sack rush, was then instituted, but eventually, in 1914, Illinois students discontinued these dangerous traditional rivalry games.

1905–1914

1905–06

AMERICA'S TIME CAPSULE

September 22, 1905 — Willie Anderson won his third consecutive U.S. Open golf championship.

October 14, 1905 — The New York Giants beat the Philadelphia Athletics to win baseball's second World Series.

April 7, 1906 — The first successful transatlantic wireless transmission was made from New York City to a receiving station in Ireland.

April 18, 1906 — A massive earthquake rocked San Francisco, killing three thousand and leaving more than half the city's inhabitants homeless.

August 1906 — The Victor Talking Machine Company began shipping the Victrola, revolutionizing the phonograph industry.

ILLINI MOMENT

Illini's First Basketball Game

The first official intercollegiate basketball game occurred at the University of Illinois some fifteen years after the sport was introduced in Springfield, Massachusetts, by Dr. James Naismith. Three hundred twenty-five fans, many of whom were probably watching the game for the first time, saw their Fighting Illini defeat Indiana, 27–24. When a goal was made, a spectator had to retrieve the ball out of the closed basket so that the game could resume. The Illini starting lineup featured center Roy Riley at the center position, forwards Floyd Talmage and V. C. Kays, and guards E. G. Ryan and Arthur Ray. Indiana jumped off to a 5–0 lead before Talmage finally scored Illinois's historic first basket. Talmage continued his sharp shooting, scoring seven field goals and two free throws for sixteen of UI's twenty-seven total points.

UI's first men's basketball team

I on 1905–06

The newfangled Model T

Life on campus for student-athletes at the University of Illinois in 1905-06 was simple. They could buy a pound of sugar, a dozen eggs, and a pound of coffee for 33 cents. Some of them had never ridden in an automobile—there were only eight thousand cars in the United States—or talked on a telephone; only 8 percent of their homes had a phone. While the average U.S. worker made between $200 and $400 per year, U of I students were studying to become accountants ($2,000 per year), veterinarians ($4,000), and mechanical engineers ($5,000).

ILLINI ITEM

The University of Illinois Water Polo Team (later called water basketball) made its debut February 17, 1906, by defeating the University of Chicago, 2–1. For the next thirty-three years, the Illini dominated the sport in the Midwest, winning ten Big Ten championships and registering a dual-meet record of 95-39-3. The sport discontinued competition at Illinois during the war years of 1941 to 1946 and was never resumed.

UI's 1906 water polo team

ILLINI LISTS

MARCHING ILLINI BAND HIGHLIGHTS

1872: The UI band performed for the first time.

1892: UI military band presented its first annual concert.

1906: "Illinois Loyalty" first performed.

1910: Debut of "Oskee-Wow-Wow" and "Hail to the Orange."

1910: Band first formed "Block I."

1922: First mass bands performance at Illinois.

1923: Band first formed the word "Illini."

1926: First performance of Chief Illiniwek.

1943: Idelle Stitch became first female to portray Chief Illiniwek.

Band director Austin Harding

One of UI's earliest bands

1948: Austin Harding, director of bands, retired, ending forty-three-year career at UI.

1952: UI band's first performance in Tournament of Roses Parade.

1970: First female members of Marching Illini.

1976: Debut of Illinettes, Big Ten's first women's dance team.

1977: Deborah Soumar became first female drum major in Big Ten.

1994: First collegiate band with a Web site

ILLINI LEGEND

The composer of "Illinois Loyalty," Thatcher Guild

Thatcher Guild

It's a name even the most avid Fighting Illini fan doesn't know. But when the University of Illinois establishes an athletic hall of fame, Thatcher Howland Guild's name needs to be included. Guild didn't score any touchdowns or hit any homeruns, but his contribution to the university—"Illinois Loyalty"—has been sung thousands of times during home Illini football and basketball game for more than ninety years. Much like Schubert's "Unfinished Symphony," Guild brought the lyrics and melody to the Urbana-Champaign campus with him from his alma mater, Brown University. His original first line ran: "We're loyal to you, men of Brown." A newly hired English instructor, Guild took his tune to UI's longtime band director Austin Harding, and the two men refined the now legendary melody. After more than six months of work, "Illinois Loyalty" was finally performed before the UI student body at Harding's First Anniversary Concert on March 3, 1906. Guild died at the tender age of thirty-five in 1914 from a heart attack while playing tennis on a hot summer's day.

Original sheet music for "Illinois Loyalty"

ILLINI LORE

On October 16, 1905, the University of Illinois's Women's Building was dedicated. Designed by the celebrated architectural firm of McKim, Mead, and White, it became a stately element along the university's principal mall. The $330,000 structure, now known as the English Building, features a central colonnade and twin-domed towers.

The Women's Building was dedicated in 1905

1906–07

AMERICA'S TIME CAPSULE

October 14, 1906   The Chicago White Sox beat the Chicago Cubs to win the third World Series.

November 9, 1906   Theodore Roosevelt became the first president to travel abroad, journeying to Panama to inspect the progress on the Panama Canal.

December 24, 1906   Reginald Fessenden made the first known radio broadcast of voice and music from his Branch Rock, Massachusetts, experiment station.

February 20, 1907   President Roosevelt signed the Immigration Act of 1907, restricting immigration by Japanese laborers.

March 21, 1907   U.S. Marines were sent to Honduras to quell a political disturbance.

ILLINI MOMENT

Illinois's First Big Ten Track and Field Title

The University of Illinois track and field team had traveled a rocky road during the first three seasons of the Harry Gill coaching era, finishing no higher than fifth in the Western Conference championship outdoor meet. So, on that cold first day of June 1907, the Illini could only be cautiously optimistic about what would ultimately turn out to be the greatest day in the history of the sport at Illinois. Illini football star Wilbur Burroughs was the star of the day, capturing individual titles in both the shot put and the hammer throw and accounting for nearly one-third of the team's points. Billy May finished first in the 100-yard dash and second in the 220-yard dash, which gave the Illini eight more valuable points, allowing Illinois to edge host Chicago, 31–29, for the school's very first conference championship in track and field.

UI's 1907 track-and-field team

I on 1906–07

George Huff called Forest Van Hook "the best offensive guard in our history." At six feet tall and weighing 295 pounds, the farm boy from Mt. Pulaski was the University of Illinois's first three-time All-Western pick (1906–1908), but there was much more to the Illini captain than just football. Van Hook graduated with high honors, finishing first in his class, then attended medical school at Northwestern. In 1914 he returned to Mt. Pulaski, serving as a medical practitioner for the remainder of his life. He died in 1937 at age fifty-one.

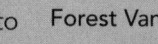

Forest Van Hook

ILLINI ITEM

The Illini baseball team won its second consecutive Western Conference title in 1907, capturing all seven of its league games. On April 14, just three days before the regular season was to begin, Coach George Huff accepted an offer from the Boston Americans to manage that professional club, so Louis Cook hastily took over for Huff to direct Illinois to its fourth conference baseball title in five years.

Jake Stahl (left) and George Huff

After only thirteen days in Boston, Huff sent a telegram to UI President Edmund James, stating, "Have received my release. Will be back Saturday. This is final and positive."

ILLINI LISTS

ILLINI COACHES WITH THE LONGEST REIGNS
(through 2015–16 season)

Gary Wieneke, cross-country	35 years	(1967–2002)
Yoshi Hayasaki, gymnastics	33 years	(1973–1993, 1996–2009)
Ed Manley, swimming	33 years	(1920–1952)
Bob Zuppke, football	29 years	(1913–1941)
Leo Johnson, track	28 years	(1938–1965)
Max Garret, fencing	27 years	(1941–1972)*
Lee Eilbracht, baseball	27 years	(1952–1978)
Harry Gill, track	26 years	(1904–1929)
George Huff, baseball	24 years	(1896–1919)

Don Sammons, swimming	23 years	(1971–1993)
Ralph Fletcher, golf	23 years	(1944–1966)
Leo Johnson, cross-country	23 years	(1938–1960)

*UI did not sponsor fencing from 1943 to 1946, and Garret did not coach in 1970.

ILLINI LEGEND

Avery Brundage

He was best known for his twenty-year reign as the controversial president of the International Olympic Committee (IOC), but few know that Avery Brundage began his career in the world of sports at the University of Illinois as an athlete. Brundage, a native of Detroit, earned varsity letters with the Fighting Illini basketball team and track squad. He was the center for the 1908 basketball squad that won twenty of twenty-six games, and an outstanding shot-putter and discus thrower for the Illini thinclads, winning an individual title in the latter event at the 1909 Western Conference track meet. Brundage competed in the 1912 Olympic decathlon with the legendary Jim Thorpe. In 1916 and 1918 he won the national all-around decathlon championship. Brundage served as president of the Amateur Athletic Union from 1928 to 1935 and for the U.S. Olympic Committee from 1929 to 1933. As the IOC's most famous administrator, he fought a fierce battle to maintain the Olympic ideals of amateurism. A longtime member of the UI President's Club, he established a scholarship bearing his name in 1974. Brundage died of a heart attack May 8, 1975, at age eighty-seven. His papers in the University Archives continue to attract scholars from around the world.

UI senior Avery Brundage, future president of the International Olympic Committee

ILLINI LORE

In May 18, 1907, the last saloon in Champaign-Urbana closed. The editor of the University of Illinois Alumni Quarterly applauded the move. "Though it cannot be expected that the closing of the saloons will put an end to drinking in the two cities," he said, "it must, in a large degree, mitigate the effect. With the saloons gone, Champaign and Urbana are undoubtedly safer places for young men than they have previously been."

The cap worn by UI freshmen in 1907

1907—08

AMERICA'S TIME CAPSULE

September 12, 1907   The *Lusitania*, the world's largest steamship, completed its maiden voyage between Ireland and New York.

October 12, 1907   The Chicago Cubs swept the World Series from the Detroit Tigers.

November 16, 1907   Oklahoma became the forty-sixth state.

December 6, 1907   In what some have called the worst mining disaster in American history, 361 miners were killed in explosions at the Fairmont Coal Company's No. 6 and No. 8 coal mines in Monongah, West Virginia.

May 10, 1908   Mother's Day was first celebrated.

ILLINI
MOMENT

Illini Defeat Minnesota to Win Title

Winning Western Conference baseball titles had become commonplace for the University of Illinois, but the game that clinched the Illini's 1908 championship was one of the most decisive victories ever registered at Illinois Field. Minnesota, which eventually wound up as the conference's runner-up, was the Illini victim on that twenty-third day of May. To say that Illinois merely won that day would be an understatement, for the 16–0 romp over the Gophers was never competitive. Pitcher Ernie Ovitz not only blanked Minnesota on the mound, allowing just one hit, he also scored runs in all four of his official times at the plate. The deadly combination of fourteen Illini hits and nine Gopher errors resulted in an average of two runs every inning and the most lopsided shutout victory in four conference seasons.

Ernie Ovitz

I on 1907–08

On January 14, 1908, the University of Michigan withdrew from the Conference in protest against guidelines to govern the then-dangerous game of football. One of the restrictions with which Michigan vehemently disagreed would have reduced player eligibility to three years. Every school except Michigan agreed with the guideline, so when forced to choose between the rule and conference membership, U-M President James Angell advocated that Michigan become a football independent. After ten years of begging for games to fill out its schedule, Michigan resumed conference membership on November 20, 1917.

University of Michigan President James Angell

ILLINI ITEM

Twenty victories in a season is the benchmark of success for collegiate basketball teams, and it only took the University of Illinois basketball program three years to reach that plateau. The 1907–08 Illini squad, coached by Fletcher Lane, accumulated a 20–6 record, a feat that wasn't accomplished again until forty-one years later, when Harry Combes's 1948–49 team went 21-4.

1908 Illini basketball team

ILLINI LISTS

ILLINOIS'S MOST DOMINANT FOOTBALL TEAMS

1910	7-0-0, outscored its opponents 89–0
1914	7-0-0, outscored its opponents 224 to 22
1915	5-0-2, outscored its opponents 183 to 25
1923	8-0-0, outscored its opponents 136 to 20
1927	7-0-1, outscored its opponents 152 to 24
1951	9-0-1, outscored its opponents 220 to 83

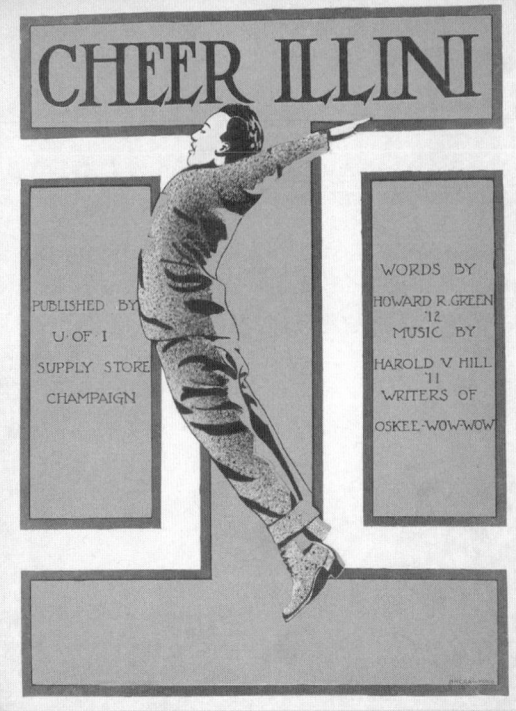

"Cheer Illini"
sheet music

ILLINI LEGEND

Coach Arthur Hall

Arthur Hall

The architect of the University of Illinois's first-ever Big Ten football title was Coach Arthur Hall, an Illini athlete himself from 1898 to 1900. Hall's greatest season came in 1910, when his Fighting Illini team became only the second conference team, and only the thirteenth in college football history, to be undefeated and to have allowed no opponent to score. In six seasons at Illinois from 1907 to 1912, Hall coached the Illini gridders to a record of 27-10-3. Incredibly, coaching football wasn't Hall's only profession. His "day" job was practicing law in Danville, Illinois. At the end of the 1912 season, Hall decided that the pace was too hectic, so he resigned his position at the University of Illinois and went into law full time. Athletic Director George Huff replaced Hall with the immortal Bob Zuppke. Artie Hall served as Vermilion County (Illinois) probate court judge until his retirement in 1954. He was also instrumental in developing the State of Illinois's "hard road" system. Hall died in 1955 at age eighty-six.

ILLINI LORE

On November 4 and 5, 1907, the University of Illinois dedicated its new $152,000 auditorium, which provided an adequate place for convocations, lectures, concerts, and other large gatherings. Constructed of brick and Indiana limestone, the facility was remodeled in 1915 to correct its acoustical deficiencies. The structure was rededicated as the Foellinger Auditorium on April 26, 1985, named for benefactor Helene Foellinger (1932). Among those who have performed or lectured at the auditorium are John Phillip Sousa (1909), Amelia Earhart (1935), Duke Ellington (1948), and Eleanor Roosevelt (1956).

A big crowd gathers for a concert in front of UI's auditorium

1908–09

AMERICA'S TIME CAPSULE

October I, 1908   Henry Ford introduced the Model T. It originally sold for $825.
November 3, 1908   William Howard Taft was elected president of the United States.
December 26, 1908   Jack Johnson became the first black world heavyweight boxing champion.
April 6, 1909   Robert Peary reached the North Pole.
July 12, 1909   Congress proposed an amendment to authorize a national income tax.
July 27, 1909   Orville Wright set a flight-duration record of just longer than one hour.

ILLINI MOMENT

Gill's Men Romp Away with Track Title

On June 5, 1909, at Chicago's Marshall Field, Coach Harry Gill directed the University of Illinois track and field squad to its second Western Conference title in three years. Though it was the official conference meet, nonconference schools such as Stanford, Michigan Agricultural College, and Notre Dame also participated in the festivities. Illinois won three individual firsts, including Roger Stephenson in the broad jump (22'6¼"), Lud Washburn in the high jump (5'10"), and Avery Brundage in the discus throw (43'2½"). The meet was clinched by the Illini mile relay team. Altogether, Illinois athletes scored in eleven of the fifteen events, claiming four firsts, four seconds, and four thirds.

Champions of the Western Conference

I on 1908–09

George Goodenough served as the University of Illinois Faculty Representative from 1906 until his death in 1929 at age sixty-one. He acquired the nickname "Steamer" from his position as professor of thermodynamics at the U of I, a field in which he became a worldwide authority. During the 1910–11 academic year, Goodenough was chairman of what was then the Western Athletic Conference. Said George Huff about Goodenough, "In all Conference legislation, he never raised the question of how it would affect Illinois. He considered it solely from the viewpoint as to whether or not the legislation was for the best interest of athletics."

Faculty representative George Goodenough

ILLINI ITEM

Though Purdue denied Illinois its fourth consecutive Western Conference baseball title, the 1909 season was nevertheless considered a grand success. The Boilermakers' 7-2 conference record was just a few percentage points better than the Illini's 9-3 league mark. Coach George Huff issued a challenge to Purdue to determine a true champion, but the Boilermakers reportedly refused.

UI's 1909 baseball team

ILLINI LISTS

BEST ILLINI DEFENSIVE PERFORMANCES
(vs. current Big Ten Basketball Opponents)

The 1909 Illini basketball team defeated Indiana, 30–2

1909	Illinois 30, Indiana 2
1909	Illinois 35, Northwestern 4
1913	Illinois 35, Iowa 9
1915	Illinois 27, Purdue 8
1914	Illinois 21, Ohio State 10
1920	Illinois 41, Michigan 14
1921	Illinois 17, Wisconsin 9
1926	Illinois 17, Minnesota 8
1993	Illinois 52, Michigan State 39
2004	Illinois 80, Penn State 37

2012	Illinois 60, Nebraska 49
2015	Illinois 64, Maryland 57
2015	Illinois 66, Rutgers 54

ILLINI LEGEND

Henry Popperfuss

Henry Popperfuss

A first-generation American, Henry Popperfuss served as captain of the 1908–09 Illini basketball team. He came to the University of Illinois as a graduate of Chicago's prestigious St. Ignatius College Prep. Popperfuss was one of Illini coach Herb Juul's best players, averaging a team-leading 15.4 points per game in 1907–08. He was also a highly successful scholar, graduating with a degree in civil engineering. Following initial employment in the railroad industry, he enlisted as a serviceman in World War I. Popperfuss became a decorated combat pilot, serving alongside Eddy Rickenbacker and Quentin Roosevelt, son of President Theodore Roosevelt. When the Great War ended in November 1918, Popperfuss rejoined his mother and brother in Chicago to operate the Hotel Newberry. Within a few years, the Popperfuss family became the proprietors of a large hotel corporation, including the twelve-story Hotel Pearson located on Chicago's Magnificent Mile. Unfortunately, the good life of the 1920s was on a collision course with the collapse of the U.S. stock market. Because the hotel's mortgage wasn't yet paid off, the bank took possession of the property. It was a devastating loss for Popperfuss, and he suffered a nervous breakdown. He died in 1938 at age fifty-one.

ILLINI LORE

The University of Illinois observed the one-hundredth anniversary of the birth of Abraham Lincoln on February 8, 1909, with a campus-wide celebration. The exercises included a convocation, an exhibit of Lincoln memorabilia, and addresses on several aspects of Lincoln's service as U.S. president.

This statue of Abraham Lincoln still stands in Urbana

1909–10

AMERICA'S TIME CAPSULE

August 2, 1909	The U.S. Mint produced the first Lincoln-head pennies.
February 6, 1910	The Boy Scouts of America organization was chartered by Chicago publisher William Boyce.
March 16, 1910	Auto racer Barney Oldfield set a land speed record of 133 miles per hour.
June 19, 1910	Spokane, Washington, became the first city to celebrate Father's Day.
January 10, 1910	Joyce Clyce Hall began America's first greeting card company. It was renamed "Hallmark" in 1954.

ILLINI
MOMENT

Illini "9" Beats Chicago in Seventeen-Inning Marathon

The May 20, 1910, baseball matchup between the Universities of Illinois and Chicago was described by the UI campus newspaper as "the most brilliant game ever played on Illinois Field." When the marathon ended after three hours and twenty minutes, Coach George Huff's Illini won their tenth consecutive game, a streak that would eventually climax at 14–0 and result in a Western Conference championship. Illinois's John Buzick went the entire distance on the mound, as did his counterpart, UC's Pat Page. With the score tied at one run apiece, Page lost the game in the bottom of the seventeenth inning when Illinois's Ray Thomas led off with a double, moved to third on a sacrifice by E. B. Righter, then scored when Page uncorked a wild pitch. The Illini went on to win their final four games and wound up as the first conference baseball team in history to finish with an unblemished overall record.

Pitcher John Buzick

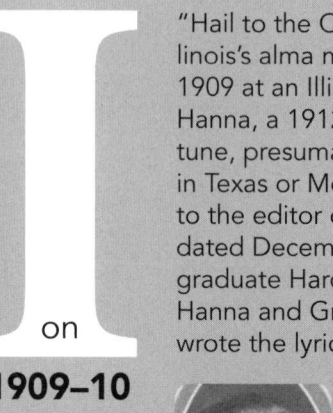

I on **1909–10**

"Hail to the Orange," the University of Illinois's alma mater, originated in the fall of 1909 at an Illinois Glee Club meeting. Paul Hanna, a 1912 UI grad, introduced the tune, presumably an old song with origins in Texas or Mexico. He indicated in a letter to the editor of the Illinois Alumni News, dated December 22, 1958, that 1911 UI graduate Harold Hill chorded the song; Hanna and Gregory Vigeant Jr. (UI '12) wrote the lyrics.

Harold Hill

Gregory Vigeant

Paul Hanna

ILLINI ITEM

The first Western Conference outdoor track and field meet held at a site other than Chicago occurred on June 4, 1910, at Champaign. Though Illinois was the top-finishing conference team, it placed third behind Notre Dame and Stanford. It wasn't until 1926 that only conference teams were allowed to participate in the outdoor championship meet.

1910 Illini track-and-field team

ILLINI LISTS

1910 BASEBALL TEAM'S PERFECT SEASON

Coach George Huff's 1910 Fighting Illini baseball team made history, finishing as the school's first unbeaten team. Included among the fourteen overall victories were eleven conference victories. It was Huff's seventh Big Ten championship club and his sixth in a span of eight years. Depending on the pitching of John Buzick, who completed all ten of the games he started, Illinois yielded just two runs per game. Huff's typical starting lineup:

Roger "Fatty" Huff

P—John Buzick	2B—Edwin "Midget" Righter, captain (.280)
P—Henry Penn	SS—Harry Weber (.200)
P—Claude Van Gundy	3B—Bobby Quayle (.244)
C—Roger "Fatty" Huff (.287 batting average)	RF—Ray Thomas (.268)
1B—Charles "Bo" Bunn (.147)	CF—Lloyd "Monk" Schwartz (.148)
	LF—Glenn Butzer (.175)

ILLINI LEGENDS

Clarence Williams and Elmer Ekblaw

Clarence Williams and Elmer Ekblaw aren't familiar names to even the most ardent Fighting Illini fans, but their accomplishment back in 1910 definitely earns them a niche in University of Illinois history. Williams, better known as "Dab," and Ekblaw, the editor of the *Daily Illini*, conceived the very first Homecoming during the fall of 1909. They presented the idea to Shield and Trident, a senior honorary society, and then called upon UI President Edmund James and Dean Thomas Arkle Clark. A year later, during that first Homecoming weekend (October 14–16, 1910) more than fifteen hundred UI graduates returned to campus, nearly one-third of the school's alumni. The culmination of the inaugural Homecoming weekend was a 3–0 victory by the Illini football team over the University of Chicago. Illinois's Otto Seiler kicked a field goal to provide the final margin.

Clarence Williams   Elmer Ekblaw

ILLINI LORE

Lincoln Hall

On August 10, 1909, President William Abbott of the Board of Trustees presided over the laying of the cornerstone for Lincoln Hall—dedicated three and a half years later, on February 12, 1913, the 104th anniversary of Abraham Lincoln's birth.

Students rub "Honest Abe's" nose in Lincoln Hall for good luck before a big test

1910–11

AMERICA'S TIME CAPSULE

November 8, 1910	In congressional elections, the Democratic party took control of Congress for the first time in sixteen years.
November 14, 1910	Civilian pilot Eugene Ely successfully launched a naval aircraft for the first time from the deck of a warship, the cruiser *Birmingham*.
March 25, 1911	New York City's Triangle Shirtwaist factory fire claimed 146 lives.
May 30, 1911	Ray Harroun won the first Indianapolis 500 automobile race.
June 16, 1911	The Computing-Tabulating-Recording (CTR) Company originated. In 1924, CTR was renamed International Business Machines (IBM).

ILLINI MOMENT

1910 Big Ten Football Champions

The University of Illinois football team's unbeaten, unscored-upon season of 1910 is a feat duplicated only nineteen times in the history of college football. Though Coach Arthur Hall's squad wasn't an offensive juggernaut, averaging just thirteen points per game, it was an immovable force when it came to playing defense. In fact, their opponents rarely crossed the Illinois fifty-yard line the entire season! The Illini opened their campaign with easy nonconference victories over Millikin and Drake before the school's historic first Homecoming game on October 15, a 3–0 win over Chicago. Two weeks later, Illinois shut out Purdue, then blanked Indiana and Northwestern on consecutive Saturdays to wrap up the school's very first Western Conference title. Otto Seiler kicked his third game-winning field goal of the year in the season finale at home against Syracuse to give the Illini a perfect 7-0 record.

This poster featured Illinois's 1910 "perfect team"

I on **1910–11**

Louis Bernstein was a two-sport star at the University of Illinois, lettering in both basketball (1910, 1911) and football (1909, 1910). A product of Chicago's Medill High School, he captained the Illini hoops squad as a senior and earned second-team All-Conference honors. Bernstein eventually became a civil engineer with the American Bridge Company in Gary, Indiana.

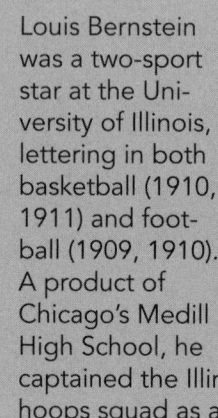

Louis Bernstein

ILLINI ITEM

The University of Illinois won its first men's Western Conference gymnastics title on April 22, 1911, over host Chicago, 1104.50 to 1016.25. Illinois's Edward Styles, R. J. Roarke, Edward Hollman, and Harry Geist all captured individual championships.

UI's 1911 gymnastics team

ILLINI LISTS

HOMECOMING THRILLERS

October 15, 1910	Illinois 3, Chicago 0
(UI's first-ever Homecoming game, the first of its kind in the nation)	
November 3, 1923	Illinois 7, Chicago 0
(UI's first-ever game at Memorial Stadium; Red Grange scored a touchdown)	
October 18, 1924	Illinois 39, Michigan 14
(Dedication game of Memorial Stadium)	
November 4, 1939	Illinois 16, Michigan 7
(UI beat UM and future Heisman Trophy winner, Tom Harmon)	

Action at Illinois's first-team Homecoming football game

October 27, 1956	Illinois 20, Michigan State 13
(UI beat ninth-ranked Spartans)	
October 26, 1968	Ohio State 31, Illinois 24
(No. 2 Buckeyes scored winning TD with 1:30 left)	
October 15, 1983	Illinois 15, Ohio State 13
(Illini beat No. 6 Buckeyes)	
October 20, 1990	Illinois 15, Michigan State 13
(Doug Higgins kicks game-winning field goal with 0:42 left)	

ILLINI LEGEND

Glenn Butzer

The premier performer during the 1910–11 athletic season at the University of Illinois was a young man whose teams tasted defeat only twice in twenty-seven contests. Not only did Glenn Butzer captain the University of Illinois's greatest football team ever in 1910, he was also the leading hitter on the 1911 Western Conference champion baseball team. On the gridiron, the Hillsdale, Illinois, native was a Walter Camp All-American as one of the game's finest linemen. The 1910 Illini football squad posted a perfect 7-0 record and never allowed its opponents to score a point. On the diamond, Butzer excelled as a left fielder. Although a large man, he possessed exceptional speed. The Illini "9" cruised to the Western Conference title, beating runner-up Purdue by five full games with a 14-1 league record. Following his athletic career at Illinois, Butzer served as city superintendent of highways of Livingston County and also for several years as city engineer in Pontiac, Illinois. He died of cancer November 13, 1935, at age forty-six.

Glenn Butzer

ILLINI LORE

U.S. President William Howard Taft visited the University of Illinois on February 11, 1911. Taft arrived at 8:50 A.M. and was driven to Illinois Field, where he reviewed the cadet regiment. He then took a tour of the campus grounds, delivered a five-minute address at the Illinois Central Station, and then left for Springfield, all in less than an hour.

President William Howard Taft

1911–12

AMERICA'S TIME CAPSULE

September 22, 1911   Pitcher Cy Young beats Pittsburgh, 1-0, for his final career victory, number 511.
November 10, 1911   Andrew Carnegie established the Carnegie Corporation with an endowment of $125 million.
February 14, 1912   Arizona was admitted to the union as the forty-eighth state.
April 12, 1912   The National Biscuit Company introduced the Oreo cookie.
April l5, 1912   About fifteen hundred people perished when the British liner Titanic struck an iceberg and
         sank off the coast of Newfoundland.

ILLINI
MOMENT

Illinois Wins Its First Swimming Title

The University of Illinois's men's swimming program had traditionally languished at or near the bottom of the Big Ten standings. But for the first three seasons of conference meets from 1911 to 1913, Coach Ed Manley's Illini set the standard of excellence. Perhaps Illinois's greatest team was its 1912 squad, winner of the Western Conference championship by seventeen points over second-place Northwestern. The Illini weren't a one-man team that year, but it would be difficult to overlook the monumental contribution by captain Bill Vosburgh. The Illini junior accounted for four individual titles—at 40, 100, 220, and 440 yards—and was the anchor of Illinois's championship relay squad. Vosburgh also took third place in a since-discontinued event called "plunge for distance," wherein swimmers dive into the water and, without taking a breath or moving arms or legs, attempt to torpedo themselves as far as possible through the pool in sixty seconds.

1912 swimming team

I on 1911–12

Paul Belting graduated from Illinois in 1912 as a twenty-five-year-old, two-time all-conference guard for Coach Bob Zuppke. But little did the Mattoon native know that his career in intercollegiate athletics was just beginning to bloom. Following thirteen years as a high-school administrator, Belting was hired as director of athletics at the University of Iowa on March 13, 1924. He became a driving force behind the construction of both the Iowa Fieldhouse and the school's new fifty-thousand-seat football stadium. Unfortunately, Belting was forced to resign from Iowa in 1929 in the wake of an alumni slush fund scandal.

Paul Belting

ILLINI ITEM

Edward Styles won his second consecutive individual all-around championship on April 11, 1911, leading the University of Illinois gymnastics squad to its second-straight team title, 1174.75 to 957.25, over Wisconsin.

Edward Styles

ILLINI LISTS

ILLINOIS'S BIG TEN MEN'S TEAM TITLES (through 2015–16)

Baseball	30 titles
Fencing	30 titles
Outdoor Track	29 titles
Gymnastics	27 titles
Indoor Track	21 titles
Tennis	18 titles
Wrestling	17 titles
Basketball	17 titles
Football	15 titles
Golf	14 titles

Illini track-and-field team of 1912

ILLINI LEGEND

Coach Ed Manley

Ed Manley

For forty-one years, the name Ed Manley was synonymous with University of Illinois swimming. He was lured to Urbana-Champaign by UI athletic director George Huff in 1912 from Springfield, Missouri, where he served as an aquatic instructor. Manley's Illini swimming teams captured Western Conference titles his first two years at Illinois and placed among the top five in the league twenty-four times. He also developed twenty conference champions in the sports of water polo and water basketball, directing those teams to dual-meet victories nearly 75 percent of the time. Manley called 1930s performer Chuck Flachmann his greatest single performer. The veteran coach was honored posthumously in 1975 when the university named the historic Huff Gym natatorium the Edwin Manley Memorial Pool. Manley died in 1962 at age seventy-five.

ILLINI LORE

In response to a request from the Athletic Department that its needs be given more consideration in future planning of the campus, Professor James White, supervising architect of the University of Illinois, submitted a new campus scheme to the board of trustees on October 5, 1911. The proposal included extensive additions to the university's land holdings, with particular view toward providing playgrounds to compensate for the utilization of the area south of the auditorium for building sites. White suggested that the entire tract of land between the campus and the Illinois Central railroad be acquired. Less than ten years later, a portion of that tract was reserved for the construction of Memorial Stadium.

UI's campus in 1912

1912–13

AMERICA'S TIME CAPSULE

November 5, 1912   Democrat Woodrow Wilson won the U.S. presidency in a landslide victory.
December 28, 1912   The first municipally owned streetcars took to the streets in San Francisco, Calif.
February 2, 1913   Grand Central Terminal, the world's largest railway station, opened in New York City.
May 31, 1913   The Seventeenth Amendment, providing for the popular election of U.S. senators,
                 went into effect.
July 28, 1913   The U.S. won the Davis Cup tennis challenge for the first time in eleven years.

ILLINI MOMENT

Illinois Wins Conference Wrestling Championship

Illinois and Minnesota shared the title at the first-ever Western Conference Wrestling Championship, held April 19, 1913, at Madison, Wisconsin. Junior lightweight G. W. Schroeder, Illinois's captain, was his team's only individual winner, defeating Albert Gran of Iowa. Illini wrestlers M. F. Leichsenring, a middleweight, and J. B. Colombo, wrestling in the "special" division, both were runners-up at their weights. It was the final season of Illinois coach Alexander Elston's brief two-year career. The Illini wrestling program went on to dominate the conference through the 1930s, capturing thirteen team titles, more than any other school.

1913 UI wrestling team

I on 1912–13

February 8, 1913: Kappa Alpha Nu, the first African American fraternity on the University of Illinois campus, was organized. The group's name was later changed to Kappa Alpha Psi. Charter member Earl B. Dickerson was influential in working with Elder Watson Diggs to expand the fraternity in its early years.

Kappa Alpha Nu was UI's first African American fraternity

ILLINI ITEM

Swimmer Bill Vosburgh

Illini swimmer Bill Vosburgh wrapped up his sensational career at the 1913 Western Conference championships by capturing three individual titles and anchoring the first-place UI relay squad. During his three years at Illinois, including his final season as team captain, Vosburgh claimed ten individual conference championships and swam on two relay winners, an all-time record at that time. He competed on the U.S. Olympic Water Polo team at Antwerp, Belgium, and was inducted into the USA Water Polo Hall of Fame in 1981. Vosburgh died in 1953 at age sixty-three.

ILLINI LISTS

WINNINGEST MARGINS BY ILLINOIS FOOTBALL TEAMS

84 pts	Illinois 87, Illinois Wesleyan 3 (October 5, 1912)
80 pts	Illinois 80, Iowa 0 (November 27, 1902)
79 pts	Illinois 79, Illinois College 0 (October 19, 1895)
73 pts	Illinois 79, Illinois Normal 6 (September 16, 1944)
68 pts	Illinois 75, Rolla Mines 7 (October 9, 1915)
67 pts	Illinois 67, Butler 0 (October 3, 1942)

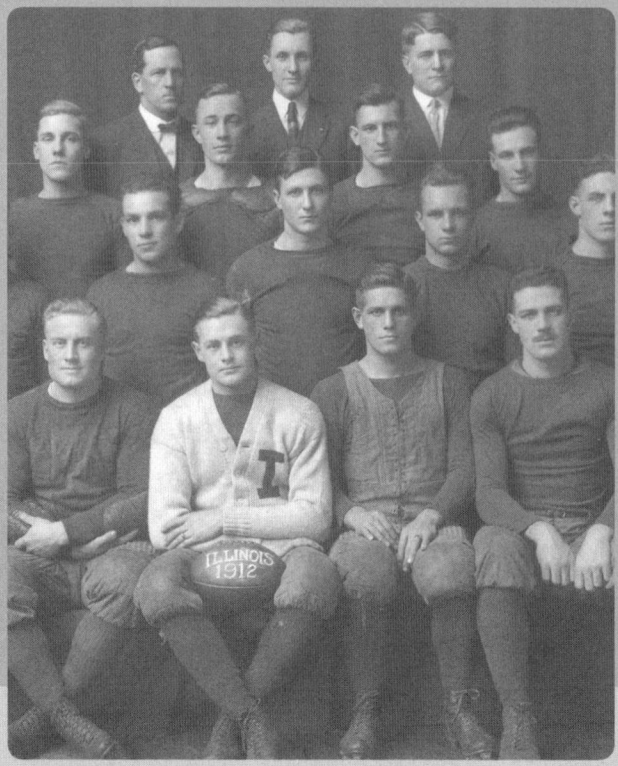

Illinois's 1912 football team

ILLINI LEGEND

Ralph Chapman

His parents presented him with the distinguished appellation of Ralph Dwyer Clinton Chapman. His classmates knew him best as "Slouie." And Bob Zuppke, the legendary coach of the Fighting Illini, touted him as one of the greatest players he ever coached. Whatever you called him, it would be difficult not to call Ralph "Slouie" Chapman the University of Illinois's best athlete of his day. A native of Vienna, Illinois, the 180-pound Chapman was named by the legendary Walter Camp as a consensus All-American performer following his sensational senior season in 1914. The captain of Illinois's first national championship club was known for his speed, aggressiveness, and fighting spirit. Following his graduation in 1915, Chapman answered the call to arms when the United States entered World War I. He was wounded in action and underwent a series of operations. Upon his discharge, Chapman entered the brokerage business in Chicago; he once served as vice president of the University of Illinois Foundation. Chapman died in 1969 at age seventy-seven.

Ralph "Slouie" Chapman

ILLINI LORE

Officials broke ground for the University of Illinois Armory on September 18, 1912. Completed in 1915 at a cost of $702,000, the ninety-eight-foot-high roof is supported by fourteen three-hinged arches. The outer section of military offices and classrooms was not completed until 1927. The Armory has been the site of Fighting Illini track meets since 1916.

The skeleton of the Armory began to appear in 1913

44

1913–14

AMERICA'S TIME CAPSULE

December 21, 1913   The first crossword puzzle (with thirty-two clues) was printed in the New York World.
December 23, 1913   President Woodrow Wilson reformed the American banking system by establishing the Federal Reserve System.
April 22, 1914   Babe Ruth played his first professional game, hurling a 6–0 shutout for the Baltimore Orioles.
May 7, 1914   A congressional resolution established the second Sunday in May to be celebrated as Mother's Day.
August 5, 1914   The first electric traffic light was installed in Cleveland, Ohio.

ILLINI MOMENT

Men's Track Team Dominates Conference Meets

The University of Illinois track and field program had become a dominant force in the Western Conference under Coach Harry Gill. It was a rare occasion when the talented Illini lost a dual meet, and equally rare when they failed to win the conference title. During the 1914 season, Illinois performed at a level that allowed the team to cruise to both the indoor and outdoor conference championships. The Illini were a superbly balanced outfit, scoring points in nearly every event. Indoors at Evanston, Illinois waltzed to a nine-point victory over Wisconsin. Outdoors at Chicago, the Illini's winning margin was twenty-two points, led by Fred Henderson's victories in the 440- and 880-yard runs. "You have a wonderful track team," wrote Cornell coach John Moakley to Gill. And who could argue with that?

Illinois's 1913 mile-relay team

I on **1913–14**

Frank Bane was a dual-sport star at Illinois, starting for both the basketball and baseball teams. A native of Chicago, he earned second-team All–Big Ten honors after leading the 1914–15 Illini basketball team to a perfect 16-0 record, the conference title, and the mythical national championship. The 1915 UI baseball team excelled as well, compiling an 18-1-1 record and capturing the league championship. Bane eventually became a farm advisor, settling with his family in Pontiac, Illinois. He died in 1969 at age seventy-six.

Frank Bane

ILLINI ITEM

Illinois's baseball team defeated league-leading Chicago, 4–3, on May 29, 1914, to win the conference title for the first time in three years. Illini pitcher Walt Halas, the older brother of football immortal George Halas, went the distance on the mound in a driving rainstorm.

Walt Halas was the younger brother of George Halas

ILLINI LISTS

ILLINI FOOTBALL COACHES' FIRST CONTRACTS

Bob Zuppke	$1,500 (1913)
Ray Eliot	$6,000 (1942)
Pete Elliott	$18,000 (1960)
Jim Valek	$18,500 (1967)
Bob Blackman	$25,000 (1971)
Gary Moeller	$35,000 (1977)
Mike White	$50,000 (1980)
John Mackovic	$70,000 (1988)
Lou Tepper	$120,000 (1992)
Ron Turner	$150,000 (1997)
Ron Zook	$5 million over five years (2005)

Bob Zuppke, the subject of this 1937 book by Red Grange, earned three-and-a-half times less in his first season as Illini coach ($1,500 in 1913) than Lovie Smith did in his first day ($5,479.45)

Tim Beckman	$9 million over five years (2012)
Bill Cubit	$2.4 million over two years (2015)
Lovie Smith	$21 million over six years (2016)

ILLINI LEGEND

Bob Zuppke

Robert Carl Zuppke was introduced to the world in 1879, just ten years after college football's inaugural game in New Brunswick, New Jersey. Thirty-five years later, the native of Berlin, Germany, would establish the University of Illinois as the home of the 1914 national football champions. By the time he retired in 1941, Zuppke's twenty-nine teams captured three more national titles—1919, 1923, and 1927—and seven Big Ten crowns. He was football's most innovative coach, being credited with such originations as the huddle, the screen pass, and the "flea flicker." Among the stars Zuppke tutored were consensus All Americans Chuck Carney, "Red" Grange, and Bernie Shively. He was honored in 1951 by being selected a charter member of college football's Hall of Fame. Zuppke died in 1957 at age seventy-eight. On November 12, 1966, Memorial Stadium's playing field was named in his honor.

Robert Carl Zuppke

ILLINI LORE

Edward A. Doisy, a 1914 graduate of the University of Illinois, shared the Nobel Prize in medicine in 1943 for isolating and determining the composition of vitamin K. This vitamin stimulates the production of prothrombin as a major element in blood clotting. Seventeen years earlier, in 1926, Doisy isolated estrone, a sex hormone. He died October 23, 1986, at age ninety-two.

Nobel Prize winner
Edward Doisy

1914–15

AMERICA'S TIME CAPSULE

October 19, 1914 — The U.S. Post Office first used an automobile to collect and deliver mail.

January 25, 1915 — Alexander Graham Bell placed the first successful transcontinental telephone call from New York City to San Francisco.

February 8, 1915 — D. W. Griffith's famous motion picture *Birth of a Nation* opened in Los Angeles.

April 5, 1915 — Jess Willard defeated Jack Johnson in twenty-three rounds to win the world heavyweight boxing title.

May 7,1915 — A German submarine sank the British steamship *Lusitania*; nearly twelve hundred passengers drowned.

ILLINI
MOMENT

Illini Basketball Team Nips Chicago

On March 6, 1915, Illinois's undefeated basketball team faced its biggest challenge of the season, a game at the University of Chicago against the second-place Maroons. Coach Ralph Jones's Illini trailed by 11–9 at the halftime intermission, and the teams traded baskets for most of the second half, with the lead going back and forth. Only a minute remained when Chicago star George Stevenson threw in a field goal, and the Maroon fans began to celebrate the apparent upset victory over their downstate rivals. However, the Illini regained the lead thirty seconds later when senior Frank Bane wove through the Chicago defense for the game-winning basket. Illinois's 19–18 triumph improved its league record to 11-0 and clinched the school's first-ever Western Conference basketball title. Their 16-0 overall record that season marks the only time in Illini history that perfection has been achieved.

UI's 1915 basketball team

I on **1914–15**

Illinois's 1914 football team was retroactively crowned the mythical national co-champion with Texas by the Billingsley Report and as a national co-champion with Army by historian Parke H. Davis. Coach Bob Zuppke's squad boasted a stcount defense, not allowing its opponents a point until game 5, when it topped Minnesota, 21-6. UI concluded its magnificent season on November 21 in Madison against Zup's alma mater, the Wisconsin Badgers, highlighted by Harold Pogue's sixty-five-yard touchdown gallop. The Illini outscored their foes by a combined total of 224 to 22, winning the Big Ten title with a perfect 6-0 record.

1914 Illini football star Harold Pogue

ILLINI ITEM

Edward Williford, leading scorer of the 1915 Fighting Illini basketball team, was the University of Illinois's first Big Ten Conference Medal of Honor recipient. The award has been given annually since that year at each conference institution to the student athlete who demonstrates proficiency in scholarship and academics.

Edward Williford was UI's first recipient of the Big Ten Conference Medal of Honor

ILLINI LISTS

ILLINOIS NATIONAL CHAMPIONS (Teams)

Men's Gymnastics	10 (1939, 1940, 1941, 1942, 1950, 1955, 1956, 1958, 1989, 2012)
Men's Track and Field	5 (1921, 1927, 1944, 1946, 1947)
Football	4 (1914, 1919, 1923, 1927)
Fencing	2 (1956, 1958)
Men's Tennis	1 (2003)

The game program from UI's 1914 Homecoming game

ILLINI LEGEND

Perry Graves

Perry Graves

At 5'6" and 148 pounds, Perry Graves looked more like a gymnast than an All-America football player. Even back when he played in 1913 and 1914, Graves was small by Big Ten standards, but all who went against him quickly realized he was a powerhouse. During Graves's senior season, Coach Bob Zuppke's Fighting Illini posted a perfect 7-0 record, won the Big Ten championship, and shared the national title with Army. A native of Rockford, Graves played freshman ball at the University of Pittsburgh but returned to his home state to compete for Illinois. He also played baseball for Coach George Huff's Illini, starring as a shortstop and a third baseman as Illinois went on to win the Big Ten title. Graves was the owner and operator of the Robinson (Illinois) Lumber and Coal Company for several years and served as a Big Ten football official for twenty-two seasons. He died in 1979 at age eighty-nine.

ILLINI LORE

During the summer of 1915, the west addition of what is now known as the Henry Administration Building was completed. The $1.45 million office space served as home of the registrar and dean of men on the first floor, as offices for the architect and the comptroller on the second floor, and as headquarters for President Edmund James and the Alumni Association on the third floor.

The University of Illinois Administration Building

1915–1924

1915–16

AMERICA'S TIME CAPSULE

October 13, 1915   The Boston Red Sox won the World Series from the Philadelphia Phillies.
December 1915   The millionth Model T rolled off Ford's assembly line in Detroit.
March 9, 1916   Legendary Mexican bandit "Pancho" Villa led fifteen hundred guerrillas across the border, killing seventeen Americans in New Mexico.
June 30, 1916   Charles Evans won the U.S. Open golf tournament.
August 4, 1916   The United States purchased the Virgin Islands from Denmark for $25 million.

ILLINI MOMENT

"Red" Gunkel's No-Hitter

Coach George Huff's 1916 Fighting Illini pitching staff was nearly flawless during its Western Conference slate, allowing a total of just ten runs in nine league games. The strongest arm belonged to a wiry, red-headed senior named Woodward "Red" Gunkel. Red's finest game came on May 5, 1916, at Illinois Field when he pitched a no-hitter against the Ohio State Buckeyes, 4–0. Gunkel pitched to only twenty-eight men in his nine innings of work, striking out twelve batters, while notching his third of four consecutive shutouts. The Illini wound up taking the conference title that season with an 8-1 record.

Woodward "Red" Gunkel

I on 1915–16

Bernhard Halstrom scored the only Illini touchdown in 1915's victory at Chicago

Playing before a crowd of 24,087 at the University of Chicago's Stagg Field on November 20, 1915, Illinois's football team beat the host Maroons, 10–0, and in the process gained a share of the Big Ten football title. Hyde Park grad Bernhard Halstrom scored the game's only touchdown in the first quarter. The Illini finished with a 3-0-2 conference record and a 5-0-2 overall mark.

ILLINI ITEM

Illinois's basketball team won twenty-five games in a row from February 21, 1914, through February 9, 1916. Included in the streak were seventeen consecutive Western Conference victories in which the Illini competition averaged fewer than fourteen points per contest. Northwestern snapped UI's nearly two-year-long skein on February 12, 1916, winning a 23–21 decision in overtime.

Action at the new gymnasium

ILLINI LISTS

LONGEST ILLINI MEN'S BASKETBALL WINNING STREAKS
IN CONFERENCE PLAY

25	January 31, 2004, through March 3, 2005
17	February 21, 1914, through February 9, 1916
15	January 20, 1951, thru February 2, 1952
14	March 7, 1942, through January 3, 1944
13	February 23, 1924, thru February 21, 1925
13	February 26, 1955, thru February 20, 1956
9	February 24, 1941, thru February 7, 1942
9	February 7, 2002, thru January 11, 2003

ILLINI LEGEND

Ray Woods

Ray Woods

Nowadays, Ray Woods's name is outshone by such basketball luminaries as George Mikan, Bill Russell, and Oscar Robertson. But in 1917 the spotlight was on Woods, when he was recognized as America's greatest college basketball player. As a three-year Fighting Illini letterman under Coach Ralph Jones from 1915 to 1917, Woods became the University of Illinois's first first-team All-American player. Though he never led his team in scoring or shooting, as did his twin brother Ralf, no one was a better allaround ball-handler or defender or leader than Ray Woods. The crafty guard from Evanston led the Illini to a cumulative record of forty-two victories against only six losses in three seasons. Two of those three teams—1915 and 1917—were Western Conference champions, while the 1916 club finished as the league runner-up. Woods died in Berwyn, Illinois, in 1965 at age seventy.

ILLINI LORE

On April 14, 1916, former University of Illinois regent Thomas J. Burrill died of pneumonia, eleven days short of his seventy-seventh birthday. He served on the UI faculty from 1868 to 1912, rising from a position as a horticulture instructor to acting head of the university in just eleven years. Burrill served as the official regent (president) from 1891 to 1894, establishing the UI's graduate school during that tenure.

Thomas Burrill

1916–17

AMERICA'S TIME CAPSULE

September 30, 1916 — The New York Giants' twenty-six-game winning streak, baseball's longest ever, was halted by the Boston Braves.

November 7, 1916 — Woodrow Wilson was reelected president of the United States.

February 3, 1917 — The United States severed diplomatic relations with Germany due to increased submarine warfare.

March 2, 1917 — The Jones Act made Puerto Rico a U.S. territory.

April 2, 1917 — President Wilson requested a declaration of war against Germany.

ILLINI MOMENT

The Illini Upset Minnesota's "Perfect Team"

The November 5 edition of the *Chicago Record-Herald* screamed out in bold type: "HOLD ON TIGHT WHEN YOU READ THIS!" And for good reason. In one of the greatest upsets in college football history, Coach Bob Zuppke's undermanned Illinois club had handed Minnesota's "perfect team" its only loss of the 1916 season, 14–9. The Illini led 14–0 at halftime on first-quarter touchdowns by captain Bart Macomber (one-yard run) and Ren Kraft (fifty-yard interception return). Minnesota narrowed the gap in the third quarter by scoring a touchdown and adding a safety, but Zuppke's men hung on in the final stanza for the victory at Minneapolis. Just how good were the Gophers? Well, other than its loss to Illinois that year, Minnesota compiled a flawless 6-0 record by outscoring its opponents 339–14.

Action from the 1916 Illinois-Minnesota game

1916 football team

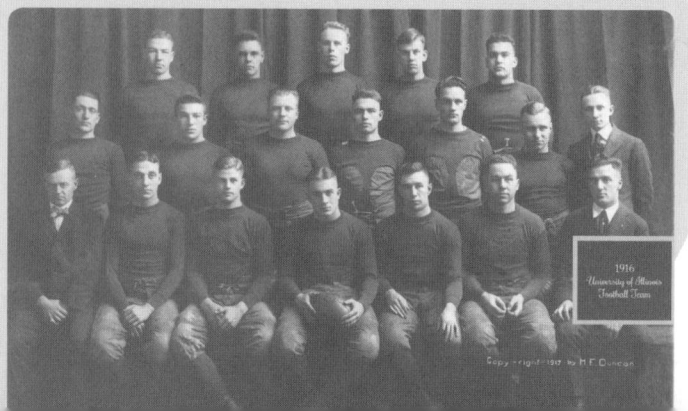

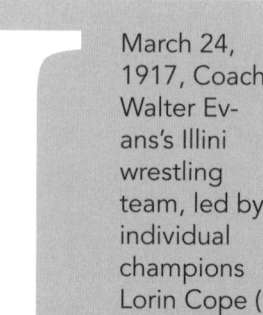 on 1916–17

March 24, 1917, Coach Walter Evans's Illini wrestling team, led by individual champions Lorin Cope (158 pounds) and E. V. Jurtzrock (145 pounds), won the Big Ten Championship in Iowa City, Iowa. Illinois scored twenty-one team points, seven more than runners-up Iowa and Indiana.

1917 Illini wrestling team

ILLINI ITEM

Illinois shared the Western Conference basketball title with Minnesota in 1917, with each team recording a mark of 10-2. Coach Ralph Jones's squad won its last six games of the season, including an 18–17 victory over the co-champion Gophers on February 10 at Urbana.

UI's 1917 basketball team

ILLINI LISTS

GEORGE HALAS CHRONOLOGY

George Halas

1895	Born February 2 in Chicago
1918	Graduated from the University of Illinois
1919	Named player of the game in the 1919 Rose Bowl, playing for Great Lakes
1919	Ended baseball career with New York Yankees (replaced by Babe Ruth)
1920	Organized the American Professional Football Association, forerunner of the NFL, which involved the Decatur Staleys
1925	Signed Red Grange from the University of Illinois
1933	Led Bears to NFL Championship
1940	Coached Bears to 73–0 massacre over Washington in NFL title game
1963	Won his final NFL championship, 14–10, over New York Giants
1968	Retired permanently as coach of the Bears
1983	Succumbed to cancer on October 31

ILLINI LEGEND

Young George Halas

George Halas

George Halas became famous for his moniker "Papa Bear," but his athletic career at the University of Illinois spanned much further than just the football field. He lettered in baseball, basketball, and football for the Illini from 1916 to 1918, starring in each sport. Halas graduated from the U of I in 1918 with a degree in civil engineering, but his life took a detour when he enlisted in the navy for service in World War I. When the war ended, he played baseball for a season with the New York Yankees. However, an injury ended his baseball career, and Halas turned to his first love—football. He was a driving force in giving birth to the National Football League in 1920, and brought credibility to the league five years later when he signed Illini running back "Red" Grange to a $100,000 Chicago Bears contract. During his forty-year coaching career with the Bears, Halas won more games (326) than any other NFL coach in history. He died October 31, 1983, at age eighty-eight.

ILLINI LORE

Nearly five million Americans served their country during World War I, including 9,442 faculty, staff, and students from the University of Illinois; 183 men and one woman from the Urbana-Champaign and Chicago campuses lost their lives in the war. The names of those 184 individuals are commemorated on the columns of Memorial Stadium.

Memorial Stadium's colonnade

AMERICA'S TIME CAPSULE

October 15, 1917	The Chicago White Sox defeated the New York Giants to win the World Series.
November 3, 1917	U.S forces engaged in their first World War I battle in Europe.
December 18, 1917	The U.S. Constitution's Eighteenth Amendment was passed, outlawing the manufacture, transportation, and sale of alcoholic liquors.
May 15, 1918	Airmail service began between New York City and Washington, D.C.
June 25, 1918	American forces halted the Germans in the Battle of Belleau Wood in France.

ILLINI
MOMENT

Fighting Illini Athletics and World War I

World War I put a crimp in the University of Illinois's athletic program during the 1917–18 season, as only football, basketball, baseball, and track were among the teams that competed on a varsity level. None of the four squads were conference champions, though baseball and outdoor track both finished runners-up to Michigan. Illinois's other sports—gymnastics, wrestling, tennis, cross-country, and fencing—were all suspended during the war years, with most not reinstated for competition until the 1919–20 season. Among Illinois's most famous World War I servicemen was three-sport star George Halas, who enlisted in the navy in January 1918. The university would later honor its war dead with the construction of Memorial Stadium.

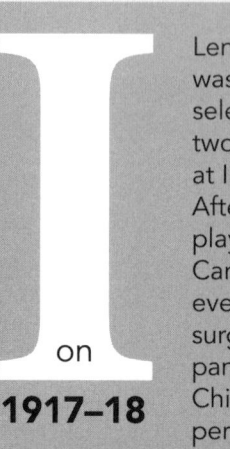 

I on 1917–18

Len "Tank" Charpier was an all-conference selection in each of the two seasons he lettered at Illinois (1916, 1917). After one season of playing for the Racine Cardinals (1920), he eventually became a surgeon at Little Company of Mark Hospital in Chicago. Charpier experimented with using blood from recently deceased cadavers for transfusions. His work didn't come to light until thirteen years after Charpier's death in 1960. Former assistant Donald Farmer, who by then was director of the Beverly Blood Center in Chicago, published an article about Charpier's work in the *Bulletin of the American Association of Blood Banks*.

Len Charpier

ILLINI ITEM

Two fighting Illini letter-winning athletes died in the service of their country during World War I. They were Homer Dahringer, who lettered for the basketball team in 1912 and 1913, and Edward Wallace, a 1911 baseball letter winner. The names of these men are engraved on two of the two hundred columns that support the east and west sides of Memorial Stadium.

This U of I service flag was located at the entrance to campus

Homer Dahringer (left) and Edward Wallace died in service during World War I

ILLINI LISTS

BOB ZUPPKE'S CONSENSUS ALL-AMERICAN
FOOTBALL PLAYERS

1914	Ralph Chapman, G
1914	Perry Graves, E
1915	Bart Macomber, HB
1918	John Depler, C
1920	Charles Carney, E
1923	Jim McMillen, G
1923–1925	Harold "Red" Grange, HB
1926	Bernie Shively, G

Ralph Chapman served
with the Marines during
World War I

ILLINI LEGEND

John Depler

One of the premier football players at the University of Illinois during the war years was a center from Lewistown, Illinois, named John Depler. Depler's All-American career with Coach Bob Zuppke's Illini was dotted with success; he was a key member of the 1918 and 1919 Western Conference champions. Illini teams won fourteen of seventeen conference games during his playing career. Following his graduation in 1919 from Illinois, Depler coached for eight seasons at Columbia University. In 1930 he organized and was co-owner of the Brooklyn Dodgers professional football team. Depler spent several years of his life operating hotels and restaurants. Upon his retirement, he wrote a newspaper column for the *Fulton County (Illinois) News* and was presented with the Illinois State Historical Society's "Individual Award for Regional History Writing." Depler died in 1970 at age seventy-one.

John Depler

ILLINI LORE

In the November 15, 1917, edition of the *Alumni Quarterly*, the University of Illinois announced that "plans for an elaborate celebration of the 50th birthday of the university have been abandoned," due to World War I. The celebration was to have centered around a "great pageant" to depict the history of the institution that opened for business March 2, 1868. Instead, the UI was asked to raise $20,000 as its share in the state's effort to collect $3 million for support of American servicemen.

World War I soldiers marching past Champaign's First National Bank

AMERICA'S TIME CAPSULE

September 11, 1918   The Chicago Cubs lost the World Series to the Boston Red Sox.
November 9, 1918   Kaiser Wilhelm II of Germany abdicated.
November 11, 1918   World War I ended on the eleventh hour of the eleventh day of the eleventh month.
June 11, 1919   Walter Hagen won the U.S. Open golf tournament.
July 4, 1919   Jack Dempsey won the world heavyweight boxing title with a technical knockout against the defending champion, Jess Willard.

ILLINI
MOMENT

Illini Gridders Claim Conference Title

Just five days after the Germans surrendered to end World War I, University of Illinois students had cause to celebrate another major event. On November 16, two-time defending Big Ten champion Ohio State came to Illinois Field to face Coach Bob Zuppke's Fighting Illini. Illinois took charge immediately, marching down the field for a touchdown on its first possession. That 7–0 halftime lead was increased to the eventual final score of 13–0 in the third quarter. The Illini wrapped up a perfect 4-0 Big Ten season (all four wins coming by shutouts) the following Saturday with a 29–0 win over Chicago. Zuppke wanted to play undefeated Michigan for an unscheduled winner-take-all game on December 7, but the proposed playoff game was vetoed by UI's Council of Administrators. Ohio State coach Jack Wilce, whose team's twenty-two-game unbeaten streak ended, told the press afterward, "We met both Illinois and Michigan, and there is no comparison. Illinois is, by far, the better."

A capacity crowd attended Illinois's 1919 Homecoming game at Illinois Field

I on 1918–19

November 11, 1918: Wrote *News-Gazette* reporter Tom Kacich in his 2002 book, *Hot Type: 150 Years of the Best Local Stories from the News-Gazette*, "The celebration of the end of the World War must have been the most jubilant and chaotic day in the history of Champaign-Urbana." University of Illinois classes were canceled so that its band could lead a 10 A.M. celebratory parade. "Oh, what a crowd," the *News-Gazette* reported. "What a seething, shouting, joy-mad mass. No pen could picture it. No man or woman who looked upon that mass will ever forget it."

ILLINI ITEM

On October 26, 1918, Illinois hosted the Municipal Pier football team in a game at Illinois Field. The Fighting Illini lost the game (7-0), but no one complained. That's because the game was played behind closed gates, due to an influenza epidemic that had begun in September in Champaign-Urbana. Throughout the state, more than thirty-two thousand people died. Champaign Township reported there were more deaths (310) than births (301) during the year.

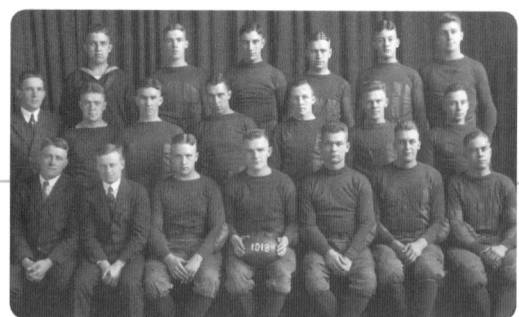

UI's 1918 football team

ILLINI LISTS

WINNINGEST ILLINI MEN'S BASKETBALL COACHES
(by percentage)

	W	L	Pct.
Bill Self (2001–2003)	78	24	.765
Ralph Jones (1913–1920)	85	34	.714
Doug Mills (1937–1947)	151	66	.696
Harry Combes (1948–1967)	316	150	.678
Bruce Weber (2004–2012)	210	101	.675
Lou Henson (1976–1996)	423	224	.654
Lon Kruger (1997–2000)	81	48	.628
Craig Ruby (1923–1936)	148	97	.604

Illini basketball coach
Ralph Jones

	W	L	Pct.
John Groce (2013–2017)	95	75	.559
Harv Schmidt (1968–1974)	89	77	.536

ILLINI LEGEND

Kenneth "Tug" Wilson

Kenneth "Tug" Wilson admitted that it was a long way from Atwood to Antwerp, but that's exactly where his athletic career led him. Born in Atwood, Illinois, a little town thirty miles south of the University of Illinois, Wilson enrolled at the UI in the fall of 1916 after two years of teaching at a country school near his home. He was a fantastic athlete, winning five varsity letters in basketball and track and field. On the hardwood, Wilson led the Illini in scoring as a junior and was the team's captain his senior year. Athletically, his greatest accomplishment came in the summer of 1920 when he was a member of the United States Olympic team, competing at Antwerp, Belgium, in the javelin and discus. Wilson began his career in athletic administration at Illinois under George Huff, then spent three years at Drake and twenty-one years at Northwestern as athletic director. In 1945 he resigned from Northwestern to become Major John Griffith's successor as commissioner of the Big Ten Conference. Tug Wilson died February 1, 1979, at age eighty-two.

Illini star "Tug" Wilson eventually became commissioner of the Big Ten Conference

ILLINI LORE

An entertaining part of campus life at the University of Illinois during the first three decades of the twentieth century was the annual Interscholastic Circus. The 1919 version of the circus, described by UI's *Alumni Quarterly* magazine as "a roaring furnace of farce," attracted more than seven thousand students, faculty, and staff. Highlights of the May 31 festivities included clowns, acrobats, and swimming coach Ed Manley's "plunge from a dizzy height of 50 feet into a shimmering, seething tank of fiery water."

The 1919 Interscholastic Circus parade

AMERICA'S TIME CAPSULE

September 26, 1919   President Wilson suffered a stroke during a national tour.

October 9, 1919   Amid a swirl of rumors about game fixing, the Chicago White Sox lost the World Series to the Cincinnati Reds.

April 20, 1920   The Olympic Games began in Antwerp, Belgium.

January 17, 1920   The Eighteenth Amendment, passed two years earlier, took effect, establishing the prohibition of alcoholic beverages in the United States.

July 5, 1920   Governor James Cox of Ohio became the Democrats' presidential nominee.

ILLINI MOMENT

Fletcher Field Goal Beats Ohio State

The Illini traveled to Ohio State for the 1919 season finale with both the Big Ten championship and the national title on the line. Coach Bob Zuppke's men trailed the Buckeyes 7–6 with just five minutes left in the game. Quarterback Lawrence Walquist and end Chuck Carney connected for three pass completions, putting the Illini deep into Ohio State territory. With only twelve seconds remaining in the game and Illinois place kicker Ralph Fletcher out with an ankle injury, Coach Zuppke called upon Ralph's younger brother, Bob, to kick a game-winning twenty-five-yard field goal—*the first field goal he'd ever attempted in a game!* The 9–7 victory gave Illinois its second national championship.

The *Ohio State Lantern* headline told the story

EXTRA **Ohio State Lantern** EXTRA

By the Students of the Ohio State University Department of Journalism

VOL. XXXIX. No. 50.   COLUMBUS, OHIO, SATURDAY, NOVEMBER 22, 1919.   PRICE FIVE

ILLINOIS DEFEATS BUCKEYE

Quarters	1	2	3	4	Total
OHIO STATE	0	0	7	0	7
ILLINOIS	6	0	0	3	9

AMES TEAM WINS RUN; OHIO FINISHES FIFTH IN FAST RACE

TRUSTEES IN FAVO OF STARTING WO ON ATHLETIC BO

I on 1919–20

Born on November 6, 1893, Clarence Applegran starred for the Illini football and basketball squads in 1915–16. Then, following service in World War I, he returned in 1919 earning All-America honors. Applegran played pro football in Detroit in 1920, then joined Washington University in 1921 as the basketball coach. Two years later, he became head coach of the Kentucky Wildcats. Applegran re-enlisted for service in World War II, rising to the rank of colonel. He returned to his hometown of Chicago and was a high school coach at Bowen, Crane Tech, Hirsch, and South Shore. Following his death in 1960 at age sixty-six, South Shore High School placed a bronze plaque on a wall that read: "CLARENCE APPLEGRAN: builder of men."

Clarence Applegran

ILLINI ITEM

On March 20, 1920, Illinois's mile-relay team of Phil Donohoe, John Prescott, Phil Spink, and Bob Emery set an indoor conference record of 3:29 in the final event, giving the Illini track team the conference title over Michigan, 31⅝ to 27½.

The baton used by the 1920 Illini mile-relay team

ILLINI LISTS

LONGEST CONTINUOUS TENURES AS ILLINI
ASSISTANT FOOTBALL COACH

Justa Lindgren	40 years (1904–1943)
Ralph Fletcher	22 years (1942–1963)
Burt Ingwersen	20 years (1945–1964)
Leo Johnson	15 years (1942–1956)
Mel Brewer	13 years (1947–1959)
Greg McMahon	13 years (1992–2004)
Robert King	11 years (1947–1957)
Milt Orlander	11 years (1924–1934)
Gene Stauber	11 years (1960–1970)
J. C. Caroline	10 years (1967–1976)

Justa Lindgren served forty
years as an assistant coach
for UI's football staff

ILLINI LEGEND

Burt Ingwersen

Burt Ingwersen

Burt Ingwersen was, literally, a man for all seasons at the University of Illinois. After the Fighting Illini football season was completed, he'd lace up his sneakers for duty with Coach Ralph Jones's basketball team. And after the basketball stopped bouncing, Ingwersen would race back out to Illinois Field to play first base for Coach George Huff's Illini baseball squad. He earned nine varsity letters altogether from 1917 to 1920, receiving all-star acclaim in football. Following graduation, Ingwersen joined the UI coaching staff, handling the freshman football and baseball squads. In 1924 Ingwersen succeeded Howard Jones as Iowa's head football coach, compiling a record of 33-27-4 in eight seasons as the Hawkeye mentor. After Iowa, he made assistant coaching stops at Louisiana State and Northwestern. In February 1943 Ingwersen was commissioned a lieutenant commander in the U.S. Navy, serving as head football coach. Two years later, he was transferred to the Naval Air Technical Training Center in Chicago, where he also served a brief stint as athletic director. Ingwersen rejoined Coach Ray Eliot's UI football staff in the fall of 1945, retiring in 1965. He died on July 17, 1969, at age seventy.

ILLINI LORE

Formal instruction in athletic coaching began during the fall of 1919 as a regular department in the University of Illinois College of Education. Athletic Director George Huff had been running successful coaching sessions for several summers, but up until this time, students in those classes never received actual course credit. Out of 136 credit hours required for graduation, students enrolled in the athletic curriculum had to complete studies in thirty-four hours of practical coaching and physical education. Among the graduates were Floyd "Shorty" Stahl, who went on to coach basketball at Ohio State; Otto Vogel, head baseball coach at Iowa; and Bernie Shively, athletic director at Kentucky for thirty years.

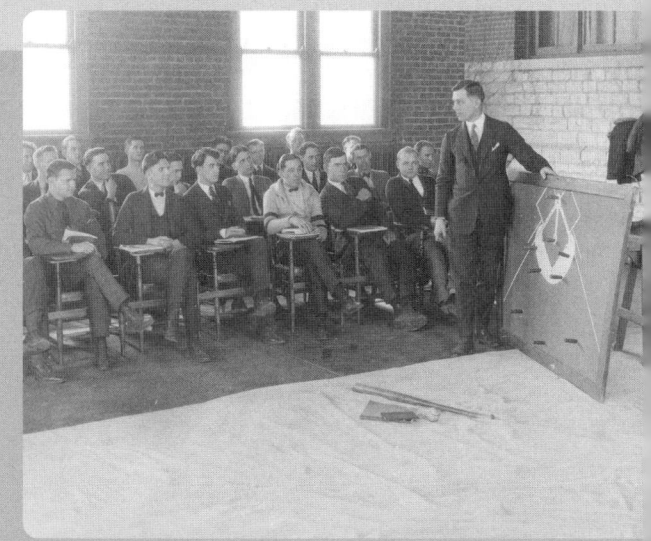

Carl Lundgren teaches a class
at UI's famous Coaching School

1920-21

AMERICA'S TIME CAPSULE

September 17, 1920	In Canton, Ohio, twelve teams paid $100 each to join the American Professional Football Association.
September 28, 1920	Eight members of the Chicago White Sox were indicted on charges of taking bribes to throw the 1919 World Series.
November 2, 1920	Warren Harding was elected U.S. president. Radio station KDKA in Pittsburgh broadcast the results of the presidential election, the first time that happened.
June 29, 1921	Elizabeth Ryan and Bill Tilden claimed Wimbledon tennis titles.
July 2, 1921	Jack Dempsey successfully defended his heavyweight boxing title.

ILLINI MOMENT

Fund Drive for New Stadium

The old gym annex looked like the Chicago Coliseum during the Republican convention on that twenty-fifth day of April, 1921. Every seat was filled as bands played and horns tooted. On the platform were university executives and distinguished Illini athletes and coaches. President David Kinley first spoke to the masses, then Athletic Director George Huff followed. When the ovation ceased, Huff said, "I want to see a great stadium at the University of Illinois. The stadium will be many things—a memorial to Illini who have died in the war, a recreational field, and an imposing place for our varsity games. But it will also be an unprecedented expression of Illinois spirit." Then football coach Bob Zuppke spoke, his hands rigidly clasped behind his back. After a few minutes, Zup ended with his request for voluntary donations of $1,000 for the stadium. Finally, following a few seconds of silence, a Latin-American student named R. L. Cavalcanti shouted out, "I will give, sir!" Within ten minutes, more than $700,000 of the $2.5 million needed to build the great structure had been pledged by the undergraduate student body.

BUILD THAT STADIUM FOR FIGHTING ILLINI

I on 1920-21

On the heels of the 1919 World Series scandal involving the Chicago "Black Sox," athletic director George Huff decided to wage an anti-betting campaign on the University of Illinois campus. "The gambler is the greatest foe of athletics that there is," said Huff to a *Daily Illini* reporter on September 28, 1920. "Gambling has ruined every sport upon which it has taken a hold." Huff then urged Champaign and Urbana business men to stop all betting on their premises and to discourage all talk of wagers. To those businessmen who agreed, a placard was posted, stating: "In order to do its part toward protecting college sport from harmful influence, this place will refuse to hold bets on University of Illinois athletic contests."

George Huff

ILLINI ITEM

First Dad's Day game: The University of Illinois hosted intercollegiate football's first "Dad's Day" on November 20, 1920. Unfortunately, Coach Bob Zuppke's Illini dropped a 7–0 decision to Western Conference champion Ohio State at Illinois Field.

Block I salutes "Dad" on Dad's Day

ILLINI **LISTS**

ILLINI NCAA TRACK AND FIELD TEAM CHAMPIONSHIPS

Illinois won the NCAA's very first outdoor track and field championship on June 18, 1921, even though the team didn't win a single individual title.

Year	Champion	Runner-Up	Site
1921	Illinois, 20¼	Notre Dame, 16¾	Chicago
1927	Illinois, 35⅖	Texas, 29½	Chicago
1944	Illinois, 79	Notre Dame, 43	Milwaukee
1946	Illinois, 78	Southern Cal, 42^{85}/$_{100}$	Minneapolis
1947	Illinois, 59⅔	Southern Cal, 34⅙	Salt Lake City

The 1921 Illinois track-and-field team won the NCAA's inaugural championship

ILLINI **LEGEND**

Chuck Carney

The greatest of athletes are honored following their careers by being selected to their particular sport's hall of fame. It's inconceivable that one man could be honored by two different sports' halls of fame, but that's exactly what former University of Illinois football and basketball star Chuck Carney could proudly claim. At 6'1" and 196 pounds, Carney was an outstanding receiver for Bob Zuppke's Illini from 1918 to 1921, earning consensus All-American honors his junior year. On the basketball court his sophomore year, he set a Western Conference record by scoring 188 points in twelve league games, a record that stood for twenty-two years. Carney also led the conference in scoring during his senior season and was named college basketball's player of the year. He coached football at Northwestern, Wisconsin, and Harvard before entering the investment banking business at the New York Stock Exchange. Carney died in 1984 at age eighty-four.

Chuck Carney starred with both the Illini football and basketball teams

ILLINI **LORE**

President David Kinley began his ten-year term at the University of Illinois on September 1, 1920. The sixty-year-old Scottish-born professor of economics was vice president and dean of the graduate school during the term of his predecessor, Edmund James. The Kinley period was highlighted by the completion of several projects begun by James. Among the facilities constructed in Kinley's decade of service were Memorial Stadium, Smith Music Hall, the Library, and McKinley Hospital.

President David Kinley

1921–22

AMERICA'S TIME CAPSULE

September 8, 1921 — Margaret Gorman of Washington, D.C., won the title of the first Miss America.
November 11, 1921 — The "Unknown Soldier" of World War I was buried at Arlington National Cemetery.
February 5, 1922 — The first *Reader's Digest* magazine was published.
May 30, 1922 — The Lincoln Memorial, designed by UI student Henry Bacon, was dedicated in Washington, D.C.
July 15, 1922 — Gene Sarazen won the U.S. Open golf tournament.

ILLINI
MOMENT

Crowd of Fifteen Thousand Sees Illini "9" Beat Michigan

The boisterous crowd of fifteen thousand gathered to watch their heroes at Illinois Field that 20th day of May, 1922, completely encircled the baseball diamond. And Coach Carl Lundgren's Illini didn't disappoint the faithful throng, pounding three Michigan hurlers for twelve hits en route to a 7–3 victory over the conference leaders. Third baseman Harry McCurdy was the hitting star for the Illini that afternoon, drilling two of Illinois's seven doubles. Wally Roettger relieved UI starter C. L. Jackson on the mound in the seventh inning, shutting out the Wolverines the rest of the way. Illinois clinched its second consecutive Western Conference title three days later at home, defeating Purdue 5–3.

Game action at Illinois Field

I on 1921–22

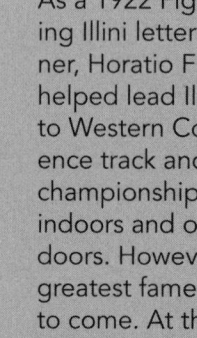

Horatio Fitch

As a 1922 Fighting Illini letter winner, Horatio Fitch helped lead Illinois to Western Conference track and field championships, both indoors and outdoors. However, his greatest fame was yet to come. At the 1924 Summer Olympics in Paris, Fitch set a record in the semifinals of the 400 meters (0:47.8). An hour later, he finished second in the finals behind Scotland's Eric Liddell, a scene that was immortalized in the movie *Chariots of Fire*. Following a lengthy career in construction engineering, Fitch died at age eighty-four in 1985.

ILLINI ITEM

Bob Zuppke first met Red Grange on May 20, 1922, when Grange was on the University of Illinois campus participating in a high school track meet. After witnessing Grange win the 220-yard dash, Zuppke commented to the youngster, "I think you have a chance to make our team.

Red Grange (left) and Bob Zuppke

ILLINI LISTS

ZUPPKEISMS

The hero of a thousand plays becomes a bum after one error.

All quitters are good losers.

A man has to lose before he can appreciate winning.

If the team wins all of its games, the alumni are loyal.

Victory in football is 40 percent ability and 60 percent spirit.

I don't care how big or how strong our opponents are, as long as they're human.

My definition of an All-American is a player who has weak opposition and a poet in the press box.

Never prophesy a great football future for any back until he has gained his first yard and taken his first bump.

No athletic director holds office longer than two unsuccessful football coaches.

Never let hope elude you. That is life's biggest fumble.

ILLINI LEGEND

Paul Prehn

The most prosperous University of Illinois coach in terms of Big Ten success was wrestling mentor Paul Prehn. During his coaching career from 1920 to 1928, Prehn's Fighting Illini grapplers dominated the sport in conference action. Illinois won Big Ten titles seven times in nine seasons and had an impressive dual-meet record of 42-5. Among Prehn's individual stars were Illini wrestling legends Allie Morrison and Hek Kenney. When he left the University of Illinois, Prehn began a highly successful restaurant business in Champaign-Urbana. He also served as chairman of the Illinois Athletic Commission for four years, a period that included the Jack Dempsey–Gene Tunney "Battle of the Century" boxing match in Chicago. Prehn also served as the state director for the Illinois Republican Party for ten years. The World War I veteran from Mason City, Iowa, died on May 10, 1973, at age eighty.

Paul Prehn

ILLINI LORE

In the spring of 1922, a four-hundred-watt transmitter using the call letters WRM went into operation in the University of Illinois Electrical Engineering Laboratory. The listeners' favorite programming included the bands, the glee clubs, and the scores of Fighting Illini athletic teams, but the few alumni who owned radio sets asked for more. In 1926 Boetius Sullivan, a wealthy UI alumnus, presented the university with a radio station in memory of his father. The station was later shifted to 890 KC, and the call letters were changed to WILL.

The original WRM-WILL radio studio

1922–23

AMERICA'S TIME CAPSULE

October 4, 1922	Famed sportswriter Grantland Rice reported the first radio play-by-play coverage of the World Series.
March 3, 1923	*Time* magazine debuted. The weekly news magazine, featuring House Speaker Joseph Cannon on its first cover, sold for fifteen cents.
March 13, 1923	Motion pictures with sound were first demonstrated in New York City.
July 15, 1923	Golf amateur "Bobby" Jones won the U.S. Open.
August 2, 1923	President Warren Harding died of an embolism while recovering from an attack of ptomaine poisoning.

ILLINOIS MOMENT

Illinois's First Conference Golf Title

The first of seven all-time Big Ten golf championships for the University of Illinois was registered by Coach George Davis's team on June 19, 1923. Evanston Golf Club was the site for Illinois's five-stroke victory over defending champ Chicago, 643 to 648. The Maroons whittled nine strokes off the Illini's firstday, fourteen-stroke lead, but the one-two punch of UI's Rial Rolfe and John Humphreys was ultimately too much to overcome. Rolfe, a product of Chicago Senn High School, also captured Illinois's first-ever individual title, defeating teammate Gustav Novotny by four strokes.

UI's 1923 golf squad

I on 1922–23

Jim McMillen was an All-American guard for Coach Bob Zuppke in 1922 and went on to a five-year career with the Chicago Bears. He transitioned into professional wrestling and, due to his notoriety as a teammate of Red Grange, participated in numerous feature bouts. During World War II, McMillen was a lieutenant commander in the U.S. Navy. His business and civic service began at the conclusion of the war; he served as the mayor of Antioch, Illinois, for six years. In his later years, McMillen was a gentleman farmer. He died at age eighty-one in 1984.

All-American guard Jim McMillen

ILLINI ITEM

Illinois's track and field squad lost the Big Ten outdoor meet to host Michigan on June 2, 1923, 57½ to 57. Despite a victory by the Illini in a record time of 3:20 in the mile relay, the referee ordered the race rerun when a misplaced hurdle caused a Michigan runner to miss a step and fall. Coach Harry Gill's Illini refused to run again, and the referee canceled the event altogether, handing Michigan the team title.

1923 Illini track-and-field team

ILLINI LISTS

ILLINI TRACK AND FIELD OLYMPIC GOLD MEDALISTS

1912	Ed Lindberg, 1,600-meter relay (second leg), 3:16.6
1924	Harold Osborn, high jump, 6'5¹⁵⁄₁₆"
1924	Harold Osborn, decathlon, 7710.755 points
1952	Bob Richards, pole vault, 14'11¼"
1952	Herb McKenley,* 1,600-meter relay (second leg), 3:03.09
1956	Bob Richards, Pole vault, 14'11½"

*Member of Jamaican Olympic team

ILLINI LEGEND

Harold Osborn

Just how outstanding a track and field athlete was the University of Illinois's Harold Osborn? He was so good that he was one of twenty-six people selected as charter members of the National Track and Field Hall of Fame, joining such greats as Ralph Boston, Bob Mathias, Wilma Rudolph, and Jesse Owens. Osborn is the only competitor in Olympic history ever to win an individual-event gold medal (the high jump), as well as the gold medal in the decathlon, registering a world record in both events! While a member of the Illini track team, Osborn led Illinois in indoor and outdoor Western Conference crowns in 1920, 1921, and 1922. From 1922 to 1933, Osborn was a coach and teacher at Champaign High School (now Champaign Central). He was an osteopathic physician in Champaign from 1939 until his retirement. Osborn died in 1975 at age seventy-five.

Harold Osborn

ILLINI LORE

During the 1922–23 school year, the University of Illinois ranked as America's third largest institution of higher learning. A total of 9,285 full-time students were enrolled at Illinois, more than at than any other U.S. university except the University of California (14,061) and Columbia University (10,308). The Universities of Michigan and Minnesota ranked fourth and fifth. At the time, Illinois had more architecture students than any other (237) and ranked second in the country in its number of commerce students (2,044).

The University of Illinois's three towers

AMERICA'S TIME CAPSULE

October 16, 1923   Brothers Walt and Roy Disney founded the Disney Cartoon Studio.
October 29, 1923   The Charleston, a dance named for the harbor city of Charleston, S.C., was introduced in the Broadway show *Runnin' Wild*.
January 25, 1924   The first Winter Olympics were held in Chamonix, France; the Americans finished fourth in the unofficial team standings.
April 17, 1924   Metro-Goldwyn-Mayer Studios (MGM) was founded in Beverly Hills, California.
June 30, 1924   The Teapot Dome oil leasing scandal indicted several oil company presidents on charges of bribery and conspiracy to defraud the United States.

ILLINI
MOMENT

Memorial Stadium Makes Its Debut

Illinois's football team made its debut at Memorial Stadium a successful one, defeating the University of Chicago, 7–0, on November 3, 1923. Construction of the stadium, begun just fourteen months before, was not totally completed, but athletic director George Huff had pledged that the imposing structure would be ready for the Illini Homecoming game of 1923. Red Grange—who else?—scored the first and only touchdown in that inaugural game, rushing twenty-four times on the muddy field for 101 yards. It rained hard all afternoon, and because the stadium's walkways weren't yet completed, several hundred of the 60,632 fans were forced to abandon their shoes and boots in the mud. Tickets, priced at $2.50

This poster promoted the first-ever game at Memorial Stadium

each, yielded record gate-sale receipts of more than $132,000 to the UI Athletic Association.

I on **1923–24**

Bernard A. Strauch isn't a name with which most Fighting Illini athletics fans are familiar, but chances are they've viewed examples of his work. In fact, not only did the 1910 UI graduate and longtime Champaign businessman (Strauch Photo Center) photograph George Huff, Red Grange, and other famous Illinois coaches and athletes for a period of more than fifty years, he also recorded thousands of images of campus and student life. A charter member of Champaign's Camera Club, Strauch died in 1967 at age eighty-four.

Photographer Bernard Strauch took this photo of The Galloping Ghost

ILLINI ITEM

Coach Craig Ruby's Illini basketball team clinched a tie for the Western Conference title on March 10, 1924, with a 31–19 victory over Minnesota. Senior Leland "Slim" Stilwell, in the final game of his career, was blanked from the field but converted eleven free throws. Stilwell later returned to the University of Illinois to serve as the school's team physician.

A capacity crowd watched this 1924 Illini basketball game

ILLINI LISTS

MEMORIAL STADIUM CONSTRUCTION STATISTICS

- 56-acre tract of land
- 2,700 tons of steel
- 800 tons of reinforcing bars
- 4.8 million bricks
- 50,000 barrels of cement
- 7,200 tons of cut stones
- 404 miles of lumber
- 17 miles of seats, covered by 21 acres of paint
- First spade of earth turned by George Huff on September 11, 1922

Director of Athletics George Huff threw the initial shovel of dirt at Memorial Stadium's ground breaking

First game in the stadium was held on November 3, 1923, 418 days after ground breaking

Final cost of construction by English Brothers of Champaign: $1.7 million (the equivalent of that amount in 2016: nearly $24 million)

ILLINI LEGEND

HAROLD "RED" GRANGE

The legendary Harold "Red" Grange

Those who call Harold Edward "Red" Grange the greatest college football player of all time have plenty of facts to back up their braggadocio. They'll point out that he was the first winner of the *Chicago Tribune*'s Silver Football Award as the Big Ten's Most Valuable Player. They'll mention that he was a charter member of both college and professional football's Hall of Fame. And they'll conclude that the Galloping Ghost was a unanimous selection on the alltime All-America team. So talented was Grange that the number 77 he wore on his back during his career at Illinois from 1923 to 1925 was immediately retired by the university. So recognizable was his name that, in his very first game as a pro, Grange turned what would have been a normal Chicago Bears' gathering of less than five thousand into a standing-room-only crowd of thirty-six thousand. Upon Grange's death in January 1991 at age eighty-seven, UI athletic director John Mackovic summed up Grange's life by saying, "Red Grange has been, and will always be, one of the largest legends in the game of football. His presence will continue to be felt as long as the game is played."

ILLINI LORE

The cornerstone for the University of Illinois's new McKinley Memorial Hospital was laid May 10, 1924. The original structure, completed in the fall of 1925 at a cost of $225,000, didn't include the north and south wings presently on the building. Senator W. B. McKinley, a student senator at the UI in the 1870s, was the benefactor of the campus's first health facility. Each student who joined the hospital association that first year paid fees of $3 per semester and was afforded a maximum of twenty-eight days' free care.

McKinley Memorial Hospital

1924–25

AMERICA'S TIME CAPSULE

November 4, 1924 — Calvin Coolidge was reelected president, defeating Democrat John Davis.

November 27, 1924 — The Macy's Christmas Parade began in New York City.

January 5, 1925 — Nellie Ross of Wyoming became the first woman governor in U.S. history.

June 2, 1925 — Manager Miller Huggins inserted Lou Gehrig into the Yankees lineup after Wally Pipp complained of a headache. That began a record consecutive-games streak of 2,130 games.

July 21, 1925 — John Scopes, a former University of Illinois student, was convicted for teaching the theory of human evolution to his public-school students.

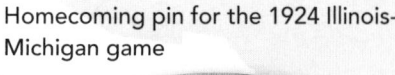

Homecoming pin for the 1924 Illinois-Michigan game

ILLINI MOMENT

The Wheaton Iceman Gallops over Michigan

October 18, 1924, is, quite understandably, the most memorable single day in University of Illinois sports history. Not only was it the afternoon the university's imposing Memorial Stadium was officially dedicated, but it was also the day when one of America's greatest football legends—Red Grange—was christened. During the first twelve minutes of the game, the Wheaton Iceman scored touchdowns the first four times he touched the ball, on runs of ninety-five, sixty-seven, fifty-six, and forty-four yards. He later returned to score a fifth TD on an eleven-yard run and also threw for a sixth Illini score. When the final gun sounded, Grange had piled up 276 yards of total offense and had 126 yards in kickoff returns. Illinois beat mighty Michigan by the unlikely score of 39–14.

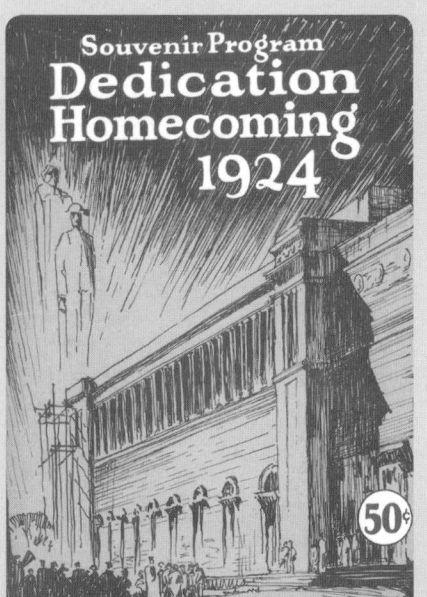

The game program for Memorial Stadium's dedication

I on **1924–25**

October 11, 1924: "Block I" initially took up its position in the east stands near the forty-yard line. Two years later, each of the four-hundred-plus members of the block was given one orange and one blue plywood card. On the command of the block leader, members held up the appropriate colored card for a particular stunt, creating simple designs. In 1984, personal computers were used for the first time to input stunt design data.

Illinois's famed "Block I"

ILLINI ITEM

The *Chicago Tribune* awarded the first Silver Football Trophy to the University of Illinois's Red Grange following the 1924 season, honoring him as the Big Ten's Most Valuable Player. Grange rushed for a career-high 743 yards on only 113 carries and scored a school-record thirteen touchdowns.

The *Chicago Tribune*'s original Silver Football Award

ILLINI LISTS

ILLINI WHO PLAYED (OR COACHED) IN THE WORLD SERIES

Fred "Cy" Falkenberg (1903, Pittsburgh)

Garland "Jake" Stahl (1903, 1912, Boston [manager])

Carl Lundgren (1906, 1907, 1908, Chicago Cubs)

Frank Pfeffer (1910, Chicago Cubs)

Wally Roettger (1928, St. Louis)

Lou Boudreau (1948, Cleveland)

John Brittin (1950, Philadelphia)

Lou Skizas (1959, Chicago White Sox)

Tom Haller (1962, San Francisco)

Ed Spiezio (1964, 1967, 1968, St. Louis)

Pitcher Frank Pfeffer

Ken Holtzman (1972, 1973, 1974, Oakland)

Scott Spiezio (2002, Anaheim Angels; 2006, St. Louis Cardinals)

ILLINI LEGEND

UI's Wally Roettger

Wally Roettger

Like George Huff and Carl Lundgren before him, the University of Illinois's Wally Roettger became the third consecutive Fighting Illini baseball coach to return to his alma mater. Roettger was an outstanding player at Illinois from 1922 to 1924, with a career batting average over .300. As a junior in 1923, he hit .409, the fifth-best single-season average ever at that time. In six big-league seasons, Roettger played for his hometown St. Louis Cardinals, the New York Giants, and the Cincinnati Reds, batting a respectable .277 in 468 games. He also helped the Cardinals win the 1931 World Series title over Philadelphia. Roettger retired from the majors following the 1932 season to coach the baseball and basketball teams at Illinois Wesleyan. In 1934 Carl Lundgren, his mentor at Illinois, died suddenly of a heart attack. Athletic Director George Huff immediately chose Roettger as Lundgren's successor. In the next seventeen years, Roettger won four Big Ten titles and finished among the top three in eight other seasons; his record with the Illini baseball team was 212-111-7. However, all was not well with Roettger, and in 1951, he took his own life at age forty-nine.

ILLINI LORE

In the fall of 1924, the University of Illinois Alumni Association conducted a random survey of its graduates, polling them regarding their occupations, incomes, and spending habits. Of the 264 people who responded, the survey concluded that the average annual income for alumni was $7,031. Graduates who went on to become manufacturers led the way with an average yearly salary of $27,100, followed by architects ($14,960), physicians ($13,831), and bankers ($12,014). Of the 264 respondents, 108 owned their homes, while eighty-six were renters. Those who owned automobiles preferred Fords (forty-seven), a choice nearly three times the total of the second-most preferred cars, Buicks and Dodges (seventeen each).

1925–1934

1925-26

AMERICA'S TIME CAPSULE

September 3, 1925	The U.S. Army dirigible *Shenandoah* was wrecked in a storm near Ava, Ohio, killing fourteen people.
November 28, 1925	The Grand Ole Opry premiered as WSM Barn Dance on WSM radio in Nashville, Tennessee.
March 7, 1926	The American Telephone and Telegraph Company successfully demonstrated the first transatlantic radio-telephone conversation between New York City and London.
May 9, 1926	Rear Admiral Richard Byrd made the first successful flight over the North Pole.
August 6, 1926	Nineteen-year-old Gertrude Ederle of New York City became the first woman to swim the English Channel.

ILLINI
MOMENT

Illini Gridders Victorious at Penn

Red Grange's long touchdown run versus Penn

Red Grange's most famous college football game, of course, was his 1924 dismantling of Michigan at Memorial Stadium. But just as impressive was his performance on October 31, 1925, against the powerful University of Pennsylvania, gridiron rulers of the East. Bolstered by the 160-man UI marching band who had made the cross-country trip to Philadelphia, Coach Bob Zuppke's Illini handed their hosts a stunning 24–2 loss. The muddy Franklin Field turf didn't slow down Grange, who rushed for 237 yards on twenty-eight carries, the best performance of his career. Besides scoring three touchdowns, Grange returned two kickoffs for seventy-nine yards and caught two passes for thirty-five yards. Wrote Walter Eckersall of the *Chicago Tribune* afterward, "Whatever doubt there was in the minds of Eastern gridiron critics and coaches regarding the quality of Red Grange was settled once and for all today."

Franklin Field Illustrated
A PERIODICAL DEVOTED TO
PENNSYLVANIA ATHLETICS

ray

ILLINOIS & PENNSYLVANIA
OCTOBER · 31 · 1925   25 · CENTS

I on 1925–26

Illinois won its third of five consecutive wrestling titles in 1926, and among the team's roster were a pair of future Fighting Illini coaches. One was Harold "Hek" Kenney; the other was Glenn "Newt" Law. Law served as Kenney's assistant coach from 1929 through 1943, then became head coach when Kenney was called into service during World War II. Of his six seasons as head coach (1944–1946 and 1948–1950), Law's '46 Illini squad was the best, winning the Big Ten title and finishing third in the NCAA championship. He died April 30, 1950, from a heart attack at age forty-eight.

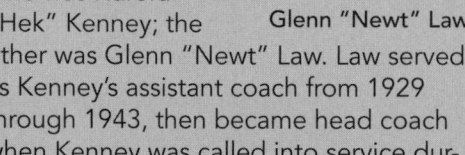

Glenn "Newt" Law

ILLINI ITEM

Two days after his final game with the University of Illinois football team on November 23, 1925, "Red" Grange signed a $100,000 contract to play football for Coach George Halas's fledgling Chicago Bears. Including his royalties for endorsements, Grange was reportedly making thousands of dollars weekly during his peak, but he asked his agent, C. C. Pyle, to limit him to a drawing account of a flat $100 per week.

Red Grange (left) and his manager C. C. Pyle

ILLINI LISTS

RED GRANGE'S BARNSTORMING TOUR

Red Grange and his stylish raccoon coat

In an effort to capitalize on the lure of their new star—Red Grange—George Halas and the Chicago Bears quickly arranged a nineteen-game nationwide barnstorming tour. Here are five memorable games that Grange and the Bears played during their sixty-six-day road trip.

November 26, 1925: Game 1—Grange made his pro debut at Cubs Park. A crowd of twenty thousand was expected, but a throng of more than seventy thousand crashed the gates to watch a 0–0 tie between the Bears and the Chicago Cardinals. (Grange: ninety-six yards rushing, intercepted pass)

December 5, 1925: Game 4—Bears top Frankford Yellow Jackets in Philadelphia before thirty-five thousand fans. (Grange: scored two TDs)

December 6, 1925: Game 5—Crowd of seventy-three thousand watched the Bears play the New York Giants at Polo Ground. (Grange: thirty-five-yard interception return for TD)

January 2, 1926: Game 13—Bears continued Florida swing with a victory over the Jacksonville All-Stars in Florida before sixty-seven hundred fans. (Grange: threw thirty-yard TD pass)

January 16, 1926: Game 15—Crowd of seventy-five thousand watched the Bears defeat the Los Angeles Tigers in California. (Grange: two TDs)

ILLINI LEGEND

UI tennis star
Tim O'Connell

Tim O'Connell

The University of Illinois's tennis program had, until recently, enjoyed only moderate team success during its history, but one Fighting Illini player still tops the Big Ten singles' list for individual achievement. Until tennis legend Marty Riessen came along at Northwestern in the early 1960s, the name Tim O'Connell of Illinois stood alone. O'Connell's serve-and-volley game won three consecutive Big Ten singles titles from 1926 to 1928, leading the Illini to team championships each of those seasons. He also was a two-time Big Ten doubles champ, giving him five individual titles altogether, second only to Riessen's six crowns. O'Connell continued his tennis pursuits after graduating from Illinois, earning amateur titles in both singles and doubles play. He worked for Union Carbide for nearly forty years. O'Connell died in June 1987 in San Mateo, California, at age eighty-two.

ILLINI LORE

The University of Illinois "New Gymnasium," later to be known as Huff Gym, opened for business with a basketball game between the Illini and Butler on December 12, 1925. The building was completed at a cost of $500,000—twenty cents per cubic foot. A $225,000 south wing, which included a swimming pool, was added a year later. Huff Gym had a capacity of seven thousand, double the size of its predecessor, the Men's Old Gym Annex. From 1925 through 1963, when the Assembly Hall opened, Illini basketball teams compiled a record of 339 victories against only 121 losses at Huff Gym.

Huff Gym hosts its first Illini basketball game

RED GRANGE AN ORIGINAL SUPERSTAR

The Legend of Harold "Red" Grange and his contributions to the University of Illinois and American society are almost larger than life. Here are some rarely seen photographs of the most famous Fighting Illini athlete of all time.

Margaret "Muggs" Grange salutes the crowd on the seventieth anniversary of Memorial Stadium's dedication

The famed "Wheaton Iceman"

Red Grange wore his famous Illini 77 jersey for the last time on November 21, 1925, at Ohio State

This Red Grange doll was a big seller in the 1920s

Red Grange (left) and Bronko Nagurski were teammates with the Chicago Bears

A poster for Red Grange's first movie, *One Minute to Play*

In the shadow of the stadium he made famous

Placed inside Zuppke Field in 1994, the Red Grange Rock came from the same stone quarry in Indiana used to form the granite columns of Memorial Stadium

The Galloping Ghost appeared on the cover of *Sports Illustrated*'s "Classic" issue in the fall of 1991

Illinois alum George Lundeen designed the twelve-foot, one-ton statue that stands on the west side of Memorial Stadium

Red Grange points to the portrait of his Illini coach, Bob Zuppke

Grange went on to become a noted broadcaster

1926–27

AMERICA'S TIME CAPSULE

September 23, 1926 — Gene Tunney defeated boxing champ Jack Dempsey in a heavyweight title fight in Philadelphia.

April 7, 1927 — Television was demonstrated for the first time in New York City, as Secretary of Commerce Herbert Hoover was seen and heard from his office in Washington, D.C.

May 20, 1927 — In a 33-hour flight, Charles Lindbergh left from Long Island, New York, for Paris, France, in his monoplane, The Spirit of St. Louis.

July 18, 1927 — Baseball's Ty Cobb collected his four-thousandth hit.

ILLINI MOMENT

Chief Illiniwek Debuts

The first appearance of the University of Illinois symbol, Chief Illiniwek, was October 30, 1926, at Memorial Stadium. Assistant marching band director Ray Dvorak is credited with starting the tradition at halftime of the 1926 Illinois-Pennsylvania football game. Sophomore Lester Leutwiler, a UI student interested in Indian lore, was the first Chief. In his recollection of that first performance, Leutwiler wrote, "As the band marched into the formation (spelling out the word "Penn"), the Chief ran from a hiding place north of the Illinois stands and led the band with his frenzied dance. The band stopped in the center of the field and played 'Hail Pennsylvania' while the Chief saluted the Penn rooters. William Penn, impersonated by (UI drum major) George Adams, came forward and accepted the gesture of friendship. Together, we smoked the peace pipe and walked arm in arm across the field to the Illinois side, amidst a deafening ovation." Leutwiler's performance was so well received that he was asked to continue his performances at future Illini football games.

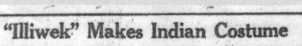

"Illiwek" Makes Indian Costume

Chief Illiniwek made his debut on October 30, 1926

I on 1926–27

Coach Carl Lundgren's 1927 Fighting Illini baseball team shared the Big Ten title with Iowa; two players who catapulted Illinois to its success were pitcher Raymond "Bud" Stewart and center fielder Ira Sweeney. Stewart was a stalwart on the mound, while Sweeney led Illini batters during conference games with a .314 average.

Bud Stewart (left) and Ira Sweeney

ILLINI ITEM

University of Illinois senior John Sittig set an American collegiate record with a time of 1:54.4 in the 880-yard run as the Fighting Illini track and field team captured the sixth annual NCAA championship in Chicago, June I, 1927.

John Sittig

ILLINI LISTS

CHIEF ILLINIWEK FACTS

Total number of Chief Illiniweks: thirty-six

First Chief Illiniwek: Lester Leutwiler, 1926–28

First Chief to appear in authentic American Indian regalia: Webber Borchers, 1930

First female Chief (Princess) Idelle Stitch, 1943

First brothers to perform as Chief: John Forsyth, 1957–59, and Ben Forsyth, 1960–63

First father-son to perform as Chief: Robert Bitzer, 1945–46, and John Bitzer, 1970–73

Most common home states of Chiefs: Illinois (thirty times) and Missouri (four times)

Chief Illiniwek's final appearance

Final Chief Illiniwek: Dan Maloney, 2006–07

Final performance: February 21, 2007

ILLINI LEGEND

Bernie Shively

When a list of the University of Illinois's finest all-around athletes is compiled, the name Bernie Shively always appears. Perhaps most famous as a guard running interference for the immortal Red Grange, Shively was selected as the Fighting Illini's eighth consensus All-America football player following the 1926 season. He was inducted into the College Football Hall of Fame in 1982. The former prep star from Paris, Illinois, also excelled on the wrestling mat, grappling to a draw with his heavyweight opponent from Indiana in the 1926 Big Ten championship match but losing on a coin toss. Shively was also a three-time letterman for the UI track and field squad, placing twice in conference championship competition as a hammer thrower. Altogether, he won eight varsity letters at Illinois. Following his graduation in 1927, Shively began a distinguished career at the University of Kentucky, culminating in a thirty-year career as director of athletics. He died in 1967 at age sixty-four.

Bernie Shively

ILLINI LORE

Famed sculptor Lorado Taft laid the cornerstone for the new $500,000 University of Illinois architecture building, November 16, 1926. In Taft's remarks at the ceremony, he paid homage to Professor Nathan C. Ricker, the father of Illinois architecture. The structure, located at the south end of the campus, brought together the instructors not only of architecture but also of art, design, sculpture, and other branches of the fine arts. The site of the three-story structure was formerly an apple orchard.

Nathan Ricker

The studio inside UI's architecture building

1927–28

AMERICA'S TIME CAPSULE

September 30, 1927 — Babe Ruth slugged his record-setting sixtieth home run for the Yankees.

October 6, 1927 — Based on a play by Illinois alumnus Samson Raphaelson, the world's first talking motion picture—*The Jazz Singer*—using the sound-on-film process was released.

November 13, 1927 — The Holland Tunnel, America's first underwater tunnel, was opened to traffic, linking New Jersey with Manhattan. Its ventilation system was designed by Illinois professor Arthur Willard.

July 30, 1928 — George Eastman demonstrated the world's first color motion pictures at Rochester, New York.

ILLINI MOMENT

Illini Gridders Claim the National Championship

A rock-ribbed defense was the hallmark of Coach Bob Zuppke's 1927 University of Illinois national championship football team. In five of its eight games, the Fighting Illini defensive unit had shutout efforts, while in two other games it yielded only a single touchdown. A 12–12 tie with Iowa State was Illinois's only flaw. The stars of Zuppke's team included All-America linemen Bob Reitsch, Russ Crane, and "Butch" Nowack. Among the key performers on the steady but unspectacular offensive team were backs Doug Mills, Frank Walker, and Fred Humbert, and end Jud Timm. Illinois's 5-0 Big Ten Conference record was good for first place ahead of 3-0-4 Minnesota.

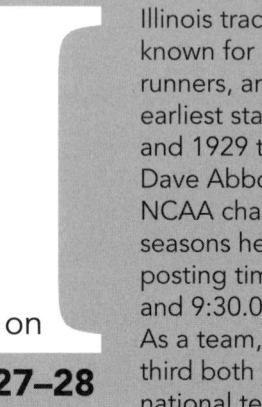

Illinois's 1927 football poster

I on **1927–28**

Illinois track and field is known for its distance runners, and one of its earliest stars was 1928 and 1929 two-mile star Dave Abbott. He was the NCAA champion both seasons he lettered, posting times of 9:28.8 and 9:30.0, respectively. As a team, Illinois placed third both years in the national team standings. Abbott also was a member of the 1928 U.S. Olympic Team, but he did not medal. He died in 1987 at age eighty-five.

Dave Abbott

ILLINI ITEM

The Fighting Illini football team made a trip to Evanston, Illinois, October 22, 1927, to take on the Northwestern Wildcats at NU's brandnew Dyche Stadium. Illinois defeated Northwestern, 7–6, on a Bud Jolley touchdown and "Butch" Nowack's successful point after touchdown. The Illini victory snapped a seven-game Wildcat winning streak.

The 1927 game program for Illinois-Northwestern

ILLINI LISTS

ILLINI ATHLETES WHO LATER BECAME
UI ATHLETIC DIRECTORS

	Years as UI athlete	Years as UI AD
George Huff	1890–1893	1896–1935
Wendell S. Wilson	1924–1926	1936–1941
Douglas R. Mills	1926–1930	1941–1966
E. E. (Gene) Vance	1942–1947	1967–1972
Raymond Eliot (interim)	1929–1931	1979
Ronald E. Guenther	1963–1966	1992–2011
Josh Whitman	1997–2000	2016–present

Wendall Wilson

ILLINI LEGEND

Allie Morrison

One of the University of Illinois's greatest athletes in the sport of wrestling was Allie Morrison, the gold medalist at 135 pounds at the 1928 Olympic Games in Amsterdam. A native of Marshalltown, Iowa, Morrison was unbeaten as a 135-pound Fighting Illini wrestler from 1928–30, compiling a perfect 22–0 record. He also won three consecutive national AAU individual titles. Team-wise, his three Illini squads won two Big Ten championships (1928 and 1930) and finished second once (1929). He began a long coaching career immediately afterward. Among his coaching stops were Penn State and Doane College, and then at the high-school level in Omaha, Nebraska, where he produced four state titles in five years. A member of the Helms Foundation Amateur Wrestling Hall of Fame, Morrison died in 1966 at age sixty-two.

Wrestling captain
Allie Morrison

ILLINI LORE

During the fall of 1927, St. John's Catholic Church was completed at the corner of Sixth Street and Armory Avenue. The church accommodated a congregation of between fifteen hundred and two thousand, and featured marble altars from Italy and stained glass windows from Germany. University of Illinois band leader Ray Dvorak served as the church's organist and choir director. Two additional residence halls, comprising 180 rooms for 360 male students, were attached to the church. The Reverend Monsignor Edward Duncan served as chaplain to the Catholic students and director of the Newman Foundation from October 1943 until 1997. He died in January 2012 at age ninety-six.

The chapel of St. John's Church

1928–29

AMERICA'S TIME CAPSULE

October 9, 1928 — The New York Yankees swept the St. Louis Cardinals in four straight games at the World Series.

November 6, 1928 — In a landslide Republican victory, Herbert Hoover defeated Alfred Smith for the presidency of the United States.

February 14, 1929 — The mass murder known as the St. Valentine's Day Massacre took place on Chicago's North Side.

May 16, 1929 — *Wings* was selected as Best Picture at the first Academy Awards.

June 30, 1929 — Bobby Jones won the U.S. Open golf tournament over runner-up Al Espinosa.

ILLINI MOMENT

Illini Clinches Big Ten Football Title with Victory Over Ohio State

November 24, 1928, was a day when Illinois's football team needed all the "ifs" to come true, and that's exactly what happened. Coach Bob Zuppke's Fighting Illini and Ohio State entered the 1928 season finale at Memorial Stadium with identical 3-1 conference records, one-half game behind undefeated Wisconsin. The combatants would need not only a victory over the other but also a win by Minnesota over the league-leading Badgers. After the dust had settled, the unlikely scenario played out perfectly to the Illini's advantage, as Illinois beat OSU, 8–0, and the Gophers beat Wisconsin, 6–0. That combination of results allowed Illinois to finish atop the Western Conference standings with a 4-1 record, its second consecutive league title. "Frosty" Peters scored the only Illini touchdown of the afternoon late in the first half on a quarterback sneak.

Forest "Frosty" Peters

I on 1928–29

Dick Oeler

Illinois made the most of hosting the Western Conference Gymnastics Championships, edging Chicago for the title, 1143.85 to 1109.85. It marked the Illini's first championship in the sport in twenty-seven years. Leading the way was pommel horse champ Richard "Dick" Oeler. He was also a standout in the classroom and, in 1930, he was named Illinois's Big Ten Conference Medal of Honor winner. Oeler died in Schaumburg in 1996 at age eighty-seven.

ILLINI ITEM

University of Illinois wrestlers Joe Sapora and George Minot won individual titles at the second annual NCAA championship, held in Columbus, Ohio. Sapora, a 115-pounder, and Minot, at 135 pounds, were Illinois's first two NCAA wrestling champs.

UI's 1929 wrestling team

ILLINI LISTS

ILLINOIS'S SPORTS INFORMATION DIRECTORS

1922–1943	L. M. "Mike" Tobin
1943–1956	Charles "Chuck" Flynn
1956–1970	Charles "Charlie" Bellatti
1970–1974	Norm Sheya
1974–1989	Tab Bennett
1980–1985	Lani Jacobsen (women's SID)
1985–1987	Tom Bobh (women's SID)
1987–1989	Mary Fowler (women's SID)
1989–1996	Mike Pearson
1996–1999	Dave Johnson

(Left to right) Charlie Bellatti, Chuck Flynn, and Tab Bennett

1999	Barbara Butler
2000–present	Kent Brown

ILLINI LEGEND

L. M. "Mike" Tobin
was Illinois's first
sports information
director

L. M. "Mike" Tobin

The greatest of Fighting Illini fans can easily recite the legends of "Red" Grange and the "Whiz Kids," but nary a one probably knows L. M. "Mike" Tobin, the man whose diligent work made those athletes household names. The Danville, Illinois, native was the first full-time collegiate athletic publicist in the country, and it was his initial task to spread the word about a red-headed youngster from Wheaton who became the most famous collegiate football player ever—Red Grange. For more than twenty years from his tiny office in Huff Gymnasium, Tobin pounded out thousands of stories about the Illini on his manual typewriter. Every sportswriter in the Midwest relied on Tobin to supply them with information about the nationally prominent University of Illinois athletic program. Upon Tobin's death in 1944 at age sixty-four, Bob Zuppke said that Illinois had lost "its most loyal of loyal friends. We owe him more than we ever could have repaid."

ILLINI LORE

Lorado Taft's *Alma Mater* statue, the $25,000 gift of the University of Illinois classes of 1923–1929, was formally dedicated June 12, 1929. Originally located just south of the Auditorium, the statue was moved to the Altgeld Hall lawn in August 1962. The central image of the three-figure bronze, inspired by Daniel Chester French's *Alma Mater* at Columbia University, welcomes visitors to the Urbana-Champaign campus. The figures at the rear, their hands clasped, represent learning and labor. Inscribed at the statue's granite base are the words, "To thy happy children of the future, those of the past send greetings."

President David Kinley (left) and sculptor
Lorado Taft stand at the base of *Alma Mater*

1929–30

AMERICA'S TIME CAPSULE

October 29, 1929   A record 16,410,000 shares were traded for whatever they would bring, signaling the beginning of the Great Depression.

November 29, 1929   Lt. Commander Richard E. Byrd completed the first flight over the South Pole.

March 13, 1930   The planet Pluto was identified from an observatory in Flagstaff, Arizona.

May 27, 1930   The Chrysler Building, at the intersection of Forty-Second Street and Lexington Avenue in New York City, opened as the world's tallest structure.

June 7, 1930   Gallant Fox captured horse racing's Triple Crown with a victory at the Belmont Stakes.

ILLINI MOMENT

"Perfect" Illini Win Big Ten Fencing Championship

Everything went "perfectly" for Coach H. W. Craig's Fighting Illini fencing team at the Western Conference's 1930 fencing championships in Chicago. Not only did Craig's squad capture the team title, all three of the young men who accompanied him on the trip to Chicago came home individual champions. Shattering all conference records as well as their own, the Illini fencing triumvirate of Otto Haier, Fred Siebert, and Chalmer "Doc" Gross recorded the league's first perfect score—a 15. Captain Haier won the foil title, his second consecutive crown in that weapon; Siebert was king of the epeeists, and Gross finished first among the sabremen. It was the second in a string of five consecutive team titles for the Illini fencers.

Illinois's 1930 fencing team

I on 1929–30

Douglas Turner of Hyde Park, Illinois, was the first black tennis player at the University of Illinois. In 1930 he took second in Western Conference singles competition. A few weeks later, Turner won the national championship of the American Tennis Association, an organization sponsoring African American competition because of the color line at United States National Lawn Tennis Association–sponsored events. He died in Chicago in 1995 at age eighty-four.

Douglas Turner was UI's first African American tennis player

ILLINI ITEM

On November 9, 1929, underdog Illinois up-ended powerful Army, 17–7, before a crowd of nearly seventy thousand in the first matchup between the two teams. Illinois's Arnold Wolgost scored the eventual game-winning touchdown on a 75-yard dash from scrimmage, while the Illini defense completely corralled Army's future Hall of Famer "Red" Cagle.

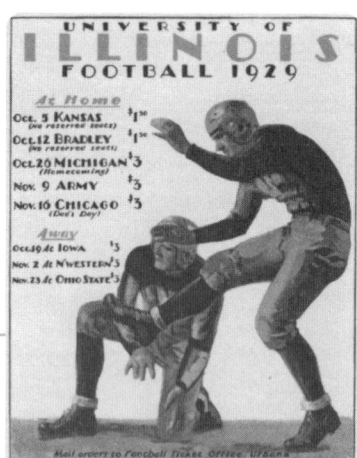

UI's 1929 football poster

ILLINI LISTS

ILLINOIS'S FIRST AFRICAN AMERICAN ATHLETES

1904	Football (Roy Young)
1904	Track and Field (Hiram Hannibal Wheeler)
1929	Tennis (Douglas Turner)
1947	Swimming (Ralph Hines)
1950	Fencing (John Cameron)
1951	Basketball (Walt Moore)
1963	Wrestling (Al McCullum)
1965	Baseball (Trenton Jackson)
1982	Gymnastics (Charles Lakes)

Walt Moore was Illinois's first African American basketball player

ILLINI LEGEND

Doug Mills

Doug Mills

The forty-year athletic career of Doug Mills at the University of Illinois must be discussed in three different chapters: as an athlete, as a coach, and as an administrator. From 1927 to 1930, Mills's career as a football and basketball athlete was highlighted by both individual and team success. He was a two-time all-conference basketball player and a three-year letterman on the gridiron, leading his teammates to a pair of Big Ten football titles. As a coach, Mills guided the Illini cagers to three conference championships in eleven seasons. Illini basketball reached its peak with Mills shortly before World War II, when four in-state athletes—Gene Vance, Ken Menke, Andy Phillip, and Jack Smiley—formed the nucleus of a team that was known simply as the "Whiz Kids." Following the 1946–47 season, Mills retired from the coaching ranks to devote himself as full-time Illinois athletic director, a job he inherited in 1941 at age thirty-three. The last years of Mills's administration were marred by a Big Ten investigation, and he gave up his post in November 1966. He died on August 12, 1983, at age seventy-five.

ILLINI LORE

The University of Illinois Library Building was dedicated October 18, 1929. The library was constructed in three sections at a cost of $1.75 million. At that time, the facility contained more than 758,000 volumes and nearly 157,000 pamphlets. In 2017, the library houses more than thirteen million volumes.

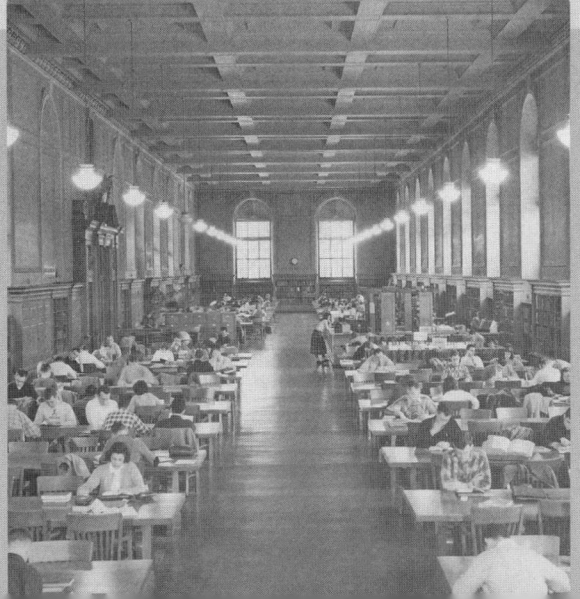

The University of Illinois Library Building opened in 1929

1930–31

AMERICA'S TIME CAPSULE

August 24, 1930   *All Quiet on the Western Front*, the first talkie war film to win an Academy Award, premiered.

September 27, 1930   Bobby Jones became the first player to capture golf's Grand Slam when he won the U.S. Amateur tournament.

January 7, 1931   The President's Emergency Committee for Unemployment Relief announced that as many as five million Americans were out of work.

March 3, 1931   President Herbert Hoover signed a congressional act making "The Star Spangled Banner" the USA's national anthem.

May 1, 1931   The Empire State Building, the world's tallest building, opened in New York City.

ILLINI
MOMENT

A "Berry" Good Performance

A young sophomore halfback from Abingdon, Illinois, wearing the number 7 on his back, stole the show for the Illinois football team on October 11, 1930, reminding fans of a redhead named Grange who had galloped the Memorial Stadium turf just five years before. Though he didn't wind up his career with as much acclaim as his famous predecessor, Gilbert Berry—for one game, at least—showed ghost-like moves on that cool autumn afternoon. His touchdown runs of sixty and eighty yards led the Fighting Illini to a 27–0 shutout of Butler. Berry touched the ball only nineteen times for 227 yards of total offense. Rushing-wise, he averaged better than twenty yards per carry, gaining 183 yards on nine attempts. The Illini victory would turn out to be one of only three for Coach Bob Zuppke's club that season.

Gil Berry

Paul Chervinko

I on **1930–31**

A sophomore on Illinois baseball's 1931 Big Ten championship team was Paul Chervinko. A native of Trauger, Pennsylvania, and a three-time letter winner, he was an excellent defensive catcher. Chervinko made it to the big leagues, playing for the Brooklyn Dodgers. Four of his teammates—Burleigh Grimes, Heinie Manush, Waite Hoyt, and Leo Durocher— all eventually were inducted into the Baseball Hall of Fame. Chervinko's shortcoming was as a hitter, batting just .147 in forty-two Major League games from 1937 to 1938. He died in Danville, Illinois, at age sixty-five.

ILLINI ITEM

Baseball standout Buster Fuzak

Coach Carl Lundgren's Fighting Illini baseball team won its Big Ten season opener April 11, 1931, crushing Northwestern 15–4 at Illinois Field. The hitting star for the Illini was senior Buster Fuzak, who hit for the cycle against the Wildcats. Fuzak connected for a single, a double, two triples, and a home run, while scoring three runs himself. Following naval service in World War II, he went on to have a distinguished career with the Chicago division of the Atomic Energy Commission. He died in 1997 at age eighty-six.

ILLINI LISTS

ILLINI CODE OF SPORTSMANSHIP

In 1930 George Huff, director of athletics at the University of Illinois, instituted the Illini Code of Sportsmanship.

Illini athletics director
George Huff

A true Illini sportsman . . .

1. Will consider all athletic opponents as guests and treat them with all of the courtesy due to friends and guests.
2. Will accept all decisions of officials without question.
3. Will never hiss or boo a player or official.
4. Will never utter abusive or irritating remarks from the sideline.
5. Will applaud opponents who make good plays or show good sportsmanship.
6. Will never attempt to rattle an opposing player.
7. Will seek to win by fair and lawful means, according to the rules of the game.
8. Will love the game for its own sake and not for what winning may bring him.
9. Will "do unto others as he would have them do unto him."
10. Will "win without boasting and lose without excuses."

ILLINI LEGEND

Dick Martin

While Walter Hagen and Bobby Jones were dominating professional golf, the kingpin of the Big Ten Conference was Illinois's Dick Martin. A letterman for Coach J. H. Utley's Fighting Illini from 1929 to 1931, Martin captured conference medalist honors as a junior in 1930 at Westmoreland Country Club in Evanston, winning by one stroke and leading his teammates to the Big Ten title. As a senior, he again became the Big Ten medalist, but he had to come from behind to do so. Martin entered the final round five strokes behind Ohio State's Johnny Florio. He played through a continual downpour to pass Florio on the twelfth hole, then had birdies on his final two holes to pull away. Once again, the Illini won the team title, by five strokes over host Michigan. Both years, Illinois placed fifth at the NCAA championships. Martin probably would have won three consecutive Big Ten titles, but Illinois did not compete in the conference meet his sophomore year due to finals scheduled on the day of the meet. Martin has been "lost" in the Alumni Association's records since graduation.

Big Ten medalist Dick Martin

ILLINI LORE

Dr. Harry Woodburn Chase assumed duties as the sixth president of the University of Illinois on July 5, 1930, taking over from David Kinley. He came from the University of North Carolina, where he had served as president from 1919 to 1930. Chase was called to assume the post at the Urbana-Champaign campus during a time that a major construction program was ending. Construction on campus during his tenure included Freer Gymnasium, the Ice Skating Rink, and the president's residence. Chase resigned July 1, 1933, to become chancellor of New York University.

President Harry Chase

1931–32

AMERICA'S TIME CAPSULE

October 25, 1931	The George Washington Bridge, connecting Manhattan with New Jersey, was opened to traffic.
March 1, 1932	Charles A. Lindbergh Jr., twenty-month-old son of the famous aviator, was kidnapped from his home at Hopewell, New Jersey.
July 2, 1932	Franklin Roosevelt accepted the Democratic Party's nomination for president, announcing his plan for a "new deal."
August 14, 1932	USA won the unofficial team championship at the Olympic games in Los Angeles by claiming the last of its sixteen gold medals. Babe Didrikson won two of the medals.

ILLINI
MOMENT

Illini Cagers Derail Boilermakers

Purdue ruled Big Ten basketball during the 1930s, but the Fighting Illini teams of Coach Craig Ruby always seemed to have the Boilermakers' number. Such was the case on January 9, 1932, when Illinois beat Purdue, 28–21, at the New Gym (soon to be called Huff Gym). Ward "Piggy" Lambert's Boilers showed a perfect 6–0 record coming into the game, relying on a fast-break style of play. However, Illinois's defense applied the brakes to the Boilermaker Express in the first half, claiming a 19–5 lead at halftime. Purdue All-American Johnny Wooden, who later became college basketball's most dominant coach at UCLA, led a strong comeback by scoring a game-high ten points. However, the Illini held on to win behind the sterling play of Cas Bennett and "Red" Owen. The loss would turn out to be the only blemish in eighteen games for Purdue that season, which ended with a 17-1 record.

UI's 1932 Illini basketball team

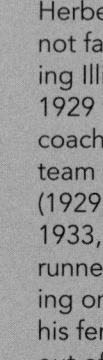 on

1931–32

Herbert Craig is a name not familiar to Fighting Illini fans. From 1929 through 1938, he coached Illinois's fencing team to six Big Ten titles (1929, 1930, 1931, 1932, 1933, and 1935) and five runner-up finishes. During one four-year stretch, his fencers won eleven out of a possible twelve individual conference titles. After turning over the coaching reigns to James Jackson in 1939, Craig joined the U.S. Navy and served as a commander during World War II. After the war, he and his wife Margaret moved to Jacksonville, Florida, where he served as a counselor for the state's Vocational Rehabilitation Service. Craig died in 1990 at age eighty-four and is buried at the Arlington National Cemetery.

Fencing coach Herbert Craig

ILLINI ITEM

Illinois's 1932 men's tennis team shared the Big Ten conference championship with Indiana in a showdown at Bloomington, Indiana, on May 18. Illini senior Eddie Lejeck beat Ohio State's Carl Dennison for the singles title, while he and Fred Hands were runners-up in doubles competition.

1932 tennis team

ILLINI LISTS

ILLINOIS'S TOP TEN CAREER BASEBALL HITTERS
(through 2001 season)

1. Darrin Fletcher, 1985–1987	.392
2. Andy Schutzenhofer, 2000–2001	.383
3. Dave Payton, 1984–1987	.374
4. Tim Richardson, 1980–1983	.372
5. Herb Plews, 1947–1950	.367
6. Ed Tryban, 1930–1932	.365
7. Sean Mulligan, 1989–1991	.364
8. Luke Simmons, 1999–2001	.362
9. Ben Lewis, 1933–1935	.361
10. Mike Murawski, 1967–1969	.356

Ed Tryban averaged .365 for the Illini from 1930 to 1932

ILLINI LEGEND

Craig Ruby

Known as one of the great basketball strategists of his time, Craig Ruby directed the University of Illinois basketball team for fourteen years (1923–1936), a span that saw the Fighting Illini claim thirteen upper-division finishes in Big Ten play. Illinois won two conference titles during that period—1923–24 and 1934–35—second only to Purdue, which won five championships during Ruby's reign in Champaign. In each of the four campaigns that Illinois played Purdue during Boilermaker championship seasons, Ruby's club upset the Riveters at least once. His teams played slow-break basketball, relying on a pivot-and-passing style. Ruby left coaching in 1936 to enter the greeting card business. He resided in Kansas City, Missouri, until his death in 1980 at age eighty-four.

Coach Craig Ruby

ILLINI LORE

James "Scotty" Reston, a 1932 graduate of the University of Illinois, is one of the school's most influential alumni. The native of Scotland worked as a student assistant in UI's sports information office and competed in varsity golf and soccer. Reston moved to the *New York Times* in 1939 following a seven-year stint with the Associated Press, becoming one of America's most noted journalists. *Time* magazine said in a 1960 edition, "Politicians and other newsmen watch Reston's tone and are influenced by it." Reston won two Pulitzer Prizes for National Reporting. He retired as vice president of the *Times* in December 1974 and died in 1995 at age eighty-six.

Illini golfer Scotty Reston became one of America's most famous journalists

1932–33

AMERICA'S TIME CAPSULE

October 2, 1932	The Chicago Cubs were swept in four straight games by the New York Yankees at the twenty-ninth annual World Series.
November 8, 1932	In a landslide victory over Herbert Hoover, Franklin Roosevelt was elected president of the United States.
March 13, 1933	United States banks began to reopen across the country, following a prolonged depression.
May 27, 1933	Chicago's Century of Progress Exposition began, in honor of that city's centennial celebration.
July 6, 1933	Babe Ruth hit a home run in Major League Baseball's first All-Star Game, as the American League defeated the National League, 4–2, at Chicago's Comiskey Park.

ILLINI MOMENT

Illini Gridders Win Doubleheader

The only football doubleheader in University of Illinois history was played at Memorial Stadium on October l, 1932. Coach Bob Zuppke divided his squad into two entirely separate units, one playing the first half of both games and one playing the second half of both. In game 1, Illinois cruised to a 20–7 victory over Miami of Ohio, thanks to a pair of touchdown passes from quarterback Jack Beynon to halfback Dave Cook. The "nightcap," which began at 3:00 P.M., resulted in a 13–0 shutout by the Fighting Illini over Coe College. Though they were blanked, Coe proved to be the tougher adversary, shutting out their hosts for most of the first half. Pete Yanuskus's touchdown just before halftime proved to be the only score the Illini would need. The biggest disappointment was that only 4,568 fans showed up on that beautiful, seventy-degree fall afternoon, causing the UI Athletic Association to incur a $3,600 loss after expenses.

Illinois's football team opened the 1932 season with doubleheader victories

I on 1932–33

Fred Frink

Frederick Ferdinand "Fred" Frink, an Illini letterman from 1932 to 1934, eventually became the twenty-ninth Illini baseball player to make it to the major leagues. On April 2, 1934, he tripled a school-record three times against Ohio. He also lettered in football under coach Bob Zuppke in 1931 and 1933. Frink made his Major League debut July 1, 1934, for the Philadelphia Phillies as an outfielder, then played a second game thirteen days later. Those were Frink's only two big-league games; he never batted. He died at age eighty-three in 1995.

ILLINI ITEM

Coach Harry Gill directed the Fighting Illini track and field squad for his thirtieth and final season in 1932–33. During those three decades, Gill led Illinois's program to eleven Big Ten outdoor team championships and eight indoor titles.

Harry Gill

ILLINI LISTS

MULTIPLE BIG TEN FENCING CHAMPIONS

Robert Tolman	3 titles (foil, 1920, 1921; sabre, 1921)
Ralph Epstein	3 titles (foil, 1932, 1934)
Francis Van Natter	2 titles (sabre, 1916; epee, 1916)
Otto Haier	2 titles (foil, 1929, 1930)
Fred Siebert	2 titles (epee, 1930; foil, 1931)
Edward Perella	2 titles (sabre, 1932, 1933)
William Chiprin	2 titles (foil, 1935, 1942)
Herman Velasco	2 titles (foil, 1954, 1956)
Larry Kauffman	2 titles (epee, 1955, 1956)
Art Schankin	2 titles (foil, 1957; sabre, 1958)

Ed Perella won Big Ten sabre titles in 1932 and 1933

Nate Haywood	2 titles (epee, 1972, 1973)
Mark Snow	2 titles (foil, 1981, 1982)
Eric Schicker	2 titles (foil, 1986, 1987)

ILLINI LEGEND

Ralph Epstein

Ralph Epstein

The only fencer in Fighting Illini history to win Big Ten individual titles in three consecutive seasons was Ralph Epstein. The foil specialist from Chicago won championships in 1932, 1933, and 1934, leading Illinois to team honors during his sophomore and junior seasons. Epstein was also a standout in the classroom, becoming the twentieth Illini athlete to be honored as the UI's Big Ten Conference Medal of Honor winner. As a serviceman in World War II, he helped the United States Air Corps design this nation's first jet airplane. After the war, Epstein returned to the Chicago architectural engineering firm of Epstein and Sons International, where he retired as president. He died on August 11, 1986, at age seventy-two.

ILLINI LORE

On December 26, 1932, President Chase announced that the University of Illinois would reduce its legislative request for operating expenses by $1 million, as compared to its last appropriation. Salaries of UI faculty and administrative staff were reduced by 10 percent, and deans and department heads were asked to boil down their budgets as never before. Ultimately, the state's appropriation to the university was reduced much more severely than expected. UI's $11.3 million budget during the 1931–32 and 1932–33 school years was cut to $7.8 million during 1933–34 and 1934–35, a reduction of 31 percent.

Campustown, circa 1930

1933-34

AMERICA'S TIME CAPSULE

December 5, 1933   Prohibition in the United States was repealed when Congress adopted the Twenty-First Amendment.

December 17, 1933   The Chicago Bears defeated the New York Giants, 23–21, winning the first National Football League championship playoff.

May 23, 1934   Dr. Wallace Carothers of DuPont Laboratories first developed a synthetic fiber called nylon.

June 14, 1934   Max Baer scored a technical knockout over Primo Camera to win the world heavyweight boxing championship.

July 22, 1934   John Dillinger, America's public enemy number one, was shot and killed in Chicago by FBI agents.

ILLINI
MOMENT

Illini Spoil Boilers' Championship Season

Coach "Piggy" Lambert's Purdue Boilermakers had wrapped up their Big Ten championship a few days before with a home-court victory over Indiana. So perhaps they had little more than pride to play for when they came to Champaign on March 5, 1934, for the season finale against Illinois. The Illini, however, had a different outlook on the game, hoping to send out their senior quartet of Huddie Hellmich, Fred Fencl, and Chin and Jake Kamm on a winning note against the 17-2 Boilermakers. The game was nip and tuck all the way and came down to the final hair-raising twenty seconds. With the Illini ahead by one point, UI's Hellmich fouled Purdue All-American Ray Eddy. Fortunately for Illinois, the Big Ten's individual scoring champion missed both of his free throws, allowing the Illini to escape with a 27–26 win.

UI's 1934 Illini basketball squad

I on 1933-34

On August 21, 1934, the Champaign-Urbana community learned about the death of veteran Illini baseball coach Carl Lundgren. "Carl was a great player and a great coach," said George Huff. "As a coach, he probably had no equal. He was kind and patient with his players, although he could be very firm if necessary. They admired him and respected him for his knowledge of the sport and idolized him for his qualities as a man, for his influence for good was tremendous. He was honest, truthful, whole-souled and genuine. In Carl Lundgren, Illinois has lost one of its foremost teachers."

Longtime baseball coach Carl Lundgren died at age fifty-four in 1934

ILLINI ITEM

Dr. Leland "Slim" Stilwell was named team physician for the University of Illinois Athletic Association in 1933. A basketball letterman for the Fighting Illini from 1922 to 1924, he was known to UI student athletes as "Doc" Stilwell for thirty-five years. He was named UI's Varsity I Award winner in 1971. Stilwell died in 1979 at age seventy-seven.

Illini basketball alum Leland Stilwell was named team physician in 1933

ILLINI LISTS

FAMOUS ILLINI "33"S

Kenny Battle, men's basketball	
Becky Beach, women's basketball	
Dusty Bensko, baseball	
Susan Blauser, women's basketball	
Kelly Bond, women's basketball	Rich McBride, men's basketball
Dee Dee Deeken, women's basketball	Ken Norman, men's basketball
Jon Ekey, men's basketball	Lonnie Perrin, football
Bill Erickson, men's basketball	Harv Schmidt, men's basketball
Chris Green, football	Kevin Turner, men's basketball
Eddie Johnson, men's basketball	John Valente, baseball
Damir Krupalija, men's basketball	Angelina Williams, women's basketball

ILLINI LEGEND

Frank Froschauer

From September 1932 through March 1935, the name Frank Froschauer dominated the sports pages at the University of Illinois. As a member of Coach Bob Zuppke's Fighting Illini football team, the Lincoln, Illinois, native was a prominent contributor from his halfback position. With Coach Craig Ruby's basketball squad, Froschauer led the team in scoring for three consecutive years, averaging eight points per game in an era when the entire team scored only thirty points a game. He also paced the Big Ten in scoring his senior season. Froschauer served as a coach and athletic director for thirty-seven years in the south suburban Chicago area. He was involved with football, swimming, and golf at Thornton Township High School in Harvey over a period of twenty-five years and became Thornridge High School's first athletic director in 1960, serving until 1972, when he was succeeded by Ron Ferguson. Froschauer died April 28, 1985, at age seventy-five.

Frank Froschauer

ILLINI LORE

Arthur Cutts Willard took over as the ninth president of the University of Illinois on July 1, 1934, succeeding Arthur Daniels. He had been head of the UI's Mechanical Engineering Department and acting dean of the College of Engineering. In 1921 Willard had received international recognition for his research work, which provided engineering principles for the ventilation system of the Holland Tunnel under the Hudson River connecting Manhattan, New York, with Jersey City, New Jersey. After twelve years of service, during a period when a depressed economy gripped his campus and the rest of America, Willard retired. On October 26, 1945, the University of Illinois Willard Airport was named in his honor. He died in 1960 at age eighty-two.

President Arthur Willard

1934–35

AMERICA'S TIME CAPSULE

October 22, 1934	Notorious bank robber "Pretty Boy" Floyd was shot and killed by FBI agents.
December 9, 1934	The Chicago Bears lost the NFL championship game to the New York Giants, 30–13.
May 6, 1935	The Works Progress Administration (WPA) began operation, giving jobs to millions of Americans.
May 24, 1935	More than twenty thousand fans at Cincinnati's Crosley Field watched their Reds beat the Philadelphia Phillies in baseball's first-ever night game.
August 14, 1935	President Roosevelt signed the Social Security Act, establishing payment of benefits to senior citizens.

ILLINI
MOMENT

Illini Cagers Beat Michigan, Claim Big Ten Title

Illinois athletic teams traveled to Ann Arbor three times during the 1934–35 season, returning each time with a victory. In football, the Illini beat Michigan, 7–6. In baseball, Illinois triumphed 1–0 at Ferry Field. But perhaps its most satisfying conquest in Michigan came on March 4, when the Illini basketball team beat their hosts, 36–22, to claim a share of the Big Ten title. Illinois exploded out of the blocks, scoring the first fifteen points of the game, behind Captain Frank Froschauer, who ended the contest with nine points. Bob Riegel (nine points), Harry Combes (eight), and Roy Guttschow (seven) tallied twenty-four of the remaining twenty-five points. Illinois wound up tying for the title with Purdue and Wisconsin, all finishing with 9–3 league records.

1935 champions of the Big Ten

I on **1934–35**

Barton Cummings, a 1935 graduate and three-time letter winner for Coach Bob Zuppke's football team, is one of the University of Illinois's most successful

Barton Cummings

graduates in the field of advertising. Following service in World War II, he joined Compton Advertising in New York City. Less than ten years later, Cummings was chief executive of the multimillion-dollar agency. Among his clients were Procter and Gamble, United States Steel, and the New York Stock Exchange. When Compton was bought by Saatchi and Saatchi in 1982, Cummings was appointed chairman emeritus, a position he held until his death in 1994.

ILLINI ITEM

President Gerald Ford was a star player for Michigan

On October 20, 1934, when Illinois squared off against Michigan's football team at Ann Arbor, Illini team members didn't realize that they were lining up against a future president of the United States. Wolverine center Gerald Ford became president forty years later in 1974, when he succeeded Richard Nixon.

ILLINI LISTS

NCAA WRESTLING CHAMPIONS

Ralph "Ruffy" Silverstein

1929	Joe Sapora, 115 pounds
1929	George Minot, 135 pounds
1930	Joe Sapora, 115 pounds
1932	Joe Puerta, 121 pounds
1935	Ralph Silverstein, 175 pounds
1938	John Ginay, 165 pounds
1938	Allen Sapora, 126 pounds
1939	Archie Deutschman 136 pounds
1946	David Shapiro, 165 pounds
1956	Larry TenPas, 157 pounds
1957	Bob Norman, heavyweight
1958	Bob Norman, heavyweight
1991	Jon Llewellyn, heavyweight
1995	Steve Marianetti, 150 pounds
1995	Ernest Benion Jr., 158 pounds
1998	Eric Siebert, 150 pounds
2000	Carl Perry, 141 pounds
2001	John Lockhart, heavyweight
2001	Adam Tirapelle, 149 pounds
2003	Matt Lackey, 165 pounds
2013	Jesse Delgado, 125 pounds
2014	Jesse Delgado, 125 pounds
2015	Isaiah Martinez, 165 pounds
2016	Isaiah Martinez, 165 pounds

ILLINI LEGEND

Charles Flachmann

One of Illinois's most brilliant athletes during the mid-1930s was swimmer Charles Flachmann. Lettering for the Fighting Illini from 1934 to 1935 for Coach Ed Manley, Flachmann dominated the freestyle events in Big Ten championship competition. He swept the 50- and 100-yard races both years and also captured the 220-yard event his junior year. Nationally, Flachmann also won titles in all three events. Following his athletic career at Illinois, he served as a captain in the army during World War II. When Flachmann returned to civilian life, he worked as an insurance broker in St. Louis and was also an amateur artist. Flachmann died in 1983 at age sixty-nine.

Charles Flachmann

ILLINI LORE

In February 9, 1935, the University of Illinois Board of Trustees approved the formation of the UI Foundation to encourage the giving of more gifts to the university, not only by alumni but by citizens in general. In 1939 the Foundation launched its first major fundraising effort, the construction and furnishing of the Illini Union. Since 1979 the UI Foundation has accepted more than $4 billion in gifts and contributions.

"To thy happy children of the future, those of the past send greetings"

1935–1944

1935–36

AMERICA'S TIME CAPSULE

September 8, 1935 — Powerful Louisiana politician Huey Long was assassinated in the corridor of the state capitol in Baton Rouge.

October 7, 1935 — The Chicago Cubs lost baseball's World Series to the Detroit Tigers, four games to two.

November 8, 1935 — *Mutiny on the Bounty*, starring Charles Laughton and Clark Gable, premiered.

June 12, 1936 — Kansas governor Alf Landon and Col. Frank Knox of Illinois were nominated by the Republican National Convention as its candidates for president and vice president.

August 16, 1936 — The Summer Olympic Games, featuring American track star Jesse Owens, ended in Berlin, Germany.

ILLINI MOMENT

Illini Bury Wolverines in Mud

The Michigan "Football Express" roared into Illinois's Memorial Stadium on a four-game winning streak, but the combination of a stingy Illini defense and a muddy field buried the Wolverines in their tracks on November 9, 1935. The mud-encrusted right foot of Illini kicker Lowell Spurgeon accounted for the only score of the day, a thirty-one-yard field goal in the second quarter, as Illinois beat Michigan, 3–0. The Wolverine offense never got started; in fact, it never carried the ball as far as the middle of the field. Gaining only sixteen total yards, the only first down Michigan managed the entire afternoon was courtesy of an Illini penalty. The mud didn't seem to bother Illini quarterback "Wib" Henry, though, as he rushed for a net gain of 123 yards.

Illini quarterback "Wib" Henry

I on 1935–36

Two-sport star Howard Braun

Howard Braun served as Illinois's basketball captain in 1936 and was a top singles player for the tennis team. He's probably best known for his coaching exploits in both sports. As assistant from 1936–47, Braun helped the Illini win three Big Ten titles, including two with the famed "Whiz Kids." Braun also coached the Illini tennis squad for 24 years. In 1967, he was dismissed from his coaching duties for the basketball team as a result of the slush fund scandal. Braun remained in Champaign, dying in 1996 at age eighty-three.

ILLINI ITEM

Coach Craig Ruby

Basketball coach Craig Ruby concluded his fourteen-year career at the University of Illinois by announcing his resignation on February 7, 1936. "My reason for resigning," said the thirty-nine-year-old Ruby, "is that I believe it is unwise for my family and myself to depend upon the game of basketball entirely in the later years of my life. I do not choose to face the prospect of coaching basketball at 50 or 60 years of age."

ILLINI LISTS

HEISMAN AWARD WINNERS WHO PLAYED AGAINST ILLINOIS
(Performances in the year they won the award)

Jay Berwanger, the first
Heisman Trophy winner

Jay Berwanger of Chicago (1935), 26 rushes,106 yards, 1 TD	Howard Cassady of Ohio State (1955), 18 rushes, 95 yards, 2 TD
Tom Harmon of Michigan (1940), 21 rushes, 58 yards, 1 TD, 1 FG	Archie Griffin of Ohio State (1974), 20 rushes, 144 yards, 2 TD
Bruce Smith of Minnesota (1941), yardage unavailable, 2 TD	Archie Griffin of Ohio State (1975), 23 rushes, 127 yards, 1 TD
Angelo Bertelli of Notre Dame (1943), 5 of 7 passes,82 yards, 1 TD pass	Desmond Howard of Michigan (1991), 7 catches, 80 yards, 1 TD
Les Horvath of Ohio State (1950), 22 rushes,109 yards, 2 TD	Eddie George of Ohio State (1995), 36 rushes, 314 yards, 3 TD
Vic Janowicz of Ohio State (1950), 21 rushes, 90 yards, 5 of 12 passes for 59 yards, 1 TD	Troy Smith of Ohio State (2006), 13 of 23 passes, 108 yards, 37 yards rushing, 0 TD

ILLINI LEGEND

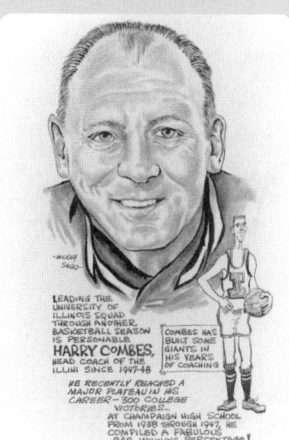

Harry Combes

For twenty-four years, the name Harry Combes was synonymous with University of Illinois basketball. The Monticello, Illinois, native played guard and forward on the Fighting Illini teams of 1935, 1936, and 1937, twice leading Illinois to Big Ten Conference titles. An All–Big Ten selection his junior and senior seasons, Combes also won the Conference Medal of Honor for proficiency in athletics and scholarship his final year. Two years after his graduation, he began a highly successful nine-year prep coaching career at Champaign High School. Combes succeeded Doug Mills as UI basketball coach in 1947 and led the Illini to Big Ten titles in three of his first five seasons. In 1949, 1951, and 1952, Illinois basketball clubs finished third at the NCAA tournament each year. Combes's twenty-year coaching record at Illinois was 316 wins and 150 losses, a mark that stood as the Illini record until it was broken by Lou Henson. He died November 13, 1977, at age sixty-two.

Illini basketball coach
Harry Combes

ILLINI LORE

In December 1935, after four months of negotiations, the State of Illinois approved an appropriation of $1.2 million to the University of Illinois for a major addition to the Medical Center on Polk Street in Chicago. For a time, the Depression halted progress on the center's east tower. But finally, in 1937, construction was eventually completed through the federal Public Works Administration.

1936–37

AMERICA'S TIME CAPSULE

November 3, 1936   Franklin Roosevelt was elected America's president in a crushing victory over Alf Landon.
May 6, 1937   The *Hindenburg* burst into flames at Lakehurst, New Jersey, marking the virtual end of lighter-than-air transportation.
May 12, 1937   Americans listened to the coronation of King George IV of England in radio's first worldwide broadcast.
January 24, 1937   Champaign radio station WDWS began broadcasting on the second floor of the *News-Gazette* building.
June 22, 1937   Joe Louis knocked out Jim Braddock to capture the heavyweight boxing title at Chicago's Soldier Field.

ILLINI
MOMENT

Illini Cagers Snap Fourteen-Year Jinx at Purdue

In one of the most raucous basketball battles ever played between Illinois and Purdue, it took a rebound basket by Illini reserve center Hale Swanson with just five seconds left to secure a 38–37 victory. The January 18, 1937, win was Illinois's first at West Lafayette in fourteen seasons and moved the Illini into a firstplace tie in the Big Ten standings. Trailing 23–11 early in the second half, Illinois steadily whittled away at the Boilermaker advantage and took the lead with six minutes remaining. Purdue regained the lead in the final minute but fouled Illini star Lou Boudreau with just five seconds left in the game. Boudreau missed both free-throw attempts, but Swanson's tip-in salvaged the Illini comeback. Illinois went on to win six of its last seven games to tie Minnesota for the Big Ten title.

Coach Doug Mills and 1938 captain Lou Boudreau

The gravesite of George Huff

I on 1936–37

At the time of George Huff's passing on October 1, 1936, hundreds of tributes poured in to honor the "Father of Illini Athletics." One came from Amos Alonzo Stagg. "As a man, George Huff was square and honest," wrote Stagg. "He had no patience with dishonesty and unfairness. With him, matters had to be decided on principle. His opinions commanded the highest respect. Mr. Huff sought no publicity and no honors for himself. If he was not met with equally fair treatment from anyone, he would not hesitate to say, 'That isn't fair.'"

ILLINI ITEM

Wendall Wilson (left) served as UI's athletics director from 1937 to 1941

Thirty-one-year-old Wendell "Weenie" Wilson, a two-time Illini football letter winner, was appointed Illinois director of athletics February 27, 1937, replacing the late George Huff. His tumultuous reign as AD lasted just more than four years, being ousted in June 1941 by the board of trustees. Wilson went on to become director of the Teton Valley Ranch Camp in Colorado and eventually retired to San Diego, California. He died in 1990 at age eighty-four.

ILLINI LISTS

ALL-TIME COLLEGE BASEBALL "DREAM TEAM"
(As selected in 1990 by *Collegiate Baseball*)

Lou Boudreau wrote
his autobiography
in 1993

Lou Boudreau, Illinois

Mickey Cochrane, Boston U.

Jackie Robinson, UCLA

George Sisler, Michigan

Eddie Collins, Columbia

Joe Sewell, Alabama

Frankie Frisch, Fordham

Thurman Munson, Kent State

Mike Schmidt, Ohio U.

Harvey Kuenn, Wisconsin

Ethan Allen, Cincinnati

Tony Gwynn, San Diego State

Lou Gehrig, Columbia

Reggie Jackson, Arizona State

Carl Yastrzemski, Notre Dame

Dave Winfield, Minnesota

Christy Mathewson, Bucknell

Eddie Plank, Gettysburg

ILLINI LEGEND

Lou Boudreau

The folks at Harvey Thornton High School probably figured it would be in the sport of basketball, not baseball, where their Lou Boudreau would make his greatest impression. He did enjoy great success on the hardcourts at Illinois, earning All-America honors as a junior. However, Major League Baseball scouts also liked what they saw of Boudreau in 1937, hitting .347 while leading the Illini to the Big Ten title. The very next spring, he joined the Cleveland Indians. At age twenty-four, Boudreau was named player-manager of the Indians. His greatest success on the baseball diamond came in 1948 when he guided Cleveland to the World Series title while earning American League MVP honors. During his fifteen-year Major League career, Boudreau hit .295 with sixty-eight home runs and 789 RBI. In addition to managing Cleveland, he also was the skipper for the Red Sox Athletics, and Cubs. He served as a television and radio announcer for the Cubs for more than two decades and was inducted into baseball's Hall of Fame in 1970. Illinois retired baseball jersey number 5 in his honor on April 18, 1992. Boudreau died in 2001 at the age of eighty-four.

Lou Boudreau

ILLINI LORE

In November of 1936, the world's longest suspension bridge, known best as the Golden Gate Bridge, opened to California motorists. A little-known fact is that a University of Illinois graduate had a great deal to do with both the design and the construction of the landmark structure. Senior engineer Charles E. Andrew (Civil Engineering, 1906), a native of Oregon, Illinois, was the principal engineer of the project, supervising one hundred designers and construction engineers. Andrew died in 1969 at age eighty-five.

Charles Andrew

1937–38

AMERICA'S TIME CAPSULE

December 12, 1937   The Chicago Bears lost the NFL championship game to the Washington Redskins, 28–21.

December 21, 1937   Walt Disney's *Snow White and the Seven Dwarfs* premiered.

May 2, 1938   Thornton Wilder's "Our Town" won a Pulitzer Prize for Drama.

June 25, 1938   President Franklin Roosevelt signed the Wage and Hours Act, raising the minimum wage for workers engaged in interstate commerce from twenty-five cents to forty cents per hour.

July 1, 1938   Don Budge and Helen Wills Moody captured Wimbledon tennis titles.

ILLINI MOMENT

Fighting Illini Battle Irish to Standstill

The scoreboard at the end of the game read Illinois-0, Notre Dame-0, but none of the forty-five thousand fans in attendance at Memorial Stadium that mild afternoon of October 9, 1937, went home disappointed. They'd just seen one of the most magnificent defensive efforts ever by their Fighting Illini, holding Coach Elmer Layden's Irish juggernaut to little more than one hundred total yards. Jack Berner, who punted ten times for an average of thirty-five yards, was also a bulwark on defense, lending a hand in stopping almost every Notre Dame run. Mel Brewer missed what would have been the game-winning field goal, a fourteen-yarder, in the first quarter, but the Illini never generated another true scoring threat. Notre Dame wound up the season with a 6-2-1 record, while Illinois finished at 3-3-2.

John Ginay

I on 1937–38

A product of Roosevelt High School in East Chicago, Indiana, John Ginay was only the fourth individual in University of Illinois wrestling history to become a two-time Big Ten champion. In 1938, his senior season, Ginay won both the conference and NCAA titles at 165 pounds. Ginay also was a member of the 1940 U.S. Olympic Team. He served in the U.S. Navy as a Lieutenant, then returned to Roosevelt High to teach and coach. Voted into the Indiana High School Wrestling Coaches Association Hall of Fame in 1973, he died at age ninety in 2004.

ILLINI ITEM

Lewis "Pick" Dehner

Illinois's Lewis "Pick" Dehner tied Big Ten basketball's individual scoring record January 15, 1938, with a twenty-nine-point performance against the University of Chicago. The record was set originally by Joe Reiff of Northwestern in 1933 and tied by Jewell Young of Purdue in 1937. Only a weakness at the free-throw line (five of ten) kept Dehner from setting a record.

NOTRE DAME

THE FIGHTING IRISH OF

ROBT. C. ZUPPKE

OFFICIAL 25¢

OCT. 9, 1937

25th Anniversary

THE FIGHTING ILLINI OF

ILLINOIS

ILLINI LISTS

FAMOUS UNIVERSITY OF ILLINOIS ALUMNI OF THE 1930S

1930	William Maxwell (fiction editor, *The New Yorker*)
1931	Nelson Algren (author, *The Man with the Golden Arm*)
1931	Charles Luckman (president, Lever Brothers, 1946–1950)
1932	James "Scotty" Reston (Pulitzer Prize, 1945 and 1957)
1932	Lee Falk (creator of *The Phantom* and *Mandrake the Magician*)
1933	Polykarp Kusch (Nobel Prize for Physics, 1955)
1933	Robert Lewis Taylor (Pulitzer Prize, 1959)
1935	J. Wayne Reitz (president, University of Florida (1955–1967)

Illinois alum Thomas Murphy became chairman of General Motors

1935	Warren Ambrose (professor of mathematics, MIT, 1957–1985)
1937	Julius Richmond (U.S. Surgeon General, 1977–1981)
1938	Thomas Murphy (chairman, General Motors, 1974–1980)
1939	Phillip Handler (president, National Academy of Sciences, 1969–1981)

ILLINI LEGEND

Hek Kenney

Harold Eugene "Hek" Kenney is remembered as the man for whom Kenney Gym on the University of Illinois campus was named. However, it was his accomplishments in the sport of wrestling that gained him his initial fame. A two-time wrestling captain during his Illini career from 1924 to 1926 under Coach Paul Prehn, Kenney succeeded his mentor as coach of UI grappling in 1929. For the next fifteen years, he guided the Illini to a dual-meet record of 91–28–2 and four Big Ten titles. It was not uncommon for Kenney's teams to wrestle before crowds of more than three thousand fans. Among his standout pupils were the Sapora brothers, Joe and Al, Ralph "Ruffy" Silverstein, and Archie Deutschman. So respected was Kenney that he served two terms as president of the National Wrestling Coaches and Officials Association. He was a member of UI's physical education faculty until his retirement in 1967. Two years later, he was honored as the first recipient of the College of Physical Education's Distinguished Alumnus Award. Kenney died in 1972 at age sixty-nine. On April 25, 1974, the building in which he had toiled for most of his life was renamed in his honor.

Harold "Hek" Kenney

ILLINI LORE

On March 11, 1938, the seventieth anniversary of the opening of the University of Illinois, workers began razing Old University Hall. The facility, completed in 1873 at a cost of $150,000, represented sixty-five years of history to UI alumni, and there was much resistance from them over tearing it down. However, building experts indicated that the cost of leveling the structure would run as much as constructing a new classroom. Salvaged from the historic building was the Memorial Clock, a gift from the class of 1878, which today graces the cupola of the Illini Union.

University Hall was razed in 1938

1938–39

AMERICA'S TIME CAPSULE

October 9, 1938	The New York Yankees defeated the Chicago Cubs in four straight games for the World Series title.
October 30, 1938	American radio listeners panicked as Orson Welles staged his play *War of the Worlds*. They mistook the realistically performed "news reports" for an actual invasion from Mars.
June 8, 1939	King George VI and Queen Elizabeth of Great Britain visited President Roosevelt at the White House.
June 28, 1939	The Pan American Airways airliner *Dixie Clipper* began regular transatlantic passenger service.
August 15, 1939	*The Wizard of Oz*, starring Judy Garland, premiered.

ILLINI MOMENT

National Champs

Coach Hartley Price's University of Illinois gymnasts were on top of the world during the 1938–39 season. They roared through their dual-meet schedule unbeaten, then hosted the Western Conference Meet at the Old Gym on March 11. The Fighting Illini didn't disappoint their hometown fans that day, outdistancing runner-up Minnesota by twenty-two points, 111.5 to 89.5. A month later came the national meet at the University of Chicago, and Illinois again wound up on top, claiming their first-ever NCAA title. Leading the way for the Illini was junior All-American Joe Giallombardo, who won the individual all-around championships at both the conference and national meets.

UI's 1939 gymnastics team reigned in NCAA champs

I on 1938–39

Paul Fina

During the 1938–39, 1939–40, and 1940–41 seasons, Paul Fina and his Illini gymnastics teammates won the NCAA championship. During the 1940s, there was perhaps no better gymnast in America, but World War II prevented his opportunity to win Olympic Gold when the games were cancelled in both 1940 and 1944. Fina medaled more than one hundred times from 1936 to 1950 and was selected as a member of the U.S. International Gymnastics Team in 1947. Among his career achievements were involvement on the Olympic Committee for both 1968 and 1972. Fina died in 2009 at age ninety-two.

ILLINI ITEM

Illini wrestler Archie Deutschman won the Big Ten Conference Medal of Honor in 1939

Fighting Illini wrestling captain Archie Deutschman was a two-way star during the 1938–39 season. On the wrestling mat for Coach Hek Kenney, he won both the Big Ten and NCAA titles at the 136-pound classification. As a reward for his proficiency in the classroom, Deutschman received Illinois's Big Ten Conference Medal of Honor. He died in 1998 at age eighty.

ILLINI LISTS

ILLINI WHOSE NUMBERS HAVE BEEN RETIRED
IN PROFESSIONAL SPORTS

No. 5	Lou Boudreau, Cleveland Indians
No. 7	George Halas, Chicago Bears
No. 22	Buddy Young, Baltimore Colts
No. 51	Dick Butkus, Chicago Bears
No. 66	Ray Nitschke, Green Bay Packers
No. 77	Red Grange, Chicago Bears

Lou Boudreau's
No. 5 has been
retired by Illini
baseball

ILLINI LEGEND

Joe Giallombardo

Joe Giallombardo

At first glance, Joe Giallombardo could hardly be mistaken for a dominant athlete. However, packed inside his stocky 5'4", 155-pound frame were tightly wound, spring-loaded muscles. While Jesse Owens, his Cleveland East Tech High School classmate, was making headlines as a track man, Giallombardo became the premier athlete in the sport of gymnastics. During his three years at the University of Illinois from 1938 to 1940, "Little Joe" won every individual title there was to win. He was a three-time all-around champion in the Big Ten, helping the Fighting Illini win the 1939 team title. Among his record seven NCAA titles were three all-around crowns, three tumbling championships, and a first-place finish on the rings. Giallombardo coached gymnastics at New Trier and New Trier West High Schools from the time he graduated until his retirement in 1975. A longtime resident of Wheeling, Illinois, he died in 2011 at age ninety-four.

ILLINI LORE

The cornerstone of Gregory Hall was laid June 10, 1939, by Alfred Gregory, son of the man for whom the memorial was being made—John Milton Gregory, first president of the University of Illinois. The structure originally housed the College of Education, the School of Journalism, and classrooms for students enrolled in Liberal Arts and Sciences. A copper box containing, among other items, the photograph and biography of President Gregory was placed inside the cornerstone.

Gregory Hall was named after UI's
first president

1939–40

AMERICA'S TIME CAPSULE

September 3, 1939   The nations of France and Great Britain declared war on Germany, while President Roosevelt said that the United States would remain neutral.

December 15, 1939   *Gone with the Wind*, starring Clark Gable and Vivien Leigh, premiered.

March 30, 1940   Indiana won its first NCAA basketball title, beating Kansas, 60–42.

May 6, 1940   John Steinbeck won a Pulitzer Prize for his book *The Grapes of Wrath*.

May 15, 1940   The first successful helicopter flight in the United States took place.

ILLINI MOMENT

Illinois Shocks Michigan

Winless Illinois wasn't given much hope against Coach Fritz Crisler's Michigan Wolverine football squad, starring eventual Heisman Trophy winner Tom Harmon. Michigan came to Champaign averaging forty-one points per game, but on that unseasonably mild November 4 afternoon, the Wolverines managed only a single touchdown. Though Harmon did net seventy-two yards rushing, his performance was stymied by a brilliant effort from Coach Bob Zuppke's defensive unit. George Rettinger

Action from the 1939 battle between Michigan and Illinois

(following a forty-eight-yard pass) and Jim Smith (on a three-yard run) scored Illinois's two touchdowns. One of the unsung heroes for the Illini was lineman Mel Brewer, who dedicated the game to his mother, who had died earlier that week. The nation's sportswriters later selected the game as the biggest upset of the 1939 season. Illinois wound up the year with a 3-4-1 record as compared with Michigan's 6-2 overall mark.

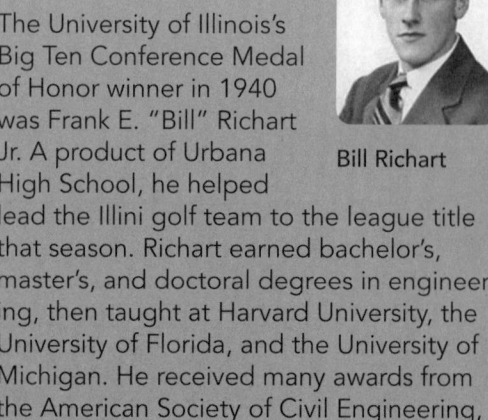

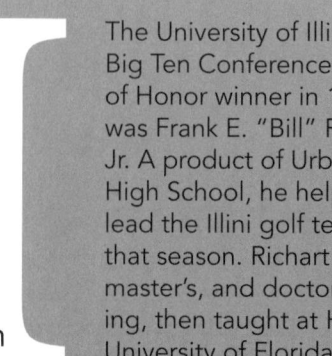

Bill Richart

I on 1939–40

The University of Illinois's Big Ten Conference Medal of Honor winner in 1940 was Frank E. "Bill" Richart Jr. A product of Urbana High School, he helped lead the Illini golf team to the league title that season. Richart earned bachelor's, master's, and doctoral degrees in engineering, then taught at Harvard University, the University of Florida, and the University of Michigan. He received many awards from the American Society of Civil Engineering, including the highest award in his specialty field, the Terzaghi Award. Richart died at age seventy-five in 1994.

ILLINI ITEM

Walter "Hoot" Evers played in the big leagues for twelve seasons

Walter "Hoot" Evers was the most versatile Fighting Illini athlete of 1939–40, lettering in basketball, baseball, and track. On the hardcourts, "Hoot" was Illinois's second-leading scorer. As a center fielder in baseball, Evers hit .353 in Big Ten play. He also competed as a javelin thrower placing second in the conference. Evers signed with the Detroit Tigers and went on to a twelve-year career, finishing with a .278 batting average. He died in 1991 at age sixty-nine.

ILLINI LISTS

SHORTEST ILLINI MEN'S BASKETBALL PLAYERS

Joe Frank, a Fighting Illini letterman from 1938 to 1940, was one of the shortest men ever to play basketball at the University of Illinois. Here's a list of the most diminutive Illini hoopsters.

5'7"	Joe Frank, Vandalia, 1940
5'7"	Seymour Gantman, Chicago, 1952
5'8"	Phil Flanigan, Tuscola, 1959
5'8"	John Easterbrook, Champaign, 1960
5'8"	Bob Meadows, Collinsville, 1965
5'9"	Bill Ridley, Taylorville, 1956
5'9"	Halim Abdullah, Jersey City, N.J., 1997
5'9"	Ahmad Starks, Chicago, 2014.

Joe Frank

5'10"	Tony Wysinger, Peoria, 1987
5'10"	P. J. Bowman, Champaign, 1990
5'10"	Jelani Boline, Chicago, 1998

ILLINI LEGEND

Bill Hapac

Bill Hapac

Quick now—What does former Illinois basketball star Bill Hapac have in common with Andy Phillip, Terry Dischinger, Jimmy Rayl, Dave Schellhase, and Rick Mount? If you guessed that they all once set the Big Ten single-game scoring record, you get the grand prize. Hapac's night in the spotlight came against Minnesota on February 10, 1940, when he scored a then-unheard-of thirty-four points. The Cicero, Illinois, native was the conference's leading scorer his senior year, averaging nearly fourteen points per game. Besides lettering three times in basketball, Hapac also earned three varsity monograms in baseball. Twice he scored five runs in a game, a mark that's still a school record. Hapac served as an officer in the air corps during World War II, then played pro basketball for several years. A consensus basketball All-American at Illinois, he coached the sport at Morton East High School until his death in 1967 at age forty-nine.

ILLINI LORE

The world's first betatron, an atom smasher for high-energy physics exploration into the nucleus of the atom, was introduced in 1940 by University of Illinois physicist Donald Kerst. Kerst's first betatron was nineteen inches long, twenty inches high, eight inches thick, and weighed two hundred pounds. It produced x-rays with an energy of 2.5 million electron volts. The electrons reached their energy by spinning around many times within a doughnut-shaped vacuum tube.

UI physicist
Donald Kerst

1940–41

AMERICA'S TIME CAPSULE

September 16, 1940   Congress passed the Selective Service Act, requiring all men between the ages of twenty and thirty-six to register for the armed services.

November 5, 1940   Franklin Roosevelt defeated Republican Wendell Willkie for a second term as president.

December 8, 1940   The Chicago Bears beat the Washington Redskins, 73–0, in the NFL championship game.

March 3, 1941   Chocolatier Forrest Mars received a patent for his manufacturing process of M&Ms.

June 22, 1941   Germany invaded the U.S.S.R.

July 17,1941   Joe DiMaggio's incredible baseball hitting streak of fifty-six consecutive games was ended by the Cleveland Indians.

ILLINI MOMENT

Illini Golfers Capture Big Ten Crown

When Coach Winsor Brown's Fighting Illini golf team captured its second consecutive Big Ten championship on June 19, 1941, it helped the University of Illinois to become the winningest confer-

UI's Alex Welsh was the Big Ten medalist in 1941

ence school ever in the sport at that time. Led by individual medalist Alex Welsh, the Illini outdistanced runnersup Ohio State and Michigan for their sixth all-time team crown. Besides Welsh, other members of the team included John Holmstrom, John Buzick, Dick Wolfley, and Bill Usinger. A week later, the Illini golf squad traveled to the NCAA championship meet and placed fourth. Since 1941, Illini golfers have won only one Big Ten team title.

The 1941 Illini won the Big Ten title

I on 1940–41

Robert "Bob" Richmond was the Most Valuable Player for the 1940–41 Illini basketball team and earned first-team All–Big Ten honor. The West Frank-

Bob Richmond

lin native was the top-scoring guard in the conference that season. In his final game for Illinois, Richmond pumped in 17 points as the Illini whipped Chicago, 52 to 33. He died tragically in a plane crash on May 16, 1941, serving with the U.S. Navy.

ILLINI ITEM

Illinois was the unofficial national champion of college ice hockey in 1941, recording a mark of 17-3-1. In competition against Big Ten foes, the Illini were 6-1-1. The stars of coach Vic Heyliger's team were Norbert Sterle, Aldo Palazarri, and Amo Bessone. Bessone later became a successful coach at Michigan State, leading the Spartans to the 1966 NCAA title.

Illinois's 1941 hockey team was the unofficial national champion

ILLINI LISTS

ILLINI MEN'S ATHLETIC TRAINERS

until 1913	William "Willie" McGill
1913–1926	Dr. Samuel Bilik
1926–1947	David M. "Matt" Bullock
1947–1951	Elmer "Ike" Hill
1951–1957	Richard Klein
1957–1969	Robert Nicollette
1969–1973	Robert Behnke
1973–1983	John "Skip" Pickering

"Wee Willie" McGill was UI's first athletic trainer

DIRECTORS OF SPORTS MEDICINE

1983–2012	Al Martindale
2012–2015	Paul Schmidt
2015–present	Randy Ballard

ILLINI WOMEN'S ATHLETIC TRAINERS

1975–1978	Dana Gerhardt
1978–1980	Ellen Murray
1980–2008	Karen Iehl-Morse

ILLINI LEGEND

Leo Johnson

Coach Leo Johnson

If the measure of success of a coach is quantified in championships, then longtime University of Illinois coach Leo Johnson was a giant of his era in the sport of track and field. From the time he was hired as coach of the Illini in 1938 until his retirement at age seventy in 1965, Johnson guided Fighting Illini teams to seventeen Big Ten titles and three national championships. Since 1944, when Johnson's Illini won the NCAA title, he is one of only four coaches outside the Sun Belt states to win a national championship. His athletes captured twenty-seven individual NCAA titles and 158 conference firsts during his twenty-eight years at Illinois. A member of numerous track and field halls of fame, Johnson was also known in Illini football history as one of the game's finest scouts. A college football and track star at Millikin College in Decatur, Johnson served as a lieutenant in World War I. When the war ended, he played pro football briefly with George Halas's Decatur Staleys, then became head coach of all sports at Millikin in 1923. Johnson died in 1982 at age eighty-seven.

ILLINI LORE

The Illini Union officially opened its doors at the University of Illinois on February 8, 1941. Interest in building a facility intensified in 1934 when A. C. Willard was inaugurated as president of the university. One of the president's first official acts was to appoint a committee to investigate construction of a Union building. When the UI decided to raze University Hall—the site on which the Illini Union was built—the decision of the committee was unanimous. An addition to the $1.2 million structure was completed at a cost of nearly $7 million in 1963. More than forty volumes of illustration of colonial architecture were used in preparing the preliminary drawings of the Illini Union. The distinctive feature of the building is a thirty-foot open-arched cupola and its eleven-foot bronze weather vane. In the belfry of the cupola is the university's historic chapel bell and, at its base, is the 124-year-old clock that once stood in University Hall.

The Illini Union is one of the University of Illinois's best-known landmarks

AMERICA'S TIME CAPSULE

December 7, 1941   About twenty-four hundred Americans lost their lives and another twelve hundred were wounded when the Japanese attacked Pearl Harbor, Hawaii.

December 11, 1941   Germany and Italy declared war against the United States.

December 21, 1941   The Chicago Bears won the NFL championship, defeating the New York Giants 37–9.

January 9, 1942   Joe Louis successfully defended his world heavyweight boxing title for the twentieth time, knocking out Max Baer in the first round.

April 18, 1942   American bombers, under the command of Maj. Gen. James Doolittle, conducted a successful air raid on Tokyo.

ILLINI MOMENT

Whiz Kids

Doug Mills coached the "Whiz Kids," which included four finely tuned athletes, all around 6'3", who formed the heart of the team. The quartet of Andy Phillip, Jack Smiley, Gene Vance, and Ken Menke, joined veteran Art Mathisen and fashioned a cumulative Big Ten record of 25–2 in 1942 and 1943, winning two conference titles. The 1943 club finished with an overall record of 17-1 and was undefeated in conference play (12-0), but didn't play in the national tournament because of service in World War II. "Uncle Sam had our draft rights," said Vance, and the war took precedence over the five-year-old NCAA championship playoffs. "I'm 99 percent sure we would have won," said Menke. When the group reunited for the 1946–47 campaign, all four players returned to starting positions, but it wasn't quite the same. "They had gone through terrible war experiences, and they had changed," recalled Mills."

(Left to right) Coach Doug Mills, Art Mathisen, Jack Smiley, Gene Vance, Ken Menke, and Andy Phillip

I on 1941–42

War hero Tom Riggs

As an Illini letter winner from 1938 to 1940, Thomas Riggs faced some fierce battles on the football field, but there was no comparison to what confronted him as a World War II soldier. Lt. Col. Riggs was captured by the Germans in 1944. A daring escape led him on a three-month, 1,000-mile trip to freedom. Riggs pleaded to rejoin his unit and he served with them until the war ended. In 1989, Riggs was presented with the University's Varsity I Award. He died in 1998 at age eighty-two.

ILLINI ITEM

Bob Zuppke (right) coached in his final game on November 17, 1941

On November 17, 1941, five days before his team's season finale at Northwestern, veteran Fighting Illini football coach Bob Zuppke announced his retirement. Under pressure from alumni and the University of Illinois Board of Trustees, Zuppke stepped down "for the good of Illinois." Unfortunately, Zuppke's team ended the season on a sour note, losing to the Wildcats, 27–0.

ILLINI LIST

THE WHIZ KIDS' 1941–42 ROSTER

The 1941–42 "Whiz Kids" are one of Illinois's most famous teams

Name	Ht.	Cl.	TP	Hometown
Bergeson, Ray	6'3"	Jr.	0	Batavia, Ill.
Dillon, Dave	6'1"	Sr.	0	Newton, N.J.
Fowler, Chuck	5'10"	So.	30	Watseka, Ill.
Fulton, Cliff	6'2"	So.	0	Mooseheart, Ill.
Grierson, Ray	6'0"	Jr.	0	Champaign, Ill.
Hocking, Bill	6'1"	Sr.	24	Braidwood, Ill.
Mathisen, Art	6'5"	Jr.	119	Dwight, Ill.
Matter, Herb	6'1"	So.	0	Naperville, Ill.
Menke, Ken	6'2"	So.	201	Dundee, Ill.
Parker, Ed (Ace)	6'3"	So.	22	Cicero, Ill.
Parker, Ken	6'4"	So.	0	Granite City, Ill.
Phillip, Andy	6'3"	So.	221	Granite City, Ill.
Sachs, Henry	5'11"	Sr.	16	Chicago, Ill.
Smiley, Arthur	6'3"	So.	89	Waterman, Ill.
Vance, Gene	6'3"	So.	100	Clinton, Ill.
Wukovits, Vic	6'3"	Sr.	128	South Bend, Ind.

ILLINI LEGEND

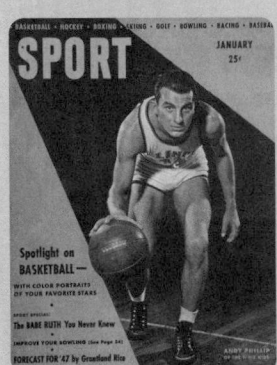

Illinois's Andy Phillip

Andy Phillip

The magnificent career of Illini basketball star Andy Phillip can be summed up in just two words: record setting. Besides establishing Illinois basketball records for points in a game, in a season, and in a career, the Granite City, Illinois, native also put his name in the record book beside several Big Ten marks. Following the 1945 season, he was named first-team All-American and was honored as the Big Ten's Most Valuable Player. Phillip and his "Whiz Kids" teammates won back-to-back Big Ten titles in 1942 and 1943. After the end of the 1943 season, Phillip was called to active duty with the Marine Corps for three years. When World War II ended, he returned to Illinois with three other "Whiz Kids" in 1947, and they settled for a second-place finish in the conference. For the next eleven years, Phillip played professional basketball in the NBA, including two seasons with the world-champion Boston Celtics. A five-time NBA All-Star, he was named to the Basketball Hall of Fame in 1961. Phillip spent all of his postbasketball life in California, retiring in 1987 after twenty-four years as supervising officer for the Riverside County Probation Department. He died on April 28, 2001, at age seventy-nine.

ILLINI LORE

During its first twelve months of operation, the $1.7 million Abbott Power Plant in 1941–42 proved to be more efficient than University of Illinois officials hoped it would be. The new plant was built adjacent to the Illinois Central railroad tracks, just northwest of Memorial Stadium, and close to the expanding university. A comparison of the facility's performance in 1921–22 to 1932–33 showed that the new plant burned nearly 10 percent less coal and heated 13 percent more cubic feet of space.

The Abbott Power Plant

1942–43

AMERICA'S TIME CAPSULE

November 26, 1942   *Casablanca*, starring Humphrey Bogart and Ingrid Bergman, premiered.
December l, 1942   Nationwide gasoline rationing went into effect.
May 1, 1943   Count Fleet, with jockey Johnny Longden, won the sixty-ninth annual Kentucky Derby.
May 5, 1943   Postmaster Frank Walker inaugurated a postal-zone numbering system to speed up
                    mail delivery.
July 19, 1943   More than five hundred Allied planes bombed Rome.

ILLINI
MOMENT

Illini End Minnesota's Eighteen-Game Winning Streak

ALERT, CHARGING TEAM OUTPLAYS NAT'L CHAMPS AT HOMECOMING, 20-13

Agase Recovers Fumble Over Goal, Steals Ball to Score Twice; Minnesota Star Returns Punt 81 Yards for Touchdown

By FRITZ JAUCH

The Fightingest Illini the University of Illinois has ever seen wrote the most glorious chapter in all Illinois football history yesterday afternoon in Memorial stadium before 24,276 wild-eyed, hysterical Homecoming fans.

Illinois upsets the defending national champs

The twenty-four thousand fans who attended Illinois's thirty-second annual Homecoming Game witnessed one of the greatest Illini football upsets ever. First-year coach Ray Eliot inspired his troops with a pregame pep talk and snapped defending national champion Minnesota's eighteen-game winning streak. The unlikely Illini hero that afternoon was junior guard Alex Agase, who scored two of his team's three touchdowns. With the score tied 13–13 late in the fourth quarter, Agase scored the game-winning TD by pouncing on an errant Gopher snap in the end zone. Illinois's 20–13 victory was its first over a Big Ten foe since 1939.

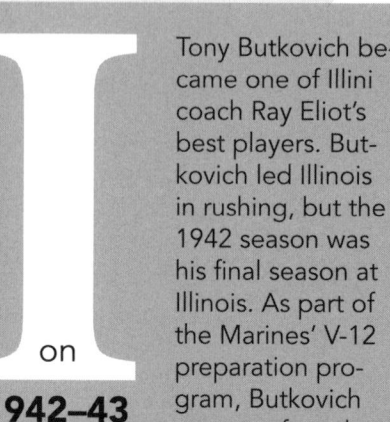

Tony Butkovich

Tony Butkovich became one of Illini coach Ray Eliot's best players. Butkovich led Illinois in rushing, but the 1942 season was his final season at Illinois. As part of the Marines' V-12 preparation program, Butkovich was transferred to Purdue to continue his Marine officer school training. As a Boilermaker in 1943, he scored four touchdowns against the Illini in a 40–21 Purdue victory. Shortly afterwards, Butkovich deployed to the Pacific as America and its allies advanced upon Japan. On April 18, 1945, during the Battle of Okinawa, he died from mortal wounds two weeks after his twenty-fourth birthday.

I on 1942–43

Illini All-American
Alex Agase

ILLINI ITEM

Illinois's "Whiz Kids" beat Northwestern, 86–44, at the Chicago Stadium on February 27, 1943, before a record crowd of 19,848. The triumph marked the school's largest margin of victory ever on the road and was the eleventh of twelve in a row as the Illini wrapped up a perfect record in conference play.

ILLINI 86, N. U. 44!
RECORD SCORE CROWD

ONLY CHICAGO BLOCKS WAY TO BIG 10 TITLE | Chicago Game Sole 'Hurdle' For Champions | Champions Wipe Out Wisconsin Mark of 74 Points | Illini Easily Shatter Old Big 10 Mar

Illinois drubbed Northwestern at the Chicago Stadium

The "Whiz Kids"

ILLINI LISTS

WHIZ KIDS' MOST MEMORABLE GAMES

In June 1994, the University of Illinois's famous Whiz Kids basketball team of the 1940s was surveyed to find out what they considered to be their most memorable games. Ken Menke, Andy Phillip, Art Mathisen, Gene Vance, and Jack Smiley were asked to rank their top ten selections in order, with ten points awarded for their first selection, nine points for their second choice, and so on. Four of the five men selected Illinois's game against Great Lakes on December 19, 1942, as their most memorable game. In that contest, the "Whiz Kids" came from behind to beat a team of former pros, 57–53.

1. December 19, 1942 vs. Great Lakes		48 pts.
2. February 27, 1943 vs. Northwestern		39 pts.

3. January 3, 1942 vs. Wisconsin		26 pts.
4. January 2, 1943 vs. Stanford		24 pts.
5. February 28, 1942 vs. Northwestern		23 pts.
6. March 1, 1943 vs. Chicago		17 pts.
7. February 23, 1942 vs. Wisconsin		16 pts.
8. January 11, 1943 vs. Wisconsin		13 pts.
9. January 13, 1947 vs. Ohio State		13 pts.
10. December 9, 1941 vs. Marquette		12 pts.

ILLINI LEGEND

Ray Eliot

During his days as a Fighting Illini football player under Bob Zuppke in the 1930s, he was listed on the roster as No. 38, Ray Nusspickle. As Zuppke's replacement from 1942 to 1959, he was introduced as head coach Ray Eliot. However, to the thousands of loyal fans who grew to love him, he was best known by the simple moniker "Mr. Illini." A football and baseball letterman at Illinois, Eliot's greatest fame came after he coached the Illini to Rose Bowl victories in 1947 over UCLA and in 1952 over Stanford. Three times, he won Big Ten championships (1946, 1951, 1953). Eliot, whose enthusiasm and vigor were trademarks, served as associate athletic director from 1960 until his retirement in 1973. He represented the Illini program in an honorary capacity after that, before being called upon in the spring of 1979 to become interim athletic director. Eliot was a dynamic speaker who was best known for his inspiring speech "The Proper State of Mind." He died on February 24, 1980, at age seventy-five, and was buried in Mt. Hope Cemetery, across Fourth Street from Memorial Stadium.

Mr. Illini: Ray Eliot

ILLINI LORE

The University of Illinois focused much of its effort toward wartime preparedness during the 1942–43 academic year. About eleven hundred people, including the physical plant staff and several faculty members, were actively engaged in a program of wartime civilian defense. University enrollment dropped 9 percent, but more than two thousand Navy School trainees were on campus, using Newman Hall and the ice rink as barracks. The UI taught forty-two special war courses, ranging from training in Red Cross and Civilian Defense to the structural design of airplanes. A total of 20,276 alumni served in the armed forces during World War 11, with twenty-nine former varsity athletes and 709 others with UI ties losing their lives in service.

UI's fraternities became army barracks during World War II

1943–44

AMERICA'S TIME CAPSULE

December 24, 1943	General Dwight D. Eisenhower was appointed Supreme Commander of Allied forces for the European invasion.
December 26, 1943	Coach George Halas's Chicago Bears won the NFL title by defeating the Washington Redskins, 41–21.
March 6, 1944	U.S. pilots dropped two thousand tons of bombs on Berlin.
June 6, 1944	More than five thousand ships, eleven thousand planes, and 150,000 servicemen began the D-Day invasion.
August 25, 1944	Paris was liberated as the German garrison surrendered the capital.

ILLINI MOMENT

Illini Athletics during the War

World War II had a dramatic effect on Illinois's athletics program. Of the eighty-one men who earned varsity letters during the 1942–43 season, only wrestling's Robert Hughes and track and field's Marce Gonzalez and Robert Phelps returned to rosters. Among the 150 eligible athletes who left school to serve in the U.S. armed forces were such stars as basketball's Andy Phillip and Gene Vance, football's Alex Agase and Tony Butkovich, and baseball's Lee Eilbracht. The war forced the Athletic Association to totally drop its gymnastics and fencing programs from 1943–46, while ice hockey was eliminated from varsity status altogether. However, Director Doug Mills decided that "athletics in wartime should be carried on in as nearly prewar fashion as possible." "Material is not plentiful, coaches may feel their task at times is insurmountable, and gate receipts may decline seriously," he said. "but none of these factors should influence us from the conviction that the basic values of the athletic program must remain alive."

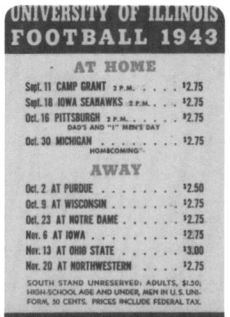

Athletics Director Doug Mills (left) and Coach Ray Eliot at the Illini Football Honor Roll

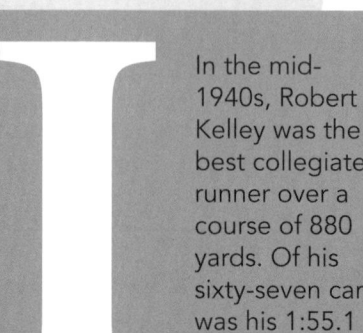
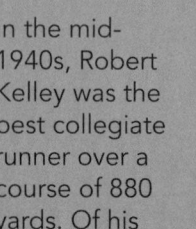

Illini sprinter Robert Kelley

I on 1943–44

In the mid-1940s, Robert Kelley was the best collegiate runner over a course of 880 yards. Of his sixty-seven career victories, the biggest was his 1:55.1 effort at the 1944 NCAA Outdoor Championships in Milwaukee. Kelley's title, combined with individual championships by Buddy Young, Dave Nichols, and Robert Phelps, helped the Illini easily capture the team crown over runner-up Notre Dame, 79–43. After Kelley graduated, he served three years in the Navy before settling in Chicago, where he was a physical education teacher. He died February 25, 2001 at age eighty.

ILLINI ITEM

Illinois lost its only opportunity to salvage a dismal football season on November 13, 1943. When Ohio State quarterback Dean Sensenbaugher's pass fell incomplete, the two teams went disappointedly to their dressing rooms, tied at 26. However, a game official had signaled the Illini off sides and put two seconds back on the clock. Both teams were brought back onto the field, and OSU placekicker John Stungis kicked a twenty-three-yard field goal to give the Buckeyes a 29–26 victory.

UNIVERSITY OF ILLINOIS
FOOTBALL 1943

· AT HOME
Sept. 11 CAMP GRANT 2 P.M. $2.75
Sept. 18 IOWA SEAHAWKS 2 P.M. . . . $2.75
Oct. 16 PITTSBURGH 2 P.M. $2.75
DAD'S AND "I" MEN'S DAY
Oct. 30 MICHIGAN $2.75
HOMECOMING

AWAY
Oct. 2 AT PURDUE $2.50
Oct. 9 AT WISCONSIN $2.75
Oct. 23 AT NOTRE DAME $2.75
Nov. 6 AT IOWA $2.75
Nov. 13 AT OHIO STATE $3.00
Nov. 20 AT NORTHWESTERN $2.75

SOUTH STAND UNRESERVED: ADULTS, $1.50;
HIGH-SCHOOL AGE AND UNDER, MEN IN U.S. UNI-
FORM, 50 CENTS. PRICES INCLUDE FEDERAL TAX.

MAIL ORDERS TO C. W. LYON
FOOTBALL TICKET OFFICE CHAMPAIGN

Buddy Young has Illini football's two longest runs ever from scrimmage

ILLINI LISTS

Buddy Young, Illinois's lightning-quick dynamo from Chicago, played more than seventy years ago but still ranks as the Fighting Illini's most electrifying running back. Of UI football's ten longest runs from scrimmage, Young owns three of those dashes, including two in the same game.

LONGEST RUNS FROM SCRIMMAGE

1.	93 yards	Buddy Young vs. Great Lakes, September 30, 1944
2.	92 yards	Buddy Young vs. Pittsburgh, October 21, 1944
3.	89 yards	Harry Jefferson vs. Syracuse, October 23, 1954
4.	86 yards	Rashard Mendenhall vs. Northwestern, November 18, 2006

5.	84 yards	Antoineo Harris vs. Purdue, October 12, 2002
6.	84 yards	Ray Nitschke vs. Northwestern, November 23, 1957
7.	83 yards	John Karras vs. Indiana, October 29, 1951
8.	82 yards	Buddy Young vs. Pittsburgh, October 21, 1944
9.	82 yards	Red Grange vs. Chicago, November 8, 1924
10.	80 yards	Daniel Dufrene vs. Ohio State, November 10, 2007
11.	80 yards	Cyril Pinder vs. Duke, October 23, 1965
12.	80 yards	Edgar Nichol vs. Coe, October 13, 1928

ILLINI LEGEND

Buddy Young sprints through the finish line

Claude "Buddy" Young

The University of Illinois's first nationally famous African American athlete stood only five feet, four inches tall, but the legacy he established is immeasurable. Claude "Buddy" Young came to Champaign-Urbana from Chicago Phillips High School, where he was a state champion sprinter and an all-star halfback in football. In his first competition with the Fighting Illini track team on February 5, 1944, Young won the 60-yard dash at New York's prestigious Millrose Games. He lost very few races that freshman year, tying the world indoor record of 6.1 seconds in the 60-yard dash and capturing two sprint titles at the NCAA outdoor meet. On the football field, little number 66 was equally magnificent. The 1944 season saw Young tie Red Grange's school record for touchdowns (thirteen) and average nearly nine yards every time he rushed the ball. He served in the navy in 1945 but was able to return to the Illini football team in 1946, winning MVP honors in the 1947 Rose Bowl. Young left Illinois after that season to sign a football contract with the New York Yankees. His Hall of Fame career in pro football ended after ten seasons, and he became the first Baltimore Colts player to have his jersey—number 22—retired. In 1964, Young became the first black executive to be hired by the National Football League. He stayed at that post until his death in an automobile accident on September 4, 1983.

ILLINI LORE

On June I, 1944, the University of Illinois Board of Trustees approved a proposal to establish a College of Veterinary Medicine and Surgery. Twenty-five years earlier, in 1919, establishment of the college had been authorized by the Illinois General Assembly, but no appropriations followed. The first course in veterinary medicine was actually taught at the U of I in 1870.

UI's Veterinary Pathology Lab

AMERICA'S TIME CAPSULE

November 7, 1944   Franklin Roosevelt was reelected America's president for a record fourth term. He died five months later and was succeeded by Harry Truman.

December 15, 1944   Big-band leader Glenn Miller died in a plane crash over the English Channel.

December 16, 1944   The last major German offensive of World War II—the Battle of the Bulge—began.

August 6, 1945   Hiroshima, Japan, was destroyed by the first atomic bomb to be used in war. Nine days later, the Japanese surrendered to the Allies.

ILLINI MOMENT

Walker Leads Illini to Track Title

Scoring in twelve of the fourteen events, Coach Leo Johnson's Fighting Illini track and field squad ended Michigan's two-year reign as Big Ten champions on May 26, 1945. Illinois's star performers included two veterans and a pair of freshmen. Junior captain Marce Gonzalez captured the 220-yard dash, while grad student Bob Kelley repeated his conference outdoor titles in the 440- and 880-yard runs. Illini rookie George Walker accounted for fifteen of his team's 65½ points, taking first place in the 100-yard dash, the 120-yard high hurdles, and the 220-yard low hurdles. Fellow freshman Henry Aihara won the broad jump and tied for fourth in the high jump. Two weeks later at the NCAA meet in Milwaukee, the Illini placed second behind Navy, 62 to 57¾. Walker captured both hurdles events, Aihara won the broad jump, and Bob Phelps took top honors in the pole vault.

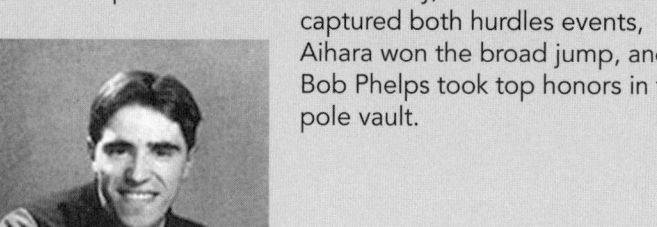

Marce Gonzalez

I on 1944–45

Ralph "Babe" Serpico

Ralph Serpico was one of Coach Ray Eliot's most beloved players. Serpico lettered all four seasons he played for the Illini (1944 to 1947). As a sophomore, he served as Illinois's captain and, as a junior, helped lead the Orange and Blue to the Big Ten title and a victory over UCLA in the 1947 Rose Bowl. Serpico unselfishly passed up coaching offers to remain in Melrose Park and tend to his wheelchair-bound father. He worked for the Cook County Assessor's office for near twenty-four years. He died in 1995 at age seventy.

Ralph "Babe" Serpico (right) captained Ray Eliot's 1945 Illini

ILLINI ITEM

Buddy Young (66) dashes around the right side

To say that the football debut of Buddy Young, September 16, 1944, was impressive would be a mammoth understatement. The nation's fastest halfback played nine and one-half minutes for Illinois against Illinois State, averaging more than twenty-eight yards every time he touched the ball. Young lost four yards on his first carry, then scored touchdowns of twenty-two and eighty-two yards on his next two attempts. He also ran fifty-one yards for a TD, only to have it called back by a clipping penalty. The final score: Illinois 79, ISU 0.

ILLINI LISTS

ILLINI FOOTBALL PLAYERS IN HEISMAN TROPHY BALLOTING

1944	Buddy Young, 5th
1951	John Karras, 6th
1953	J. C. Caroline, 7th
1959	Bill Burrell, 4th
1963	Dick Butkus, 6th
1964	Dick Butkus, 3rd
1965	Jim Grabowski, 3rd
1980	Dave Wilson 10th
1982	Tony Eason, 8th
1989	Jeff George, 35th
2001	Kurt Kittner, 12th

Illini star Buddy Young finished fifth in the Heisman Trophy voting of 1944

ILLINI LEGEND

Walton Kirk

It was a star-studded cast of nominees for the *Daily Illini*'s annual "Illini Athlete of the Year" award in 1944–45, but in the end, a junior basketball guard nicknamed "Junior" ran away from his competition. Unanimous All–Big Ten selection Walton "Junior" Kirk was the students' first choice, outdistancing two-sport standout Howie Judson by a 2:1 margin. The native of Mt. Vernon, Illinois, was the Most Valuable Player of Doug Mills's Illinois cagers, averaging nearly eleven points per game. His best effort of the 1944–45 campaign came at Michigan in a 55–37 victory when he scored a season-high twenty-one points. Kirk entered military service at Fort Lewis in June 1945, then returned to Illinois for the 1946–47 season. He subsequently signed a $10,000 NBA contract with the Fort Wayne Pistons, joining teammates Jack Smiley and Ken Menke. Kirk scored 907 points during his 163-game NBA career with Fort Wayne, TriCities, and Milwaukee. In 1952 he began a long high school career in administration and coaching, which included stops at Harvard and Salem, Illinois, and at Dubuque, Iowa. Kirk died in 2012 at age eighty-eight.

Walt Kirk

ILLINI LORE

George Dinsmore Stoddard was appointed University of Illinois's tenth president May 26, 1945, replacing Arthur Cutts Willard as the chief executive officer, a position Stoddard held during a construction boom on campus, yet he also found himself mired in controversy. The university's board of trustees and state legislators disapproved of Stoddard's frequent trips abroad and of his ongoing debates with various members of the school's faculty. Stoddard resigned July 24, 1953, under pressure from the Board of Trustees following a 6–3 vote of "no confidence."

George Stoddard (left) succeeded Arthur Willard as UI's president in 1945

1945–1954

1945-46

AMERICA'S TIME CAPSULE

September 2, 1945
October 10, 1945
February 15, 1946
June 25, 1946
July 4, 1946
August 25, 1946

Japan signed the formal document of surrender aboard the U.S.S. Missouri in Tokyo Bay.
The Chicago Cubs lost the World Series to the Detroit Tigers, four games to three.
Scientists developed the world's first electronic digital computer in Philadelphia.
Fire destroyed the LaSalle Hotel in Chicago; sixty-one people lost their lives.
President Harry Truman proclaimed Philippine independence.
Ben Hogan won the PGA championship.

ILLINI
MOMENT

Illini Teams Win Four Big Ten Titles

Though they finished second to Ohio State in the all-sports standings among Big Ten schools, Fighting Illini teams won more conference titles than any other conference member during the 1945–46 athletic season. Illinois took top honors in the sports of both indoor and outdoor track, wrestling, and tennis. The latter two were especially pleasing, since several years had lapsed in between championships. Nine years had passed since the Illini grapplers last won a title, and fourteen years had gone by since the tennis squad ended up on top of the league standings. Coach Leo Johnson's track and field team made the biggest news, however. Not only did they sweep titles in both Big Ten seasons, they also took top honors nationally, winning the NCAA outdoor title in Minneapolis.

The 1946 Illini tennis team was the Big Ten champion

I on 1945–46

Les Bingaman
When Coach Ray Eliot recruited Lester Alonza "Les" Bingaman to Illinois from Gary, Indiana, in 1944, Bingaman faced dropped-mouth

Illinois's Les Bingaman

stares from everyone he met because of his size. As a pro, the 350-pound middle guard helped the Detroit Lions reach the NFL championship game for three straight seasons in the early 1950s. "Bing" retired at age twenty-eight in 1954 following three consecutive appearances in the Pro Bowl. He then turned to coaching and, during the 1969 season, Bingaman collapsed on the sideline from a heart attack. He died a few months later at age forty-four.

ILLINI ITEM

Ray Eliot's football squad flew to Ohio State in November 1945

The very first "Flying Illini" team took to the airways November 16, 1945, when Coach Ray Eliot's football squad chartered a flight from Willard Airport to Ohio State. Eliot and nineteen of his top players departed Savoy on a TWA airliner at 1:00 P.M. It was the first large passenger takeoff from the new airport, dedicated just three weeks before. The entire squad returned to Champaign via the railways following its 27–2 loss.

ILLINI LISTS

MULTIPLE ILLINI BIG TEN INDIVIDUAL MEN'S TRACK CHAMPIONS (since 1945)

George Walker won ten Big Ten titles during his Illini track career

1. Charlton Ehizuelen (1974–1977)	12 titles
(includes one relay title)	
2. Andrew Riley (2009–2012)	12 titles
3. George Walker (1945–1948)	10 titles
4. Mike Durkin (1972–1975)	9 titles
5. Herb McKenley (1946–1947)	9 titles
(includes three relay titles)	
6. Willie Williams (1952–1954)	9 titles
7. Marko Koers (1992–1995)	9 titles
(includes one relay title)	

8. Tim Simon (1985–1988)	8 titles
(includes four relay titles)	
9. Bobby True (1996–1999)	8 titles
(includes four relay titles)	
10. Sherman Armstrong (1998–2001)	8 titles
(includes three relay titles)	
11. George Kerr (1958–1960)	7 titles
(includes two relay titles)	
12. Don Laz (1949–51)	7 titles
13. Dorian Green (1994–97)	7 titles
(includes four relay titles)	

ILLINI LEGEND

Herb McKenley

His coach, Leo Johnson, once compared Herb McKenley to "a golf ball bouncing down a concrete road." That statement probably doesn't do justice to how good Illinois's greatest quarter-miler actually was. McKenley rarely met defeat during his two-year track career at the University of Illinois, setting some sort of standard every time he ran. He ran thirty-four races as an Illini, excluding relays, winning thirty-one and setting eighteen records—three of which were world records. As a junior in 1946 and a senior in 1947, no one was ever able to beat him in a 440-yard race at the Big Ten and NCAA meets. He swept to six titles. The Jamaican speedster, who came to Illinois after a two-year stop at Boston College, also led his native country to a gold medal victory over the United States at the 1952 Olympics. McKenley later became coach and director of Jamaica's Olympic track squad. One of his athletes, George Kerr, later broke McKenley's world record at Illinois. McKenley died in his native homeland in 2007 at age eighty-five.

Jamaican sprinter Herb McKenley set a record nearly every time he ran

ILLINI LORE

Less than four years after President Arthur Willard first addressed the University of Illinois Board of Trustees about securing an appropriation of $200,000 for the purchase of land in Savoy, the University's new airport was dedicated October 26, 1945. The 762-acre airport featured three mile-long concrete runways, making it the nation's foremost university-owned facility. It was renamed UI Willard Airport on October 18, 1961, after the former president.

MRS. A. C. WILLARD

RECEPTION COMMITTEE

DEDICATION OF THE UNIVERSITY OF ILLINOIS AIRPORT OCTOBER 26, 1945

This ribbon belonged to the wife of Arthur Willard, the namesake of UI's new airport

1946–47

AMERICA'S TIME CAPSULE

December 15, 1946	Coach George Halas's Chicago Bears won the NFL championship, beating the New York Giants 24–14.
December 20, 1946	*It's a Wonderful Life*, starring Jimmy Stewart as George Bailey, premiered.
April 11, 1947	Jackie Robinson made his debut with the Brooklyn Dodgers as Major League Baseball's first black player.
April 16, 1947	Nearly six hundred people died and more than five thousand were injured in a ship explosion at Texas City, Texas.
June 23, 1947	Despite President Truman's veto, Congress passed the controversial Taft-Hartley Labor Act.

ILLINI MOMENT

Illini Smell the Roses

The road to Pasadena was a long and winding one for the University of Illinois. Illini players traveled familiar highways through such midwestern cities as Bloomington, Ann Arbor, and Iowa City, but also detoured through sites that were much less familiar, such as Germany and Okinawa. Nearly three hundred men, most of whom were returning from military duty in World War II, turned out for Coach Ray Eliot's opening practice in 1946. The Illini split their first four games but stepped on the gas at the end. Illinois consecutively disposed of Wisconsin, Michigan, Iowa, Ohio State, and Northwestern to wind up with a 6–1 Big Ten record and a berth in the Rose Bowl. It marked the first game in the pact between the Big Ten and the Pacific Eight Conferences. Though it marked UI's first-ever trip to Pasadena for the New Year's Day classic, the Illini weren't greeted with open arms. California's media didn't respect the eleven-point underdogs, predicting a huge victory by third-ranked UCLA. The Bruins led 7–6 after the first quarter, but it was all Illinois during the final three periods. Illini running backs Julius Rykovich and Buddy Young rushed for 103 yards apiece, and seven different players each scored a touchdown. The final score: Illinois 45, UCLA 14.

Illinois's starters line up in the end zone of the famed Rose Bowl

I on 1946–47

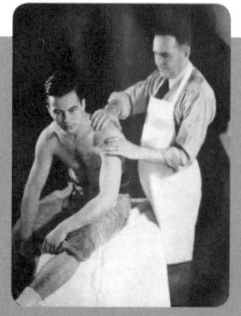

David M. "Matt" Bullock, athletic trainer from 1913 to 1947, first moved with his family to Champaign in 1907 and took a job working in the University of Illinois gymnasium in 1913. The Illini athletic trainer at the time, "Wee Willie" McGill, hired Bullock as his assistant in 1914. The affable Kentucky native became head athletic trainer and equipment manager in 1916. A charter member of the National Athletic Training Association Hall of Fame in 1962, eight former students and assistants have been similarly honored. Bullock died in 1953 at age sixty-seven.

"Matt" Bullock served as UI's athletic trainer from 1913 to 1947

ILLINI ITEM

Catcher Lee Eilbract eventually took over as coach of the Fighting Illini

In addition to the Illini football team, four other Illinois athletic teams finished on top of their respective Big Ten standings. Leo Johnson's track team swept titles, led by Bob Rehberg, Bob Richards, and Herb McKenley. The baseball team, coached by Wally Roettger, garnered big seasons from pitcher Marv Rotblatt and catcher Lee Eilbracht. Finally, the champion wrestling squad saw Dave Shapiro and Lou Kachiroubas successfully defend their Big Ten titles.

ILLINI LISTS

ILLINOIS FOOTBALL PLAYERS WHO WERE BIG TEN MVPS

The Chicago Tribune has presented the Silver Football award to the Big Ten's Most Valuable Player each year since 1924. Here are the seven Illinois gridders who've been so honored:

1924	Harold "Red" Grange, halfback
1946	Alex Agase, guard
1959	Bill Burrell, guard
1963	Dick Butkus, linebacker
1965	Jim Grabowski, fullback
1983	Don Thorp, defensive tackle
2007	Rashard Mendenhall, tailback

Alex Agase

ILLINI LEGEND

Alex Agase was an All-American at Illinois and Purdue

Alex Agase

In 1990, to commemorate the hundredth anniversary of Walter Camp's first All-American football team, the *New Haven (Connecticut) Register* selected a twenty-four-member All-Century Team. Among the two dozen players chosen, the University of Illinois led the way with three honorees. Two were predictable—Red Grange and Dick Butkus—but the third Illini—Alex Agase—was probably a surprise to some. However, when one considers that the 205-pound guard from Evanston, Illinois, was the only college player to be a three-time All-American for two different teams—Illinois and Purdue—his selection makes perfect sense. In addition to earning MVP honors at Illinois in 1946, Agase also was selected as the Big Ten's top player, leading the Illini to the 1947 Rose Bowl championship. Following a pro football career in Chicago, Cleveland, and Baltimore, Agase entered the coaching ranks. He served as head coach for both Northwestern and Purdue, earning Coach of the Year honors in 1970. Agase died at age eighty-five in 2007 at his home in Tarpon Springs, Florida.

ILLINI LORE

The University of Illinois received the largest gift in its history on June 29, 1946, when wealthy landowner Robert Allerton presented the UI with more than six thousand acres of farmland, located just west of Monticello, Illinois. The gift more than doubled UI's land holdings. Allerton Park was eventually opened to the general public, with the exception of the mansion, which Allerton stipulated be used for general university purposes. During the Bob Blackman era, the Illinois football team stayed at Allerton House the night before home games.

The Allerton House and more than six thousand acres of farmland was given to the University of Illinois in 1946

1947–48

AMERICA'S TIME CAPSULE

October 14, 1947	Captain Chuck Yeager piloted the world's first supersonic aircraft.
December 5, 1947	Heavyweight boxing champion Joe Louis earned a split decision over "Jersey Joe" Walcott.
March 8, 1948	The Supreme Court ruled that religious education in public schools was a violation of the First Amendment.
May 3, 1948:	James Michener's *Tales of the South Pacific* and Tennessee Williams's *A Streetcar Named Desire* earned Pulitzer Prizes.
August16, 1948	Babe Ruth, baseball's greatest player, died of cancer.

ILLINI MOMENT

Illini and Army Battle to Scoreless Tie

New York's historic Yankee Stadium, the site of many of baseball's greatest games, hosted one of college football's top battles on October 11, 1947. The combatants were a powerful Army team, unbeaten in thirty consecutive games, and Illinois, looking for its third win in three outings. Coach Ray Eliot's Fighting Illini carried the fight through the entire game, out-gaining their highly favored opponents 212 yards to 162. Illinois's best opportunity to score came late in the first half when it moved the ball fifty-one yards from its own 27 to the Army 22. Illini placekicker Don Maechtle came in to try a field goal, but a low snap ruined UI's only chance to score all day. Army, which had only nine total first downs, never came close to denting the Illini end zone, and the game ended in a 0–0 tie.

The game program sold at Yankee Stadium for the 1947 battle between Illinois and Army

I on 1947–48

Walt Kersulis

East St. Louis's Walter "Slip" Kersulis is the answer to a trivia question: Who's the only Illini of the modern era to have earned four varsity letters in both football and basketball? His Illini athletic career began in 1944–45, then was delayed for three years for service in World War II. Kersulis was an all-star receiver for Coach Ray Eliot, then turned his attention to the basketball court during the winter months. After graduating, he worked for Reynold Metals in Virginia. He died from leukemia at age forty-six.

Walter "Slip" Kersulis

ILLINI ITEM

Huff Gym was packed for the 1948 Illinois-Notre Dame game

The 1947–48 basketball season marked the first of twenty years in the saddle for Illinois hoops coach Harry Combes. Combes, who'd spent the year before as head coach at Champaign High School, won his first seven games as the Illini mentor. His Illini were nearly perfect in contests at Huff Gym that season, winning eleven of twelve games, losing only to eventual Big Ten champion, Michigan.

ILLINI LISTS

ILLINOIS'S GREATEST STRIKE-OUT PITCHERS (Career)
(through the 2001 season)

1. Brett Weber (1995–1998)	292
2. Marv Rotblatt (1946–1948)	286
3. John Ericks (1986–1988)	210
4. Jason Anderson (1998–2000)	197
5. Carl Jones (1984–1987)	196
6. Greg McCollum (1984–1987)	196
7. Jeff Innis (1981–1983)	178
8. Bubba Smith (1989–1991)	171
9. John Oestriech (1992–1995)	169
10. Mark Dressen (1989–1992)	162

Marv Rotblatt held UI's strikeout record for forty-seven years

ILLINI LEGEND

Illini left-hander
Marv Rotblatt

Marv Rotblatt

Though he stood only five-feet-six inches tall, southpaw Marv Rotblatt was one of college baseball's greatest pitchers in the 1940s. Relying on his wicked curve ball, Rotblatt set a plethora of records in 1947 and 1948, many of which still stand. In six Big Ten appearances during the 1947 campaign, the lefty from Chicago's Von Steuben High School compiled a perfect 6–0 record, striking out forty-nine batters in fifty-four innings. Rotblatt's finest single game effort was an eighteen-strikeout gem against Purdue on April 30, 1948. Career-wise, from 1945 to 1948, he won twenty-five of twenty-nine decisions for the Illini and registered a school-record 286 Ks. Rotblatt signed with the Chicago White Sox for a $3,000 bonus and pitched in the major leagues for three seasons, during which his ERAs led the league. He died in Evanston, Illinois, on July 16, 2013, at age eighty-five.

ILLINI LORE

During the 1947–48 academic year, Professor Albert Austin Harding completed forty-three years as director of University of Illinois bands. A 1906 UI graduate, Harding helped "Illinois Loyalty" composer Thatcher Howland Guild arrange the school's fight song. Harding was widely acclaimed for his work with university bands, and due to his admiration of Harding's work, famed "March King" John Philip Sousa donated his massive band collection to the university.

Longtime UI Director of Bands A. A. Harding (right) and the famous John Philip Sousa

1948–49

AMERICA'S TIME CAPSULE

November 2, 1948	In a major upset, Harry Truman defeated Thomas Dewey for the U.S. presidency.
December 15, 1948	State Department official Alger Hiss was indicted by a federal grand jury on two counts of perjury.
April 4, 1949	NATO was formed when member nations signed the North Atlantic Treaty.
April 20, 1949	The discovery of cortisone, the hormone promised to bring relief to sufferers of rheumatoid arthritis, was announced.
June 22, 1949	Ezzard Charles defeated "Jersey Joe" Walcott to become the new heavyweight boxing champion.

ILLINI MOMENT

Illini Need Two Overtimes to Beat Hoosiers

Fred Green needed nearly fifty minutes to score his only basket of the game, but it proved to be the biggest one of his career and the biggest shot of the 1948–49 Illini basketball season. Playing before a sellout crowd in Bloomington on January 8, 1949, Illinois and Indiana battled back and forth through a 37–37 tie at regulation time and 40–40 at the end of the first overtime. With fourteen seconds left in the second OT and the ball belonging to the Illini out of bounds under Indiana's goal, Bill Erickson slowly brought the ball down the court and shot a pass in to Green, deep in the lane. The 6'7" senior from Urbana wheeled to his left and shot with his right hand, threading the ball through the hoop with just four seconds remaining. Illinois's 44–42 victory was its second of what would eventually be a league-leading ten wins that season, enough for the school's first Big Ten title in six years.

Fred Green (front row, fifth from left) led the Illini past Indiana to win the Big Ten championship

Herb Plews

I on 1948–49

A two-time baseball MVP, Herb Plews was signed by the Yankees in 1950. Following two years of service during the Korean War, then two years in the minors, Plews was called up to the big leagues by the Washington Senators. His rookie season in 1956 included ten doubles, seven triples, and one home run among his sixty-nine hits. The left-handed hitter played three more seasons, ending his career with a lifetime average of .262 after the 1959 season. He passed away in 2014 at the age of eighty-six.

Illini baseball's Herb Plews went on to play Major League Baseball

ILLINI ITEM

Though it was the only time in his first dozen seasons that he didn't win the Big Ten title, Charlie Pond made his debut as head coach of the Illini gymnastics team in 1948–49. Pond's success with at Illinois was accentuated by eleven conference championships and four NCAA titles. He coached the Illini until 1973, then served as an Olympic coach and judge. Pond died in 2003 at age eighty-seven.

Coach Charlie Pond's Illini gymnasts won four NCAA titles

ILLINI LISTS

LONGEST ILLINI PUNTS

1.	88 yards	Dike Eddleman vs. Iowa, November 6, 1948
2.	86 yards	Dike Eddleman vs. Ohio State, November 13, 1948
3.	86 yards	Bill Butkovich vs. Michigan, October 27, 1945
4.	85 yards	Ryan Tabloff vs. Purdue, October 25, 1997
5.	85 yards	Phil Vierneisel vs. Michigan State, October 19, 1974
6.	82 yards	Phil Vierneisel vs. Ohio State, November 2, 1974
7.	80 yards	Brett Larsen vs. Arizona, September 16, 1995
8.	79 yards	Steve Weatherford vs. Michigan State, October 9, 2004
9.	78 yards	Steve Fitts vs. Wisconsin, October 17, 1998
10.	75 yards	Steve Fitts vs. Minnesota, October 16, 1999

Dike Eddleman
was a punter
extraordinaire

ILLINI LEGEND

Dike Eddleman

In the fall of 1992 the University of Illinois honored the greatest all-around athlete in its history by naming its "Athlete of the Year" award after the incomparable Dike Eddleman. No other man can claim the amazing feats accomplished by the pride of Centralia, Illinois, during his Illini career. Not only was Eddleman a member of Illinois's first Rose Bowl championship team in 1947 and the leading scorer on UI's first Final Four basketball team in 1949, he also won a silver medal as a high-jumper in the 1948 Olympic games. Dike's eleven varsity letters at Illinois also stand as a record. He starred in the classroom as well, earning the Big Ten Conference Medal of Honor as an Illini senior. Following his graduation, Eddleman played in the NBA with the Tri-City Blackhawks and the Fort Wayne Pistons. In 1970 Dike returned to Illinois as the executive director of the Athletic Association's Grants-in-Aid program, retiring in 1992. He died on August 1, 2001, at age seventy-nine.

Dike Eddleman starred
with UI's basketball team

ILLINI LORE

Professor Joseph Tykociner, developer of movies with sound, retired in 1949 after twenty-seven years at the University of Illinois. He was born in Russian Poland in 1877 and studied in German technical institutes before coming to the United States in 1920. Following a year with Westinghouse, Tykociner joined the UI staff, and a year later, on June 9, 1922, gave his first public demonstration of movies with sound. Tykociner's developmental budget was less than $1,000. By coincidence, the first full-length sound picture, *The Jazz Singer*, was written by UI alumnus Samson Raphaelson.

Professor Joseph Tykociner retired from
the University of Illinois in 1949

1949–50

AMERICA'S TIME CAPSULE

October 9, 1949	The New York Yankees beat the Brooklyn Dodgers to win baseball's World Series.
October 24, 1949	The United Nations' headquarters were dedicated in New York.
February 8, 1950	The first credit card charge (Diners Club) was made by founder Frank McNamara.
April 23, 1950	The Minneapolis Lakers, starring George Mikan, beat the Syracuse Nationals to win the first NBA championship.
June 27, 1950	President Truman ordered U.S. armed forces to Korea to help South Korea repel the North Korean invasion.

ILLINI MOMENT

The Argo Express

Johnny Karras originally reported to the University of Illinois football camp in the fall of 1946, but he quickly discovered that his opportunity to be a first-team running back was limited by the presence of an abundance of returning war veterans, including Buddy Young and Paul Patterson. Karras decided to return to his hometown of Argo, Illinois, and enlist in the army, spending eighteen months in the service. It turned out to be one of the smartest decisions he ever made, for when he came back to Illinois in 1949 as a mature, twenty-year-old sophomore, he exploded into prominence, earning first-team All–Big Ten honors. In nine games that season, the Argo Express averaged 6.5 yards per rush and thirty-one yards per kickoff return, scoring an Illini high seven touchdowns. For that performance, he was named Illinois's Most Valuable Player. Karras's success continued in 1950 and 1951, as he eventually earned All-American laurels his senior year.

Johnny Karras

I on 1949–50

Sam Rebecca

Few individuals invested their lives more into the University of Illinois than Sam Rebecca. He came to Urbana-Champaign as a quarterback and placekicker, then spent thirty-two more years as an administrator.

Sam Rebecca (17) went on to a long career at his alma mater

A letter winner in 1950 and 1951, it was Rebecca's game-winning field goal against Northwestern that vaulted the Illini into the 1952 Rose Bowl. In 1970 Rebecca was selected as the university's director of housing; ten years later he was appointed assistant vice chancellor for administrative affairs. He finished his career in 1992 as administrative assistant to athletic director John Mackovic.

ILLINI ITEM

Dick "Rocky" Raklovits starred in football and baseball at Illinois

Dick "Rocky" Raklovitz Dick "Rocky" Raklovits starred on both the football field and the baseball diamond. He led the Big Ten in rushing in 1950; the following spring he led the Fighting Illini in batting average (.387), hits, runs, and steals. He earned first-team All–Big Ten honors in both of those sports in the same season. He has served as a coach and physical education instructor at Western Michigan University. He turned eighty-eight years old in 2016.

ILLINI LISTS

ILLINI ATHLETES WHO BECAME MEMBERS OF
THE BOARD OF TRUSTEES

*James W. Armstrong, football/track	1923–1935	
David J. Downey, basketball	1991–1993	
Harold E. Grange, football	1951–1955	
Wirt Herrick, track	1949–1961	
Robert Z. Hickman, football	1949–1955	
*Harold A. Pogue, football/track	1935–1941	
Russell W. Steger, football/baseball	1969–1975	
Frederick L. Wham, football	1925–1927	

*Served as president of the board

Wirt Herrick lettered in
track and field for Illinois
from 1909 to 1911

ILLINI LEGEND

Russell "Ruck"
Steger was UI's
Athlete of the
Year in 1950

"Ruck" Steger

Russell "Ruck" Steger was a born entertainer. As an athlete, he thrilled Fighting Illini fans with battering-ram runs and tape-measure clouts. Off the field, Ruck mesmerized his audience by strumming a guitar and singing "The Wabash Cannonball." In addition to combining brawn and charm, the native of St. Louis also had his share of brains, maintaining a B average in the classroom and eventually earning the Big Ten Conference Medal of Honor. Uncle Sam put the finger on Ruck for two years before he could begin his athletic career at the University of Illinois. But once he put on an Illini uniform, there was no holding him back. In football, Steger was a first-team All–Big Ten running back, leading Illinois rushers in 1947 and 1948. As an outfielder for Wally Roettger's UI baseball squad, Ruck had a career .317 average, en route to winning all-conference and Illini Athlete of the Year honors in 1950. His success didn't stop there, as he enjoyed a prosperous career in insurance and other businesses. Steger also served as a member of the University of Illinois Board of Trustees. He died in 2011 at age eighty-five.

ILLINI LORE

The University of Illinois's new eighteen-hole golf course, built at a cost of $250,000 entirely from Athletic Association funds, opened May 13, 1950, in Savoy. Constructed on 170 acres of rich farmland donated by Hartwell Howard, the 6,884-yard course was designed and built by C. D. Wagstaff, a 1918 UI alumnus.

UI's eighteen-hole golf course in
Savoy opened on May 13, 1950

1950–51

AMERICA'S TIME CAPSULE

September 26, 1950 — U.S. troops recaptured Seoul, the capital of South Korea.

October 7, 1950 — The New York Yankees defeated the Philadelphia Phillies to win the World Series, four games to none.

February 26, 1951 — Congress adopted the Twenty-Second Amendment to the U.S. Constitution, stipulating that no person may be elected to the presidency for more than two terms.

April 11, 1951 — President Truman relieved Gen. Douglas MacArthur of his post as supreme commander.

June 25, 1951 — The Columbia Broadcasting System (CBS) presented commercial television's first color broadcast.

ILLINI MOMENT

Fletcher's Heroics Lead Illini to Big Ten Title

Trailing by four points in the Big Ten season finale with only four and a half minutes left on the Jenison Field House clock, Illinois's prospects for an undisputed conference basketball crown certainly didn't look very promising . . . that is, until Rod Fletcher stepped forward to put on a dazzling one-man show for the Illini. During the ensuing sixty seconds, he picked the pockets of two Michigan State dribblers and cashed them into baskets, tying the score at 43. With 3:30 left, the backcourt whiz from Champaign rose at the free-throw line to can a jumper, and a minute later tapped in a left-handed rebound to give Illinois a four-point lead and its eventual 49–43 victory. Fletcher's heroics gave Harry Combes's troops a nearly perfect 13-1 record in Big Ten play, a half game better than runner-up Indiana, sending them to the NCAA tournament. In postseason play, the Illini lost the opening-round game at New York's Madison Square Garden to Kansas State, then rebounded in game two to defeat Columbia. Illinois then beat North Carolina State and lost to champion-to-be Kentucky by two points. The Illini salvaged third place in the Final Four by beating Oklahoma A&M at Minneapolis, giving them a final overall record of 22-5.

Rod Fletcher

I on 1950–51

Ted Beach

Champaign's Ted Beach

Ted Beach's name was synonymous with basketball in Champaign-Urbana. Ted's mid-1940s Champaign High teams reached the state championship game three years in a row, winning it his junior year (1946). Ted set a three-year tournament scoring record with 195 points. He attended the U of I in 1946 and played on Big Ten championship teams in 1949 and 1951. In 1964, Beach became the backup timer for Illini games, and he stayed on in varying roles for the next forty years. Beach is a member of the Illinois Basketball Hall of Fame (2011).

ILLINI ITEM

Pole vaulter Don Laz

On May 25, 1951, Don Laz's unusual double victory in the pole vault and the broad jump led Illinois to the Big Ten Outdoor Track and Field Championships at Dyche Stadium in Evanston, Illinois. Laz's amazing feat marked the first time in the fifty-one-year history of the conference championships that the same man had captured individual titles in those two events in the same meet. Laz died in 1997 in Champaign at age sixty-seven.

ILLINI LISTS

ILLINI FOOTBALL'S GREATEST PERFORMANCES
VERSUS NO. 1–RANKED TEAMS

October 28, 1944 at Notre Dame 13, Illinois 7
October 30, 1948 at Michigan 28, Illinois 20
November 18, 1950 at Illinois 14, Ohio State 7
October 27, 1956 at Illinois 20, Michigan State 13
November 11, 2006 Ohio State 17, at Illinois 10
November 3, 2007 Illinois 28, at Ohio State 21

The Illini football team upset No. 1 Michigan State in 1956

ILLINI LEGEND

Don Sunderlage

The 1951 Big Ten basketball season featured an abundance of stars, including Indiana's Bill Garrett and Minnesota's Whitey Skoog, but the league's Most Valuable Player that year was a senior guard from the University of Illinois named Don Sunderlage. The Illini captain led the conference in scoring with an average of 17.4 points per game. Many of Sunderlage's points came from the charity stripe, setting Illini records for both free throws made (171) and attempted (218). Those marks stood for forty-two years at Illinois until Kiwane Garris broke them in 1993–94. Sunderlage wound up his college career as Illinois's all-time scoring leader, tallying 777 points in three seasons. He spent two seasons in the NBA, one year each with Milwaukee and Minnesota, averaging nearly eight points per game. Sunderlage was a member of the West squad in the 1954 NBA AllStar Game. His life came to a tragic end at age thirty-one on July 15, 1961, when he and his wife, Janice, were killed in an automobile crash.

Don Sunderlage

ILLINI LORE

The first coed cheerleaders for a University of Illinois athletic event appeared September 30, 1950, when the Fighting Illini football team hosted Ohio University at Memorial Stadium. The group included Marilyn Lowe of Springfield, Dorothy Rich of Manteno, Mary Lou Schaeflein of Chicago, and Marilyn Berger of Chicago.

Illinois's cheerleading squad became coed in 1950

1951–52

AMERICA'S TIME CAPSULE

November 10, 1951	The first transcontinental direct-dial telephone call was placed from New Jersey to California.
December 20, 1951	A station in Idaho began producing electricity from the first atomic-powered generator.
March 27, 1952	*Singin' in the Rain*, starring Gene Kelly, Donald O'Connor, and Debbie Reynolds, premiered.
April 8, 1952	A presidential order prevented a shutdown of the nation's steel mills by strikers.
July 11, 1952	Gen. Dwight Eisenhower and Sen. Richard Nixon were nominated as the presidential ticket for the Republicans.

ILLINI MOMENT

More Roses

Coach Ray Eliot's 1951 squad is the last University of Illinois football team to be undefeated during an entire season. They won their first seven games of the campaign, then played to a score-

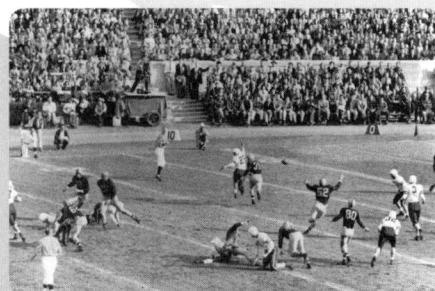

Action at the 1952 Rose Bowl game between Illinois and Stanford

less tie at Ohio State. Illinois's Rose Bowl-clinching victory came in the regular-season finale at Northwestern, thanks to the toe of Sammy Rebecca, who kicked a sixteen-yard field goal. The New Year's Day showdown against Stanford, America's first college football game to be nationally telecast, proved to be a defensive struggle through the first half, with the Indians leading the Illini by a single point, 7–6. However, Illinois exploded for thirty-four unanswered points in the second half, capitalizing on a pair of Stan Wallace defensive interceptions and a strong running attack from game MVP Bill Tate (150 yards) and Johnny Karras. The 40–7 victory capped a 9-0-1 season and allowed the Illini to finish third in the national rankings.

The Marching Illini in the 1952 Rose Parade

I on 1951–52

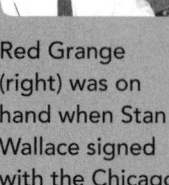

Stan Wallace

Stan Wallace had sports dreams. One of his best was his interception in the 1952 Rose Bowl, setting up Bill Tate's go-ahead touchdown run. After his Illinois career, Wallace played in the Senior Bowl and the College All-Star Game. He was then chosen in the first round (sixth selection overall) of the 1954 NFL draft by the Chicago Bears. Wallace played safety for the Bears from 1954 to 1958, then played for the Toronto Argonauts in the Canadian Football League. In 1990, Wallace was selected to the Illinois All-Century Football Team. Wallace died in December 1999 at age sixty-eight.

Red Grange (right) was on hand when Stan Wallace signed with the Chicago Bears in 1954

ILLINI ITEM

UI's Bob Richards won Olympic gold medals in both 1952 and 1956

On January 2, 1952, former University of Illinois pole vaulter Bob Richards was named winner of the Sullivan Award, symbolic of the nation's top amateur athlete. The twenty-five-year-old preacher was the first choice cast by a nationwide panel of sports authorities. Richards was the reigning Olympic champion in both the pole vault and the decathlon events, and the only two-time gold medal winner in his event (1952, 1956) in Olympic competition.

The Illini basketball team celebrated its
Big Ten championship in 1952

ILLINI LISTS

MOST BIG TEN MEN'S TEAM CHAMPIONSHIPS IN A SINGLE SEASON (through the 2014–15 season)

8	Illinois, 1951–52
8	Michigan, 1943–44
6	Illinois, 1921–22
6	Michigan, 1922–23
6	Illinois, 1923–24
6	Michigan, 1960–61
6	Indiana, 1972–73
6	Indiana, 1973–74
5	Michigan, 8 times
5	Illinois, 6 times
5	Michigan State, 1970–71

ILLINI LEGEND

Chuck Boerio

Linebacker Chuck Boerio typified the group of players who made up the University of Illinois's 1952 Rose Bowl team. At 5'11" and 190 pounds, Boerio was Coach Ray Eliot's star linebacker, earning first-team All–Big Ten honors. As the Illini's defensive signal caller, the Kincaid, Illinois, walk-on was the leader of a unit that allowed its six Big Ten foes an average of only five points per game during the 1951 campaign. Boerio, named Illini Athlete of the Year for 1951–52, was selected defensive captain of the 1952 College All-Stars in their game against the NFL champion Los Angeles Rams. His pro football career lasted only half a season with the Green Bay Packers, primarily due to his lack of size and speed. Boerio returned to the U of I in 1956 and coached under Eliot for three seasons. He served as an assistant at the University of Colorado from 1959 to 1961, helping guide the Buffaloes to the school's first Big Eight title in 1961. Boerio was a teacher and coach in the Boulder, Colorado, school district for twenty-eight years, retiring in 1990. He died at age eighty-one in 2011.

Chuck Boerio

ILLINI LORE

The University of Illinois School of Journalism celebrated its silver anniversary May 9, 1952. Among the individuals who have studied journalism at Illinois are *Chicago Sun-Times* movie critic Roger Ebert, *New York Times* columnist and former Illini golfer James "Scotty" Reston, *Sports Illustrated*'s William Nack, the *Wall Street Journal*'s Frederick Klein, and WNBC-TV's general manager Dennis Swanson.

Dennis Swanson

1952-53

AMERICA'S TIME CAPSULE

September 23, 1952 — Rocky Marciano stayed undefeated, beating "Jersey Joe" Walcott for the world heavyweight boxing title.

November 4, 1952 — Dwight Eisenhower defeated Illinois governor Adlai Stevenson for the U.S. presidency.

January 2, 1953 — Wisconsin senator Joseph McCarthy, known for his charges of communist infiltration in various organizations, was accused by a senate subcommittee of "motivation by self-interest."

March 18, 1953 — Baseball's Boston Braves moved to Milwaukee.

May 4, 1953 — Ernest Hemingway was awarded a Pulitzer Prize for his book *The Old Man and the Sea*.

ILLINI MOMENT

More Titles in 1952–53

At no time in University of Illinois history was its athletic program prospering more than in the early 1950s under Athletic Director Doug Mills. In fact, from the 1950–51 season through the 1953–54 campaign, Fighting Illini teams captured twenty-three of the Big Ten Conference's possible forty-eight championships—nearly 50 percent! The 1952–53 athletic year saw Illinois ring up five titles. Lee Eilbracht's baseball team averaged only .223 at the plate in thirteen conference games that season, but the strong pitching of Clive Follmer, Carl Ahrens, and Gerry Smith rang up a combined record of 9-2 on the mound as Illinois tied Michigan. Charlie Pond's Illini gymnastics team reigned as Big Ten champs for the fourth consecutive season and placed second in the NCAA meet, behind the consistent performances of Frank Bare, Jeff Austin, and Bob Sullivan. The Illini track teams, directed by Leo Johnson, once again dominated the conference cinders both indoors and out, thanks to sprinter Willie Williams, middle-distance star Stacey Siders, and high hurdler Joel McNulty. In fencing, it was business as usual, with Illinois winning its fourth consecutive Big Ten crown under Coach Max Garret. Sabreman John Cameron slashed his way to an individual title in his specialty.

UI track star Stacey Siders

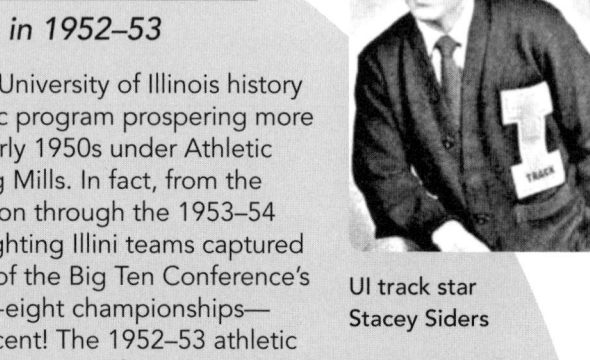

Gymnast Frank Bare

I on 1952–53

World-record sprinter Willie Williams

Willie Williams

Willie Williams enjoyed success during his college career (1952–1954), winning seven individual Big Ten sprint titles, but his greatest notoriety came later. On August 3, 1956, at the National Military Track Meet in Berlin, Germany, Williams made history, breaking his hero Jesse Owens's world record in the 100-meter dash in 10.1 seconds, in the same stadium and in the very same lane that Owens had run as a gold medal winner at the 1936 Olympic Games. One more thing that Williams shares with his hero: they have the same birth date, September 12.

ILLINI ITEM

Clive Follmer

Illinois's top two-sport athlete of 1952–53 was Clive Follmer. He averaged 11.8 points per game in basketball as a senior starter, helping the Illini to an 18–4 overall record and a second-place finish in the Big Ten. As a baseball pitcher that season, he had a 6-1 overall record, striking out fifty-one batters in sixty-eight innings. The longtime attorney was a member of four Big Ten championship clubs. He died in 2016 at age eighty-four.

ILLINI LISTS

ILLINI ON ALL-TIME PRO BASKETBALL SCORING LIST*
(through 2015–16 season)

1.	19,202	Eddie Johnson (1982–1999)
2.	16,006	Derek Harper (1984–1999)
3.	13,103	Deron Williams (2005–2016)**
4.	12,914	Kendall Gill (1991–2005)
5.	12,480	John "Red" Kerr (1955–1966)
6.	12,233	Don Freeman (1968–1976)
7.	11,549	Don Ohl (1961–1970)
8.	11,529	Nick Anderson (1990–2002)
9.	8,717	Ken Norman (1988–1997)

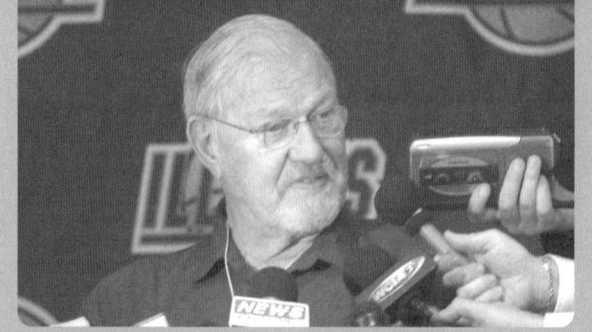

UI's Johnny "Red" Kerr scored 12,480 points during his twelve-year NBA career

10.	7,922	Rich Jones (1970–1977)
11.	6,384	Andy Philip (1948–1958)

*includes NBA, ABA, NPBL
**still active

ILLINI LEGEND

Al Brosky

The record Al Brosky achieved as a defensive back for the Fighting Illini football team is difficult to measure accurately. It might be akin to Joe DiMaggio hitting in fifty-six consecutive games or Harry Broadbent's record of scoring a goal in sixteen straight National Hockey League contests. However, Brosky's NCAA record of an interception in fifteen consecutive games is significantly more impressive in that opposing quarterbacks purposely threw their passes away from him, knowing his proficiency as a defender. The youngest of twelve children of immigrant Czechoslovakian parents, Brosky attended Harrison Tech High School in Chicago. Upon his graduation, he enlisted in the army and served for more than fifteen months. He was discharged in 1948 and enrolled at St. Louis University, but he left after a semester and came to the University of Illinois. During the next three seasons, Brosky was simply amazing, developing into the greatest Illini pass defender ever. In twenty-eight career games at Illinois, he picked off a national-record thirty interceptions. Besides being captain and Most Valuable Player of the 1952 squad, Brosky also was an All–Big Ten and All-American selection. A severe back disorder as well as other complications never allowed him to pursue a career in professional football, so he went into business for himself. Brosky died in Naperville at age eighty-two in 2010.

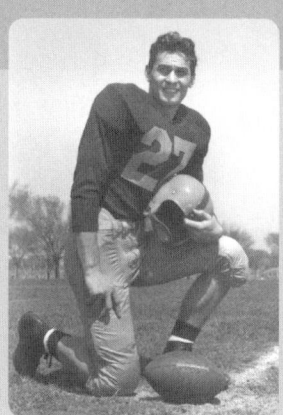

Al Brosky intercepted at least one pass in fifteen consecutive games

ILLINI LORE

In February 1953 the Federal Communications Commission assigned television channel 12, later to become WILL-TV, to the University of Illinois. Coordinated by the UI's new TV-Motion Picture unit, channel 12's original studio was located just inside gate 24 on the west side of Memorial Stadium. Also located in the southwest tower of the stadium were the station's offices, control room, projection booths, and film-editing facility. Often, Fighting Illini fans who were unable to secure a ticket to sold-out basketball games at Huff Gym were given the opportunity to watch the events on closed-circuit TV inside the Great West Hall of the stadium. WILL-TV officially began TV broadcasts August 1, 1955, as the nation's fourteenth educational station. The broadcasts were initially limited from 6:45 P.M. to 8:30 P.M., Monday through Friday.

A scene at WILL-TV's studios in the 1950s

1953–54

AMERICA'S TIME CAPSULE

August 5, 1953 — *From Here to Eternity*, starring Burt Lancaster, Montgomery Clift, and Frank Sinatra, premiered.

August 16, 1954 — Time-Life Inc. introduced *Sports Illustrated*.

February 23, 1954 — Inoculation of school children against polio began for the first time.

March 1, 1954 — An explosion of a hydrogen bomb in the Marshall Islands exceeded all estimates of its power.

May 17, 1954 — The Supreme Court declared racial segregation in public schools unconstitutional.

ILLINI MOMENT

Caroline, Bates, and Company Jet Past Buckeyes

One veteran Ohio sportswriter said that Illinois's October 10, 1953, performance against Ohio State was "the wildest first half in Ohio Stadium history, leaving Buckeye fans stunned." Though Illinois led by only one point at halftime, 21–20, it was all Illini in the second half, with the final score showing them on top, 41–20. Two jet-powered halfbacks, J. C. Caroline and Mickey Bates, combined for an unheard-of 339 yards rushing from scrimmage, 192 by Caroline and 147 by Bates. Afterward, bewildered OSU coach Woody Hayes said, "They just ran us to death, that's the whole story." Illinois continued its rampage through the Big Ten, with the no. 3–ranked Illini stumbling only at Wisconsin and tying Michigan State for the conference football title.

Since the Illini and the Spartans hadn't faced each other in 1953, Big Ten athletic directors were forced to choose the league's Rose Bowl representative. Unfortunately, they picked MSU, and the Illini spent their holidays at home.

Mickey Bates rushed for 147 yards against Ohio State in Illinois' 41–20 victory

I on 1953–54

Bob Lenzini (right) served as Coach Ray Eliot's Illini football captain in 1953

Bob Lenzini

Illinois's 1953 football captain Bob Lenzini combined excellence on the football field with a sterling effort as a civil engineering major, becoming the university's first Academic All-American in 1952. Lenzini also earned the Big Ten Conference Medal of Honor. Following his graduation, he served three years as an aviator in the U.S. Army Corps of Engineers, stationed in Germany. Lenzini co-founded a civil engineering firm in St. Charles, Illinois. The UI's Civil and Environmental Engineering honored Lenzini in 2002 with its Distinguished Alumni Award in 2002. He died in 2013 at age eighty.

ILLINI ITEM

UI's John Kerr was the Big Ten's Most Valuable Player in 1954

Johnny "Red" Kerr   John Kerr was selected as the conference's Most Valuable Player following the 1954 basketball season. He established single-season (556) and career scoring records (1,299) from 1952 to 1954, then went on to the NBA. Kerr played in three NBA All-Star Games and won an NBA championship ring for the Syracuse Nationals in 1955. After four years as an NBA coach, he became a commentator for Chicago Bulls games. In 2009, Kerr died at the age of seventy-six.

ILLINI LISTS

ILLINOIS'S FIRST-ROUND NFL/AFL DRAFT PICKS

1944	Tony Butkovich, RB, Los Angeles Rams, 11th pick
1954	Stan Wallace, DB, Chicago Bears, 6th pick
1954	John Bauer, G, Cleveland Browns, 12th pick
1959	Rich Kreitling, WR, Cleveland Browns, 11th pick
1961	Joe Rutgens, DT, Oakland Raiders, AFL, 4th pick
1961	Joe Rutgens, DT, Washington Redskins, 3rd pick
1965	Dick Butkus, LB, Chicago Bears, 3rd pick
1965	George Donnelly, DB, San Francisco 49ers, 13th pick
1966	Jim Grabowski, RB, Green Bay Packers, 9th pick
1966	Jim Grabowski, RB, Miami Dolphins, AFL, 1st pick
1981	Dave Wilson, QB, New Orleans Saints, 1st pick*
1983	Tony Eason, QB, New England Patriots, 15th pick
1988	Scott Davis, DE, Los Angeles Raiders, 25th pick
1990	Jeff George, QB, Indianapolis Colts, 1st pick
1991	Henry Jones, DB, Buffalo Bills, 26th pick 1992
1992	Brad Hopkins, OT, Houston Oilers, 13th pick
1996	Kevin Hardy, LB, Jacksonville Jaguars, 2nd pick
1996	Simeon Rice, LB, Arizona Cardinals, 3rd pick
2008	Rashard Mendenhall, RB, Pittsburgh Steelers, 23rd pick
2009	Vontae Davis, CB, Miami Dolphins, 25th pick
2011	Corey Liuget, DT, San Diego Chargers, 18th pick
2012	Whitney Mercilus, DE, Houston Texans, 26th pick

John Bauer

*supplemental draft

ILLINI LEGEND

J. C. Caroline

Though he played for only two seasons at Illinois, J. C. Caroline ultimately earned College Football Hall of Fame honors. He rushed for a Big Ten record 1,256 yards in 1953, shattering Red Grange's Illini single-season mark. Of the myriad stars Ray Eliot coached at Illinois, the veteran mentor rated Caroline at the very top. Caroline's All-America career at Illinois ended when he dropped out of school before his senior season to sign with the Canadian Football League. In 1956 coach George Halas of the Chicago Bears inked Caroline and converted him into a defensive back. He retired as a player in 1965 after ten seasons with the Bears. Caroline served as an assistant coach at Illinois from 1967 to 1976, then coached briefly at Urbana High School. Following a long career as a teacher in Urbana's school system, he continues to live in his adopted hometown. Caroline turned eighty-four in January 2017.

J. C. Caroline

ILLINI LORE

On February 1, 1954, Dr. Lloyd Morey became the seventh president and eleventh chief executive officer of the University of Illinois. Morey had been appointed acting president five months earlier when President George Stoddard was forced to resign by the University of Illinois Board of Trustees. Morey had been on the staff for forty-two years and held the position of comptroller at the time of his appointment. He died at age seventy-nine in 1965.

President Lloyd Morey

1954–55

AMERICA'S TIME CAPSULE

October 15, 1954	Hurricane Hazel killed ninety-nine Americans and 249 Canadians.
November 8, 1954	Baseball's Philadelphia Athletics moved to Kansas City.
December 2, 1954	In a vote by U.S. Senators, Sen. Joseph McCarthy was condemned for activities in his anticommunist witch hunt.
April 12, 1955	Dr. Jonas Salk's vaccine against polio was released to the public.
April 15, 1955	Ray Kroc's first McDonald's restaurant opened at 400 N. Lee Avenue in Des Plaines, Illinois.
May 2, 1955	Tennessee Williams received the Pulitzer Prize for his drama *Cat on a Hot Tin Roof*.

ILLINI MOMENT

Illini Gymnasts Claim First of Two Consecutive National Titles

Coach Charlie Pond's outstanding Illini gymnastics teams of the 1950s strung together a since unmatched chain of eleven consecutive Big Ten crowns, but the pinnacle of their success came during the 1955 and 1956 seasons when Illinois won back-to-back NCAA championships. The first of the two national titles in 1955 at Los Angeles was achieved without one single Illini gymnast winning an individual championship. Illinois placed at least two scorers in every event with the exception of the rings, with Jeff Austin coming the closest to a title with a runner-up finish on the trampoline. Illini captain Tom Gardner (fifth), Tony Hlinka (sixth), and Dick Jirus (seventh) all placed among the top seven all-arounders, as Illinois clipped second-place Penn State, 82.5 to 69, for the team crown. Pond's Illini traveled to Chapel Hill, North Carolina, for the 1956 team title, nearly doubling runner-up Penn State's score, 123.5 to 67.5. Illinois's fifty-six-point decision still is the second-greatest margin of victory ever for a gymnastics team in an NCAA championship meet. Don Tonry in the all-around and Dan Lirot in the tumbling event claimed individual championships that year.

UI's 1955 gymnasts were NCAA champs

I on 1954–55

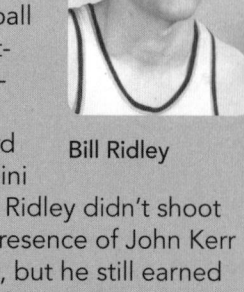

Bill Ridley

Bill Ridley was a "tornado" on the basketball court. At just five-feet-seven-inches, the Taylorville Tornados star scored a school-record 1,752 points. As an Illini player from 1954–56, Ridley didn't shoot as much due to the presence of John Kerr and George BonSalle, but he still earned first-team All–Big Ten honors as a junior and senior. Illinois compiled an impressive 52–14 record and finished among the nation's top twenty ranked teams each year. Ridley was inducted into the Illinois Basketball Coaches Association Hall of Fame in 1973.

Bill Ridley

ILLINI ITEM

Galva, Illinois's favorite son, Will Thomson

Willard Thomson of the Fighting Illini track team hurdled his way to three Big Ten championships during the 1954–55 season. Altogether during his career at Illinois, Thomson accounted for six individual conference hurdles titles and an NCAA championship (120 hurdles) in 1954. In 1957 Thomson returned to his hometown of Galva, Illinois, to work in his grandfather's company, Dixline Corporation. Eventually, Will replaced his father, Willard, and spent forty-five years as chairman of the company. In April 2017, he turned eighty-four years old.

ILLINI LISTS

TOP TEN RUSHING PLAYS AT MEMORIAL STADIUM

Harry Jefferson

1. 89 yards	Harry Jefferson of Illinois vs. Syracuse, October 23, 1954	
2. 84 yards	Antoineo Harris of Illinois vs. Purdue, October 22, 2002	
3. 84 yards	Ray Nitschke of Illinois vs. Northwestern, November 23, 1957	
4. 84 yards	Billy Taylor of Michigan, November 8, 1969	
5. 83 yards	Brian Leonard of Rutgers, September 3, 2005	
6. 83 yards	Emil Sitko of Notre Dame, September 28, 2046	
7. 80 yards	Cyril Pinder of Illinois vs. Duke, October 23, 1965	
8. 80 yards	Edgar Nichol of Illinois vs. Coe, October 13, 1928	
9. 78 yards	Howard Griffith of Illinois vs. Utah, September 17, 1988	
10. 78 yards	Keith Jones of Illinois vs. Nebraska, September 20, 1986	

ILLINI LEGEND

Paul Judson

Paul Judson

Four different members of Clarence and Jesse Judson's family wore Fighting Illini basketball uniforms during a thirty-six-year period, starting in 1944 with son Howard and ending in 1980 with grandson Rob. The Judsons' twin boys, Paul and Phil, also lettered during the mid-1950s for Coach Harry Combes's Illini cagers, starring first on the University of Illinois campus in 1952 when they led tiny Hebron High to the state championship at UI's Huff Gym. Who was the best Judson athlete of them all? Well, Clarence and Jesse would never say, but objective observers would probably choose Paul. The 6'4" guard was Illinois's Most Valuable Player in 1955 as a junior and was later selected by the *Daily Illini* as the school's Athlete of the Year. During his career from 1954 to 1956, Paul tallied 1,013 points, a total second only in Illini annals at the time to John Kerr. Though none of the three Illini teams with which Paul Judson played ever won a Big Ten championship, they did have a combined record of fifty-two victories against only fourteen losses, a winning percentage of .788. Today, Paul lives in Florida, having retired following a thirty-year high-school basketball coaching career at Dundee High School and a short stint as athletic director at Hampshire High School. He turned eighty-three years old in April 2017.

ILLINI LORE

On December 14, 1954, David Dodds Henry accepted an offer from the University of Illinois Board of Trustees to succeed Dr. Lloyd Morey as the school's president. The forty-nine-year-old Henry, a graduate of Pennsylvania State University, came to Urbana-Champaign from New York University, where he had served as that institution's vice chancellor since 1952. Henry began his appointment at the University of Illinois on September 1, 1955, at a salary of $30,000.

President David Henry

Longtime Fighting Illini photographer Mark Jones has graciously contributed several of his favorite images for inclusion in the third edition of *Illini Legends, Lists and Lore*. He and his wife, Beth, operate Tintype Shoppe of Photography in Arthur, Illinois. A protégé of the famous Ansel Adams, Mark has served as the University of Illinois "official sports photographer" since 1988.

For more information, visit THETINTYPE.com or illiniphoto.com, or call 217-543-2233.

Mark and Beth Jones

J Leman (47) celebrated with teammate Mike Ware following Illinois's upset victory over top-ranked Ohio State in 2007.

Revelry ensued in the stands of the Big House in 2008 when the Illini football team walloped Michigan.

The greatest quarterbacks in Illini history assembled at Memorial Stadium in 2008. The group included (left to right) Jeff George, Mike Wells, Tommy O'Connell, Jason Verduzco, Kurt Kittner, and Jack Trudeau.

Four of the finest running backs in Illinois football history gathered in 2008, including (left to right) Jim Grabowski, Howard Griffith, Robert Holcombe, and J. C. Caroline.

Illini fans spilled onto the court following Illinois's 78–73 victory over Michigan State in 2010.

In 1990, Illinois selected its All-Century Football Team. Those who appeared at Memorial Stadium included (left to right) Mike Bass, Alex Agase, Doug Dieken, John Karras, Ed O'Bradovich, J. C. Caroline, Dick Butkus, (partially hidden) Dike Eddleman, Al Brosky, Don Thorp, Jeff George, and Jim Grabowski.

Andy Kaufmann (34) launched a miraculous game-winning shot against Iowa in 1993.

The 2015 Illini baseball team, coached by Dan Hartleb (24), finished eighth in the national rankings and compiled an amazing 21-1 record against Big Ten opponents en route to its thirtieth conference championship.

Illini athletes Tonja Buford-Bailey (left), Marko Koers (middle), and Kirsten Gleis all competed in the 1992 Summer Olympic Games.

A banner honoring women's basketball standout Ashley Berggren resides in the rafters of the State Farm Center.

Second baseman Allie Bauch hit .320 for the 2016 Fighting Illini softball team and also earned the Big Ten Conference Medal of Honor.

Angela Bizzarri won the 2009 NCAA individual championship.

Illinois's fabulous cheerleading squad has won numerous national awards.

Basketball's Deon Thomas (left) and football's Dana Howard starred during the 1990s for the Fighting Illini.

Vanessa DiBernardo (20) starred for UI's soccer team from 2010 to 2013.

Howard Griffith (29) powered up the middle for one of his NCAA-record eight touchdowns against Southern Illinois in 1990.

Head coach Lovie Smith took direction of the Illini football program in 2016.

Illinois gymnast Melissa Fernandez displayed her grace on the balance beam from 2008 to 2011.

Illini hurdler Perdita Felicien was UI's Female Athlete of the Year three times (2001, 2002, 2003).

Members of the 1988–89 Flying Illini basketball team gathered to remember their appearance in the NCAA Final Four.

Frank Williams's (30) driving layup at Minnesota in 2002 helped Illinois win the 2002 Big Ten title.

UI softball's Jenna Hall set records for both single-season and career batting average.

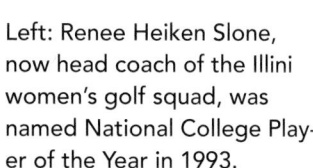

Right: Illinois's greatest collection of linebackers was this 1994 group featuring Kevin Hardy (51), Dana Howard (40), Simeon Rice (97), and John Holecek (52).

Left: Renee Heiken Slone, now head coach of the Illini women's golf squad, was named National College Player of the Year in 1993.

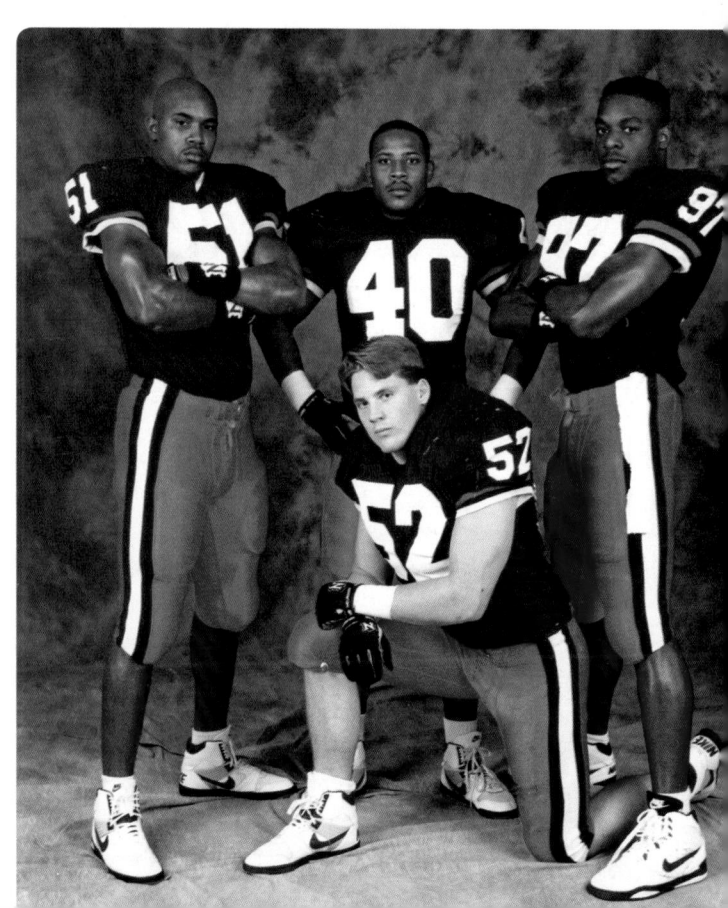

Wrestler Isaiah Martinez claimed NCAA championships in each of his first two seasons at Illinois (2015 and 2016).

Illini basketball's Orange Krush is widely acclaimed as one of the nation's premier student-run organizations.

This group of 2004–05 Illini basketball players led Illinois to a 37-2 overall record and a berth in the NCAA Championship Game.

Wearing his trademark headband, Dee Brown (11) is recognized as Illinois's most exciting player ever.

Where were you on March 26, 2005, when Deron Williams stroked this memorable shot against Arizona to help send Illinois to the Final Four?

Illinois's Yvonne Mensah won fifteen Big Ten titles as a member of the track and field team from 2004 to 2007.

Whitney Mercilus (85) became a first-round NFL draft pick of the Houston Texans in 2012.

The 2012 Illini men's gymnastics team won both the Big Ten and NCAA team championships.

Members of this Illini tennis team celebrated wildly after their victory.

Illini runners battled for the lead at the Big Ten Cross Country Championship.

A keen batting eye helped Justin Parr win the Big Ten batting title in 2011.

UI's Andrew Riley was the first male athlete in NCAA history to win national titles in the 100-meter dash and the 110-meter hurdles in the same year.

Men's golf coach Mike Small (right) helped Scott Langley (left) win individual medalist honors at the 2010 NCAA Championship.

The greatest Illini gymnast ever? Many would argue it's Justin Spring, now the head coach at Illinois.

Volleyball's Betsy Spicer Brookbank twice won first-team All–Big Ten honors.

Steve Stricker has played on the PGA Tour since 1990 and has won nearly $50 million in prize money.

Longtime men's tennis coach Craig Tiley discussed strategy with Rajeev Ram and Brian Wilson during the 2003 NCAA Championship.

A record crowd packed Huff Hall in 2010 to watch the Illini and Penn State volleyball match.

The 2011 Illini finished as runner-up in the NCAA Volleyball tournament.

UI's Colleen Ward was a first-team All-American in 2011.

2008 Illini women's basketball seniors (left to right) Danyel Crutcher, Rebecca Harris, Audrey Tabon, and Stephanie Chellen.

Jenna Smith accumulated a school-record 2,160 points for the Illini women's basketball team from 2006 to 2010.

Illini tennis star Michelle Webb Voss was awarded the Big Ten Conference Medal of Honor in 2003.

Alina Weinstein set UI gymnastics records and scored a perfect 10 on the vault.

Elise Gill (top left), Jacqueline Kantecki Weist (top right), Macy Hyatt (lower left) and Alina Weinstein (lower right) made up Illini gymnastics' 2013 senior class.

The Illini swimming team traditionally sings the fight song after a victory.

February 21, 2007: The final performance of Chief Illiniwek.

Memorial Stadium.

UI's Assembly Hall was renamed the State Farm Center on April 29, 2013.

The Red Grange statue welcomes Illini fans to Memorial Stadium.

University of Illinois Director of Athletics Josh Whitman.

Kendall Gill

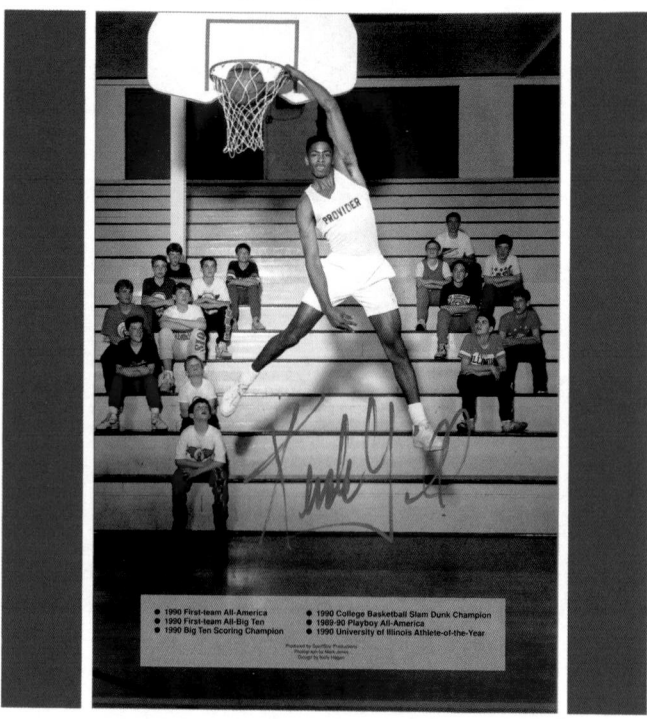

Dream It.

Kendall Gill

ILLINOIS

KENNY BATTLE

Flying Illini star Kenny Battle

In February 1999, Illini wrestling coach Mark Johnson savored Illinois's first victory over Iowa in thirty-nine years.

1955–56

AMERICA'S TIME CAPSULE

September 21, 1955 — Rocky Marciano defeated Archie Moore to retain the heavyweight boxing title.

October 4, 1955 — The Brooklyn Dodgers beat their crosstown rivals, the Yankees, in game 7 of the World Series.

October 27, 1955 — *Rebel Without a Cause*, posthumously starring twenty-four-year-old James Dean, debuted. He had died just four weeks earlier.

April 19, 1956 — American actress Grace Kelly married Prince Rainier of Monaco.

June 16, 1956 — Dr. Cary Middlecoff defeated Ben Hogan and Julius Boros by one stroke to win the U.S. Open golf tournament.

ILLINI
MOMENT

Illini Gridders Up-End No. 1 Michigan

Illini football fans who attended the November 5, 1955, matchup at Memorial Stadium between 3-3 Illinois and 6-0 Michigan were probably pessimistic about their hometown heroes' chances against the nation's No. 1–rated team. However, when the Illini battled the Wolverines on even terms after the first half, 6–6, there was a little more cause for optimism. A fake field-goal attempt that turned into a screen pass to Abe Woodson late in the third quarter gave the Illini a 12–6 lead. Then Illinois put its bag of tricks away to rely upon its fleet-footed halfback, Bobby Mitchell. The speedy sophomore from Hot Springs, Arkansas, who accounted for 173 rushing yards on only ten attempts that afternoon, nailed the Michigan coffin shut with a sixty-four-yard sprint to the end zone, giving the Illini an insurmountable lead and their eventual 25–6 upset win. Afterward, Illini coach Ray Eliot called his squad's effort "a great team victory." "It best exemplified what is meant by the words Fighting Illini," he said. "Every kid did a magnificent job. They were all heroes."

The game football from Illinois's 1955 victory over Michigan

I on 1955–56

Hiles Stout

Hiles Stout

Coaches from Notre Dame, Georgia, Miami, Kansas, and elsewhere made the trek to Peoria to talk to Hiles Stout about attending their university, but the multisport star made it clear that he wasn't about to pick one of his specialty sports over the other. Illini coaches, however, came with the right pitch: play whatever you want, just come to Illinois. Stout started at quarterback for Ray Eliot, leading the team in passing in 1956. For Harry Combes, the six-foot-four-inch whirlwind also wore jersey number 10, lettering in 1955, 1956, and 1957. After graduation, Stout served for the Marine Corps, then returned to his hometown to enter a fifty-year career in insurance. The Peoria hall of famer died on October 31, 2016, at age eighty-one.

ILLINI ITEM

Em Lindbeck was UI's Athlete of the Year in 1956

Emerit "Em" Lindbeck was selected as the University of Illinois's Athlete of the Year for 1955–56. He earned MVP honors in both football and baseball. As a quarterback, Lindbeck led the 1955 Illini past No. 3–ranked Michigan, earning honorable mention All–Big Ten acclaim. On the baseball diamond, he batted .382 as a center fielder. Lindbeck eventually played Major League Baseball in 1960, albeit for only two games. He passed on his seventy-fourth birthday in 2008.

ILLINI LISTS

MEN'S BASKETBALL SCORING LEADERS
OF THE 1950S (points per game)

1949–50	15.1	Wally Osterkorn
1950–51	17.4	Don Sunderlage
1951–52	13.7	John Kerr
1952–53	17.5	John Kerr
1953–54	25.3	John Kerr
1954–55	16.5	Paul Judson
1955–56	22.9	George Bon Salle
1956–57	18.8	Harv Schmidt
1957–58	19.6	Don Ohl
1958–59	17.9	Roger Taylor

George BonSalle

ILLINI LEGEND

Art Schankin

If you asked the man on the street to name the world's most famous fencer, you might end up with a blank stare. But if you asked a sports trivia expert about the greatest fencer in the history of the U of I, Art Schankin's name would probably be at the top of the list. Though toiling in relative anonymity, Schankin ruled the world of collegiate fencing from 1956 through 1958. He tied for fifth nationally in the sabre event as a sophomore, finished third in foil as a junior, and swept the NCAA sabre title as a senior, becoming the first intercollegiate fencer to win a national championship with an unbeaten mark. Schankin continued to compete in the sport after his graduation in 1958, being nationally ranked. In 1964, six weeks before his wedding day, he was in an automobile accident that ended his fencing career but began his highly successful coaching tenure with the Illini. From 1973 to 1993, Schankin's UI teams amassed a dual-meet record of 391 wins and fifty-one losses, including seven Big Ten champions. In addition to being Illini fencing coach, Schankin was also a sales supervisor for Collegiate Cap and Gown. A longtime resident of Champaign, he died in 2014 at age eighty-seven.

Star fencer Art Schankin

ILLINI LORE

A pair of distinguished University of Illinois alumni—Dr. Vincent du Vigneaud and Dr. Polykarp Kusch—were awarded Nobel Prizes in November of 1955. Dr. du Vigneaud, who received his bachelor's degree in 1923 and his master's in 1924 from the U of I, won the $36,720 award for chemistry for his work on two hormones that assist in childbirth and keep a check on vital organs. He was on the staff of Cornell University's medical college at the time. Dr. Kusch, who earned his master's in 1933 and his doctorate in 1936 from the U of I, split the Nobel physics award with Dr. W. E. Lamb of Stanford. Kusch, who then taught at Columbia University, won his prize for work in calculating the properties of the atom.

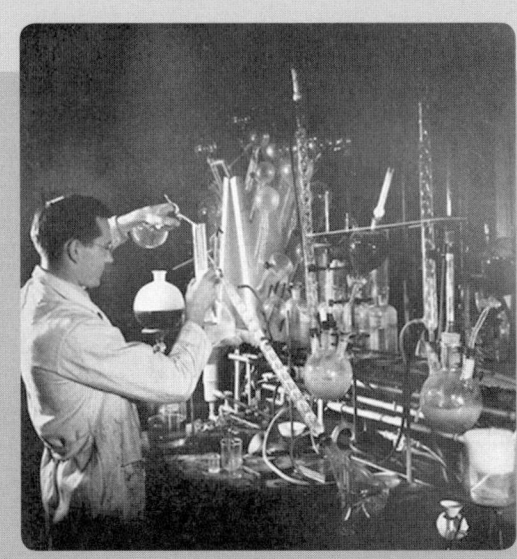

Dr. Polykarp Kusch in the lab

1956–57

AMERICA'S TIME CAPSULE

October 8, 1956   Don Larsen of the New York Yankees hurled the first perfect game in World Series history.
November 6, 1956   Dwight Eisenhower defeated Illinois governor Adlai Stevenson in the presidential election.
January 21, 1957   NBC carried the first nationally televised videotaped broadcast, a recording of the
                     presidential inauguration ceremonies.
July 12, 1957   Surgeon General Leroy Burney reported that a link between cigarette smoking and lung
                 cancer had been established.

ILLINI MOMENT

No. 1 Falls Again to Illini

For the second consecutive season, a highly rated football team from the state of Michigan was brought to its knees at Memorial Stadium, as Illinois beat top-ranked Michigan State, 20–13, on October 27, 1956. As big a thorn as Bobby Mitchell was to Michigan in 1955, so was Abe Woodson to the Spartans in 1956. Trailing 13–0 at halftime, prospects for another Fighting Illini upset looked bleak. But that's when the Austin Express got rolling. Woodson narrowed the margin to 13–6 midway through the third quarter on a two-yard touchdown. Then, in the fourth quarter, he tied the game with 1:42 gone on a seventy-yard gallop around right end. Nine minutes later,

Woodson scored the game winner when he grabbed a screen pass from sophomore quarterback Bill Offenbecher on the eighteen-yard line and dashed eighty-two yards. All told, Woodson touched the ball twenty times for 271 yards, marking an individual performance that ranks among Illinois's best ever.

Abe Woodson

I on 1956–57

Bobby Mitchell

For Robert Conelius Mitchell, his ground-breaking thirty-year journey from Hot Springs, Arkansas, to the Pro Football Hall of Fame is one that younger Illini fans should know. Convinced by Coach Ray Eliot to attend the University of Illinois instead of signing a minor league baseball contract, Mitchell starred in football and track for the Illini. The Cleveland Browns signed him in 1958 to team up with Jim Brown. Mitchell eventually became the Washington Redskins' first African American star. In 1983, Mitchell was inducted into the Pro Football Hall of Fame.

Bobby Mitchell starred on the track as well as on the football field

ILLINI ITEM

The University of San Francisco's basketball team tasted defeat for the first time in more than two years on December 17, 1956, when Illinois beat the defending national champions, 62–33, at Huff Gym. Coach Harry Combes's Illini broke USF's national-record sixty-game winning streak behind a strong defensive effort and nineteen points from center George Bon Salle.

ILLINI LISTS

ILLINI'S FOOTBALL RUSHING LEADERS OF THE 1950S

1950	Dick "Rocky" Raklovits	709 yards
1951	John Karras	650 yards
1952	Pete Bachouros	484 yards
1953	J. C. Caroline	1,256 yards
1954	J. C. Caroline	440 yards
1955	Harry Jefferson	514 yards
1956	Abe Woodson	599 yards
1957	Ray Nitschke	514 yards
1958	Marshall Starks	303 yards
1959	Bill Brown	504 yards

Running back
Ray Nitschke

ILLINI LEGEND

Abe Woodson

Abe Woodson starred in the NFL
with the San Francisco 49ers

Abe Woodson had a lot to live up to when he inherited football jersey number 40 at the University of Illinois. The two men who wore those numerals before him were Dike Eddleman, Illinois's greatest all-time athlete, and Stan Wallace, a gridiron star in his own right at Illinois. Well, when Woodson's eligibility expired in 1956, the former star from Chicago's Austin High School had proved he was more than worthy. Woodson, of course, is best known for his role in Illinois's 1956 upset of no. 1 ranked Michigan State. He wound up his three-year career as the school's fifth leading rusher, with 1,276 yards, and twice led Illinois in pass receiving. Abe was also a terror on the track, winning two Big Ten titles as a 50-yard hurdler and tying the world's indoor mark twice in that event. After being selected as UI's Athlete of the Year in 1956–57, Woodson enjoyed a nine-year career in the National Football League with San Francisco and St. Louis. He hung up his cleats in 1967 and worked briefly for S&H Green Stamps. Woodson then began a twenty-year career as a life insurance agent in the San Francisco area. In 1991 he enrolled as a student at the Southern California School of Evangelism. Woodson became a Church of Christ minister in Las Vegas, Nevada, and developed a prison ministry in Indian Springs, Nevada. He died in February 2014, seven days shy of his eightieth birthday.

ILLINI LORE

The University of Illinois's John Bardeen was one of three American scientists to be awarded the 1956 Nobel Prize in physics for their development of the transistor. Bardeen, a professor of electrical engineering and physics since 1951, perfected the micro-amplifiers with William Shockley of Pasadena, California, and Walter Brattain of Murray Hill, New Jersey, at the Bell Telephone Laboratories. In 1972, he again shared a Nobel Prize for a theory on superconductivity.

John Bardeen

1957–58

AMERICA'S TIME CAPSULE

September 25, 1957 — President Eisenhower sent one thousand army paratroopers to Little Rock, Arkansas, to enforce the desegregation of Central High School.

October 4, 1957 — The Soviet Union launched Sputnik 1, the first Earth satellite.

December 14, 1957 — *The Bridge on the River Kwai*, winner of Best Picture at the Academy Awards, premiered.

January 31, 1958 — The U.S. launched its first Earth satellite, Explorer I, from Cape Canaveral, Florida.

March 25, 1958 — Sugar Ray Robinson regained the world middleweight boxing title for an unprecedented fifth time, defeating Carmen Basilio.

ILLINI MOMENT

Illini Fencers and Gymnasts Win NCAA Crowns

University of Illinois athletes captured a pair of national team championships during the 1957–58 season, with Illini fencers and gymnasts bringing home top honors. Coach Mac Garret's swordsmen traveled all the way to Lubbock, Texas, on March 21–22, edging Columbia, Yale, and Navy for the NCAA title. Illinois's fencers earned forty-seven points altogether, including twenty-one in sabre from individual champion Art Schankin, fourteen in foil from Abbey Silverstone, and twelve in epee from Lee Sentman. The Illini gymnasts tied Michigan State for the national title on April 11–12, with each team scoring seventy-nine points at MSU's Jenison Field House. Illinois garnered predicted individual championships in the horizontal bars and free exercise events from Abie Grossfeld, but it was a junior tumbler named Allan Harvey who provided the Illini with their biggest surprise. For the first time in his competitive career, Harvey executed the difficult double back somersault, a performance that netted him second place in tumbling. A shoulder injury suffered by UI's Bob Diamond on the first night of competition probably cost Illinois an undisputed team title, as Diamond was counted on to place well on the side horse.

Allen Harvey

Mannie Jackson (left) and Govoner Vaughn

I on 1957–58

Mannie Jackson and Govoner Vaughn

Racial integration of the Illinois basketball program made a real impact on December 11, 1957, when Govoner Vaughn and Mannie Jackson made their debut with respective 26 and 15-point performances. They finished their Illini careers among the top five scorers in school history. Following brief flings as players for the Harlem Globetrotters, they began careers in business. When Jackson purchased the Globetrotters in 1993, Vaughn became the team's director of alumni relations. Jackson's $3 million gift to the university supported the opening of the Mannie L. Jackson UI Basketball Hall of Fame in 2016.

ILLINI ITEM

Pro Football Hall of Famer Bobby Mitchell

Illini in Pro Football Hall of Fame (year inducted, years lettered)

*Harold "Red" Grange	1963	1923–25
*George Halas	1963	1917
#Hugh "Shorty" Ray	1966	—
Ray Nitschke	1978	1955–57
Dick Butkus	1979	1962–64
Bobby Mitchell	1983	1955–57

*Charter member
#Supervisor of NFL officials

Werner Holzer won Big Ten titles in 1957 and 1958

ILLINI LISTS

ILLINOIS'S MULTIPLE BIG TEN WRESTLING CHAMPIONS

3 Jon Llewellyn, heavyweight (1989, 1990, 1991)	2 Dave Shapiro, 165 pounds (1943, 1947)
3 Bob Emmons, 126 pounds (1931, 1932, 1933)	2 Norm Anthonisen, 165 and 175 pounds (1942, 1946)
2 Isaiah Martinez, 165 pounds (2015, 2016)	2 Archie Deutschman, 135 pounds (1938, 1939)
2 Jesse Delgado, 125 pounds (2013, 2014)	2 John Ginay, 165 pounds (1937 1938)
2 Mike Poeta, 157 pounds (2008, 2009)	2 Jack McIlvoy, 145 pounds (1935, 1937)
2 Alex Tirapelle, 157 pounds (2004, 2005)	2 Ralph Silverstein, 175 pounds and heavyweight (1935, 1936)
2 Matt Lackey, 165 pounds (2002, 2003)	
2 Bob Norman, heavyweight (1957, 1958)	2 Pete Pakutinsky, 118 and 126 pounds (1934, 1935)
2 Werner Holzer, 147 and 157 pounds (1957, 1958)	2 Barney Cosneck, 165 pounds and heavyweight (1932, 1934)
2 Norton Compton, 137 pounds (1952, 1953)	
2 Lou Kachiroubas, 128 pounds (1946, 1947)	2 Joe Sapora, 115 pounds (1929, 1930)

ILLINI LEGEND

Bob Norman

Bob Norman

His dream was to play varsity football for the University of Illinois, but a knee injury during his freshman year never allowed Bob Norman to realize his boyhood ambition. So after sitting out the balance of that season and all of his sophomore year, Norman turned to his second love—the sport of wrestling. What resulted were two consecutive Big Ten and NCAA heavyweight championships and a nearly perfect 36-0-1 record. The 6'4" 225-pounder's senior campaign in 1958 was particularly impressive, recording fourteen pins during a flawless 21-0 performance. Norman earned entrance into the Amateur Wrestling Hall of Fame in 1978. Following his graduation from Illinois with a degree in horticulture, Norman entered the construction business in Chicago. He worked several years as an engineer for Cook County and the State of Illinois; he currently owns his own carpentry business in Winfield, Illinois. His son, Tim, lettered in football at Illinois from 1977 to 1980, and his grandson, Jake, won monograms from 2007 to 2010.

ILLINI LORE

Details of a ten-year, $198.5 million building program for the University of Illinois were announced at a July 1957 meeting of the board of trustees. The previous comprehensive building program for the U of I took place more than a quarter-century earlier, when, during the 1920s, the university expanded its facilities to handle rising enrollments. Among the facilities planned were plant services buildings. More than $5 million of the 1957 request was for remodeling and renovation of existing structures.

The Fine Arts Building was part of UI's building plan in 1957

1958–59

AMERICA'S TIME CAPSULE

September 30, 1958   Arkansas governor Orval Faubus defied the Supreme Court's ruling against racial segregation in public schools.

January 3, 1959   President Dwight Eisenhower proclaimed Alaska the forty-ninth state.

February 3, 1959   Rock and roll stars Buddy Holly and Richie Valens died in an airplane crash.

March 9, 1959   The first Barbie doll went on display at the American Toy Fair in New York City.

July 28, 1959   American spy thriller *North by Northwest* debuted.

August 21, 1959   Hawaii was admitted to the union as the fiftieth state.

ILLINI
MOMENT

Illini Rally Derails First-Place Hoosiers

The odds seemed overwhelming against Illinois's basketball team derailing league-leading Indiana at Bloomington, February 9, 1959. The ninth-place Illini, mired in the throes of a five-game losing streak, faced a Hoosier club that featured 6'11" center Walt Bellamy and an array of other talented sophomores. During the first four and a half minutes, Indiana ran off to a 15–0 lead and had visions of resetting the single-game scoring record of 122 points it had compiled one week before at Ohio State. The Hoosiers lost their momentum, however, and the Illini played on even terms for the balance of the first half. In the last period, Illinois rode the hot shooting of Govoner Vaughn to finally take the lead, 68–67. From that point on, Illinois never trailed, winding up with a come-from-behind 89–83 victory.

Govoner Vaughn

I on 1958–59

Bobby Klaus

Illini baseball star Bobby Klaus

One of Coach Lee Eilbract's most talented players was an infielder named Bobby Klaus. From 1957 to 1959, the second baseman hit .317. Klaus was signed by the Cincinnati Reds immediately after his collegiate career ended. After starring in the Pacific Coast League, he got the call up from the Reds to replace a struggling young Pete Rose. Rose eventually regained his hitting form, so Bobby was dealt to the New York Mets. He stayed in the majors for one more season, finishing with a career batting average of .208.

ILLINI ITEM

UI's 1959 track and field team won the Big Ten title

The Illini track and field team successfully defended its Big Ten outdoor title in the spring of 1959, outdistancing runner-up Michigan, 65.5 points to 45. George Kerr set a conference record while winning the 880-yard run; Ernie Haisley defended his high-jump title; and John Lattimore, Ted Beastall, Del Coleman, and Kerr captured the mile relay crown. But the real hero was Ward Miller Jr., who swept the 100- and 220-yard dashes.

ILLINI LISTS

ILLINOIS GYMNASTICS BIG TEN ALL-AROUND CHAMPIONS

E. B. Styles	1910, 1911, 1912
A. W. Ziegler	1920
Joe Giallombardo	1938, 1939
Frank Dolan	1950
Bob Sullivan	1952
Don Toney	1956
Abie Grossfeld	1957, 1958, 1959
Ray Hadley	1960, 1962
Charles Lakes	1984, 1985
Dominick Minicucci	1988

Gymnast Ray Hadley

Justin Spring	2006
C. J. Maestas	2012

ILLINI LEGEND

Abie Grossfeld

Abie Grossfeld was a Big Ten champion, a national champion, and a two-time Olympian, but he said that being chosen as UI's Athlete of the Year marked one of the most special moments in his gymnastics career. "In 1959, when I received that award from the *Daily Illini*, I was the first person to win who wasn't a football or a basketball player. I was very proud to be picked as Illinois's Athlete of the Year." From 1957 to 1959, Grossfeld won seven Big Ten titles and was a member of three conference championship teams. Grossfeld also earned the Big Ten Conference Medal of Honor as Illinois's top scholar-athlete.

Chosen as UI's Athlete of the Year in 1959 was gymnast Abe Grossfeld

After earning his bachelor's and master's degrees at Illinois, Grossfeld entered the coaching world and was the head coach at Southern Connecticut State University from 1963 to 2004. Grossfeld directed SCSU to three national titles and twenty-nine individual national titles. His greatest athlete at SCSU was Peter Kormann, a bronze medalist in the 1976 Olympics. Grossfeld was the head coach of the U.S. Olympic Gymnastics Team in 1972, 1984, and 1988, and was an assistant coach in 1964 and 1968. In 2015 he received the Frank Bare Award from the International Gymnastics Hall of Fame, emblematic of individuals who have made exceptional contributions in growing the sport. Celebrating his eighty-second birthday in March 2016, the gymnastics hall of famer resides in Woodbridge, Connecticut.

ILLINI LORE

Charles "Chilly" Bowen stepped down from his post as executive director of the Alumni Association in June 1959 following seventeen years of service for the organization. A 1922 graduate of the University of Illinois, Bowen began his thirty-two-year stint with the U of I as ticket manager and business manager for the Athletic Association. In 1942 he was appointed as the Alumni Association's first executive director. Alumni membership grew from less than three thousand to more than nineteen thousand during Bowen's eighteen years in that position. In 1979 the university awarded him the Distinguished Service Medallion. He died in 1980 at age eighty.

Charles "Chilly" Bowen

1959–60

AMERICA'S TIME CAPSULE

October 18, 1959   The Los Angeles Dodgers beat the Chicago White Sox for the World Series title.

January 4, 1960   The United Steel Workers and the nation's steel companies agreed on a wage increase to settle a six-month strike.

May 1, 1960   A U.S. U-2 reconnaissance plane was shot down inside the U.S.S.R., causing the Soviets to cancel a planned summit meeting in Paris.

June 20, 1960   Floyd Patterson knocked out Ingemar Johansson to become the first boxer in history to regain the heavyweight title.

ILLINI
MOMENT

Illini End Eliot Era with Victory

The Ray Eliot era at Illinois concluded with a storybook finish November 21, 1959, as the Fighting Illini football team swept past Northwestern, 28–0, at Memorial Stadium. Playing against the school that had inflicted so many thorns in his side during eighteen years on the sidelines, Eliot and his charges were in control all the way, out-gaining the Wildcats 365 yards to 142. Nearly all of Illinois's yards—348—came on the ground as fullback Bill Brown (164 yards) and halfback Mel Counts (109 yards) averaged more than eight yards a carry. The Illini defensive unit, led by Bill Burrell, allowed Northwestern to penetrate the fifty-yard line only once all day. When the final gun sounded, UI students rushed the field and, along with Illini players, hoisted the broadly smiling Eliot and carried him off the field.

Ray Eliot finished his Illini coaching career in 1959

I on 1959–60

George Kerr

The winner of seven Big Ten titles and back-to-back NCAA championships, George Kerr rarely experienced defeat at Illinois. Nearly sixty years after he last competed, Kerr's school-record marks in the 440 (0:45.98) and the 880 (1:46.40) still rank among the best in Illini annals. He competed in the 1960 Rome Olympic Games and won a pair of bronze medals for the West Indies team in the 800-meter run and the 4x400. At the Tokyo Olympics in 1964, he broke the Olympic record for the 800 in the semifinals yet narrowly lost the bronze in the finals. Kerr died in 2012 at age seventy-four.

George Kerr

ILLINI ITEM

Fighting Illini basketball star Govoner Vaughn saved his best for last, scoring a career-high thirty points in his final game at Huff Gym, February 29, 1960. The senior forward from Edwardsville hit fourteen of seventeen shots from the field, including all nine of his attempts in the second half, to lead Illinois to a 90–61 victory over Michigan.

Govoner Vaughn

ILLINI LISTS

LEO JOHNSON'S ALL-TIME ILLINI TRACK TEAM

Leo Johnson coached the University of Illinois track and field squad for twenty-eight years, from 1938 to 1965. Here, based on the Big Ten championship titles they won, are the athletes Johnson might have chosen to compete on his Fighting Illini outdoor track and field "Dream Team" (two men per individual event):

Cirilo McSween

- 100-yard dash: Willie Williams and Claude "Buddy" Young
- 220-yard dash: Herb McKenley and Willie Williams
- 440-yard run: Cirilo McSween and Herb McKenley
- 880-yard run: Stacey Siders and George Kerr
- 1-mile run: Bob Rehberg and Jim Bowers
- 2-mile run: Waldemar Karkow and Ken Brown

- 120-yard high hurdles: George Walker and Willard Thomson
- 220-yard low hurdles: George Walker and Willard Thomson
- High jump: Dike Eddleman and Al Urbanckas
- Pole vault: Don Laz and Bob Richards
- Discus: Bogie Redmon and Marv Berschet
- Shot put: Bill Brown and Norm Wasser
- Long jump: Paul Foreman and Don Laz
- 1-mile relay team: Herb McKenley, Bob Rehberg, Cirilo McSween, and Stacey Siders

ILLINI LEGEND

Bill Burrell

The 1959 Heisman Trophy balloting, long recognized as a barometer of individual greatness in college football, ranked Bill Burrell as the nation's fourth-best overall player and No. 1 defensive performer his senior year. He was named a consensus All-American linebacker and was a three-time first-team all-conference selection. The *Chicago Tribune* even named Burrell as Big Ten football's Most Valuable Player in 1959. But today, despite all those laurels, Bill Burrell probably still doesn't receive the credit he is due. Ray Nitschke, a teammate and one of the Illini linebackers ranked above Burrell, recently called him Illinois's "forgotten man." The fact that he was one of only a handful of black men playing college football in the late 1950s lends credence to the charge that racism has robbed Burrell of his recognition. However, to his Illini teammates, it is impossible to masquerade number 68 as anything less than the best UI player of his time. Burrell became a successful realtor in Rockford; he died in 1998 at age sixty-two.

Bill Burrell (right) was one of
Ray Eliot's greatest players

ILLINI LORE

Two weeks and one day before the presidential election—October 24, 1960—Democratic candidate John F. Kennedy campaigned on the front steps of the University of Illinois Auditorium. It was the first time since 1890 that a presidential candidate was allowed to speak on university premises. Addressing a throng of ten thousand students, Kennedy said, "I come to this university, which is a center of knowledge and a center of truth, and you cannot possibly tell me that in 1960 that the American people are going to sit still. The kind of country we build here is the test of our ability to lead around the world. What we are speaks far louder than what we say. I come here today and ask you to join rebuilding the strength and image of the United States as a progressive society. I want the people of the world to wake up in the morning and wonder what the United States is doing, not what Mr. Khrushchev is doing." JFK wound up carrying the state of Illinois over Vice President Richard Nixon, winning the state's twenty-seven electoral votes.

Thousands of UI students
turned out to see Democratic
presidential nominee John
Kennedy on October 24, 1960

1960-61

AMERICA'S TIME CAPSULE

October 13, 1960   Bill Mazeroski's game-winning home run against the New York Yankees gave the Pirates the World Series championship.

November 8, 1960   John Kennedy was elected America's president in a narrow victory.

April 17, 1961   Two thousand CIA-trained anti-Castro Cuban exiles landed in Cuba, in what came to be known as the Bay of Pigs invasion.

May 5, 1961   Alan Shepard made a successful flight aboard the capsule Freedom Seven to become the first American in space.

ILLINI MOMENT

Elliott Debuts as Winner

On September 24, 1960, just ten months after the Eliot era had concluded, the Elliott era began at the University of Illinois's Memorial Stadium. And as Ray Eliot's career had ended, so too did Pete Elliott's career begin—with an Illini football victory. Illinois's victim on this warm September afternoon was Indiana, recently suspended from conference competition due to its violation of recruiting rules. For the first seven minutes of the game, Indiana appeared to be in complete control, marching for an eighty-yard touchdown on the opening drive. Thereafter, it was all Illinois, as Elliott's option attack punctured the Hoosier defense for two touchdowns and a field goal while the Illini defense limited IU to just two first downs the balance of the game. Illinois's individual star was Champaign senior quarterback Johnny Easterbrook, who twice ran options around left end for TDs and led the team in rushing with seventy-four yards. The final score: Illinois 17, Indiana 6.

Coach Pete Elliott

I on 1960-61

Joe Rutgens

Joe Rutgens was a first-round pick in the 1961 NFL Draft

One of Illinois's greatest but least-publicized football stars was 6-foot-2, 245-pound tackle Joe Rutgens. Rutgens twice earned first-team All–Big Ten honors. He was a first-round pick in the 1961 NFL and AFL drafts, chosen third by the Washington Redskins and fourth by the Oakland Raiders. He chose to sign with Washington and was twice selected to play in the Pro Bowl. Today, he resides in Spring Valley with his wife, Donna.

ILLINI ITEM

Jerry Colangelo

Jerry Colangelo Jerry Colangelo chose the Illini to play basketball and baseball. Upon his graduation, he began his ascension as a sports executive. By age twenty-nine, he became the youngest general manager in professional sports, hired to direct the newly franchised Phoenix Suns. He eventually followed up by bringing pro baseball and hockey to Phoenix. In 2005, Colangelo became director of the newly organized USA National Basketball Team program. Today, he's a special advisor for the Philadelphia 76ers. Through it all Colangelo has remained loyal to the Illini, presenting his alma mater with several generous donations.

ILLINI LISTS

PETE ELLIOTT'S CAPTAINS

Pete Elliott coached Illinois's football team from 1960 through 1966, compiling a 31–34–1 record. Two of his captains—Dick Butkus in 1964 and Jim Grabowski in 1965—both finished third in Heisman Trophy balloting, and both were voted Big Ten Players of the Year. The Illini All-Americans went on to careers in the NFL—Butkus with the Chicago Bears and Grabowski with the Green Bay Packers—and met each other on the professional gridiron ten times (Packers eight wins, Bears two).

Former Illini teammates Dick Butkus (Bears) and Jim Grabowski (Packers) met on the NFL gridiron

1960	Bill Brown
1961	Gary Brown
1962	Bob Scharbert and Ken Zimmerman
1963	Mike Taliaferro and Dick Deller

1964	Dick Butkus and George Donnelly
1965	Jim Grabowski and Don Hansen
1966	Bo Batchelder and Kai Anderson

ILLINI LEGEND

Bill Brown

Bill Brown

The term "battering ram" probably never more aptly described a football player than it did Illinois's Bill Brown. At 5'11", 210 pounds, the all-state fullback from Mendota, Illinois, was never known as a flashy player, but there were few who were more productive. From 1958 to 1960, Brown ground out a total of 1,269 yards to become Illinois's sixth-leading rusher of all time. When his Illini offensive unit ran out of downs, Brown stayed on the field as a defensive linebacker. And when he wasn't playing offense or defense, Brown starred as a punter, winding up his career with a UI-record average of more than forty yards per punt. When football season ended, Brown headed for the Armory to compete for Leo Johnson's track team as a shot putter. He lettered twice in track, holding the school's outdoor record in the shot put (54'8 ½") and winning the 1960 Big Ten indoor title. Brown was drafted by the NFL's Chicago Bears in 1961 but spent twelve of his thirteen years in the pros with the Minnesota Vikings. He led the Vikings in rushing five times and played in three Super Bowls. After hanging up his cleats, Brown worked in the insurance business for ten years, but for the last twenty-five years he has directed the sales force of John Roberts Printing Company in Minneapolis, Minnesota.

ILLINI LORE

On May 20, 1961, the University of Illinois's Krannert Art Museum was dedicated. Mr. and Mrs. Herman Krannert, benefactors of $430,000, were on hand to open the university's first real home for UI's permanent art collection. Previously the Architecture Building was the campus site for art displays.

UI's Krannert Art Museum opened in 1961

1961–62

AMERICA'S TIME CAPSULE

October 1, 1961	Roger Maris of the New York Yankees hit his sixty-first home run, breaking Babe Ruth's single-season record.
February 10, 1962	Jim Beatty became the first American to break the four-minute mile indoors (3:58.9).
February 20, 1962	Astronaut John Glenn became the first American to orbit the Earth, circling the globe three times aboard Friendship 7.
March 2, 1962	Wilt Chamberlain became the first NBA player to score one hundred points in a game.
August 5, 1962	Actress Marilyn Monroe, age thirty-six, died in her Los Angeles home of an overdose of sleeping pills.

ILLINI MOMENT

Illini Baseball Team Is Undisputed Champion

Behind the flawless pitching of Tom Fletcher and Doug Mills and the timely hitting of Lloyd Flodin and Tony Eichelberger, Illinois's 1962 baseball team captured its first undisputed Big Ten title in fifteen years. Only Indiana and Northwestern were able to hand the Fighting Illini losses in fifteen Big Ten games, as Illinois finished a half-game better than runner-up Michigan. The clincher came on May 19 at Illinois Field when the Illini swept a doubleheader from Iowa, while the league-leading Wolverines were dropping a pair at Wisconsin. Fletcher and Mills both went to the mound five times during the Big Ten season, and each man recorded a perfect 5-0 win-loss mark. Illinois's top hitters were Flodin (.370), the team's catcher, and shortstop Eichelberger (.365). Right fielder Bud Felichio led the Illini in home runs and runs batted in during conference play, with two and thirteen, respectively. In NCAA tournament action, Coach Lee Eilbracht's troops beat the University of Detroit in their opening game (2–1), but lost their next two to Western Michigan (10–2) and Michigan (5–1) to be eliminated.

1962 Big Ten baseball champs

I on 1961–62

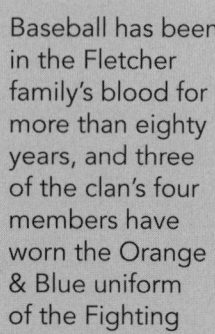

Tom Fletcher

Baseball has been in the Fletcher family's blood for more than eighty years, and three of the clan's four members have worn the Orange & Blue uniform of the Fighting Illini. In the spring of 1962, left-handed pitcher Tom Fletcher posted a nearly perfect 5–0 record and an earned run average of 0.40 in the Big Ten play, leading all conference pitchers. He pitched one Major League game for the Detroit Tigers. Tom's son, Darrin (1985–87), and his grandson, Casey (2014–15), eventually followed in his footsteps at Illinois.

ILLINI ITEM

Mike Toliuszis

Senior Mike Toliuszis became the first University of Illinois golfer since 1942 to win medalist honors at the Big Ten Championships, May 18–19, 1962. Toliuszis trailed Purdue's Steve Wilkinson by five strokes after thirty-six holes but pulled into a first-place tie after the third round. In the fourth and final round, the Illini star shot a 73 to wind up six strokes better than the second-place Wilkinson. Today, Toliuszis is a financial advisor in Kankakee.

ILLINI LISTS

MOST POINTS BY BIG TEN BASKETBALL
PLAYERS VS. ILLINOIS

49 points	Glenn Robinson, Purdue (March 13, 1994)
49 points	Gary Bradds, Ohio State (February 10, 1964)
48 points	Mike Woodson, Indiana (March 3, 1979)
45 points	Terry Dischinger, Purdue (January 8, 1962)
45 points	Terry Dischinger, Purdue (February 17, 1962)
43 points	Robin Freeman, Ohio State (February 25, 1956)
43 points	Terry Dischinger, Purdue (January 11, 1960)
42 points	Walt Bellamy, Indiana (February 22, 1960)
41 points	Dave Schellhase, Purdue (February 6, 1965)
41 points	Steve Downing, Indiana (February 12, 1973)

Purdue's Terry
Dischinger

ILLINI LEGEND

Three-sport star
Doug Mills

Doug Mills

Though he is no relation to his namesake, Douglas C. Mills had a lot in common with the longtime Illini athlete, coach, and athletic director. Both men were multi-sport stars as undergraduates, and both were huge successes after their playing days were through. The younger Mills lettered in football, basketball, and baseball during his career at the UrbanaChampaign campus, earning six monograms altogether. His greatest individual achievements came as a pitcher for Coach Lee Eilbracht's UI baseball squad. As a senior, Mills appeared on the mound five times in Big Ten play and won all five decisions, helping Illinois capture its first undisputed conference baseball title in fifteen years. Illinois's 1962 Athlete of the Year has enjoyed a remarkable career in the banking industry, rising to chairman of the board of Urbana's First Busey Corporation. After forty years with Busey, Mills resigned in 2010, having taken it from a $40 million bank to a $4 billion traded company with operations in three states. In 1998, Mills, his late wife, Linda, and their children, David and Rob, gave a gift that endows the salary of the head football coach at the University of Illinois.

ILLINI LORE

James Brady, former press secretary to President Ronald Reagan, earned a degree in journalism in 1962. The Centralia, Illinois, native served as president of Sigma Chi fraternity as a University of Illinois student and also wrote for the *Daily Illini*. Just three months after his appointment as the presidential press secretary, Brady was critically injured in the March 1981 assassination attempt on the president. He received the UI Alumni Association's Alumni Achievement Award in 1991 and served as vice chairman of the National Organization on Disability in Washington, D.C. In 2000 the Press Briefing Room at the White House was named the James S. Brady Press Briefing Room. Brady died in 2014 at age seventy-three.

Illinois alum Jim Brady ('62)

1962–63

AMERICA'S TIME CAPSULE

October 1, 1962 — James Meredith, escorted by U.S. marshals, became the first black student to attend classes at the University of Mississippi.

December 10, 1962 — *Lawrence of Arabia*, winner of seven Academy Awards, premiered.

May 7, 1963 — The communications satellite Telstar 2 was launched and began relaying television signals between the United States and Europe.

August 28, 1963 — Dr. Martin Luther King Jr. presented his "I Have a Dream" speech to a crowd of two hundred thousand from the steps of the Lincoln Memorial.

ILLINI MOMENT

Illini Cagers Clinch Big Ten Title at New Assembly Hall

The 1962–63 basketball season was an unforgettable one for the University of Illinois. First, the Fighting Illini played their thirty-eighth and final season at Huff Gym, winning all nine of their games in that storied facility. Second, Illinois opened its futuristic new palace, the Assembly Hall, on March 4, 1963, with a nail-biting 79–73 victory over Northwestern. But the most thrilling chapter of 1962–63 came on March 9, when, in the regular-season finale at Champaign, Illinois defeated Iowa, 73–69, to claim a share of the Big Ten title. Illinois went on to the NCAA tournament for the first time since 1952. Illinois traveled up to East Lansing, Michigan, for the Mideast Regional games, defeating Bowling Green in the opener, then losing to eventual champ Loyola in game 2. The Illini heroes that season included starting forwards Bob Starnes and Dave Downey, center Bill Burwell, and guards Bill Small and Tal Brody. Skip Thoren, Bill Edwards, and Bogie Redmon were valuable members of the team off the bench for Coach Harry Combes's 20-6 club.

Illini warm up before first game in Assembly Hall

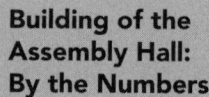

I on 1962–63

Building of the Assembly Hall: By the Numbers

Assembly Hall construction in 1962

3.5: In inches, the thickness of the concrete dome.

8.35: In millions, the cost of the project.

128: In feet, the height of the roof.

400: In feet, the diameter of the building.

614: Miles of one-quarter-inch steel wire wrapped around the dome.

1,379: Days from groundbreaking (May 25, 1959) to first game.

16,137: Attendance at first game (March 4, 1963).

130,000: Pounds per square inch of tension on the concrete, causing it to squeeze inward and rise upward.

ILLINI ITEM

1962 Illini Football schedule

On November 3, 1962, the Illini football team broke the longest losing streak in modern Big Ten history—15 in a row—with a 14–10 upset victory over at Purdue. Coach Pete Elliott's Illini shocked the Homecoming crowd when they took the lead on a twenty-three-yard pass from Mike Taliaferro to Thurman Walker in the second quarter. When the team returned, they were greeted by thousands of fans lined up on Cunningham and Florida Avenues

ILLINI LISTS

PRO FOOTBALL HALL OF FAME

The Pro Football Hall of Fame in Canton, Ohio

On January 29, 1963, the National Football League elected its charter class for the new Pro Football Hall of Fame in Canton, Ohio. Two men with Illini ties were among the group of sixteen:

Sammy Baugh, QB	Don Hutson, E
Bert Bell, contributor	"Curly" Lambeau, player/coach
Joe Carr, contributor	Tim Mara, contributor
"Dutch" Clark, QB	George Marshall, contributor
Harold "Red" Grange, RB	Johnny "Blood" McNally, RB
George Halas, player/coach	"Bronko" Nagurski, RB
Mel Hein, C	Ernie Nevers, RB
Cal Hubbard, T	Jim Thorpe, RB

ILLINI LEGEND

Dave Downey, on the fiftieth anniversary of his scoring record

Dave Downey

Dave Downey's association with the University of Illinois has seen him rise from the status of student athlete to that of assistant coach, then to a role as a color analyst on the Illini basketball telecasts, and, finally, to an appointment from the governor as a member of the university's board of trustees. For Downey, the challenge of combining a career of athletics and academics was seemingly never difficult, as witnessed by his earning the prestigious Big Ten Conference Medal of Honor as a senior in 1963. He was best known for his Illini exploits on the basketball court, a three-year stretch from 1960 to 1963 in which he was named team MVP every season. Downey set nearly every UI scoring record, including marks for a single game (fifty-three points versus Indiana on February 16, 1963) and for a career (1,360 points). A charter member of the Illinois Coaches Association High School Hall of Fame, the Canton (Illinois) High School graduate earned All–Big Ten and All-American honors at Illinois. Downey received of the Varsity "I" Award in 1988, saluting his marvelous performance as an athlete and his successful career as president of The Downey Group in Champaign. In 2015, he and his family and friends donated $2 million toward a lounge for Courtside Club members, named Club 53, during the renovation of the State Farm Center.

ILLINI LORE

A massive building program begun in 1958 at the University of Illinois saw the completion of numerous structures during the 1962–63 school year. Among the facilities opened to students were the $1.35 million Student Services Building, the $1.96 million Entomology Building, the $2.3 million Physics Building, the $5.75 million Pennsylvania Residence Halls, the $6.9 million Illini Union addition, and the $8.3 million Assembly Hall.

Pennsylvania Residence Halls

1963–64

AMERICA'S TIME CAPSULE

October 2, 1963   Pitcher Sandy Koufax of the Los Angeles Dodgers set a World Series record by striking out fifteen New York Yankees in the opening game.

November 22, 1963   President John F. Kennedy was killed by an assassin's bullet in Dallas, Texas.

December 31, 1963   The Chicago Bears won the NFL championship by defeating the New York Giants, 14–0.

February 7, 1964   The Beatles arrived in New York City for an appearance on the *Ed Sullivan Show*.

March 30, 1964   TV game show *Jeopardy!* debuted on NBC-TV.

July 2, 1964   President Lyndon Johnson signed the Civil Rights Act of 1964.

ILLINI MOMENT

President's Assassination Delays Illini Championship

For the University of Illinois football team, it was the worst of times and it was the best of times. Forced to postpone its season-ending showdown at Michigan State for five days due to the shocking assassination of President John Kennedy, Coach Pete Elliott's Illini made a second trip to East Lansing to play the fourth-ranked Spartans on Thanksgiving Day 1963. State's roster was stocked with All-Americans, such as halfback Sherman Lewis, but the Illini countered with a stifling defense led by the incomparable Dick Butkus.

In the end, Illinois's defenders were the difference, causing the Spartans to cough up three fumbles and throw four interceptions, resulting in a 13–0 Illini victory. UI's offensive attack was led by sophomore fullback Jim Grabowski, who rushed for eighty-five yards against the previously impenetrable Spartan defense. The triumph gave Illinois its twelfth football championship and its third trip to the Rose Bowl.

1963 Illinois-MSU football program

I on **1963–64**

Allen Carius

In 1962 and 1963, Al Carius became the Illini's first-ever two-time Big Ten cross-country champion. He was a three-time two-mile champ in the Big Ten. He ran competitively until 1968. Carius eventually became a mentor, taking over head coaching duties for cross-country and as track and field coach at North Central College, continuing for forty-four years. Sixteen times his cross-country teams won NCAA Division III titles, and ten times NCU captured indoor and outdoor team championships. Carius is a member of numerous halls of fame, including the Chicagoland Sports Hall of Fame.

Al Carius

ILLINI ITEM

1964 Rose Bowl ticket

The Fighting Illini football team made it three Rose Bowl victories in a row on January 1, 1964, by defeating Washington 17–7. In a game witnessed by nearly ninety-seven thousand fans, including former president and Tournament of Roses Grand Marshal Dwight Eisenhower, the Illini rebounded from a 7–3 halftime deficit behind the defensive expertise of Dick Butkus (fumble recovery and interception) and the methodical running of game MVP Jim Grabowski (125 yards rushing).

ILLINI LISTS

ILLINI COACHING STAFF AT 1964 ROSE BOWL

UI's 1964 Rose Bowl coaching staff

Position	Name (Hometown; alma mater; today's whereabouts)
Head Coach:	Pete Elliott (Bloomington, Illinois; Michigan '49; died January 4, 2013)
Assistant Coaches:	Jim Brown (Mendota, Illinois; Illinois '61; resides in Geneva, Illinois.)
	Ralph Fletcher (Morris, Illinois; Illinois '21; died January 4, 1967)
	Bob Herndon (Medford, Oklahoma; Oklahoma '55; died December 30, 2012)
	Burt Ingwersen (Clinton, Iowa; Illinois '21; died July 15, 1969)
	Coleman "Buck" McPhail (Oklahoma City, Oklahoma; Oklahoma '53; died March 4, 2005)
	Gene Stauber (Gary, Indiana; Toledo '47; died September 1985)
	Bill Tate (Mattoon, Illinois; Illinois '53; resides in Omaha, Nebraska)
	Bill Taylor (Kimball, Nebraska; Nebraska '56; resides in San Diego, California)

ILLINI LEGEND

Coach Pete Elliott (left) and Dick Butkus

Pete Elliott

One of the most popular men ever to don Fighting Illini coaching apparel, Pete Elliott took his team from the brink of destruction to the pinnacle of success during his career from 1960 to 1966. Elliott's initial years at the University of Illinois were clouded with failure, losing a modern Big Ten record fifteen games in a row from November 19, 1960, to October 27, 1962. But in 1963 Elliott's troops made Cinderella's story pale in comparison, capturing the 1963 Big Ten title and defeating Washington in the 1964 Rose Bowl. "We knew as we went through the losses that we didn't have a good team," Elliott told the *Champaign News-Gazette* in 1977. "But we were confident because our athletes were devoted and they helped us recruit top prospects. They were tremendous emissaries for the school." On March 18, 1967, Elliott and basketball coach Harry Combes resigned from the U of I staff as a result of the "slush fund" scandal. Elliott served as head football coach, then athletic director at the University of Miami from 1973 to 1978. He later was executive director of the Pro Football Hall of Fame from 1979 until he retired on October 31, 1996. Elliott died in Canton, Ohio, in 2013 at age eighty-six.

ILLINI LORE

A 1964 graduate of the University of Illinois and a native of Urbana, famed film critic Roger Ebert had his first professional newspaper job when he was fifteen years old, as a sportswriter for the *News-Gazette* in Champaign. An employee of the *Chicago Sun-Times* since 1967, he was the first-ever recipient of a Pulitzer Prize for Film Criticism (1975) and is best known for his TV work with the late Gene Siskel on the shows *At the Movies* and *Siskel and Ebert*. Ebert authored numerous books about the cinema and was a highly acclaimed screenwriter. On April 24, 2014, a year after his death at age seventy, Champaign-Urbana organizers unveiled a life-size bronze statue of Ebert in front of the Virginia Theatre at the communities' annual Ebertfest.

1964 Daily Illini editor
Roger Ebert

1964–65

AMERICA'S TIME CAPSULE

September 27, 1964   The Warren Commission on the assassination of John Kennedy reported that Lee Harvey Oswald alone was responsible for the shooting of the president.

November 3, 1964   Lyndon Johnson defeated Barry Goldwater in the presidential election.

March 2, 1965   *The Sound of Music*, starring Julie Andrews and Christopher Plummer, debuted.

March 8, 1965   The first United States combat forces landed in South Vietnam.

June 5, 1965   Astronaut Edward White successfully completed a twenty-minute walk in space, the first by an American.

ILLINI MOMENT

Grabowski Sets Big Ten Record

Jim Grabowski is grateful to the numerous teammates who opened the holes for his 239-yard rushing performance against Wisconsin, November 14, 1964. But the man to whom number 31 owes the greatest debt of gratitude might be Illini publicity man Charlie Bellatti. It was Bellatti who sent word to his sideline spotters that Grabowski needed only nineteen more yards in the final quarter to set a Big Ten record. "I wasn't going to put Jim back in the next series," head coach Pete Elliott told reporters afterward, "but a man deserves a shot at a record like that." He needed only thirty-three attempts to set the record, two of which resulted in touchdowns. In 1965 he received the Chicago Tribune Silver Football as the Big Ten's Most Valuable Player and finished third in the Heisman Trophy voting. He then went on to a six-year NFL career, including two Super Bowl performances with Green Bay in 1967 and 1968.

Jim Grabowski

I on 1964–65

In 1965, Ken Holtzman earned third-team All–Big Ten honors, assembling a record of 4–2 in seven Conference games. He was selected by the Chicago Cubs in the 1965 draft; three months later, he was called up to the big leagues. Holtzman's most spectacular efforts with the Cubs occurred in 1969 and '71, when he spun respective no-hitters against the Atlanta Braves and Cincinnati Reds. He went to the Oakland Athletics in 1971. Holtzman's fifteen-year big league record was 174-150, excluding a 4-1 mark in World Series action. He returned to St. Louis and became a successful stockbroker.

Ken Holtzman's 1967 baseball card

ILLINI ITEM

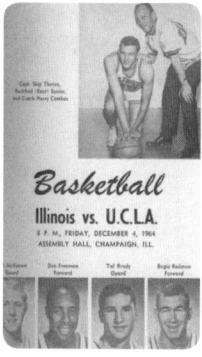

Game program for UI's big upset

Coach Harry Combes's Fighting Illini basketball team demolished defending national champion UCLA, 110–83, on December 4, 1964, severing the Bruins' thirty-game-winning streak. Though UCLA guard Gail Goodrich tossed in a game-high twenty-five points, the Illini countered with a balanced attack that had six men score in double figures, paced by twenty points from center Skip Thoren. The 1964–65 Illini would finish with an overall record of 18-6 and place third in the Big Ten standings.

ILLINI LISTS

LEADING SINGLE-GAME RUSHERS IN BIG TEN HISTORY

When Jim Grabowski broke the Big Ten's single-game football rushing record on November 14, 1964, he put his name atop a list that included many of the conference's greatest stars.

239 yards	Jim Grabowski of Illinois, vs. Wisconsin, 1964
216 yards	Bill Daley of Michigan, vs. Northwestern, 1943
212 yards	Harold "Red" Grange of Illinois, vs. Michigan, 1924
207 yards	Tony Butkovich of Purdue, vs. Illinois, 1943
205 yards	J. C. Caroline of Illinois, vs. Minnesota, 1953
200 yards	Alan Ameche of Wisconsin, vs. Minnesota, 1951
199 yards	Dick Gordon of Michigan State, vs. Wisconsin, 1964

Jim Grabowski

ILLINI LEGEND

Dick Butkus

Dick Butkus

Just how good was Illinois linebacker Dick Butkus? Consider the following:

- He was a two-time consensus All-American and All–Big Ten selection for the Fighting Illini from 1962 to 1964.
- He was the Big Ten's MVP in 1963.
- He finished third in the Heisman Trophy balloting as a senior, unheard of for a defensive player.

- His jersey, number 50, was retired at Illinois alongside Red Grange's immortal 77.
- He's a member of every all-time all-star squad in existence and was a first ballot selection into the College and Pro Football Halls of Fame.
- An award in his name is given annually to the nation's top college football linebacker.
- During his nine-year career with the Chicago Bears, he was an All-Pro pick eight times.
- Butkus has fifty-one credits during his career as a TV and movie actor from 1971 to 2014. His Butkus Foundation has supported several charitable causes, including The Dick Butkus Center for Cardiovascular Wellness, a nonprofit organization in Orange County, California. He and his wife, Helen, reside in Rancho Mirage, California.

ILLINI LORE

The U of I College of Education dedicated its new $3.3 million building November 6–7, 1964, before an overflow group of students, alumni, and other guests. The facility brought together departments that had been spread out over twenty-seven campus locations. The education building was one of the first structures on campus to feature extensive use of glass and to be fully air-conditioned.

The College of Education's new facility

1965–1974

1965–66

1965–66

AMERICA'S TIME CAPSULE

October 28, 1965   Workers topped out the Gateway Arch in St. Louis, Missouri.
January 31, 1966   President Lyndon Johnson announced that American pilots had resumed their bombing raids on North Vietnam after a thirty-eight-day hiatus.
April 28, 1966   The Boston Celtics beat the Los Angeles Lakers in game 7 of the NBA championship series, enabling coach Red Auerbach to retire with his eighth successive title.
June 8, 1966   The National and American Football Leagues merged, effective in 1970, setting up a Super Bowl game between the league champions.

ILLINI MOMENT

Combes Wins His Three-Hundredth Illini Victory over Michigan

Illinois's most memorable basketball victory of the 1965–66 season came on February I, 1966, before a sellout crowd of 7,350 at Michigan's Yost Field House. The 99–93 triumph not only got Illinois back in the Big Ten race, it also marked UI's first win in Ann Arbor in eleven years and gave Coach Harry Combes his three-hundredth win as Illini coach. Trailing by three points at the half, Illinois shot a school-record .697 from the field in the second half (twenty-three of thirty-three) to create a three-team log jam atop the conference standings. Illinois's offensive heroes were Don Freeman (thirty-three points) and Rich Jones (thirty-one points), while defensive kudos went to Preston Pearson, who, despite playing the entire second half with four fouls, "held" Michigan's Cazzie Russell to thirty-three points.

Basketball

U of M Basketball

M

ILLINOIS

DAVE STRACK, Basketball Coach University of Michigan

**February 1, 1966
8:00 P.M.**

M

||||| |||||||||
15 Cents

Oliver Darden

Program for Harry Combes's 300th coaching victory

I on 1965–66

Don Freeman, 1966 All-Big Ten honoree

Don Freeman's senior-year performance was mighty impressive. The 6'3" jumping jack from Madison, Illinois, averaged 27.8 points per game, establishing Illini single-season and career records, and earning first-team All–Big Ten honors. As a pro in the old American Basketball Association, he played for seven different teams, averaging nearly nineteen points per game and appearing in five ABA All-Star Games. When his playing career ended, he launched a career in banking. Today, Freeman is senior examiner for the Federal Reserve Bank of Kansas City, based in Omaha, Nebraska.

ILLINI ITEM

Bruce Capel

Illini football player, John "Bruce" Capel, has lived in honor at the University of Illinois for fifty years. Capel enlisted with the Marine Corps at age twenty-three, and in March 1966, Lt. Capel was sent to Vietnam. On May 12, he and his men were ambushed by Viet Cong. Only two members of the patrol survived. Each year, the Illinois football team recognizes their most courageous player with the Bruce Capel Award for Courage.

ILLINI LISTS

TOP BIG TEN TITLE WINNERS AMONG ILLINI COACHES

Track-and-field coach Leo Johnson retired in 1965

20 titles	Harry Gill, track and field (1904–1929, 1931–1933)
18 titles	Leo Johnson, cross-country (1938–1960) and track and field (1938–1965)
17 titles	Maxwell Garret, fencing (1941–1972)
12 titles	Gary Wieneke, cross-country (1967–2002) and track and field (1974–2002)
11 titles	George Huff, baseball (1896–1919)
11 titles	Charlie Pond, gymnastics (1949–1961, 1962–1973)

11 titles	Gary Winckler, women's track and field (1986–2008)
8 titles	Art Schankin, fencing (1973–1993*)
8 titles	Craig Tiley, tennis (1993–2005)
7 titles	Bob Zuppke, football (1913–1941)
6 titles	Paul Prehn, wrestling (1921–1928)
6 titles	Hek Kenney, wrestling (1929–1943, 1946–1947)

*Fencing was discontinued as a Big Ten–sponsored sport following the 1985–86 season.

ILLINI LEGEND

The Jim Grabowski family

Jim Grabowski

He broke nearly all of Red Grange's rushing records and played in the first two Super Bowls during a six-year career in the National Football League, but Jim Grabowski will be remembered for much more than just his prowess on the athletic field at the University of Illinois. The personable Chicago native was an all-star in the classroom as well, earning Academic All-America acclaim in 1964 and 1965 and the Big Ten Conference Medal of Honor in 1966. Grabowski was inducted into the Academic All-America Hall of Fame in 1993, joining such notables as Princeton's Bill Bradley, Notre Dame's Joe Theismann, and Southern Cal's Pat Haden. Number 3 in the Heisman Trophy balloting of 1965, Grabowski finished his brilliant Illini career as the Big Ten's career rushing leader with 2,878 yards. He was the first-round pick of the Green Bay Packers in 1966, retiring after the 1971 season following a series of knee injuries. Grabowski is a member of the College Football Hall of Fame (1995), the Academic All-America Hall of Fame, the Rose Bowl Hall of Fame, and the National Polish-American Sports Hall of Fame. Grabowski was an analyst on Illini football radio broadcasts for nearly thirty years. Today, he and his wife, Kathleen, reside in Inverness, Illinois.

ILLINI LORE

Early in 1966, wrecking crews began to remove the University of Illinois's temporary housing units known to their tenants as Illini Village and Stadium Terrace. The buildings, which once served as housing at an Indiana plant during World War II, provided homes for 762 families of married students. War veterans attending school on the G.I. Bill, and many others over the next two decades, remember these hastily built structures as brutally hot in the summer and bone-chillingly cold in the winter.

Stadium Terrace, just west of Memorial Stadium, was torn down in 1966

1966–67

AMERICA'S TIME CAPSULE

October 13, 1966 U.S. bombers made their heaviest air strike of the war on North Vietnam.
November 11, 1966 The last mission of the Gemini space series was launched as astronauts Jim Lovell and "Buzz" Aldrin successfully rendezvoused with an Agena target vehicle.
January 15, 1967 The Green Bay Packers defeated the Kansas City Chiefs in the first-ever Super Bowl, 35–10.
March 25, 1967 Sophomore center Lew Alcindor led UCLA to the NCAA basketball championship over Dayton, 79–64.
July 23, 1967 Forty-three people were killed in Detroit as the worst race riot in U.S. history erupted.

ILLINI MOMENT

Slush Fund Scandal Rocks Illinois

March 19, 1967: "I have received today and have accepted the resignations of Pete Elliott, head football coach, Harry Combes, head basketball coach, and Howard

Champaign *News-Gazette*'s headline tells the story

Braun, assistant basketball coach." With those twenty-six words, U of I President David Dodds Henry brought an end to one of the darkest sagas in Fighting Illini athletic history. Henry's actions came three months after he had asked the Big Ten Conference to make an investigation of alleged irregularities in assistance to athletes. On December 23, 1966—two days before Christmas—Big Ten Commissioner Bill Reed announced confirmation that illegal funds did exist. "These funds were completely apart from the operation of the University's grants-in-aid program," Reed said. "They were created with the knowledge of the director of athletics (Doug Mills) and of the assistant director of athletics (Mel Brewer), and disbursements were made at the direction of the respective head coaches." Twelve Illini football and basketball athletes were identified by the Big Ten and suspended from any further intercollegiate competition. It would take Illinois sixteen years to win its next Big Ten football title and seventeen years to claim its next conference basketball championship.

Game program for the first Super Bowl

I on **1966–67** On January 15, 1967, the Los Angeles Memorial Coliseum hosted the first AFL-NFL World Championship Game, eventually to be known as Super Bowl I. Coach Vince Lombardi's Green Bay Packers roster included a pair of Illini: linebacker Ray Nitschke and running back Jim Grabowski. The Packers led the Kansas City Chiefs 14–7 at halftime, then poured it on in the second half, winning by a score of 35–10. With the victory, both Nitschke and Grabowski earned a bonus of $15,000 each, but just a pittance of the $97,000 that the 2016 Super Bowl winners received.

ILLINI ITEM

Coach Max Garret

Illini fencing coach Maxwell Garret, born Max Goldstein, was inducted into the Helm's Fencing Hall of Fame on April l, 1967. He won seventeen Big Ten titles and NCAA titles in 1956 and 1958, serving as Illinois's head coach from 1941 to 1972, excluding three years when he was in the army. His Illini teams finished in the top ten of NCAA competition nineteen times during his twenty-seven years. Garret died in Florida in 2013 at age ninety-five.

ILLINI LISTS

ILLINI WHO HAVE PLAYED IN THE SUPER BOWL

The first Super Bowl was played in January 1967 between the Green Bay Packers and the Kansas City Chiefs. Two former Illini, Ray Nitschke and Jim Grabowski, played in that inaugural battle between the American and National Football Leagues. Here's a list of all the Illinois football players who have Super Bowl experience:

Jim Grabowski played in Super Bowls I and II

Ed Brady, Cincinnati—XXIII
Bill Brown, Minnesota—IV, VII, IX
Michael Buchanan, New England—XLIX
Darryl Byrd, L.A. Raiders—XVIII
Jameel Cook, Tampa Bay—XXXVII
Carey Davis, Pittsburgh—XLIII

Dave Diehl, N.Y. Giants—XLII, XLVI
Ken Dilger, Tampa Bay—XXXVII
Tony Eason, New England—XX
Greg Engel, San Diego—XXIX
Jim Grabowski, Green Bay—I, II
Howard Griffith, Denver—XXXII, XXXIII
Kelvin Hayden, Indianapolis—XLI, XLIV
Nathan Hodel, Arizona—XLIII
Robert Holcombe, St. Louis—XXXIV, XXXVI

ILLINI LEGEND

Jim Dawson's number 24 banner resides in the rafters of the State Farm Center

Jim Dawson

His selection as the Big Ten's most valuable basketball player in March 1967 was a curious one. Illinois's Jim Dawson wasn't the league's top scorer (25.5 points per game); that distinction belonged to Minnesota's Tom Kondla. He wasn't the conference's best rebounder or shooter; Ohio State's Bill Hosket easily won those titles. And he didn't lead his team to the Big Ten championship, as had Indiana's Butch Joyner. What earned Dawson the MVP title was his ability to perform in the face of adversity, and no one endured more adversity than did the University of Illinois at that time. The "slush fund" scandal had brought about the ineligibilities of a trio of exceptional Illini players—Rich Jones, Steve Kuberski, and Ron Dunlap—and stripped away Illinois's opportunity at a national title. Big Ten coaches clearly recognized the fact that, without Dawson, the Illini, at 6–8, might not have won a conference game. Following a one-year stint with the ABA's Indiana Pacers, the six-foot guard from Elmhurst York High School took that same determined approach in the business world, moving from New York's Wall Street to California, and, in 1982, to a securities position in Winnetka, Illinois. In 2008 a banner with Dawson's name and jersey number 24 was raised to the rafters of the State Farm Center. He retired in 2010 and now resides in Savannah, Georgia.

ILLINI LORE

The University of Illinois observed its centennial celebration beginning February 28, 1967. The university's board of trustees met at the state capitol in Springfield to witness the issuance of an executive proclamation by Governor Otto Kerner. On campus that morning, the Altgeld Hall chimes played a brief anniversary concert, followed by the band's performance of the *National Anthem* and *Illinois Loyalty*. A total of 3,567 UI students received degrees in June 1967, as compared with twenty in the first senior class of 1872.

A commemorative button from UI's Centennial celebration

1967–68

AMERICA'S TIME CAPSULE

October 2, 1967 — Thurgood Marshall was sworn in as the United States' first black Supreme Court justice.

January 23, 1968 — North Korea seized the naval intelligence ship U.S.S. Pueblo off its coast.

April 4, 1968 — Dr. Martin Luther King Jr. was assassinated by a sniper in Memphis, Tennessee, setting off a week of rioting in several urban black ghettos.

June 5, 1968 — Presidential candidate Robert Kennedy was fatally shot in Los Angeles after delivering a speech to acknowledge his victory in the California primary.

ILLINI MOMENT

Valek Wins Home Debut

It would prove to be one of only four home-field victories he'd capture over the ensuing four years, but new Fighting Illini football coach Jim Valek truly enjoyed his first appearance on the sidelines of Memorial Stadium, September 30, 1967. Valek's troops had lost their debut a week earlier at Florida, but this one belonged to the Illini from start to finish, defeating Pittsburgh, 34–6. Quarterback Bob Naponic directed Illinois to scoring drives of forty-six, seventy-one, and sixty yards as the Illini beat Pitt for the sixth time in as many meetings. U of I's workhorse out of the backfield was junior fullback Rich Johnson, who gained 116 yards in just seventeen attempts. Illinois's defense, bolstered by interceptions from Ron Bess and Ken Kmiec, halted Panther runners to an average of less than two yards per try and allowed only eight receptions of twenty-three passes. It would be more than a year later— November 16, 1968—before Illinois would win again at home. Jim Valek died in 2005 at age seventy-seven.

Rookie coach Jim Valek

I on 1967–68

Mike Murawski was UI baseball's Most Valuable Player in 1967 and 1968

Mike Murawski was originally recruited to Illinois to play football, but his real passion was baseball. Murawski never did play football for the Illini, but he sparkled in baseball. As a sophomore outfielder/catcher in 1967, Murawski led Illinois in hitting with a .375 average. He followed up by hitting .348 as a junior, winning team MVP honors for a second straight season, but was sidelined for the entire 1969 Big Ten season with an injury. Today, Murawski still ranks among the school's top ten in average at .356. He passed away on his sixty-third birthday in 2010.

ILLINI ITEM

Ron Bess, 1967 Illini co-captain

Ron Bess served as an Illinois football co-captain in 1967, displaying the leadership that would eventually make him one of Chicago's premier advertising executives. He became a master brand builder, founding Bayer Bess Vanderwarker in Chicago. BBV would go on to win AdWeek's "Agency of the Year" award in 1988, serving such clients as Gatorade, Campbell's, and Motorola. Bess next moved to New York then returned to Chicago to become CEO of Havas Chicago. Today, he serves as a consultant.

ILLINI LISTS

ILLINI WHO HAVE PLAYED IN THE SUPER BOWL
(continued from 1966–67 List)

Green Bay Packer
legend Ray Nitschke

Michael Hoomanawanui, New England—XLIX	Preston Pearson, Baltimore—III; Pittsburgh—IX; Dallas—X, XII, XIII
Brad Hopkins, Tennessee—XXXIV	Neil Rackers, Arizona—XLIII
A.J. Jenkins, San Francisco—XLVII	Simeon Rice, Tampa Bay—XXXVII
Henry Jones, Buffalo—XXVI, XXVII, XXVIII	Jack Squirek, L.A. Raiders—XVIII
Jim Juriga, Denver—XXIV	Calvin Thomas, Chicago—XX
Greg Lewis, Philadelphia—XXXIX	Pierre Thomas, New Orleans—XLIV
Adam Lingner, Buffalo—XXV, XXVI, XXVII, XXVIII	Steve Weatherford, N.Y. Giants—XLVI
Rashard Mendenhall, Pittsburgh—XLIII, XLV	Eugene Wilson, New England—XXXVIII, XXXIX, XLII
Aaron Moorehead, Indianapolis—XLI	Tavon Wilson, New England—XLIX
Ray Nitschke, Green Bay—I, II	Walter Young, Carolina—XXXVII; Pittsburgh—XLIII, ILV

ILLINI LEGEND

John Wright set Big Ten
records for receptions

John Wright

It was during of his junior season against Indiana that John Wright became the leading pass receiver in University of Illinois football history. From that point on, every time he caught a pass, he set a record. From 1965 to 1967, the split end from Wheaton set Big Ten records of 159 catches for 2,284 yards, more than twice the previous UI record totals of Rex Smith (seventy catches) and John "Rocky" Ryan (1,041 yards). Wright also lettered twice in track as a hurdler. Academically, he earned even more honors, including Academic All-American laurels in 1966. Following college, Wright played for the NFL's Detroit Lions but sustained a career-ending injury in his third season. Today, he is CEO and former managing partner of the Wright Financial Group, a member of the Northwestern Mutual Financial Network. Wright also is a popular speaker among corporate leaders and was voted the top speaker at the NFL National Rookie Symposium six times. His St. Joseph estate has become a renowned training center for a variety of Fortune 500 CEOs and professional athletes. John and his son Johnny are the only father-son duo in NCAA football history to have earned First-Team Academic All-America laurels.

ILLINI LORE

On June 15, 1966, the University of Illinois Board of Trustees formally approved the establishment of the administrative post of chancellor for the Urbana-Champaign campus. Chosen as UIUC's first chancellor was forty-three-year-old Jack Peltason, who previously served as vice chancellor for academic affairs at the University of California Irvine. Peltason remained at Illinois until August 1977, when he became president of the American Council on Education. He returned to UCI in 1984 to become its chancellor. Eight years later Peltason became president of the University of California. In retirement, he was presented with UC's President's Medal, the university's highest honor. Peltason died in 2015 at age ninety-one.

Jack Peltason served as
UI's president until 1977

1968–69

AMERICA'S TIME CAPSULE

October 10, 1968   The Detroit Tigers won the World Series for the first time since 1945, defeating the St. Louis Cardinals in seven games.

November 5, 1968   Republican Richard Nixon won the presidential election, beating Hubert Humphrey by a half million votes.

July 16, 1969   U.S. space capsule Apollo 11 landed on the moon at 4:17 P.M. EDT. Astronaut Neil Armstrong became the first person to set foot on the moon.

August 15, 1969   The Woodstock Music and Art Fair began, drawing half a million people.

ILLINI MOMENT

Illini Cagers Battle for Big Ten Crown

Coach Harv Schmidt's 1968–69 basketball team fought to an impressive 19–5 overall record and a spot in the top-twenty national ranking, but could do no better than finish four games behind champion Purdue in the Big Ten standings. Illinois won its first ten in a row before losing to Rick Mount's juggernauts at West Lafayette in game 2 of the conference season. The Illini turned a disappointing 4-4 conference start into a 9-5 final league record by winning five of its last six Big Ten games. The U of I's balanced attack was paced by senior forward Dave Scholz (19.1 points per game) and sophomore center Greg Jackson (16.4). Guards Mike Price (12.4) and Jodie Harrison (10.6) also were consistent scorers for the Illini. Illinois's nineteen victories were the most since the 1962–63 season, when that club won the Big Ten title with twenty overall wins.

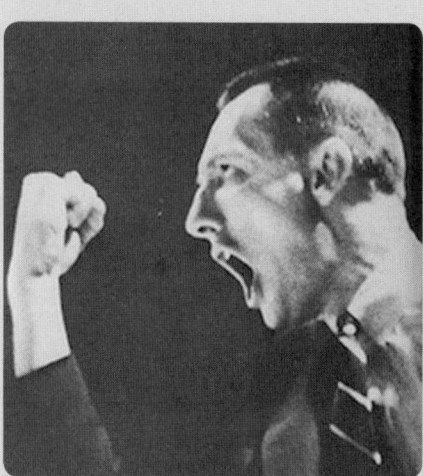

Coach Harv Schmidt

I on 1968–69

The Most Valuable Player of Illinois's 1969 baseball team was Rich Binder. Drafted in 1965 by the Los Angeles Dodgers, he instead committed to pitch for the Illini and won varsity letters from 1967 to 1969. As a senior, Binder dominated Big Ten hitters, spinning a perfect 6-0 record and earning first-team All–Big Ten honors. Binder served the Belleville school district as a teacher and a principal. He also taught at McKendree University. A charter member of the Waterloo High School Hall of Fame, he and his wife, Portia, currently reside in Smithton, Illinois.

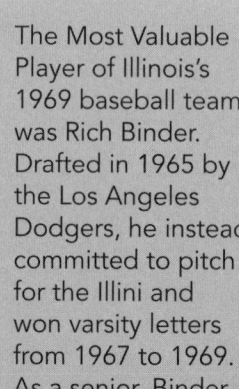

Left-hander Rich Binder was baseball's MVP for 1969

ILLINI ITEM

An indoor track and field dual meet against Wisconsin at the University of Illinois Armory on February 22, 1969, was the site for a recordbreaking performance by Illini pole vaulter Ed Halik. Halik cleared the bar at 16'¾", becoming the first Illinois vaulter and only the third Big Ten athlete to clear a height over sixteen feet. He graduated with a degree in education but chose to serve in the air force for twenty years. Halik resides in Colorado Springs and is currently a first officer for American Airlines.

Ed Halik

ILLINI LISTS

IF ILLINI ATHLETES WERE KNOWN
BY THEIR GIVEN FIRST NAMES

Duane "Skip" Thoren

Nelison (Nick) Anderson

Theodore (Tab) Bennett

Daniel (Dee) Brown

George (Potsy) Clark

Talib (Ty) Douthard

Charles (Tony) Eason

Thomas (Dike) Eddleman

Walter (Hoot) Evers

Morris (Moe) Gardner

Harold (Red) Grange

Rausell (Rocky) Harvey

Richard (Itch) Jones

Harold (Hek) Kenney

Jeremy (J) Leman

Charles (Bubba) Smith

Russell (Ruck) Steger

Duane (Skip) Thoren

Thomas (T. J.) Wheeler

Isiah (Juice) Williams

Kenneth (Tug) Wilson

Claude (Buddy) Young

ILLINI LEGEND

Dave Scholz

A humble Dave Scholz used to tell his friends, "I really didn't have the ability to play major college basketball." So how did the six-eighter from Decatur end up as the University of Illinois's all-time leading scorer? "I was on the receiving end of a lot of good passes," he says. Still, scoring a total of 1,459 points against such superstars as Lew Alcindor and Rudy Tomjanovich takes some coordination. In fact, of the nearly five hundred men who've lettered in basketball at Illinois, only Scholz (20.5 points per game), Nick Weatherspoon (20.9), and Don Freeman (20.1) have averaged better than twenty points per contest. Number 40's biggest night came on February 24, 1968, when he drilled home forty-two points against Northwestern, a single-game total second only to Dave Downey's fifty-three-point masterpiece versus Indiana. Following a brief tour of the pros, Scholz returned to the U of I to obtain his master's degree in accountancy. In 1980 he began the first of six years in Saudi Arabia with the Arabian American Oil Company. Scholz died in 2015 in Nashville, Tennessee, at age sixty-seven.

Dave Scholz

ILLINI LORE

The $21 million Krannert Center for the Performing Arts opened its doors to the University of Illinois community in April 1969. Donated to the U of I by philanthropists Mr. and Mrs. Herman C. Krannert, the center was conceived with a twofold purpose. First, it would provide the most up-to-date facilities for the training of UI students in the performing arts; second, it would provide a modern cultural center for the community. The facility features three auditoriums: Foellinger Great Hall, seating twenty-one hundred, designed for music presentations; the Tryon Festival Theatre, with a capacity of 974, planned for singing performances; and the Colwell Playhouse, seating nearly seven hundred, designed specifically as a venue for acting. Among the notables who have performed at Krannert over the years: Luciano Pavarotti (1980), Yo-Yo Ma (2006), the Russian National Ballet Theatre (2011), and the Chinese National Symphony Orchestra (2013).

The Krannert Center for the
Performing Arts opened in 1969

1969–70

AMERICA'S TIME CAPSULE

October 24, 1969   *Butch Cassidy and the Sundance Kid* debuted at movie theaters.
November 16, 1969   As many as five hundred Vietnam villagers were slain by a U.S. infantry unit in what would be known as the My Lai Massacre.
March 18, 1970   The first major postal workers' strike began in the United States.
April 29, 1970   U.S. and South Vietnamese troops invaded Cambodia.
May 4, 1970   Four Kent State University students were killed by National Guard troops during an antiwar demonstration.

ILLINI MOMENT

Illini Shatter Shooting Record

Coach Harv Schmidt's 1969–70 Fighting Illini basketball squad, known more for its defensive prowess, shot the proverbial lights out against Indiana on January 6, 1970, at Illinois's Assembly Hall. With a .679 shooting performance from the field (forty of fifty-nine), the Illini obliterated their former high mark of .613, set against Iowa in 1967. Individually, the Illinois's outside shooters were paced by Rick Howat and Mike Price, who hit sixteen of their twenty-four long-bomb attempts. Inside, the triumvirate of Randy Crews, Fred Miller, and Greg Jackson connected on nearly 71 percent of their shots. Illinois's 94–74 victory over the Hoosiers was the second of the young Big Ten season. Illinois went on to win three more games in a row to improve its record to 12-2. They couldn't keep up their momentum, however, winding up with an overall mark of 15-9.

Rick Howat

I on 1969–70

At a time when individual championships were infrequent for University of Illinois athletes, Champaign High School graduate Mark Koster was an exception to the rule. Illini coach Bob Wright and assistant coach Gary Wieneke helped turn Koster into a champion hurdler at Illinois. His photo-finish victory in the 440-yard intermediate hurdles at the 1970 Big Ten Outdoor Championships in Bloomington, Indiana, was the Illini's only individual title that spring. Following his graduation, Koster volunteered in the Peace Corps for two years in Vietnam. Eventually, he moved back to his hometown and had a successful career in construction.

Mark Koster

ILLINI ITEM

Lou Boudreau (left) and MLB Commissioner Bowie Kuhn

On July 27, 1970, former Fighting Illini baseball and basketball standout Lou Boudreau was inducted into Cooperstown's Baseball Hall of Fame. Said Boudreau in his speech, "This is the happiest day of my life. There can be no greater reward for a player. My prayers have been answered." Also included in Cooperstown's class of 1970 with the former Cleveland Indians star were pitcher Jesse Haines, outfielder Earl Combs, and former baseball commissioner Ford Frick.

ILLINI LISTS

ILLINI FOOTBALL ACADEMIC ALL-AMERICA AWARDS
(first-team selections)

1952	Bob Lenzini, OT
1964–65	Jim Grabowski, FB
1966	John Wright Sr., E
1970	Jim Rucks, DE
1971	Bob Bucklin, DE
1980–82	Dan Gregus, DL
1991	Mike Hopkins, DB
1992	John Wright Jr. WR
1994	Brett Larsen, P

Jim Rucks earned
Academic All-America
honors in 1970

1999–00	Josh Whitman, TE
2007	Ryan McDonald, C

ILLINI LEGEND

Randy Crews was Illinois's
defensive stopper

Randy Crews

The University of Illinois may never honor Randy Crews with a spot in its Hall of Fame, but the kid from Bradley-Bourbonnais High School will definitely get some write-in votes for his athletic versatility. Crews received more than one hundred athletic scholarship offers and could have signed to a bonus with the San Francisco Giants, but he instead decided to attend Illinois. Crews wore jersey number 30 from 1968 to 1970 for Coach Harv Schmidt's Illini basketball team and was noted for his defense rather than his offense, frequently being assigned to the opponent's top scorer. The 6'5" first baseman was even more intimidating on the baseball diamond, finishing his career among Illinois's top-ten all-time hitters, with a .315 batting average. He was chosen to the Big Ten's 1970 all-star baseball squad his senior year, hitting .361 for the season. Crews played four seasons in minor-league baseball for the Chicago Cubs organization, totaling thirty-seven home runs and 166 RBI with a .295 average. In 1975 he was inducted into the Illinois Basketball Coaches Association Hall of Fame. Today, Crews resides in Momence, Illinois.

ILLINI LORE

The month of May, 1970, will be remembered by students and faculty as a period of great unrest at American universities. Stoked by President Nixon's announcement that American troops would be sent to Cambodia and ignited by the killing of four Kent State University students on May 4, UI students and thousands of others at campuses across the country called for a nationwide strike. A rally jammed the UI Auditorium on May 5, and action began the moment the gathering ended. The "trashing" of the campus business district and some university buildings started soon after UI Chancellor Jack Peltason denounced the violence and refused to close the university, but only 60 percent of the classes went on as scheduled. From May 5 to May 10, police made 221 arrests, and damage totaled more than $26,000.

Police and the National Guard
protected Campustown in May 1970

1970–71

AMERICA'S TIME CAPSULE

November 8, 1970	Tom Dempsey of the New Orleans Saints kicked an NFL-record sixty-three-yard field goal.
December 2, 1970	The Environmental Protection Agency, established in July, was activated.
December 23, 1970	The World Trade Center was topped in New York City to become the world's largest building.
January 25, 1971	Charles Manson and three of his followers were convicted of the 1969 murders of actress Sharon Tate and six others.
March 29, 1971	William Calley was convicted of the murder of twenty-two unarmed South Vietnamese civilians at My Lai.

ILLINI MOMENT

Illini Gridders End Losing Streak

It had been nearly two years since Illinois had won a Big Ten Conference football game, so the odds of coach Jim Valek's squad beating Purdue in the Boilermakers' Homecoming game (October 31, 1970) would have tested even the bravest gambler. Purdue jumped off to a 14–0 lead at halftime, thanks to a sixty-two-yard touchdown pass from quarterback Gary Danielson to halfback Otis Armstrong. Illinois bounced back to take a 17–14 advantage early in the fourth quarter, but Purdue regained the lead, 21–17, with 4:01 remaining. Illini quarterback Mike Wells then engineered a game-winning, seven-play, sixty-nine-yard drive, combining his own passes to Doug Dieken with the brilliant running of Darrell Robinson. The 23–21 Illinois victory brought an end to the school's eleven-game Big Ten losing streak. It would be the last win in Valek's Illini coaching career.

Jim Valek and his 1970 captains, Doug Dieken (left) and Kirk McMillin

I on 1970–71

From 1968 to 1970, Fighting Illini football was struggling with a 2-19 record for the period, but Doug Dieken was Illinois's silver lining. A native of Streator, Illinois, Dieken primarily played tight end for the Illini. The co-captain was Illinois's only representative on the 1970 All–Big Ten team. Dieken played fourteen NFL seasons for the Cleveland Browns, playing in 203 consecutive games. When he retired, Dieken became the Browns' color commentator on radio broadcasts and, in 2016, he completed his twenty-ninth season in that role.

Doug Dieken was an All–Big Ten selection in 1970

ILLINI ITEM

Illini football letterman Tim McCarthy

Tim McCarthy, who used to deliver hard hits as a safety on the Fighting Illini football team, stepped in front of a bullet aimed at President Ronald Reagan and was wounded in the abdomen on March 30, 1981. On January 11, 1982, the National Collegiate Athletic Association honored him with its Award of Valor. McCarthy retired from the Secret Service in 1993. He has served as chief of police for Orland Park since 1994.

ILLINI LISTS

NAISMITH AWARD WINNERS' PERFORMANCES VERSUS ILLINOIS

James Naismith, the inventor of basketball

1971	Austin Carr, Notre Dame, 23 points on January 30, 1971 (Illinois won, 69–66)
1973	Bill Walton, UCLA, 20 points on December 30, 1972 (UCLA won, 71–64)
1976	Scott May, Indiana, 27 points on January 17, 1976 (IU won 83–55); and 6 points on February 4, 1976 (IU won, 58–48)
1988	Danny Manning, Kansas, 28 points on November 29, 1987 (Illinois won, 81–75)
1993	Calbert Cheaney, Indiana, 30 points on January 16, 1993 (IU won, 83–79); and 29 points on February 17, 1993 (IU won, 93–72)
1994	Glenn Robinson, Purdue, 49 points on March 13, 1994 (PU won, 87–77)
2001	Shane Battier, Duke, 11 points on November 28, 2000 (Duke won, 78–77)
2010	Evan Turner, Ohio State, 16 points on March 2, 2010 (OSU won 73–57); and 31 points on March 13, 2010 (OSU won 88–81)
2013	Trey Burke, Michigan, 19 points on January 27, 2013 (UM 74–60); and 26 points on February 24, 2013 (UM won 71–58)
2015	Frank Kaminsky, Wisconsin, 23 points on February 15, 2015 (UW won, 68–49)

ILLINI LEGEND

Lee LaBadie

Lee LaBadie was the first Illini to break four minutes in the mile run

Though he won only one individual conference title during his three-year career at the University of Illinois, Lee LaBadie's name will always have a prominent place in Big Ten track and field lore. On May 11, 1971, in a dual meet against Southern Illinois, he became the first Big Ten Conference undergraduate to break the four-minute barrier in the mile run. LaBadie ran his first 440 yards in sixty seconds, but his pace slowed to 2:03 after the first half mile. Then he began to pour on the coals, touring the next quarter mile in 0:57.5. LaBadie ran the final 440 yards in 0:58.3, finishing in a record time of 3:58.8. He was also a key member of a world-record-tying two-mile relay squad at Illinois, a unit that won the 1972 NCAA indoor title. He served as cross-country and track coach at Parkland College from 1976 to 1985, and in 1985 LaBadie became head coach of Bowling Green State's women's cross-country and track programs. From 1989 to 1993, he was Ohio State's assistant men's cross-country and track coach and helped Buckeye runner Mark Croghan to the NCAA steeplechase title. He served a second stint with the Buckeyes from 2006 to 2008, then took over as head coach at the University of Akron. LaBadie completed his ninth season at Akron in 2016. He and his wife reside in Cuyahoga Falls, Ohio.

ILLINI LORE

On February 13, 1971, the U of I Board of Trustees elected forty-six-year-old Dr. John "Jack" Corbally as the university's thirteenth president, replacing the retiring David Henry. The six-foot-four-inch Corbally came to the Urbana-Champaign campus from Syracuse University, where he had served as president and chancellor. He remained at UI until September l, 1979. Corbally became the first president of the MacArthur Foundation in 1980, then served as board chairman of the foundation until 2002. He died at age seventy-nine in 2004.

John Corbally

1971–72

AMERICA'S TIME CAPSULE

September 13, 1971   A prison riot at Attica State Correctional Facility in New York ended after claiming thirty-nine lives.

February 21, 1972   President Nixon began his historic visit to mainland China.

May 26, 1972   Soviet General Secretary Leonid Brezhnev and President Nixon signed the Anti-Ballistic Missile Systems.

June 17, 1972   Police arrested five men involved in a burglary of Democrat Party headquarters, beginning the famed Watergate affair.

ILLINI MOMENT

Bob Blackman Hired

The hiring of Bob Blackman as the Fighting Illini football coach on December 23, 1970, was greeted with open arms by the Champaign-Urbana community and University of Illinois fans all around the state. The entire Illini athletic program had been submerged in the dregs of the infamous "slush fund" scandal, and Blackman's glowing sixteen-year record at Dartmouth, everyone hoped, would be the antidote that would cure the school's football ills. The Blackman era began slowly. After losing their first six games of 1971, including their first three by shutouts, the Illini bounced back to win their last five in a row. Again, in 1972, Blackman's squad began poorly, losing its first seven games, before salvaging three of its last four contests. That mediocre trend continued for the balance of Blackman's six-year career at Illinois, with only 1974's record, 6-4-1, breaking the sub-.500 pattern. There were several bright spots, however, during Blackman's reign. Despite going 0-12 against the Big Ten's "Big Two" of Michigan and Ohio State during his Illini career, Blackman's Illini amassed a cumulative record of 24-11-1 against the other seven conference opponents. Blackman died in 2000 at age eighty-one.

Bob Blackman coached the Illini from 1971 to 1976

I on 1971–72

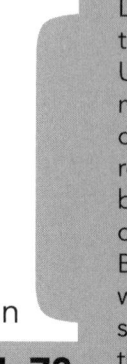

Coach Don Sammons

Don Sammons took over as the University of Illinois's swimming coach in 1971. During his twenty-two-year reign, the 1955 UI graduate's swimmers broke every school record. Sammons coached seven All-Americans and seven Big Ten Conference champions. Sammons won the Illinois Swimming and Diving Association's John Newman Award in 1974, the highest award presented in Illinois aquatics, and is also a member of the Illinois Swimming Hall of Fame. The university dropped men's swimming from varsity status on May 7, 1993. Today, Sammons and his wife, Marilyn, reside in Gilbert, Arizona.

ILLINI ITEM

Rick Gross, an All-American and 1971 Big Ten runner-up in cross-country, was also successful in track and field at the University of Illinois. He set records in the steeplechase (8:41.8) and the 10,000-meter run (29:17.4), and nearly broke the magic four-minute barrier in the mile run (4:00.4). Earning both his bachelor's and master's degree in finance, Gross oversees a team that provides capital and investment advice for Barclays Capital. He and his wife, Cynthia, split their time between Colorado and South Carolina.

Rick Gross

ILLINI LISTS

ILLINOIS'S FASTEST MILERS

1.	3:53.47		Marko Koers, 1996
2.	3:56.7		Mike Durkin, 1975
3.	3:58.8		Lee LaBadie, 1971
4.	4:00.17	indoors	Graham Morris, 2013
4.	4:00.4		Rick Gross, 1972
5.	4:00.56	indoors	Len Sitko, 1991
6.	4:00.68	indoors	Tom Stevens, 1982
7.	4:00.8		Jeff Jirele, 1976
8.	4:00.94	indoors	Greg Domantay, 1983
9.	4:01.49	indoors	Jon Schmidt, 1982
10.	4:02.30	indoors	Mike Patton, 1985

Lee LaBadie

ILLINI LEGEND

Tab Bennett

To become a college football All-American, it is almost always necessary that one's team be ranked among the nation's elite. But that certainly wasn't the case in 1972 for Illinois's standout defensive end Theodore Anthony "Tab" Bennett. The Illini's 3-8 mark didn't draw attention to Bennett's individual talent as Nebraska's nearly perfect record had done for All-American middle guard Rich Glover, but it was difficult to disguise Bennett's outstanding abilities. The native of Miami, Florida, lettered once under Coach Jim Valek and twice for Bob Blackman, and earned All–Big Ten honors both his junior and senior seasons. Bennett's 231 career tackles ranked second only to Dick Butkus's record at the time. An ankle injury prevented him from continuing his career in the NFL, so Bennett turned his sights toward a profession in college athletic administration at his alma mater. A meteoric rise saw him named as Illinois's sports information director in 1974, becoming the Big Ten Conference's first-ever African American SID. Bennett continued in that role until 1989, when a life-threatening automobile accident forced him to retire. He died March 13, 1994, at age forty-two.

Tab Bennett signs autographs for young admirers

ILLINI LORE

The $11.2 million Intramural–Physical Education Building opened for use at the University of Illinois during the fall semester of the 1971–72 academic year. University students paid the major portion of the bill—$9.1 million—through an activity fee of $18 per semester. Highlighting the facility were four large gymnasiums, indoor and outdoor swimming pools, a three-court tennis complex, twenty-three handball courts, and seven squash courts. Estimated usage by students that first year was more than 548,000, with a record 734,000 student usage in 1987–88. In March 2006, a $54 million renovation and expansion began. Twenty-nine months later, in August 2008, the renamed Activities and Recreation Center (ARC) was dedicated. It features a 150-person auditorium, a wellness center, a thirty-four-thousand-square-foot strength and conditioning area, and a thirty-four-foot climbing wall.

An outdoor pool was a popular part of the new IMPE facility

1972–73

AMERICA'S TIME CAPSULE

November 7, 1972 — The Republican Party enjoyed its greatest landslide victory ever with the reelection of President Richard Nixon.

January 22, 1973 — Representatives of the United States and North and South Vietnam, meeting in Paris, signed an agreement to end the war in Vietnam.

April 3, 1973 — Motorola introduced the first handheld cellular telephone.

June 9, 1973 — Secretariat, called the greatest race horse ever, won the Belmont Stakes to become the ninth Triple Crown winner.

July 16, 1973 — The existence of the Watergate tapes was revealed.

ILLINI MOMENT

Perrin Puts on a Show as Illini Dazzle Indiana

November 11, 1972, marked one of the greatest individual performances in Fighting Illini football history, as Illinois's Lonnie Perrin set a Big Ten total-offense record against the Indiana Hoosiers. The sophomore halfback from Washington, D.C., rushed 142 yards in twelve carries, completed two passes to Garvin Roberson for ninety-four yards, and grabbed three aerials from Mike Wells for an additional thirty-five yards. Perrin's fourteen rushes and passes averaged 16.86 yards per play, erasing a four-year-old mark held by Iowa's Ed Podolak. The most exciting play in Illinois's 37–20 victory over the Hoosiers was Perrin's long, cross-field lateral to George Uremovich, who sprinted down the west sideline to complete a ninety-six-yard kickoff return. "I really didn't feel up for the game," said Perrin afterward in the locker room, "but after my first play [a sixteen-yard gain] I was ready." Perrin was an NFL running back from 1976 to 1979 and played for Denver in Super Bowl XII. He and his wife, Karen, now live in Clinton, Maryland.

Lonnie Perrin

I on 1972–73

Rob Mango

From 1970–73, Rob Mango's two passions were running and painting, which he frequently combined during his lengthy training sessions. "As the pain from running became excruciating, I would visualize my paintings, usually works in progress," explained the former Big Ten Medal of Honor winner. Mango's unusual technique made him a highly successful middle-distance runner, yielding three Big Ten individual (880-yard run) and relay championships, and a 1972 NCAA two-mile relay title. Since 1977, he has operated a gallery and studio and has written a book, *100 Paintings: An Artist's Life in New York City*.

ILLINI ITEM

The University of Illinois's fencing team became the only Illini unit to win a Big Ten championship March 3, 1973, when Coach Art Schankin's swordsmen captured the conference title at East Lansing, Michigan. Led by epee champion Nate Haywood and sabre titlist Alan Acker, Illinois easily outdistanced second-place Ohio State, 37–25, to win its second consecutive team title.

1972–73 fencing team

ILLINI LISTS

GREATEST MEN'S BASKETBALL DEBUTS

Points		
30	Jeff Dawson vs. DePauw, December 2, 1972	
23	Govoner Vaughn vs. Marquette, December 2, 1957	
22	Brandon Paul vs. SIU-Edwardsville, November 13, 2009	
21	Deon Thomas vs. American-Puerto Rico, November 23, 1990	

Rebounds		
13	Greg Jackson vs. Butler, December 2, 1968	
12	Bill Burwell vs. Creighton, December 1, 1960	
11	Dave Downey vs. Creighton, December 1, 1960	
11	Don Freeman vs. Butler, November 30, 1963	

Jeff Dawson

ILLINI LEGEND

Nick Weatherspoon

Team-wise, Nick Weatherspoon's college basketball career at the University of Illinois was only moderately successful, but individually, very few Fighting Illini basketball players were more proficient than "The Spoon." The former Ohio Prep Player of the Year from Canton McKinley High School ruled Coach Harv Schmidt's Assembly Hall court from 1971 to 1973, setting Illini records for points (1,481) and rebounds (806). His career averages of 20.9 points and 11.4 rebounds per game are still tops at Illinois. Weatherspoon seemed to peak when the Illini played Michigan, averaging nearly twenty-six points and fourteen rebounds in his five career games against the Wolverines. "Spoon" was the thirteenth pick in the first round of the 1973 NBA draft, going to the Washington Bullets. His eight-year NBA career also included stints with the Seattle Supersonics, the Chicago Bulls, and the San Diego Clippers. The 6'7" forward scored 4,086 points and grabbed 2,232 rebounds in 453 career NBA games. A member of Illinois's All-Century team and the owner of the Weatherspoon Insurance Agency in Canton, Weatherspoon died in 2008 at age fifty-eight.

Nick Weatherspoon

ILLINI LORE

The Levis Faculty Center began operation during the 1972–73 academic year. Made possible by a $1.2 million gift from Margaret Levis, a 1914 graduate, the center's primary purpose was to serve as an intellectual gathering place for the faculty and staff of the University of Illinois. The facility replaced the University Club on Oregon Street that UI faculty had previously used.

The Levis Faculty Center on the UIUC campus

1973–74

AMERICA'S TIME CAPSULE

December 6, 1973	Following Spiro Agnew's resignation, Gerald Ford was sworn in as vice president.
December 16, 1973	O. J. Simpson of the Buffalo Bills set an NFL single-season rushing record.
February 5, 1974	Patricia Hearst was kidnapped from her California apartment by a group calling itself the Symbionese Liberation Army.
April 8, 1974	Hank Aaron of the Atlanta Braves hit his 715th career home run, breaking Babe Ruth's legendary record.
August 8, 1974	President Richard Nixon announced his resignation. Gerald Ford was sworn in as president the following day.

ILLINI
MOMENT

The Harv Schmidt Era Ends

Harv Schmidt's University of Illinois basketball coaching career ended in 1973–74 as stormily as it began. The former Illini standout from Kankakee was hired as his alma mater's head coach in 1967, taking over for Harry Combes, who resigned in the aftermath of the infamous "slush fund" scandal. Schmidt's first team, headed by Dave Scholz, Randy Crews, and Mike Price, managed an overall record of only 11-13. Illinois's success under Schmidt reached its zenith in 1968–69, streaking to a second-place finish in the Big Ten and a 19-5 season mark. The Illini fans fondly embraced their coach, rising to their feet at his mere appearance from the Assembly Hall tunnel. Harv's third Illini team, 1969–70, jumped off to a terrific 12-2 start but managed only three more wins in its final ten games that season. Despite that late-season slump, Illinois basketball fans turned out in record numbers during the 1970–71 campaign, setting an NCAA-record attendance average of 16,128 per game. Schmidt's final four Illini teams from 1970–71 to 1973–74 compiled a sub-.500 mark of forty-four wins and fifty losses, and he was replaced in 1974 by Gene Bartow.

Harv Schmidt (right) and assistant Dick Campbell

I on **1973–74**

On May 15, 1974, the University of Illinois Board of Trustees, chaired by Earl Hughes, took action to put intercollegiate athletics for women under the auspices of the Athletic Association. Dr. Karol A. Kahrs became the Illinois's first assistant director for women's athletics on June 1, 1974.

Dr. Karol Kahrs

ILLINI ITEM

Dan Beaver

On September 29, 1973, a redheaded missionary's son from Africa began his assault on the University of Illinois's football record book. Dan Beaver's thirty-seven-yard field goal against West Virginia was the first of thirty-eight three-pointers he'd kick during his career from 1973 to 1976. Two weeks later against Purdue, the soccer-style kicker booted a Big Ten-record five field goals. Beaver kicked four placements of fifty yards or more, including a conference-record-tying fifty-seven-yarder versus Purdue his junior year. He became Illinois's all-time leading scorer on November 20, 1976, breaking Red Grange's fifty-one-year-old record with a four-year total of 198 points. For more than twenty-five years, Beaver and his wife, Tory, have served as Christian missionaries on Boracay Island in Manila, Philippines.

ILLINI LISTS

ILLINOIS'S LONGEST FIELD GOALS (in chronological order)

50 yards	by Earl Britton vs. Iowa, October 23, 1923
51 yards	by Dan McKissic vs. Purdue, November 4, 1967
52 yards	by Lonnie Perrin vs. Penn State, October 7, 1972
57 yards	by Dan Beaver vs. Purdue, October 18, 1975

OPPONENTS' LONGEST FIELD GOALS VS. ILLINOIS (in chronological order)

57 yards	by Pat O'Dea of Wisconsin, November 11, 1899
59 yards	by Tom Skladany of Ohio State, November 18, 1975
61 yards	by Ralf Mojsiejenko of Michigan State, September 11, 1982

Dan Beaver

ILLINI LEGEND

Charlton Ehizuelen

Charlton Ehizuelen

More than forty years have passed, but Big Ten track and field aficionados can still find Charlton Ehizuelen's name at the top of the conference's all-time lists in the long jump. The "kangaroo" from Benin City, Nigeria, dominated the conference competition during his career from 1974 to 1977 at Illinois. Ehizuelen missed the 1974 Big Ten meet due to a bout with malaria and was absent from the 1976 conference championships due to his suspension from the team. However, in the six Big Ten track meets in which he did compete, the amazing African captured eleven of a possible twelve conference titles. Ehizuelen also won four NCAA championships, including three long-jump titles. After graduating in 1977 Ehizuelen held all-time Big Ten best performances in both the long jump (27'1¼" indoors, 26'10" outdoors) and the triple jump (54'9½" indoors, 55'-2¼" outdoors), breaking Jesse Owens's record on one occasion. Though he performed for Coach Gary Wieneke, the 6'0", 160-pound Ehizuelen was actually recruited by Wieneke's predecessor, Bob Wright, who brought him to Champaign-Urbana with the help of Nigerian coach Awoture Eleyae, a UI postgraduate student. In 1976 Ehizuelen made the Nigerian Olympic Team, but he was denied his chance to perform when his country boycotted the games. Today, Ehizuelen lives with his family in Surulere, Lagos, Nigeria.

ILLINI LORE

A $1.65 million capital fund campaign "to keep Memorial Stadium beautiful for the next 50 years" was announced by the University of Illinois at a meeting of the UI Foundation in October 1973. Priorities for the campaign were to replace Zuppke Field's natural grass with an artificial turf, to install lighting for night activities at the stadium, and to renovate the locker rooms and training facilities. Directing the "Golden Anniversary Fund Campaign" were chairman William Karnes and honorary chairman Harold "Red" Grange.

William Karnes (left) and Jack Chamblin directed UI's 1973 fundraising effort for Memorial Stadium

1974–75

AMERICA'S TIME CAPSULE

September 8, 1974	President Ford pardoned former President Nixon for any crimes he may have committed while in office, calling for an end to the Watergate episode.
October 30, 1974	Muhammad Ali recaptured the heavyweight boxing title with an eighth-round knockout of George Foreman in Zaire.
February 21, 1975	Former White House aides H. R. Haldeman and John Ehrlichman and former attorney general John Mitchell were each sentenced to thirty months' imprisonment for their roles in the Watergate affair.
July 5, 1975	Arthur Ashe became the first African American to win the men's singles title at England's Wimbledon tennis championships.
July 31, 1975	Former Teamsters leader James Hoffa was reported missing.

MEN'S ILLINI MOMENT

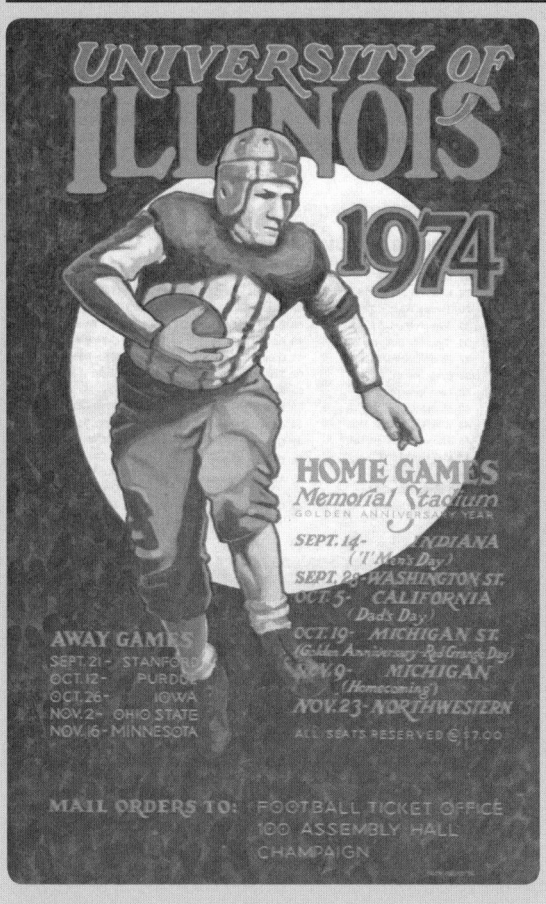

1974 Illini football poster

The Ice Man Returneth

Fifty years to the day after his greatest Illinois triumph, October 18, 1974, Harold "Red" Grange returned to Memorial Stadium. A half-century earlier, he'd galloped against Michigan, leading Illinois to a 39–14 victory. But on this afternoon, the seventy-one-year-old football legend spoke to Coach Bob Blackman's 1974 Illini squad. "Football is a game that demands teamwork," Grange told the young Illini. "It is natural, I suppose, for the scorer to get all the publicity. But it isn't fair. At Illinois, I was just a cog in a good machine." That evening, the Galloping Ghost was feted by a packed house of nearly seven hundred fans at the Ramada Inn's Convention Center. George Halas, Grange's coach with the Chicago Bears, told the twenty-dollars-a-plate crowd that "Red Grange had more impact on the game of football than any single individual in this century." The next day at Memorial Stadium, between halves of the Illinois-Michigan State game, which ended in a 21–21 tie, Grange was presented the UI Board of Trustees' highest award, the Trustee Medallion. Then the Wheaton Iceman addressed his adoring fans. "I've always said that this is the most beautiful stadium in the world and that Illinois fans are the most beautiful people in the world."

OTHER TOP MOMENTS

1. Gene Bartow's only season with Illini ends with 8-18 record
2. Junior football star Greg Williams murdered on Homecoming eve
3. Tennis team posts 14-5 dual-meet record

MEN'S ILLINI LIST

ILLINI CAREER TACKLES—LEADERS (through 1974 season)

1.	374	Dick Butkus (1962–1964)
2.	274	Tom Hicks (1972–1974)
3.	231	Tab Bennett (1970–1972)
4.	231	Ty McMillin (1972–1974)

Ty McMillin

MEN'S ILLINI ITEM

The University of Illinois's twelve-year drought without a Big Ten championship in any sport other than fencing ended on May 17, 1975, when the Illini track and field squad nipped runner-up Indiana by one-and-a-half points. Senior captain Mike Durkin paved the way with a double victory in the steeplechase and the 880-yard run. The meet was undecided heading into the triple-jump finals, but Illini star Charlton Ehizuelen sewed up the team championship with a title-winning 50'6¼" leap. Up to then—dating all the way back to a football title by the 1963 Illini—eleven UI athletic teams, with the exception of the fencing squad, had entered 130 consecutive Big Ten championship competitions without a victory.

Mike Durkin

MEN'S ILLINI LEGEND

Tom Hicks

Tom Hicks

As a tackler, there were few better than Illini linebacker Tom Hicks. Number 99 had a fabulous senior season in 1974 for Coach Bob Blackman, recording 116 stops against Big Ten offensive stars like Archie Griffin, Gordon Bell, Mike Pruitt, and Rick Upchurch. Hicks was the team's defensive MVP as a senior and earned first-team All–Big Ten accolades. A native of Villa Park, Hicks was selected in the sixth round of the 1975 NFL draft by his hometown Chicago Bears, adding him to a group that included Walter Payton, Bob Avellini, and Illini teammate Revie Sorey. From 1976 through 1980, Hicks started forty-two of the sixty-four games in which he appeared, playing alongside Doug Plank and Doug Buffone for defensive coordinator Buddy Ryan. His most memorable individual highlight as a Bear was a sixty-six-yard touchdown interception that beat Green Bay at Lambeau Field in 1979. Hicks was a commodities trader at the Chicago Mercantile Exchange for seventeen years, then later became a tech consultant and mortgage broker. He still resides in Chicagoland.

OTHER TOP MEN'S ATHLETES

1. Howard Beck, gymnastics (pommel horse champ, Big Ten Medal of Honor in 1974, 1975)
2. Craig Virgin, cross-country/track and field (sophomore wins his second Big Ten cross-country title)
3. Charlton Ehizuelen, track and field (two Big Ten triple-jump titles, one long-jump championship)

1974–75

WOMEN'S ILLINI MOMENT

Chancellor Appoints Committee to Study Women's Athletics

In 1973, among growing pressure from campus faculty and staff, Chancellor J. W. "Jack" Peltason appointed a committee to study to future of women's sports at the University of Illinois. The group was directed by Dr. Laura Huelster, a retired physical education instructor. She was joined on the committee by Illini athletic director Cecil Coleman, associate professor of physical education Phyllis Hill, and Department of Physical Education head Dr. Rollin Wright. Huelster, a native of Mason City, Iowa, earned a degree in physical education from Illinois in 1927 and had just retired after forty-three years on UI's staff when Peltason approached her. Following a thorough study, the committee's recommendations were approved on May 15, 1974. Nineteen days later, Coleman hired Dr. Karol Anne Kahrs, assistant professor in physical education, to oversee the women's intercollegiate program. Kahrs, a former volleyball coach, immediately began her search for coaches.

Retired physical-education instructor Laura Huelster was a standout athlete during her days as an undergraduate

OTHER TOP MOMENTS

1. Illinois Tennis posts a perfect 6-0 dual record.
2. Five Illini track and field athletes—Liz Sharp, Barb Grider, Diana Kummer, Nessa Calabrese, and Sue Bowker—traveled to Texas for Illinois's first-ever AIAW national competition. Calabrese placed seventh in the javelin event.
3. Volleyball began the season with four consecutive victories.

WOMEN'S ILLINI LIST

Dr. Karol Kahrs was hired in 1974

WOMEN'S ATHLETICS TIMELINE

1899:	The Women's Basketball Committee became the first national body to regulate sports for women.
1941:	The American Association for Health, Physical Education, and Recreation organized the first national collegiate championship (golf).
1957:	The National Joint Committee on Extramural Sports (NJCES) was formed to guide and administer women's intercollegiate athletic programs.
1971:	The Association for Intercollegiate Athletics for Women (AIAW) came into existence. Its first eight national championships took place during the 1972–73 season.
1972:	The United States Congress passed Title IX of the Education Amendments.
1974:	UI Board of Trustees approved the AA's recommendation to include women's athletics.
1974:	Dr. Karol Kahrs was hired to oversee UI's seven-sport program.
1981:	The first Big Ten championship event for women's athletics was held (field hockey at Iowa).

WOMEN'S ILLINI LEGEND

Karol Kahrs

When the United States Congress passed Title IX regulations in 1972, mandating equal opportunity for women, the face of intercollegiate athletics began to change at the University of Illinois. On June 1, 1974—just nine days after the University of Illinois Board of Trustees approved the Athletic Association's recommendation to include women's athletics—Athletic Director Cecil Coleman hired Dr. Karol Kahrs to oversee Illinois's seven-sport women's program. Kahrs's initial budget was $82,500 in 1974–75. Women's athletics were incorporated into the Big Ten Conference during the 1981–82 season, and since that time, Illini teams have won fifteen league titles in four different sports. In 1988 Kahrs served as director of internal affairs for the AA, helping with its merger into the university in 1989 as the Division of Intercollegiate Athletics (DIA). In 1992 the National Association of College Women Athletic Administrators recognized Kahrs's contributions to intercollegiate athletes, naming her NACWAA Administrator of the Year for District V. Her last two years at the DIA were spent in the Development Office. Kahrs retired from the University of Illinois on August 31, 2000, after thirty-six years of service. She now lives in North Carolina.

Dr. Kahrs is presented with a plaque from Athletics Director Ron Guenther

OTHER TOP WOMEN'S ATHLETES

1. Mary Patterson, swimming (All-American)
2. Sue Bochte, volleyball (spiking specialist)
3. Colleen McNamara, tennis (top singles player)

ILLINI LORE

The University of Illinois student body was treated to a plethora of talented musicians during the 1974–75 school year. Among the individuals and groups providing entertainment at the Assembly Hall and Krannert Center were John Sebastian, The J. Geils Band, The Eagles, The Guess Who, Fleetwood Mac, Stevie Wonder, The Carpenters, Billy Joel, Mac Davis, Gregg Allman, and Jethro Tull.

Stevie Wonder was one of many talented musicians who performed at the University of Illinois during the 1974–75 school year

1975–1984

1975–76

AMERICA'S TIME CAPSULE

September 5, 1975   President Gerald Ford escaped the first of two assassination attempts in a little more than two weeks. Lynette "Squeaky" Fromme was apprehended.

September 18, 1975   A nineteen-month FBI search ended when Patricia Hearst was captured in San Francisco.

October 1, 1975   Heavyweight boxing champion Muhammad Ali defeated Joe Frazier in the "Thrilla in Manilla."

April 1, 1976   Steve Jobs, Steve Wozniak, and Ronald Wayne founded Apple Computer Inc.

July 4, 1976   The United States celebrated the bicentennial of its independence.

MEN'S ILLINI MOMENT

Illini Cagers Upset Michigan

Illinois's 1975–76 basketball poster

Fourteenth-ranked Michigan came to Urbana-Champaign with a nearly perfect 6–1 Big Ten record. Coach Johnny Orr's lineup included future NBA stars Phil Hubbard and Rickey Green, plus former Chicago prep star John Robinson. "I've never seen a line-up with the speed and quickness that Michigan has," said first-year Illini coach Lou Henson, who countered with blue-collar seniors like Nate Williams, Mike Washington, and Otho Tucker. Despite a subpar shooting performance, Michigan controlled play for the first thirty-nine minutes and led 75–72 following a Wayman Britt jumper with fifty-five seconds left. Illinois's Williams was fouled seventeen seconds later when his fifteen-foot turnaround jumper cut the Michigan lead to 75–74. And when he missed the free-throw attempt, 6'9" sophomore Rich Adams soared high to tip in the ball for what would ultimately be the winning goal. Orr's talented Wolverines had a flurry of attempts in the closing seconds, but a tip-in by Robinson came a split second after the final buzzer.

Michigan bounced back from that defeat to become an NCAA finalist, while Henson's Illini were limited to four victories in their last ten games.

OTHER TOP MOMENTS

1. Illini baseball's Bob Harold and Dan Ingram threw back-to-back no-hitters in April 1976.
2. Junior Craig Virgin captured his third consecutive Big Ten cross-country title.
3. Football team topped No. 16 Michigan State, 21–19, at East Lansing.

MEN'S ILLINI LIST

LOU HENSON'S ALL-OPPONENT TEAM (1975–1996)

Earvin "Magic" Johnson

Starting Five:	Bench:
G-Magic Johnson, Michigan State	Juwan Howard, Michigan
G-Isiah Thomas, Indiana	Jimmy Jackson, Ohio State
C-Mychal Thompson, Minnesota	Ronnie Lester, Iowa
F-Glen Rice, Michigan	Shawn Respert, Michigan State
F-Glenn Robinson, Purdue	Jalen Rose, Michigan
	Steve Smith, Michigan State
	Chris Webber, Michigan

MEN'S ILLINI ITEM

The University of Indiana completely dominated the sport of swimming and diving during the 1970s, and that was the case in the 1976 Big Ten championship meet as Hoosier swimmers captured ten of the thirteen events. One of those three non-IU winners was an Illini freshman named Jim Schanel. He captured the 100-yard breaststroke in a winning time of 0:58.913. It was the first time an Illinois swimmer won an individual event since Kip Pope in 1969.

Jim Schanel

MEN'S ILLINI LEGEND

Lou Henson

Lou Henson

It took University of Illinois athletic director Cecil Coleman just three days to name a basketball coaching successor for Gene Bartow, and his April 5, 1975, announcement of Lou Henson stunned the media gathered that day at the U of I Varsity Room. Among the names the press bandied about were those of Barrow's assistants, Tony Yates and Leroy Hunt, plus Virginia Tech's Don Devoe and Kansas State's Jack Hartman, but never once mentioned was the forty-three-year-old head coach from New Mexico State. In 1975–76, Henson's first season as the Illini mentor, Illinois won its first five games en route to posting a 14-13 record. His first big year in Urbana-Champaign was 1978–79, when the Illini started out 15-0, including a two-point thriller over Magic Johnson and Michigan State. Henson's Illini made it to the semifinals of the NIT in 1979–80, while the 1980–81 club qualified for the NCAA tournament for the first time in eighteen years. Henson's other major accomplishments since coming to Illinois include an NCAA Final Four appearance in 1989, eleven seasons of twenty or more victories, eleven NCAA tournament appearances, and Big Ten Coach of the Year honors in 1993. He retired as head coach of the Illini following the 1995–96 season and accumulated a record of 423-224 in twenty-one seasons. He was head coach at New Mexico State from 1997 until midway through the 2004–05 season to enter treatment for non-Hodgkin's lymphoma. He currently acts as special advisor to the NMSU basketball program.

OTHER TOP MEN'S ATHLETES

1. Craig Virgin (Big Ten cross-country champ and two-time winner in track)
2. Joe Smalzer, football (first-team All-Big Ten)
3. Glenn Hummel, tennis (Big Ten Conference Medal of Honor recipient)

1975–76

WOMEN'S ILLINI MOMENT

Nancy Thies

Thies Leads Gymnastics Team to Big Ten Title

December 4–5, 1975: The University of Illinois women's gymnastics team, coached by New Zealand native Allison Milburn, won the first unofficial Big Ten women's championship in any sport. The Fighting Illini edged runner-up Michigan State, 102.55 to 97.10. Illinois's Nancy Thies won not only the all-around title (36.55) but also each of the other four events (9.10 in vaulting, 9.20 on uneven parallel bars, 9.25 in floor exercise, and 9.0 on the balance beam). Other key performers included Patti Carmichael, Sarah Roska, and Maria Salinas.

OTHER TOP MOMENTS

1. Tennis won Illinois AIAW championship
2. Women's golf team placed second in Big Ten Tournament
3. Volleyball was runner-up to Michigan State at conference meet

WOMEN'S ILLINI LIST

FIRST WOMEN'S COACHES

Basketball: Steve Douglas (1974–1975)
Cross-Country: Jessica Dragicevic (1977–1981)
Golf: Betsy Kimpel (1974–1978)
Gymnastics: Kim Musgrave (1974–1975)
Soccer: Jillian Ellis (1997–1998)
Softball: Terri Sullivan (2000–2015)
Swimming and Diving: Jeanne Hultzen (1974–1975)
Tennis: Peggy Pruitt (1974–1975)
Track and Field: Jerry Mahew (1975)
Volleyball: Kathleen Haywood (1974–1975)

Kathleen Haywood

Becky Beach

WOMEN'S ILLINI ITEM

Under the coaching direction of former Kansas State player Steve Douglas, the Fighting Illini women's basketball team went from a 2-9 record to 8-7 in 1975–76. Mary Pat Travnik and Becky Beach, a pair of talented freshmen, complemented returnees Betty Anderson, Marjo Dluzak, and senior guard Linda Roberts.

WOMEN'S ILLINI LEGEND

Becky Beach

Becky Beach was one of the University of Illinois's premier female athletes during the infancy of women's intercollegiate athletics. She had been a dominant athlete at nearby Champaign High School, lettering in five different sports. Besides winning golf-medalist honors at the 1976 Big Ten championships and winning two state collegiate titles, Beach also starred on the basketball court from 1976–78, finishing as the Illini's all-time leader in points, assists, and rebounds. Today, the daughter of former Illini basketball star Ted Beach is the first assistant golf professional at Lincolnshire Fields Country Club in Champaign.

Champaign's
Becky Beach

OTHER TOP WOMEN'S ATHLETES

1. Nancy Thies, gymnastics (freshman captured individual championships in every event)
2. Nessa Calabrese, track and field (records in javelin and discus)
3. Mary Patterson, swimming (All-American)

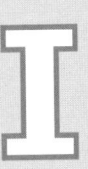

ILLINI LORE

The Medical Sciences building made its debut at the University of Illinois campus during a dedication ceremony on October 15, 1975. The ultramodern, $10 million facility became the newest structure in the Life Sciences complex, joining Morrill and Burrill Halls. The School of Basic Medical Sciences, while located at the Urbana-Champaign campus, actually is a part of the College of Medicine at the Medical Center in Chicago.

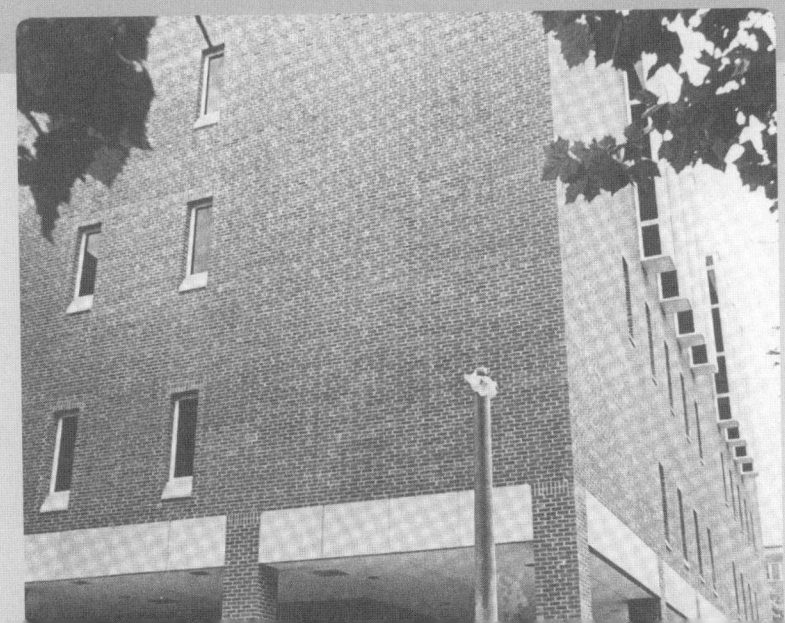

1976-77

AMERICA'S TIME CAPSULE

September 12, 1976   Jimmy Connors and Chris Evert were crowned U.S. Open tennis champions.
November 2, 1976   Jimmy Carter defeated incumbent Gerald Ford in the presidential election.
December 14, 1976   ABC-TV aired Barbara Walters's first special, featuring interviews with Jimmy Carter
                      and Barbra Streisand.
January 17, 1977   *Rocky*, eventual winner of the Academy Award for Best Picture, premiered.
May 25, 1977   The epic American movie series *Star Wars*, directed by George Lucas, debuted.
August 10, 1977   New York City police arrested David Berkowitz, known as the Son of Sam killer.

MEN'S ILLINI MOMENT

Illini Host 1977 NCAA Track Meet

For five days in the spring of 1977 the University of Illinois's Memorial Stadium became the mecca for track and field fans. The fifty-sixth annual NCAA championship drew a talented field of competitors, including lightning-fast sprinters such as Harvey Glance of Auburn, Johnny Jones of Texas, and Herman Frazier of Arizona State. Illinois native Gregory Foster, who wore the blue and gold uniform of UCLA, was the meet's most celebrated hurdler. Africans Samson Kimombwa and Henry Rono paced the distance runners, while 5'5" high jumper Franklin Jacobs of Farleigh Dickinson and pole vaulter Earl Bell of Arkansas State were premier performers in the field events. The Illini contingent was led by distance star Craig Virgin, who placed second in the 10,000-meter run and fourth in the 5,000; pole vaulter Doug Laz, who finished fourth with a respectable effort of 16'6"; and Charlton Ehizuelen, who placed second in the long jump and third in the triple jump. Arizona State beat runner-up Texas-El Paso, 64–50, for the team title on June 4 before a crowd of between fifteen thousand and twenty thousand fans at Memorial Stadium.

Illinois meet officials so impressed their guests and NCAA officials that the meet was granted again to the U of I in 1979.

Program for the 1977 NCAA championship

OTHER TOP MOMENTS

1. Bob Blackman's Illini football team shocked sixth-ranked Missouri at home, winning 31–6.
2. Tennis team snapped host Michigan's forty-eight-match winning streak with a 5–4 victory.
3. Basketball team upset Purdue at home on Audie Matthews's fifteen-foot jumper with one second left.

MEN'S ILLINI LIST

ILLINI BIG TEN CROSS-COUNTRY CHAMPIONS

1928	David Abbott
1945	Victor Twomey
1962	Allen Carius
1963	Allen Carius
1973	Craig Virgin
1974	Craig Virgin
1975	Craig Virgin
1976	Craig Virgin

Four-time Big Ten champion Craig Virgin

MEN'S ILLINI ITEM

Scott Studwell

There was no stronger or more aggressive player among Big Ten linebackers in 1976 than 6'3", 235-pound Scott Studwell. And nobody had more tackles than the senior from Evansville, Indiana. Studwell had a school-record 177 stops in just eleven games, including fifteen more in conference games than Ohio State All-American Tom Cousineau. "Stud's" single-game bests were twenty-three tackles versus Purdue, twenty-one versus Michigan State, and twenty versus Ohio State. Studwell's exceptional production continued in the NFL during a fourteen-season career with the Minnesota Vikings, finishing as the team's all-time leading tackler. In 2010 he was named as one of the fifty greatest Vikings ever, and his name graces the team's Ring of Honor. Studwell has been Minnesota's director of college scouting since 2002. In 1990 he was a top-voted member on Illinois's All-Century Team.

MEN'S ILLINI LEGEND

Craig Virgin (right) and Coach Gary Wieneke

Craig Virgin

It's shocking to learn that Craig Virgin, the University of Illinois's greatest distance runner ever, almost never made it past age five. Following surgery for a bladder ailment, the young farm boy's condition worsened, affecting his kidneys. Doctors weren't optimistic, but, slowly, Virgin got stronger. As a scrawny high school freshman, his fame as a distance runner began to grow, luring Illini cross-country coach Gary Wieneke to Virgin's hometown of Lebanon, Illinois. Virgin ultimately ended up at the UI, enjoying a four-year career that included every honor imaginable. He became the Big Ten's first four-time cross-country champion from 1973 to 1976 and captured the NCAA title in that sport his junior year. On the track, he became America's premier distance runner, setting the U.S. collegiate record for the 10,000-meter run in 1976 (27:59.4). Following his graduation from UI's College of Communications in 1977, Virgin continued to run. He was a member of the U.S. Olympic Team in 1976, 1980, and 1984, and competed for the U.S. International Cross-Country Team from 1978 to 1988, twice winning the world title. Virgin launched an unsuccessful campaign for the Illinois State Senate in 1992; he currently serves as president of Front Runner Inc., a sports-marketing company based in Lebanon, Illinois.

OTHER TOP MEN'S ATHLETES

1. Doug Laz, track and field (indoor and outdoor Big Ten pole-vault champion)
2. Charlton Ehizuelen, track and field (three Big Ten titles: long jump (twice) and triple jump)
3. Dan Beaver, football (first-team All–Big Ten)

1976–77

WOMEN'S ILLINI MOMENT

Linda Thiel

Illinois Swimmers Capture State Championship:

Coach Ann Pollock's Illini women's swimming team won the IAIAW state title, defeating Southern Illinois, 655 to 577. Mary Paterson led the way by winning individual titles in the 50-yard freestyle, the 50- and 100-yard butterfly, and the 100-yard individual medley, as well as anchoring the 200- and 400-yard freestyle relay championships. Becky McSwine captured the 100- and 200-yard backstroke titles. Other point producers for the Illini included Linda Thiel.

OTHER TOP MOMENTS

1. Gymnastics won second consecutive unofficial Big Ten title.
2. Golf captured IAIAW team championship.
3. Basketball topped Iowa, 53–40, in opening round of conference tournament.

WOMEN'S ILLINI LIST

ILLINI OLYMPIANS SINCE 1972

1972	Nancy Thies Marshall, gymnastics
1992	Tonja Buford-Bailey, track and field, and Kirsten Gleis (Holland), volleyball
1996	Tonja Buford-Bailey, track and field
2000	Ilkay Dikman (Turkey), swimming; Perdita Felicien (Canada), and Karen Brems Kurreck*, cycling
2004	Jenny Kallur and Susanna Kallur (Sweden), track and field
2008	Susanna Kallur (Sweden), track and field, and Emily Zurrer (Canada), soccer
2012	Gia Lewis, track and field, and Nikkita Holder (Canada), track and field

*Brems was a gymnast as an undergrad

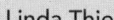

1972 Olympian
Nancy Thies

A trio of Illini women's athletes qualified for the Association of Intercollegiate Athletics for Women national meet, Illinois's biggest representation ever. High-jumper Bev Washington, champion in that event at the Big Ten championships, placed tenth nationally with a 5'2" leap. Nessa Calabrese, winner of the javelin competition at the conference meet, posted a personal best but didn't reach the finals. Speedy Linn Grieb ran both the 100- and 200-yard dashes but failed to place.

Bev Washington
clears the bar

WOMEN'S ILLINI LEGEND

Nancy Thies was
an NBC analyst
for the 1976
Olympics

Nancy (Thies) Marshall

Perhaps the greatest female gymnast in University of Illinois history grew up in Urbana. Nancy (Thies) Marshall competed for the Fighting Illini gymnastics squad in 1976 and 1977. She won the Big Ten's all-around title both years, as well as individual championships on the vault, the uneven parallel bars, the balance beam, and the floor exercise.

Thies also served as the U of I's Homecoming Queen in 1978. As a member of the 1972 United States Olympic team, her team placed fourth behind Olga Korbut's gold-medal-winning Soviet squad. It was USA's highest finish since 1948. Individually, fifteen-year-old Nancy, the youngest American Olympian, tied for thirty-sixth place. When the gymnastics competition concluded, Nancy and her family flew home and, upon arrival, were told by her

OTHER TOP WOMEN'S ATHLETES

1. Becky Beach, golf and basketball (leading hoops scorer)
2. Mary Patterson, swimming (Big Ten 50 freestyle and butterfly champ)
3. Diane Miller, golf (AIAW national participant)

grandparents about the tragic terrorist act that saw eleven Israeli hostages killed. In May 1973, Thies competed in a landmark diplomacy meet between China and America. She enrolled at the University of Illinois and competed for the Illini, but a severe ankle injury ended her career following her sophomore year. NBC-TV invited her to become an analyst for the 1976 Olympic Games, where she worked with veteran broadcasters Jim Simpson, Charlie Jones, and Bryant Gumbel, as well as fellow gymnast Bart Conner. In 1988 she authored a book titled *Women Who Compete*. Today, Marshall serves as the director of human services at Corban University in Salem, Oregon.

ILLINI LORE

James R. Thompson, a former student at the University of Illinois's Chicago Undergraduate Division at Navy Pier, became the first UI alumnus to win election as the state's governor, November 2, 1976. One other alumnus, Samuel Shapiro (class of 1929), advanced from lieutenant governor to the governorship when Gov. Otto Kerner resigned to become a federal judge in 1968.

1977–78

AMERICA'S TIME CAPSULE

September 13, 1977   General Motors introduced the first diesel-engine automobiles.
February 8, 1978   Egyptian President Anwar el-Sadat began a six-day visit to the United States to hasten a Middle East peace settlement.
February 15, 1978   Leon Spinks won a fifteen-round decision over Muhammad Ali to capture the heavyweight boxing title.
June 10, 1978   Affirmed, ridden by jockey Steve Cauthen, won horse racing's Triple Crown with a victory at the Belmont Stakes.
August 4, 1978   Evacuation of the Love Canal area of Niagara Falls, a dumping ground for toxic waste in the 1940s and 1950s, began.

MEN'S ILLINI MOMENT

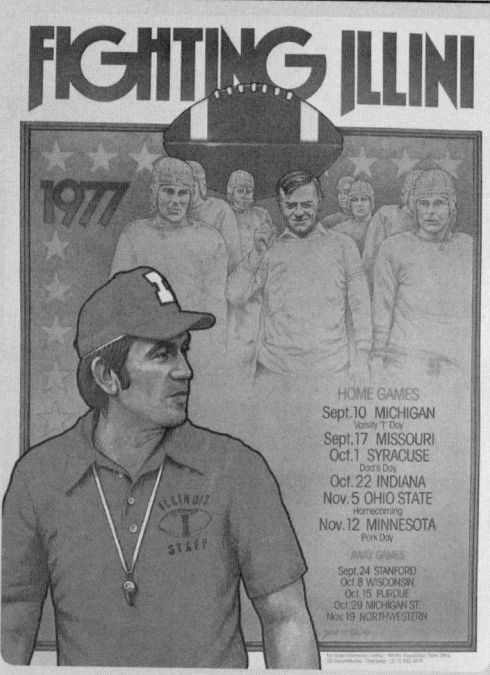

UI's 1977 football poster featured new coach Gary Moeller

Moeller Replaces Blackman

Just thirteen days after Bob Blackman received word that his six-year reign as Illinois's head football coach had ended, the University of Illinois secured one of its archenemies' brightest young assistants. On December 2, 1976, thirty-five-year-old Michigan defensive coordinator Gary Moeller became Illinois's third coach in seven seasons. Illini athletic director Cecil Coleman interviewed eight men for the position, including Chuck Studley, Don James, and Jim Young, but settled on Bo Schembechler's top assistant. "I want to have a winning program and see the players benefit from it," said Moeller at his introductory press conference. "We will throw the ball, if I feel we can do it successfully, but very few passing teams are consistent winners." Moeller's christening as a head coach came September 10, 1977, against Michigan and his former mentor. The Illini took a 3–0 lead that afternoon, but ended up losing, 37–9. Unfortunately, Moeller's luck at Illinois never changed, as his teams struggled to consecutive records of 3-8, 1-8-2, and 2-8-1. On November 20, 1979, he was fired by Athletic Director Neale Stoner. From 1990 to 1994, Moeller served as Michigan's head football coach, winning Big Ten Coach of the Year honors in both 1991 and 1992. In January 2016, he turned seventy-five.

OTHER TOP MOMENTS

1. U of I Gymnastics finished runner-up to Minnesota (Butch Zunich, John Davis and Steve Yasukawa won individual titles).
2. Five clutch free throws by Rob Judson helped Illinois upset defending Big Ten champion Michigan, 65–61.
3. Seniors Rich Adams and Audie Matthews finished their basketball careers as UI's sixth and seventh leading career scorers, respectively.

MEN'S ILLINI LIST

TOP MEMORIAL STADIUM RUSHING PERFORMANCES

1. 289 yards Ron Dayne, Wisconsin, November 23, 1996
2. 266 yards Kent Kitzmann, Minnesota, November 12, 1977
3. 263 yards Howard Griffith, Illinois vs. Northwestern, November 24, 1990
4. 251 yards Jason Wright, Northwestern, November 22, 2003
5. 246 yards Carlos Hyde, Ohio State, November 16, 2013
6. 239 yards Jim Grabowski, Illinois vs. Wisconsin, November 14, 1964

At Memorial Stadium in 1977, Minnesota's Kent Kitzmann rushed for 266 yards

7. 231 yards Leroy Keyes, Purdue, November 14, 1967
8. 228 yards Anthony Thomas, Michigan, September 23, 2000
9. 215 yards Rocky Harvey, Illinois vs. Middle Tennessee, September 12, 1998
10. 212 yards Red Grange, Illinois vs. Michigan, October 18, 1924

MEN'S ILLINI ITEM

Linebacker John Sullivan was Most Valuable Player of the 1977 and 1978 Illini football teams. He finished his career as Illinois's all-time leading tackler, breaking Dick Butkus's fourteen-year-old record. As an NFL player, Sullivan played two seasons with the New York Jets. Now known as John Patrick Sullivan, he authored two books, *Complete Stretching: A New Exercise Program for Health and Vitality* and *No End Zone*, which centers on liberation, openness, and the love of truth.

John Sullivan

MEN'S ILLINI LEGEND

Coach Lee Eilbracht

Lee Eilbracht

From 1952 to 1978, fourteen different men served as manager of the Chicago Cubs. During that same twenty-seven-year span, the University of Illinois had one baseball coach: Lee "Swami" Eilbracht. Appointed acting head coach in 1952 following the death of Wally Roettger, Eilbracht's position was made permanent at the end of the season. "The Swami," as he was affectionately called by his players, recorded more coaching victories than any of his five Illini predecessors. His career record of 519–397–6 included Big Ten championships in 1952, 1953, 1962, and 1963. Eilbracht coached two athletes to All-American honors, twelve to first-team All–Big Ten laurels, and thirty-four others to All-Star mention. Catcher Tom Haller and pitcher Ken Holtzman, who went on to the major leagues, were two of his most famous pupils. Eilbracht earned three varsity letters at Illinois and was named the Illini's Most Valuable Player in 1946 and 1947. He hit .484 during the 1946 Big Ten season, the fourth-best average in conference history, and had a career average of .330. After his retirement following the 1978 season, Eilbracht served as the executive director of the American Association of College Baseball Coaches. He died in January 2013 at age eighty-eight.

OTHER TOP MEN'S ATHLETES

1. Steve Yasukawa and John Davis, gymnastics (won Big Ten horizontal bar and still rings titles, respectively)
2. Kevin Pancratz, football (first-team All–Big Ten)
3. Ken Kellaney, golf (first-team All–Big Ten)

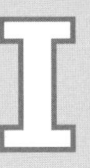

1977–78

WOMEN'S ILLINI MOMENT

Coach Jessica Dragicevic

Outdoor Track Shines

Following a disappointing performance during the indoor season, Coach Jessica Dragicevic's marked improvement once her team was able to breathe the fresh air outdoors. Record-breaking performances in eight events occurred at the Illini Invitational, leading to a first-place team finish. Success continued at the IAIAW state championship with Bev Washington, Nessa Calabrese, and Dorothy Carver winning individual titles in the high jump, discus, and pentathlon, respectively. At the national AIAW meet, six athletes represented the Orange and Blue. Washington's sixth-place was Illinois's top effort.

OTHER TOP MOMENTS

1. Debut of women's cross-country as a varsity sport.
2. Illinois basketball topped perennial state champ Illinois State, shutting down 6'2" Olympic center Charlotte Lewis.
3. Volleyball finished 38–17–6, qualifying for the AIAW national tournament.

WOMEN'S ILLINI LIST

WINNINGEST VOLLEYBALL COACHES (by winning percentage)

.718	Mike Hebert (323-127), 1983–1995
.691	Kevin Hambly (161-72), 2009–2015
.679	Kathleen Haywood (19-9), 1974
.592	Chris Accornero (84-51-7), 1977–1979
.589	Don Hardin (234-163), 1996–2008
.588	Terry Hite (40-28), 1975–1976
.415	John Blair (56-79), 1980–1982

Coach Chris Accornero

Many of the Fighting Illini's pioneering women's athletes typically participated in more than one sports, and Vanessa "Nessa" Calabrese was no exception. As a track-and-field athlete, the former Forest View High School star broke UI records in both the discus and javelin. And in volleyball, she was one of Illinois's first eleven varsity letter winners.

Vanessa Calabrese

WOMEN'S ILLINI LEGEND

Beverly Washington

Beverly Washington

One of the University of Illinois's earliest stars in women's athletics was track-and-field All-American Beverly Washington. The self-labeled tomboy from North Babylon, New York enjoyed a wide variety of sports as a youngster, including volleyball, basketball, tennis, softball, and, of course, track and field. "I've always been very athletic," she said. As Coach Jessica Dragicevic's most accomplished Illini athlete, Washington performed as a sprinter, a hurdler, and a jumper. Her expertise as a high jumper netted her Big Ten outdoor titles as both a sophomore and junior, then both indoor and outdoor championships in 1978, topping out at the 5'10" mark. She spent 1979 with the U.S. Olympic training team. Washington earned a bachelor's degree in dance education from Illinois, then took her confident personality into fashion merchandising for several companies, including Marshall Field's, Hart Schaffner Marx, and others. She's since written a book—*Don't Call Me Bev: Things That Work My Last Nerve*—and conducted numerous training seminars through her Chicago-based company, Image Factor Inc. Washington also has expanded her talents to include acting in television commercials and producing and hosting her cable TV show, *Stop the Drama*.

OTHER TOP WOMEN'S ATHLETES

1. Dorothy Carver, track and field (IAIAW pentathlon champ)
2. Mary Pat Travnik, basketball (team's top scorer in 1977–78)
3. Becky Beach, basketball (all-time leading scorer and rebounder)

ILLINI LORE

On his forty-eighth birthday, September 9, 1977, William P. Gerberding was introduced as the new chancellor for the University of Illinois at Urbana-Champaign. He came from UCLA, where he served for sixteen years, first as a faculty member and then as executive vice chancellor. Gerberding left the U of I in 1979 to become president at the University of Washington.

President William Gerberding

1978-79

AMERICA'S TIME CAPSULE

September 15, 1978 | Muhammad Ali regained the heavyweight boxing title with a fifteen-round decision over Leon Spinks.

November 18, 1978 | More than nine hundred people, including 211 children, were found dead in Guyana. Jim Jones, leader of a religious sect, led the group in a mass suicide by poison.

March 26, 1979 | Magic Johnson and Michigan State defeated Larry Bird and Indiana State in the NCAA basketball championship game at Salt Lake City.

March 28, 1979 | Three Mile Island, near Harrisburg, Pennsylvania, was the site of a nuclear near-disaster.

May 25, 1979 | An American Airlines DC-10 jet crashed shortly after takeoff in Chicago, killing all 272 passengers on board and three other people on the ground.

MEN'S ILLINI MOMENT

Eddie Johnson launches one of Illinois's most memorable shots

Illini Victory Proves to Be Better than Magic

A record Assembly Hall crowd of 16,209 was on hand January 11, 1979, to watch its third-ranked Fighting Illini (14-0) against No. 1 Michigan State (9-1). The Johnson boys—MSU's Earvin and Illinois's Eddie—were their respective teams' stars, but despite his opponent's famous nickname, it was Eddie who was "magic" on this particular night. The Spartans vaulted off to a 24–13 lead after the first ten minutes of play, but the Illini sizzled in the last ten minutes, outscoring their guests 19–4. The second half was like a seesaw, as the lead changed hands eight times. A Mike Brkovich jumper with 2:27 left pulled State even at 55–55, and Illini coach Lou Henson called time out with just 0:37 left on the clock to set up his team's final shot. UI's Steve Lanter penetrated the lane, forcing MSU's Greg Kelser to abandon Eddie Johnson. Lanter then dished the ball out to the right baseline where number 33 was in position for an uncontested eighteen-footer. Johnson set himself, flicked his wrist, and sent the ball arcing toward the hoop. Nothing but net! The 57–55 victory improved the Illini record to 15-0, but, unfortunately, that perfection would last only for another thirty-six hours.

OTHER TOP MOMENTS

1. Lee Eilbracht's earned his five-hundredth career victory in his final season as Illini coach.

2. Marty Schiene finished fourth at the Big Ten golf championship. Only future PGA stars John Cook, Rick Born, and Tom Lehman placed ahead of him.

3. Memorial Stadium's hosted the NCAA track and field championships for the second time in three years.

I

MEN'S ILLINI LIST

ALMOST NO. 1

Lou Henson's club of 1978–79 started the season with fifteen consecutive victories, including its monumental win over Magic Johnson's No. 1–rated Michigan State team at the Assembly Hall on January 11, 1979. Illinois's streak was finally snapped by a talented Ohio State team, two days after the Illini victory over the Spartans. Here's how the season's streak played out:

1. Illinois 109, Texas-Arlington 74 (H-November 24)
2. Illinois 81, Denver 57 (H-November 28)
3. Illinois 65, Tulane 60 (A-December 2)
4. Illinois 69, Missouri 57 (A-December 5)
5. Illinois 64, South Carolina 57 (H-December 8)
6. Illinois 86, Centenary 60 (H-December 9)
7. (#18) Illinois 82, Kent State 44 (A-December 16)
8. (#15) Illinois 82, (#8) Syracuse 61 (N-December 22)
9. (#15) Illinois 71, (#17) Texas A&M 57 (N-December 23)
10. (#6) Illinois 84, Western Michigan 79 (N-December 28)
11. (#6) Illinois 88, Ozarks 82 (N-December 29)
12. (#6) Illinois 92, Alaska-Anchorage 80 (A-December 30)
13. (#4) Illinois 65, Indiana 61 (H-January 4)
14. (#4) Illinois 74, Northwestern 56 (A-January 6)
15. (#4) Illinois 57, (#1) Michigan State 55 (H-January 11)
16. Ohio State 69, (#4) Illinois 66 (OT) (H-January 13)

MEN'S ILLINI ITEM

Cecil Coleman was dismissed as athletic director at the University of Illinois on April 27, 1979. Hired in 1972 to improve the school's image with the NCAA and to balance a budget that had a $1 million deficit, Coleman achieved both of those objectives. He received minimal credit for other accomplishments, including the hiring of basketball coach Lou Henson and the establishment of UI's women's athletic program. Coleman died in February 1988 at age sixty-three.

Cecil Coleman

MEN'S ILLINI LEGEND

Mark Smith

Mark Smith

Even though he was voted Most Valuable Player of the 1978–79 Fighting Illini basketball squad, Mark Smith could have easily developed a Rodney Dangerfield complex. Classmate Eddie Johnson got the bulk of the publicity during their four years together at Illinois from 1978 to 1981, but Smith's accomplishments were nothing short of sensational. It's true that Eddie wound up as UI's all-time leading scorer, with 1,692 points, but there was Mark with just thirty-nine fewer points. Johnson was the Illini's career rebounding leader, but Mark averaged just one rebound less per game. Though Johnson was considered the better shooter, it was Smith who posted better percentages both from the field (.525 to .454) and at the free-throw line (.781 to .671). And when it came to passing the ball, the former Peoria Richwoods High School star had nearly twice as many career assists (350 to 209). During Smith's four years at Illinois, the Illini won nearly 62 percent of their games. He died in June 2001 at age forty-one in his hometown of Peoria.

OTHER TOP MEN'S ATHLETES

1. Gail Olson, track and field (set Big Ten record in high jump with leap of 7'3" as freshman)
2. Kevin Cawley, fencing (Big Ten sabre champion)
3. John David, gymnastics (Big Ten Conference Medal of Honor recipient)

1978–79

WOMEN'S ILLINI MOMENT

Gymnastics coach Bev Mackes

No Big Ten Title, but Gymnasts Continue Run of Success

All in all, Illinois's women's gymnastics team couldn't complain about its 1978–79 season. The Illini, coached by second-year mentor Bev Mackes, stunned the experts by defeating perennial powerhouse Southern Illinois at the state championship meet, 130.95 to 130.70. It was the first defeat SIU had suffered at home in eleven years. Mary Charpentier led the way for the Illini, finishing first in the vault (8.80), second on the beam (8.55), and fourth in the all-around competition (33.25). Next up was the Big Ten Conference meet, but the competition was particularly rugged, paced by undefeated Michigan State, plus talented Michigan and Ohio State squads. Illinois had experienced success in recent seasons at the Big Ten Conference meet, winning the 1976 and 1977 titles under Allison Milburn, but this time around Mackes wouldn't have any superstars to score big points. However, the determined Illini still had a strong cast, including Gayle Fleischman, Gaye Johnson, Charpentier, and freshman Lisa Howell. Unfortunately, less than spectacular scores saw the host Illini finish just eighth-tenths of a point behind MSU in the final team standings.

OTHER TOP MOMENTS

1. Freshman Lisa Robinson led the women's basketball team in scoring.
2. Volleyball won the IAIAW championship.
3. Rookie golf coach Paula Smith began her twenty-eight-year career at Illinois.

WOMEN'S ILLINI LIST

LONGEST WOMEN'S COACHING REIGNS (through 2016)

28 years	Paula Smith, golf (1978–2006)
23 years	Gary Winckler, track and field (1985–2008)
15 years	Bev Mackes Stevens, gymnastics (1978–1993)
15 years	Janet Rayfield, soccer (2002–present)
13 years	Don Sammons, swimming (1980–1993)
12 years	Don Hardin, volleyball (1996–2008)
12 years	Mike Hebert, volleyball (1983–1995)
12 years	Theresa Grentz, basketball (1995–2007)
10 years	Jennifer Roberts, tennis (1988–1998)
10 years	Bob Starkell, gymnastics (2000–2010)

Coach Paula Smith (left) and her star Renee Heiken

On May 2, 1978, Lisa Robinson and Lynette Robinson of Annawan, Illinois, became the first women athletes in University of Illinois history to sign full scholarships. Four years later, they ended their careers as Illinois's top two career basketball scorers of all time. By the time Lisa and Lynette played their last games in Illini uniforms, the twins ranked as UI's Nos. 1 and 2 career scorers and Nos. 1 and 4 career rebounders, respectively.

Lynnette and Lisa Robinson

WOMEN'S ILLINI LEGEND

Mary Pat (Travnik) Connelly

Mary Pat (Travnik) Connelly

When Mary Pat (Travnik) Connelly was a young girl, basketball was considered as a "boy's sport." "We even played with a men's basketball," she remembered. "We were just happy that the girl's game was being acknowledged." The recruiting process for women athletes was in its infancy. Mary Pat's coach at Lourdes High School, Bob Lenihan, contacted Illini coach Steve Douglas to tell him that he had a six-foot post player who was pretty good. There was no videotape presentation, no in-home recruitment. In Connelly's freshman season, she received tuition. The Title IX legislation then kicked in and she was rewarded with a full scholarship for her final seasons in 1977, 1978 and 1979. Number 42 twice led the Illini in rebounding and, as a junior, paced the team in scoring. Connelly finished her career No. 1 on UI's career rebounding list, with 564. She was drafted by the Women's Professional Basketball League's Chicago Hustle and played for two seasons in the league. In 1986 she married and then began her family. Connelly decided in 1990 to pursue a career in coaching, first in the high school ranks, then at the college level. Marist High School hired her in 2001 to start the girls' basketball program; 2016–17 is her fifteenth season at the school located on 115th Street in Chicago. Ten of Connelly's players have gone on to earn either Division I or II basketball scholarships. Her family includes her husband, Mike, and four sons.

OTHER TOP WOMEN'S ATHLETES

1. Mary Charpentier, gymnastics
2. Anita Moyer, track and field
3. Gayle Fleischman, gymnastics

ILLINI LORE

On May 4, 1979, John E. Cribbet, dean of UI's College of Law, was named interim chancellor at the Urbana-Champaign campus of the University of Illinois, replacing William Gerberding, who had left to become president at the University of Washington. Seven months later, December 12, 1979, Cribbet was chosen from a field of 114 candidates to become the full-time chancellor.

John Cribbet was UI's interim chancellor for seven months

1979-80

AMERICA'S TIME CAPSULE

September 9, 1979   John McEnroe and Tracy Austin won singles tennis titles at the U.S. Open.
November 4, 1979   Iranian revolutionaries seized the U.S. embassy in Teheran, taking ninety hostages, including sixty-five Americans.
February 22, 1980   At the Olympics, the U.S. hockey team beat the heavily favored Soviet Union, 4-3, then defeated Finland for the gold medal.
May 18, 1980   Mount St. Helens, a volcano that had been dormant since 1857, erupted in Washington.
May 22, 1980   The Pac-Man arcade game debuted in Japan.

MEN'S ILLINI MOMENT

Neale Stoner meets the Illini media for the first time

Stoner Begins Initial Season as Athletic Director

Californian Neale Stoner became athletic director of the University of Illinois on September 27, 1979, boldly proclaiming that "the '80s belong to the Illini." Stoner had extraordinary success as AD at Cal State–Fullerton, but rebuilding Illinois into an athletic power would be the most challenging task of his career. After less than three months on the job, he replaced Gary Moeller as head football coach with another Californian, Mike White. White's successful passing attack helped raise Illinois's average football attendance from forty-five thousand per game in 1979 to more than seventy-six thousand in 1984. Grant-in-aid support rose from around $400,000 annually in the 1970s to between $2 million and $3 million in the mid-1980s. Other accomplishments during the Stoner era included a capital campaign that produced new offices for the football staff and new facilities for baseball and outdoor track and field. The beginning of the end for Stoner came during the summer of 1988 when media questioned his use of Athletic Association funds and his miscalculation of AA income and expenses, which had resulted in a $1.45 million shortfall during the 1987–88 fiscal year. On July 12, 1988, Stoner submitted his resignation as UI's athletic director "so that accusations [would] no longer interfere with the effective operation of the Athletic Association." From 1993 to 2000, he served as San Diego State's men's golf coach.

OTHER TOP MOMENTS

1. Illini basketball advanced to the Final Four of the NIT, taking third at Madison Square Garden.
2. Coach Art Schankin's fencing team won the 1980 Big Ten championship.
3. "Mr. Illini," former football coach Ray Eliot, died at age seventy-four in February 1980.

MEN'S ILLINI LIST

ILLINI MEN'S BASKETBALL SINGLE-GAME SCORING LEADERS

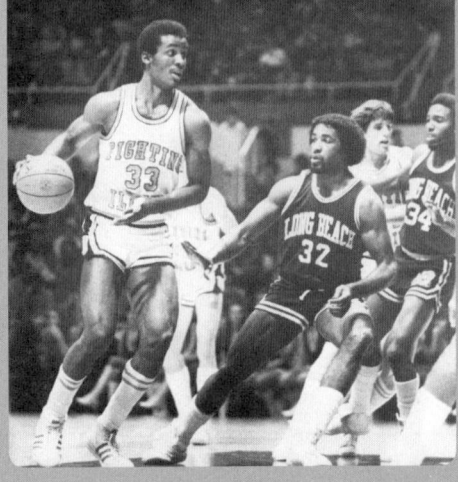

1.	53 points	Dave Downey at Indiana, 1963
2.	46 points	Andy Kaufmann vs. UW-Milwaukee, 1990
3.	43 points	Brandon Paul vs. Ohio State, 2012
4.	42 points	Dave Scholz vs. Northwestern, 1968
5.	40 points	Andy Kaufmann vs. Eastern Illinois, 1990
	40 points	Andy Phillip at Chicago, 1943
	40 points	Malcolm Hill vs. Northern Kentucky, 2016
8.	39 points	Rich Adams vs. Arizona, 1977
	39 points	Deon Thomas vs. Illinois-Chicago, 1991

Eddie Johnson scored thirty-eight points versus Long Beach State in 1979

10.	38 points	John Kerr at Ohio State, 1954
	38 points	Eddie Johnson vs. Long Beach State, 1979
	38 points	Dave Scholz at Northwestern, 1968

MEN'S ILLINI ITEM

Illinois's basketball team qualified for postseason play for the first time in seventeen years during the 1979–80 season. Coach Lou Henson's squad finished the regular season at 18-12. The Illini won their first three games of the NIT, qualifying for a Final Four trip to New York City. Minnesota beat Illinois in the semifinals, 65–63, but Henson's Illini ended their season on an up note by defeating UNLV in the consolation game.

Illinois basketball's 1979–80 poster

MEN'S ILLINI LEGEND

Eddie Johnson

Eddie Johnson

Eddie Johnson's record-breaking career at the University of Illinois from 1978 to 1981 resulted in excellent team success as well. Though Johnson and his teammates registered a sub-.500 record during his freshman season, results dramatically improved during his last three campaigns. Illinois nearly grabbed the nation's No. 1 ranking during his sophomore year, winning its first fifteen games in a row before finally winding up with a 19-11 record. The Illini qualified for the NIT his junior year and, in Johnson's senior season, Illinois made it to the NCAA tournament, the first time it had accomplished that since 1963. Number 33 did become the school's all-time leading scorer (1,692 points) and rebounder (831 rebounds) and will be best remembered in Illini history for his shot that beat No. 1 Michigan State in 1979. Chosen in the 1981 NBA draft by the Kansas City Kings, he completed a seventeen-year career with an average of seventeen points per game. Johnson's total of more than nineteen thousand points placed him thirtieth on the NBA's all-time scoring list, making him the highest-ranked NBA scorer who never played in an All-Star game. For nearly twenty years, Johnson has served as an analyst for Fox Sports Arizona.

OTHER TOP MEN'S ATHLETES

1. Paul Marsillo, baseball (first-team All–Big Ten)
2. Mike Lehmann, track and field (earned Big Ten titles, indoors and outdoors, in shot put)
3. Dave Stoldt, gymnastics (Big Ten Conference Medal of Honor recipient)

1979–80

WOMEN'S ILLINI MOMENT

Mary Charpentier

Illini Gymnasts Edged Out for Title

The University of Illinois's Kenney Gym was the site of the1980 Big Ten meet, and Coach Bev Mackes's Fighting Illini squad couldn't have come any closer to sending the home fans happy. Unfortunately, the Orange and Blue lost to Michigan State by just one-tenth of a point, 138.35 to 138.25. Three Illinoisans placed among the top six in the all-around: freshman Mimi Eberle was second, Mary Charpentier was fifth, and Gayle Fleischman was sixth.

OTHER TOP MOMENTS

1. St. Charles freshman Sue Westhoff set records in both 200-meter breaststroke and 200-meter butterfly.
2. Pam York shattered UI's 50- and 100-meter breaststroke records.
3. Sophomore Lisa Robinson scored at a record pace for Coach Jane Schroeder's first Illini basketball team.

WOMEN'S ILLINI LIST

PROGRESSION OF ILLINI BASKETBALL'S
SINGLE-GAME SCORING RECORDS

26 points	Betty Anderson vs. Western Illinois, 1975
32 points	Liz Brauer vs. Western Illinois, 1980
33 points	Lisa Robinson vs. Miami (Ohio), 1980
40 points	Lisa Robinson vs. Southern Illinois, 1981
49 points	Kendra Gantt vs. Kent State, 1983

Liz Brauer scored a UI record thirty-two points on January 17, 1980

It was her only season of lettering for the Illini gymnastics team, but Hanover Park freshman Mimi Eberle made the most of her time in Champaign-Urbana. At the 1980 Big Ten meet, she won the vaulting event and placed second in the all-around competition. Amazingly, Eberle accomplished everything despite performing with a severe ankle injury.

Freshman Mimi Eberle

WOMEN'S ILLINI LEGEND

Becky (Kaiser) Clayton

In 1980, long-jumper Becky (Kaiser) Clayton became the University of Illinois's first female athlete to win All-American honors. The sophomore from Charleston, Illinois, went 20'5½" to place second at the Association of Intercollegiate Athletics for Women indoor track and field championships. Clayton also helped score points as a sprinter, qualifying for the AIAW meet in the 60-yard dash. Additionally, she led off an 880-meter relay team that ran a 1:46.3 at the Big Ten meet, two seconds faster than the previous Illini record. A three-time All-American at Illinois, Kaiser married former Illini men's track athlete and coach Jerry Clayton. In 2003 she graduated from Auburn University in nursing. Her two sons also became collegiate athletes: Zach was a member of Auburn's 2010 national championship football team, and Nicholas was a member of Air Force's track-and-field squad.

OTHER TOP WOMEN'S ATHLETES

1. Liz Brauer, basketball (set UI single-game scoring mark with thirty-two points vs. Western Illinois)
2. Lisa Robinson and Lynnette Robinson, basketball (sophomore twins combined to average 30.7 points and 12.7 rebounds per game).
3. Robin Duffy, diver (set and re-set her own diving records twelve times).

Becky Kaiser

ILLINI LORE

Forty-four-year-old Stanley O. Ikenberry began what was to become a sixteen-year term as the president of the University of Illinois on September 1, 1979, replacing Dr. John Corbally. The university's fourteenth chief executive officer came from Pennsylvania State University, where he had served for eight years as senior vice president. Ikenberry was a catalyst behind the move by the Big Ten in 1990 to add Penn State as the eleventh conference member. He retired from the UI presidency in 1995 but returned in 2010 to serve as interim president. The university recognized his loyalty in 2008 when it named the Stanley O. Ikenberry Commons and Ikenberry Dining Hall in his honor. He celebrated his eighty-first birthday in 2016.

President Stanley Ikenberry

1980–81

AMERICA'S TIME CAPSULE

November 4, 1980   Ronald Reagan won the presidential election in a landslide over incumbent Jimmy Carter.
November 21, 1980   More than half of America's television audience tuned in *Dallas* to see "Who Shot J. R.?"
January 20, 1981   The Iranian hostage crisis ended when Iran released American captives who were seized at
    the U.S. embassy in Teheran fourteen months before.
April 14, 1981   The space shuttle *Columbia* successfully touched down on Earth following a fifty-four-hour
    maiden flight in space.
June 12, 1981   *Raiders of the Lost Ark*, starring Harrison Ford, premiered.

MEN'S ILLINI MOMENT

Quarterback Dave Wilson

Wilson Sets NCAA Passing Mark

One Chicago sportswriter called it "the most incredible passing performance in collegiate history." That phrase, as well as any, accurately summed up the effort put forth by Illinois's senior quarterback Dave Wilson at Ohio State on November 8, 1980. In setting and tying forty-four different Illini, Big Ten, and NCAA records, Wilson completed forty-three of sixty-nine passes to ten different receivers for an amazing 621 yards and six touchdowns against a Buckeye team that had ranked first in the league in pass defense. Following Wilson's sixth TD pass with eleven seconds left that made the final score Ohio State 49, Illinois 42, Buckeye fans rose from their seats to give the Illini signal-caller a standing ovation. One loyal OSU fan even handed Wilson his Scarlet and Gray hat as a souvenir. "What makes it such a tremendous accomplishment," said Illini coach Mike White afterward, "was that it came against a quick, aggressive Ohio State defense. Maybe Dave just plain wore them out."

Highlighted by his effort against the Buckeyes, Wilson had three of the Big Ten's top four passing efforts in his only season at Illinois. Facing NCAA eligibility issues again in 1981, Wilson turned to the NFL. He was chosen No. 1 in the 1981 supplemental draft by the New Orleans Saints and threw for nearly seven thousand yards during a nine-year NFL career. Today, Wilson is a pro scout in Southern California.

OTHER TOP MOMENTS

1. Brian Bock, baseball (All-Big Ten designated hitter)
2. Mark Snow, fencing (undefeated Big Ten foil champion)
3. Efrem Stingfellow, track and field (Big Ten outdoor triple jump champ with leap of 50'9")
4. Eddie Johnson, basketball (first-team All-Big Ten)

MEN'S ILLINI LIST

CAREER BIG TEN YARDS GAINED PASSING (through 2015)

1.	621	Dave Wilson, Illinois at Ohio State (43–69), 1980
2.	558	Chuck Hartlieb, Iowa at Indiana (44–60), 1988
3.	546	Curtis Painter, Purdue vs. Central Michigan (35–54), 2007
4.	532	Mike Kafka, Northwestern vs. Auburn (47–78), 2010
5.	522	Drew Brees, Purdue vs. Minnesota (31–36), 1998
	522	Kyle Orton, Purdue vs. Indiana (33–54), 2004
7.	520	C. J. Bacher, Northwestern at Michigan State (38–48), 2007

Dave Wilson

8.	516	Scott Campbell, Purdue vs. Ohio State (31–52), 1981
9.	513	Brett Basanez, Northwestern at Texas Christian (39–62), 2004
10.	509	Drew Brees, Purdue vs. Michigan State (40–57), 1999

— MEN'S ILLINI ITEM —

Illinois's men's gymnastics team won its first Big Ten conference title in twenty-one years March 14, 1981, at Columbus, Ohio, outscoring five-time defending champion Minnesota by just one-tenth of a point, 539.50 to 539.40. Coach Yoshi Hayasaki's Illini built up a six-point lead during the first day's optional competition, behind the impressive performances of Kevin McMurchie (rings), Gilberto Albuquerque (vault), Gilmarcio Sanches (floor exercise), Kari Samsten (parallel bars), and Steve Lechner (horizontal bar).

1981 Illini gymnastics team

MEN'S ILLINI LEGEND

Coach Mike White

Mike White

On December 14, 1979, forty-three-yearold Mike White began his tempestuous career as head football coach at the University of Illinois. Compared to the "vanilla" offensive system of his predecessor, Gary Moeller, White's style was strictly "neapolitan." In White's first season alone, Illinois had an eleven-game passing yardage total of 3,227, compared to Moeller's thirty-three-game total of 3,300 aerial yards. His best team was the 1983 Big Ten championship club, which registered ten victories, including a record 9-0 mark against conference foes. For that performance, White was recognized as college football's Coach of the Year. His Illini appeared in the Liberty Bowl (1982), the Rose Bowl (1984), and the Peach Bowl (1985) but never won a post-season game. Attendance at Illini football games averaged nearly sixty-nine thousand during White's reign from 1980 to 1988. However, despite all of the successes, Mike White's career was also marred by controversy with the NCAA. And on January 18, 1988, he tendered his resignation to Athletic Director Neale Stoner. White later became head coach of the Oakland Raiders (1995–96). Today, he resides on Balboa Island in Newport Beach, California. White celebrated his eighty-first birthday in 2017.

OTHER TOP MEN'S ATHLETES

1. Eddie Johnson, basketball (first-team All-Big Ten)
2. Brian Bock, baseball (first-team All-Big Ten)
3. John Kakacek, wrestling (Big Ten Conference Medal of Honor recipient)

1980–81

WOMEN'S ILLINI MOMENT

NCAA member schools voted for inclusion of women's athletics

History Made at NCAA Convention

In January 1981, the agenda at the seventy-fifth annual NCAA convention at Miami, Florida, featured the landmark decision to include women's athletic programs within the NCAA governing structure, sounding a death knell for the Association for Intercollegiate Athletics for Women. Some in attendance called the NCAA's action to bring women's athletics into the fold "a blitzkrieg" and "a power play." A prolonged debate on the constitutional amendment first resulted in a 128–127 tally against sponsoring women's championships in Division I. A second vote's result was 137–117 in favor of the NCAA. "It was dramatic," said Ruth Berkey, the NCAA's director of women's championships at the time. "It was pretty euphoric for those people who were excited about the opportunity and pretty devastating for those people who were opposed to it." It took some time for the bitterness of AIAW supporters' feelings to pass, but eventually many of their leaders became involved in NCAA committees. During the 1981–82 academic year, the NCAA sponsored twenty-nine championships for women.

OTHER TOP MOMENTS

1. Volleyball received an at-large berth to the Midwest Regional meet.
2. Marianne Dickerson, cross-country, placed first at state AIAW meet.
3. Freshmen Karen Brems and Heidi Helmke, gymnastics, were event title leaders in 1980–81.

WOMEN'S LIST

WOMEN'S BASKETBALL SINGLE-SEASON
SCORING LEADERS (through 2015–16)

Lisa Robinson scored an Illini record in 1980–81

689 points	Ashley Berggren, 1995–96 (28 games, 24.6 ppg)
658 points	Lisa Robinson, 1980–81 (31 games, 21.2 ppg)
640 points	Jenna Smith, 2007–08 (35 games, 18.3 ppg)
633 points	Karisma Penn, 2012–13 (33 games, 19.2 ppg)
627 points	Jonelle Polk, 1986–87 (29 games, 21.6 ppg)
624 points	Jonelle Polk, 1985–86 (30 games, 20.8 ppg)
615 points	Jenna Smith, 2009–10 (34 games, 18.1 ppg)
599 points	Allison Curtin, 1999–00 (34 games, 17.6 ppg)
588 points	Kendra Grant, 1982–83 (28 games, 21.0 ppg)
573 points	Jenna Smith, 2008–09 (31 games, 18.5 ppg)

Due to the new Title IX regulations, the budget for Illini women's athletics dramatically increased from 1979–80 to 1980–81. A total of $224,093 was spent in 1979–80; the budget was increased by 60.3 percent to $359,334 in 1980–81. The most dramatic jumps came in women's basketball (101 percent), swimming (91.4 percent), tennis (56.7 percent), golf (49.6 percent), gymnastics (40.8 percent), and track and field (36.6 percent).

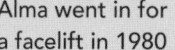

Women's funds less than most of Big Ten

The budget for women's athletics began to climb in 1980–81

WOMEN'S ILLINI LEGEND

Lynnette Robinson

Lynnette Robinson

At that point in history, she was one half of the University of Illinois's greatest sister act ever. Lynnette Robinson came with her sister, Lisa, from tiny Annawan High School in the fall of 1978. Throughout her career, Lynnette never scored as many points as her sister, but her true specialty was rebounding the basketball. Lynnette's hallmark season came during her junior year (1980–81) when, in addition to scoring 16.3 points per game, she also snared 10.8 rebounds per game. To date, it's one of only four occasions in history that an Illini women's player has averaged a double-double during a season. After graduating from Illinois in 1982, Lynnette turned to coaching. Though she's never been a collegiate head coach, she's been a superb assistant, particularly at Missouri State. From 1987 through 2002, the Lady Bears enjoyed national prominence in both prestige and attendance. Robinson's highlight came in her fifth season at MSU, 1991–92, when the Bears made it all the way to the NCAA semifinals. She's also been an assistant coach for four seasons at Michigan and for three years at Missouri. In 2015 Robinson was inducted into the Missouri State Athletics Hall of Fame. Today, in semi-retirement, she's an administrator at Target Inc. in Columbia, Missouri.

OTHER TOP WOMEN'S ATHLETES

1. Lisa Robinson, basketball (averaged 21.2 points per game to lead the Illini)
2. Mary Ellen Murphy, golf (top Illini finisher at the Big Ten meet)
3. Terrie Berto, golf (AIAW All-State selection)

ILLINI LORE

The *Alma Mater* sculpture made only its second journey in fifty-two years on August 11, 1980, when the campus landmark was removed from its base for a ten-day respite of restoration at the Physical Plant Services Building. Its first trip came in 1962 when the campus icon was transferred from a grove of evergreens south of the Auditorium to its present site north of Altgeld Hall. Nature's elements had rusted the iron bolts that secured the sections, so art professor Robert Youngman and his team of workers replaced what they could reach with stainless steel bolts and sprayed the remainder of the bronze sculpture with rust inhibitor. Physical Plant workers returned the refurbished *Alma Mater* by crane to her granite base on August 21, 1980.

Alma went in for a facelift in 1980

1981–82

AMERICA'S TIME CAPSULE

September 21, 1981   Sandra Day O'Connor became the first female member of the Supreme Court.
January 8, 1982   An eight-year antitrust suit by the Justice Department ended when the American Telephone
                      and Telegraph Company (AT&T) agreed to divest itself of its twenty-two Bell Telephone
                      operating systems.
March 29, 1982   Michael Jordan and North Carolina defeated Patrick Ewing and Georgetown in the NCAA
                      basketball finals.
June 25, 1982   *E.T.: The Extra-Terrestrial*, the highest grossing film of the 1980s, premiered.
July 3, 1982   Martina Navratilova won her first Wimbledon tennis championship.

MEN'S ILLINI MOMENT

Rick Filippo

Illini Baseball Wins the Big Ten West

Illinois's 1982 baseball season was one of multiple winning streaks, leading to a school-record forty-nine victories and a Big Ten West Division championship. Coach Tom Dedin's starting lineup was sprinkled with seven Illini players who earned all-conference honors, more than any other team. Two of the seven all-stars were pitchers, left-hander Rick Filippo and right-hander Randy Conte. Filippo was nearly perfect on the mound during the league season, hurling three complete games while not allowing a single earned or unearned run in twenty-one innings. Conte completed two of the three Big Ten games he started, posting a 3-0 record and a 2.45 ERA. Overall, Conte broke a fifty-three-year-old school record with thirteen overall wins. A third pitcher, Dan Hamstra, also went 3-0, and had a 1.29 ERA. At the plate, Illini hitters finished third in league games with a .315 average, including a league-leading seven triples and twenty-five stolen bases. First baseman Tim Richardson, a first-team All–Big Ten selection, batted .353 in sixteen Big Ten games and hit better than .400 over the course of the year. Other Illini sluggers included three second-team all-conference picks—second baseman Brian White, designated hitter Ken Warmbler (.409 average), and shortstop Rob Pullen (.354)—and a third-team choice, left fielder Todd Schmitke (.357). One thing that Illini fans would rather forget about the 1982 season is that their favorites crumbled in the Big Ten playoffs, losing two straight games in the double-elimination tournament.

OTHER TOP MOMENTS

1. A record average home crowd of 62,365 watched the Illini win all five of their home games for the first time since 1951.

2. Led by freshman phenom Derek Harper, UI's basketball team posted its second consecutive winning record in Big Ten play (10–8) for the first time since 1969 and 1970.

3. UI's Tom Stevens wins the Big Ten's 1,000-yard run (indoors) and 3,000-meter steeplechase (outdoors).

MEN'S ILLINI LIST

BASEBALL'S BEST BIG TEN SEASONS (minimum ten games, by percentage)

1.000	1910, Coach George Huff (11-0*)
.955	2015, Coach Dan Hartleb (21-1*)
.933	1911, Coach George Huff (14-1*)
.917	1903, Coach George Huff (11-1*)
.909	1921, Coach Carl Lundgren (10-1*)
.900	1934, Coach Carl Lundgren (9-1*)
.900	1937, Coach Wally Roettger (9-1*)
.875	1982, Coach Tom Dedin (14-2**)

Tom Dedin

.866	1962, Coach Lee Eilbracht (13-2*)
.864	1915, Coach George Huff (9-1-1*)

*Big Ten champions
**First place, Big Ten West

MEN'S ILLINI ITEM

Fighting Illini first baseman Tim Richardson amassed terrific statistics during his junior baseball season in 1982. Playing a record seventy-two games, he batted .400, becoming the first Illinois player since Ruck Steger in 1952 to crack that magic average. Additionally, Richardson stroked school records for hits (104), triples (11) and total bases (163). At the end of the season, Big Ten coaches accorded him first-team all-conference honors. Richardson now is vice president of sales and development at United Displaycraft in Chicagoland.

Tim Richardson

MEN'S ILLINI LEGEND

Tony Eason

Tony Eason

The name Charles Carroll Eason IV sounds more as if it belongs to a Bostonian socialite than to a quarterback from Walnut Grove, California. However, the guy his Illini teammates called "Tony" was very much a quarterback; in fact, he was one of the greatest signal-callers in University of Illinois football history. Eason was recruited in 1980 by Coach Mike White along with another junior college QB, Dave Wilson. Wilson beat out Eason for the starting job that first season, but "Champaign Tony" was a smash hit in 1981, breaking nine Big Ten records by passing for 3,360 yards and twenty touchdowns. His senior season in 1982 was even more brilliant, accounting for 3,671 yards and earning first-team All–Big Ten honors for a second consecutive year as the Illini qualified for the Liberty Bowl. Named the Fighting Illini Player of the Decade for the 1980s, Eason enjoyed a successful career in the National Football League, quarterbacking the New England Patriots to a berth against the Chicago Bears in Super Bowl XX. He stayed with the Patriots for seven seasons (1983–89), ranking as that franchise's third-leading passer of all-time, with 10,732 yards and sixty TD passes. Eason retired from the NFL following the 1990 season with the New York Jets. He started a business called Athletic Enhancements, training athletes to be more proficient. He lives in San Marcos, California.

OTHER TOP MEN'S ATHLETES

1. Greg Boeke, football (first-team All–Big Ten)
2. Rick Filipo, baseball (first-team All–Big Ten)
3. Randy Conte, baseball (Big Ten Conference Medal of Honor recipient)

1981–82

WOMEN'S ILLINI MOMENT

Women's Athletics Begin in Big Ten

Until May 15, 1974, women's athletics were under the auspices of the Department of Physical Education at the U of I. At that time, the budget for the women's program amounted to $14,110. Nearly twenty-six months after the Equal Rights Amendment was passed by the U.S. Senate, the University of Illinois Board of Trustees placed intercollegiate athletics for women under the auspices of the Athletic Association. Seventeen days later, on June l, the AA hired Dr. Karol Kahrs to be the first assistant director for women's athletics. Immediately, the recruitment of part-time coaches began. There were no scholarships in the 1974–75 season, but steps were taken the following year to upgrade to tuition and fees. Finally, in May 1978, the first full-scholarship athletes began signing. On August 1, 1981, after much discussion, the UI women's athletic program officially became part of the Big Ten Conference, and competition began in 1981–82. In March 1982, the women's basketball team finished second in the conference standings and qualified for the first NCAA women's basketball championship. Through the first thirty-four seasons of Big Ten competition, Fighting Illini women's teams won or shared eighteen conference titles.

OTHER TOP MOMENTS

1. Illinois's basketball team qualified for the NCAA tournament but loses at No. 13 Kentucky, 88–80.

2. Marianne Dickerson finished sixth at AIAW national cross-country championship, becoming UI's first woman to earn All-American honors in that sport.

3. Freshman Kim Nicholson set UI swimming records in the 100-meter freestyle, 200-meter backstroke and the 100-, 200- and 400-meter individual medleys.

WOMEN'S ILLINI LIST

FIRST OFFICIAL BIG TEN CHAMPIONSHIPS

1981: Field hockey (hosted by Iowa; won by Iowa)

1981: Volleyball (won by Michigan; UI tied for ninth of ten teams)

1981: Cross-country (hosted by Michigan State; won by Michigan State; UI placed ninth of ten teams)

1982: Gymnastics (hosted by Michigan; won by Michigan; UI placed sixth of eight teams)

1982: Basketball (won by Ohio State; UI tied for second among ten teams)

1982: Swimming and diving (hosted by Wisconsin; won by Ohio State; UI placed seventh of ten teams)

1982: Indoor track and field (hosted by Indiana; won by Wisconsin; UI placed seventh of ten teams)

1982: Softball (hosted by Michigan; won by Michigan)

1982: Tennis (hosted by Wisconsin; won by Indiana; UI placed eighth of ten teams)

1982: Golf (hosted by Minnesota; won by Michigan State; UI placed fourth of eight teams)

1982: Outdoor Track and Field (hosted by Illinois; won by Michigan State; UI tied for sixth of ten teams)

Illinois hosted the first official Big Ten women's track and field championship in 1982

TITLE IX

WOMEN'S ILLINI LEGEND

Lisa Robinson, Basketball

Lisa Robinson

The Village of Annawan, Illinois is a sleepy little town off Interstate 80, where, back in the mid-1970s, young basketball players flocked to Clarence and Priscilla Robinson's backyard basketball court at 508 South State Street. Teenagers Lisa and Lynnette Robinson were the court's hostesses. The 5'11" twins regularly played hoops with boys, readying them for the tougher, more physical play they'd soon face. Dr. Clarence "Pete" Hughes, the Robinsons' prep coach, had been a doctoral student at the University of Illinois. "We were probably leaning toward Illinois State because they were offering us a scholarship-and-a-half, but Dr. Hughes urged us to consider the Illini," said Lisa. Prompted by Illini women's coach Carla Thompson, the twins got a telephone call from Lou Henson. "Coach Henson, along with Dr. Hughes, asked us to visit the University of Illinois. Our campus visit included an inspirational conversation with Ray Eliot, and we immediately knew that Illinois was where we wanted to be." In the summer of 1978 the Robinsons became the first female athletes to receive full scholarships from the U of I. In four years, Lisa became the Illini's all-time leading scorer (1,906 points), while sister Lynnette finished atop the career rebounding list (894). Lisa was a highly decorated player, earning All–Big Ten kudos and winning the 1982 Big Ten Conference Medal of Honor. Upon Lisa's graduation, she began a thirty-year coaching career that included stops at ISU, Augustana College, Wyoming, Air Force, and Bradley. Today, Lisa resides in Colorado Springs, Colorado, where she works at the Air Force Academy as an academic advisor and learning-strategies instructor.

OTHER TOP WOMEN'S ATHLETES

1. Sue Arildsen, tennis (team MVP)
2. Sandy Sutton, golf (All–Big Ten)
3. Robin Duffy, swimming (All-American)

ILLINI LORE

The Big Ten Conference began one-year sanctions against the University of Illinois's intercollegiate football program on August 6, 1981. The original penalties, imposed in May, were partially a result of Illini quarterback Dave Wilson's legal struggle against the conference. The Big Ten faculty representatives voted to prohibit the Illini from playing in a postseason bowl game in 1981 and denied the university a share of the conference receipts from televised football games. On September 3, Governor James Thompson signed into law a bill that created a special lottery that helped offset an estimated $500,000 loss in football TV revenue. The lottery, originally sponsored by State Senator Stanley Weaver of Urbana and State Representative Virgil Wikoff of Champaign, eventually netted UI's Athletic Association $850,000.

Thompson Signs Lottery Bill

A special lottery that helped offset a half-million-dollar loss in Illini football TV revenue

1982–83

AMERICA'S TIME CAPSULE

September 29, 1982	Seven people in the Chicago area died from cyanide placed in Tylenol capsules.
October 20, 1982	The St. Louis Cardinals won the seventh and deciding game of the World Series, defeating the Milwaukee Brewers.
December 2, 1982	Barney Clark was the first successful recipient of an artificial heart transplant. He died on March 23, 1983.
March 2, 1983	More than 125 million viewers watched the final television episode of *M*A*S*H*.
April 12, 1983	Democratic congressman Harold Washington became the first African American mayor of Chicago.

MEN'S ILLINI MOMENT

Liberty Bowl coaches Mike White and Paul "Bear" Bryant

Illini Gridders Battle the Bear

The 1982 Fighting Illini football season will be remembered for many reasons. The year began with a highly successful "Tailgreat" promotion and a big win over Northwestern in Memorial Stadium's first ever night game. It was the season Tony Eason established an all-time record for passing proficiency. And it was the year that Illinois went "bowling" for the first time in nineteen years, meeting Alabama at the Liberty Bowl December 29 in Memphis, a game that would turn out to be the final one for the Crimson Tide's legendary Paul "Bear" Bryant. Bryant, who won more games than any other coach in college football, announced his retirement two weeks before, making the otherwise second-rate bowl game one of the season's top attractions. The night was clear, and the thirty-four-degree weather favored Alabama's wishbone attack. Illinois trailed the Tide by 7–6 at the half, as Alabama defenders repeatedly pummeled Eason with a ferocious pass rush. On three occasions, crushing Alabama tackles forced Eason from the game. "My eyes were bobbing up and down," the Illini quarterback said afterward. "I couldn't even find the ground." Despite a record 423 yards passing by Eason, Illinois dropped a 21–15 decision, giving the Bear his 323rd and final collegiate victory.

OTHER TOP MOMENTS

1. Derek Harper's buzzer-beater topped Minnesota and sent Illinois to the NCAA tournament.
2. Illini fencers captured the Big Ten championship; UI's Edward Kaihatsu captured foil title.
3. Men's gymnastics squad shared the conference title with Ohio State, finished sixth at NCAA.

MEN'S ILLINI LIST

GAME-WINNING FIELD GOALS IN THE LAST SIXTY SECONDS SINCE 1980

September 13, 1980: Mike Bass, 38 yards at 0:00 to beat Michigan State, 20–17.

October 22, 1982: Mike Bass, 46 yards at 0:03 to beat Wisconsin, 29–28.

October 5, 1985: Chris White, 38 yards at 0:00 to beat Ohio State, 31–28.

October 17, 1987: Doug Higgins, 34 yards at 0:54 to beat Wisconsin, 16–14.

October 29, 1988: Doug Higgins, 44 yards at 0:01 to tie Minnesota, 27–27.

October 20, 1990: Doug Higgins, 48 yards at 0:42 to beat Michigan State, 15–13.

October 12, 1991: Chris Richardson, 41 yards at 0:36 to beat Ohio State, 10–7.

September 30, 2006: Jason Reda, 39 yards at 0:06 to beat Michigan State, 23–20.

November 1, 2008: Matt Eller, 46 yards at 0:24 to beat Iowa, 27–24.

November 22, 2014: David Reisner, 36 yards at 0:08 to beat Penn State, 16–14.

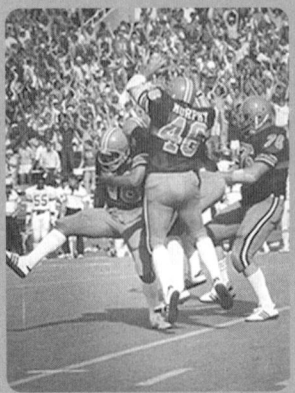

Teammates rush Mike Bass after his 1980 game-winning field goal versus Michigan State

MEN'S ILLINI ITEM

Nothing was more dramatic for Illini place kicker Mike Bass in 1982 than his forty-three-yard field goal to beat host Wisconsin. Bass was a nearly perfect twenty-three of twenty-six on his place kicks in '82, earning second-team All-American honors. Not only did his school-record 101 points that year break Red Grange's fifty-eight-year-old record, he also bested UI's career mark with 209 points. Today, he's senior associate vice president and deputy comptroller at the University of Illinois.

Mike Bass

MEN'S ILLINI LEGEND

Derek Harper was Illinois's star player in 1982–83

Derek Harper

From 1981–83, Derek Harper, the 6'4" guard from West Palm Beach, Florida, was the Big Ten's top defender, leading the conference in steals his sophomore and junior seasons. Though he wasn't known as a shooter, Harper set a Big Ten record by making nineteen consecutive field goal attempts during his final campaign in 1983. His best single effort was a twenty-nine-point outing against Michigan that season. During his three years at Illinois, the Illini averaged twenty victories per season and qualified twice for the NCAA tournament. Harper left Illinois following the 1982–83 season and was a first-round pick for the Dallas Mavericks in the 1983 NBA draft. He played in Dallas for twelve seasons, winding up as the Mavericks' No. 3 all-time scorer (12,597 points), No. 1 all-time assist man (5,111), and No. 1 in career steals (1,841). Harper also played with the Knicks, Magic, and Lakers during his sixteen-year NBA career and retired in 1999, placing eleventh for most steals and seventeenth for most assists in league history. He now serves as the Mavs' television color commentator.

OTHER TOP MEN'S ATHLETES

1. Mike Martin, football (first-team All–Big Ten)
2. Rich Baader, track and field (Big Ten Medal of Honor)
3. Tony Eason, football (Athlete of the Year)

1982–83

WOMEN'S ILLINI MOMENT

Kendra Gantt

Gantt Explodes for Forty-Nine

It was a historic night at the Assembly Hall on January 3, 1983, and the Illini sophomore from Peoria said afterward that she never knew she was close to a record. With thirty-two points in the first half on fifteen-of-seventeen shooting, Kendra Gantt remained focused—not on herself, but on winning the game. Gantt continued her unwitting assault on the Illini record book in the second half, missing only three of the ten shots she attempted and ending with a school-record forty-nine points, nine more than the previous Illini mark, held by Lisa Robinson. The 6'3" center's twenty-one field goals broke the existing NCAA record, while her forty-nine-point mark was only one shy of the women's collegiate high score. When Gantt's Illini career ended in 1985, only Robinson had scored more than her 1,526 points. Today, she works for a private security firm in Kuwait City, Kuwait.

OTHER TOP MOMENTS

1. Gretchen Grier earned UI's first official Big Ten track title (600-yard run).
2. Track's 400-meter relay team (Kim Dunlap, Yvonne Oldham, Rolanda Conda, Rachel Bass) won the Big Ten outdoor title.
3. Tennis team set a single-season record for victories (twenty-two).

WOMEN'S ILLINI LIST

ILLINOIS'S INDIVIDUAL SINGLE-GAME SCORING BESTS

49 pts	Kendra Gantt vs. Kent State, January 3, 1983
43 pts	Ashley Berggren vs. Minnesota, January 14, 1996
41 pts	Kris Dupps vs. Kent State, January 2, 1994
40 pts	Lisa Robinson vs. Southern Illinois, February 19, 1981
39 pts	Sarah Sharp vs. Northwestern, January 27, 1991
39 pts	Kendra Gantt vs. Bradley, December 22, 1982
38 pts	Ashley Berggren vs. Northwestern, February 23, 1996
37 pts	Jonelle Polk vs. Nebraska, December 30, 1986
36 pts	Ashley Berggren vs. Purdue, February 18, 1996
36 pts	Ashley Berggren vs. Northwestern, December 29, 1995

Kendra Gantt

Mary Ellen (Murphy) Martin was an Illini junior when she realized she could compete with the best. A product of Driscoll High School in Addison, Illinois, Martin was twice a national qualifier, but she also excelled in the classroom. She became the first Illini female athlete to earn an NCAA postgraduate scholarship and was awarded the 1983 Big Ten Conference Medal of Honor. Martin is still a dominant player, having won several women's club championships and some Chicago District Golf Association events. Her son, Kyle, played college golf at Indiana Wesleyan University.

Mary Ellen Murphy

WOMEN'S ILLINI LEGEND

Marianne Dickerson (Athlete of the Year)

One of the greatest women's distance runners in Illinois history, Marianne Dickerson was the Fighting Illini Female Athlete of the Year for 1982–83. She set numerous records in cross-country and track and field, and she twice won All-American honors. During her Fighting Illini career, Dickerson recorded eight of the top ten cross-country marks and set UI varsity records in the two- and three-mile runs and 5,000- and 10,000-meter runs. She was also an excellent student, graduating with a 4.5 grade-point average (on a 5.0 scale) in engineering. After her collegiate career ended, Dickerson won the 1988 Baltimore Marathon. She passed away in October 2015 at age fifty-four.

OTHER TOP WOMEN'S ATHLETES

1. Laurie Watters, volleyball (led the Big Ten in spiking percentage)
2. Julie Lantis (set records in both the 1,500-mter run and the mile)
3. Cindy Stein, basketball (Illini assists leader set career record in just two seasons)
3. Gayathri DeSilva, tennis (career record for singles victories)

Marianne Dickerson

ILLINI LORE

Following two years of intense debate and examination, the Circle and Medical Center campuses at Chicago began a unified effort during the 1982–83 academic year. University of Illinois President Stanley Ikenberry, in his recommendation to the board of trustees for acceptance of the consolidation, said the merger would give the new UI Chicago "the ability to compete in the Chicago-area academic arena and contribute to the strengthening of the university as a whole."

President Stanley Ikenberry

1983–84

AMERICA'S TIME CAPSULE

September 1, 1983 — A Soviet fighter plane shot down a South Korean airliner, killing all 269 people aboard.

October 23, 1983 — A truck laden with explosives blew up outside the U.S. Marine headquarters in Beirut, Lebanon, taking the lives of 241 Marines and Navy personnel.

April 23, 1984 — Federal researchers announced the identification of a virus thought to cause acquired immune deficiency syndrome (AIDS).

May 8, 1984 — The U.S.S.R. Olympic Committee withdrew from the 1984 Summer Olympics, to be held in Los Angeles, California.

July 28, 1984 — The Summer Olympic Games began in Los Angeles, highlighted by the performances of Carl Lewis and Mary Lou Retton.

MEN'S ILLINI MOMENT

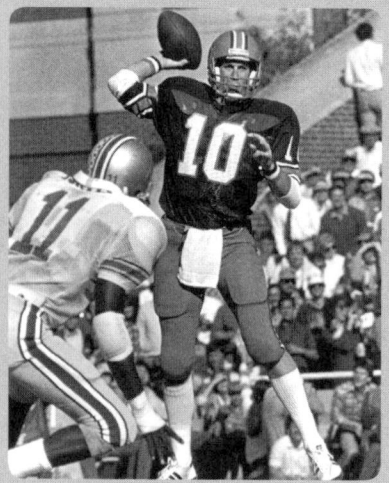

Quarterback Jack Trudeau

Illini Football Team Wins Big Ten

Between 1896 and 1982, fifty of the first eighty-seven Big Ten championship teams wound up unbeaten and untied. In 1983 Coach Mike White's Fighting Illini football team defied the odds by becoming the first Big Ten club ever to post victories over all nine of its conference foes. Game by game, momentum stayed in Illinois's corner. First, unbeaten Michigan State bit the dust (20–10), then fourth-ranked Iowa (33–0) and rugged Wisconsin (27–15) were history. Sixth-ranked Ohio State battled the Illini tooth and nail at Memorial Stadium before finally succumbing, 17–13. Illinois improved its conference mark to 5-0 with a 35–21 win at Purdue, setting up its showdown against unbeaten Michigan before a record crowd at Champaign. The bonecrushing Illini defense was at its best that day, holding the eighth-ranked Wolverines without a touchdown en route to a 16–6 victory. All that separated Illinois from the Rose Bowl were a trio of conference doormats: Minnesota, Indiana, and Northwestern. Despite a lackluster effort at the Metrodome, the Illini disposed of the Golden Gophers, 50–23, to improve their conference record to 7-0. On November 12, more than seventy-three thousand fans were on hand at Memorial Stadium to see their Illini clinch their first Rose Bowl berth in twenty years, with a convincing 49–21 triumph over Indiana. About thirty thousand Illini faithful showed up at Northwestern's Dyche Stadium for the regular-season finale, and White's troops toyed with the Wildcats, 56–24, to post their Big Ten-record ninth victory. Before Illinois's Rose Bowl battle against Pac-10 champion UCLA, the team collected a bushel of accolades. Six Illini players earned first-team all-conference honors, including defensive tackle Don Thorp, who was named the Big Ten's Most Valuable Player. White was honored by nearly everyone as their Coach of the Year. On January 2, 1984, a lovely eighty-four-degree day welcomed the teams to Pasadena. Unfortunately, the weather was the high point of the day for Illinois. UCLA built up a 28–3 lead and wound up with a 45–9 victory over the fourth-ranked Illini, the most lopsided Rose Bowl score since 1960. An otherwise sweet season had been marred by one very sour performance.

OTHER TOP MOMENTS

1. Safety David Edwards stunted a late Ohio State drive with an interception, helping Illinois top No. 6 Buckeyes, 17–13.

2. An emotional four-overtime thriller saw Illinois basketball team survive against Michigan, 75–66.

3. Coach Art Schankin's Illini fencing team captured first place at the Big Ten championships, then later placed eleventh at the NCAA meet.

MEN'S ILLINI LIST

ILLINOIS FOOTBALL'S MOST PROLIFIC SCORING TEAMS

The 1983 Fighting Illini football team is the school's most prolific scoring squad ever in terms of Big Ten Conference games. Here's the entire list:

Thomas Rooks

	Points per game	Team (leading passer/receiver/rusher)		Points per game	Team (leading passer/receiver/rusher)
1.	35.8	2010 (Scheelhaase/Jenkins/Leshoure)	6.	29.9	1989 (George/Bellamy/Griffith)
2.	33.7	1983 (Trudeau/D. Williams/Rooks)	7.	29.3	1981 (Eason/D. Smith/Thomas)
3.	32.4	2001 (Kittner/Lloyd/Harvey)	8.	27.6	2007 (J. Williams/Benn/Mendenhall)
4.	30.4	1984 (Trudeau/D. Williams/Rooks)	9.	26.5	2002 (Beujter/Lloyd/Harris)
5.	30.3	1982 (Eason/Martin/Beverly)	10.	25.8	1995 (Johnson/Dulick/Holcombe)
				25.8	1947 (Moss/Zatkoff/Steger)

MEN'S ILLINI ITEM

Illinois (26–5) claimed a share of the Big Ten basketball title in 1983–84 by winning fifteen of eighteen conference games. Highlighting the regular season was a four-overtime victory at the Assembly Hall on January 28 over Michigan, 75–66. The Illini won their first two games in NCAA tournament play, advancing to a quarterfinal showdown against host Kentucky. The Wildcats had beaten Illinois in an earlier game, 56–54, and the Illini lost the rematch, too, 54–51.

The 1983–84 Big Ten champs

MEN'S ILLINI LEGEND

Don Thorp

Don Thorp

As a youngster, Don Thorp attended Chicago Bears games with his father, idolizing their star linebacker, Dick Butkus. So, in 1983—exactly twenty years after Butkus was named the Big Ten's Most Valuable football player—the University of Illinois's defensive tackle from Buffalo Grove appropriately matched his hero's accomplishment, capturing the *Chicago Tribune*'s Silver Football Award. Ever the big-play specialist, he registered seventeen tackles for losses his senior year, bringing his career total to a school-record thirty-seven. Thorp was the stalwart for a defensive unit that was primarily responsible for his team's perfect 9–0 Big Ten record. He was rewarded with first-team All-American laurels and, more important to him, Most Valuable Player honors from his teammates. Thorp played in the NFL for three seasons for the New Orleans Saints, Indianapolis Colts, and Kansas City Chiefs. Today, he is in his twenty-first year as president at Prinova Group, a food and beverage company located in Carol Stream, Illinois.

OTHER TOP MEN'S ATHLETES

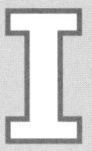

1. Bruce Douglas, basketball (first-team All–Big Ten selection)
2. Efrem Winters, basketball (first-team All–Big Ten selection)
3. Craig Swoope, football (second-team All-American)
4. Efrem Winters, basketball (first-team All–Big Ten)
3. Kerry Dickson, track and field (Big Ten Conference Medal of Honor recipient)

1983–84

WOMEN'S ILLINI MOMENT

Karen Brems

Brems Sweeps Top Illini Awards

In 1983–84, University of Illinois women's gymnast Karen Brems became the first Fighting Illini athlete to be named as the school's Athlete of the Year and the Big Ten Conference Medal of Honor Award winner in the same season. As a youngster in Urbana, she idolized gymnasts like Olga Korbut and Nadia Comaneci, dreaming of becoming an Olympic competitor herself one day. Under the tutelage of Coach Bev Mackes at Illinois, Brems qualified for the NCAA championships as a sophomore in 1982 but eventually realized that she would probably fall short of her aspirations to become an Olympian. "I thought I was pretty much done in competitive sports," she said. Brems continued to be a fitness enthusiast, so she took up running and cycling, then competing in triathlons. Cycling turned out to be much kinder to her body, and she quickly advanced from regional and national meets to the Tour de France and world championship competition. In 2000 Brems accomplished her Olympic dream, competing in the Sydney Games. At the 2016 USA Cycling Cyclocross National Championships in Asheville, North Carolina, Brems won the Master Women's 50–54 title, riding for SunPower Racing. She now lives in Palo Alto, California, working for Hewlett Packard as a software engineer.

OTHER TOP MOMENTS

1. Illini basketball topped Indiana, 73–62, shooting conference-game record .627 (thirty-two of fifty-one) from the field.
2. Mike Hebert's initial Illini volleyball team beat Wisconsin in the team's first conference game.
3. Tragic death of gymnast Cindy McGee occurred on November 4, 1983.

WOMEN'S ILLINI LIST

FOUR- AND THREE-TIME WOMEN'S TEAM MVPS

Megan Fudge, tennis (2007, 2008, 2009, 2010)

Jenna Smith, basketball (2008, 2009, 2010)

Jennifer McGaffigan, tennis (2001, 2002, 2004)

Perdita Felicien, track and field (2001, 2002, 2003)*

Ashley Berggren, basketball (1996, 1997, 1998)

Kim Berres, gymnastics (1996, 1997, 1998)

Lindsey Nimmo, tennis (1991, 1992, 1993)

Mary Eggers (1986, 1987, 1988)

*Track and field does not select a team MVP, but Felicien was UI's three-time Female Athlete of the Year.

Kim Berres

Maureen McNamara was a two-time Most Valuable Player for the University of Illinois tennis team (1983 and 1984). The Peoria native finished her career as the Illini's career leader in singles victories (89-60) and also held the single-season mark for wins (28-16 in 1981–82). In 1992 McNamara was voted to UI's Women's Tennis Team of the Decade. After a few years in in the business world, she joined Notre Dame as its assistant tennis coach. She has remained on the Fighting Irish staff and is now assistant athletics director at Notre Dame.

Maureen McNamara

WOMEN'S ILLINI LEGEND

Michelle Vossen

Michelle Vossen

Off the court, Lisa Robinson called her former Illini basketball teammate Michelle Vossen a giver. "She has a great heart," she said, "a wonderful giving person." On the court, the dynamo from St. Louis was also a giver, setting UI single-season (173) and career (391) records for assists. The former Visitation Academy star battled shin splints throughout her career but fought through the pain to help lead the Illini to back-to-back twenty-win seasons in 1980–81 and 1981–82. Vossen's senior-year team was especially successful, earning a berth in the 1982 NCAA tournament. Today, she's a senior manager at Accenture, a global professional services company based in St. Petersburg, Florida.

OTHER TOP WOMEN'S ATHLETES

1. Laurie Walters, volleyball (team Most Valuable Player)
2. Heidi Helmke, gymnastics
3. Sandy Sutton, golf (team Most Valuable Player, first-team All–Big Ten)

ILLINI LORE

William Warfield, University of Illinois professor of voice from 1974 to 1990, received a Grammy Award in April 1984 for his narration of Abraham Lincoln in Aaron Copland's composition, "A Lincoln Portrait." Warfield, a bass baritone, became nationally recognized for his role as Porgy in George Gershwin's *Porgy and Bess* and for his rendition of "Ol' Man River" in the 1951 movie *Showboat*. He died in 2002 at age eighty-two.

William Warfield

1984–85

AMERICA'S TIME CAPSULE

October 7, 1984	Steve Garvey led the San Diego Padres to the National League pennant over the Chicago Cubs.
November 6, 1984	Ronald Reagan was reelected president over Walter Mondale in the greatest Republican landslide ever.
March 4, 1985	The Environmental Protection Agency ordered a ban on leaded gasoline.
April 8, 1985	The government of India sued the Union Carbide Corporation in connection with a plant disaster that killed seventeen hundred and injured as many as two hundred thousand others.
July 13, 1985	President Reagan underwent surgery to remove a cancerous tumor from his colon.

MEN'S ILLINI MOMENT

Efrem Winters helped lead Illinois past Indiana in 1985

Illini Bid Bobby "Good Night"

Illinois took advantage of a freshman-dominated Indiana lineup January 27, 1985, and administered a 52–41 spanking to Coach Bobby Knight's young Hoosiers. The perfection-driven coach from Bloomington brought only twelve players with him on the bus to Champaign, leaving veterans Winston Morgan and Mike Giomi at home because he was so disgusted with their performance in a two-point loss at Ohio State a few nights before. Knight even left All-American Steve Alford on the bench all afternoon, underlining his slightly bizarre statement to his team. Fortunately for the Illini, Knight's psychological ploy backfired. So dominating was the Illini defensive effort that night at the Assembly Hall that Indiana managed only five baskets and two free throws in the first half. The final box score showed Efrem Winters and George Montgomery pacing Illinois with twelve and ten points, respectively, while Anthony Welch grabbed ten rebounds. Aside from 7'2" Uwe Blab, the six Hoosiers in the game were freshmen. Afterward, Illini guard Doug Altenberger summed up the afternoon: "The game was just weird." Was Illini coach Lou Henson disappointed he didn't get a chance to coach against Indiana's best? "It would suit me fine if they didn't play when we go over to Bloomington," he said. As it turned out, the Illini won again on February 21 at IU, 66–50, propelling them to a second-place finish in the Big Ten in 1985.

OTHER TOP MOMENTS

1. Cross-country team captured its first Big Ten title in thirty-seven years.
2. Baseball rode the pitching staff to Big Ten West division title.
3. Illini basketball squad reached NCAA Sweet Sixteen, sweeping Northeastern and Georgia in opening games.

MEN'S ILLINI LIST

FIRST-TEAM ALL–BIG TEN BASEBALL PITCHERS (since 1951)

1951	George Maier
1961	Doug Mills
1962	Tom Fletcher
1963	Jerry Weygandt
1969	Rich Binder
1982	Rick Filipo
1985	Donn Pall
1996	Brett Weber
1998	Brett Weber
	Jim Journell

1999	Jason Anderson
2001	Andy Dickinson
2002	Andy Dickinson
2005	Brian Blomquist
2015	Kevin Duchene
2015	Tyler Jay

Donn Pall earned first-team All–Big Ten honors in 1985

MEN'S ILLINI ITEM

Fighting Illini men's teams completed one of their finest overall seasons in school history during the 1984–85 campaign, outscoring Michigan for an overall first-place finish in the Big Ten's twelve championships. The Illini cross-country squad was the only team to win a title, but four other sports—football, indoor track, fencing, and basketball—placed second. The Illini men's gymnastics team was ranked among the nation's Top 20 and the baseball team won the Big Ten West division title.

Ty Wolf led the Illini cross-country team to a 1984 Big Ten title

---

MEN'S ILLINI LEGEND

Charles Lakes

Charles Lakes

One of the greatest Illini athletes of the 1980s was gymnast Charles Lakes. He's remembered for his stylish flair on the high bar and parallel bars, his spectacular leaps on the vault, and his overall consistency in the all-around competition. But, historically, Lakes will forever hold the title as the first African American gymnast at the University of Illinois and in the Olympic Games. As a junior in 1984, he became the first Illini to win NCAA gold on the high bar since Abe Grossfeld's similar accomplishment in 1958. Lakes had captured six Big Ten championships when he was selected as Illinois's 1985 Male Athlete of the Year. He left the Illini in 1986 to concentrate on making the Olympic team in 1988. There he was the highest-ranked American in the all-around finals, placing nineteenth. "I think of myself as a gymnast first," he told NBC. "But I am black, and, as a result, I am a role model for younger minority athletes." In 2003 Lakes was inducted into the USA Gymnastics Hall of Fame. Today, he resides in Grenada Hills, California.

OTHER TOP MEN'S ATHLETES

1. Graeme McGufficke, swimming (conference title in 1650-yard freestyle)
2. Lane Lohr, track and field (Big Ten indoor pole-vault champion)
3. Peter Bouton, tennis (Big Ten Medal of Honor)
4. Donn Pall, baseball (first-team All–Big Ten pitcher)

1984-85

WOMEN'S ILLINI MOMENT

Kelly McNee (155) and Margaret Vogel (159)

Illini Harriers Post Best Finish

The Fighting Illini women's cross-country team placed second at the Big Ten championship meet on October 27, its highest finish of all time. Illinois, directed by interim coach Patty Bradley, was runner-up to defending champion Wisconsin, 27–79. Junior Kelly McNee earned All–Big Ten honors by placing sixth individually. Three other Illini runners—Ruth Sterneman, Margaret Vogel, and Colleen Hackett—all finished among the meet's top seventeen. McNee went on to represent Illinois at the NCAA championship, where she finished twenty-first of 150 runners and earned All-American honors.

OTHER TOP MOMENTS

1. UI's 4x800-meter relay team (Ann Henry, Cheryl Ward, Kelly McNee, and Margaret Vogel) set a Big Ten championship record.

2. Laura Golden began her six-year stint as Illini basketball coach.

3. Cross-country finished runner-up at the Big Ten meet, best finish ever.

WOMEN'S ILLINI LIST

MIKE HEBERT'S VOLLEYBALL MVPS

Denise Fracaro was UI's Most Valuable Player in 1984 and 1985

1983	Laurie Watters
1984	Denise Fracaro
1985	Denise Fracaro
1986	Mary Eggers
1987	Mary Eggers and Nancy Brookhart
1988	Mary Eggers
1989	Laura Bush
1990	Petra Laverman
1991	Lorna Henderson
1992	Kirsten Gleis

1993	Tina Rogers
1994	Julie Edwards
1995	Erin Borske

In cross-country, Kelly (McNee) Innis earned All–Big Ten honors in 1984, leading the Illini to a second-place finish at the conference meet. Her time in the 5,000 meters (16:36) as a junior at the NCAA Midwest regionals continues to stand as Illinois's best time at that distance. Her greatest individual honor came in 1985, when she was named the Illini Female Athlete of the Year. Today, Innis lives in Chicago and works for Selective Search.

Kelly (McNee) Innis

WOMEN'S ILLINI LEGEND

Mike Hebert

While the Fighting Illini football and men's basketball teams were winning Big Ten championships during the 1983–84 season, a thirty-nine-year-old volleyball coach named Mike Hebert was in the early stages of his career at the University of Illinois. Hebert's first season started unceremoniously with just five victories in thirty matches, but more than a decade later the California native had proved to be one of the Illini's winningest coaches ever. From 1983 through 1995 Hebert's Illini captured 323 victories against only 127 losses, a winning percentage of .718. That's more efficient than Lou Henson or Bob Zuppke or most any other Illini coaching legend. Including the 1994 season, Hebert's teams qualified for the NCAA tournament ten consecutive years, including back-to-back Final Four appearances in 1987 and 1988, and have won four Big Ten championships. Such success made Illini volleyball an NCAA leader

Mike Hebert

OTHER TOP WOMEN'S ATHLETES

1. Denise Fracaro, volleyball (team MVP)
2. Sue Arildsen, tennis (Big Ten Conference Medal of Honor recipient)
3. Ruth Sterneman, cross-country (second-team All–Big Ten)

in attendance, tops in both 1992 and 1993. Several of Hebert's athletes have earned All-American acclaim, including first-teamers Mary Eggers and Kirsten Gleis. The Illini mentor was named National Volleyball Coach of the Year in 1985. He left Illinois to become Minnesota's head coach and retired after fifteen seasons in December 2010. At the time, Hebert's 892 career victories ranked fourth all-time in Division I women's volleyball history. He was inducted into the American Volleyball Coaches Association Hall of Fame in 2006.

ILLINI LORE

At a news conference on May 22, 1984, President Stanley Ikenberry introduced Thomas Everhart, age fifty-two, as the chancellor-elect of the Urbana-Champaign campus. Everhart, dean of Cornell University's College of Engineering, succeeded John Cribbet, who returned to teaching in UI's College of Law. "This is truly a great university," Everhart told the media, "one of the four or five premier public campuses in the country. The opportunity to assume the chancellorship of this distinguished campus is compelling." Everhart presided at the U of I until 1987, then became president at the California Institute of Technology in Pasadena, serving until 1997. In 2002 the Institute of Electrical and Electronics Engineers awarded him its Founder's Medal, and he was honored with the Okawa Prize. Everhart turned eighty-four in February 2016.

President Thomas Everhart

1985-86

AMERICA'S TIME CAPSULE

September 9, 1985	President Reagan announced trade sanctions against South Africa to protest that country's policy of apartheid.
September 11, 1985	Cincinnati's Pete Rose broke Ty Cobb's Major League Baseball record for hits when he collected his 4,192nd hit, against San Diego.
October 27, 1985	The Kansas City Royals defeated the St. Louis Cardinals, four games to three, to win the World Series.
January 26, 1986	Mike Ditka's Chicago Bears beat the New England Patriots, 46–10, to win Super Bowl XX.
January 28, 1986	Seven astronauts were killed when the space shuttle *Challenger* exploded just seventy-four seconds after liftoff at Cape Canaveral, Florida.

MEN'S ILLINI MOMENT

Chris White

Chris White's Field Goal Beats Ohio State

Illinois coach Mike White called it "the sweetest victory I can remember in my coaching career," and none of the 76,343 Illini fans assembled at Memorial Stadium that windy October 5th afternoon could argue with his statement. Shouldering the burden of both a disappointing 1-2 start and a 28–14 second-half deficit to their guests from Ohio State, the Fighting Illini football team rose from the dead to register a stunning 31–28 win over the fifth-ranked Buckeyes. The decisive play came when the coach's son, Chris White, drilled a thirty-eight-yard field goal as the clock ran out. However, there were more Illini heroics prior to that, and quarterback Jack Trudeau was primarily responsible for the stunning rally. Completing twenty-eight of his forty passes, Trudeau relied on a short passing game against the wind. His quick shovel passes to fullback Thomas Rooks and Stephen Pierce's timely catches for 131 yards nickel-and-dimed the traditionally tough Buckeye defense to death. Chris White's game-winning kick came following a pair of timeouts, the second called by Ohio State in an attempt to unnerve the senior placekicker. "I've got a lot of faith in that son of mine," the elder White told the media afterward. "His temperament is unbelievable. I don't think that ball was six inches off center." Following nearly twenty years in San Francisco as a real estate agent, Chris White now resides in Sacramento, California.

OTHER TOP MOMENTS

1. Steve Stricker tied for Big Ten golf championship medalist honors with Northwestern's Jim Benepe.
2. Illini pole vaulter Lane Lohr swept Big Ten indoor and outdoor titles.
3. In December 1985 the soon-to-be World Champion Chicago Bears practiced at Memorial Stadium, preparing for the Super Bowl.

MEN'S ILLINI LIST

FOOTBALL'S BIG TEN CONFERENCE MEDAL OF HONOR RECIPIENTS

Jim Juriga, 1986 Conference Medal of Honor recipient

1918	Leo Klein, end
1919	George Bucheit, end
1923	Otto Vogel, center
1925	Gilbert Roberts, center
1949	Dwight "Dike" Eddleman, halfback
1950	Russell "Ruck" Steger, fullback
1954	Robert Lenzini, guard
1964	Richard Deller, tackle
1966	James Grabowski, fullback

1972	Robert Bucklin, end
1986	James Juriga, guard
1989	Peter Freund, quarterback
1992	Michael Hopkins, defensive back
1994	Forrest "Forry" Wells III, punter
2008	Jeremy "J" Leman, linebacker
2010	Jon Asamoah, guard
2014	Nathan Scheelhaase, quarterback

MEN'S ILLINI ITEM

On April 15, 1985, construction began on $34 million worth of athletic facility improvements. Of the total, $7 million was targeted toward upgrading the football plant, including the resurfacing of Zuppke Field, expansion of the football headquarters, and installation of an air-support structure that was eventually nicknamed "The Bubble." Construction on the new track and baseball stadiums began in June 1985 and commenced hosting competition in 1987 and 1988, respectively.

Illinois Field for baseball (foreground) and the Illinois Track Stadium

MEN'S ILLINI LEGEND

College Football Hall of Famer David Williams

David Williams

The soft hands of All-American receiver David Williams were once described by a sportswriter as "bean bags used to catch bullets." During his career at the University of Illinois from 1983 to 1985, Williams caught 262 passes for 3,392 yards, mostly from Illini quarterback Jack Trudeau. Williams's top effort came in 1984 when he became the first (and only) Illini receiver to catch more than one hundred passes (101). Statistically, Illinois's No. 1 had his best individual game on October 12, 1985, against Purdue, when he set an Illini record with sixteen catches for 164 yards. Williams, one of three brothers who played for the Illini during the 1980s, was picked up in the third round of the 1986 NFL draft by the Chicago Bears, played with Tampa Bay and the Los Angeles Raiders his first two seasons as a pro. In 1988 he began a seven-year career in the Canadian Football League. In the fall of 1995 he returned to the University of Illinois to complete his bachelor's degree. Williams was inducted into the College Football Hall of Fame in 2005. Today, Williams is the manager at Jacquet West in Carson, California.

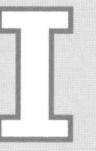

OTHER TOP MEN'S ATHLETES

1. Terry Dixon, swimming (Big Ten champion in 100-yard breaststroke)
2. Ken Norman, basketball (first-team All–Big Ten)
3. Guy Teafatiller, football (first-team All–Big Ten)
4. Steve Juengert, gymnastics (Big Ten champion on still rings)
5. Brad Wentz, baseball (first-team All–Big Ten)

1985–86

WOMEN'S ILLINI MOMENT

One of many celebrations at Kenney Gym in 1985

Volleyball's 1985 Season

No doubt about it, creaky old Kenney Gym on West Green Street in Urbana was the place to be in the fall of 1985. Behind the high-energy play of Lockport senior and first-team All–Big Ten pick Denise Fracaro and Aurora's conference Freshman of the Year Mary Eggers, Illinois's volleyball team streaked to thirty consecutive victories to open the season. The best crowd came on October 4, when a Big Ten attendance record crowd of 2,632 watched the Illini sweep Iowa. Two of only three losses for Big Ten Coach of the Year Mike Hebert's squad (39-3) came within a five-day stretch, including one to eventual Big Ten champ Purdue, 3–2. The Illini went on to win its next seven matches, gaining a berth in the 1985 NCAA tournament. Illinois disposed of host Western Michigan in its first appearance, 3–1, but was beaten in straight sets in Sweet Sixteen action against Southern California. Other key contributors to the Illini's success were sophomore Disa Johnson, a second-team all-conference selection, sisters Chris and Rita Schwarz, and kills specialists Sally Rea, Elizabeth Binkley, Sandy Scholtens, and Lori Anderson.

OTHER TOP MOMENTS

1. In record-setting performances at the 1986 Big Ten outdoor meet, Leticia Bevery won the 100-meter hurdles (0:13.48) and ran a leg on the 400-meter relay team (0:44.87).
2. Kelly McNee won Big Ten indoor mile title (4:48.64).
3. Illinois hosted the 1986 Big Ten golf championship.

WOMEN'S ILLINI LIST

BASKETBALL'S FIRST-TEAM ALL–BIG TEN HONOREES

1986, 1987	Jonelle Polk
1991	Sarah Sharp
1996, 1997, 1998	Ashley Berggren
1999	Susan Blauser
2000	Tauja Catchings
2000, 2001	Allison Curtin
2002	Iveta Marcauskaite
2005	Angelina Williams
2008, 2010	Jenna Smith
2013	Karisma Penn

Jonelle Polk

When Coach Mike Hebert took over Illinois's volleyball program in 1983, he inherited a roster that was, for the most part, devoid of Big Ten-caliber talent. Sophomore Denise (Fracaro) Juriga proved to be an exception. By the time her senior year rolled around in 1985, the program had evolved from "doormat" to "dominant." Juriga was a record-setting blocker from Lockport, Illinois, setting single-game (7), single-season (44) and career marks (499) for blocks. Additionally, she was named to UI's Senior 100 Class, a special award that honors students for leadership and academic qualities. It was at Illinois where she met her future husband, Illini football player Jim Juriga. Today, Denise manages the Valley Animal Hospital in Geneva, Illinois, where Jim serves as the chief veterinarian. She and Jim have three children.

Denise Fracaro

WOMEN'S ILLINI LEGEND

Jonelle (Polk) McCloud

Junior center Jonelle (Polk) McCloud became the first University of Illinois women's basketball player to earn first-team honors on the All–Big Ten squad. McCloud led the conference in scoring, with an average of 21.9 points per game, and also ranked among the leaders in numerous other statistical categories.

Despite being named Big Ten Player of the Week four times in 1985–86, McCloud was edged out by Ohio State's Tracy Hall as league Player of the Year. When she graduated from Illinois in 1987, the former Manual High School standout stood atop UI women's all-time scoring (1,984) and rebounding (833) records. Until Deon Thomas surpassed two thousand points in 1993–94, McCloud remained Illinois's all-time scoring leader for both men and women. She now manages Peoria's Proctor Recreation Center. McCloud, her husband, Daniel, and their two children reside in Peoria.

Jonelle Polk was Illinois's initial first-team All–Big Ten selection

OTHER TOP WOMEN'S ATHLETES

1. Mary Eggers, volleyball (first-team All–Big Ten)
2. Brenda Macconnachie, golf (first-team All–Big Ten)
3. Christy Flesvig, tennis (Big Ten Conference Medal of Honor recipient)
4. Kathy Neil, tennis (team MVP, set single-season record for doubles wins with 30)

ILLINI LORE

It wasn't a university-sponsored event, nor was it an athletic event, but probably the most noteworthy campus event of 1985–86 occurred at Memorial Stadium, September 22, 1985. The event's official name was "Farm Aid," and it was undoubtedly one of the most diversified collections of musical talent ever to gather at the Urbana-Champaign campus. The fourteen-hour concert was marred by rain and cold temperatures, but that didn't much bother the seventy-eight thousand fans who filled the stadium. Among the more than fifty stars of rock and roll, blues, and country who performed on the giant stage located at the north end of Zuppke Field were Willie Nelson (the event's co-organizer), Johnny Cash, Alabama, Billy Joel, the Beach Boys, Van Halen, B. B. King, and Kenny Rogers. More than $9 million in ticket sales, corporate donations, and private pledges was eventually used for cash grants to needy farmers.

Willie Nelson headlined "Farm Aid" in 1985 at Memorial Stadium

1986–87

AMERICA'S TIME CAPSULE

November 3, 1986   The Iran-Contra affair became public when a Lebanese magazine revealed that the United States had been secretly selling arms to Iran in hopes of securing the release of hostages held in Lebanon.

November 22, 1986   Twenty-year-old Mike Tyson became the youngest heavyweight boxing champion in history when he knocked out Trevor Berbick.

April 12, 1987   Larry Mize sank a fifty-yard wedge shot on the second hole of a three-way playoff against Greg Norman and Seve Ballesteros to win the Masters golf tournament.

August 16, 1987   A Northwest Airlines jet crashed on takeoff from the Detroit Metropolitan Airport, killing 156 of 157 passengers.

MEN'S ILLINI MOMENT

Douglas Sets Big Ten Assists Record

The Good Book clearly states, "Thou shalt not steal." However, former Illinois basketball star Bruce Douglas, a devout Christian, knew that the sixth of the Ten Commandments had nothing to do with what he did on the basketball court. The Quincy Blue Devils all-star used his nearly forty-inch sleeve length to regularly swipe the ball from his opponents, setting Illini single game (8), season (88) and career (324) totals in that category. Others who watched Douglas play might argue that his ability to pass the ball was his strength, as witnesses those UI records he set from 1983 to 1986. His individual success led to marvelous team results, including a Big Ten title (1984) and four consecutive appearances in the NCAA Tournament. Douglas became a minister shortly after his professional playing career ended. Today, Pastor Douglas serves Walking in Grace Community Church in Plainfield, Illinois. He is also president of "Shooting for Christ Ministry," a basketball camp and community outreach program. Bruce and his wife, Madge, have four sons.

Bruce Douglas deals a wrap-around assist

OTHER TOP MOMENTS

1. At the Big Ten indoor championships, Lane Lohr became the first Illini pole vaulter to top eighteen feet (18'1¼").
2. Illini football team upset sixteenth-ranked Iowa, 20–16.
3. The men's cross-country team placed seventh at the NCAA meet, its best finish in seventeen years.
4. Illinois retired football jersey number 50 in honor of Dick Butkus.
5. Gary and Carlotta Bielfeldt pledge $5 million for the Athletic Administration Building.

MEN'S ILLINI LIST

MEN'S BIG TEN GOLF MEDALISTS

1923	Rial Rolfe
1930, 1931	Richard Martin
1941	Alex Welsh
1942	James McCarthy
1962	Mike Toliuszis
1982	Mike Chadwick
1986,* 1988, 1989	Steve Stricker
1993	Jamie Fairbanks
1999*	Larry Nuger
2011, 2012	Luke Guthrie

Steve Stricker was a three-time Big Ten medalist

2013	Thomas Pieters
2014*	Charlie Danielson
2015*	Nick Hardy
2016	Thomas Detry

*Co-medalist

MEN'S ILLINI ITEM

Lou Henson's 1986–87 basketball team will forever be linked with a one-point loss to Austin Peay in the first-round of the NCAA tournament, but it was an outstanding team (23-8). The regular lineup featured three guards—Doug Altenberger, Tony Wysinger, and Glynn Blackwell—and big men Lowell Hamilton and Jens Kujawa, along with 6'8" forward Ken Norman, a second-team All-American honors and the Illini MVP. Norman was the nineteenth pick in the first round of the 1987 NBA draft.

Ken Norman and Doug Altenberger headlined the 1986–87 Illini

MEN'S ILLINI LEGEND

Darrin Fletcher

Darrin Fletcher excelled as a catcher, but his greatest notoriety came as a batsman, hitting a school-record .392 from 1985 to 1987, including a stunning .497 average his junior year. Fletcher held eight UI marks altogether and was named the 1986–87 Fighting Illini Male Athlete of the Year. He was chosen as the Big Ten's baseball Player of the Year, hitting .432 in conference play. Darrin was a sixth-round draft choice of the Los Angeles Dodgers in 1987, earning a spot on the parent club late in the 1989 season. He was traded to Philadelphia in 1990, and a year later was dealt from the Phillies to the Montreal Expos. The crowning moment of Fletcher's MLB career came in 1994, when he was selected as a member of the National League all-star team. When his fourteen-year big-league career ended in 2002 fol-

Darrin Fletcher

OTHER TOP MEN'S ATHLETES

1. Dave Halle, cross-country (All–Big Ten)
2. Phil Callahan, wrestling (earned All-American honors)
3. Graeme McGufficke, swimming (Big Ten Conference Medal of Honor recipient)

lowing five seasons with the Toronto Blue Jays, Fletcher's statistics included a .269 batting average, 124 home runs and 583 RBI. His son, Casey, was a 2015 All–Big Ten outfielder for the Illini. Darrin and his wife, Sheila, now reside in Oakwood.

1986–87

WOMEN'S ILLINI MOMENT

Nancy Brookhart (17) and Disa Johnson (10) were two of the stars of the 1986 Illini

Volleyball Wins Big Ten Title

Perfection in an eighteen-match, round-robin format had never before been accomplished by a Big Ten volleyball team, but that all changed in 1986. Coach Mike Hebert's Fighting Illini sailed through the conference portion of the season, sweeping to victory an unprecedented eighteen straight times, including three-games-to-none shutouts in thirteen of those matches. During the regular season, the Illini dropped matches only to fourth-ranked San Jose and sixth-ranked Nebraska.

Heading into the NCAA tournament with its 34-2 record, Illinois sported a twenty-four-match winning streak. The Mideast region's No. 2 seed easily disposed of Northern Iowa and Western Michigan in the first two rounds, but the Illini were eliminated in the semifinals by Nebraska in three consecutive games. Illinois athletes dominated the All–Big Ten squad as Player of the Year Mary Eggers, Disa Johnson, and Sally Rea all were named as first-teamers. Eggers also won first-team All-American honors.

OTHER TOP MOMENTS

1. Track and field team placed second at 1987 Big Ten outdoor championships, its best finish in official conference competition.
2. Basketball (19-10) qualified for the NCAA tournament, beating Bowling Green in the first round.
3. Gymnastics (11-6) set a record for victories in dual meets.

WOMEN'S ILLINI LIST

ILLINI WOMEN'S TRACK AND FIELD MULTIPLE BIG TEN INDIVIDUAL TITLISTS (through 2015)

25 titles	Tonja Buford (1990–1993)
20 titles	Tonya Williams (1993–1996)
19 titles	Celena Mondie-Milner (1987–1990)
15 titles	Yvonne Mensah (2004–2007)
14 titles	Renee Carr (1986–1990)
12 titles	Ashley Spencer (2012–2013)
11 titles	Leticia Beverly (1986–1989)
9 titles	Angela McClatchey (1986–1989)
8 titles	Carmel Corbett (1992–1995)
8 titles	Benita Kelley (1995–1998)

Renee Carr won fourteen Big Ten titles from 1986 to 1990

WOMEN'S ILLINI ITEM

May 23–24, 1987 The Fighting Illini track team placed second to Purdue at the Big Ten outdoor track and field championships in Iowa City, Iowa, its highest finish ever to that point. Coach Gary Winckler's squad racked up a school-record 112 points—just three points behind the Boilermakers. Sophomore Leticia Beverly claimed two individual titles, winning the 100-meter hurdles and the long jump, as well as leading off the victorious 400-meter relay unit. Victoria Fulcher was the only other Illini athlete who captured an individual championship, winning the 400-meter hurdles.

Victoria Fulcher takes the handoff

WOMEN'S ILLINI LEGEND

Denise (Lamborn) Van Horn

Fighting Illini freshman gymnast Denise (Lamborn) Van Horn made a bit of history in April 1987. The star from South Bend, Indiana's John Adams High School was the first Illinois women's gymnast to qualify for the national championships since women's athletes were recognized by the NCAA. Unfortunately, Van Horn was ill when she competed, and she struggled physically throughout the meet in Salt Lake City, Utah. Said Van Horn afterward, "I'm glad that I got to go even though I wasn't at my best."

She was a three-time All–Big Ten performer, winning the conference's vault title as a senior. It was one of thirty-eight individual events she won during three letter-winning seasons in 1987, 1988, and 1990. Today, Denise Van Horn resides in Southwest Florida.

Denise Lamborn

OTHER TOP WOMEN'S ATHLETES

1. Liz Grant, swimming (set school records in 200-meter, 500-meter, and 1,000-meter freestyle)
2. Jonelle Polk, basketball (Big Ten Conference Medal of Honor recipient)
3. Angie McClellan, basketball (single-season and career leader in steals)

ILLINI LORE

On November 8, 1986, a gala ball at Lincoln Hall capped off a week of festivities that marked the seventy-fifth anniversary of the World Heritage Museum. The museum's early development occurred under curators Neil Brooks and Arthur Pease. Its first full-time director was Oscar Dodson in the 1960s. Among the museum's most notable pieces are an original fragment from the Bible's Book of James, a large display of medieval and Renaissance armor, a page from the Gutenberg Bible, and Olympic memorabilia from the collection of University of Illinois graduate and track star Avery Brundage.

A scene at UI's World Heritage Museum

1987-88

AMERICA'S TIME CAPSULE

October 19, 1987	The worst stock-market crash in the recent history of the New York Stock Exchange occurred when the Dow Jones industrial average fell 508 points.
November 18, 1987	President Reagan was blamed for failing in his constitutional duty by the congressional committee report on the Iran-Contra affair.
February 5, 1988	A federal grand jury in Miami indicted Panamanian General Manuel Noriega in connection with illegal drug dealings.
April 23, 1988	A ban on smoking in passenger planes went into effect.
August 8, 1988	The first night baseball game in the history of Chicago's Wrigley Field took place, though it was rained out.

MEN'S ILLINI MOMENT

John Mackovic (center) with Chancellor Morton Weir (left) and Neale Stoner

White Out, Mackovic In

Just sixteen days separated the firing of Fighting Illini head football coach Mike White and the hiring of his replacement, John Mackovic. The furious chain of events began January 18, 1988, when White submitted his resignation to Director of Athletics Neale Stoner. An NCAA investigation into alleged recruiting violations prompted White's action. Said Interim Chancellor Morton Weir, "The Athletic Association's Board of Directors and I believe that Coach White has responded appropriately by tendering his resignation." The search for White's replacement began immediately, with a list of candidates that included Illini defensive coordinator Howard Tippett, former Northwestern coach Dennis Green, Boston College's Jack Bicknell, and Stoner's personal choice, ex–Kansas City Chiefs coach John Mackovic. The AA's board convened for more than three hours on February 2 before arriving at the decision to hire Mackovic. The forty-four-year-old Wake Forest graduate immediately went about hiring a staff and salvaging a nearly impossible recruiting scenario by signing eventual Illini standouts Brad Hopkins, Jason Verduzco, and John Wright.

OTHER TOP MOMENTS

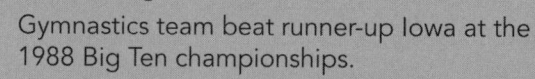

1. Illinois track-and-field squad swept indoor and outdoor Big Ten titles.
2. Gymnastics team beat runner-up Iowa at the 1988 Big Ten championships.
3. Illini basketball team won at Indiana, 75–65, giving Lou Henson his five-hundredth coaching-career win.

Lee Bridges

MEN'S ILLINI LIST

1988 TRACK AND FIELD CHAMPIONS

Rod Tolbert	55-meter dash (indoors)
Tim Simon	300-dash (indoors) and 400-meter dash (indoors and outdoors)
Lee Bridges	500-meter run (indoors) and 200-meter dash (outdoors)
Tolbert, Simon, Troy Heitmeyer and Bridges	1,600-meter relay (indoors)
Dean Starkey	Pole vault (indoors)
Charlton Hamer	800-meter run (outdoors)
Jon Thanos	3,000-meter steeplechase (outdoors)
Bryan Benso, Bridges, Hamer, and Simon	4x400-meter relay (outdoors)
Jerome Jenkins	Triple jump (outdoors)

MEN'S ILLINI ITEM

Illinois's men's golf team ended a forty-seven-year championship drought on May 16, 1988, when it defeated six-time Big Ten titlist Ohio State by twenty strokes. Illini junior Steve Stricker was named the conference's Player of the Year for firing a seventy-two-hole total 279 to outdistance teammate Mike Small and OSU's Chris Smith by fourteen shots. The triumph by Ed Beard's squad came at home on Savoy's Orange Course.

Steve Stricker captured Big Ten medalist honors by fourteen strokes in 1988

MEN'S ILLINI LEGEND

Tim Simon on the cover of *Athletic Journal* in May 1986

Tim Simon

Coach Gary Wieneke knew he had something special when he convinced Proviso East High School star Tim Simon to attend the University of Illinois. Not only was the sprinter/jumper an athlete with Olympic-caliber talent, he also was a brilliant student in the classroom. As an Illini freshman, Simon won All-American honors at the 1985 NCAA indoor championships when he finished third in the 400-meter run. He had a remarkable senior season at the national level, placing second in the 400 indoors and third outdoors. In Big Ten indoor competition, Simon won three individual titles and was a member of two first-place relays. Amazingly, Simon swept the Big Ten's Athlete of the Championship and won both of Illinois's top end-of-the-year awards, receiving the Dike Eddleman Male Athlete of the Year and the Big Ten Conference Medal of Honor. He earned a medical degree from Howard University in 1993, then performed his internship and residency in general surgery at Emory University. Dr. Simon has been a physician with Georgia Colon and Rectal Surgical Associates in metro Atlanta since 2002.

OTHER TOP MEN'S ATHLETES

1. Scott Davis, football (first-team All–Big Ten)
2. Dominick Minicucci, gymnastics (Big Ten all-around champion)
3. Kirk Azinger, wrestling (142-pound senior became UI's first individual Big Ten champion since 1961)

1987–88

WOMEN'S ILLINI MOMENT

Heather Singalewitch

Big Ten Gymnast of the Year

Heather (Singalewitch) Endre became the first Illinois women's athlete to be honored as the Big Ten Conference's Gymnast of the Year. The sophomore from Edison, New Jersey, shared the honor in 1988 with Minnesota's Marie Roethlisberger. At that meet, Endre also tied Minnesota's Lisa Wittwer for the all-around championship, with a 38.10 score, tied for second on the uneven bars (9.40), took third on the balance beam (9.60), and tied for third in the vault (9.50). One week prior to the 1990 Big Ten meet, Endre developed a lump on her neck, restricting her movement. Doctors in Champaign ultimately drained her neck of fluid on Wednesday of that week and released her to fly to Ann Arbor for Friday's championships. Somewhat miraculously, Heather helped her team not only win the Big Ten team title but also capture the individual floor exercise crown, with a 9.7 score. The Athletics Department rewarded her effort by naming her winner of the first-ever Female Illini Spirit Award. Today, she and husband, Mark Endre, reside in Leland, North Carolina, with their two sons.

OTHER TOP MOMENTS

1. Volleyball won Big Ten title, advanced to NCAA's Final Four.
2. Illinois track and field squad placed third in the Big Ten; five athletes earned All-American status.
3. Basketball upset No. 12 Vanderbilt and No. 13 Southern California.

WOMEN'S ILLINI LIST

BASKETBALL VICTORIES AGAINST HIGHLY RANKED TEAMS

vs. No. 3 Long Beach State, 97–91 (3OT) (January 13, 1982)
vs. No. 5 Georgia, 82–67 (January 2, 2000)
vs. No. 6 Georgia, 70–59 (December 28, 2012)
vs. No. 6 Notre Dame, 77–67 (November 27, 1999)
vs. No. 9 Kentucky, 77–71 (November 27, 2014)
vs. No. 10 Minnesota, 94–80 (January 1, 2003)
vs. No. 10 Penn State, 75–71 (January 1, 2001)
vs. No. 10 Arkansas, 100–81 (January 1, 1997)
vs. No. 11 Wisconsin, 83–75 (December 30, 1997)
vs. No. 12 Michigan, 85–81 (December 28, 2001)

vs. No. 12 Penn State, 88–80 (December 6, 1986)
vs. No. 12 Iowa, 78–68 (March 6, 1986)

Letecia Beverly

WOMEN'S ILLINI LEGEND

Mary Eggers

Mary (Eggers) Tendler

Wrote one sports journalist, Mary Eggers "stalks the court with an icy look of controlled violence that combines the cool of Star Trek's Mr. Spock with the rage of a pit bull." That analogy aptly described the woman who went on to become the most prolific player in University of Illinois volleyball history.

From Big Ten Freshman of the Year in 1985 to conference MVP from 1986 to 1988, no one individual dominated the court quite like Tendler. She led the nation in hitting percentage her sophomore and senior seasons and set Fighting Illini career records for aces, blocks, kills, and attack percentage. The four Illini teams on which she played had a cumulative record of 136 victories against only seventeen losses for a winning percentage of .889. Tendler's crowning glory came following her senior season in 1988, when she earned the Honda Broderick Award as the nation's top collegiate volleyball player. Following her graduation in 1991, she played professional volleyball in Europe. Since 2003 Tendler has been the head volleyball coach at Elon University. She and her husband, Blaine, reside in Burlington, North Carolina.

OTHER TOP WOMEN'S ATHLETES

1. Justi Rae Miller, golf (All–Big Ten)
2. Victoria Fulcher, track and field (Big Ten champion in 400-meter dash and 400-meter high hurdles)
3. Disa Johnson, volleyball (Big Ten Conference Medal of Honor recipient)
4. Melissa Straza, cross-country (All–Big Ten)

ILLINI LORE

Chancellor Morton Weir

Morton W. Weir, interim chancellor at the Urbana-Champaign campus since August 1987, was unanimously approved as permanent chancellor by the University of Illinois Board of Trustees on April 14, 1988. His appointment vacated the post left by former chancellor Thomas Everhart, who left the U of I to become president of Cal Tech. Weir also served as Illinois's acting chancellor between the terms of former chancellors Jack Peltason and William Gerberding. Among the previous positions held by Weir at the U of I were head of the Psychology Department, vice chancellor of administrative affairs, and vice president of academic affairs. He stepped down as chancellor in 1992 to return to classroom duties and part-time service with the University of Illinois Foundation.

1988–89

AMERICA'S TIME CAPSULE

September 29, 1988   NASA launched its first manned space flight in thirty-two months, carrying a $100 million communications satellite.

November 8, 1988   Vice President George Bush defeated Governor Michael Dukakis of Massachusetts in the presidential election.

January 22, 1989   The San Francisco 49ers defeated the Cincinnati Bengals, 20–16, in Super Bowl XXIII. Joe Montana passed for a record 357 yards as the 49ers won their third Super Bowl title.

March 24, 1989   The oil tanker Exxon Valdez struck a reef in Prince William Sound, Alaska, leaking more than a million barrels of crude oil into the water.

MEN'S ILLINI MOMENT

(Left to right) Lowell Hamilton, Stephen Bardo, Kenny Battle, Kendall Gill, and Nick Anderson

The Flying Illini

To Many Illini fans, the 1988–89 men's basketball squad is the standard by which other Illini teams are measured. Coach Henson's athletes rolled through the regular season with a 27-4 record, including victories in their first seventeen games. That seventeenth win, a 103–92 double-overtime victory against Georgia Tech at the Assembly Hall on January 22, catapulted the Illini to the top of the national rankings. Unfortunately, the bad news in that contest against the Yellowjackets was an injury to Kendall Gill, which triggered three Illinois losses in the next four games. Strong play by fellow all-star Nick Anderson, co-captains Kenny Battle and Lowell Hamilton, and sophomore Marcus Liberty kept the Illini going until Gill returned with two games left in the regular season. The Illini beat Iowa and Michigan, finishing with a 14-4 conference record, and entered the NCAA tournament as the No. 1 seed in Midwest regional play. There they easily disposed of McNeese State and Ball State. In the third-round battle against Louisville, a strong effort by Liberty helped Illinois overcome an injury to Hamilton, and the Illini beat the Cardinals, 72–60. In the regional finals against Syracuse, Anderson came up with his most impressive game, scoring twenty-four points and grabbing sixteen rebounds as Illinois beat the Orangemen, 89–86, to qualify for the Final Four in Seattle. The April 1 semifinal pitted the Illini against Michigan, a team they had already overcome twice during the regular season. Unfortunately, the third time was a charm for the Wolverines, and Michigan prevailed 83–81 to knock the Illini out of their chance to win a national title. After the season, Anderson, Illinois's Most Valuable Player, announced that he was going to forego his final year of college eligibility to enter the NBA draft.

OTHER TOP MOMENTS

1. Coach Gary Wieneke's track-and-field squad won both the indoor and outdoor Big Ten championships for the third consecutive season.
2. Baseball claimed its first Big Ten title since 1953.
3. Gymnastics won its second-straight conference championship.

MEN'S ILLINI LIST

JIMMY COLLINS AND DICK NAGY'S TOP FIVE MEMORIES OF THE 1988–89 SEASON

Lou Henson's longtime assistants, Jimmy Collins and Dick Nagy, chose their top five memories of the 1988–89 "Flying Illini."

Assistant coaches Jimmy Collins (left) and Dick Nagy (center)

1. March 26 vs. Syracuse: The Illini earned a spot in the Final Four.

2. December 19 vs. Missouri: Kenny Battle scored twenty-eight points as UI improves record to 8–0. The Illini overcame an eighteen-point deficit.

3. March 4 at Indiana: Nick Anderson hit a miracle three-pointer to beat the Hoosiers.

4. March 24 vs. Louisville: Illinois won its thirtieth game behind Anderson's twenty-four points.

5. January 22 vs. Georgia Tech: Illini earned No. 1 ranking with a two-overtime win.

MEN'S ILLINI ITEM

With Illinois trailing Indiana by eleven points (20–9), Fighting Illini football fortunes looked hopeless at Memorial Stadium on November 5, 1988. Coach John Mackovic's squad narrowed the Hoosier lead to 20–15 on a grab by Shawn Wax from quarterback Jeff George with 1:27 remaining. Then, Illini linebacker Julyon Brown picked off an interception. With just twenty-six ticks left, George threw a game-winning TD pass to Mike Bellamy, helping the Illini escape, 21–20.

Mike Bellamy makes the game-winning catch vs. Indiana

MEN'S ILLINI LEGEND

David Zeddies

David Zeddies

The most well-known individual athletic award presented to an intercollegiate athlete during any given year is undoubtedly the Heisman Trophy, symbolic of the outstanding college football player in America. Perhaps one of the least-known single prizes in college athletics is the Nissen Award, emblematic of the top male gymnast. So, during the 1988–89 season, while Oklahoma State gridiron star Barry Sanders was picking up his hardware in New York City, Illinois gymnast David Zeddies was doing much the same on April 12, 1989, in Lincoln, Nebraska. Zeddies, a native of Union Springs, New York, became the Illini's first Nissen Award winner since the prize was initiated in 1966. He combined his marvelous athletic ability with sportsmanship and leadership and was also an outstanding scholar. Zeddies excelled on the rings and the parallel bars, earning 1988 Big Ten Gymnast of the Year honors and helping to lead Coach Yoshi Hayasaki's Illini squad to the 1989 NCAA title. He earned his doctorate at Northwestern University and currently serves as a senior scientist for JASCO Applied Sciences in Silver Spring, Maryland.

OTHER TOP MEN'S ATHLETES

1. Bubba Smith, baseball (Big Ten Player of the Year and Freshman of the Year)

2. Moe Gardner, Darrick Brownlow, and Glenn Cobb, football (first-team All–Big Ten)

3. Steve Stricker, golf (Big Ten medalist)

1988–89

WOMEN'S ILLINI MOMENT

Illini Win Title with Record Point Total

Illinois's women's track-and-field squad captured the 1989 outdoor title at IUPUI Track Stadium in Indianapolis with a record-setting 169 points, thirty-one more than any other previous champion had registered in the eight-year history of the meet. Fighting Illini athletes captured titles in eleven of the nineteen events, including four by Celena Mondie-Milner (100- and 200-meter dashes and 400- and 1,600-meter relays). Predictably, eight of the sixteen athletes who earned All-Big Ten honors were Illini. Joining Mondie-Milner were Shayla Baine, Lisa Balagtas, Leticia Beverly, Renee Carr, Cindy Lawrence, Angela McClatchey, and Debbie Smith.

(Clockwise from left) Celena Mondie-Milner, Letecia Beverly, Renee Carr, and Angela McClatchey

OTHER TOP MOMENTS

1. Volleyball posted a perfect 18-0 record and won its third consecutive Big Ten title.
2. Senior golfer Justi Rae Miller earned All-Big Ten honors for second-straight season.
3. Basketball upset twentieth-ranked Illinois State, 74–70.

WOMEN'S ILLINI LIST

VOLLEYBALL ALL-AMERICANS

Nancy Brookhart (background)

First Team

Mary Eggers, 1986, 1987, 1988

Kirsten Gleis, 1992

Erin Borske, 1995

Laura DeBruler, 2009

Colleen Ward, 2011

Second Team

Nancy Brookhart, 1987, 1988, 1989

Laura Bush, 1989

Second Team, continued

Tina Rogers, 1992

Laura DeBruler, 2008

Colleen Ward, 2010

Jocelynn Birks, 2014

WOMEN'S ILLINI ITEM

Theodore Roosevelt High School in Gary, Indiana, has had a history of producing amazing athletes. NBA stars such as Dick Barnett and Glenn Robinson, football greats like George Taliaferro and Gerald Irons, and Olympic gold medal winners Charles Adkins and Lee Calhoun. In the mid-1980s, future Illini Angela McClatchey had her time in Roosevelt High's spotlight. As a sprinter extraordinaire at Illinois, the 4x100- and 4x400-meter relay teams with whom she ran won an amazing nine Big Ten titles. Those same teams won All-American acclaim seven times at NCAA meets. Today, McClatchey lives in North Carolina and serves as the banquet captain at the Charlotte Convention Center.

Angela McClatchey

WOMEN'S ILLINI LEGEND

Gary Winckler

Gary Winckler

Arguably, Gary Winckler is the greatest women's team coach in University of Illinois history. On three different occasions, he's been chosen as NCAA Coach of the Year (1984, 1985, and 1989), and eleven times his peers have selected him as Big Ten Coach of the Year. From 1985 through 2008 Winckler's Illini athletes won 266 individual conference titles. Fifty-one competitors earned All-American recognition 188 times. Thirteen different ladies qualified for the Olympic Games in the sprints, hurdle relays and won gold, silver, and bronze medals. Ninety-seven percent of his student-athletes graduated; seventy-four of them received Academic All–Big Ten awards 156 times. The list of individuals Winckler tutored reads like a "Who's Who" of track and field. The group includes Tonja Buford-Bailey, Perdita Felicien, Celena Mondie-Milner, Aspen Burkett, Yvonne Harrison, Susanna Kallur, and Tonya Williams. In 2009 Winckler was inducted into the Hall of Fame for the United States Track and Field Coaches Association. Raised as a farmer and rancher in central Washington state, and today he designs and produces handmade saddles at WS Saddles in Couer d'Alene, Idaho.

OTHER TOP WOMEN'S ATHLETES

1. Mary Eggers, volleyball (first-team All-American and Athlete of the Year)
2. Nancy Brookhart, volleyball (second-team All-American)
3. Chris Schwarz, volleyball (Big Ten Conference Medal of Honor recipient)

ILLINI LORE

The Beckman Center was dedicated April 7, 1989, just two-and-one-half years after the groundbreaking ceremonies. The new home for the executive and scientific staffs of the National Center for Supercomputing Applications had a $50 million price tag, $40 million of which was donated by philanthropist Arnold Beckman ('22). Located on University Avenue between Wright Street and Mathews Avenue, the 310,000-square-foot facility is on the same site as Illinois Field, home of Illini football through most of 1923 and Illini baseball through 1987.

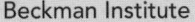
Beckman Institute

1989-90

AMERICA'S TIME CAPSULE

September 21, 1989 — Hurricane Hugo ravaged Charleston, South Carolina, causing more than $1 billion in damage.

October 17, 1989 — An earthquake measuring 6.9 on the Richter scale hit the San Francisco Bay area, killing more than sixty people.

February 28, 1990 — African National Congress leader Nelson Mandela met with President George H. W. Bush just two weeks after Mandela's release from a twenty-seven-year imprisonment in South Africa.

May 31, 1990 — Mikhail Gorbachev met with President Bush in a Washington summit.

August 7, 1990 — American troops, responding to the crisis in the Middle East, left for Saudi Arabia as Operation Desert Storm began.

MEN'S ILLINI MOMENT

Mike Bellamy (2) and Jeff George (11) celebrated after the 31–21 Florida Citrus Bowl victory

Illini Bowl Over Virginia

For the first time in more than a quarter-century, Illinois's football team began its season with a win and ended it with a bowl-game victory. At one time, the 1989 campaign was scheduled to begin several thousand miles away in Moscow, Russia, with the first-ever Glasnost Bowl, but a last-minute change in plans placed the Fighting Illini instead at the Los Angeles Coliseum against highly ranked Southern Cal. A national television audience on Labor Day night witnessed one of the most exciting comebacks in UI history when quarterback Jeff George tossed a pair of fourth quarter touchdowns to Shawn Wax and Steven Williams. The 14–13 triumph over the Trojans began a string of seven Illini successes in its first eight games, highlighted by Illinois's second-straight win over Ohio State, George's triumphant return to Purdue, a miracle victory at Michigan State, and a decisive 31–7 pasting of the Iowa Hawkeyes at Kinnick Stadium. On November 11 at Memorial Stadium, Illinois hosted Michigan for the inside track to the Big Ten championship. However, for the second year in a row the Illini stumbled, forcing them to refocus their sights on a second-place conference finish and a berth in the Florida Citrus Bowl. Mackovic's talented troops, led by a defensive unit that featured five future pros (Moe Gardner, Henry Jones, Mel Agee, Chris Green, and Darrick Brownlow), easily disposed of Indiana and Northwestern, and the Illini began packing for Orlando. The team climbed on the plane at Champaign, where the wind chill was a brutal fifty degrees below zero, and were similarly greeted by Florida's worst cold snap in years. But, like the weather, the Illini eventually warmed up to their task, defeating 10–1 Virginia by a score of 31-21. The pinpoint passes of game MVP George to his trusty receiver, Mike Bellamy, ended a twenty-six-year bowl victory drought and lifted the Illini to tenth in the final national rankings with a 10-2 record. It would prove to be the final time that Jeff George would wear an Illini uniform, as he declared for the NFL draft and became the first overall pick of his hometown Indianapolis Colts.

OTHER TOP MOMENTS

1. Coach Augie Garrido's Illini baseball team won the Big Ten Tournament title.

2. Heavyweight Jon Llewellyn captured the Big Ten wrestling championship for second consecutive year.

3. No. 5 Illinois topped No. 4 Missouri in basketball's Braggin' Rights Game.

I

MEN'S ILLINI LIST

ILLINI WHO WERE FIRST-ROUND NBA DRAFT PICKS

1951	Don Sunderlage, 9th pick, Philadelphia Warriors
1954	John Kerr, 6th pick, Syracuse Nationals
1957	George BonSalle, 7th pick, Syracuse Nationals
1970	Mike Price, 17th pick, New Jersey Knicks
1973	Nick Weatherspoon, 13th pick, Washington Bullets
1983	Derek Harper, 11th pick, Dallas Mavericks
1987	Ken Norman, 19th pick, Los Angeles Clippers
1989	Nick Anderson, 11th pick, Orlando Magic
1989	Kenny Battle, 27th pick, Detroit Pistons
1990	Kendall Gill, 5th pick, Charlotte Hornets

Nick Anderson

2002	Frank Williams, 25th pick, Denver Nuggets
2003	Brian Cook, 24th pick, Los Angeles Lakers
2005	Deron Williams, 3rd pick, Utah Jazz
2005	Luther Head, 24th pick, Houston Rockets
2012	Meyers Leonard, 11th pick, Portland Trail Blazers

MEN'S ILLINI ITEM

A finalist for both the Outland Award and the Lombardi Trophy, Moe Gardner was a fourth-round pick of the Atlanta Falcons in 1991. After his six-year NFL career ended, Gardner went back to school at Georgia State Community College, studying African American Culture. Eventually, he became manager and senior librarian at Atlanta's Auburn Avenue Research Library on African American Culture and History, where he arranges lectures, events, and exhibitions.

Moe Gardner

MEN'S ILLINI LEGEND

Kendall Gill

Kendall Gill

Kendall Gill joined Coach Lou Henson's Illini basketball team as the sleeper of Illinois's 1985 recruits, but left as the Big Ten's scoring leader (1990) and a first-team All-American. Gill proved to be one of the sparkplugs on Illinois's famed "Flying Illini" team of 1988–89. That squad glided to a 17-0 start and the nation's No. 1 ranking, but a broken bone in his foot sidelined Gill for twelve games. Upon Gill's return to the lineup, the Illini quickly regrouped and rolled through Indianapolis and Minneapolis into the Final Four. Upon completion of his UI career in 1989–90, Gill wound up his career as the school's seventh all-time leading scorer, with 1,409 points. Selected in the first round of the 1990 NBA draft by the Charlotte Hornets, he played through the 2004–05 season for eight different teams, scoring 12,914 points. Gill now works for Comcast Sports Net and serves as an analyst for Chicago Bulls telecasts. He's raised millions of dollars for the Cunningham Children's Home in Urbana.

OTHER TOP MEN'S ATHLETES

1. Darrick Brownlow, football (runner-up for the Butkus Award)
2. Mark Dalesandro, baseball (Big Ten Player of the Year)
3. John Murray, tennis (Big Ten Conference Medal of Honor recipient)
4. Brian Roberts, baseball (first-team All–Big Ten)
5. Len Sitko, cross-country (All–Big Ten)
6. Trevor Beard, golf (All–Big Ten)
7. Andy McVea, swimming (All–Big Ten)

1989–90

WOMEN'S ILLINI MOMENT

Peggy Pullman

Illini Gymnasts Reach the Summit

In March 1990 the Fighting Illini women's gymnastics team captured its first-ever official Big Ten title, nipping Michigan State and Minnesota in a championship where only four points separated the first- and last-place teams. Coach Bev Mackes's squad boasted four individual titlists, including Denise Lamborn in the vault, Peggy Pullman and Laura Knutson on the balance beam, and Heather Singalewitch in floor exercise. Mackes earned honors as Big Ten Coach of the Year.

OTHER TOP MOMENTS

1. Volleyball beat No. 1 Ohio State in NCAA Mideast regional semifinal at Kenney Gym.
2. Track and field finished runner-up at Big Ten indoor and outdoor championships.
3. Basketball squad upset No. 18 St. Joseph's, 78–65.

WOMEN'S ILLINI LIST

WOMEN'S BIG TEN COACHES OF THE YEAR

Tonja Buford-Bailey, track and field (2013)

Theresa Grentz, basketball (1997, 1998)

Don Hardin, volleyball (2001, 2003)

Mike Hebert, volleyball (1985, 1986, 1988)

Bev Mackes, gymnastics (1990)

Janet Rayfield, soccer (2011)

Bob Starkell, gymnastics (2005, 2009, 2010)

Terri Sullivan, softball (2010)

Mary Tredennick, tennis (1987)

Gary Winckler, track and field (indoors—1989, 1992, 1993, 1995, 1996; outdoors—1988, 1989, 1992, 1995, 2005, 2007)

UI's Gary Winckler was named Big Ten Coach of the Year eleven times

University of Illinois track-and-field alum Celena Mondie-Milner won 19 Big Ten titles and 18 All-America honors during her spectacular career (1987–1990). As a freshman, she ran a leg on Illinois's indoor and outdoor 4x100-meter relay teams. Four more conference titles came her way in 1988. As a junior, Mondie-Milner added six more Big Ten titles as a sprinter. Finally, in 1990, she won four individual and three relay championships. Mondie-Milner earned her PhD in educational leadership from Mercer University in May 2016.

Celena Mondie-Milner

WOMEN'S ILLINI LEGEND

Laura Bush

The numbers tell the story about Laura Bush's volleyball career. As a player from 1987 to 1990, her Illini teams won nearly 82 percent of their Big Ten matches (59–13), earned a pair of Big Ten championships, and racked up an 8–4 record in four consecutive NCAA tournament appearances. She's gone to the Final Four a total of four times with three different Big Ten programs, including once each as an assistant coach with Michigan State (1995) and Minnesota (2009). As a junior middle blocker in 1989, Bush won first-team All–Big Ten and second-team All-American laurels, then was accorded Female Athlete of the Year honors for the 1989–90 season. Between assistant coach stints with the Spartans (1993–1998) and Golden Gophers (2008–2015, including interim head coaching duties from 2011 to 2012), she was head coach at Marquette (1999–2002) and Auburn (2002–2007). Since 2015, Bush has been an executive coach and consultant for the LB Group and a color analyst for ESPN. She currently resides in Minneapolis, Minnesota.

Laura Bush

OTHER TOP WOMEN'S ATHLETES

1. Laura Knutson and Peggy Pullman, gymnastics (co-champs, Big Ten balance beam)
2. Lia Biehl, golf (All–Big Ten)
3. Renee Carr, track and field (three-time Big Ten champion)

ILLINI LORE

Celebrating its 120st anniversary in 2016, the University of Illinois Observatory earned the designation of a National Historic Landmark in December of 1989, placing it alongside the Brooklyn Bridge, Carnegie Hall, and the Alamo. The observatory's twelve-inch refracting telescope, first used in 1896, is still being used by UI students for viewing the heavens and for instruction in general astronomy. In 2013 and 2014 the observatory's telescope and dome were refurbished.

The University of
Illinois Observatory

1990–91

AMERICA'S TIME CAPSULE

November 8, 1990	President Bush doubled U.S. forces in the Persian Gulf region to nearly half a million troops.
January 16, 1991	U.S. and allied planes attacked Iraq's communications systems and chemical weapons plants.
February 27, 1991	The United States and Allied forces claimed an overwhelming victory, pushing back the Iraqi Republican Guard during the Gulf War.
March 3, 1991	Los Angeles policemen stopped and beat African American motorist Rodney King; an observer recorded the event on videotape.
June 12, 1991	Michael Jordan led the Chicago Bulls to their first-ever NBA championship, beating the Los Angeles Lakers, four games to one.

MEN'S ILLINI MOMENT

(Left to right) Marlon Primous, Henry Jones, Moe Gardner, Coach John Mackovic, Darrick Brownlow, Curt Lovelace, and Mel Agee

Illini Football Celebrates Its Centennial Season

Coach John Mackovic's Fighting Illini shared the Big Ten football title with Iowa, Michigan, and Michigan State in 1990, but that championship isn't what that season will be remembered for by most University of Illinois gridiron fans. The 1990 season was highlighted by the centennial celebration of Illini football, the largest athletic promotion ever staged at the Urbana-Champaign campus. The symbol of the event was a logo designed by UI student Rebecca Byrne, depicting a silhouette of Red Grange and the columns of Memorial Stadium. Among the key elements of the centennial were a traveling display of Illini football memorabilia that visited forty-four locations around the state of Illinois; a historical book and video; banners on the street lights surrounding and leading to the stadium that featured each of the one hundred years of Illini football; and a twenty-five-man All-Century Team that was selected by more than ten thousand UI fans. Each of the six home games in 1990 honored a different segment of Illini football, with more than five hundred former UI gridiron stars ultimately returning to their alma mater and being individually introduced to their adoring fans. Said one Illini football alumnus, "It was a thrill to once again walk onto the field, this time in the presence of my wife, son, and daughter."

OTHER TOP MOMENTS

1. Senior nose tackle Moe Gardner was named a consensus All-American for the second straight year.

2. Golf's Trevor Beard shot a record-low sixty-four at the Big Ten championship.

3. Basketball's Andy Kaufmann posted consecutive forty-point games, missing UI's single-season points record by eight.

4. On April 30, 1991, against UI-Chicago, junior first baseman Bubba Smith collected six hits in seven at-bats, including a record four home runs and ten RBI.

MEN'S ILLINI LIST

HOWARD GRIFFITH'S NCAA RECORD EIGHT TOUCHDOWNS

On September 22, 1990, Illinois's Howard Griffith became the first player in NCAA Division IA football to score eight touchdowns in a single game. He broke the record of seven TDs by Mississippi's Arnold Boykin, set against Mississippi State in 1951. Here's a score-by-score description of Griffith's explosion versus Southern Illinois at Memorial Stadium:

The record-breaking performance of Howard Griffith

First TD: 5-yard burst off right tackle, 10:06 left in 1st quarter.

Second TD: 51-yards up the middle, 8:50 left in 2nd quarter.

Third TD: 7-yard up-the-middle run, 4:53 left in 2nd quarter.

Fourth TD: 41-yard dash, left side, 3:10 left in 2nd quarter.

Fifth TD: 5-yard run off right tackle, 12:34 left in 3rd quarter.

Sixth TD: 18-yard, tackle-breaker, 10:10 left in 3rd quarter.

Seventh TD: 5-yard run off right tackle, 6:07 left in 3rd quarter.

Eighth TD: 3-yard dive off right tackle, 1:25 left in 3rd quarter.

MEN'S ILLINI ITEM

His offensive-line mentor, Mike Deal, called Tim Simpson the best run-blocker he'd ever coached. Simpson, offensive tackle Brad Hopkins, and center Curt Lovelace systematically opened gaping holes for UI's record-setting running back Howard Griffith. Simpson's NFL career included his appearance in the Pittsburgh Steelers' 1994 AFC championship game. In addition to a supervisory career with Caterpillar since 1997, he continued to play professionally and eventually got into coaching.

Tim Simpson

MEN'S ILLINI LEGEND

Jon Llewellyn

As a freshman wrestler at Hinsdale Central High School in suburban Chicago, Jon Llewellyn was a ninety-eight-pound weakling. But seven years later, he rose to the title of NCAA heavyweight champion. "I took my lumps as a 98-pounder," Llewellyn confessed. "I never dreamed of becoming a national champion. I put in my time lifting weights and working out. I would eat all the time, even when I didn't want to." From 1988 to 1991, the 240-pound heavyweight was the only shining light in the Illini wrestling program. Three times—as a sophomore, junior, and senior—Llewellyn won the league title, setting an Illinois record in that weight class. His most glorious season came as a senior in 1990–91 when he rolled through his competition with a perfect 33–0 record, boosting his career record to ninety-seven wins against only twenty-three losses and three draws. Llewellyn's ultimate accomplishment came March 13, 1991, when he beat defending champion Kurt Angle of Clarion State, 6–3, at the NCAA championships in Iowa City, Iowa. Later that spring, he was honored as Illinois's Male Athlete of the Year, beating out two-time football All-American Moe Gardner. Today, Llewellyn, his wife, Kara, and four children reside in Perrysburg, Ohio.

Jon Llewellyn

OTHER TOP MEN'S ATHLETES

1. Ricardo Cheriel, gymnastics (All–Big Ten)
2. Aaron Mobarek, track and field (Big Ten Conference Medal of Honor recipient)
3. Scott Turner, track and field (Big Ten Freshman of the Year)

1990-91

WOMEN'S ILLINI MOMENT

UI volleyball's first match at Huff Hall

Magic Returns to Huff Hall

Long known as the home of "March Madness" when it served as the site for Illinois's annual high school basketball championships, Huff Hall became the home of Illini volleyball on September 4, 1990. On hand for the opening festivities were the five men who provided the old gymnasium with its greatest basketball memories—Illinois's famed "Whiz Kids." The quintet of Jack Smiley, Ken Menke, Andy Phillip, Art Mathiesen, and Gene Vance joined volleyball co-captains Barb Winsett and Laura Bush, plus coach Mike Hebert, at center court for the traditional ribbon cutting. The Illini spikers then disposed of Southern Illinois in four games. Through the 2016 season, Illinois's volleyball team has won 281 of 392 matches at Huff Hall.

OTHER TOP MOMENTS

1. At the Outdoor Track and Field Championship, sophomore Tonja Buford was named Big Ten Athlete of the Year.
2. Tennis sophomore Lindsey Nimmo earned her first of three Illini MVP awards.
3. Track and field's Laura Simmering won the one-mile run at the Big Ten indoor championship.

WOMEN'S ILLINI LIST

GOLF'S ALL–BIG TEN SELECTIONS

Sandy Sutton, 1982, 1984

Brenda Macconnachie, 1986

Justie Rae Miller, 1988, 1989

Lia Biehl, 1990, 1991

Renee Heiken, 1991, 1992, 1993

Becky Biehl, 1992, 1993, 1994, 1995

Seul Ki Park, 2008 (second team)

Ember Schuldt, 2014 (second team)

Bing Singhsumalee 2016 (second team)

Renee Heiken (left) and Becky Biehl

An All–Big Ten performer in both 1990 and 1991, Lia (Biehl) Lukkarinen was also a star in the classroom, earning Academic All–Big Ten honors three times. Now married to Mike Lukkarinen, Lia spent two years on the Future's Tour, where she won one tournament and placed among the top six in earnings. In 1994 she played as an exempt player on the LGPA tour, including the 1994 U.S. Women's Open. In 2001 she returned to Illinois and served as Paula Smith's assistant. Lukkarinen became head coach at WIU in 2005. She and her husband have two children.

Lia Biehl

WOMEN'S ILLINI LEGEND

Sarah Sharp

Sarah Sharp was Chicago Robeson High School's go-to scorer. Of the Public League record 2,574 points she scored as a prep, sixty-two came in a single game vs. Bogan High in December 1985. Illini coach Laura Golden started her only twice during her freshman season at Illinois, instead relying on the point production of Lisa Bradley and Dee Dee Deeken. After that first year, however, Sharp regained her status as a shooter, averaging 16.7 points per game as a sophomore, then 15.5 and 18.0 averages in her final two seasons. When she finished her Illini career in 1991, Sharp ranked fourth on the school's all-time list, with 1,516 points, fourth in rebounding (644) and third in steals (180).

Sarah Sharp

OTHER TOP WOMEN'S ATHLETES

1. Renee Heiken, golf (Athlete of the Year and Big Ten medalist)
2. Petra Laverman, volleyball (team MVP)
3. Lynn Devers, gymnastics (Big Ten uneven parallel bars champ and Big Ten Conference Medal of Honor recipient)

She was accorded Most Valuable Player honors as a junior and senior, and she shared Illinois's Female Athlete of the Year honors in 1991 with golfer Renee Heiken. In 2009 Sharp was inducted into the Illinois Basketball Coaches Association Hall of Fame.

ILLINI LORE

On November 7, 1990, despite finding Illinois not guilty of any of the original charges brought against the men's basketball program, the NCAA levied harsh penalties against the university. Based on what it called "lack of institutional control" and a third appearance by the school in the previous six years before the infractions committee, the NCAA issued a three-year probation for Coach Henson's program. The coaching staff was originally accused of offering money and a car to recruit Deon Thomas, but they were eventually exonerated of any unethical conduct. Chancellor Morton Weir acknowledged some procedural and administrative shortcomings in the basketball program but was disturbed by the NCAA's labeling of "lack of institutional control." "Over the past five years or so," said Weir, "the university has taken extraordinary measures to ensure the integrity of intercollegiate athletics on this campus. Our record in recent years demonstrates that we do not hesitate to take the strongest actions when they are warranted."

Deon Thomas (left) and attorney Steve Beckett

1991–92

AMERICA'S TIME CAPSULE

September 9, 1991   Boxing champ Mike Tyson was indicted on rape charges by a Marion County (Indiana) grand jury.

November 7, 1991   Basketball's Magic Johnson retired after announcing that he had tested positive for HIV.

December 25, 1991   Mikhail Gorbachev resigned his position as leader of the Soviet Union.

May 1, 1992   President George H. W. Bush ordered federal troops to enter riot-torn Los Angeles. The unrest was triggered when a jury acquitted four policemen charged with beating Rodney King.

May 22, 1992   More than fifty million television viewers tuned in to watch Johnny Carson's final appearance on *The Tonight Show*.

MEN'S ILLINI MOMENT

Tepper Promoted after Mackovic Leaves for Texas

Lou Tepper's first game as the Illini coach was at the John Hancock Bowl

In a whirlwind twenty-four-hour period, Illinois's football program lost one head coach and hired another. Rumors had constantly circulated around the status of Athletic Director/Head Coach John Mackovic, and on December 12, 1991, the highly regarded Illini mentor was hired by the University of Texas. Quickly, Chancellor Morton Weir and interim AD Bob Todd promoted Lou Tepper the very next day as Mackovic's replacement. "We knew we had the right person right here on campus," said Weir. "Lou is a man of integrity, with a strong orientation toward the academic success of student athletes." The forty-six-year-old Tepper pledged his long-term commitment toward the university, saying, "If I had just wanted to be a head coach, I could have done so several years ago. That was not my goal. My goal was to be a head coach at a prestigious institution and to be at one institution for a very long time." Tepper didn't need to wait the customary nine months to coach his first game, as he directed the Illini eighteen days later in their December 31 John Hancock Bowl matchup against UCLA. The Illini lost to the Bruins, 6–3. Tepper would coach five full seasons at Illinois, recording a 25-31-2 mark. Today, Lou and his wife, Karen, reside in Lake Oconee, Georgia, near their daughter Stacy and son Matt.

OTHER TOP MOMENTS

1. Ron Guenther was named director of athletics, replacing interim AD Bob Todd (May 14, 1992).

2. Illinois hired Mark Johnson as its wrestling coach.

3. Deon Thomas's twenty-six points, plus seventeen points and ten assists from Rennie Clemons, led the Illini past No. 12 Michigan State, 80–71.

MEN'S ILLINI LIST

FIRST-TEAM ALL–BIG TEN OFFENSIVE LINE (since 1990)

1990	Curt Lovelace, center
1991	Tim Simpson, guard
1992	Brad Hopkins, tackle
2001	Jay Kulaga, guard
2001, 2002	Tony Pashos, tackle
2007	Martin O'Donnell, guard

Tony Pashos

MEN'S ILLINI ITEM

No. 11 Ohio State and No. 20 Illinois squared off at Memorial Stadium for what turned out to be a defensive struggle. The Illini had racked up a surprising three-game winning streak against the Buckeyes, and a fourth victory would constitute an all-time record in the longtime series. With the score tied at 7–7, placekicker Chris Richardson kicked a career-best forty-one-yard field goal, and the Illini had beaten the mighty Buckeyes again.

1991 Illinois–Ohio State souvenir program

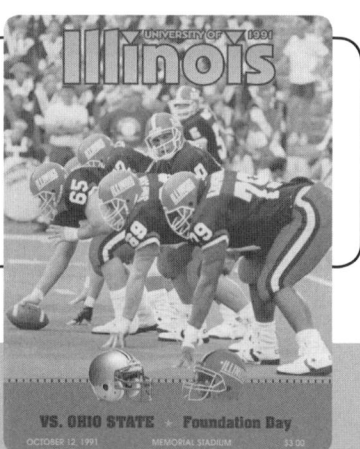

MEN'S ILLINI LEGEND

Brad Hopkins

Brad Hopkins

One of the most underrated offensive linemen in University of Illinois history is Brad Hopkins, an honorable mention All-American honoree as a senior in 1992. As the Illini left tackle, he anchored an offensive line that helped generate more than 360 yards per game and a trip to the Holiday Bowl. After graduating with a degree in speech communications, Hopkins was the thirteenth overall pick in the first round of the 1993 NFL draft by the Houston Oilers (now the Tennessee Titans). That first season in the pros saw him win first-team All-Rookie honors. When he wrapped up a thirteen-year NFL career following the 2005 season, Hopkins had been in the starting lineup in 188 of his 194 games (97 percent), protecting such stars as Steve McNair and Eddie George. Perhaps his best season came in 2000, when he earned his first Pro Bowl invitation and was named All-AFC by *Pro Football Weekly*. Hopkins pursued a career in broadcasting following his playing days; he currently works as an analyst for SiriusXM's Bleacher Report Radio, College Sports Nation, and NFL Radio. He and his wife, Ellen, have two sons and a daughter and live in Nashville, Tennessee. One son, Brycen, now plays football at Purdue.

OTHER TOP MEN'S ATHLETES

1. Len Sitko, cross-country/track and field (co-Athlete of the Year)
2. Scott Turner, track and field (Big Ten 400-meter dash champion)
3. Marko Koers, track and field (Big Ten Big Ten Freshman of the Year and 800-meter run champion)

1991—92

WOMEN'S ILLINI MOMENT

The 1992 Illini women's golf team

Illini Golf Notches Best Finish

The University of Illinois women's golf team took advantage of its role as host of the 1992 Big Ten Golf Championship by achieving its best finish ever. Though finishing third as a team at the Savoy Golf Course, thirteen strokes behind champ Indiana, the Illini had two of the top four individual finishers. Rookie Becky Biehl won individual medalist honors with a seventy-two-hole total of 317, three strokes fewer than Indiana's Amy McDonald. Biehl was named the conference's Freshman of the Year and earned All–Big Ten honors. Teammate Renee Heiken placed fourth overall, shooting 324, including 80s in her final three rounds. After the tournament, she was named Big Ten Player of the Year. Other Illini finishers include Jennifer Lynch (sixteenth), Stacey Pirk (thirtieth), and Christine Garrett and Wendy Evans (tie for forty-first).

OTHER TOP MOMENTS

1. Illinois's volleyball team sold out Huff Hall for the first time, packing in 4,050 fans to see the Ohio State match.
2. Coach Kathy Lindsay's basketball squad upset eighteenth-ranked Northwestern at the Assembly Hall, 70–58.
3. The new Atkins Tennis Center opened in October 1991, hosting both women's and men's matches.

WOMEN'S ILLINI LIST

ILLINOIS'S ALL-STAR ALL-DECADE TEAM

As part of the celebration of ten years of women's athletics in the Big Ten Conference in 1991–92, the University of Illinois selected an allstar, all-decade team for its entire women's program.

Illini diver
Robin Duffy

Leticia Beverly, track	Renee Heiken, golf	Petra Laverman, volleyball
Nancy Brookhart, volleyball	Heidi Helmke, gymnastics	Celena Mondi-Milner, track
Tonja Buford, track	Disa Johnson, volleyball	Mary Ellen Murphy, golf
Laura Bush, volleyball	Becky Kaiser, track	Lindsey Nimmo, tennis
Robin Duffy, swimming and diving	Lynette Robinson, basketball	Jonelle Polk, basketball
*Mary Eggers, volleyball	Heather Singalewitch, gymnastics	Lisa Robinson, basketball
Kendra Gantt, basketball	Denise Lamborn, gymnastics	*Athlete of the Decade

WOMEN'S ILLINI ITEM

Coach Gary Winckler's women's track and field team swept to Big Ten championships both indoors and out during the 1992 season. At the indoor meet in Columbus (February 28–29), Illinois outlasted Wisconsin, 81–76, in a meet that went down to the final event, the 4x400-meter relay. Outdoors at Minneapolis (May 22–23), the Illini cruised to a 122–99 victory over the runner-up Badgers. Just as she had been indoors, junior Tonja Buford was selected as the Big Ten Athlete of the Championship, again winning three individual events.

Tonja Buford

WOMEN'S ILLINI LEGEND

Renee Heiken

Renee (Heiken) Slone

Renee (Heiken) Slone, the greatest golfer in the twenty-year history of women's athletics at the University of Illinois, began honing her skills on the links at the tender age of six. The only child of John and Ronda Heiken of Metamora, Illinois, didn't have the luxury of having a course in her hometown, so dad had to cart young Renee to a nine-hole course in nearby Eureka. In high school she played on the boys' team and was the most valuable player each year. Slone came to Illinois after graduating early from high school. Her winning ways continued with the Illini as she claimed a total of fifteen tournament championships during her career, including eight in 1992–93 alone. Twice, in 1991 and 1993, she earned honors as the Big Ten championship medalist. Slone played three consecutive years in the NCAA tournament, placing among the tournament's top six golfers each time. Over 118 career rounds, Slone amazingly averaged just more than seventy-five strokes per eighteen holes, including a varsity-record sixty-eight at Hawaii's Rainbow Wahine Invitational in 1993. The two-time Illini co-Female Athlete of the Year (1992 and 1993) and 1993 National Golf Coaches Association Player of the Year was inducted into both the National Golf Coaches Association Players Hall of Fame and the Greater Peoria Sports Hall of Fame in 2004. Slone concluded her eleventh year as head coach at Illinois in 2017.

OTHER TOP WOMEN'S ATHLETES

1. Tonja Buford, track and field (Big Ten Track and Field Athlete of the Year)
2. Laura Simmering, cross-country (All–Big Ten)
3. Kate Riley, basketball (Big Ten Conference Medal of Honor recipient)

ILLINI LORE

The University of Illinois's sixty-eight-year-old Memorial Stadium received an $18 million facelift between November 1991 and August 1992. Among the project's main objectives was the replacement of all the concrete bleachers in both upper decks, as well as the replacement of the uppermost twenty-five rows of the main stands. The stadium's electrical and drainage systems were also brought up to code. The UI Auxiliary Facilities System Funds issued revenue bonds to raise money for the project.

Memorial Stadium got a facelift in 1992

1992–93

AMERICA'S TIME CAPSULE

November 3, 1992	Bill Clinton won the presidential election, defeating incumbent George H. W. Bush and independent candidate Ross Perot.
December 8, 1992	The first United Nations-authorized troops landed in Somalia to assist the starving populace.
February 26, 1993	Terrorists bombed New York City's World Trade Center.
April 19, 1993	Nearly one hundred people perished at David Koresh's Branch Davidian compound in a fire that ended a fifty-one-day standoff against federal agents in Waco, Texas.
June 20, 1993	The Chicago Bulls defeated the Phoenix Suns, 99–98, to win their third consecutive NBA championship.

MEN'S ILLINI MOMENT

Kaufmann's Buzzer-Beater Upsets Iowa

Andy Kaufmann (34) launched one of the most dramatic shots in Illini history

High-flying Iowa, led by lanky Acie Earl, invaded Illinois's Assembly Hall February 4, 1993, with soaring hopes, but a miracle shot by Andy Kaufmann instead sent the Hawkeyes home minus a few tail feathers. The Illini had not defeated an opponent ranked in the top ten in its last twelve tries, but this night belonged to the Orange and Blue. Freshman sharpshooter Richard Keene kept Illinois close throughout the game by connecting on five three-pointers, but he saved the dramatics for his senior teammate from Jacksonville. After a fluke basket by Iowa with just two seconds left gave the Hawkeyes a two-point lead, Illinois immediately called time out. Illini coach Lou Henson drew up his team's last-gasp shot, calling for T. J. Wheeler to heave a three-quarter-court pass in the direction of the Illini basket. Kaufmann hauled in the pass in front of the Illinois bench, then spun, squared up, and lofted a twenty-three-footer toward the iron rim. The ball passed cleanly into the net as the buzzer sounded, sending a tumultuous throng of Illini fans onto the court in celebration of a 78–77 Illinois victory. Today, Kaufmann lives in Winchester, Illinois. He has three children.

OTHER TOP MOMENTS

1. The Division of Intercollegiate Athletics announced that varsity programs for men's swimming, fencing, and men's and women's diving would be eliminated, effective July 1, 1993.

2. Playing for an invitation to San Diego's Holiday Bowl, Illinois held off a late Michigan State rally and beat the Spartans, 14–10.

3. Jamie Fairbanks won individual medalist honors at the Big Ten golf championship.

4. Craig Tiley was named head coach of the Illini tennis team.

MEN'S ILLINI LIST

ILLINI BASEBALL CAREER-HOME-RUN
LEADERS (through 2015 season)

48	Scott Spiezio (1991–1993)
40	Sean Mulligan (1989–1991)
39	Drew Davidson (2002–2005)
39	D.J. Svihlik (1997–2000)
38	Craig Marquie (1997–2000)
38	Josh Klimek (1993, 1995–1996)
38	Forry Wells (1991–1994)
38	Darrin Fletcher (1985–1987)

Scott Spiezio hit a career-record forty-eight home runs at Illinois

| 35 | Brian McClure (1993–1996) |
| 33 | Bubba Smith (1989–1991) |

MEN'S ILLINI ITEM

In 1992 the University of Illinois made the claim of having both a father and a son earn first-team Academic Football All-America honors. When John Wright II was accorded that distinction, he joined his dad, John, a 1966 recipient. Will a third-generation Wright garner Academic All-America kudos? Possibly, but not in the sport of football. You see, John II and his wife, Laura, have four daughters. Today, he's managing partner of the Goodwin-Wright Northwestern Benefit Corporation of Georgia, located in Atlanta.

John Wright Jr. (left) and John Wright Sr.

MEN'S ILLINI LEGEND

Marko Koers

Marko Koers

A quick glance through the University of Illinois men's track-and-field record book emphasizes why Marco Koers, the 1993 Illini Male Athlete of the Year, is considered one of the school's greatest middle-distance runners. Born in Molenhoek, Limburg, Netherlands in 1972, he was recruited to Urbana-Champaign in 1991 by Coach Gary Wieneke. When Koers's collegiate career ended in 1996, he had won three NCAA championships, including two as a sophomore (800 meters indoors and 1,500 meters outdoors) and one as a senior (1,500 meters). Nine times he earned All-American acclaim. His eight individual Big Ten titles—two indoors and six outdoors—make him only one of seven Illini athletes to win at least that many non-relay championships since 1945. Twenty years after he last wore the Orange and Blue, Koers still has the best times for 800 meters (1:44.49), 1,500 meters (3:33.05), and the mile run (3:53.47). Three times he competed in the Olympic Games for the Netherlands (1992, 1996, and 2000). Today, his Holland-based company, Marko Koers Sports, develops and organizes company sports activities and events.

OTHER TOP MEN'S ATHLETES

1. Brad Hopkins, football (first-team All–Big Ten and first-round pick in 1993 NFL draft)
2. Baseball's Forry Wells registers a slugging percentage of .726 (.385 average, twelve home runs, fifty-four RBI).
3. Brad Lawton, track and field (Big Ten Conference Medal of Honor recipient)

WOMEN'S ILLINI MOMENT

Kirsten Gleis

A Season of Superstars

A conference-record four University of Illinois women's stars earned Big Ten Athlete of the Year honors during the 1992–93 season, a feat that may never be duplicated. Volleyball All-American Kirsten Gleis dominated that sport in what would turn out to be her only season as an Illini. Tonja Buford ruled Big Ten track and field, winning nine indoor and outdoor conference titles altogether as a senior. Golfer Renee Heiken was the medalist in the 1993 conference championship, repeating as her sport's Player of the Year. Finally, on the tennis courts, no Big Ten player was better than Lindsey Nimmo. She also captured Player of the Year honors.

OTHER TOP MOMENTS

1. Illinois won the Big Ten Indoor Track and Field Championship.
2. Basketball upset No. 18 Purdue, 84–78.
3. Illini hired Lynn Crane to replace Bev Mackes as gymnastics coach.

WOMEN'S ILLINI LIST

WINNINGEST BIG TEN VOLLEYBALL SEASONS

18-0	(1.000)	1988 (Big Ten champs)
18-0	(1.000)	1986 (Big Ten champs)
19-1	(.950)	1992 (Big Ten co-champs)
17-1	(.944)	1987 (Big Ten champs)
16-2	(.889)	1985 (2nd place, Big Ten)
16-4	(.800)	2014 (3rd place, Big Ten)
16-4	(.800)	2011 (2nd place, Big Ten)
16-4	(.800)	2009 (3rd place, Big Ten)
15-5	(.750)	2008 (3rd place, Big Ten)
15-5	(.750)	2003 (2nd place, Big Ten)

Kristen Henriksen and her 1992 Illini teammates won nineteen of their twenty Big Ten matches

WOMEN'S ILLINI ITEM

Volleyball tied for the Big Ten title with Penn State, recording a nearly perfect 19-1 conference record and finishing 32-4 overall. Illinois started hot in September, winning five consecutive victories against ranked teams, then ended the regular season with eighteen consecutive wins. In the NCAA tournament, the Illini disposed of No. 22 Ohio State and No. 7 Nebraska in straight sets, setting up a home-court match against No. 2 Stanford. Before a Huff Hall record crowd of 4,316, the Cardinals prevailed, 3–1.

A record crowd of 4,316 watched Illinois play Stanford

WOMEN'S ILLINI LEGEND

Tonja Buford-Bailey

Tonja Buford-Bailey

Tonja Buford-Bailey's magnificent career at the University of Illinois is underlined by the fact that she won not only more individual Big Ten track titles than any other Illini athlete, but also more titles than any other women's or men's athlete in the history of the conference. Her total of twenty-five championships broke the record of twenty-three by Wisconsin distance star Suzy Favor. From 1990 to 1993, Buford-Bailey dominated hurdles competition at league track-and-field meets. Buford-Bailey's eight individual titles and two relay championships during her senior season may never be broken. She was a four-time Big Ten Track Athlete of the Year honoree and was named Athlete of the Championship three times. Buford-Bailey shared Illinois's Female Athlete of the Year award in 1992 and won it outright in 1993. The Dayton, Ohio, native became the first Illini women's track runner ever to compete in the Olympic Games when she qualified for the 400-meter hurdles at the 1992 Summer Games in Barcelona, Spain. At the 1996 Olympics in Atlanta, Buford-Bailey won a bronze medal in that event. She was also a member of the 2000 Olympic squad. Buford-Bailey returned to coach the Illini in 2004, first as an assistant then as head coach from 2008 to 2014. In 2016 Tonja Buford-Bailey completed her second season as associate head coach of the University of Texas track-and-field program. She and her husband, Victor, have two children.

OTHER TOP WOMEN'S ATHLETES

1. Carmel Corbett, track and field (Big Ten pentathlon champion)
2. Tonya Williams, track and field (Big Ten Freshman of the Year, 100-meter and 400 intermediate hurdles titles)
3. Jill Estey, basketball (team's Most Valuable Player)

ILLINI LORE

Michael Aiken, sixty-year-old provost at the University of Pennsylvania since 1987, was chosen as chancellor for the University of Illinois at Urbana-Champaign in early February 1993. The Arkansas native and University of Mississippi graduate replaced Morton Weir, who stepped down to return to the classroom. "Though some board members had emphasized a search for women and minority candidates," said Board of Trustees President Judith Calder, "we were satisfied that Aiken's experience showed his commitment to equal opportunity." Aiken retired as chancellor in 2001.

Chancellor Michael Aiken

1993–94

AMERICA'S TIME CAPSULE

October 6, 1993	Michael Jordan shocked professional basketball by announcing his retirement from the Chicago Bulls.
November 30, 1993	*Schindler's List*, winner of seven Academy Awards, premiered. It earned $321 million on a $22 million budget.
January 17, 1994	An earthquake in southern California killed fifty-seven people.
June 17, 1994	Former football star O. J. Simpson, charged with two counts of murder, led a convoy of police cars on a sixty-mile chase before returning to his home.
August 12, 1994	Major League Baseball players went on strike. The balance of the season, including the World Series, was cancelled on September 14.

MEN'S ILLINI MOMENT

Quarterback Johnny Johnson

Jim Klein caught the game-winning touchdown at Michigan in 1993

Illini Surprise Michigan

Winning football games at Michigan has never been an easy chore for Illinois, so the Fighting Illini victory at Ann Arbor October 23, 1993, was especially gratifying for Coach Lou Tepper's troops. As had been the case so many times before in contests at mammoth Michigan Stadium, Illinois trailed the thirteenth-ranked Wolverines entering the fourth quarter. A Ty Douthard touchdown with 11:37 remaining narrowed the Illini deficit to 21–17, but Illinois's task appeared hopeless with just more than a minute remaining and Michigan in control of the ball. Suddenly, UI's Simeon Rice stripped the ball away from Maize and Blue running back Ricky Powers at the Michigan forty-four-yard line, and a confident Illini offense raced back onto the field. Quarterback Johnny Johnson methodically guided Illinois into the end zone in six plays, capped by a fourth-down, fifteen-yard touchdown pass to Jim Klein. The 24–21 Illini victory at Ann Arbor snapped a twenty-seven-year road jinx and presented Illinois with one of its most satisfying victories of the 1990s.

OTHER TOP MOMENTS

1. Track and field sprinter Anthony Jones won Illini Athlete of the Year honors.
2. Illini basketball team upset No. 11 Indiana before a national TV audience on Super Bowl Sunday.
3. Baseball's Tom Sinak led the Illini with .418 average and finished second in Big Ten hitting at .458.

MEN'S ILLINI LIST

ORIGINAL COSTS OF ILLINOIS'S CURRENT
ATHLETIC FACILITIES

Donated by Gary
and Carlotta Biel-
feldt, the Bielfeldt
Athletic Admin-
istration Building
opened in 1996

*$40,000	Kenney Gym (1902)
$702,000	Armory (1915)
$2.5 million	Memorial Stadium (1923)
$725,000	Huff Hall (1925)
$250,000	Savoy Golf Course (1950, original 18 holes)
$8.35 million	Assembly Hall (1963)
$2.2 million	Outdoor Track and Field Stadium (1987)
$1.64 million	Illinois Field (1988)
$5.3 million	Atkins Tennis Center (1991)

$7.2 million	Bielfeldt Athletic Administration Building (1996)
$1.2 million	Illinois Soccer–Track and Field Stadium (1999)
$12.5 million	Irwin Indoor Practice Facility (2000)
$2 million	Eichelberger Field (2001)
$5.1 million	Demirjian Golf Practice Facility (2007)
$5.3 million	Khan Outdoor Tennis Complex (2011)
$5.5 million	Lauritsen/Wohlers Golf Practice Facility (2015)

*Estimated cost, due to the gymnasium being included in a bid of three
different buildings

MEN'S ILLINI ITEM

Only a 74–70 loss to Michigan spoiled an otherwise perfect men's basketball season at the Assembly Hall in 1993–94. Coach Lou Henson's Fighting Illini scored victories in fifteen of sixteen games at home, including a shiny 8-1 mark in Big Ten contests. Among Illinois's highlights were a triumph over Indiana, UI's thirteenth consecutive home-court win over a talented Wisconsin club, and a senior-night victory by Deon Thomas, T. J. Wheeler, and Tommy Michael over Minnesota.

(Left to right): T. J. Wheeler, Deon Thomas, Gene Cross, and Tom Michael

MEN'S ILLINI LEGEND

Deon Thomas

Deon Thomas

As a youngster, Deon Thomas survived the brutal experiences of growing up on the streets of Chicago's West Side to become one of the city's finest prep players at Simeon High School, ultimately earning an athletic scholarship at the University of Illinois. Just a few months later, false allegations of NCAA recruiting violations, based on audiotapes obtained by an assistant coach at Iowa, turned Thomas's future down a road of despair. After sitting out his freshman season, Thomas began a brilliant career at Illinois during the 1990–91 campaign by averaging fifteen points per game.

His senior year, 1993–94, saw him break Fighting Illini records nearly every time he played. Not only did Thomas become the school's all-time leading scorer, with 2,129 points, he also set UI marks for blocked shots, and ranked second-best in rebounds and field-goal percentage. Thomas was the first pick in the second round of the NBA draft by the Dallas Mavericks, and he played professional ball overseas for fourteen seasons in six different countries. He currently serves as the color analyst for the Illini Basketball Radio Network.

OTHER TOP MEN'S ATHLETES

1. Daren McDonough, track and field (pole vaults 18'5¼" at the Big Ten outdoor meet, a championship record)
2. Forry Wells, football/baseball (Big Ten Conference Medal of Honor recipient)
3. Brian Kobylinski, gymnastics (Big Ten still-rings champion)

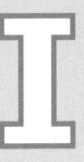

1993–94

WOMEN'S ILLINI MOMENT

Tonya Williams

Hurdling Success

She originally played soccer and field hockey but didn't take up the sport that would bring her the most fame until the spring of her junior year at Norview High School in Norfolk, Virginia. Tonya Williams was fortunate to have two great coaches to tutor her at the University of Illinois. Coach Gary Winckler taught her the fundamentals of hurdling. "When I was young, I was just running and jumping over the hurdle," Williams said. "Gary taught me all about steps, timing, and technique." Her other coach was a fellow athlete, Tonja Buford-Bailey. "Tonja was the big sister I never had," Williams intimated. "Some great athletes don't want to take on younger people as protégés. Tonja never turned me away." Williams said she always had confidence that she could win, and the statistics within Illinois's track-and-field record book bear that out. She won two national championships in the 400-meter hurdles in 1995 and 1996 and an unbelievable twenty Big Ten titles, ten each in individual events and ten with relay teams. Twice, Williams earned Illinois's Female Athlete of the Year award. She relocated to Florida in 2001 and today coaches the North Miami Beach Sundevils Track Club. Williams and her daughter, Sienna, reside in Pembroke Pines, Florida.

OTHER TOP MOMENTS

1. Mandy Cunningham finished her career in third place on basketball's all-time scoring list, with 1,536 points.

2. Illinois volleyball won the NCAA attendance title for the second consecutive year.

3. Illini track-and-field team finishes runner-up to Michigan, indoors and outdoors.

4. Basketball's Kris Dupps scores forty-one points, second-most ever, in a loss against Kent State.

WOMEN'S ILLINI LIST

CAREER THREE-POINT FIELD GOAL PERCENTAGE
(minimum 125 attempts)

.403	Allison Curtin, 1998–2001 (114/283)
.395	Kyley Simmons, 2015–2016 (149/377)
.372	Lori Bjork, 2005–2008 (214/576)
.369	Rebecca Harris, 2006–2008 (58/157)
.359	Mandy Cunningham, 1990–1994 (168/468)
.357	Jenna Smith, 2006–2010 (46/129)
.348	Amber Moore, 2009–2014 (295/848)
.344	Aminata Yanni, 2000–2004 (99/288)

Mandy Cunningham

.341	Janelle Hughes, 2002–2006 (78/229)
.339	Brooke Kissinger, 2015–2016 (53/156)

WOMEN'S ILLINI ITEM

Becky (Biehl) Sabbert's sister, Lia, was her role model. "When she earned a scholarship to Illinois, it helped me to see the potential that golf could play in my future," said Sabbert. Becky won medalist honors as a freshman at the 1992 Big Ten championship meet. That success helped Biehl earn All–Big Ten honors all four years, 1992–1995. She is currently working as a registered nurse near her home in Fenton, Missouri.

Becky Biehl

WOMEN'S ILLINI LEGEND

Tina Rogers (12)

Tina (Rogers) Smith

At 6'3", longtime Illini mentor Mike Hebert called Tina (Rogers) Smith "the most dominating outside hitter I've ever coached." She missed two weeks of her sophomore season following knee surgery, but a more serious injury occurred in late November 1992 at Michigan State when she broke a joint in her ankle. Through therapy and rehab, she made it through the balance of the season, one in which Illinois won the Big Ten title and she earned second-team All-American honors. More in-depth surgery followed; her recovery was long and arduous. "It was a long road and it troubled the beginning of my senior season," said Smith. "That was both a physical and emotional struggle." Still, she fought through the pain and repeated as an All–Big Ten selection. Her crowning achievement came in the spring of 1994 when she was named Illinois's Female Athlete of the Year. Most of Smith's professional career has centered around the banking, finance, and mortgage industry, and today she is a correspondent mortgage banking underwriter for the State Bank of Lincoln. Her family includes a daughter who plays basketball at Millikin University and a young son.

OTHER TOP WOMEN'S ATHLETES

1. Kristin Henriksen, volleyball (All–Big Ten, third consecutive conference hitting title)
2. Kristen Jones and Kristi Meola, tennis (All–Big Ten)
3. Tonya Booker, basketball (Big Ten Conference Medal of Honor recipient)

ILLINI LORE

On April 24–25, 1994, Monsignor Edward J. Duncan was honored for his fifty years of service as chaplain and director of the Newman Foundation on the U of I campus. Among the guests honoring Monsignor Duncan at a gala luncheon included retired General Motors chairman Thomas Murphy and former Illini football great Dick Butkus. During the festivities, University of Illinois Director of Athletics Ron Guenther announced that the Illini football team would institute a special citizenship award to honor its longtime team chaplain. Monsignor Duncan became chaplain at St. John's Catholic Church in 1943. He died in January 2012 at age ninety-six.

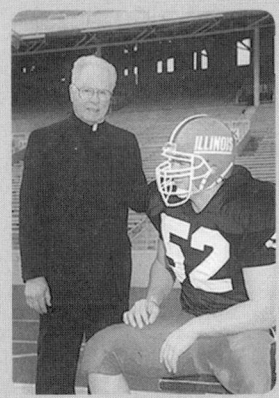

Monsignor Edward Duncan (left)

1994–95

AMERICA'S TIME CAPSULE

November 5, 1994 — Forty-five-year-old George Foreman became boxing's oldest heavyweight champion.

November 8, 1994 — The Republicans won control of both houses of Congress for the first time in forty years, rebuking Democratic president Bill Clinton.

January 29, 1995 — The San Francisco 49ers won an unprecedented fifth Super Bowl title, beating San Diego 49–26.

July 16, 1995 — Amazon.com opened for business. During 2015 Amazon's sales soared to $88 billion.

April 19, 1995 — Terrorists bombed the Alfred P. Murrah Federal Building in Oklahoma City, killing 168 people, including several children. It was, at the time, the deadliest terrorist attack ever on U.S. soil.

MEN'S ILLINI MOMENT

(From top, clockwise): Co-captains Dana Howard, Jon Kerr, John Holecek, and Pete Gabrione

Liberty Bowl Champs

Lou Tepper's third full season as head football coach at the University of Illinois was just twenty-two agonizing points away from being a banner year. And though the painful sting of narrow losses to four bowl-qualifying teams was eased a bit in the finale when Illinois won the Liberty Bowl, Illini fans couldn't help but think about what might have been during this rollercoaster season. The campaign began disappointingly at Chicago's Soldier Field with a one-point loss to Washington State, 10–9, but Illinois rebounded well by demolishing their next two nonconference foes, Missouri and Northern Illinois, by a cumulative score of 76–10. In week four, the Illini came up thirty-six inches shy of a victory in the Big Ten opener against Purdue, as the game ended with tight end Ken Dilger stacked up at the one-yard line. Tepper's crew shocked Ohio State in Columbus for a fourth consecutive time the following week, 24–10, helping linebacker Dana Howard live up to his bold prediction of a victory. Illinois then won three of its next four games, sandwiching a difficult 19–14 loss to Michigan between victories over Iowa, Northwestern, and Minnesota. The most exciting game of 1994 came November 12, when No. 2 Penn State traveled to Memorial Stadium. A 28–14 halftime lead by the Illini ultimately evaporated into a 35–31 loss to the eventual Rose Bowl champs. A defeat in the regular season finale at Wisconsin backed the Illini into the Liberty Bowl, and doomsayers weren't optimistic that Illinois could beat pesky East Carolina in the December 31 game at Memphis. However, a dominating offensive performance by quarterback Johnny Johnson and an equally sterling defensive effort from Simeon Rice and company made New Year's Eve especially sweet for the Orange and Blue.

OTHER TOP MOMENTS

1. Illini hosted the Big Ten indoor track-and-field championship but fell short of a title by a point-and-a-half to Michigan.

2. Robert Bennett scored a career-high twenty-four points in Illinois's 94–88 overtime win versus No. 22 Minnesota.

3. Tom Sinak achieved a Big Ten record six-for-six at the plate in a 22–10 Illini win at Michigan State.

MEN'S ILLINI LIST

TRACK AND FIELD INDIVIDUAL BIG TEN TITLES (since 1945)

12	Andrew Riley (5 indoors/7 outdoors)
12	Charlton Ehizuelen (8 indoors/4 outdoors)
10	George Walker (5 indoors/5 outdoors)
9	Marko Koers (3 indoors/6 outdoors)
9	Mike Durkin (5 indoors/4 outdoors)
9	Willie Williams (4 indoors/5 outdoors)
8	Bobby True (5 indoors/3 outdoors)
8	Dorian Green (6 indoor/2 outdoors)
8	Sherman Armstrong (4 indoors/4 outdoors)

Marko Koers won nine Big Ten titles at Illinois

8	Tim Simon (5 indoors/3 outdoors)
8	Herb McKenley (3 indoors/5 outdoors)

MEN'S ILLINI ITEM

Illinois's wrestling program's thirty-seven-year dormancy got the boost it was looking for March 18, 1995, when senior Steve Marianetti (150 pounds) and sophomore Ernest Benion (158) both captured individual NCAA crowns. Third-year Illini coach Mark Johnson led his team to a top-ten finish (ninth) for the first time since 1958. It was the first time since 1938 that two UI wrestlers won national titles in the same year.

National champions Steve Marianetti and Ernest Benion

MEN'S ILLINI LEGEND

Dana Howard

Dana Howard

Illinois's reputation as "Linebacker U" gained considerable punch on December 9, 1994, when Illini senior Dana Howard earned the Butkus Award as college football's top linebacker. It was the first major individual award ever won by an Illini football player. Presenting the prize that night in Orlando, Florida, was its namesake, former UI star Dick Butkus, who was celebrating his fifty-second birthday. In accepting the award, Howard said, "I'd like to thank Dick Butkus for bringing that great linebacker tradition to Illinois. It gave me something to measure myself by." Howard's second consecutive All-American season was highlighted by two memorable events. First was his daring public prediction of victory and his subsequent performance at Ohio State in a 24–10 Illini win. Howard nailed down the Butkus Award in a 35–31 loss to second-ranked Penn State when he became the Big Ten's all-time leading tackler. Number 40 topped the century mark in tackles all four seasons he played for the Illini, finishing with 595 stops, twenty-three more than previous record-holder Marcus Marek of Ohio State. Howard was a fifth round draft pick of the Dallas Cowboys and later played for the St. Louis Rams and Chicago Bears. Today, Howard is the owner of Dana Howard Construction Company, based in Belleville, Illinois. His family includes his wife, Patrice, and two children.

OTHER TOP MEN'S ATHLETES

1. Josh Klimek, baseball (All-Big Ten)
2. Kiwane Garris, basketball (Illini Most Valuable Player)
3. Jeremiah Landry, gymnastics (Big Ten pommel horse champ)

1994—95

WOMEN'S ILLINI MOMENT

Carmel Corbett

Illini Sweep Big Ten Meets

For the third time in the fourteen-year history of Big Ten women's track and field, Illinois swept both the indoor and outdoor conference titles. Indoors at Ann Arbor, the Illini blew by runner-up Wisconsin, 132–83. Carmel Corbett's double-victory effort (long jump and pentathlon) led the way; she got support from Collinus Newsome's win in the shot put and Tonya Williams victory in the 55-meter hurdles. Outdoors at Minneapolis, the Illini had an overwhelming fifty-one-point margin over second-place Wisconsin, 163–112. There were eight titles by Illinois, including two each by Aspen Burkett (100 and 200) and Dawn Riley (100 hurdles and triple jump).

OTHER TOP MOMENTS

1. Volleyball made a tenth-straight appearance at the NCAA tournament.
2. Kris Dupps led the Illini basketball team to a 68–54 victory over No. 24 Minnesota.
3. Illinois's track-and-field squad finishes twenty-fourth at the NCAA indoor championship, including a fourth-place finish in the 800-meter run from Hope Sanders.

WOMEN'S ILLINI LIST

KAROL KAHRS'S MOST OUTSTANDING WOMEN ATHLETES

Dr. Karol Kahrs, longtime associate director of athletics, chose the most outstanding Illini women athletes of her twenty-five years at Illinois (1974–1999). Here are her selections, sport by sport:

Lindsey Nimmo

Basketball:	Lisa Robinson
Cross-Country:	Kelly McNee
Golf:	Renee Heiken
Gymnastics:	Nancy Thies
Swimming and Diving:	Mary Paterson
Tennis:	Lindsey Nimmo

Track and Field:	Tonja Buford
Volleyball:	Mary Eggers

At the University of Tennessee's Tom Black Track in Knoxville, the Fighting Illini women's team enjoyed its best performance to date with a fourth-place at the 1995 NCAA outdoor track-and-field championship. UI scored its first six points on a third-place finish in the 4x100-meter relay (Benita Kelley, Terra Crutchfield-Tyus, Tonya Williams, and Aspen Burkett). After six events, the Orange and Blue stood in first place, thanks to strong efforts in the 800-meter run by Tama Tochihara (fifth place) and Williams's victory in the 400-meter hurdles. The Illini got additional team points from Williams in the 100-meter hurdles (third place), Burkett in the 200-meter dash (fifth place) and Carmel Corbett in the high jump (tied for seventh).

Aspen Burkett

WOMEN'S ILLINI LEGEND

Theresa Grentz

Coach Theresa Grentz

Theresa Grentz, the seventh-winningest women's basketball coach in NCAA history and head coach of the 1992 United States Olympic Team, was selected as the University of Illinois's sixth head women's basketball coach on May 15, 1995. The twenty-year coaching veteran from Rutgers University saw the Lady Knights rise toward the top of women's intercollegiate basketball, compiling a record of 434-150 (.743), including nine consecutive NCAA tournament appearances from 1986 to 1994. Grentz's 1981–82 Rutgers team captured the AIAW national championship with a 25-7 record. During her collegiate playing career at Immaculata (she was then known as Theresa Shank), she helped establish the first national power in women's collegiate basketball. The Mighty Macs won seventy-four games and captured three consecutive national titles (1972, 1973, and 1974) during her career. Grentz was named a first-team All-American each season and had her number (12) retired by Immaculata. Following twelve seasons at Illinois, where she compiled a record of 210-156, she served as the vice president at Immaculata. Grentz recently completed her second season as head coach at Lafayette College in Easton, Pennsylvania.

OTHER TOP WOMEN'S ATHLETES

1. Erin Borske, volleyball (Big Ten Freshman of the Year)
2. Carmel Corbett, track and field (Big Ten Indoor Track Athlete of the Championship, Big Ten Conference Medal of Honor recipient)
3. Danyel Crutcher, basketball (Big Ten All-Freshman Team)
4. Camille Baldrich, tennis (first-team All–Big Ten)

ILLINI LORE

Within a period of just seventy-two hours, the University of Illinois merged a Springfield-based university into its system, saw the structure of its governing board change, and gained a new president. The tumultuous three-day period began on February 28, 1995, when Governor James Edgar signed legislation to merge Sangamon State University in Springfield with the University of Illinois in January 1996, as well as give the governor power to appoint UI trustees. Two days later, on March 2, UI-Chicago Chancellor James Stukel was named the university's fifteenth president, replacing the retiring Stanley Ikenberry.

President James Stukel

1995–2004

1995—96

AMERICA'S TIME CAPSULE

September 6, 1995 — Baltimore Orioles shortstop Cal Ripken Jr. played his 2,131st consecutive game before a sold-out crowd at Oriole Park at Camden Yards, breaking the record set by baseball legend Lou Gehrig in 1939.

October 3, 1995 — The "Trial of the Century" came to an end in Los Angeles when a jury, sequestered for 266 days, deliberated for less than four hours and found O. J. Simpson not guilty of double murder.

April 3, 1996 — Identified by his brother, alleged "Unabomber" Theodore Kaczynski was arrested by FBI agents at his tiny, isolated cabin in Montana.

July 17, 1996 — TWA's Flight 800 mysteriously exploded moments after taking off from New York's Kennedy International Airport, killing all 230 people on board.

August 4, 1996 — The Summer Olympic Games, held in Atlanta, came to a close. Highlights included Carl Lewis's fourth consecutive gold medal in the long jump, Michael Johnson's victories in the 400-meter and 200-meter races, and Muhammad Ali's lighting of the Olympic flame.

MEN'S ILLINI MOMENT

Kevin Hardy Wins Butkus Award

Kevin Hardy (left) and Dick Butkus

To become the best at one's craft, a person often needs to be challenged, and former Illini football great Kevin Hardy was always surrounded by people who tested him. At Harrison High School in Evansville, Indiana, Hardy's basketball teammates included Calbert Cheaney and Walter McCarty. At the University of Illinois, his fellow linebackers were John Holecek, Dana Howard, and Simeon Rice. And in the NFL, his teammates included myriad Hall of Famers. Hardy was an exceptional athlete, but knew that his 6'4", 250-pound frame was better suited to football than basketball. As an Illini senior in 1995, his collegiate career reached its zenith when he received the Dick Butkus Award as college football's premier linebacker. Hardy was selected second overall by Jacksonville in the 1996 NFL draft and played six seasons for the Jaguars, one for the Dallas Cowboys, and three years for the Cincinnati Bengals. In 2007 he built a nightclub in South Beach, Florida, called Dream Nightclub, and it flourishes today. Kevin and his wife, Terrie, have two children.

OTHER TOP MOMENTS

1. Marko Koers won at both 800 and 1,500 meters, earning the Big Ten outdoor track-and-field championship's Athlete of the Year honors. He also received the Big Ten Conference Medal of Honor.

2. Josh Klimek slammed an Illini-record twenty-six home runs, ten more than any other Big Ten player.

3. Illinois's athletics staff moved into the new Bielfeldt Athletic Administration Building.

4. Illini football team defeated No. 17 Arizona, 9–7.

5. The Big Ten Conference celebrated its centennial anniversary.

6. Wrestling placed third at Big Ten Championship, its best finish since a second-place finish in 1958.

MEN'S ILLINI LIST

UI SINGLE-SEASON HOME-RUN LEADERS

Josh Klimek

Illinois's Josh Klimek led the nation in home runs during the 1996 baseball season and was chosen Big Ten Player of the Year. His twenty-six round-trippers that year still top the Illini single-season list.

26	Josh Klimek, 1996		16	Brian McClure, 1996
19	Forry Wells, 1994		16	Scott Spiezio, 1993
19	Scott Spiezio, 1992		16	Mark Dalesandro, 1990
18	Bubba Smith, 1991		15	D. J. Svihlik, 1999
16	David Kerian, 2015		15	D. J. Svihlik, 1998
16	Dusty Bensko, 2005		15	Sean Mulligan, 1990
			15	Darrin Fletcher, 1987
			15	Darrin Fletcher, 1986

MEN'S ILLINI ITEM

Lou Henson stunned Illinois fans on February 24, 1996, by announcing that he would step down at the end of the season after a school-recordbreaking twenty-one years on the job. Athletic Director Ron Guenther responded quickly by luring Lon Kruger to Urbana-Champaign from the University of Florida. In January 2017, Henson celebrated his eighty-fifth birthday, while Kruger serves as head coach of the Oklahoma Sooners.

Surrounded by his family, Lou Henson announced that he would step down as Illini coach

MEN'S ILLINI LEGENDS

Simeon Rice graced the front of this 1995 game program

Simeon Rice

"There's no such thing as an easy thing if you want to be successful." That was a life lesson impressed upon Mount Carmel High School junior Simeon Rice by his father, Henry. Simeon was frustrated, ready to transfer to another school so that he could be a running back, but dad refused. "I sent you there to go to school and get an education, not to play football," said Henry. "If you were good, you wouldn't be on the bench." From that point on, Simeon's attitude about life totally changed. At Rice's first Illini practice, then defensive-line coach Denny Marcin knew he had something special in the 6'5", 240-pound physical freak. Number 97 went on to become a two-time All-American, obliterating Illinois's records for career tackles for loss (sixty-nine) and quarterback sacks (44.5). Rice was drafted third overall in the first round in 1996 by the Arizona Cardinals. Through twelve NFL seasons, he was a three-time Pro Bowl selection. In 2015 Rice, a longtime movie buff, chased his next dream: he wrote, produced, and directed a movie thriller titled *Unsullied*. Today, he splits his time between homes in Phoenix and Tampa.

OTHER TOP MEN'S ATHLETES

1. Brian McClure, baseball (.418 average, 16 HR, 65 RBI)
2. Jeremy Sutter, tennis (All–Big Ten)
3. Dorian Green, track and field (Athlete of the Championship, Big Ten indoor meet)
4. Kiwane Garris, basketball (First-Team All–Big Ten)

271

1995-96

WOMEN'S ILLINI MOMENT

(Front, left to right) Aspen Burkett, Benita Kelley, Kerry Ann Richards, and Tonya Williams. (Back) Terra Crutchfield-Tyus, Collinus Newsome, Dawn Riley, and Stacy Ann Grant.

Women's Track-and-Field Squad Tops Illini Fortunes

Coach Gary Winckler's women's track-and-field squad captured Illinois's lone Big Ten team title during the 1995–96 season. Amazingly, UI's victory at the indoor championships was achieved without the benefit of an individual title by its star performer, Tonya Williams, who was weakened by the flu and nagging injuries. Fortunately, Winckler got record-setting efforts from teammates Dawn Riley (triple jump), Collinus Newsome (shot put), and Benita Kelley (55 dash). It was the fourth team title for the Illini in five years. At the Big Ten outdoor meet, Illinois lost the team championship by just one point, 149–148, despite capturing nine of the twenty events, primarily in the sprints and the hurdles. Williams, who had recuperated from her maladies at the winter meet, bounced back strong in the spring championships. She was part of four different Big Ten titles and ultimately claimed UI's Female Athlete of the Year award.

OTHER TOP MOMENTS

1. Shot putter Collinus Newsome notched a fifty-three-foot toss, breaking the Big Ten championship record by 11.5 inches.
2. Volleyball ended its regular season with victories at No. 10 Penn State and No. 7 Ohio State.
3. Theresa Grentz's first season included wins over No. 14 Arkansas and No. 23 Florida.

WOMEN'S ILLINI LIST

TRACK AND FIELD'S BEST FINISHES AT THE NCAA CHAMPIONSHIPS

Coach Tonya Buford-Bailey's 2009 Illini tied for twelfth place at the 2009 NCAA Outdoor Championships

4th outdoors	1996 (Eugene, Oregon)
4th outdoors	1995 (Knoxville, Tennessee)
6th indoors	1996 (Indianapolis, Indiana)
7th outdoors	1993 (New Orleans, Louisiana)
7th outdoors	1989 (Provo, Utah)
8th indoors	1997 (Indianapolis, Indiana)
(T) 10th outdoors 2002	Baton Rouge, Louisiana)
(T) 12th outdoors 2009	(Fayetteville, Arkansas)
12th indoors	1994 (Indianapolis, Indiana)
12th outdoors	1990 (Durham, North Carolina)

Mike Hebert departed the University of Illinois athletic scene in the spring of 1996 after a sparkling thirteen-year career as head coach of the women's volleyball squad. From 1983 through 1995, Hebert's spikers won an unprecedented 72 percent of their games, finishing in the upper half of the Big Ten for eleven consecutive years. He was named National Coach of the Year in 1985 after leading the nation with a 39-3 record, and he won Big Ten Coach of the Year honors in 1985, 1986, and 1988. Hebert became head coach at the University of Minnesota and retired at the end of the 2010 season with an additional Big Ten title and a total of five appearances in the NCAA volleyball's Final Four. In 2006 he was inducted into the American Volleyball Coaches Hall of Fame. Hebert and his wife, Sherry, currently reside in Minneapolis.

Mike Hebert

WOMEN'S ILLINI LEGEND

Erin (Borske) Gray

Erin Borske

Though she only played for the Fighting Illini volleyball team for two seasons, Erin (Borske) Gray more than made her mark in Illinois's record book. The product of Stagg High School in Palos Heights quickly made an immediate impact, earning Big Ten Freshman of the Year honors in 1994, amassing 478 kills and 355 digs. More than twenty years later, her sophomore season total of 714 kills still stand as UI's record. That effort earned her first-team All-America honors. Of Illinois's top-ten single-game performances for kills, Gray holds the top two marks in that category (forty-four against Penn State and forty-one against Minnesota) plus three others. Her hopes to transfer to Arizona State never materialized, so she instead pursued a professional career in beach volleyball. Gray was Rookie of the Year and Player of the Year on the EVP Tour in 1998 and 1999, respectively. She retired in 2015 following several years on the circuit. Today, she resides in Redondo Beach, California, and serves as assistant coach for that city's sand beach team. Gray and her husband have five children.

OTHER TOP WOMEN'S ATHLETES

1. Tonya Williams, track and field (Female Athlete of the Year)
2. Ashley Berggren, basketball (leads Big Ten in scoring, first-team All–Big Ten)
3. Dawn Riley, track and field (Big Ten Conference Medal of Honor recipient)

ILLINI LORE

Soon after he assumed the school's top leadership post in 1995, James J. Stukel made clear his four-point presidential vision for the University of Illinois: to enrich undergraduate education; to enhance quality throughout the University; to strengthen the university's ties to the citizens of the state of Illinois; and to free more money for academic purposes by streamlining business operations. Thanks in part to a $1 billion capital campaign, the university thrived under Stukel's direction. He served as UI's president until 2005, when Joseph White succeeded Stukel. In 2007 a new residence hall on the University of Illinois-Chicago's campus, located on the corner of Roosevelt Road and Halstead Street, was named in Stukel's honor.

Joseph White

1996–97

AMERICA'S TIME CAPSULE

November 5, 1996 — Bill Clinton was elected to a second term as U.S. president, easily defeating former Kansas senator Bob Dole. Clinton won thirty-one states.

April 13, 1997 — Twenty-one-year-old Tiger Woods became the youngest and the first minority golfer to win the Masters, outdistancing Tom Kite by twelve shots.

June 2, 1997 — Timothy McVeigh was found guilty for his part in the 1995 bombing of the Alfred P. Murrah Federal Building in Oklahoma City that killed 168 people.

August 31, 1997 — Americans and people all over the world mourned the passing of England's Princess Diana, who died in a Paris automobile crash.

MEN'S ILLINI MOMENT

Lon Kruger (left) and Kiwane Garris

Lon Kruger's First Season

Based on a top-twenty finish in the polls, the school's first twenty-win campaign, and a berth in the NCAA tournament, Lon Kruger's initial season as Fighting Illini head basketball coach could be considered a major success. His 1996–97 squad was led by point guard Kiwane Garris, a senior captain who was not only the team MVP but also a near unanimous first-team All–Big Ten selection. He ranked second in Big Ten scoring behind Iowa's Andre Woolridge and was runner-up in both assists and free throw percentage. Garris was joined in the starting lineup by backcourt stars Matt Heldman and Kevin Turner, in the frontcourt by Chris Gandy and Jarrod Gee. Following a victory over Missouri in the Braggin' Rights Battle, the Illini entered conference play

OTHER TOP MOMENTS

1. Illinois prevailed over Indiana, 46–43, in the Big Ten's first-ever overtime football game.
2. On December 2, 1996, Ron Guenther named Chicago Bears offensive coordinator Ron Turner as replacement for Lou Tepper.
3. Illini placed two of the top five finishers at the Big Ten Cross-Country Championship (Barry Pearman, fourth, and Jason Zieren, fifth).

with a 10-2 record. Illinois then ran off an impressive 11-7 Big Ten record, highlighted by a 96–90 win over eventual Final Four participant Minnesota, plus victories against nationally ranked Indiana, Iowa, and Michigan. The Illini won their first-round NCAA tournament game against Southern California but lost in the second round to Chattanooga.

MEN'S ILLINI LIST

THE INCREDIBLE HOLC

Despite a disappointing performance by the team, Illinois running back Robert Holcombe had an all-star season in 1996. His 315-yard rushing effort against Minnesota on November 16, 1996, set an all-time Illini record.

Robert Holcombe

1.	330	Mikel Leshoure at Northwestern, Nov. 20, 2010
2.	315	Robert Holcombe at Minnesota, Nov. 16, 1996
3.	263	Howard Griffith vs. Northwestern, Nov. 24, 1990
4.	239	Jim Grabowski vs. Wisconsin, Nov. 14, 1964
5.	237	Red Grange, at Pennsylvania, Oct. 31, 1925
6.	215	Rocky Harvey vs. Middle Tennessee, Sept. 12, 1998

7.	214	Rashard Mendenhall vs. Indiana, Oct. 22, 2007
8.	212	Red Grange, Michigan, Oct. 18, 1924
9.	208	Howard Griffith vs. Southern Illinois, Sept. 22, 1990
8.	206	Robert Holcombe vs. Minnesota, Nov. 18, 1995

MEN'S ILLINI ITEM

For the first time since Franklin Delano Roosevelt reigned in the White House, Illinois's men's tennis team captured the Big Ten title, beating top-seed Northwestern, 4–2. As the league's Freshman of the Year, Cary Franklin keyed UI's title run by beating Conference Player of the Year Alex Witt of Northwestern in the championships. The Illini wound up the 1996–97 campaign with an overall record of 18-10, including a 10-3 mark in Big Ten matches.

Illini players raise their trophies

MEN'S ILLINI LEGEND

Ernest Benion

Ernest Benion

Whether it was as a wrestler or as an a cappella singer, Ernest Benion had a starspangled career at Illinois. On the mat, the Bolingbrook native was an all-star, becoming one of only a handful of Illini grapplers to finish among the top three in the NCAA meet three different times. Benion racked up a win-loss record of 121-40 in four seasons at Illinois, but no victory was more important than the final match of his sophomore season, when he won the national 158-pound crown. He placed second in the NCAA meet his junior year and was third as a senior, but Benion's most memorable work came outside the gymnasium. He was co-chair of the student athlete advisory board and an active member of the Fellowship of Christian Athletes. Said Johnson, "He was a son every parent would love to have." Benion also loved to sing. On numerous occasions before a variety of Illini athletic events, he used his beautiful baritone voice to sing the national anthem. Benion is now a minister at the Church of God in Greenville, Ohio.

OTHER TOP MEN'S ATHLETES

1. Chris Jones, track and field (Big Ten Freshman of the Year)
2. Travis Romagnoli, gymnastics (Big Ten vault champion)
3. Seth Brady, wrestling (Big Ten Conference Medal of Honor recipient)

1996–97

WOMEN'S ILLINI MOMENT

Raising the championship banner

Women's Basketball Wins First-Ever Big Ten Title

In seasons prior to Theresa Grentz's arrival, the attendance at Fighting Illini women's basketball games could easily have been counted at a distance by the ticket manager's index finger rather than by a turnstile. On Sunday, February 23, 1997, the record-breaking crowd of 16,050 that saw UI's home game against Purdue was larger than the *total* season attendance at Illinois for every year prior to 1995. The reason? Winning basketball! The 1996–97 Illini compiled an overall record of 24-8 and tied Michigan State and Purdue for their first-ever Big Ten title. Grentz's troops were nearly perfect on the home court (11-1) and put together an impressive 4-1 record against ranked teams. Five Illini players were accorded post-season honors, including junior Ashley Berggren, who was picked by the media as Conference Player of the Year. Also chosen as Big Ten all-stars were Alicia Sheeler (third team), Krista Reinking (honorable mention), and Tauja Catchings and Katie Coleman (all-freshman team). Grentz won Big Ten Coach of the Year. In NCAA tournament play, Illinois made it to the Sweet Sixteen for the first time and nearly upset top-ranked Connecticut in the NCAA regional semifinal.

OTHER TOP MOMENTS

1. First-year volleyball coach Don Hardin beat his former team, No. 15 Louisville, 3–0.
2. Jillian Ellis was named as Illinois's first women's soccer coach.
3. Illinois's women's gymnastics team sets a school record for dual meet victories (13-5).

WOMEN'S ILLINI LIST

VOLLEYBALL: DON HARDIN VS. THE BIG TEN

22-4	(.846)	Iowa
20-6	(.769)	Indiana
17-9	(.654)	Northwestern
17-9	(.654)	Purdue
13-13	(.500)	Michigan
13-13	(.500)	Michigan State
9-17	(.346)	Ohio State
7-18	(.280)	Minnesota
7-20	(.259)	Wisconsin
2-25	(.074)	Penn State

Don Hardin

Tisha Ponder was the freshest of the freshmen in the Big Ten track-and-field class of 1996–97. The young lady from Delmar High School in San Jose, California, made a huge splash at the championship level, winning the Big Ten indoor title at Illinois's Armory with a long jump of 20'1¾". That performance landed her Freshman of the Year honors indoors. Three months later, again on her home turf in Champaign—but this time outdoors—Ponder added 8.5 inches in her specialty event, winning the championship by nearly six inches. Once again, she was Freshman of the Year. When the University of Illinois handed out its end-of-the-year awards, Ponder was a shoo-in as Newcomer of the Year.

Tisha Ponder

WOMEN'S ILLINI LEGEND

Ashley Berggren

Ashley Berggren

After having suffered through a brutal freshman season in which her team had posted a 10-17 record, Ashley Breggren blossomed beautifully under Theresa Grentz's system, setting an Illini single-season scoring record in 1995–96 while averaging 24.6 points per game. That season included a forty-three-point game against Minnesota, thirty-eight points versus Northwestern, and thirty-six points against Purdue, three of the top efforts in Illini history. During Berggren's junior season, Illinois captured the school's first Big Ten title in women's basketball and advanced to the Sweet Sixteen, taking top-ranked Connecticut to the limit in a five-point loss. As a senior, Berggren and the Illini again won their first two NCAA tournament games, and she became UI's all-time leading scorer (2,089 points) and a third-team All-American. Her crowning glory came in 1998, when she was named Illinois's Female Athlete of the Year and winner of the Big Ten Conference Medal of Honor. Berggren went on to play professional basketball and has coached at both the prep and collegiate levels in Illinois and Colorado. A banner with her jersey (32) hangs in the rafters of the State Farm Center.

OTHER TOP WOMEN'S ATHLETES

1. Stacy Ann Grant, track and field (Big Ten high-jump champ)
2. Kelly Buszkiewicz, golf (team Most Valuable Player)
3. Kelly Scherr, volleyball (Big Ten Conference Medal of Honor recipient)

ILLINI LORE

In September 1996, the University of Illinois opened its beautiful new Campus Recreation Outdoor Center and multiplex fields. Located west of the Activities and Recreation Center (ARC) at First Street, the amenities featured six lighted basketball and tennis courts, three lighted sand volleyball courts, and four lighted turf fields.

Beach volleyball courts

1997—98

AMERICA'S TIME CAPSULE

November 19, 1997	Seven babies—four boys and three girls—were delivered by doctors to Bobbi and Kenny McCaughey in Iowa.
March 23, 1998	*Titanic* beat out *Good Will Hunting* and *As Good as It Gets* as Best Picture at the seventieth annual Academy Award ceremonies in Hollywood.
May 15, 1998	Frank Sinatra died of a heart attack at age eighty-two.
June 16, 1998	In what many people thought would be his final game, Michael Jordan hit the game-winning shot with just 0:05.2 left and led the Chicago Bulls to an 87–86 victory over the Utah Jazz in the deciding game of the NBA Finals.
August 17, 1998	In a televised address to the nation, President Bill Clinton admitted to an affair with White House intern Monica Lewinsky.

MEN'S ILLINI MOMENT

Coach Itch Jones

DJ Svihlik

Illini "9" Come within Two Outs of College World Series Berth

Illinois's 1998 baseball season was truly a rollercoaster ride, ranging from a series of steep hills and sharp curves to a heart-pounding finish. As it had done in previous seasons, Coach Itch Jones's squad got off to a painfully slow start, losing its first six games. Thanks to steady pitching and the powerful bats of second baseman D. J. Svihlik (fifteen home runs) and third baseman Craig Marquie (fifty-eight RBI), the Fighting Illini methodically improved, winning thirteen of their first fourteen games at Illinois Field. In Big Ten play, Illinois got off to a marvelous 9-1 start and came up big at the end as well, sweeping four home games against Iowa and four road games at Purdue to claim its first regular-season Big Ten championship in thirty-five years. The Illini placed second behind Minnesota in the conference tournament yet earned a berth in NCAA south regional play. In the opener at Gainesville, Florida, Wake Forest outslugged Illinois, 14–12, but the Illini won their next three against Monmouth, Baylor, and Wake Forest to qualify for the title game against host Florida. The winner would earn a spot in the College World Series. UI senior All-American Brett Weber, the Big Ten's Pitcher of the Year, hurled 7.2 gutsy innings on two days' rest against the Gators, and the game eventually went to extra innings. Illinois took a 6–5 lead into the bottom of the eleventh but surrendered two runs to Florida, losing by a score of 7–6 to bring a disappointing end to an otherwise storybook season (42-21 overall).

OTHER TOP MOMENTS

1. Illinois topped Northwestern, 4–1, to win the Big Ten tennis tournament finals at the Atkins Tennis Center.

2. Travis Romagnoli won the NCAA gymnastics championship all-around title and Big Ten Gymnast of the Year honors.

3. Six baseball players—D. J. Svihlik, Craig Marquie, Dan O'Neil, Aaron Nieckula, Brett Weber, and Jim Journell—were named first-team All–Big Ten.

4. Senior Kevin Turner hit a spinning bank shot at the end of regulation, then Illini the outscored Wisconsin in overtime to win their first game at UW's new Kohl Center.

5. Kevin Rudden blasted three home runs in Illinois baseball's 20–3 win over Michigan.

MEN'S ILLINI LIST

MARK JOHNSON'S NCAA WRESTLING CHAMPS

1995	Ernest Benion, 158 pounds
1995	Steve Marianetti, 150 pounds
1998	Eric Siebert, 150 pounds
2000	Carl Perry, 141 pounds
2001	John Lockhart, heavyweight
2001	Adam Tirapelle, 149 pounds
2003	Matt Lackey, 165 pounds

2000 NCAA champion Carl Perry

MEN'S ILLINI ITEM

Anchored by the upper-class starting five of Jerry Hester, Brian Johnson, Jarrod Gee, Kevin Turner, and Matt Heldman, Illinois captured the school's thirteenth Big Ten title in 1997–98. It rolled through the conference schedule with a 13-3 record. The most exciting game came on February 12, when the Illini blasted co-champion Michigan State, 84–63. The seniors, paced by Turner's 17.7 points per game, provided an amazing 84 percent of the team's total scoring.

(Left to right) Kevin Turner, Jerry Hester, Brian Johnson, Jarrod Gee, Matt Heldman, and Coach Lon Kruger

MEN'S ILLINI LEGEND

Eric Siebert

During every stage of his life, former Illini wrestler Eric Siebert has made an impact. As a prep at LaSalle-Peru High School, Siebert won the first state title in Cavaliers wrestling history. At the University of Illinois from 1995 to 1998, he was a four-time NCAA tournament qualifier. Siebert's senior season was particularly impressive, finishing with a perfect 36-0 record at 150 pounds, including Illinois's sixteenth national individual title. Furthermore, Siebert, with a 112-30 career record, received UI's 1998 Male Athlete of the Year award and the prestigious Big Ten Conference Medal of Honor, symbolic of achievement on the mat and in the classroom. In 2001 Siebert was inducted into the Illinois Wrestling

Eric Siebert

Coaches and Officials Association Hall of Fame. Seven years later, he became head wrestling coach at Carl Sandberg High School in Orland Park, taking over for legendary coach Mike Polz. An eighth Siebert protégé earned a state championship in 2015–16, and his teams have won a pair of state titles. He and his wife have two children.

OTHER TOP MEN'S ATHLETES

1. D. J. Svihlik, baseball (Big Ten Player of the Year)
2. Robert Holcombe, football (team MVP, five 100+ rushing games)
3. Kevin Turner, basketball (first-team All–Big Ten, team co-MVP with Jerry Hester)

1997–98

WOMEN'S ILLINI MOMENT

Coach Theresa Grentz (left) and
Ashley Berggren

Basketball Makes Sweet Sixteen

While it didn't win a Big Ten championship as it did in 1996–97, Coach Theresa Grentz's squad was able to play its way into the NCAA's Sweet Sixteen. Illinois began the year ranked seventh in the preseason poll and advanced two more spots following its November 30 defeat of No. 15 Duke at the San Juan Shootout. However, a three-game losing streak, including consecutive losses at No. 1 Tennessee and to No. 18 Stanford at home, forced the Illini to regroup. Behind the steady scoring of Ashley Berggren, the aggressive rebounding of Alicia Sheeler, and the pin-point assists from sophomore Tauja Catchings, the Illini won their first seven Big Ten games. Illinois did have the advantage of playing its first two NCAA tournament games at home, then took on No. 7 North Carolina at Nashville in the third round. An 80–74 loss resulted, and the Illini finished with a 20-10 record.

OTHER TOP MOMENTS

1. Illini women's basketball was ranked fifth in the nation by Associated Press (December 8).
2. Stacy Ann Grant placed fourth in the high jump at the NCAA track-and-field championships.
3. Illinois volleyball team defeated three Top 25 teams en route to posting 17-13 overall record.

WOMEN'S ILLINI LIST

LONG-DISTANCE MARKSWOMEN (career three-point field goals of total attempts)

1.	295 (of 848)	Amber Moore, 2009–2014
2.	214 (of 576)	Lori Bjork, 2005–2008
3.	194 (of 582)	Krista Reinking, 1994–1998
4.	168 (of 468)	Mandy Cunningham, 1990–1994
5.	149 (of 377)	Kyley Simmons, 2012–2016
6.	133 (of 416)	Melissa Parker, 1996–2000
7.	114 (of 283)	Allison Curtin, 1998–2001
8.	103 (of 343)	Ivory Crawford, 2011–2015

Krista Reinking

9.	99 (of 288)	Aminata Yanni, 2000–2004
10.	96 (of 339)	Jere Issenmann, 2001–2005

Illinois's first women's soccer team

WOMEN'S ILLINI ITEM

Soccer Joins Varsity Sports The University of Illinois's first new varsity sport in nineteen years made its debut in 1997. Coach Jill Ellis's soccer roster was primarily made up of freshmen and sophomores. After winning its opening four games, the Illini struggled, losing seven games in a row, including six to Big Ten opponents. Illinois won two of its last five games to finish 7-10 overall and 1-8 in Big Ten games.

WOMEN'S ILLINI LEGEND

Yvonne Harrison

Yvonne Harrison

From 1996 to 1998, one of the prominent faces of University of Illinois women's track and field was Yvonne Harrison. Each season she competed, Harrison won at least one Big Ten championship, either on a 4x400-meter relay team or as an individual sprinter and hurdler. Three times she won All-American laurels at the NCAA meet, including a second-place finish in the 400-meter intermediate hurdles during her senior year. That performance earned Harrison Female Athlete of the Year honors, which she shared with co-honoree Ashley Berggren (basketball). She served as Illinois's volunteer assistant coach for one season, then represented Puerto Rico as a professional athlete, which afforded her the opportunity to compete in three World Championships (Edmonton 2001, Paris 2003, and Helsinki 2005) and to appear in the 2004 Olympic Games in Athens, where she finished as a semifinalist. Harrison then joined the track-and-field staff at St. John's University. Today, she is the senior pastor of Restoration Temple Ministries in Bronx, New York. She's currently pursuing her DMin in Homiletics at New York Theological Seminary.

OTHER TOP WOMEN'S ATHLETES

1. Kim Berres, gymnastics (All–Big Ten)
2. Aspen Burkett, Collinus Newsome, Benita Kelley, Lyria Martin, and Aleisha Latimer, track and field (All–Big Ten)
3. Cristy Chapman and Tracey Marshall, volleyball (first-team All–Big Ten)

ILLINI LORE

On January 28, 1998, the day after his State of the Union address, President Bill Clinton spoke to an enthusiastic, standing-room-only crowd at the Assembly Hall. Four hundred media members accompanied the president and vice president on their visit. Air Force One, which had delivered the Washington celebrities, made additional news afterward, getting stuck in the mud at Willard Airport in Savoy.

President Bill Clinton visited the University of Illinois in January of 1998

1998-99

AMERICA'S TIME CAPSULE

September 8, 1998	Mark McGwire broke one of baseball's most revered records when he slugged his sixty-second home run, topping the thirty-seven-year-old mark of sixty-one homers by Roger Maris.
October 29, 1998	Seventy-seven-year-old John Glenn returned to space thirty-six years after becoming the first American in orbit.
December 19, 1998	The United States House of Representatives impeached President Clinton on charges of perjury and obstruction of justice in the White House sex scandal.
April 20, 1999	Two Littleton, Colorado, students went on a shooting rampage at Columbine High School, killing fifteen, including themselves.

MEN'S ILLINI MOMENT

Illinois's 1999 Big Ten champs

Tennis Wins Again

It was déjà vu for the Fighting Illini men's tennis team in 1999. Not only did the team roll over its Big Ten competition to the tune of a perfect 13-0 record for a second consecutive season, head coach Craig Tiley also repeated as Big Ten Coach of the Year. The biggest improvement from the previous season was the team's record-setting 28-4 dual-meet mark and its advancement to the NCAA tournament's Elite Eight. Though the season ended on a sour note when fifth-seed Mississippi's 4–3 victory spoiled third-seed Illini's hopes of a national championship, it remained an unforgettable year. Individually, senior Oliver Freelove from England won Big Ten Athlete of the Year honors. Team-wise, Illinois eventually extended its Big Ten dual-meet winning streak to fifty-seven consecutive matches, dating from April 16, 1997, to April 29, 2001.

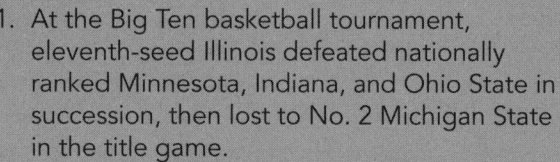

OTHER TOP MOMENTS

1. At the Big Ten basketball tournament, eleventh-seed Illinois defeated nationally ranked Minnesota, Indiana, and Ohio State in succession, then lost to No. 2 Michigan State in the title game.
2. Rocky Harvey rushed for 215 yards as the Illini snapped an eighteen-game losing streak, beating Middle Tennessee, 48–20.
3. Track and field's Bobby True was named Big Ten Indoor Athlete of the Championship and received the Big Ten Conference Medal of Honor.

Itch Jones won Big Ten Coach of the Year honors in 1998 and 2005

MEN'S ILLINI LIST

BIG TEN COACHES OF THE YEAR

Baseball	Richard "Itch" Jones (1998, 2005)	Men's Golf	Ed Beard (1988)
	Dan Hartleb (2015)		Mike Small (2002, 2009, 2010, 2011, 2012, 2013, 2015, 2016)
Men's Basketball	Lou Henson (1993)	Men's Gymnastics	Yoshi Hayasaki (1988, 1989, 2004, 2009)
	Bruce Weber (2005)		Justin Spring (2010, 2011, 2012)
Football	Mike White (1983)	Men's Tennis	Craig Tiley (1998, 1999, 2000, 2002, 2003, 2004, 2005)
	John Mackovic (1988, 1989)	Men's Track and Field	Gary Wieneke (1988, 1989, 1994)
	Ron Turner (2001)		Mike Turk (2015)
	Ron Zook (2007)	Wrestling	Mark Johnson (2001, 2005)

MEN'S ILLINI ITEM

It had been 39 years since Illinois's wrestling team last beat the Iowa Hawkeyes, so it wasn't shocking to see Illini coach Mark Johnson's so emotional on February 19, 1999. With its 20–16 win, the eighth-ranked Illinois ended a dual-meet streak of thirty-two losses to their gold-and-black-clad neighbors. Though the Illini never trailed in the meet, the outcome wasn't decided until the final match won by redshirt freshman Griff Powell over eighth-ranked Jamie Heidt.

Illinois wrestling posted its first victory over Iowa in thirty-nine years

MEN'S ILLINI LEGEND

Oliver Freelove

Oliver Freelove

He traveled more than four thousand miles from his home in Bromley, England, to walk-on at the University of Illinois, but Oliver Freelove will tell you that his experience in the states was well worth the trip. The university's 1999 Male Athlete of the Year was rarely absent from the tennis courts, becoming the first Illini player to crack the century mark in both singles (119-62) and doubles (115-37). As a senior in 1999, Freelove was 34-14 by himself (10-2 Big Ten) and 37-8 (12-1) with doubles partner Cary Franklin, earning himself the conference's Player of the Year award. As a professional, the 6'4" right-hander was most successful as a doubles player, competing twice at Wimbledon.

OTHER TOP MEN'S ATHLETES

1. Sherman Armstrong, track and field (Big Ten Track Athlete of the Year)
2. Jon Anderson, baseball (All–Big Ten)
3. Cory Bradford, basketball (first-ever freshman player to be named Illini MVP)
4. Larry Luger and D. A. Points, golf (All–Big Ten)
5. Leo Oka, gymnastics (All–Big Ten)

1998—99

WOMEN'S ILLINI MOMENT

Terri Sullivan

Sullivan Joins Illini Family

On July 12, 1999, Fighting Illini Director of Athletics Ron Guenther named Terri Sullivan as the university's first softball coach. A product of Chicago's Madonna High School, Sullivan pitched for Loyola, a university where her father, Gene, once served as basketball coach. She joined the Illini staff from UI-Chicago, where she served as the Flames' assistant coach from 1993 to 1999.

OTHER TOP MOMENTS

1. Illini men's basketball defeated a school-record five ranked opponents (No. 17 Stanford, No. 13 Florida, No. 18 Penn State, No. 24 Ohio State, and No. 15 Penn State).
2. Sujay Lama began an eight-year stint as tennis coach.
3. Soccer posted a winning record (12-8) in only its second season.

WOMEN'S ILLINI LIST

FEMALE ATHLETES OF THE YEAR (by sport)

18	Track/Cross-Country
8	Volleyball
3	Basketball
2	Gymnastics
2	Golf
2	Soccer
1	Swimming

Track and field's Tonya Williams was UI's Female of the Year in 1995 and 1996

WOMEN'S ILLINI LEGEND

Christy Chapman

Christy (Chapman) Uhrig

First, she was an Eagle at Newton High School in Jasper County, Illinois. Then she became a Cardinal at the University of Louisville for two years. But when Don Hardin was hired to coach Illinois's volleyball team, Christy (Chapman) Uhrig just couldn't resist the opportunity to become a member of the Fighting Illini. It didn't take long for her to make an impact at Illinois, starting twenty-nine of the team's thirty matches as a middle blocker and ranking among the top three Illini in total blocks, kills, and hitting percentage. As a senior in 1998, Uhrig paced the team with twenty-nine solo blocks and 145 total stops, earning her a second-straight All–Big Ten honor. An even higher award came her way at the end of UI's 1998–99 athletics season, when she was named Illini Female Athlete of the Year. Uhrig played professionally from 1999 to 2003, then embarked on a coaching career that has taken her to California, then Louisville, then back to the West Coast, where she now coaches the Laguna Beach Volleyball Club. She, her husband, Jeff Uhrig, and their four sons reside in Coto de Caza, California.

OTHER TOP WOMEN'S ATHLETES

1. Gina Weichmann, gymnastics (All–Big Ten, co–Big Ten balance-beam champ)
2. Kerry Ann Richards, track and field (set Big Ten indoor championship record in 60-meter dash)
3. Stacy Schapiro, tennis (Big Ten Conference Medal of Honor recipient)
4. Simone Kung and Stacy Shapiro, tennis (All–Big Ten)

ILLINI LORE

The east entryway to the Urbana-Champaign campus at the corner of Lincoln Avenue and Illinois Street got a something-old-something-new look on October 8, 1998, when the Hallene Gateway Plaza was dedicated. Alumni Alan and Phyllis Hallene contributed the funds for the construction, which features the stone portal from the entrance to the first university-built classroom building, University Hall.

UI's Hallene Gateway Plaza

1999–2000

AMERICA'S TIME CAPSULE

September 18, 1999 — Hurricane Floyd, reduced to a tropical storm as it moved up the eastern United States, left thirty-four dead and thousands homeless.

November 12, 1999 — Judge Thomas Jackson handed down a 412-paragraph decision that Bill Gates's Microsoft had an illegal monopoly over personal-computer operating systems.

January 1, 2000 — The much-awaited turn of the century arrived with considerable celebration around the world—but without the violence or massive computer glitches that had been feared.

March 26, 2000 — At the Academy Awards, *American Beauty* won five awards, including Best Picture and Best Actor (Kevin Spacey).

MEN'S ILLINI MOMENT

Illinois Football Gets Offensive

Quarterback Kurt Kittner and Coach Ron Turner

For the first time in a long while, the 1999 Fighting Illini football team was positively offensive, and not negatively offensive. That is to say, Illinois fans weren't offended by the performance of its team, but its opponents' defensive units definitely were. Perhaps the best way to describe the Illini offense, led by recordsetting quarterback Kurt Kittner and a bevy of receivers and running backs, was by its splashy statistics. In 1999 Illinois scored a total of 388 points in twelve games (32.3 per game), more than any other team in Illini history. Coach Ron Turner's previous two squads (1997 and 1998) scored a cumulative total of 268 points in twenty-two games (12.2). And, in the sport of football, lots of points normally mean lots of victories, and that was the case in 1999, as Illinois went 8-4 and ranked tenth in the final Associated Press poll. With the exception of a heartbreaking 34–31 overtime loss at Indiana, Illinois posted wins each time it scored twenty-nine or more points. By far, the most satisfying triumphs were at Ann Arbor against ninth-ranked Michigan, where it came back from a record 27–7 deficit to beat the Wolverines, 35–29, and at Columbus versus Ohio State, where Illinois handed the Buckeyes their worst home loss in fifty years, 46–20. In fact, no team had beaten those two schools on the road in the same season since Michigan State won a national championship in 1951. Illinois's crowning jewel came at the Micronpc.com Bowl in Miami, where the Illini topped Virginia, 63–21, scoring the second-most points ever in a bowl game by any NCAA team.

OTHER TOP MOMENTS

1. After basketball's Lon Kruger left Illinois to become head coach of the Atlanta Falcons, Bill Self joined the Illini.

2. Illinois beat Penn State, 5–3, to win the Big Ten Tournament championship for the first time since 1990.

3. Craig Tiley was named Big Ten Tennis Coach of the Year.

4. Illini baseball team pounded out thirty-nine hits in a 32–0 win over St. Joseph's. Andy Schutzenhofer and Luke Simmons both were six-for-eight at the plate.

5. Wrestling's Carl Perry won the NCAA title at 141 pounds.

MEN'S ILLINI LIST

ACCURATE QUARTERBACKS

Kurt Kittner enjoyed the greatest season ever among Fighting Illini quarterbacks in 1999. In leading Illinois to an 8-4 record, he averaged 225 passing yards per game. Perhaps Kittner's most impressive statistic was his touchdown-to-interception ratio. UI's leaders in that category:

Kurt Kittner

Rank	TD	INT	DIFF	Player, Season
1.	24	5	+19	Kurt Kittner, 1999
2.	27	14	+13	Kurt Kittner, 2001
	19	6	+13	Johnny Johnson, 1994
4.	14	3	+11	Wes Lunt, 2014

Rank	TD	INT	DIFF	Player, Season
5.	21	11	+10	Jon Beutjer, 2002
	18	8	+10	Kurt Kittner, 2000
	22	12	+10	Jeff George, 1989
8.	17	8	+9	Nathan Scheelhaase, 2010
9.	21	13	+8	Nathan Scheelhaase, 2013
	18	10	+8	Jack Trudeau, 1984

MEN'S ILLINI ITEM

Cary Franklin and Graydon Oliver captured Illinois's first-ever national tennis championship on May 28, 2000, at the University of Georgia's Dan Magill Tennis Complex, breezing past Southern California's Ryan Moore and Nick Rainey by scores of 6–4 and 6–2. The victory earned Franklin and Oliver a berth in the prestigious U.S. Open in New York later that year.

Graydon Oliver (left) and Cary Franklin

MEN'S ILLINI LEGEND

Jason Anderson

The case for calling Jason Anderson the greatest pitcher in Illini baseball history is convincing. There's his cumulative 29-5 win-loss record from 1998 to 2000 or his 197 strikeouts in 287.1 innings, his pick to the All-American first team in 2000 and his two first-team All–Big Ten selections. But beyond his on-field accomplishments, the Danville, Illinois, star had equally impressive credentials in the classroom. As a junior, Anderson earned first-team Academic All-America honors with B+ grades in his accounting major. During his final season at Illinois, he had a 14-3 record, setting Illini single-season marks for victories and innings pitched (134.1), while leading UI to its fifth-consecutive postseason berth. That effort earned Anderson Illini Athlete of the Year honors, outpolling fellow athletic greats such as football quarterback Kurt Kittner, national doubles tennis champion Cary Franklin, and NCAA wrestling champ Carl Perry. The New York Yankees chose Anderson in the tenth round of the 2000 MLB draft; he played portions of three big-league seasons with the Yankees, Mets, and Indians (career record of 2-0 from 2003 to 2005). In 2017 he completed his third season as head baseball coach at Eastern Illinois University.

Jason Anderson

OTHER TOP MEN'S ATHLETES

1. Fred Wakefield, football (first-team All–Big Ten)
2. Travis Romagnoli, gymnastics (Big Ten Conference Medal of Honor recipient)
3. Andy Schutzenhofer, baseball (All–Big Ten)

1999–2000

WOMEN'S ILLINI MOMENT

The 2000 team created the foundation for Illinois's softball program

Softball Makes Its Debut

The University of Illinois softball team made its varsity debut in 2000, but due to the lack of a home field, Coach Terri Sullivan's players were never seen by their Illini faithful. Instead, the squad of twenty-four, stocked primarily with freshmen, played all thirty of its games on the road. Surprisingly, the results were anything but disastrous, as Illinois produced a respectable 13-17 record. The team lost a 3–2 decision to host Coastal Carolina in its first game, but the Illini women rallied in the nightcap of the double-header for their first-ever victory by the same score. The team's leaders were sophomore Heather Black (.391 average) and freshman pitcher Pam Almanza (7-8 record with a 3.02 ERA).

OTHER TOP MOMENTS

1. The Illini basketball won twenty-three games, second most in its twenty-six-year history, and made its fourth-straight appearance in the NCAA tournament.
2. In Tricia Taliaferro's first season as Illini soccer coach, UI compiled a 15-12-3 record.
3. The UI women's hoopsters defeat sixth-ranked Notre Dame, 77–67, at the Assembly Hall.

WOMEN'S ILLINI LIST

BASKETBALL PLAYERS WITH 1,000 POINTS AND 750 REBOUNDS

2,160 pts and 1,217 rebs	Jenna Smith (2007–2010)
1,965 pts and 1,043 rebs	Karisma Penn (2010–2013)
1,346 pts and 1,014 rebs	Cindy Dallas (1999–2004)
2,089 pts and 779 rebs	Ashley Berggren (1995–1998)
1,984 pts and 933 rebs	Jonelle Polk (1984–1987)
1,526 pts and 803 rebs	Kendra Gantt (1982–1985)
1,502 pts and 825 rebs	Tauja Catchings (1997–2000)
1,373 pts and 823 rebs	Kris Dupps (1992–1995)
1,322 pts and 894 rebs	Lynnette Robinson (1979–1982)
1,166 pts and 900 rebs	Lacey Simpson (2006–2010)

Tauja Catchings (12)

WOMEN'S ILLINI ITEM

Two seniors and a junior lifted the Fighting Illini volleyball team to their second consecutive invitation to the NCAA tournament. Illinois was sent to Gainesville, Florida, and won its opening match against Wisconsin-Milwaukee. However, the host Gators nipped the Illini, 3–2, in a hard-fought five-set battle, ending UI's season at 17-11. Veteran setter Melissa Beitz broke UI's all-time career-assists record (5,797), and fellow senior Tracey Marshall became the school's all-time digs leader—1,426 over four years. Junior middle blocker Betsy Spicer received first-team All–Big Ten honors, as well as All-District 2 kudos from the AVCA.

Melissa Beitz   Tracey Marshall

WOMEN'S ILLINI LEGEND

Jessica Aveyard-Sayers

Jessica Aveyard

In 2000, for the first time in history, a Fighting Illini women's swimmer was honored as the Dike Eddleman Female Athlete of the Year. Though only a sophomore, Jessica Aveyard-Sayers beat out Illini seniors Kerry Ann Richards and Tauja Catchings, plus juniors Tara Mendozza, Betsy Spicer, and Emily Brown for the prize. Aveyard-Sayers was Illinois's most versatile swimmer, competing in a variety of distance freestyle and backstroke events. She was best at the 200-meter backstroke, obliterating the team record by more than two seconds. At the time, Aveyard-Sayers's 1:57.90 swim at the NCAA championships was the fastest time ever among Big Ten swimmers. Her junior season at Illinois saw her repeat as an All-American in the 200-meter backstroke, finishing sixth at the NCAA meet.

OTHER TOP WOMEN'S ATHLETES

1. Emily Brown, soccer (All–Big Ten)
2. Tisha Ponder, track and field (All–Big Ten)
3. Tara Mendozza, track and field (Big Ten Conference Medal of Honor recipient)
4. Tauja Catchings, basketball (team Most Valuable Player)

Aveyard-Sayers competed at the World Championships during the summer of 2002, then sparkled again for the Illini as a senior. When she graduated in 2003, she had the best times in UI history in both the 200-meter backstroke and the 500-meter freestyle. Aveyard-Sayers went on to earn an MBA at Illinois in 2005, then began work as a sales manager at Archer Daniels Midland in Decatur. She spent two years in Minnesota with Land O'Lakes, then six more in Denver with Trinidad Benham. She and her husband have two children.

ILLINI LORE

There was a historic gathering of Chief Illiniwek supporters and detractors on April 14, 2000, at the University of Illinois's Foellinger Auditorium. Louis Garripo, former circuit court judge in Cook County, presided over the spirited dialogue, which featured anti-Chief groups from as far away as Oklahoma, as well as legions of supportive alumni and friends. Six months later, Garripo's statistical findings were presented to the University of Illinois Board of Trustees, but it did not settle the longstanding argument over the university's seventy-five-year-old symbol.

Judge Louis Garippo

2000–01

AMERICA'S TIME CAPSULE

October 26, 2000	The Yankees won the Subway Series by beating the Mets, claiming their third-consecutive world championship.
November 7, 2000	Texas Governor George W. Bush and Vice President Al Gore squared off in the closest presidential election ever, so close that a winner wasn't declared until thirty-six days later, on December 13.
December 12, 2000	Twenty-five-year-old free agent Alex Rodriguez signed a record-high ten-year, $252 million baseball contract with the Texas Rangers.
February 18, 2001	NASCAR legend Dale Earnhardt died in a crash on the final lap of the Daytona 500.
June 11, 2001	Convicted Oklahoma City bomber Timothy McVeigh was put to death, becoming the first federal prisoner to be executed in thirty-eight years.

MEN'S ILLINI MOMENT

The 2001 Big Ten champions

Men's Basketball Shares Big Ten Title, Earns No. 1 Seed

It is true that when Lon Kruger departed Illinois to become head coach of the Atlanta Hawks, he left the cupboard overflowing with talent for incoming coach Bill Self. Ready for action were Peoria seniors Sergio McClain and Marcus Griffin, junior three-point specialist Cory Bradford, and super sophs Frank Williams and Brian Cook. But as the old saying goes, "Championships are won on the court, not on paper," so there was plenty of pressure on the Fighting Illini to produce positive results in 2000–01. Illinois faced a very difficult nonconference schedule but wound up posting victories over powerhouses Maryland, Seton Hall, Arizona, and Missouri. The Big Ten portion of the slate was filled with highlights as well, including wins in six of its first seven conference games, a scintillating eleven-point victory over fourth-ranked Michigan State at the Assembly Hall, and triumphs over Iowa and at Minnesota to end the regular season that allowed the Illini to share the regular-season crown. Though UI slipped unexpectedly at the Big Ten tournament, it was still rewarded with a No. 1 seed in the NCAA tournament. Northwestern State and Charlotte were Illinois's first two victims, then, at the Midwest regional in San Antonio, Illinois opened play by spanking Kansas by sixteen points, setting up a regional finals game against Arizona. However, foul problems plagued the Illini, and they missed out on the Final Four by just six points. UI's twenty-seven victories were the second-most in its history, and Frank Williams became the first Illini player since 1967 to earn Big Ten Most Valuable Player honors. Also during the 2000–01 season, Cory Bradford extended his consecutive-games streak (with a threepointer) to eighty-eight.

OTHER TOP MOMENTS

1. Tennis went undefeated (10-0) in Big Ten dual meets.

2. Illinois handed Purdue its worst-ever defeat at Mackey Arena, winning 82–61. Cory Bradford hit a three-pointer in his eighty-eighth straight game.

3. Wrestling finished second in Big Ten Championships; Mark Johnson was conference Coach of the Year.

4. No. 7 Illini got a triple-double (ten points/eleven rebounds/eleven assists) from Sergio McClain in an 80–51 win against Michigan.

5. Former Illini baseball star Darrin Fletcher presented a gift of $50,000 to the Fighting Illini Scholarship Fund.

6. Marcus Griffin scored the last of his eighteen points off an inbounds pass from Sean Harrington with eight-tenths of a second left as No. 4 Illinois beat No. 19 Wisconsin, 68–67.

MEN'S ILLINI LIST

MOST SUCCESSFUL FIRST-YEAR MEN'S BASKETBALL COACHES

Coach Bill Self

Bill Self's debut in 2000–01 as the Fighting Illini men's basketball coach was a spectacular one, joining Doug Mills as the only UI coaches who won Big Ten titles in their inaugural seasons.

Rank	Pct. (W-L)	Coach, First Season	Rank	Pct. (W-L)	Coach, First Season
1.	.788 (26-7)	Bruce Weber, 2003–04*	6.	.688 (22-10)	Lon Kruger, 1996–97
2.	.778 (14-4)	Doug Mills, 1936–37*	7.	.639 (23-13)	John Groce, 2012–13
3.	.771 (27-8)	Bill Self, 2000–01*	8.	.625 (10-6)	Ralph Jones, 1912–13
4.	.769 (20-6)	Fletcher Lane, 1907–08	9.	.611(11-7)	Frank Winters, 1920–21
5.	.750 (15-5)	Harry Combes 1947–48	10.	.600 (9-6)	Craig Ruby, 1922–23

*Big Ten Champion

MEN'S ILLINI ITEM

Illinois lost three of its most legendary athletes within a 105-day span when Andy Phillip (April 28, 2001), Dike Eddleman (August 1, 2001), and Lou Boudreau (August 10, 2001) all died. Phillip, age seventy-nine, was a member of the Basketball Hall of Fame and Illinois's Whiz Kids; Eddleman, age seventy-eight, was generally recognized as UI's greatest all-around athlete; and Boudreau, age eighty-four, was Illinois's only former athlete inducted into the Baseball Hall of Fame.

Dike Eddleman (center) with Jason Anderson (left) and Jessica Aveyard

MEN'S ILLINI LEGENDS

Adam Tirapelle   John Lockhart

Adam Tirapelle and John Lockhart

On March 17, 2001, individual national championships by Adam Tirapelle at 149 pounds and by John Lockhart at heavyweight boosted Illinois's total to six NCAA titles since 1995. Tirapelle and Lockhart were both runners-up at the 2001 Big Ten meet, but they advanced all the way to the top step of the awards stand at the national championships in Iowa City. Tirapelle faced Lehigh's Dave Esposito and posted a 5–3 win. As for Lockhart, he consistently used overtime to his advantage. The junior from Mahomet, Illinois, used two overtimes in his first-round match, a single overtime in his second-round match, a single-point victory in the quarterfinals, a two-overtime victory in the semis, and two overtimes in the final. He escaped with eleven seconds remaining in the thirty-second sudden-victory period to claim his crown. Team-wise, Illinois finished fifth nationally, its best placing since 1946. Tirapelle is now an advisor in the Hobbs, Conner, and Tirapelle Wealth Management Group in Clovis, California. Lockhart is a pediatric primary-care sports-medicine specialist for Seattle Children's Hospital and also a clinical assistant professor at the University of Washington.

OTHER TOP MEN'S ATHLETES

1. Andy Dickinson, baseball (Big Ten Pitcher of the Year)
2. Fred Wakefield, football (first-team All–Big Ten)
3. Graydon Oliver, tennis (Big Ten Conference Medal of Honor recipient)

2000–01

WOMEN'S ILLINI MOMENT

NCAA Record

It was a world-record-setting performance for four Fighting Illini women's track hurdlers at the Drake Relays in Des Moines, Iowa, on April 27, 2001. The 4x100-meter shuttle hurdle relay quartet of Jenny Kallur, Camee Williams, Susanna Kallur, and Perdita Felicien streaked around the track in an all-time-best clocking of 52.85 seconds, shattering LSU's ten-year-old record of 53-flat. "The record had been a goal of ours," said head coach Gary Winckler. "We executed very well. I couldn't be happier."

The world record-breaking shuttle-hurdle relay team of (left to right) Jenny Kallur, Camee Williams, Perdita Felicien, and Susanna Kallur

OTHER TOP MOMENTS

1. Illinois's softball complex, Eichelberger Field, was dedicated on March 27, 2001. Longtime Illini women's athletics advocate Lila Jeanne "Shorty" Eichelber threw out the ceremonial first pitch.
2. Coach Theresa Grentz's basketball team beat two ranked teams (No. 14 Auburn and No. 10 Penn State).
3. The U of I volleyball squad beat No. 13 and two-time defending Big Ten champion Wisconsin.

WOMEN'S ILLINI LIST

SUE NOVITSKY'S SWIMMING ALL-AMERICANS

2001	Jessica Aveyard, 200-meter backstroke
2001	Anna Christiansen, 400-meter individual medley (honorable mention)
2002	Jessica Aveyard, 200-meter backstroke (honorable mention)
2002	Ilkay Dikmen, 200-meter breaststroke (honorable mention
2004	Ilkay Dikmen, 200-meter breaststroke (honorable mention)
2005	Barbie Viney, 100-meter freestyle (honorable mention)

Coach Sue Novitsky

For six straight years the Bettendorf Bulldogs won the girls state tennis championship, and each team's roster included at least one young lass named McGaffigan. Jenny McGaffigan eventually found her way to Champaign-Urbana and enjoyed major success. As a first-year player for the Illini in 2001, she won honors as the Big Ten's Freshman of the Year and also as the school's Newcomer of the Year. That season and for the next three years, McGaffigan earned All–Big Ten laurels. She ended her Illini career as the school's top winner in both singles (105-58) and doubles (104-49). She received what is perhaps her greatest award in 2004, when McGaffigan won the Big Ten Conference Medal of Honor.

Jenny McGaffigan

WOMEN'S ILLINI LEGEND

Betsy (Spicer) Brookbank

Betsy Spicer

Illini volleyball alum Betsy (Spicer) Brookbank loved her home away from home, Huff Gym. "Huff was one of the greatest places to play," said Brookbank. "The crowd was so much fun and every match felt special." And she loved her coach, Don Hardin. "He was like another parent. Don not only cared about the program and making sure it was successful, but he cared about making sure you had the best college experience."

From 1997 to 2000, Brookbank experienced personal success, twice winning first-team All–Big Ten honors. She'll also be remembered for her triple-double against Kansas State in 1998: thirteen kills, thirteen digs and eleven blocks. As a senior, Brookbank received the prestigious Big Ten Conference Medal of Honor, awarded for proficiency in athletics and academics. She played three years of professional volleyball and spent several more as a coach. She met her husband, Wade, in Grand Rapids, Michigan, and has followed him during his National Hockey League stops in Nashville, Vancouver, Boston, and Carolina, and many other minor league destinations. Today, he's a professional scout for the Chicago Blackhawks. The Brookbank family includes two children.

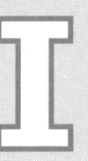

OTHER TOP WOMEN'S ATHLETES

1. Perdita Felecien, track and field (Female Athlete of the Year)
2. Cecelia Williams, cross-country (All–Big Ten)
3. Emily Brown, soccer (first-team All–Big Ten)
4. Gia Lewis, track and field (Big Ten discus champ)

ILLINI LORE

Where, for years, sheep and other livestock roamed in 138 acres of grassy fields, the University of Illinois's newest research park began to sprout on the southwest corner of St. Mary's Road and First Street in the summer and fall of 2000. Officially known as the Science and Technology Engineering Technology Communications Center, these impressive structures of brick and mortar send a strong message about the U of I's support of economic development. Motorola, long a corporate partner of the university, became the park's first official tenant. Today, the Research Park includes more than one hundred companies that employ students and full-time technology professionals.

University of Illinois Research Park

2001–02

AMERICA'S TIME CAPSULE

September 11, 2001 — Nineteen foreign terrorists hijacked four American passenger jets, crashing two of them into the north and south towers of New York's World Trade Center, another into the Pentagon, and a fourth plane into a vacant field southeast of Pittsburgh. A total of 3,056 people died.

October 5, 2001 — Barry Bonds of the San Francisco Giants broke Mark McGwire's single-season home run record by hitting his seventy-first homer against Los Angeles Dodgers pitcher Chan Ho Park. He would eventually hit seventy-three home runs during the 2001 season.

February 8, 2002 — The nineteenth Olympic Winter Games opened in Salt Lake City, Utah. Among the ten American gold medal winners were figure skater Sara Hughes, sledder Jack Shea, and speed skater Derek Parra.

MEN'S ILLINI MOMENT

Captains Bobby Jackson (2), Kurt Kittner (15), Brandon Moore (96), and Luke Butkus (71), and Coach Ron Turner accept the 2001 Big Ten championship trophy

Illinois Football Enjoys a Sweet Season

Highlighted by victories over three Top 25 teams and a perfect 6-0 record at home, Big Ten Coach of the Year Ron Turner and the Fighting Illini football team made school history in 2001, qualifying for their first-ever appearance in the Bowl Championship Series. A record-setting offensive effort and a surprisingly stingy defense yielded Illinois's first Big Ten championship since 1990 and a 10-1 regular-season record. Spoiled only by a game 4 loss at seventeenth-ranked Michigan, the Illini swept the remaining seven games of their schedule, averaging more than thirty-four points per game. One by one, Illinois defeated Minnesota, Indiana, Wisconsin, fifteenth-ranked Purdue, Penn State, twenty-fifth-ranked Ohio State, and Northwestern. Two days after UI's thrilling 34–28 win over the Wildcats at Memorial Stadium on Thanksgiving Day, Ohio State did the Illini a favor by defeating Michigan at Ann Arbor, thus handing Illinois its first outright Big Ten title since 1983. UI's individual heroes included All-Big Ten first-teamers Tony Pashos (tackle) and Jay Kulaga (guard), center Luke Butkus, senior quarterback Kurt Kittner, who passed for 3,256 yards and a single-season record twenty-seven touchdowns, and receiver Brandon Lloyd, who caught ten TDs. Defensively, the stars included linebacker Jerry Schumacher, cornerbacks Eugene Wilson and Christian Morton, and safety Bobby Jackson. Punter Steve Fitts and placekicker Peter Christofilakos also were key contributors. Though the season ended disappointingly on New Year's Day at the Sugar Bowl in a 47–34 loss to Louisiana State, Illini fans still had a lot to smile about.

OTHER TOP MOMENTS

1. Illini tennis recaptured Big Ten title for its fourth championship in the last five seasons.

2. Golfers finished four strokes behind team titlist Minnesota at the Big Ten championship. James Lepp and Geoff Lound were selected to the All–Big Ten team.

3. The Big Ten cancelled the men's indoor track-and-field championships after the completion of four events due to the death of Penn State pole vaulter Kevin Dare.

MEN'S ILLINI LIST

BIG TEN CHAMPIONSHIPS BY ILLINI FOOTBALL AND
MEN'S BASKETBALL TEAMS IN THE SAME SEASON

1914–15	Football (outright), Basketball (outright)
1923–24	Football (shared with Michigan), Basketball (shared with Chicago and Wisconsin)
1951–52	Football (outright), Basketball (outright)
1983–84	Football (outright), Basketball (shared with Purdue)
2001–02	Football (outright), Basketball (shared with Indiana, Ohio State, and Wisconsin)

2001 Big Ten
football trophy

MEN'S ILLINI ITEM

Coach Bill Self's Fighting Illini repeated as Big Ten co-champions in 2002, but it took something like a miracle to record that achievement. In its final win of eight in a row, 67–66 at Minnesota, a shot by Frank Williams with three seconds left enabled the Illini to win back-to-back Big Ten titles for the first time in fifty years. Illinois won its first- and second-round NCAA tournament games at Chicago but fell to Kansas in the third game, ending its season with a record of 26-9.

Frank Williams's historic shot at Minnesota

MEN'S ILLINI LEGEND

Kurt Kittner

Since 1980, the list of University of Illinois football quarterbacking greats rivals that of any other school in the Big Ten. Starting with Dave Wilson, Tony Eason, and Jack Trudeau in the early 1980s and continuing with Jeff George, Jason Verduzco, and Johnny Johnson into the 1990s, this illustrious group of Illini triggermen was joined in the twenty-first century by a right-handed slinger from Schaumburg named Kurt Kittner. Statistically speaking, Kittner's numbers glowed as bright as any of his fellow Illini. Though he fell just nine feet short of Trudeau's career record of 8,725 passing yards, Kittner demolished Jack's mark for touchdown passes with seventy. Kurt's finest hour may have been as a sophomore in 1999 when he led Illinois to victories at Michigan and at Ohio State, the first time

Kurt Kittner

OTHER TOP MEN'S ATHLETES

1. Patrick Arlis and Andy Dickinson, baseball (All–Big Ten)
2. John Kronforst, cross-country (All–Big Ten)
3. Phil Stolt and Brian Wilson, tennis (All–Big Ten)
4. John Lockhart, wrestling (Big Ten Conference Medal of Honor recipient)

any Big Ten school had pulled off that feat in nearly half a century.
After a career from 2002 to 2005 with five pro teams, including four NFL clubs, he served as the color analyst on Illini radio broadcasts (2007–2015). Today, Kittner is senior vice president at Jones Lang LaSalle, a commercial real estate company in Chicago.

2001–02

WOMEN'S ILLINI MOMENT

Shadia Haddad

Volleyball's Exciting Ride

The 2001 season was a bit of a rollercoaster ride. Coach Don Hardin's sixth Illini team raced off to a 6-0 start, then faced a tough seven-game stretch, including matches against No. 11 Florida and four nationally ranked Big Ten opponents. Illinois stood 8-5 after the first week of October but then turned its season around by winning twelve of its last fifteen, including a 3–2 thriller versus No. 13 Penn State on November 9 at Huff Gym. UI was chosen to host the opening rounds of the NCAA tournament. It beat Missouri in the first match, 3–1, but lost by the same score to No. 4 Arizona. Illinois collected several individual honors from the Big Ten at season's end. Hardin was chosen as Coach of the Year, while senior Shadia Haddad was named the conference's Defensive Player of the Year. Additionally, sophomore Lisa Argabright joined Haddad as first-team All–Big Ten honorees.

OTHER TOP MOMENTS

1. For the second consecutive season, track and field star Perdita Felecien won UI's Female Athlete of the Year award.

2. On December 28, Illinois's basketball team began its Big Ten season with an 85–81 victory at Michigan.

3. Following the tragic September 11 attack on the World Trade Center, the Big Ten cancelled all athletic events for the following weekend.

WOMEN'S ILLINI LIST

ALL-TIME BIG TEN WOMEN'S SPORTS CHAMPIONSHIPS
(through 2015–16)

1.	Michigan	103
2.	Penn State	61
3.	Ohio State	58
4.	Wisconsin	38
5.	Indiana	37
6.	Northwestern	32
7.	Minnesota	29
8.	Iowa	27
9.	Michigan State	26

10.	Illinois	18
	Purdue	18
12.	Nebraska	8
13.	Maryland	5
14.	Rutgers	0

A quartet of stars led Illinois's second-year softball program to a 49-23 record in 2002. Both sophomore shortstop Lindsey Hamma and freshman outfielder LeeAnn Butcher were selected to the conference's first-team All–Big Ten squad, while sophomore catcher Janna Sartini was a third-team choice. Hamma hit a school-record .429 while Butcher batted .336. Sherri Taylor paced the Illini pitching staff with twenty wins and a 1.99 earned run average.

LeeAnn Butcher

WOMEN'S ILLINI LEGEND

Gia Lewis

Gia Lewis-Smallwood

As a youngster, Gia Lewis-Smallwood fancied herself a sprinter and a basketball player, eventually participating in both sports at Champaign's Centennial High School. During her senior year, the Chargers track coach encouraged Lewis to try the discus event as a way of scoring additional points for the team. College coaches began to seek her out because of her skills as a thrower, but she instead chose to walk on with the University of Illinois's basketball team. It became apparent that her dream of playing in the WNBA wasn't going to happen, so after one year she traded the twenty-two-ounce basketball for the 2.2-pound discus. Lewis had made a decision to maximize her enormous potential. "You have to practice a skill, then practice it some more," she said. Her hard work resulted in a Big Ten championship and a fifth-place finish at the NCAA meet in 2001, but Lewis wanted more. Over the course of a dozen years, she raised her personal best from 180 feet to an American best throw of 217.5 feet in 2013. Lewis's career was topped off by a trip in 2012 to the Olympic Games in London, where she placed fifteenth. Today, she resides in Champaign with her husband, Tim.

OTHER TOP WOMEN'S ATHLETES

1. Ashley Williams, gymnastics (All–Big Ten and Freshman of the Year)
2. Michelle Webb, tennis (Big Ten Conference Medal of Honor recipient)
3. Colleen Joyce, soccer (first-team All–Big Ten)
4. Jennifer McGaffigan, tennis (All–Big Ten)
5. Nicole Whitman and Camee Williams, track and field (All–Big Ten)

ILLINI LORE

On October 22, 2001, Chicago Bears President and CEO Ted Phillips and University of Illinois Director of Athletics Ron Guenther announced that the National Football League team would play its 2002 schedule at UI's Memorial Stadium. The move was made to allow the construction and renovation of Chicago's Soldier Field. As part of the deal, a number of major improvements were made at Memorial Stadium, including new training facilities and a state-of-the-art video scoreboard. One final note: the Bears went on to compile a disappointing record of 3-7 at their temporary home.

Chicago Bears CEO Ted Phillips announced that his NFL team would play its 2002 home games at UI's Memorial Stadium

2002-03

AMERICA'S TIME CAPSULE

September 24, 2002　The stock market sunk as the Dow Jones fell to a four-year low of 7,683.
November 25, 2002　President George W. Bush signed legislation creating the Department of Homeland Security.
February 1, 2003　The Space Shuttle Columbia disintegrated over Texas and Louisiana as it reentered the
　　　　　　　　　　Earth's atmosphere, killing all seven crew members.
March 20, 2003　The U.S. launched the country's first preemptive war, invading Iraq.
April 9, 2003　Baghdad fell, ending Saddam Hussein's twenty-four-year reign of Iraq.
June 26, 2003　Cleveland Cavaliers selected LeBron James No. 1 in the NBA draft.

MEN'S ILLINI MOMENT

The 2003 NCAA tennis champions

Men's Tennis Wins NCAA Championship

When Craig Tiley was named men's tennis coach in 1992, he put together a masterplan to build the University of Illinois into a national champion. On May 20, 2003, against 27-3 Vanderbilt at Dan Magill Tennis Complex in Athens, Georgia, his ultimate dream became a reality. Tiley's Illini headed into its biggest match in its ninety-four-season history with a perfect 31-0 record, but after losing a doubles point Illinois dropped two of three singles matches to fall into a 3–1 hole. With three singles matches remaining, the Illini had no margin for error. First, Illinois junior Michael Calkins prevailed at No. 5 singles, closing out Vandy's Zach Dailey and narrowing UI's deficit to 3–2. Eyes then turned to No. 4 singles where Illinois junior Phil Stolt won in three sets, tying the score at 3-all. Immediately, both teams descended to the winner-take-all match between UI's Chris Martin and VU's Lewis Smith. The score was tied at one set apiece, and Martin led the third set at 5–4; Martin rifled the match point shot past his opponent. Smith called the ball out, but the chair umpire overruled him, and the NCAA championship belonged to the Orange and Blue. For the first time since 1972, a team other than Georgia, Southern California, UCLA, or Stanford was sitting on top of the collegiate tennis world. Said Tiley afterward, "I wanted an opportunity to build a program with American players and sell it as a development program. With a little bit of luck, everything has fallen into place."

OTHER TOP MOMENTS

1. Illini swept Big Ten honors when Perdita Felicien won the Suzy Favor Female Athlete of the Year award, while tennis champ Amer Delic and wrestling titlist Mack Lackey shared the Jesse Owens Male Athlete of the Year prize.

2. Jerry Colangelo presented a gift of $1.25 million as an endowment for five men's basketball scholarships.

3. Football lost in overtime to eventual national champ Ohio State.

4. Craig Tiley was named Big Ten and NCAA Coach of the Year.

5. Brian Cook scored a career-high thirty-one points to lead tenth-ranked Illinois past Wisconsin, 69–63.

6. Gymnastics placed fifth at NCAA championship.

MEN'S ILLINI LISTS

BRIAN COOK, BIG TEN SCORING CHAMP

Illinois senior Brian Cook earned Big Ten Most Valuable Player honors in 2003, leading the conference in points (20.0), finishing third in rebounding (7.6), eighth in free throw percentage (.820), and tenth in field-goal percentage (.479). The Big Ten's top ten scoring leaders of 2003:

Brian Cook

1.	20.0	Brian Cook, Illinois	6.	16.2	LaVell Blanchard, Michigan
2.	18.3	Brent Darby, Ohio State	7.	15.8	Chauncey Leslie, Iowa
3.	17.8	Willie Deane, Purdue	8.	15.6	Rick Rickert, Minnesota
4.	16.2	Kirk Penney, Wisconsin	9.	15.2	Daniel Horton, Michigan
5.	16.2	Bracey Wright, Indiana	10.	14.9	Jeff Newton, Indiana

MEN'S ILLINI ITEM

Matt Lackey   As a teenager at Moline High School, Matt Lackey won two state titles and was a perfect 77-0 his last two seasons. At Illinois, from 2000 to 2003, he was victorious in 120 of his 134 matches, including a perfect 38-0 record as a senior. Lackey finished third at the 2001 NCAA Championships, improved to second at the 2002 meet, then won it all in 2003, earning honors as UI's Male Co-Athlete of the Year. Illini coach Mark Johnson told the *Quad City Times* that Lackey was the best athlete he'd coached in his seventeen seasons at Illinois. Today, he works for Stryker Orthopaedics in Lincoln, Nebraska.

Matt Lackey

MEN'S ILLINI LEGEND

Amer Delic

Born in Tuzla, Yugoslavia, Illini tennis star Amer Delic's family immigrated to Jacksonville, Florida, where he attended Samuel Wolfson High School and won the state championship. Amer was recruited to the University of Illinois by Coach Craig Tilley and eventually helped lead the Illini to the 2003 NCAA team title. That season, he won the NCAA singles championship, adding to his All-American and All-Big Ten honors. He also shared 2003 Illini Athlete of the Year honors with wrestler Matt Lackey. Delic's collegiate record in singles was 92-33 and he won twenty-six of his twenty-eight Big Ten singles matches. As a doubles player at Illinois, he was 89-31 overall and 26-6 against conference competition.

Delic turned pro in 2003 after his junior year at Illinois and played on the professional circuit for nine years. In 2009 Delic reached the Round of 32 at the Australian Open, losing to third-ranked Novak Djokovic in four sets. He reached the second round in a Grand Slam on five other occasions, including three other times at the Australian Open (2006, 2007, 2008). In 2015 Delic joined Meritage Capital, an investment management firm located in Austin, Texas.

Amer Delic

OTHER TOP MEN'S ATHLETES

1. Antoineo Harris, football (team Most Valuable Player)
2. James Lepp, golf (All–Big Ten)
3. Tony Pashos, football (first-team All–Big Ten)
4. Andy Schutzenhoffer, baseball (Big Ten Conference Medal of Honor recipient)
5. David Diehl and Eugene Wilson, football (second-team All–Big Ten)

2002-03

WOMEN'S ILLINI MOMENT

Amanda Fortune

Rachelle Coriddi

Softball Goes to NCAA Tournament for First Time

After two years of being spurned by the NCAA Softball Tournament Committee, Illinois was finally chosen to participate in 2003. Coach Terri Sullivan's team entered the Big Ten season on March 28 with a 19-5. After two narrow losses to U-M and Michigan State, the Illini won ten of their next eleven league games and rose to twenty-second in the national rankings. Despite a subpar performance at the Big Ten tournament, Illinois got the opportunity to play in the NCAA regional at Tuscaloosa, Alabama. It opened with a 5–3 win versus George Tech but was eliminated with losses in its next two games. Junior pitcher Amanda Fortune won twenty-four games and posted 123 strikeouts and a 1.89 ERA. Freshman Rachelle Coriddi led the Illini in hitting with a .357 average, while junior power-hitter Erin Montgomery paced the team with twelve home runs, fifteen doubles, and forty RBI. Jenna Hall, first base, was UI's lone first-team All–Big Ten selection.

OTHER TOP MOMENTS

1. Volleyball team beat No. 6 Minnesota and former Illini coach Mike Hebert.
2. The Illini basketball squad defeated a ranked team for the tenth straight year, 52–51, over No. 20 Ohio State.
3. In Janet Rayfield's first season, UI soccer topped No. 13 Purdue and No. 11 Penn State within a four-day span.

WOMEN'S ILLINI LIST

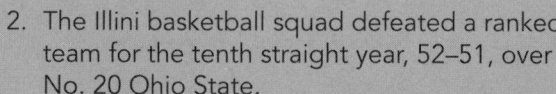

SOFTBALL'S HIGHEST SEASON BATTING AVERAGE
(min. 100 at-bats)

.481	Jenna Hall (63/131), 2006
.429	Lindsey Hamma (75/175), 2002
.425	Danielle Zymkowitz (71/167), 2011
.418	Meredith Hackett (64/153), 2010
.411	Hope Howell (74/180), 2010
.409	Danielle Zymkowitz (76/186), 2010
.401	Danielle Zymkowitz (63/157), 2009
.399	Allie Bauch (71/178), 2015

Lindsey Hamma

.383	Kylie Johnson (44/115), 2014
.376	Alyssa Gunther (65/173), 2015

Four-time Academic All–Big Ten tennis athlete Michelle (Webb) Voss earned the prestigious Big Ten Conference Medal of Honor in 2003, an award given to the individual with the greatest proficiency on the court and in the classroom. Her 32-10 doubles record in 2003 still stands as Illinois's record. Dr. Voss (PhD) now is an assistant professor in the Department of Psychological and Brain Sciences at the University of Iowa.

Michelle Webb

WOMEN'S ILLINI LEGEND

Perdita Felicien

Perdita Felicien

Perdita Felicien's track and field career would have never occurred had it not been for the constant urging of her mother. As an athlete for Coach Gary Winckler at the University of Illinois, Felicien accumulated myriad achievements. The ten-time All-American won three NCAA titles, one in the 60-meter hurdles (2002) and two in the 100-meter hurdles (2002, 2003), setting national marks in both events. Felicien won four Big Ten championships and, three times, was the Illini Female Athlete of the Year (2001, 2002, 2003). Her success carried on to the realm of professional sport. In 2003 Felicien won gold in the 100-meter hurdles at the IAAF world outdoor championships, and in 2004 she won the IAAF world indoor title. She has represented Canada at five world championships and a pair of Olympic Games (2000, 2004). Felicien had a busy year in 2016: on July 6 she was inducted into Athletic Canada's Hall of Fame; then, a month later, she served as a reporter for Canada's CBC Television Network at the Olympic Games in Rio de Janeiro. She's now writing a book about her life and her extraordinary relationship with her mother.

OTHER TOP WOMEN'S ATHLETES

1. Angelina Williams, basketball (team's leading scorer)
2. Tara Hurless and Meghan Kolze, soccer (second-team All–Big Ten)
3. Ilkay Dikmen, swimming (participated in two events at NCAA meet)
4. Ashley Williams and Kara Kapernekas, gymnastics (second-team All–Big Ten)

ILLINI LORE

The fifty-five-thousand-square-foot Spurlock Museum opened in 2002 at 600 South Gregory Street on the University of Illinois campus. Originally established in 1911 and housed on the fourth floor of Lincoln Hall, the extensive collection of cultural and archaeological collections became known as the World Heritage Museum in 1971. Spurlock Museum includes nine permanent exhibits that represent historical and contemporary peoples from around the world. Its visitors number more than fifty thousand each year, including thousands of schoolchildren and dozens of university classes.

UI's Spurlock Museum

2003-04

AMERICA'S TIME CAPSULE

October 7, 2003	Arnold Schwarzenegger was elected governor of California.
December 13, 2003	American troops capture Saddam Hussein.
January 27, 2004	*Lord of the Rings: Return of the King* won the Oscar for Best Picture.
February 4, 2004	Founder Mark Zuckerberg launched his *Facebook* website.
August 13, 2004	At the Olympic Games in Greece, American swimmer Michael Phelps won six gold and two bronze medals.

MEN'S ILLINI MOMENT

Luther Head's game-winning put-back at Purdue

Men's Basketball Wins Outright Big Ten Title

Bruce Weber's first season as head coach of the Fighting Illini basketball team was a smashing success, winning the school's first outright Big Ten title in fifty-two years. The Illini stood 3-3 after its first six Conference games, but went on to win its last ten games of the regular season to finish 13-3. The overtime finale at Purdue was won on a buzzer-beating put-back by Luther Head. Though the team lost the title game of the Big Ten tournament, the NCAA selection committee still rewarded the Illini with a No.

OTHER TOP MOMENTS

1. Illinois wrestling won the Midlands tournament for the first time.

2. A two-out RBI single by Dusty Bensko in the bottom of the seventh gave Illini baseball a 6–5 win over eventual Big Ten champ Minnesota.

3. Deron Williams scored a game-high thirty-one points against Coach Bob Huggins's Cincinnati Bearcats.

4. Track and field's Wayne Angel became Illinois's first African American male coach.

5 seed. Traveling three hundred miles east to Columbus and Ohio's Nationwide Arena, the Illini dispatched Murray State and higher-seed Cincinnati in consecutive games. However, top-seed Duke popped Illinois's postseason bubble in Atlanta, 72–62. The sophomore trio of Deron Williams (team MVP), Dee Brown, and James Augustine, plus juniors Roger Powell and Luther Head, accounted for 78 percent of the scoring. Though the Sweet Sixteen loss to the Blue Devils was painful, even more fruitful days were just ahead.

MEN'S ILLINI LIST

COLANGELO ELECTED TO BASKETBALL HALL OF FAME

On April 4, 2004, former Illini basketball and baseball letter winner Gerald J. "Jerry" Colangelo was inducted into the James Naismith Memorial Basketball Hall of Fame. Here is a timeline of his life and achievements:

1939	Born in Chicago Heights, Illinois
1960	Earned the first two of his four University of Illinois varsity letters in basketball and baseball
1966	Began his career in professional basketball with the Chicago Bulls
1968	Hired as the first general manager of the Phoenix Suns

1970	Became head coach of the Suns
1995	Granted (with his investment group) a Major League Baseball expansion team, the Arizona Diamondbacks
1996	Instrumental in relocating the NHL's Winnipeg Jets to Phoenix (Arizona Coyotes)
1997	His women's NBA team, the Phoenix Mercury, began playing
2004	Sold controlling interest to the Diamondbacks, Suns, and Mercury
2005	Named director of USA Basketball
2015	Became Chairman of Basketball Operations for the Philadelphia 76ers

---

MEN'S ILLINI ITEM

Tennis Wins Sixty-Four Straight Dual-Meet Matches With four All–Big Ten players on his roster, Coach Craig Tiley had almost forgotten what it felt like to lose. Beginning with a season-opening win versus Ball State on January 26, 2003, and continuing through an NCAA quarterfinal match against Vanderbilt on May 25, 2004, Illinois tennis assembled sixty-four consecutive dual-meet victories. Led by two-time Illini MVP Brian Wilson and fellow all-conference selections Michael Calkins, Ryler De-Heart, and Phil Stolt, Illinois only lost two or more sets twelve times during their amazing streak.

Brian Wilson

MEN'S ILLINI LEGEND

Justin Spring

Justin Spring's name aligns perfectly with his chosen sport. He inherited his athletic ability from his parents, Woody and Debbie, both former gymnasts. His older sister, Sarah, was a gymnast as well, performing for the Ohio State Buckeyes. Justin's specialties were the high bar and the parallel bars, and he won two NCAA titles in each event. During his four-year career at Illinois (2003–2006), he earned three individual Big Ten championships. As a senior in 2006, Spring received the Conference's Gymnast of the Year accolades. Twelve times he won All-American honors and twice received the Dike Eddleman Male Athlete of the Year award. Spring's spectacular career continued after his graduation in 2006. At the 2007 and 2008 national competitions, he won gold on the high bar (2007) and parallel bars (2008). He took first on the parallel bars at the 2008 Olympic trials, earning a spot on the United States team that eventually won bronze medals in Beijing. Spring concluded his seventh season as head coach at Illinois in 2017, highlighted in 2012 when he guided the Illini to its tenth NCAA team title and won National Coach of the Year honors.

Justin Spring

OTHER TOP MEN'S ATHLETES

1. Deron Williams, basketball (first-team All–Big Ten)
2. Alex Tirapelle, wrestling (157-pounder was NCAA semifinals, ended with 35-2 record)
3. Phil Stolt, tennis (Big Ten Conference Medal of Honor recipient)

2003-04

WOMEN'S ILLINI MOMENT

Tara Hurless

Illini Soccer Tops Michigan to Win BTT Final

Entering the 2003 Big Ten soccer tournament, Coach Janet Rayfield's Illini soccer team was riding a sea of positives. It had the premier goalkeeper in Leisha Alcia, and it had a powerhouse of a goal scorer in Tara Hurless. In the opening game at the University of Wisconsin's McClimon Soccer Complex, No. 2–seed Illinois blanked Michigan State, 2–0. The Illini duplicated that effort in game 2, topping Purdue by the same score in the semifinal round. That set up a match against Michigan. Illinois applied considerable pressure in the first half, but intermission arrived without any goals being scored. The Illini would score the game-winner with just more than ten minutes left, as Hurless found herself alone with the ball at the side of the box. She drew Michigan's keeper out of the net before putting it in the left side of the goal to give the Illini a 1–0 lead. Exactly three minutes later, Illinois boosted its lead to 2–0, when Jessica Bayne blasted a shot from the same spot as Hurless. Time eventually ran out on the Wolverines, and the championship belonged to Illinois.

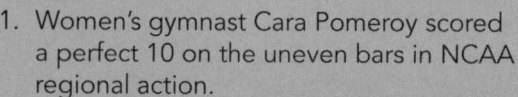

OTHER TOP MOMENTS

1. Women's gymnast Cara Pomeroy scored a perfect 10 on the uneven bars in NCAA regional action.
2. Volleyball topped Louisville in the second round of the NCAA tournament, sending it to Hawaii for a Sweet Sixteen game.
3. At Waco, Texas, the Illini softball team made its first appearance in an NCAA regional championship game, losing to LSU, 4–1.
4. Softball notched its first victory against a Top 10 foe, beating ninth-ranked Michigan, 3–2.

WOMEN'S ILLINI LIST

WINNINGEST WOMEN'S TENNIS PLAYERS (W-L)

105-38	Jennifer McGaffigan, 2000–2004
103-33	Lindsey Nimmo, 1990–1993
97-44	Megan Fudge, 2006–2010
89-60	Maureen McNamara, 1980–1984
87-55	Tiffany Eklov, 2000–2004
84-64	Marisa Lambropoulos, 2007–2012
83-79	Stacy Schapiro, 199519–99
83-37	Carla Rosenberg, 1997–2001
82-68	Gayathri DeSilva, 1979–1983
82-63	Sue Hutchinson, 1980–1984

Tiffany Eklov

WOMEN'S ILLINI ITEM

In only the program's fifth season, two Fighting Illini softball players earned first-team All–Big Ten honors, and three others got third-team mention. Sophomore first-baseman Jenna Hall was such a menacing hitter (.313, six HR, thirty-five RBI) that opposing pitchers walked her a record thirty times. Senior pitcher Amanda Fortune allowed opponent batters to hit only .195 against her, helping set an Illini ERA record of 1.24. Third-teamers Erin Jones at third base, Lindsey Hamma at shortstop, and Rachelle Coriddi combined to hit .308 with twenty-seven extra-base hits and fifty-eight RBI. Illinois finished second in the Big Ten behind Michigan.

Amanda Fortune

WOMEN'S ILLINI LEGEND

Leisha Alcia

On December 12, 2003, without having to take a U.S. citizenship test, Canadian Leisha Alcia became an All-American. That's not nearly as confusing at it sounds. Originally recruited from Mississauga, Ontario, by then Illini coach Tricia Taliaferro, Alcia pondered transferring to another school when Janet Rayfield was hired at Illinois. Thankfully, she stayed in Champaign. From 2001 to 2004, she starred as a goalkeeper, starting eighty-three of eighty-five matches. Cumulatively, Alcia gave up just ninety goals in more than seventy-seven hundred minutes between the posts, recording a microscopic goal-against average of 1.05. Her numerous school records also included twenty-four shutouts in forty-eight total victories, resulting in first-team All-American and

Leisha Alcia

OTHER TOP WOMEN'S ATHLETES

1. Lindsey Hamma, softball (hit .463 in her final fifteen games of the season).
2. Ilkay Dikman, swimming (All-American, set UI record in 100-meter breaststroke)
3. Lisa Argabright, volleyball (third-team All-American)
4. Cindy Dallas, basketball (earned Big Ten rebounding crown for a third time)

UI Female Athlete of the Year honors. Alcia debuted for the Canadian National Team in 2006, helping her country win a silver medal at the Women's Gold Cup. After concluding her playing career, she coached at Western Kentucky and Illinois. Alcia is now an academic coordinator with the University of Nevada athletics staff.

ILLINI LORE

Perhaps you've never heard of 2004 University of Illinois graduate Jawed Karim, but chances are you've used the products he's invented hundreds, maybe even thousands of times. Born in 1979 to a Bangladeshi father and a German mother, Karim is one of the co-founders of the *YouTube* video-sharing Web site. In fact, he uploaded *YouTube*'s first-ever video—"Me at the Zoo"—on April 23, 2005. Today, more than a billion users consume hundreds of millions of hours of video on the world's most popular online site.

YouTube co-founder Jawed Karim graduated from the University of Illinois in 2004

2004–05

AMERICA'S TIME CAPSULE

October 27, 2004 — The Boston Red Sox won the one hundredth World Series, its first championship since 1918.

November 2, 2004 — George W. Bush is reelected president, defeating John Kerry.

April 23, 2005 — *YouTube* first appeared on the internet.

June 27, 2005 — The Supreme Court ruled that the Ten Commandments cannot be displayed on government property.

August 25, 2004 — Hurricane Katrina made landfall in Louisiana, ultimately killing 1,833 people.

MEN'S ILLINI MOMENT

Jim Delaney congratulates the 2005 Big Ten Tournament champions

Basketball to Final Four

Describing Illinois's amazing men's basketball season of 2004–05 in less than a thousand words is nearly impossible. You can't leave out the pummeling No. 1 Wake Forest endured at the Assembly Hall in December (91–73), or the Illini road victory (75–65) at Wisconsin's seemingly unwinnable arena. Who remembers Illinois's home-court Big Ten win against No. 12 Michigan State (81–68) and the final home-game victory versus Purdue (84–50)? And, oh yes, Matt Sylvester's game-winning shot at Ohio State that snapped UI's record twenty-nine-game winning streak. A string of fifteen consecutive weeks as college basketball's top-ranked teams has to be mentioned when telling the story of 2004–05 as do the championships during the Big Ten regular season and at the conference tournaments. That success enabled Illinois to gain the No. 1 overall seed in the NCAA's "Big Dance." Illini fans traveled en masse for the opening-round wins at the RCA Dome (Fairleigh Dickinson and Nevada), Chicago's Sweet Sixteen victory over Bruce Pearl and Wisconsin-Milwaukee, and the unforgettable overtime thriller over Arizona that saw UI cutting down Final Four nets afterward. It was a festival in St. Louis, with Illini Nation overwhelming the Gateway City. They cheered the Orange and Blue when they beat Louisville in the semifinals and shed a few tears after the championship game against North Carolina. But, as head coach Bruce Weber reminded us, "If you're not happy with this [37–2], I feel sorry for you, because life ain't getting any better."

OTHER TOP MOMENTS

1. Baseball won the Big Ten title in Itch Jones's final season.

2. Ron Turner was fired, Ron Zook was hired.

3. Illinois basketball celebrated its centennial with a win versus Minnesota. More than three hundred former Illini coaches and players—including Harv Schmidt, Gene Bartow, and Lou Henson—attend the festivities.

4. Dee Brown appeared on the cover of the March 7 *Sports Illustrated*.

MEN'S ILLINI LIST

MARK JOHNSON'S COACHING HIGHLIGHTS

Mark Johnson

On March 2, 2005, wrestling coach Mark Johnson achieved one of the greatest goals of his coaching career, leading Illinois to its first Big Ten title in fifty-three years. His other achievements, by the numbers:

.818	His winning percentage with the Illini in dual-meet matches
1	National ranking his 2004 team achieved
2	Times named Big Ten Coach of the Year (2001, 2005)
4	Number of UI wrestlers who won the Big Ten Conference Medal of Honor

7	Number of individuals who won NCAA individual titles
8	Best finish at the NCAA Championships (2009)
17	Seasons he coached at Illinois
18	Number of wrestlers who earned Academic All-America honors
45	Total of Illini wrestlers who were All-Americans
120	Number of UI wrestlers who competed at the NCAA Championships
203	Dual-meet victories at Illinois (203-44-3)

MEN'S ILLINI ITEM

He brought unimaginable success to the University of Illinois and, on June 8, 2005, Craig Tiley felt the urge to take on a new challenge, that of reviving Australia's national tennis program. "I am looking forward to taking on a significant leadership role in international tennis," he said. Tiley's decision ended a magnificent thirteen-year run with Fighting Illini tennis. His first Illinois squad in 1992–93 went 4-23 but then amassed a record of 274-76, including a 32–0 record during the national championship season of 2003. Said athletic director Ron Guenther, "Thanks in large part to Craig, Illinois's tennis program operates from a position of strength."

Craig Tiley

MEN'S ILLINI LEGEND

(Left to right) Dee Brown, Luther Head, and Deron Williams

Deron Williams, Dee Brown, and Luther Head

They were the three-headed backcourt of college basketball's most exciting team of the 2004–05 season. As a trio, Deron Williams, Dee Brown, and Luther Head cumulatively averaged forty-two points and fifteen assists per game, starting all thirty-nine contests in a 37-2 season. They made up three-fifths of the 2005 All–Big Ten first team and three-tenths of the first- and second-team All-American squads. Brown was the *Sporting News* National Player of the Year, Williams was Illinois's Male Athlete of the Year, and Head was an Oscar Robertson Player of the Year finalist. Brown, labeled the "poster child of Illinois basketball," probably said it best. "Opponents tend to pay attention to me because it's my face on the national magazines, but I'm *nothing* without Deron and Luther."

OTHER TOP MEN'S ATHLETES

1. Justin Spring, gymnastics (won second NCAA title)
2. Drew Davidson, baseball (Big Ten Most Valuable Player)
3. Jack Ingram, basketball (Big Ten Conference Medal of Honor recipient)
4. Dusty Bensko, Ryan Rogowski, Chris Robinson, and Brian Blomquist, baseball (first-team All–Big Ten)
5. Zach Glavash, track and field (All-American)
6. Kyle Ott, wrestling (NCAA finalist for second consecutive year at 125 pounds)
7. Pierre Thomas, football (team Most Valuable Player, rushed for 1,126 yards)

2004–05

WOMEN'S ILLINI MOMENT

The celebration after Illinois's victory over No. 1 Southern California

Volleyball Stuns No. 1 USC at Huff

Top-rated Southern California came to Huff Hall as the two-time undefeated national champion and owners of an NCAA-record fifty-two-match winning streak. Host Illinois won game 1, 30–24, but the Trojans bounced back in game 2, winning by the same score. USC totally dominated game 3, 30–12, but Coach Don Hardin's team amazingly maintained its composure. Meghan Macdonald and Jen Hynds registered nine kills between them in game 4 and Illinois evened the match at 2–2 with a 30–27 victory. The Illini used Macdonald's powerful serve to take charge in the fifth game and, buoyed by the fervent home crowd of nearly three thousand fans, momentum took over. Tournament MVP Rachel VanMeter closed out the comeback for the Illini by scoring three of the final points with powerful swings, sending Huff into a sea of pandemonium.

OTHER TOP MOMENTS

1. Track and field won the Big Ten outdoor championship behind Cassie Hunt's two individual titles.
2. Volleyball qualified for its sixteenth NCAA tournament.
3. Illini basketball upset No. 21 Louisiana Tech and No. 16 UCLA in December.
4. Tennis has a record-best 18-5 dual-meet record.
5. Gymnastics' Bob Starkell was named Big Ten Coach of the Year.

WOMEN'S ILLINI LIST

CROSS-COUNTRY'S BEST NCAA CHAMPIONSHIP FINISHES

1st (19:46)	Angela Bizzarri, 2009
6th (19:59)	Angela Bizzarri, 2008
6th (18:10)	Marianne Dickerson, 1981
11th (20:05)	Cassie Hunt, 2005
14th (20:35)	Angela Bizzarri, 2007
21st (16:57)	Kelly McNee, 1984
24th (21:18)	Angela Bizzarri, 2006

Angela Bizzarri

Illini tennis star Cynthia Goulet had a special season in 2005. Not only did she claim a 29-7 record as a singles player, her twenty-seven doubles victories were just five fewer than the school mark in that category. In the classroom, Goulet earned a bachelor's degree in accounting and finance with Bronze Tablet distinction. Her exceptional performance on and off the court earned her the Big Ten Conference Medal of Honor. Goulet is now vice president at Chicago's Lincoln International, focusing on global heathcare and industrials.

Cynthia Goulet

WOMEN'S ILLINI LEGEND

Cassie (Hunt) Busch

Cassie Hunt

The year 2005 is one that naturally stands out in Cassie (Hunt) Busch's memory bank. On May 14, at Ohio State University's Jesse Owens Memorial Stadium, the conditions for the physically exhausting Big Ten 3,000-meter steeplechase finals were ideal. The native of Roachdale, Indiana, stayed with the pack, then broke away to finish in convincing fashion with a time of 10:14.02. The following afternoon, she gained another ten points for her team with a first-place performance in the 5,000-meter run, finishing five seconds ahead of her runner-up. With those twin victories, Big Ten coaches selected Busch as the conference's Outdoor Athlete of the Year. After a summer of rest, she competed in the fall with the Illini cross-country team. On October 30 Busch won her third Big Ten title in six months, holding off Michigan sophomore Alyson Kohlmeier down the final stretch to win by ten yards. She was clocked with a time of 21 minutes, 0.54 seconds. Today, the two-time Illini Female Athlete of the Year (2005, 2006), her husband, Roger, and two daughters reside in Crawfordsville, Indiana.

OTHER TOP WOMEN'S ATHLETES

1. Jessica Belter, volleyball (first-team All–Big Ten)
2. Angelina Williams, basketball (ended career at No. 4 scorer in Illini history)
3. Tara Hurless, soccer (second-team All-American)
4. Yvonne Mensah, track and field (won three Big Ten titles)
5. Cara Pomeroy, gymnastics (first-team All–Big Ten)

ILLINI LORE

On October 14, 2004, engineering's quadrangle, stretching from Engineering Hall to the Grainger Engineering Library, was dedicated as Bardeen Quad, in honor of John Bardeen, the only person to win the Nobel Prize twice in the same field, physics. The landscaping and concrete terrace on the north side of Engineering Hall were funded by the Grainger Foundation as part of the dedication. Bardeen Quad anchors north campus, home to the UI's renowned engineering program. Buildings on the quad include Grainger Engineering Library, Mechanical Engineering Laboratory, Materials Science Engineering, Engineering Hall, Everitt Lab, and Talbot Lab.

Bardeen Quad

2005–2014

2005–06

AMERICA'S TIME CAPSULE

October 26, 2005	The Chicago White Sox won the World Series for the first time in eighty-eight years.
March 20, 2006	Baseball Commissioner Bud Selig launched an investigation about the use of performance enhancing drugs.
March 21, 2006	New York University graduate student Jack Dorsey sent out his first "tweet," launching the social media phenomenon called *Twitter*.
April 17, 2006	A federal grand jury found former Illinois governor George Ryan guilty of racketeering.
June 20, 2006	Dwyane Wade led the Miami Heat past Dallas to win the franchise's first NBA title.

MEN'S ILLINI MOMENT

James Augustine (left) and Dee Brown

Senior Night for Dee Brown and James Augustine

Love was in the air at the Assembly Hall the night of February 25, 2006, and it was definitely a two-way affair. Nerves got the best of veterans Dee Brown and James Augustine, and they didn't play as well on Senior Night as they would have liked. However, their teammates came to the rescue as No. 8 Illinois topped first-place Iowa, 71–59. Brown, Illinois's head-banded senior guard, was just two of twelve from the field, while Augustine spent much of the game on the bench with foul trouble, so the rest of the Illini starters and bench players had to step up. Scoring a total of fifty-three points, the subs eventually opened Illinois's lead up to 63–47. Said teammate Rich McBride afterward, "Dee and James both had special careers here, so we wanted to send them out with a bang on their last night at Assembly Hall." When Coach Bruce Weber pulled his senior stars off the floor in the final minute, the sellout crowd rose to its feet. It was the 111th victory for Brown and Augustine, setting a school record that still stands today.

OTHER TOP MOMENTS

1. Justin Spring received the Nissen Emery Award as college gymnastics premier senior performer.
2. Tennis beat No. 1 Virginia.
3. Football bounced back from deficit to beat Rutgers in Ron Zook's coaching debut, tying the Illini record for the biggest comeback victory.
4. Dee Brown scored career-high thirty-four points, as No. 6 Illinois (15-0) topped No. 7 Michigan State, 60–50.
5. Wrestling won the Midlands tournament.
6. Illini hoopsters beat North Carolina at the Dean Dome.

MEN'S ILLINI LIST

DEE BROWN'S BEST STATISTICAL PERFORMANCES

Score (Date)	Points-Assists-Rebounds-Steals
UI 60, Michigan State 50 (Dec. 5, 2006)	34p-3a-1r-2s
UI 70, Michigan State 40 (Feb. 18, 2003)	24p-5a-5r-5s
UI 89, Oregon 59 (Dec. 10, 2005)	26p-7a-4r-1s
UI 83, Penn State 63 (Feb. 16, 2005)	19p-11a-4r-2s
UI 78, Iowa State 59 (Feb. 25, 2004)	18p-10a-7r-1s
UI 80, Eastern Illinois 68 (Dec. 10, 2002)	25p-4a-5r-2s
UI 65, Xavier 62 (Dec. 3, 2005)	20p-7a-5r-3s
UI 71, Texas–Pan American 59 (Nov. 20, 2005)	20p-4a-7r-4s
UI 79, Michigan 74 (Jan. 14, 2006)	26p-5a-2r-1s

Dee Brown

MEN'S ILLINI ITEM

Monday, May 29, 2006, was a special day for the Illini doubles team of sophomores Kevin Anderson and Ryan Rowe. In Palo Alto, California, the third-seed duo successfully completed their climb to an NCAA championship by defeating Pepperdine's twosome of Andre Begemann and Scott Doerner. It was the third doubles title in school history, joining the teams of Graydon Oliver and Cary Franklin in 2000 and Rajeev Ram and Brian Wilson in 2003.

Ryan Rowe (left) and Kevin Anderson

MEN'S ILLINI LEGEND

Sports Illustrated celebrated the 2004–05 Illini by featuring Dee Brown on its cover

Dee Brown

Daniel "Dee" Brown inherited many nicknames during his four years with the University of Illinois's basketball program, including "the one-man fast break" and "Illinois's poster child." Fans especially loved it when Assembly Hall public address announcer Jim Sheppard would croon, "Deeee for Threee!" after one of his 299 career three-pointers. Brown's career statistics—13.2 points, 4.9 assists, and 1.7 steals per game—are impressive. His awards—Sporting News National Player of the Year, Big Ten Player of the Year, and Illini Male Athlete of the Year—are also worth admiring. But his greatest accomplishments were achieved off the court, where his personality and grace impressed people of all ages. Brown played professionally in the NBA and internationally for nine seasons. He served as special assistant to Illinois's director of athletics from July 2015 until May 2016 when he became the Illini basketball program's director of player development and alumni relations. Today, Brown's family, including his wife, Delores, two sons, and two daughters, reside in Chicago.

OTHER TOP MEN'S ATHLETES

1. Abe Jones, track and field (won Big Ten 400-meter hurdles for a second time)
2. Alex Tirapelle, wrestling (became winningest wrestler in UI history)
3. James Augustine, basketball (All–Big Ten, UI's all-time leading rebounder)

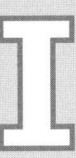

2005—06

WOMEN'S ILLINI MOMENT

Illinois's Cassie Hunt (far right) won the 2005 Big Ten individual championship

Cross-Country's Magical Season

Rain fell upon the University of Minnesota's Les Bolstad Golf Course on October 30, 2005, making the footing treacherous for the Big Ten women's cross-country championship. Defending three-time champion Michigan was picked as the favorite for the team crown, while the Wolverines' Rebecca Walter was tabbed to win her second individual title. But Coach Karen Harvey's Illini harriers had other plans. Illinois's junior superstar Cassie Hunt did her part, breaking away from the pack early and holding that lead through the finish line, clocking in with a top time of twenty-one minutes flat. She became the first Illini runner in history to win a Big Ten individual championship. Junior Stephanie Simms finished eleven seconds later, placing fourth. Freshman Katie Engel (thirteenth) and sophomore Katie Coppin (eighteenth) also had Top 20 finishes. Teamwise, Michigan was able to edge out Illinois for the team title, 42–60, with its top four runners, finishing second, seventh, eighth, and eleventh. Illinois's Hunt went on to place fifth at the NCAA meet.

OTHER TOP MOMENTS

1. Barbie Viney became first UI swimmer to win a title in twenty-four years.
2. Renee Heiken Slone began as golf coach.
3. Tennis standout Macall Harkins upsets seventh- and eighth-ranked foes in a late-season surge.

WOMEN'S ILLINI LIST

PAULA SMITH, BY THE NUMBERS

Paula Smith

After twenty-eight years, Paula Smith stepped down from her post as head coach of the Fighting Illini women's golf program following the 2006 season. Her career highlights, by the numbers:

2	As a player, number of Illinois Women's amateur championship titles she won (1971, 1972)
2	Big Ten Tournament medalists she coached (Renee Heiken, 1991, 1993; Becky Biehl, 1992)
6	All–Big Ten players she coached (thirteen occasions)
10	Times Smith's team won the Illini Classic Tournament

12	Illini players who were tournament medalists under Smith (thirty-three occasions)
60	Academic All-America honorees during her twenty-eight seasons
1978	Began her career at Illinois
1994	Inducted into the Southern Illinois Golf Association Hall of Fame
1997	Inducted into the National Golf Coaches Association Hall of Fame

Rachel (VanMeter) McClellan brought some southern charm to Illinois's volleyball program when she arrived from South Carolina's Dorman High School in the fall of 2002. Already a formidable front-line player, the 6'3" attacker had the good fortune of polishing her skills at Illinois with such players as Lisa Argabright, Sue Webber, and classmate Jessica Belter. When McClellan's senior season rolled around in 2005, Coach Don Hardin had established her as the Illini's go-to attacker. Her 672 kills that year nearly set a UI record, falling just shy of Erin Borske's 714 blasts set ten seasons earlier. She concluded her college career as a unanimous All–Big Ten selection, then began a professional volleyball career overseas. Now married and living in Chicagoland, McClellan is manager of U.S. collegiate operations at Elite Volley Agency.

Rachel VanMeter

WOMEN'S ILLINI LEGEND

Jenna Hall

Jenna Hall

The pride of Channahon, Illinois, and Minooka High School, Jenna Hall was one of the most influential players in the early history of Illinois softball. As a freshman in 2003, she displayed an incredible flair at first base, committing only one error in 365 chances. Hall, a left-handed hitter, swatted nine home runs and had forty-three RBI as a junior. Her monumental performance as a senior in 2006 was literally record breaking: Hall's .481 batting average, .651 on-base percentage, and .847 slugging percentage obliterated all existing marks and still remain today. Another Illini record that belongs to Hall is her .357 career batting average. She was a member of the All–Big Ten team all four years, earning first-team honors in 2003 and 2004. Hall played professionally for the Philadelphia Force of the National Pro Fastball League. In her first year with the Force, she was selected to the NPF All-Star team. She concluded her fourth season as an assistant coach with Ohio State in 2016.

OTHER TOP WOMEN'S ATHLETES

1. Yvonne Mensah, track and field (Big Ten Athlete of the Indoor Championship)
2. Christen Karniski, soccer (Big Ten Conference Medal of Honor recipient)
3. Cara Pomeroy, gymnastics (first-team All–Big Ten selection for second year in a row)
4. Christina Brunka, swimming (school records in 50- and 100-meter butterfly, and member of 200- and 400-meter freestyle relay record-holders)

ILLINI LORE

In August 2005 the NCAA announced that it was banning "hostile and abusive" school nicknames and Native American imagery within its membership, essentially putting an end to the presence of the University of Illinois's nearly eighty-year-old school symbol, Chief Illiniwek. About eight months later—April 28, 2006—the NCAA rejected the university's appeal that would have allowed the Chief to perform. "Our decision is final," said Walter Harrison, NCAA Executive Committee chairman. Added UI athletic director Ron Guenther, "The inability to host NCAA championship competition would have an unbelievably negative effect on our program."

2006–07

AMERICA'S TIME CAPSULE

October 17, 2006	The population of the United States reached 300 million.
December 30, 2006	Former Iraq dictator Saddam Hussein was hanged for crimes against humanity in the mass murder of Shiite men and boys in the 1980s.
February 4, 2007	At Super Bowl XLI, Peyton Manning quarterbacked the Indianapolis Colts past the Chicago Bears, 29–17.
April 16, 2007	In Blacksburg, Virginia, a deranged shooter killed thirty-three people on the campus of Virginia Tech University.
August 7, 2007	Barry Bonds surpassed Hank Aaron's record to become the new home-run king.

MEN'S ILLINI MOMENT

Chief Illiniwek made his final appearance on February 21, 2007

Chief's Last Dance

It was a debate that pitted tradition against political correctness. To a large segment of University of Illinois alumni and Illini faithful, Chief Illiniwek stood as a beloved eighty-year-old symbol honoring the Native American tribe that once resided in the state. However, in the view of vocal critics, the Chief spewed racism. When the NCAA announced in 2006 that it would bar the university from hosting national tournament play on campus as long as administrators allowed Chief Illiniwek's performances to continue, the writing was on the wall. Fast forward to February 21, 2007, the Chief's final official dance at the Assembly Hall. A sellout crowd of more than sixteen thousand people, primarily attired in orange garb, was in attendance to watch Illinois's basketball team play Michigan. The real drawing card that night, though, was Chief Illiniwek's final appearance. Those with sideline seats stood three deep as the "Three-in-One" began and graduate student Dan Maloney, portraying the Chief, emerged from the north tunnel. After the singing of "Hail to the Orange," the Chief continued his performance. When the Illini band struck the final note, Maloney strode off the court but instead of continuing down the tunnel, he pivoted and returned to center court to salute the crowd for a final time. Said Illini coach Bruce Weber afterward, "Even though he's gone, we'll always love what the Chief stands for, and he'll stay in the heart of Illini Nation forever."

OTHER TOP MOMENTS

1. Tennis advanced to the NCAA title match versus Georgia.
2. Jamar Smith and Brian Carlwell escaped serious injuries in a single-car accident on First Street in Champaign.
3. Jason Reda's last-second field goal beat MSU.
4. Brad Dancer's NCAA Elite Eight victory over Ohio State kept Illini alive.

MEN'S ILLINI LIST

TENNIS SINGLES LEADERS, BY CLASS

Aleks Vukic compiled a 45-5 record as an Illini freshman

Freshmen:		Juniors:	
45-5	Aleks Vukic, 2014–15	42-10	Ryler DeHeart, 2004–05
32-17	Phil Stoldt, 2000–01	40-11	Gavin Sontag, 1997–98
29-7	Aron Hiltzik, 2014–15	36-5	Amer Delic, 2002–03
Sophomores:		Seniors:	
37-10	Mike Kosta, 1999–00	39-8	Ryler DeHeart, 2005–06
32-10	Chris Martin, 2002–03	37-16	Oliver Freelove, 1998–99
32-17	Mark Spicijaric, 2008–09	35-15	Jakub Teply, 1998–99

MEN'S ILLINI ITEM

Illinois's men's basketball team suffered through a barrage of injuries in 2006–07 but overcame that adversity to post twenty-three victories. Two of those wins came against archrival Indiana. On March 9, in the quarterfinals of the Big Ten tournament at the United Center, Shaun Pruitt (eighteen points) and Warren Carter (seventeen points) tallied 60 percent of Illinois's points in a 58–54 overtime decision. It marked the senior duo's seventh-win at the UC without a loss.

Shaun Pruitt   Warren Carter

MEN'S ILLINI LEGEND

Kevin Anderson

Kevin Anderson

Standing 6'8", South African Kevin Anderson is perhaps the most physically imposing tennis player in Fighting Illini history. Recruited by Craig Tiley out of Johannesburg, Anderson stepped away from his lifelong plan to turn pro and instead enrolled at the University of Illinois, where he earned All-American honors all three of his seasons. As a sophomore, he won the NCAA doubles title with teammate Ryan Rowe, then advanced to the national semifinals in 2007 singles and to the finals round in doubles competition. Anderson swept all of the individual honors, being named the Big Ten Player of the Year, UI's Most Valuable Player, and the school's Dike Eddleman Male Athlete of the Year. He's excelled as a professional at well, reaching the fourth round in each of 2014's tennis majors. As of the summer of 2016, Anderson was ranked fifteenth in the world in singles and seventieth in doubles, and has had career earnings of more than $7 million. Kevin and his wife, Kelsey, a former Illini golfer, currently reside in Miami, Florida.

OTHER TOP MEN'S ATHLETES

1. Wes Haagensen, gymnastics (Big Ten Gymnast of the Year)
2. Mike Poeta, wrestling (placed third at 157 pounds in the NCAA Championships)
3. Lars Davis, baseball (batted .400 with thirteen homers and fifty-six RBI)

2006–07

WOMEN'S ILLINI MOMENT

Jolette Law

Illini Hire Jolette Law

On May 11, 2007, Jolette Law became the University of Illinois's seventh head women's basketball coach, replacing Theresa Grentz. The former Iowa Hawkeye star had been Vivian Stringer's associate head coach at Rutgers before assuming the Illini position. Law, a native of Florence, South Carolina, and a former member of the Harlem Globetrotters, successfully recruited such standout players as Karisma Penn, Amber Moore, Adrienne Godbold, and Ivory Crawford to the Urbana-Champaign campus. During her five seasons at Illinois, Law's teams won sixty-nine games and twice qualified for the WNIT. In 2016–17 she began her fifth season as assistant coach at the University of Tennessee.

OTHER TOP MOMENTS

1. Illini softball rallies for three in the seventh and beat Michigan on Sarah Beyers two-run long ball in the eighth.
2. Big Ten launched its celebration of the twenty-fifth anniversary of Big Ten women's championships.
3. Michelle Dasso took over as head coach of the tennis team.
4. Two goals by Ella Masur rallied Illini to an upset win over No. 9 Penn State, 3–2.

WOMEN'S ILLINI LIST

ILLINOIS SOCCER'S UPSETS VERSUS TOP-FIFTEEN TEAMS

1999	Illinois 3, #12 Wisconsin 2
2002	Illinois 3, #13 Purdue 2
2002	Illinois 4, #11 Penn State 3
2003	Illinois 2, #11 Ohio State 0
2004	Illinois 1, #8 Kansas 0
2004	Illinois 2, #7 Texas A&M 1
2006	Illinois 1, #13 Auburn 0
2006	Illinois 4, #12 Utah 1
2006	Illinois 3, #9 Penn State 2
2007	Illinois 1, #9 Florida 0

The Illini celebrated after their 2015 victory over No. 11 Rutgers

2011	Illinois 1, #11 Penn State (OT)
2012	Illinois 1, #3 Penn State 0
2013	Illinois 4, #7 Portland 3 (OT)
2015	Illinois 2, #11 Rutgers 1

History was made in University Park, Pennsylvania, on May 13, 2007, when, for the first time in history, the Big Ten women's outdoor track-and-field championship ended in a 129–129 tie. Senior Yvonne Mensah had built a comfortable margin earlier in the meet with top performances in the 100- and 200-meter dashes and the triple jump. She also anchored the title-winning 4x400-meter relay that included Carlene Robinson and Camille Robinson plus Tiara Armstrong.

Illini Track and Field's 2007 seniors

WOMEN'S ILLINI LEGEND

Yvonne Mensah

Yvonne Mensah

In the history of University of Illinois athletics, there have been only four women who have earned the school's Athlete of the Year Award and the Big Ten Conference Medal of Honor in the same year. In 2007 Yvonne Mensah joined that special group. Hailing from Vancouver, British Columbia, her Illini track-and-field career progressively got better and better. Mensah won two individual Big Ten championships as a freshman (2004), three as a sophomore (2005), four as a junior (2006), and six as a senior (2007). Seven of her titles were as a sprinter, six came as a long- and triple jumper, and two others were as a hurdler. Mensah went on to become the Canadian 400-meter hurdles champion and won that event at her country's 2008 Olympic trials. But as good as she was on the track, Mensah was equally proficient in the classroom, earning a bachelor's degree in kinesiology. She had her eyes set on understanding the role of the nervous system and the biomechanics of the body and eventually attended Parker University in Dallas, Texas. Mensah's career has focused on chiropractic adjustments, and she now practices complete family wellness, treating everyone from newborns to the elderly at Providence Chiropractic in Surrey, B.C.

OTHER TOP WOMEN'S ATHLETES

1. Ella Masur, soccer (second-team All-American)
2. Shanna Diller, softball (sixteen home runs, tied UI record)
3. Barbie Viney, swimming (competed in three events at NCAA meet)
4. Angela Bizzarri, cross-country (first-team All–Big Ten as freshman)

ILLINI LORE

Initially chartered by the State of Illinois in 1911, the Illini Publishing Company became the Illini Media Company in 1984, helping University of Illinois students prepare for careers in print media and broadcasting. IMC's location moved to 512 East Green Street in 2007 and houses the *Daily Illini*, WPGU Radio and the *Illio* yearbook.

Headquarters of the *Daily Illini*

2007–08

AMERICA'S TIME CAPSULE

October 12, 2007	Al Gore and the U.N. Panel on Climate Change shared the Nobel Peace Prize.
December 13, 2007	George Mitchell's report on steroids rocked baseball. Accused players included Roger Clemens.
March 16, 2008	Bear Stearns was rescued from impending bankruptcy by a deal with J. P. Morgan Chase.
June 3, 2008	Barack Obama secured the Democratic nomination.
June 5, 2008	Khalid Shaikh Mohammed was arraigned for his role as the mastermind of the September 11 attacks.

MEN'S ILLINI MOMENT

Football Upsets Top-Ranked Ohio State

J Leman (47) and Mike Ware (76) celebrated their upset of top-ranked Ohio State

In the wide world of sports, there are upsets and there are *shocking* upsets. Illinois's victory over OSU on November 10, 2007, easily qualifies as the latter. Entering the game at the Horseshoe in Columbus, no one expected Coach Ron Zook's 7-3 Illini to provide much of a challenge to top-ranked and undefeated Ohio State. The stingy Buckeye defense had held their previous ten opponents to two touchdowns or less, including only five total touchdown passes. Illini quarterback Juice Williams, though, wasn't the least bit intimidated. Using an effective running game, including 124 yards by Rashard Mendenhall and 136 by himself, to set up Illinois's passing game, Williams tossed TD passes to Michael Hoomanawanui, Jacob Willis, Brian Gamble, and Marques Wilkins. Illinois's key drive occurred late in the fourth quarter. While the sixteen-play drive didn't produce any points, it did milk the final 8:09 off the clock to seal Illini victory. It marked Illinois's first win over a No. 1-ranked team since 1956 and ultimately catapulted the Orange and Blue to a second-place finish in the Big Ten and a berth in the 2008 Rose Bowl.

OTHER TOP MOMENTS

1. Big Ten Coach of the Year Ron Zook led the Illini to a Rose Bowl berth; Illini lost to Southern Cal, 49–17.

2. Basketball upset Purdue in overtime.

3. The Big Ten Network launched its broadcasts on August 30, 2007.

4. Illini gymnasts placed third at NCAA meet.

MEN'S ILLINI LIST

ILLINOIS'S GREATEST FOREIGN ATHLETES

Iveta Marcauskaite came to play for the Illini from her native Lithuania

The University of Illinois's grand tradition in athletics has been bolstered by several athletes who were products of foreign countries:

Robert Archibald, basketball, Scotland	Kirsten Gleis, volleyball, Holland	Graeme McGufficke, swimming, Australia
Darren Boyer, football, Canada	Jens Kujawa, basketball, Germany	Iveta Marcauskaite, basketball, Lithuania
Carmel Corbett, track, New Zealand	Jenny and Susanna Kallur, track, Sweden	Herb McKenley, track, Jamaica
Thomas Detry, golf, Belgium	George Kerr, track, Jamaica	Cirilo McSween, track, Panama
Charlton Ehizuelen, track, Nigeria	Marko Koers, track, Holland	Lindsey Nimmo, tennis, England
Victor Feinstein, gymnastics, Israel	Andy Kpedi, basketball, Nigeria	Thomas Pieters, golf, Belgium
Perdita Felicien, track, Canada	Damir Krupalija, basketball, Yugoslavia	Andrew Riley, track, Jamaica
Oliver Freelove, tennis, England	Petra Laverman, volleyball, Holland	Kari Samsten, gymnastics, Finland
		Gilmarcio Sanches, gymnastics, Brazil
		Pedrya Seymour, track, Bahamas

MEN'S ILLINI ITEM

Rushing for a UI single-season best of 1,681 yards, Rashard Mendenhall, the junior from Niles West High School, broke Antoineo Harris's mark by an amazing 351 yards. Mendenhall chose to turn pro after his junior season and was the twenty-third overall pick in the 2008 NFL draft by the Pittsburgh Steelers. He rose to stardom following back-to-back seasons of one thousand yards rushing in 2009 and 2010, then a near-thousand-yard effort in 2011. Mendenhall retired from the NFL at age twenty-six in March 2014. He now is a staff writer for the HBO football show *Ballers*.

Rashard Mendenhall

MEN'S ILLINI LEGEND

J Leman

J Leman

Illini linebacker Jeremy "J" Leman has deep roots in Champaign-Urbana. He played football at Champaign Central High School and worked around the community for his family-owned lawn service. Leman's parents, Happy and Dianne, were senior pastors at the Urbana-based Vineyard Church, and J was an active member. "Faith was always first in our family," Leman said, "but sports were second. Dad would tell me, 'You always have to pray for the Holy Spirit to fill you up before a game, ask Him to empower you.'" Leman's senior-season statistics—132 tackles and 10.5 tackles for loss—reflected his emotion on the field. He wasn't overt about his faith, but he believed that he had supernatural insight against his opponents. "Some of the instinctual plays I made, I believe I knew were coming," he said. "Yes, some of it was preparation, but sometimes something would kick in that was just another level." Following his senior season, Leman collected three of UI's top awards: the Dike Eddleman Male Athlete of the Year, the Big Ten Medal of Honor, and the Fighting Illini Spirit Award. The consensus All-American played briefly in the NFL, but now he is best known as a Big Ten Network football analyst.

OTHER TOP MEN'S ATHLETES

1. Paul Ruggeri, gymnastics (won NCAA high-bar champ as freshman)
2. Ryan Rowe and Ruben Gonzales, tennis (All–Big Ten)
3. Mike Poeta, wrestling (runner-up in NCAA meet at 157 pounds)
4. Kyle Hudson, football/baseball (All–Big Ten on baseball diamond)
5. Arrelious Benn, football (Big Ten Freshman of the Year)
6. Martin O'Donnell, football (first-team All-American)
7. Trent Hoerr, cross-country (first-team All-American)

2007–08

WOMEN'S ILLINI MOMENT

(Left to right): Illinois's 2008 senior class included Danyel Crutcher, Rebecca Haris, Audrey Tabon, and Stephanie Chelleen

Basketball Upsets Top-Seeded Ohio State

Upon entering the 2008 Big Ten women's basketball tournament, Coach Jolette Law implored her Illini to ignore seeding numbers. Though an 8-10 record in Big Ten tagged the Orange and Blue with a No. 9 seed, Law preached a step-by-step, game-by-game approach. After comfortably beating Wisconsin in the opening round, top-seed Ohio State was the opponent in game 2. Five weeks earlier, Illinois had beaten the nationally ranked Buckeyes by four points in Champaign, so the team played with a quiet confidence. The game was nip and tuck at halftime, with OSU leading, 28–27. The Illini bounced out of the locker room with a 15-6 run, using a grind-it-out style. "It was the pace we wanted," Law said. "We knew we had to stop their transition game." With less than a minute remaining, OSU cut UI's lead to 60–58, but clutch free throws by Lori Bjork (sixteen points) and Rebecca Harris (twenty-two points) clinched the game for the Illini. Said Harris after the 68–64 victory, "We know we can beat any of these teams because we've already seen them. If we were the underdog, then I guess it was an upset."

OTHER TOP MOMENTS

1. Illini softball upset UCLA, 6–2, one of only nine games the Bruins lost all year.
2. Gymnastics team barely misses out on its first-ever NCAA championship appearance.
3. Tennis squad posted 7-3 Big Ten record, most improved among women's teams.

WOMEN'S ILLINI LIST

SINGLE-SEASON HOME-RUN LEADERS

24	Angelena Mexicano, 2008
19	Nicole Evans, 2015
16	Meredith Hackett, 2010
16	Shanna Diller, 2007
16	Angelena Mexicano, 2007
15	Lana Armstrong, 2007
14	Jessica Davis, 2011
13	Jenna Hall, 2006
12	Nicole Evans, 2016
12	Allie Bauch, 2015
12	Erin Montgomery, 2003

Angelena Mexicano

WOMEN'S ILLINI LEGEND

Jenna Smith

Jenna Smith

Though her secret passion was soccer, Jenna Smith knew that her height fit another game more appropriately. The 6'3" center from Bloomington, Minnesota, was her state's "Ms. Basketball" as a high school senior so, when she chose to play at Illinois over Minnesota, Iowa, and Nebraska, much was expected. Smith impressed from the very beginning, breaking the Illini's freshman record for rebounding. As a sophomore, she earned first-team All–Big Ten and team MVP honors after averaging seventeen points and nine rebounds per game. Smith duplicated those honors during her junior and senior seasons, contributing more than eighteen points, ten rebounds, and two blocked shots over two campaigns. Careerwise at Illinois, she wound up No. 1 in each of those statistical categories and became only the fourth player in Big Ten history with more than two thousand points (2,160) and more than one thousand rebounds (1,217). Smith was chosen as the November 14 overall pick in the 2010 WNBA draft, but instead played in basketball in France, Slovakia, Israel, and Romania. "Overseas, I have been in the best places and I have been in the worst," Smith said. "I'm so much more open-minded to life and different ways of living." She's still playing professionally today but has targeted a coaching career in college as her future objective.

OTHER TOP WOMEN'S ATHLETES

1. Julie Crall, gymnastics (Big Ten balance-beam champion)
2. Shanna Diller, softball (first-team All–Big Ten)
3. Allison Buckley, gymnastics (sport's sixth All-American)
4. Mary Therese McDonnell, soccer (Big Ten Conference Medal of Honor recipient)

ILLINI LORE

In May 2009, the *Chicago Tribune* revealed that University of Illinois administrators helped admit underqualified students with political connections. This scandal resulted in the resignations of President Joseph B. White, Chancellor Richard Herman, and all but two members of the UI Board of Trustees.

2008–09

AMERICA'S TIME CAPSULE

September 29, 2008	The Dow Jones Industrial Average dropped a record 778 points because of financial turmoil.
November 4, 2008	In an historic election, Illinois Senator Barack Obama became the first African American president.
December 19, 2008	President George W. Bush unveiled a $17.4 billion rescue of America's auto industry.
January 29, 2009	The Illinois State Senate voted to remove Governor Rod Blagojevich from office.
June 25, 2009	Michael Jackson, the King of Pop, died at age fifty. It would later be ruled a homicide by drug overdose.

MEN'S ILLINI MOMENT

Night of Legends, Basketball

Kenny Battle's family saw their dad's banner raised in 2008

On a September evening in 2008, more than fifteen thousand fans inside the Assembly Hall had the opportunity to relive the entire 103-year history of Fighting Illini basketball. The event was titled "A Night of Legends," and it undeniably lived up to its lofty billing. The program began with a game between the 2005 Final Four team and a squad of Illini all-stars that included players from the 1989 "Flying Illini" and other UI championship units. During the game's timeouts, fans relived a bevy of magic moments that included Deron Williams's three-pointer against Arizona in 2005 and Nick Anderson's game-winning shot at Indiana in 1989. Halftime featured a 2008 Olympic tribute to Williams and Jerry Colangelo and remarks from both men. The pièce de résistance was the unveiling of thirty honored-jersey banners. That group was limited to men who had achieved National Player of the Year, enshrinement in the National Basketball Hall of Fame, Olympic status, Big Ten Player of the Year, consensus first- or second-team All-American status, or who were members of Illinois's All-Century Team.

OTHER TOP MOMENTS

1. Illini golf won Big Ten title for first time since 1988.
2. Illini football team scores forty-five points against Michigan.
3. Gymnastics team rallied in their final event to earn share of the Big Ten title with Michigan.
4. Mike Small was named Big Ten Coach of the Year.
5. More than five thousand fans attended the baseball opener versus Ohio State.
6. No. 23 Illinois won at No. 12 Purdue, 66–48, behind a fourteen-point/sixteen-rebound performance by Mike Davis.
7. Justin Spring was named gymnastics coach, replacing Yoshi Hayasaki.
8. Illini teams finished historical-best twentieth place in NACDA Directors' Cup Standings.
9. Baseball's Willie Argo slammed three home runs in his first collegiate start, against No. 1 LSU.

MEN'S ILLINI LIST

GRAND RE-OPENING OF MEMORIAL STADIUM

On September 6, 2008, the University of Illinois unveiled a completed $123 million renovation of Memorial Stadium that represented more than two years of work. Directed by Associate Athletics Director Warren Hood and featuring the design of HNTB of Kansas City, Missouri, and the construction of Hunt Construction Managers, the west side of the eighty-five-year-old structure received a facelift that included the addition of luxury suites, indoor and outdoor club areas, and refurbishment of the concourses. From the west balcony sprouted a three-level structure that featured a new press box, two floors of suites, and an indoor space named the "77 Club" to honor Illinois's gridiron legend Red Grange. The north end of the stadium also was reworked to feature bleacher seating, expansion of the weight room, plus training facilities and meeting space. In attendance for the festivities was a galaxy of former Illini stars dating back to the 1940s; they were treated to a 47–21 Illini victory over Eastern Illinois.

Memorial Stadium's new look

MEN'S ILLINI ITEM

Athletic director Ron Guenther had his hands full when Yoshi Hayasaki, Mark Johnson, and Don Hardin all retired following the 2008–09 season. Hayasaki's thirty-five-year gymnastics reign included an NCAA title in 1989, six Big Ten championships, and three Olympians. Johnson's seventeen seasons as the Illini head coach completely transformed the wrestling program, advancing it to a Big Ten championship in 2005. Hardin had an especially tough act to follow. As Mike Hebert's replacement, three of the six Illini teams he coached made the NCAA Sweet Sixteen. Hardin's Illini posted a 234-163 overall record he was named the conference's Coach of the Year twice.

MEN'S ILLINI LEGEND

Paul Ruggeri

Paul Ruggeri, gymnastics

Paul Ruggeri's success at Illinois for Coach Yoshi Hayasaki was immediate and substantial. As a freshman in 2008, Rugerri won the NCAA high-bar title, becoming the first Illini gymnast to win a national championship in his first year of competition since 1960. He doubled his achievements as a sophomore, capturing NCAA titles in two events, and was named UI's Dike Eddleman Male Athlete of the Year. In his senior year Ruggeri captured what was, in his mind, the crown jewel: it wasn't his fourth individual national championship (vault) or the Nissen-Emery Award he won as his sport's top performer—it was his team's NCAA title over host Oklahoma that Ruggeri will remember most. His personal performance was subpar, and he felt as if he had let his team down. "It was an incredible feeling to be able to rely on my teammates and to see how much gratification winning the title brought to everyone," said Ruggeri. "In that moment, I learned a lot about life. Ups and downs are unavoidable. You just have to hang on and give it your best shot." Rugerri is currently a member of Team USA.

OTHER TOP MEN'S ATHLETES

1. Gakologelwang Masheto, track and field (finished three-year career with six Big Ten titles)
2. Arrelious Benn, football (team Most Valuable Player)
3. Mike Poeta, wrestling (two-time NCAA runner-up, finished with .882 winning percentage)

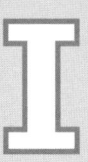

2008-09

WOMEN'S ILLINI MOMENT

Illinois's 2008 cross-country team

Women's Cross-Country Top Ten Again

The span from 2005 through 2009 could easily be referred to as the golden age of Illini women's cross-country. Beginning with Coach Karen Harvey's last two teams and continuing through Coach Jeremy Rasmussen's first three squads, Illinois made history, placing among the top twelve teams at the NCAA championship. On November 24, 2008, the Illini competed in the wet and windy conditions at Indiana State's course. Led by junior Angela Bizzarri's sixth-place finish and senior Katie Engel's twenty-second-place clocking, Illinois ended tenth in the final team standings behind champion Washington. "This is a great feat for our program," said Rasmussen. "Through all of the ups and downs this season, it took a lot of convincing to let the girls know that we would be good when we needed to be, and we are. We are definitely looking to continue that tradition of success down the road."

OTHER TOP MOMENTS

1. The (Shadid) Khan Outdoor Tennis complex opened in the spring of 2009.
2. Soccer earned its third NCAA Sweet Sixteen berth in five years.
3. Bob Starkell won gymnastics national Coach of the Year honors, leading the Illini to their first-ever NCAA appearance.

WOMEN'S ILLINI LIST

GYMNASTICS INDIVIDUAL CAREER EVENT TITLES LEADERS

62	Allison Buckley, 2008–2011
58	Nancy Thies, 1976–1977
43	Alina Weinstein, 2010–2013
41	Cara Pomeroy, 2004–2007
38	Denise Lamborn, 1987–1990
34	HeatherSingalewitch, 1987–1990
33	Kelsey Joannides, 2009–2012
32	Kim Berres, 1996–1999
29	Sarah Schmidt, 2007–2010
27	Amber See, 2011–2014

Sarah Schmidt

In 2008 Illinois's soccer team advanced to the NCAA Tournament's Sweet Sixteen for the third time in five years. Coach Janet Rayfield's Illini opened against Memphis and battled to a scoreless tie until the second overtime, when UI sophomore Jordan Hilbrands broke the stalemate. Illinois won game two against Missouri on penalty kicks, with Kapicka recording a career-best eleven saves. UI's season ended when they lost to eventual champion North Carolina, losing 3–0.

The Illini celebrate after an NCAA Tournament win over Missouri

WOMEN'S ILLINI LEGEND

Laura DeBruler

Laura DeBruler

At the end of the 2010 season, Laura DeBruler's name was listed throughout the Illini volleyball record book, ranking at the top of both career kills (1,833) and career attacks (4,806), and in the top ten of several other categories. But the truth is, her individual statistics and UI's team victory total could have been considerably larger had it not been for a college-career-ending injury that caused DeBruler to miss her team's final seventeen matches, including a 3–2 loss to Texas in the third-round of the NCAA tournament. She and her Illini teammates will probably always wonder what might have been. Still, DeBruler is one of the most celebrated volleyball players in UI history. She was a first-team All-American as a junior in 2009, a second-teamer in 2008, and a three-time All–Big Ten selection. A native of Downers Grove, Illinois, DeBruler was a volunteer assistant for Illinois in 2012, launching a coaching career that has taken her to stints at Western Illinois, Bowling Green, and, currently, Oregon State.

OTHER TOP WOMEN'S ATHLETES

1. Angela Bizzarri (second time as UI Athlete of the Year)
2. Emily Zurrer, soccer (three-time All-American; Big Ten Conference Medal of Honor recipient)
3. Jenna Smith, basketball (repeated as first-team All–Big Ten selection)
4. Danielle Zymkowitz, softball (All-American at second base)
5. Deserea Brown, track and field (Big Ten champion in 400-meter hurdles)
6. Megan Fudge, tennis (All–Big Ten for third consecutive year)

ILLINI LORE

A great majority of University of Illinois students and alumni wouldn't know Albert Marion and Susanne Wood, but they certainly would recognize their musical talents. You see, Marion and Wood served as the campus's chimemasters for a period of nearly sixty years, playing the fifteen-bell carillon in Altgeld Hall's tower. Their renditions of "Hail to the Orange," "Illinois Loyalty," and a wide selection of other familiar songs echoed across the North Quad for decades. They dreamed of a full forty-nine-bell, full-octave presence in the tower, but that just wasn't feasible for cramped Altgeld. In 2008 Marion and Wood's vision became a reality, though, when the McFarland Memorial Bell Tower was erected on the South Quad. The funding for the $1.5 million structure came from a donation by 1952 grad H. Richard McFarland, in memory of his wife Sarah "Sally" McFarland. The current carillon is controlled by a computer with five hundred pre-programmed songs, or it can be played directly from a keyboard.

McFarland Memorial Bell Tower

2009–10

AMERICA'S TIME CAPSULE

December 24, 2009	By a partisan vote of 60–39, the U.S. Senate passed the Health Care Reform Bill.
February 7, 2010	The New Orleans Saints beat the Indianapolis Colts in their first-ever Super Bowl appearance.
April 5, 2010	Duke ended Butler's twenty-five-game winning streak, claiming the NCAA basketball title with a 61–59 victory.
June 9, 2010	For the first time in forty-nine years, the Chicago Blackhawks won the Stanley Cup, defeating Philadelphia.
August 31, 2010	President Barack Obama announced an end to combat missions in Iraq.

MEN'S ILLINI MOMENT

ESPN's College GameDay's crew of (left to right) Rece Davis, Hubert Davis, Digger Phelps, and Jay Bilas entertained the Orange Krush on February 6, 2010

Home Basketball Win versus MSU Following ESPN GameDay

Ignited by the Orange Krush, the inside of the University of Illinois's Assembly Hall figuratively resembled a plasma globe the day of February 6, 2010. The electricity began to spark in mid-morning when Rece Davis, Digger Phelps, Jay Bilis, and Hubert Davis hosted *ESPN College GameDay* in front of the Krush and several thousand of their friends. Then, a few hours later, Illinois's basketball team took center stage, hosting No. 5 Michigan State. The Illini jumped out to an early ten-point lead; however, the Draymond Green–led Spartans whittled the margin to just one point by halftime. MSU rallied to take a brief lead early in the second period, but UI junior guard Demetri McCamey countered by scoring ten of his game-high twenty-two points to regain the edge. The Spartans kept battling and got within a point with 3:44 remaining. Fortunately, that's when Coach Bruce Weber's Illini took over. McCamey hit a huge three-pointer with thirty-seven seconds to play, forcing State to foul. Freshman D. J. Richardson hit three free throws in the last twenty-six seconds and slammed home a dunk at the buzzer to make the final score 78–73. Illini students stormed the court, ending a perfect day.

OTHER TOP MOMENTS

1. UI captured its second consecutive Big Ten golf title on Chris DeForest's eagle.
2. The Illini gymnasts won the Big Ten championship.
3. A twelve-foot-tall, two-thousand-pound bronze statue of Red Grange was unveiled on the west side of Memorial Stadium.
4. Illinois basketball won at Indiana in consecutive seasons for the first time since 1998.
5. The $5.3 million Shahid and Ann Kahn Outdoor Tennis Complex opened.
6. Basketball rallied from twenty-three down to stun host Auburn.

MEN'S ILLINI LIST

FOOTBALL CAREER TOTAL YARDS LEADERS

Total Yards	Player (passing yards/rushing yards), years
10,634	Nathan Scheelhaase (8,568/2,066), 2010–2013
10,594	Juice Williams (8,037/2,557), 2006–2009
8,880	Kurt Kittner (7,722/158), 1998–2001
8,640	Jack Trudeau (8,725/–85), 1981–1985
7,256	Jason Verduzco (7,532/–276), 1989–1992
7,002	Tony Eason (7,031/–29), 1981–1982
5,612	Wes Lunt (5,900/–298), 2014–2016
5,358	Johnny Johnson (5,293/65), 1992–1994

Illini quarterback
Nathan Scheelhaase

5,158	Jon Beutjer (5,190/–32), 2002–2004
4,767	Jeff George (5,189/–422), 1988–1989

MEN'S ILLINI ITEM

On Halloween Day 2009 at Memorial Stadium a momentum-changing tackle stole the headlines. Leading by six at intermission, Michigan scored a seventy-six-yard touchdown. However, officials reviewed the play and determined that Illini freshman defensive back Terry Hawthorne had stopped Roundtree just short of the end zone. The Illini defense stonewalled four consecutive Michigan runs and turned the ball over to their offense. UI went on to score twenty-four more unanswered points to win, 38–13.

Terry Hawthorne's touchdown-saving tackle of Michigan's Roy Roundtree

MEN'S ILLINI LEGEND

Scott Langley

Scott Langley

Former Fighting Illini star Scott Langley can do a lot more than hit a little white ball around a golf course. He is a multitalented guy. His parents encouraged him to play the violin, a talent he's had since the third grade. He's also an accomplished juggler. "I can't juggle chickens or anything like that, but I can juggle." And he can cook. "I'm not Emeril Lagasse, but I do make some pretty mean pasta dishes." As a golfer, Langley is as good as the University of Illinois has ever had. In 2010 at the NCAA men's golf championship in Ooltewah, Tennessee, he won national medalist honors, shooting 206 over fifty-four holes. From there Langley went on to become the low amateur at the 2010 U.S. Open. During his four years at Illinois (2008–2011), he won All-American kudos twice and finished with a school-record average of 72.5 strokes through 166 rounds. Langley recently concluded his fifth season on the PGA Tour and has earned more than $3 million.

OTHER TOP MEN'S ATHLETES

1. Paul Ruggeri, gymnastics (two Big Ten titles)
2. John Dergo, wrestling (Big Ten title)
3. Casey McMurray, baseball (led Illini in batting average, home runs, and RBI)
4. Jon Asamoah, football (Most Valuable Player; Big Ten Conference Medal of Honor recipient)
5. Abe Souza, tennis (35-6 record)
6. Chad Wiest, gymnastics (most outstanding, most improved Illini gymnast)

2009–10

WOMEN'S ILLINI MOMENT

Senior Kylie McCulley (15) goes high for a kill versus Minnesota

7,632 See Illini Volleyball Beat Hebert's Gophers

One of Illinois volleyball's most memorable home matches of the past ten years was a spectacle that took place not at Huff Hall but at the Assembly Hall. The meeting between No. 10 Illinois and No. 6 Minnesota included several angles. It was the school's first match in the Hall in twenty-eight years. The opposing coach was Mike Hebert, a man who's directed the Illini through their most successful years. And a UI-record 7,632 fans were on hand to witness the action. What was expected to be a defense-oriented affair turned out to be one of offensive fire power. Illinois's right-side hitter Michelle Bartsch stood out in the first set, belting seven kills, and UI jumped out to a 1–0 lead. The Illini had to dig deep in set 2 of a side-out affair, depending on the sensational digs of Ashley Eddinger, but ultimately prevailed and led 2–0. All-American Laura DeBruler and senior Kylie McCulley were particularly impressive in the victorious third set, knocking down sixteen kills. "With the students surrounding the court, this was a fun event to play in," said first-year Illini coach Kevin Hambly. "We were entirely focused on the match, though, and in the end it all worked out great."

OTHER TOP MOMENTS

1. Softball's Meredith Hackett earned first-team All-America accolades.
2. Volleyball's Laura DeBruler was honored as a first-team All-American.
3. Kim Landrus was named gymnastics coach.
4. Basketball turned a seventeen-point deficit into a fifteen-point victory at Wake Forest.
5. Softball's Terri Sullivan was named Big Ten Coach of the Year.

WOMEN'S ILLINI LIST

FIRST-TEAM ACADEMIC ALL-AMERICA HONOREES

1980	Liz Brauer, basketball
1982	Lisa Robinson, basketball
1989	Laura Bush, volleyball
1990	Laura Bush, volleyball
1996	Renee Gamboa, swimming
2010	Angela Bizzarri, track and field/cross-country
2010	Johannah Bangert, volleyball

Illinois's Johannah Bangert

Ashley Buckley

WOMEN'S ILLINI LEGEND

UI's Angela Bizzarri was the 2009 Honda Award winner for cross-country

Angela Bizzarri

Angela Bizzarri made an instant impression in cross-country at Illinois, finishing fifth at the Big Ten meet and twenty-fourth at the NCAA championship. She continued her improvement as a sophomore, placing third and fourteenth at those same events. As a junior, she earned All-American honors for a third time, finishing sixth at the national meet. Then, in her senior season, Bizzarri became the individual national champion, smashing her previous personal-best and school-record time by thirteen seconds. That, she says, was her most memorable race as an Illini. "I did a good job of focusing on the positives, staying in the moment and remaining confident in myself and my abilities. I won't ever forget how surprised I was after finishing first." She also earned All-American honors in track and broke numerous Illinois distance events records. Bizzarri was the 2009 NCAA champ at 5,000 meters, then captured the 3,000-meter national title in 2010. At Big Ten meets, she won five times. All of that success earned her three Dike Eddleman Female Athlete of the Year awards. Bizzarri, who hopes to become a sports medicine physician, currently runs professionally for Brooks Sports in Seattle, Washington.

OTHER TOP WOMEN'S ATHLETES

1. Jenna Smith, basketball (UI career leader in points, rebounds, and steals)
2. Danielle Zymkowitz, softball (first-team All–Big Ten)
3. Megan Fudge, tennis (All–Big Ten four straight years)
4. Pepper Gay, softball (UI Newcomer of the Year)
5. Lacey Simpson, basketball (broke UI career records for games played and steals)

ILLINI LORE

Chosen from more than two hundred candidates for the University of Illinois's top administrative post, Michael Hogan was named UI's eighteenth president on May 12, 2010. Myriad challenges, including state funding woes and fallout from the recent admissions controversy, didn't deter the sixty-six-year-old Hogan from accepting the offer. "If there weren't any challenges, it wouldn't be any fun," he joked. Hogan had been president at the University of Connecticut since 2007.

President Michael Hogan

2010–11

AMERICA'S TIME CAPSULE

November 1, 2010 — The San Francisco Giants beat the Texas Rangers and claimed their first World Series title since 1954.

December 22, 2010 — President Barack Obama officially repealed the "Don't Ask, Don't Tell" military policy, forbidding discrimination against openly gay men and women in the services.

January 6, 2011 — U.S. Representative Gabrielle Giffords was among nineteen people shot in an assassination attempt in Arizona.

March 12, 2011 — The National Football League shut down when owners and players could not come to terms for a new collective-bargaining agreement.

May 2, 2011 — Osama bin Laden, the FBI's most wanted man, was killed by U.S. Special Forces in Pakistan.

MEN'S ILLINI MOMENT

Illinois Beats Northwestern at Wrigley Field

Mikel Leshoure rushed for 330 yards vs. Northwestern in 2010

When a fan mentions Chicago's Wrigley Field, his or her thoughts immediately are transported to Cubbie blue and the legendary ivy-covered outfield walls. However, on November 20, 2010, "The Friendly Confines" hosted a football game, marking the first time in eighty-seven years—since 1923—that the Fighting Illini gridders had convened at the ballpark bounded by Clark and Addison Streets and Waveland and Sheffield Avenues. Because the 120-yard football field barely squeezed into the park built for baseball, Illinois and Northwestern agreed that, for safety reasons, all offensive plays would head toward the west end. The game itself was a blowout, won by the Illini, 48–27. Illinois's primary offensive weapon was junior running back Mikel Leshoure, who ran around, over, and through the Wildcat defense for a school-record 330 yards. In the first quarter alone, No. 5 accumulated a whopping 153 yards and two touchdowns. Junior Jason Ford added three more TDs as the Illini scored more than forty points for the fourth time in five consecutive games.

OTHER TOP MOMENTS

1. Matt Dittman's home run clinched a share of the Big Ten title. UI also won the Big Ten tournament and played in the NCAA tournament.

2. Mike Thomas was named Illinois's athletic director in August 2011.

3. Gymnastics won its third consecutive Big Ten title. Justin Spring was named conference Coach of the Year.

4. In a shootout at the "Big House," UI lost in three overtimes to Michigan, 67–65.

5. Illini basketball beat UNLV in the NCAA tournament.

6. Nate Bussey's interception helped UI football post its first-ever win at Penn State.

7. The Big Ten Network chose Red Grange as the conference's No. 1 historical icon.

8. Illinois won its third-straight Big Ten golf title.

MEN'S ILLINI LIST

BIG TEN BATTING CHAMPIONS

1943	Boyd Bartley, SS	(.400)
1946	Lee Eilbracht, C	(.484)
1948	Herb Plews, 2B	(.404)
1987	Dave Payton, 3B-OF	(.460)
2001	Luke Simmons, 3B	(.426)
2011	Justin Parr, DH	(.411)

Justin Parr

MEN'S ILLINI ITEM

As a basketball rookie, Demetri McCamey set a Big Ten tournament record for single-game three-point field goal percentage by hitting six-of-six against Purdue. During his sophomore year, he led all Big Ten players in assists. McCamey won first-team All–Big Ten acclaim as a junior. Finally, as a senior, he was one of ten finalists for the Bob Cousy Award and became only the second player in Big Ten history to reach sixteen hundred career points and seven hundred assists.

Demetri McCamey

MEN'S ILLINI LEGEND

Ron Guenther

Ron Guenther's service to the University of Illinois dates to the 1960s

During the nineteen years of Ron Guenther's term as director of intercollegiate athletics, the 1966 University of Illinois football MVP and 1967 graduate paid back the scholarship he was granted in a variety of ways. He guided the DIA's nineteen varsity sports to a total of thirty-four Big Ten championships, including a rarely achieved conference title sweep by both football and basketball in 2001–02. In terms of bricks and mortar, thanks to Guenther, the campus's athletic facilities are among the Big Ten's best. Included among the additions to the Illini landscape under Guenther's administration are a $121 million renovation of Memorial Stadium, construction of UI's Irwin Indoor Football Facility, the Ubben Basketball Practice Facility, the Bielfeldt Athletic Administration Building, the Irwin Academic Center, Eichelberger Field (softball), a track-and-field and soccer stadium, the Atkins Tennis Center, the Khan Outdoor Tennis Complex, and the Demirjian Indoor Golf Facility. And as a result of Guenther's leadership, Illinois is bringing in millions of dollars from licensing and a marketing/equipment agreement with Nike. Guenther retired from Illinois on June 30, 2011, and now serves as a consultant for the Big Ten Conference.

OTHER TOP MEN'S ATHLETES

1. Andrew Riley, track and field (first of two Athlete of the Year awards)
2. Luke Guthrie, golf (record 71.36 average)
3. Nathan Scheelhaase, football (rushed for a UI-quarterback record 868 yards)

2010–11

WOMEN'S ILLINI MOMENT

The scene at Huff Gym when Illinois ended Penn State's streak

Volleyball Ends Penn State's Sixty-Five Match Big Ten Winning Streak

There were abundant storylines the evening of September 24, 2010, when Illinois's ninth-ranked volleyball team hosted No. 2 Penn State. On self-proclaimed "History at Huff" night, the Illini marketing staff aimed at selling out Huff Gym for the first time in eighteen years. There was the much-anticipated return of senior All-American Laura DeBruler from a bout with mononucleosis, and Illinois would need her best effort and that of many others in order to defeat the Nittany Lions, unbeaten in their previous sixty-five Big Ten matches. PSU quieted the standing-room-only crowd of 4,141 with a 25–17 win in the opening set, but Michelle Bartsch's serving sparked the Illini to back-to-back victories in sets 2 and 3. Penn State won set 4, setting up a classic rubber match. Colleen Ward, Hillary Haen, Jennifer Bonilla, Johannah Bangert, and Erin Johnson all contributed key plays, and victory belonged to Illinois, 17–15.

OTHER TOP MOMENTS

1. Elizabeth Boyle's school-record 10,000-meter time surpassed a twenty-nine-year-old Illini mark.
2. Rookie Stephanie Richartz became first Illini pole vaulter to clear thirteen feet.
3. Nebraska was admitted membership to the Big Ten Conference.
4. Danielle Zymkowitz became UI's first two-time All-American.

WOMEN'S ILLINI LIST

SINGLE-GAME SOCCER GOALS

4	Vanessa DiBernardo vs. Purdue, Oct. 1, 2010
3	Janelle Flaws vs. St. Louis, Aug. 30, 2015
3	Jannelle Flaws vs. Purdue, Sept. 21, 2014
3	Jannelle Flaws at Nebraska, Oct. 17, 2013
3	Jannelle Flaws vs. Illinois State, Sept. 1, 2013
3	Vanessa DiBernardo vs. Michigan State, Sept. 4, 2013
3	Niki Read vs. Ball State, Aug. 26, 2011
3	Chichi Nweke vs. Utah, Sept. 17, 2006
3	Tara Hurless vs. Iowa, Nov. 8, 2001
3	Emily Brown at Louisville, Sept. 13, 1998

Vanessa DiBernardo's four goals against Purdue in 2010 stands as the Illini record

3	Sarah Aberle at Louisville, Sept. 13, 1998
3	Lisa Baldwin at Ohio State, Sept. 18, 1998
3	Emily Brown vs. Washington U., October 28, 1998
3	Rachel Smith vs. Aurora, October 13, 1997

WOMEN'S ILLINI ITEM

Ashley Kelly had watched Marion Jones perform in the 2000 Sydney Olympic Games and decided to trade her softball glove for a pair of track cleats. At the 2011 Big Ten indoor championships, she won the 400-meter run; then, outdoors, she placed eighth at the NCAA meet, accomplishing her goal of becoming an All-American. In April 2016, Kelly realized her lifelong dream, qualifying for the Rio de Janeiro Olympic Games for her native Virgin Islands.

Ashley Kelly

WOMEN'S ILLINI LEGEND

Melissa Fernandez

Melissa Fernandez, Gymnastics

Melissa Fernandez was one of those fun-loving, furniture-jumping, lawn-cartwheeling kids. Her mother, Tami Klinedinst, decided to enroll six-year-old Melissa in a gymnastics class. The little dynamo immediately fell in love with the sport and its demand for perfection. Little did Tami know that she was launching a career that would allow Melissa to earn an athletic scholarship at the University of Illinois and eventually give her the opportunity to travel around the world with Cirque du Soleil. From 2008 to 2011, Fernandez performed spectacularly for the Illini, earning a bevy of awards. As a sophomore, she became the first Illini gymnast to become an All-American on the balance beam. She continued to excel throughout her senior season, setting a UI record by earning three All-American honors at the NCAA championships, picking up first-team honors on beam and the all-around, plus second-team accolades in floor exercise. In June 2011, Fernandez received the Dike Eddleman Award as Illinois's premier Female Athlete of the Year. "It's my most cherished award," she says. Fernandez recently rejoined Cirque du Soleil following the birth of her daughter, Zoey. She performs in a production called "Amaluna," consisting of both gymnastics elements and dance choreography. Fernandez's family is currently based in Atlanta, Georgia.

OTHER TOP WOMEN'S ATHLETES

1. Karisma Penn, basketball (led UI in scoring and four other categories)
2. Ashley Buckley, gymnastics (surpassed Nancy Thies Marshall's record for career event titles)
3. Colleen Ward, volleyball (first-team All–Big Ten, second-team All-American)

ILLINI LORE

The University of Illinois's Nugent Hall opened in the fall of 2010 as part of the Ikenberry Commons North community. Its first floor serves as home to the Beckwith Residential Support Service program for students with severe physical disabilities. Named for Timothy Nugent, the pioneering founder of UI's Disability Resources and Education Services, each floor of the facility alternates rooms for men and women, as opposed to other halls that may have men on one end of a floor and women on the other.

Tim Nugent was the founder of UI's Disability Resources and Education Services

2011–12

AMERICA'S TIME CAPSULE

November 5, 2011   Former Penn State football coach Jerry Sandusky was arrested on forty counts of sexual abuse. Four days later, head coach Joe Paterno was fired.

December 11, 2011   Pop superstar Whitney Houston died at age forty-eight of a drug overdose.

May 9, 2012   President Barack Obama declared his support for same-sex marriage.

July 20, 2012   Twelve people were killed and seventy others were injured in a Colorado theater shooting.

July 27, 2012   The Thirtieth Olympic Games opened in London. Sprinter Usain Bolt starred.

MEN'S ILLINI MOMENT

The 2012 Illini gymnastics team won both the Big Ten and NCAA titles

Men's Gymnastics Wins NCAA Team Title

University of Illinois men's gymnastics dominated the headlines on back-to-back days in April 2012. Competing at the University of Oklahoma's Lloyd Noble Center, Coach Justin Spring's Illini rallied from a two-point deficit in the final two rotations to capture the 2012 NCAA team championship. Illinois's school-record-breaking 60.750 points on pommel horse proved to be the difference, pushing the Illini past host and No. 1-ranked Oklahoma, 358.850 to 357.450. It was Illinois's tenth championship and its first since 1989. "This team is one that truly took ownership of the details," said Spring, "and that's not easy to do when you're in a sport that's based off perfection." Less than twenty-four hours later, senior Paul Ruggeri and freshman C. J. Maestas both stood on the award stands as individual champions, Ruggeri for the vault and Maestas as UI's first-ever still-rings titlist.

OTHER TOP MOMENTS

1. Paul Ruggeri won gymnastics' Nissen-Emery Award.

2. Brandon Paul scored forty-three points against No. 5 Ohio State.

3. Thomas Pieters won the NCAA golf title.

4. Men's tennis stunned Ohio State in the Big Ten Tournament final

5. Luke Guthrie repeated as Big Ten golf medalist.

6. Football came from behind to beat UCLA in the Kraft Bowl.

7. A.D. Mike Thomas fired Bruce Weber and hired John Groce as basketball coach.

8. Division alignment begins in Big Ten football (Legends and Leaders), resulting in a season-ending league championship game.

MEN'S ILLINI LIST

WHITNEY MERCILUS, BY THE NUMBERS

Whitney Mercilus was the 2011 National Defensive Performer of the Year

In 2011, Illini defensive end Whitney Mercilus became UI football's twenty-fifth consensus All-American. The story of his career, by the numbers:

4.5	In millions, his base salary with the Houston Texans in 2016.
4.68	His 40-yard dash time at the 2012 NFL combine.
9	Forced opponent fumbles—best in the nation for 2011.
10	He became the tenth player to win the Ted Hendricks Award as college football's top defensive end.

18	Number of quarterback sacks he totaled from 2009 to 2011.
26	He was the twenty-sixth overall pick in the 2012 NFL draft.
30	Whitney's NFL career sack total in four years with the Texans.
59	The jersey number he wears for Houston.
85	His jersey number at Illinois.
265	Pounds on his 6'4" frame.

MEN'S ILLINI ITEM

Entering the 2012 Big Ten men's tennis championships, Coach Brad Dancer knew that his Illini were facing a tall task against Ohio State. OSU jumped off to a 3-1 advantage. Illini victories by junior Stephen Hoh and freshman Ross Guignon evened the score at 3–all. UI's Roy Kalmanovich and OSU's Blaz Rola battled in the decider, and the Illini senior prevailed in three sets, giving Illinois its first victory over Ohio State since 2007.

Senior Roy Kalmanovich hoisted the 2012 Big Ten championship trophy

MEN'S ILLINI LEGEND

Andrew Riley won the NCAA's 100-meter dash

Andrew Riley

In Jamaican slang, Illini track and field star Andrew Riley had every reason to "big up his chest." In four record-setting seasons at Illinois, the native of Kingston rarely disappointed his coaches, becoming a twelve-time All-American. Just two months after first arriving in Champaign-Urbana from Jamaica, he was named Big Ten track's Freshman of the Year, then later Illinois's Male Newcomer of the Year. In 2010 at the NCAA outdoor championships, Riley won the 110-meter hurdles in a school-record time of 0:13.45. Success continued in his junior season, when he won a second national title in the 60-meter hurdles and just missed a repeat championship outdoors. That earned him the Dike Eddleman Male Athlete of the Year award. As a senior, Riley became the first male athlete in NCAA history to win national titles in the 100-meter dash and the 110-meter hurdles during the same year. He also competed for Team Jamaica at the 2012 London Olympics and earned a second consecutive Eddleman Award. In 2016, Riley once again represented his native country in the Olympics, teaming up with Usain Bolt.

OTHER TOP MEN'S ATHLETES

1. A. J. Jenkins, football (ninety receptions)
2. Dennis Nevolo, tennis (four-time All–Big Ten honoree)
3. Jordan Parr, baseball (leader in seven statistical categories)
4. Mario Gonzalez, wrestling (Big Ten's 197-pound champ)

2011-12

WOMEN'S ILLINI MOMENT

The 2011 Illini volleyball team was the NCAA runner-up

Volleyball Is NCAA Runner-Up

Coach Kevin Hambly's 2011 Illini volleyball team won its first twenty matches of the year, rising to No. 1 in the AVCA To 25 Coaches Poll. Their 16-4 record tied for second-place in the Big Ten standings behind Nebraska. As the No. 3 seed in the NCAA tournament, superstars Colleen Ward, Michelle Bartsch, and Annie Luhrsen led the Illini into the Final Four, facing top-ranked Southern California in the semifinals. Play came down to a fifth and final set. On match point, both teams took turns making huge digs until finally USC flinched and hit the ball out of bounds. "That last point defined the whole match in itself, just how tough of a match it was, how big of a battle it was," said Hambly. Two nights later in the national championship match, Illinois was pitted against UCLA. Regrettably, the Bruins' big block prevailed in four sets and Illinois's season ended with a 32-5 record.

OTHER TOP MOMENTS

1. Basketball topped No. 10 Ohio State.
2. Track and field's Ashley Spencer won the NCAA 400-meter dash on her nineteenth birthday.
3. Track's 1,600-meter relay team broke a nineteen-year-old record.
4. Kevin Hambly was honored as *Volleyball Magazine*'s National Coach of the Year.
5. Matt Bollant was hired to replace Jolette Law as Illini women's basketball coach.

WOMEN'S ILLINI LIST

BIG TEN COACHES OF THE YEAR

Basketball	Theresa Grentz (1997, 1998)
Gymnastics	Bob Starkell (2005, 2010)
Soccer	Janet Rayfield (2011)
Softball	Terri Sullivan (2010)
Tennis	Mary Tredennick (1987)
Track and Field	Gary Winckler (1989, 1992, 1993, 1995, 1996)
	Tonja Buford-Bailey (2013)
Volleyball	Mike Hebert (1985, 1986, 1988)
	Don Hardin (2001, 2003)

UI's Janet Rayfield was Big Ten Coach of the Year in 2011

WOMEN'S ILLINI ITEM

Sophomore Vanessa DiBernardo was the clear-cut star of the 2011 Illini soccer team, but she was surrounded by an experienced cast that included seniors Marissa Mykines, Julie Ewing, Jackie Guerra, and Jenna Carosio, juniors Niki Reed, Steph Panozzo, Shayla Mutz and Marissa Holden, sophomore Megan Pawloski, and freshman Jannelle Flaws. Illinois won the Big Ten Tournament, but fell to Notre Dame in the first round of the NCAA tournament, 1–0. They ended with a record of 17-5-2.

A trio of Illini celebrates its team's 1–0 victory over Notre Dame

WOMEN'S ILLINI LEGEND

Colleen Ward

Colleen Ward spent her first two seasons with the Florida Gators, but her experience in Gainesville didn't completely fill her needs. So, following the 2009 campaign, Ward decided to move back to Illinois. "Choosing the U of I was one of the best decisions I've ever made," she said. Ward moved into Coach Kevin Hambly's starting lineup in 2010 and became an instant star for the Illini, winning first-team All–Big Ten and second-team All-American accolades. Everything came together in 2011, her senior year, one in which Ward was selected as a first-team All-American and as Illinois's Female Athlete of the Year. However, it was her team's success that stands out most for her. "We unfortunately lost that national championship match, but it was one of the most memorable moments in my life," she said. "I consider myself fortunate to have that experience. It has kept me motivated to reach for the highest level in all that I do." Today, Ward is back in Florida, serving as an underwriter for Northern Trust Corporation in Miami. In her spare time, she enjoys playing beach volleyball and serving her community.

Colleen Ward

OTHER TOP WOMEN'S ATHLETES

1. Vanessa DiBernardo, soccer (second-team All-American)
2. Adrienne GodBold, basketball (Big Ten Sixth Player of the Year)
3. Michelle Bartsch, volleyball (third-team All-American)
4. Kelsey Joannides, gymnastics (two-time Big Ten champ)
5. Jenna Carosio, soccer (Big Ten Conference Medal of Honor recipient, Big Ten Defensive Player of the Year)
6. Ashley Spencer, track and field (Big Ten Outdoor Athlete of the Championships)

ILLINI LORE

Michael Hogan's twenty-month tenure as the University of Illinois president ended on March 22, 2012, when he submitted his letter of resignation to board of trustees chairman Christopher Kennedy. A faculty group at the flagship Urbana-Champaign campus was concerned that Hogan's actions to "brand" the university system as a whole would lead to a loss of distinction and autonomy at each of the individual campuses. Kennedy said that Hogan had "moved a number of tough initiatives forward," including chancellor hires at the UIUC and Springfield campuses, plus $30 million in administrative cost savings. However, it became clear that Hogan could no longer weather the discontent of the faculty. Robert Easter was chosen as his successor.

President Robert Easter

2012–13

AMERICA'S TIME CAPSULE

October 29, 2012   Hurricane Sandy makes landfall in New Jersey, resulting in 110 deaths and $50 billion in damages.

November 6, 2012   By a popular vote advantage of 50 percent to 48 percent, Barack Obama defeated Mitt Romney and won a second term as president.

December 14, 2012   A deranged gunman killed twenty-six people, including twenty children, at Sandy Hook Elementary School in Newtown, Connecticut.

January 19, 2013   Cyclist Lance Armstrong admitted to doping in all seven of his Tour de France victories.

April 15, 2013   Multiple bombs exploded near the finish line of the Boston Marathon. The surviving suspect was apprehended four days later.

MEN'S ILLINI MOMENT

Basketball Tops No. 1 Indiana on Griffey Layup

Tyler Griffey's uncontested layup beat top-ranked Indiana, 74–72

Newly minted No. 1 Indiana came to the State Farm Center on February 7, 2013, with a lineup that included future first-round draft picks Cody Zeller and Victor Oladipo. Predictably, IU led the underdog Illini by twelve at halftime, but D. J. Richardson and Brandon Paul's second-half jump-shooting kept UI in the game. Illinois had the ball with only 0.9 seconds remaining and the score tied, though overtime seemed certain. Instead, Paul's spotted a curl-cutting Tyler Griffey for an uncontested layup, and Illini fans instantaneously streamed onto the floor. Illinois had beaten a top-ranked team for the first time since 2004.

OTHER TOP MOMENTS

1. Illinois hosted the NCAA Men and Women's NCAA Tennis Championships at the four-year-old Khan Outdoor Tennis Complex.
2. Baseball ended Indiana's eighteen-game winning streak.
3. In the fiftieth-anniversary year of the indoor arena, the University of Illinois and State Farm announced a thirty-year, $60 million naming-rights agreement, changing the Assembly Hall to the State Farm Center.
4. Mike Small was named NCAA Coach of the Year.
5. Coach Mike Turk's team barely missed a team title at the Big Ten indoor meet.

MEN'S ILLINI LIST

BASKETBALL ROAD WINS VS. TOP-TEN OPPONENTS

December 8, 2012	Illinois 85, at #10 Gonzaga 74
December 30, 2008	Illinois 71, at #9 Purdue 67 (OT)
March 11, 1989	Illinois 89, at #8 Michigan 83
March 5, 1989	Illinois 70, at #3 Indiana 67
March 1, 1986	Illinois 59, at #4 Georgia Tech 57
January 23, 1982	Illinois 64, at #5 Minnesota 57
February 1, 1966	Illinois 99, at #4 Michigan 93
December 19, 1964	Illinois 91, at #8 Kentucky 86
February 20, 1954	Illinois 74, at #10 Iowa 51

Brandon Paul (center) scored thirty-five points in Illinois's win at No. 10 Gonzaga on December 8, 2012

MEN'S ILLINI ITEM

Illini golf coach Mike Small called upon his quintet of Thomas Detry, Thomas Pieters, Brian Campbell, Alex Burge, and Charlie Danielson in the semifinal match against top-seed California. In a two-hole playoff in the deciding individual match, Pieters, the 2012 NCAA champ, ultimately defeated Cal's Max Homa to give Illinois the victory. Luck didn't stay on Illinois's side, however, as Alabama beat the Illini for the NCAA title, 4–1.

There were hugs all around following Illinois's NCAA semifinal victory over top-seed California

MEN'S ILLINI LEGEND

Justin Parr (left) with his twin brother, Jordan

Justin Parr, Baseball (Athlete of the Year, Big Ten Player of the Year, first-team All-American, thirty-three-game hitting streak)

Fans of Illini baseball star Justin Parr might be surprised by what he considers his greatest accomplishment. From 2011 to 2013, his career was jam-packed with honors, including national accolades and winning the University of Illinois 2013 Dike Eddleman Male Athlete of the Year award. "It was a great honor to be an All-American," said Parr, "but, for me, holding the record for the longest hitting streak in Illinois history is the thing that really stands out." During his senior season, UI's No. 15 strung together at least one hit in thirty-three consecutive games, smashing the previous school mark by eight games. Just as impressive was the fact that Parr had a hit in forty-nine of the fifty-five games he played in 2013 and was errorless as a center fielder, earning him Big Ten Player of the Year honors. Justin admitted that his favorite individual season was 2011 when the Illini roster also included his twin brother Jordan, and his older brother, Josh. Today, Parr works in Chicago for C. H. Robinson, one of the world's largest third-party logistics providers.

OTHER TOP MEN'S ATHLETES

1. Jesse Delgado, wrestling (wins 125-pound NCAA title)
2. Thomas Pieters, golf (Big Ten medalist)
3. Fred Hartville, gymnastics (wins Big Ten and NCAA vault championships)

2012–13

WOMEN'S ILLINI MOMENT

The 2012 Illini fell just short of repeating at Big Ten Tournament champions

Soccer Advances to Big Ten Tournament Finals

For the Illini women's soccer, a fifth-seed going into the 2012 Big Ten tournament, the odds repeating as champs were slim. Their chances appeared even gloomier when Minnesota jumped off to a 2–0 advantage just fifteen minutes into the quarterfinal game. Miraculously, the Illini rallied to win a 3–2 penalty-kick shootout. Next up for Illinois in the semifinals was third-ranked Penn State, the best offensive team in the nation. Clearly, the key to Illini victory would lay on the shoulders of goalkeeper Steph Panozzo. Just two minutes into the game, off a Nittany Lion corner kick, she leaped high above a legion of players to snatch the ball and prevent a probable goal. On a couple of other occasions, Panozzo cut off oncoming attackers, forcing wide shots. Finally, with just five minutes left in the first half, Illinois got a rare opportunity to score. Triggered by Megan Pawloski's classic flip throw-in from the right side of the field, the ball took two big bounces toward the far post. Sophomore Nicole Breece out-sprinted her defender and kicked the ball into the back of the net. It would turn out to be the only goal of the game and send the Illini to the championship game for the fifth time in their history. Unfortunately, Illinois fell short in the title tilt, losing at the hands of Ohio State, 2–1.

OTHER TOP MOMENTS

1. Track and field won indoor Big Ten title.
2. Basketball upset undefeated and No. 6 Georgia, 70–59.
3. Volleyball topped Texas, 3–2. Longhorns went on to win the NCAA championship.

WOMEN'S ILLINI LIST

WOMEN'S TRACK AND FIELD: BIG TEN FRESHMEN OF THE YEAR

1990	Tonja Buford (outdoors)
1993	Tonya Williams (indoors and outdoors)
1995	Collinus Newsome (indoors)
1995	Aspen Burkett (outdoors)
1996	Kerry Ann Richards (outdoors)
1997	Tisha Ponder (indoors)
2001	Perdita Felicien (indoors)
2001	Susanna Kallur (outdoors)
2004	Yvonne Mensah (indoors)

Morolake Akinosun was Track and Field's 2013 Big Ten Freshman of the Year

2012	Ashley Spencer (indoors and outdoors)
2013	Morolake Akinosun (indoors)

A first-generation American, former University of Illinois gymnast Alina Weinstein has packed a lot of great experiences into her twenty-seven-year-old life. She became one of the most decorated gymnasts in Illini history, achieving UI record scores in all-around competition (39.625) and floor exercise (9.975). She's traveled around the world as a cast member of Cirque du Soleil and currently works in San Francisco's high-tech community for Yelp.

Alina Weinstein

WOMEN'S ILLINI LEGEND

2013 NCAA 400-dash champion Ashley Spencer

Ashley Spencer

Though she competed at the University of Illinois for only two seasons, the accomplishments that Ashley Spencer compiled were staggering. The sprinter from Lawrence North High School in Indianapolis established six different UI records, including marks at 200, 300 and 400 meters, then two more as a member of 4x400-meter relay teams both indoors and outdoors. Twice she won NCAA titles in the 400-meter dash. During her freshman campaign in 2012, Spencer was Illinois's Female Newcomer of the Year. Her greatest individual award came in 2013, when she received UI's Dike Eddleman Female Athlete of the Year Award. She transferred to the University of Texas for her final two collegiate seasons, training with former Illini great Tonja Buford-Bailey. The 2016 Olympic bronze medalist in the 400-meter hurdles is now a professional sprinter for Nike.

OTHER TOP WOMEN'S ATHLETES

1. Vanessa DiBernardo, soccer (All-American)
2. Stephanie Richartz, track and field (three-time pole-vault champs)
3. Alina Weinstein, gymnastics (Big Ten Conference Medal of Honor recipient)
4. Morolake Akinosun, track and field (Big Ten [indoor] Freshman of the Year)
5. Karisma Penn, basketball (honorable mention All-American)
6. Rachael White and Melissa Kopinski, tennis (NCAA doubles All-Americans)

ILLINI LORE

On March 28, 2013, the University of Illinois's National Center for Supercomputing Applications formally launched its Blue Waters supercomputer, one of the most powerful in the world for open scientific research. It is also the fastest supercomputer on a university campus. Using Blue Waters, scientists will create breakthroughs in nearly all fields of science, design new materials at the atomic level, predict the behavior of hurricanes and tornadoes, and simulate complex engineered systems like the power-distribution system in airplanes and automobiles. Blue Waters has more than twenty-five petabytes of disk storage, enough to store all of the printed documents in all of the world's libraries.

The home of UI's Blue Waters supercomputer

2013–14

AMERICA'S TIME CAPSULE

October 1, 2013	Largely due to a standoff over Obamacare, Congress failed to agree on a budget. The government shutdown ended fifteen days later.
December 11, 2013	Pope Francis was named *Time*'s Person of the Year.
February 6, 2014	Jay Leno ended his reign as host of The Tonight Show. Jimmy Fallon took over eleven days later.
March 22, 2014	Thirty people were killed by a mudslide in Oso, Washington.
August 10, 2014	Following the death of African American Michael Brown, who was shot by a policemen, unrest broke out in Ferguson, Missouri.
August 11, 2014	Actor and comedian Robin Williams committed suicide at age sixty-three.

MEN'S ILLINI MOMENT

Illini football alum Mike Hopkins spent nearly six months in space on the International Space Station

An Illini in Space

Born on a farm outside Richland, Missouri, Mike Hopkins has been on a journey that has taken him from relative obscurity to worldwide fame. He joined Coach Mike White's football Illini as a walk-on in 1987, then slowly worked his way up the chart. As a sophomore for Coach John Mackovic, Hopkins was named Special Teams Player of the Year. In 1989 he became a starter at free safety and won UI's Bruce Capel Award, symbolic of the player who displays courage and determination. As a senior co-captain, Hopkins helped lead the Illini to the 1990 Big Ten co-championship. His time at Illinois included four consecutive bowl-game appearances and four victories over Ohio State in as many years. However, there was much more to Mike Hopkins than just football. He earned a bachelor's degree in aerospace engineering, served in UI's Reserve Officers Training Corps, and won first-team Academic All-America honors.

Hopkins's achievements over the ensuing years included a master's degree at Stanford, training and missions as a U.S. Air Force test pilot, a stint with the Canadian Flight Test Center, and foreign-language coursework at Italy's Università degli Studi di Parma. He applied for nearly twelve years before being accepted into the NASA astronaut program and was serving as special assistant to the vice chairman of the Joint Chiefs of Staff in the Pentagon prior to his selection to NASA. Hopkins was sent on his first space mission in the fall of 2013 on board the Soyuz TMA-10M spacecraft. He was launched into space from the Baikonur Cosmodrome in Kazakhstan on September 25, 2013, and returned to earth on March 10, 2014, after spending nearly six months in space on the International Space Station, orbiting Earth 2,656 times and traveling more than seventy million miles. Today, he's a U.S. Air Force colonel and resides in Houston with his wife, Julie, and two sons.

OTHER TOP MOMENTS

1. Brian Campbell led the Illini golf team to NCAA quarterfinals.
2. Tennis made the NCAA quarterfinals.
3. Yoshi Hayasaki was inducted into USA Gymnastics Hall of Fame.
4. Players and fans enjoyed the twenty-fifth reunion of the "Flying Illini."
5. Track and field claimed team championship at Drake Relays.
6. Jon Ekey's deep three sent Hawkeye fans home sad, 66–63.

MEN'S ILLINI LIST

BASKETBALL'S FIRST-SEASON SCORING LEADERS
(average points per game)

20.478	Dave Scholz, 1966–67
18.625	Jeff Dawson, 1972–73
16.750	Dave Downey, 1960–61
16.565	Nick Weatherspoon, 1970–71
16.417	Greg Jackson, 1968–69
15.928	Kiwane Garris, 1993–94
15.909	Nick Anderson, 1987–88
15.857	Rayvonte Rice, 2013–14

Basketball standout
Rayvonte Rice

15.636	Kenny Battle, 1987–88
15.438	Cory Bradford, 1998–99

MEN'S ILLINI ITEM

The annual "Braggin' Rights" basketball game in St. Louis between unbeaten Missouri against 9-2 Illinois came down to the last few seconds. With the Tigers on top, 64–63, Illinois got the ball into the hands of Tracy Abrams at the top of the key. He spun and drove the lane but was fouled by Mizzou with 0:04.6 left. Abrams calmly sank both free throws, putting the Illini in front for good, 65–64.

Rayvonte Rice exits the court to the cheers of Illini fans

MEN'S ILLINI LEGEND

Two-time NCAA champion Jesse Delgado

Jesse Delgado

In NCAA wrestling history, Illinois's Jesse Delgado became only the one-hundredth athlete to have accomplished back-to-back national titles, joining such other collegiate legends as Cael Sanderson and Lee Kemp. The 125-pounder from Gilroy, California, began making a splash on Illini wrestling from the very start, placing seventh at the 2012 NCAA meet as a freshman. As a sophomore in 2013, Delgado first defeated Iowa's top-seed Matt McDonough for the Big Ten title, then followed it up with a 7–4 win over Penn State's Nico Megaludis in the finals of the national championships. In 2014 he defeated Megaludis a second time at the conference meet, then became Illinois's first back-to-back national champion in fifty-six years, defeating Cornell's Nahshon Garrett in a thrilling 3–2 match that was scoreless for much of the bout. Delgado once again qualified for the NCAAs as a senior in 2015, but he injured his right knee during the second period of his consolation match against Virginia's Nick Hermann. That ended his collegiate career with a 101-16 record, making him just the twenty-second Illini wrestler to top the century mark. Today, Delgado is pursuing his dream of becoming a mixed-martial-arts fighter.

OTHER TOP MEN'S ATHLETES

1. Farris Gosea, tennis (Big Ten Player of the Year)
2. Jordan Valdez, gymnastics (NCAA high bar title)
3. Nathan Scheelhaase, football (career total offense leader, Big Ten Conference Medal of Honor recipient)

2013–14

WOMEN'S ILLINI MOMENT

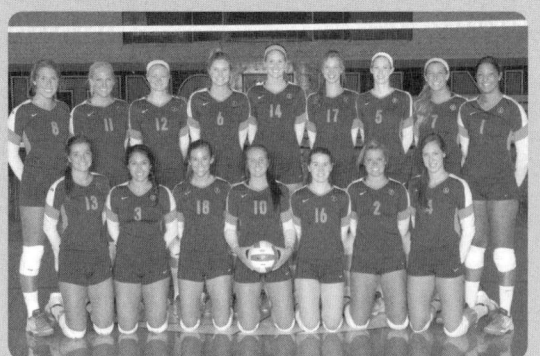

The 2013 Illini volleyball squad

Volleyball Reaches the Sweet Sixteen

The 2013 Fighting Illini volleyball team was determined that it would rebound from a sub .500 season the year before. It achieved its goal, returning to the NCAA Sweet Sixteen for the fifteenth time in school history, placing fourth following a rugged Big Ten schedule. After an October 30 loss at Nebraska, UI's ninth defeat at the hands of a nationally ranked team, its record fell to 9-12, and it didn't appear that the Illini would qualify for the postseason. However, Coach Kevin Hambly's troops bounced back with a vengeance, capturing seven of their last nine regular-season matches. The NCAA committee rewarded Illinois with a No. 13 seed and home games for every match prior to the Final Four. UI swept Morehead State in the opener in Huff Gym, then discarded No. 22 Marquette in game 2. Illinois's home venue switched to the State Farm Center on December 13, but Purdue swept the Orange and Blue, ending UI's season at 18-15.

OTHER TOP MOMENTS

1. Women gymnasts finished 11th at NCAA meet.
2. Volleyball topped Iowa, 3–0, before 7,061 at the State Farm Center.
3. Soccer rallied from 2–0 deficit to beat Portland and advanced to Sweet Sixteen.
3. Maryland and Rutgers were admitted to membership in the Big Ten Conference.

WOMEN'S ILLINI LIST

SOCCER'S CAREER GOAL LEADERS

54	Jannelle Flaws, 2011–2015
47	Tara Hurless, 2001–2004
46	Emily Brown, 1998–2000
43	Vanessa DiBernardo, 2010–2013
30	Jessica Bayne, 2003–2006
27	Ella Masar, 2004–2007
23	Lisa Baldwin, 1998–1999
21	Colleen Joyce, 2000–2001
20	Tiffani Walker, 2000–2003

Jannelle Flaws

18	Chichi Nweke, 2006–2009
18	Lindsay Johnson, 1998–2000

WOMEN'S ILLINI ITEM

Vanessa DiBernardo's four years in Urbana-Champaign (2010–2013) resulted in a number of records and achievements. She finished her Illini career with forty-three goals and twenty-two assists, and Illinois's 2011 Big Ten Tournament title remains as her favorite team memory. DiBernardo's career culminated when she received the Big Ten Conference Medal of Honor, a prize that symbolizes excellence in both athletics and academics. In 2016 DiBernardo played for the Chicago Red Stars of the National Women's Soccer League.

Vanessa DiBernardo

WOMEN'S ILLINI LEGEND

Jannelle Flaws

Jannelle Flaws

With fifty-four goals, Jannelle Flaws finished her Illini career in rarified air. Not only did the former Glenbrook South star obliterate Illinois's record, she became the first non–Penn State player to crack Big Ten history's fifty-goal plateau. Flaws's UI career began quietly, redshirting in 2010, then tallying just three goals in season 2. But for the next three seasons, she scored virtually at will. Flaws's twenty-three goals in twenty-three games during the 2013 campaign set an Illini single-season record and was sixth-most by any Big Ten player. For that performance, she was named Illinois's Female Athlete of the Year. Flaws tallied seventeen goals in 2014, earning third-team All-American accolades. She wrapped up her sensational career in 2015 with eleven goals and six assists. Flaws is now a member of the Chicago Red Stars Reserves, the backup squad for the Red Stars of the National Women's Soccer League.

OTHER TOP WOMEN'S ATHLETES

1. Jennifer Beltran, volleyball (UI's all-time digs leader)
2. Amber Moore, basketball (career three-point field-goal leader)
3. Jocelynn Birks, volleyball (All–Big Ten)
4. Kandie Bloch-Jones, track and field (Newcomer of the Year)
5. Amber See (recorded a perfect 10 on the vault)
6. Alex Booker, softball (.371, three home runs, twenty-seven RBI)

ILLINI LORE

Timothy L. Killeen was named the twentieth president of the University of Illinois in November 2014 following a nationwide search. A native of Wales, Killeen had been serving as vice chancellor for research and president of the Research Foundation at the State University of New York. He received his doctoral degree in atomic and molecular physics from University College of London at age twenty-three.

President
Timothy Killeen

2014–15

AMERICA'S TIME CAPSULE

November 3, 2014	New York City's 104-story One World Trade Center opened, thirteen years after the September 11 attacks.
April 12, 2015	Twenty-one-year-old Jordan Spieth wins the Master's golf tournament.
May 20, 2015	David Letterman hosted CBS's *The Late Show* for the last time.
June 6, 2015	American Pharaoh became the first horse in thirty-seven years to win the Triple Crown.
June 26, 2015	U.S. Supreme Court ruled 5–4 that same-sex marriage is a legal right across all states.
July 1, 2015	United States and Cuba announced an agreement to reopen embassies and establish full diplomatic ties.

MEN'S ILLINI MOMENT

Baseball Sets Big Ten Record for Victories

History will always remember the achievements of the 2015 Fighting Illini baseball team:

- A season of fifty victories—to break the previous record of forty-nine (1982).

- A Big Ten record twenty-seven-game winning streak from March 30 to May 20, just seven shy of the collegiate record.

- An outright Big Ten title, the thirtieth in school history, second only to Michigan's thirty-five.

- A nearly perfect 21-1 conference record (.955 winning percentage).

- A Big Ten record twenty consecutive conference wins, including a record seven-straight conference series sweeps.

- A record of 25-4 at Illinois Field, played before an average of 1,721 fans.

- A national ranking of No. 2, the highest in program history.

- Hosting its first-ever NCAA Regional, going 3-0.

- Participation in its first-ever NCAA super regional. Eventual national runner-up Vanderbilt beat Illinois in consecutive games.

- A sweep of the Big Ten's individual awards: first baseman David Kerian as Player of the Year; left-hander Tyler Jay as Pitcher of the Year; and Dan Hartleb as Coach of the Year.

- First-team All-American honors to Jay and second-team kudos to Kevin Duchene.

- Jay's selection at No. 6 in the Major League Baseball draft.

The 2015 Big Ten champions

OTHER TOP MOMENTS

1. Rayvonte Rice shot beat Mizzou in the "Braggin' Rights" game.

2. The Lauritsen/Wohlers Outdoor Golf Facility opened.

3. Golfer Nick Hardy won Big Ten Championship's individual medalist honors and was named Freshman of the Year.

4. Illini Football played in the Heart of Dallas Bowl against Louisiana Tech, losing 35–18.

5. A record crowd of 17,087 saw the Illini basketball team beat Michigan in overtime.

MEN'S ILLINI LIST

BIG TEN WON-LOST RECORD PITCHING LEADERS

Illini pitcher Kevin Duchene compiled a perfect 7-0 record in Big Ten play

1940	John Pacotti, R (5-1)		
1941	Alan Grant, R (5-1)		
1943	Al Scharf, R (3-0)		
1947	Marv Rotblatt, R (6-0)		
1951	George Maier, L (5-1)	1969	Rich Binder, L (6-0)
1952	Garry Smith, L (5-0)	1985	Donn Pall, R (4-0)
1959	Terry Gellinger, R (5-0)	1996	Brett Weber, R (6-1)
1961	Doug Mills, R (4-0) and Ron Johnson, R (4-0)	1998	Brett Weber, R (6-0)
1962	Tom Fletcher, L (5-0) and Doug Mills, R (5-0)	2001	Andy Dickinson, L (5-1)
1963	Jerry Weygandt, R (5-0)	2015	Kevin Duchene, L (7-0)

MEN'S ILLINI ITEM

Sitting in third place at the Big Ten Track and Field Championships, Illinois had eleven qualifiers in fourteen events for the May 17, 2015 finals. Bookending the day with ten-point victories in the 4x100-meter and 4x400-meter relays, Coach of the Year Mike Turk also got first-place finishes from Athlete of the Championships D. J. Zahn (400 dash) and Cam Viney (400 hurdles). The Illini had won their forty-ninth Big Ten team title.

A jubilant Illini track-and-field squad celebrates its 2015 outdoor Big Ten championship

MEN'S ILLINI LEGEND

Left-hander Tyler Jay was UI's 2015 Dike Eddleman Athlete of the Year

Tyler Jay

Taught to him by his dad, Brian, Fighting Illini left-hander Tyler Jay has had the same pitching wind up since he was seven years old. He fingers his grip on the ball in his glove, keeping it chest high. Jay's right knee rises to the uniform's letters, and his willowy left arm stays hidden until he snaps his wrist and follows through. From his senior year at Lemont High School, when he posted 102 strikeouts in seventy-five innings, through his three seasons at Illinois, when he accounted for 143 Ks in 129 frames, Jay's cobra-like wind up has served him well. In seventy-one career appearances on the mound for the Orange and Blue, all but two in relief, he recorded a miniscule earned run average of 1.68. Jay's 2015 pitching statistics were particularly impressive, striking out seventy-six batters and walking only seven in 66.2 innings. The awards rolled in for No. 11, including those as Big Ten Pitcher of the Year, first-team All-American and Dike Eddleman Male Athlete of the Year. On June 8, 2015, Jay became a first-round pick in the Major League Baseball draft, selected sixth by the Minnesota Twins. He signed a $3.9 million contract and currently pitches in the Twins' minor league system.

OTHER TOP MEN'S ATHLETES

1. Isaiah Martinez, wrestling (undefeated NCAA champion, UI Newcomer of the Year)
2. Jared Hiltzik, tennis (All-American)
3. Rayvonte Rice, basketball (leading scorer and rebounder)

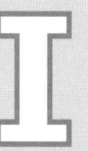

2014–15

WOMEN'S ILLINI MOMENT

Coach Kevin Hambly exhorts his Illini

Volleyball Stuns Penn State

Perhaps it's not as rare as a visit from Halley's Comet, but winning a Big Ten volleyball match at Penn State certainly qualifies as extraordinary. On October 11, 2014, the Recreation Hall crowd of 3,594 expected their defending national champion Nittany Lions to beat Illinois. After all, Penn State had won ninety-four of their previous ninety-six home matches, including nineteen in a row. In the first set, the Illini's confidence that they could compete successfully was boosted when they rallied from a 19–8 deficit to win 26–24. "That was pretty miraculous," admitted UI coach Kevin Hambly afterward. PSU bounced back to convincingly win the second set, tying the match at 1–1. Illinois opened up an early 5–2 lead to start the third set and continued to hold the lead throughout, with Katie Roustio sewing up a 25–23 victory with her powerful kill shot. In the fourth set, the Illini used the effective serving of Brandi Donnelly and Jocelynn Birk's offensive net dominance to win 25–22, tying a bow on the 3–1 upset. "I was proud of the kids for the way they fought," said Hambly.

OTHER TOP MOMENTS

1. Gymnasts Mary Jane Horth, Sunny Kato, and Giana O'Connor won All-America accolades.
2. Soccer coach Janet Rayfield won her two-hundredth career match.
3. Basketball's Chatrice White broke UI's freshman record for points and blocked shots.

WOMEN'S ILLINI LIST

TERRI SULLIVAN, BY THE NUMBERS

On June 4, 2015, longtime Illini softball coach Terri Sullivan announced her retirement. A look at her career, by the numbers:

Coach Terri Sullivan

2	Highest Illini finish in the Big Ten (2004, 2010)
4	UI appearances in the NCAA tournament
6	Illini players who won All-Big Ten accolades in 2010
7	Number of NCAA tournament victories
10	No-hitters recorded by Sullivan's pitchers
15	Longest Big Ten winning streak
16	Number of seasons she coached at Illinois
17	UI's ranking in the final 2004 national poll
22	Most runs in a game by the Illini (vs. Indiana, 2015)
43	Number of players who won All–Big Ten honors
45	Victories won by the Illini in 2010 (45-8)
84	Home runs hit by the Illini in 2007 to lead the nation
859	Total games she coached at Illinois (488-369-2)

Illini volleyball's three-time All-American Jocelynn Birks was an anomaly, preferring a good defensive play over offense. "I love being able to run and chase down a ball or getting a really good dig to extend a rally," she said. Birks wrapped up her career in 2015 as Illinois's all-time leader for kills (1,972). She graduated in May 2016 with a degree in elementary education and, following a professional career in volleyball overseas, will become a teacher.

Jocelynn Birks

WOMEN'S ILLINI LEGEND

Stephanie Richartz

Michael and Cindy Richartz always encouraged their daughter, Stephanie, to aim high. At Carmel High School in Mundelein, she was a member of the National Honor Society and an accomplished athlete who became a state finalist in the pole vault. At the University of Illinois, Richartz studied industrial engineering and earned an international study scholarship, but she was best known for her accomplishments

Stephanie Richartz displays her perfect form as a pole vaulter

in track and field. She steadily improved her vaulting skills, going from 11'6" as a prep to 13'1¾" as a college freshman in 2011. Richartz increased her height to 14'2¾" as a sophomore, becoming UI's first Big Ten pole-vault champion. She added yet another foot as a junior in 2013, winning conference titles both indoors and outdoors, and placing sixth at the NCAA outdoor meet. An injury sidelined Richartz for most of 2014, but she rebounded for two more Big Ten championships as a senior in 2015 and finished third at the NCAA Championships with a personal best jump of 14'7¼". Today, Richartz is a business and systems integration analyst at Accenture in Chicago.

OTHER TOP WOMEN'S ATHLETES

1. Ivory Crawford, basketball (team Most Valuable Player)
2. Allie Bauch, softball (.399, twelve HR, thirty-eight RBI)
3. Liz McMahon, volleyball (Big Ten Conference Medal of Honor recipient)
4. Giana O'Connor, gymnastics (first-team All-American)
5. Alison Meng, swimming (set records in 100-meter butterfly, 100-meter backstroke, 200-meter medley relay, and 400-meter medley relay)
6. Carly Thomas, softball (first-team All–Big Ten, .365, nine home runs, forty-two RBI)

ILLINI LORE

On March 12, 2015, the University of Illinois Board of Trustees voted unanimously to create the nation's first college of medicine that would focus connecting engineering and medicine. It was the first new college created at UIUC in sixty years. The college is a partnership between the university and Carle Health System, integrating the university's long-established assets in engineering, technology, and supercomputing with Carle's nationally acknowledged comprehensive healthcare system.

2015–2016

2015–16

AMERICA'S TIME CAPSULE

September 22, 2015	Pope Francis arrived in the United States for his six-day tour, including addressing Congress.
December 15, 2015	The mayor of Flint, Michigan, declared a state of emergency over contaminated water supplies.
January 6, 2016	*Star Wars: The Force Awakens* broke U.S. box-office record ($750.5 million), previously held by *Avatar*.
November 2, 2016	The Chicago Cubs won their first World Series championship in 108 years, defeating the Cleveland Indians, 8–7, in game 7.
November 8, 2016	Despite Democrat Hillary Clinton collecting nearly three million more votes, Republican Donald Trump won more electoral votes and was elected president of the United States.

MEN'S ILLINI MOMENT

Illini Merry-Go-Round Finishes on High Note

From May of 2015 through March of 2017, Illinois's Division of Intercollegiate Athletics was in a period of continuous change. The timeline of events:

- May 7, 2015: Former Illinois offensive tackle Simon Cvijanovic accused football coach Tim Beckman and the U of I Athletic Department of creating a culture of abuse and mistreatment of players.

- August 28, 2015: One week before Illini football's season opener, Athletic Director Mike Thomas terminated Beckman's contract and named offensive coordinator Bill Cubit interim coach.

- February 17, 2016: Thirty-seven-year-old Illinois alum and former football player Josh Whitman was hired as Illinois's Director of Athletics.

- March 5, 2016: Whitman dismissed Cubit as football coach.

- March 8, 2016: Lovie Smith was announced as Illinois's new head coach.

- February 10, 2017: Chris Tamas named UI's head volleyball coach, replacing Kevin Hambly.

- March 11, 2017: Illinois fired head basketball coach John Groce.

- March 20, 2017: Whitman named Oklahoma State's Brad Underwood as Groce's replacement.

Director of Athletics Josh Whitman (left) and Head Football Coach Lovie Smith

OTHER TOP MOMENTS

1. Seventeen-year-old sophomore Brandon Ngai became the youngest person ever to win an NCAA gymnastics title (pommel horse).

2. Illini wrestling tied for ninth place at the NCAA championships.

3. Men's golf battled its way to the NCAA semifinals, losing to eventual champion Oregon.

4. Grange Grove, a park setting on the west side of Memorial Stadium, opened to the public.

MEN'S ILLINI LIST

MEN'S OLYMPIANS SINCE 1988

2008 Olympian Justin Spring and his medal

1988	Charles Lakes and Dominic Minicucci, gymnastics; Bob Espeseth, rowing
1992	Dominic Minicucci, gymnastics; Marco Koers, track and field (Holland); Jens Kujawa (Germany), basketball
1996	Marco Koers, track and field (Holland)
2000	Marco Koers, track and field (Holland); Bobby True (Liberia), track and field
2008	Deron Williams, basketball; Kevin Anderson (South Africa), tennis; Chris Robinson (Canada), baseball; Gakologelwang Masheto (Botswana), track and field; Justin Spring, gymnastics

2010	Jonathan Kuck, speed skating
2012	Deron Williams, basketball; Robert Archibald, basketball (Great Britain); and Andrew Riley (Jamaica), track and field
2014	Jonathan Kuck, speed skating
2016	Thomas Pieters, golf (Belgium); Rajeev Ram, tennis; Andrew Riley, track and field (Jamaica)

Durkin, Virgin, and Espeseth also qualified for the 1980 Olympic team, but did not compete due to the U.S. boycott; Espeseth, Millns, and Kuck were students at University of Illinois but were not varsity student-athletes.

MEN'S ILLINI ITEM

On November 22, 2015, eighty-four-year-old Lou Henson was inducted into the National Collegiate Basketball Hall of Fame, joining classmates Don Donoher, Quinn Buckner, John Havlicek, and Charlie Scott. Eleven days later—December 2—the playing floor at State Farm Center was officially dedicated as Lou Henson Court, accented by his patented orange blazer and a pair of wings as a tribute to the Flying Illini of 1989.

Former players and staff members joined Lou and Mary Henson for the unveiling of Lou Henson Court

Lou Henson's famous orange blazer is represented on the State Farm Center playing court

MEN'S ILLINI LEGEND

Isaiah Martinez

Isaiah Martinez

It's arguable that Illini junior Isaiah Martinez is the University of Illinois's greatest wrestler ever. Through his first three seasons, the 157-pounder from Lemoore, California, was virtually unstoppable. In 2014–15, Martinez was undefeated as a freshman (35-0), becoming the first NCAA rookie to do so since Iowa State's Cael Sanderson in 1999. He faced personal tragedy just before his sophomore season when his stepfather, Alfred, passed away. With a heavy heart but fully determined, Martinez wheeled through his competition at the 2016 NCAA meet, setting up a rematch at New York City's Madison Square Garden with Penn State's Jason Nolf who had pinned him in a mid-season bout. With the score tied at 4–4 and only twenty seconds left in regulation, Martinez ducked under Nolf and drove through for the winning takedown, then rode out his opponent for the remaining ten seconds to seal his second national crown. After the referee raised his hand, Martinez walked away, pointing to his heart. In March of 2017, he reached the NCAA finals for a third time, but was pinned, suffering only his second loss in 100 collegiate matches.

OTHER TOP MEN'S ATHLETES

1. Charlie Danielson, golf (Big Ten Conference Medal of Honor recipient)
2. Clayton Fejedelem, football (Big Ten's leading tackler, with 11.7 per game)
3. Malcolm Hill, basketball (first-ever UI player to top 600 points, 200 rebounds and 100 assists in a single season)

2015–16

WOMEN'S ILLINI MOMENT

Jordyn Poulter (on knee) had 1,088 assists in 2015

The Future Is Bright

A bevy of talented freshmen who starred during their rookie seasons in 2015–16 will lead Illinois into a promising future era of Illini women's athletics. Six were finalists for UI's 2016 Newcomer of the Year Award, a prize ultimately won by volleyball's Jordyn Poulter.

Achievements by four of the Illini super-frosh:

Jordyn Poulter, volleyball: She started twenty-nine of thirty-two contests as a true freshman and chosen as a member of the Big Ten's All-Freshman team.

Alex Wittinger, basketball: After averaging ten points and nearly seven rebounds per game, she earned a spot on the conference's All-Freshman Team.

Bing Singhsumalee, golf: The rookie star began her collegiate career impressively, breaking UI's all-time record for single-season stroke average (73.94).

Lizzie Leduc, gymnastics: She qualified for the 2016 NCAA championships with her nearly perfect 9.950 performance in floor exercise at the regional meet.

OTHER TOP MOMENTS

1. Senior gymnasts Sunny Kato and Giana O'Connor won All–Big Ten accolades.
2. Cross country's Alyssa Schneider earned All–Big Ten and All-American honors.
3. Chatrice White tallied a career-high thirty-five points at Michigan.

WOMEN'S ILLINI LIST

JERSEY NUMBERS OF THE GREATEST ILLINI WOMEN ATHLETES

No. 6 Danielle Zymkowitz

1	Leisha Alcia, soccer
1	Erin Borske, volleyball
1	Laura DeBruler, volleyball
3	Laura Bush, volleyball
3	Jannelle Flaws, soccer
4	Colleen Ward, volleyball
4	Jenna Hall, softball
6	Kirsten Gleis, volleyball
6	Danielle Zymkowitz, softball
7	Cristy Chapman, volleyball

8	Mary Eggers, volleyball
9	Meredith Hackett, softball
12	Tina Rogers, volleyball
13	Jenna Smith, basketball
24	Jonelle Polk, basketball
31	Sarah Sharp, basketball
32	Ashley Berggren, basketball

Tyra Perry's first Illini softball team flirted with school history in 2016, ending the campaign with a 36-23 record. Despite a mediocre start, Illinois finished the regular season by winning each of its last four Big Ten series, making its fourth-straight Big Ten tournament appearance and advancing to the NCAA regionals for the first time in six years. Perry's senior class of Allie Bauch, Kylie Johnson, Remeny Perez, Danielle Trezzo, and Nicole Tobon combined to hit .314, just above the team's .306 season average. Junior Nicole Evans also had a solid performance at the plate, batting .328 with a team-best twelve home runs and fifty RBI. Together, the pitching twosome of juniors Breanna Wonderly and Jade Vecvanags started fifty-four of UI's fifty-six games while limiting opposing batters to just three earned runs per contest.

Coach Tyra Perry

WOMEN'S ILLINI LEGEND

Academic All-American Allie Bauch

Allie Bauch

University of Illinois softball's Allie Bauch was one of those special people who ultimately rose to the top. A star at Conant High School in Hoffman Estates, she chose to walk on for the Illini. It didn't take long for Illini coach Terri Sullivan to conclude that Bauch could help her team, and the rookie infielder eventually started forty of forty-nine games in 2013. Bauch continued to improve as a sophomore, hitting eight home runs and averaging .347. Her .399 average and twelve homers in 2015 earned Bauch first-team All–Big Ten accolades as a junior. The left-handed hitter's average dipped to a still-respectable .320 in her final season, but she helped lead the Illini to the NCAA tournament and a tourney victory over Butler. Though Bauch's name will be heavily sprinkled in the Illini record book for her exploits on the diamond, it's her classroom achievements and community service that deserve more attention. The math major posted an impressive 3.78 cumulative grade point average and became softball's first two-time Academic All-American. Bauch also received the prestigious Big Ten Conference Medal of Honor, emblematic of the university's premier female student-athlete.

OTHER TOP WOMEN'S ATHLETES

1. Jocelynn Birks, volleyball (UI's all-time kills leader and 2016 Female Athlete of the Year)
2. Pedrya Seymour, track and field (All-American hurdler)
3. Kandie Bloch-Jones, track and field (NCAA championships competitor)

ILLINI LORE

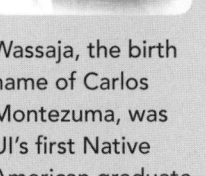

Wassaja Hall

Named after its first Native American graduate, Wassaja Hall opened in the fall of 2016 at the corner of First Street and Gregory Drive. As part of the State of Illinois's Art-in-Architecture program, the residence facility features Native American art. Wassaja (pronounced WAHS-as-ja) was the birth name of 1884 UI medical school graduate Carlos Montezuma. Stolen from his family as a small boy and later sold, Wassaja spent his early childhood on the road performing with Buffalo Bill's Wild West Show. After serving as a reservation doctor for the Bureau of Indian Affairs, he fought tirelessly for Native American rights and citizenship.

Wassaja, the birth name of Carlos Montezuma, was UI's first Native American graduate

THE DIVISION OF DISABILITY RESOURCES AND EDUCATIONAL SERVICES (DRES)

(COLLEGE OF APPLIED HEALTH SCIENCES AT THE UNIVERSITY OF ILLINOIS AT URBANA-CHAMPAIGN)

In 1947, as a response to the Servicemen's Readjustment Act of 1944—also known as the G.I. Bill—the University of Illinois converted a former Veterans Administration Building in Galesburg into a satellite campus to accommodate the education of disabled veterans.

However, what's forgotten is, but for the self-advocacy of many UI students with disabilities, this noble idea almost never developed. When it was decided in 1949 that the Galesburg campus would close, those individuals who were affected set off for Springfield to request that Governor Adlai Stevenson intervene to stop the closure. Their chivalrous effort fell on deaf ears, so they took the road again, this time to Champaign-Urbana. There the disabled students demonstrated to the UI administration that with minimal architectural and personal assistance they could navigate the campus and achieve the same success as the fully abled students.

Begrudgingly, UI administrators acquiesced to this "experiment." For nearly a decade, those students and others who followed continued to advocate for the disabled. Finally, in 1954, they convinced Illinois Governor William Stratton to use his political clout and significantly advance their cause.

Since then, UI's Division of Disability Resources and Educational Services (DRES) has helped thousands of disabled students earn college degrees. Today, the Urbana-Champaign campus is a world leader in postsecondary education for people with disabilities. It has established the first wheelchair-accessible bus system, developed architectural accessibility standards, and offered the first collegiate sports and recreation program for athletes with disabilities.

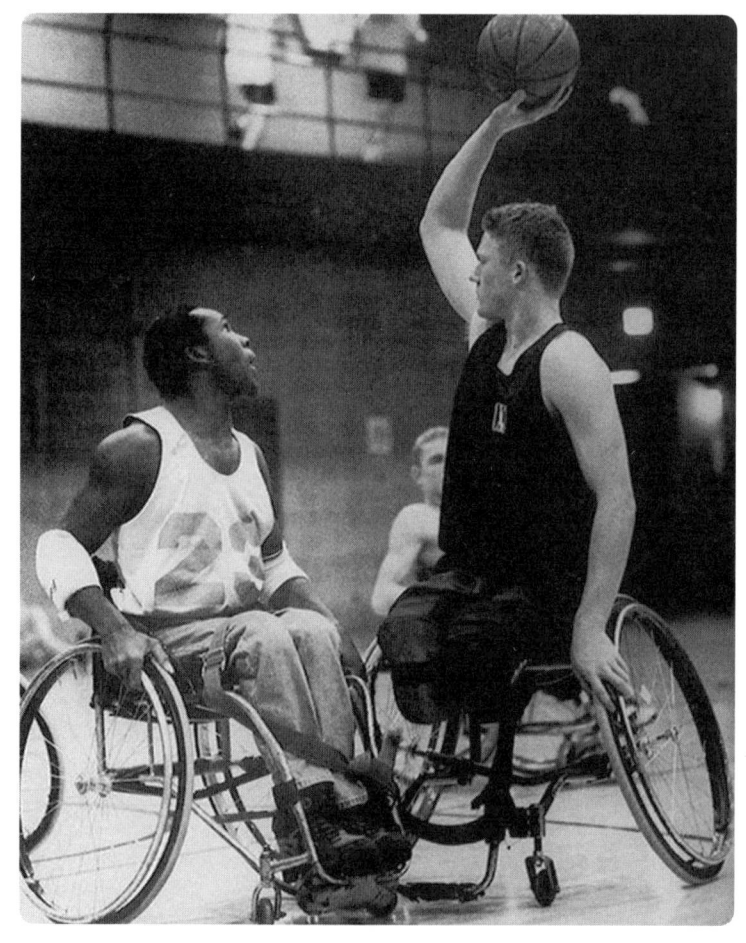

HISTORICAL TIMELINE OF DRES ATHLETICS

1949 Tim Nugent and UI students with disabilities hosted the first National Wheelchair Basketball Tournament at Galesburg and established the National Wheelchair Basketball Association, the first wheelchair-sports organization in the United States. Nugent created the Illinois "Gizz Kids" men's wheelchair basketball team in 1948. The term "Gizz" (short for "Gizzmo") was a nod to the 1940's Fighting Illini Whiz Kids.

1960 The first Paralympic Games were held in Rome. Jack Whitman, an Illinois student, won the first Paralympic Gold Medal for the USA in archery. The Illinois Gizz Kids traveled to South Africa to perform sports demonstrations for a racially integrated population of South Africans with disabilities.

1968 Illinois's Gizz Kids traveled to Hawaii to perform wheelchair sports demonstrations at rehabilitation centers on Oahu.

1974 The Illinois Ms. Kids women's wheelchair basketball team was established. The Ms. Kids prevailed in the first-ever game between two women's teams in the United States, defeating the SIU Squidettes, 34–14.

1976 The Illinois Gizz Kids were a founding member of the Central Intercollegiate Conference of the NWBA, the nation's first collegiate wheelchair basketball division.

1977 Illinois finished second to SIU in the first National Intercollegiate Wheelchair Basketball Tournament. Illinois wheelchair athletes were the first on any campus to be awarded varsity letters. Gunnar Arlind of Sweden was the first athlete to receive a varsity I letter award.

1978 Both the Illinois Gizz Kids and Illinois Ms. Kids won their first national wheelchair basketball tournaments.

1980 Illinois hosted the National Wheelchair Games. The members of the Tribe of Illini, composed of all Illinois varsity athletes, selected Sharon Rahn Hedrick and Dave Wilson as the university's Most Outstanding Athletes.

1984 Two wheelchair track events were added as exhibition events to the Summer Olympic Games in Los Angeles. Two Illini, Ann Cody and Sharon Hedrick, advanced to the final, and Hedrick won the internationally televised women's 800-meter track event in a world-record time of 2:12.

1988 Alumnus Sharon Hedrick and Illinois student Jean Driscoll advanced to the finals of the women's 800-meter track event at the Seoul Olympics. Hedrick won in world record time. Illinois student Scot Hollonbeck advanced to the finals of the men's Olympic 1,500-meter track event and finished second.

1990 Jean Driscoll won the 1990 Boston Marathon, beginning a seven-year winning streak. She won her eighth and final Boston title in 2000, giving her more victories than any other person.

2014 The USOC/USP established its first national training site for wheelchair racing at the University of Illinois Division of Disability Resources and Educational Services.

2016 Tatyana McFadden won the Boston Marathon, the London Marathon, the Los Angeles Marathon, and the New York Marathon for the second consecutive year. She is the only individual to have won all four in a single year.

At the 2016 Paralympic Games in Rio de Janeiro, Brazil, thirteen different Illinois alumni won medals. UI's ten gold medal winners included: Ray Martin (400 and 1,500 meters) and McFadden (400, 800, 1,500 and 5,000 meters) in track and field; Gail Gaeng, Megan Blunk, Christina Schwab, and Stephanie Wheeler (head coach) in women's basketball; Brian Bell and Steve Serio in men's basketball; Kari Miller in sitting volleyball; and Dylan Alcott in tennis (both singles and doubles).

TIMOTHY J. NUGENT (1923–2015)

Nugent founded the first comprehensive program of higher education for individuals with disabilities in 1948. He served as professor of rehabilitation education and director of the Rehabilitation Education Center and the Division of Rehabilitation Education Services at the University of Illinois, retiring in 1985. He founded the National Wheelchair Basketball Association in 1949 and served as its commissioner for the first twenty-five years.

Tim Nugent

ILLINOIS'S GREATEST DISABLED ATHLETES

JACK WHITMAN

A 1960 Paralympic athlete, Whitman won a total of eleven gold medals in Paralympic archery competitions. He was inducted into the U.S. Wheelchair Sports Hall of Fame in 1971 and was regarded as "America's Father of Wheelchair Archery."

Jack Whitman

SHARON RAHN HEDRICK

A six-time MVP for UI's wheelchair basketball team, Hedrick also was an outstanding competitor in track, winning gold, silver, and bronze medals in three different Paralympic Games. She was inducted into the Wheelchair and Ambulatory Sports Hall of Fame in 1992.

Sharon Hedrick

JEAN DRISCOLL

A competitor at four Summer Paralympic Games, Driscoll won a total of five gold medals, three silvers, and four bronzes in events ranging from 200 meters to the marathon. She also won the women's wheelchair division of the Boston Marathon eight times, including seven consecutive first-place finishes from 1990 to 1996.

Jean Driscoll

SCOT HOLLONBECK

Both an Olympic and Paralympic wheelchair track athlete, Hollonbeck won two gold medals and a silver in Barcelona, then two silver medals in Atlanta.

Scot Hollonbeck

TATYANA McFADDEN

The 2016 Boston Marathon champion, McFadden has won ten Paralympic medals in multiple Summer Paralympic Games. She also competed in the 2016 Paralympic Games in Rio de Janeiro.

Tatyana McFadden

PATRICK ANDERSON

Anderson helped Canada win back-to-back Paralympic gold medals (Sydney 2000 and Athens 2004) and a silver medal in Beijing in 2008.

Patrick Anderson

RAY MARTIN

Martin won Paralympic gold medals at the 2012 games in London in four different events: 100 meters, 200 meters, 400 meters, and 800 meters. He also competed in the 2016 Paralympic Games in Rio de Janeiro.

Ray Martin

BARBARA YOSS

Yoss, a 1982 Urbana High School graduate, competed in Paralympic wheelchair basketball in 1984 and 1988. The team won a gold medal in 1988.

Thank you to Dr. Brad Hedrick, who helped with the text and photos for this chapter about the University of Illinois's disabled athletes. He earned his PhD at Illinois in 1984 in the Department of Leisure Studies, now Recreation, Sport, and Tourism. From 1981 to 1996, Hedrick served as head coach of UI's varsity athletic teams for students with disabilities, as well as an administrator, researcher, and educator within the Division of Disability Resources and Educational Services (DRES). In 2005 he was inducted into the National Wheelchair Basketball Association Hall of Fame for his contributions. In 2006 Hedrick received the University of Illinois Chancellor's Academic Professional Excellence Award. His wife, Sharon (Rahn) Hedrick, is one of UI's most accomplished wheelchair athletes.

Dr. Brad Hedrick

FIGHTING ILLINI ATHLETES OF THE YEAR

Initiated in 1940, the award was named after Dwight "Dike" Eddleman in 1993. Eddleman is generally considered the greatest athlete in the history of University of Illinois athletics.

1940	William J. Hapac, basketball and baseball
1941	John Drish, basketball and baseball
1942	Andy Phillip, basketball and baseball
1943	Andy Phillip, basketball and baseball
1944	Claude "Buddy" Young, football and track and field
1945	Walton "Junior" Kirk, basketball
1946	Herbert McKenley, track and field
1947	Alex Agase, football and wrestling
1948	Dwight "Dike" Eddleman, football, basketball, and track and field
1949	Dwight "Dike" Eddleman, football, basketball, and track and field
1950	Russell Steger, football and baseball
1951	Don Sunderlage, basketball
1952	Charles Boerio, football
1953	Clive Follmer, basketball and baseball
1954	J. C. Caroline, football
1955	Paul Judson, basketball
1956	Em Lindbeck, football and baseball
1957	Abe Woodson, football and track and field
1958	Bob Mitchell, football and track and field
1959	Abe Grossfeld, gymnastics
1960	Bill Burrell, football
1961	Bill Brown, football and track and field
1962	Doug Mills, football, basketball, and baseball
1963	Harold Holmes, gymnastics
1964	Dick Butkus, football
1965	Dick Butkus, football
1966	Jim Grabowski, football
1967	Jim Dawson, basketball
1968	Dave Scholz, basketball
1969	Dave Scholz, basketball
1970	Mike Price, basketball
1971	Lee LaBadie, track and field /cross-country
1972	Rick Gross, track and field /cross-country
1973	No award conferred
1974	No award conferred
1975	No award conferred
1976	No award conferred
1977	Craig Virgin, track and field/cross-country
	Nancy Thies, gymnastics
1978	No award conferred
1979	No award conferred
1980	No award conferred
1981	No award conferred
1982	Tony Eason, football
	No women's award conferred
1983	Tony Eason, football
	Marianne Dickerson, track and field / cross-country
1984	Don Thorp, football
	Karen Brems, gymnastics
1985	Charles Lake, gymnastics
	Kelly McNee, track and field /cross-country
1986	David Williams, football
	Jonelle Polk, basketball
1987	Darrin Fletcher, baseball
	Mary Eggers, volleyball
1988	Tim Simon, track and field
	Mary Eggers, volleyball
1989	David Zeddies, gymnastics
	Mary Eggers, volleyball
1990	Kendall Gill, basketball
	Laura Bush, volleyball

1991	Jon Llewellyn, wrestling
	Sarah Sharp, basketball; Renee Heiken, golf
1992	Tim Simpson, football; Len Sitko, track and field / cross-country
	Renee Heiken, golf; Tonja Buford, track and field
1993	Marko Koers, track and field
	Tonja Buford, track and field
1994	Anthony Jones, track and field
	Tina Rogers, volleyball
1995	Dana Howard, football; Steve Marianetti, wrestling
	Tonya Williams, track and field
1996	Kevin Hardy, football
	Tonya Williams, track and field
1997	Ernest Benion, wrestling
	Ashley Berggren, basketball
1998	Eric Siebert, wrestling
	Ashley Berggren, basketball; Yvonne Harrison, track and field
1999	Oliver Freelove, tennis
	Cristy Chapman, volleyball
2000	Jason Anderson, baseball
	Jessica Aveyard, swimming
2001	Adam Tirapelle, wrestling
	Perdita Felicien, track and field
2002	Kurt Kittner, football
	Perdita Felicien, track and field
2003	Amer Delic, tennis; Matt Lackey, wrestling
	Perdita Felicien, track and field

2004	Justin Spring, gymnastics
	Leisha Alcia, soccer
2005	Deron Williams, basketball
	Cassie Hunt, track and field/cross-country
2006	Justin Spring, gymnastics
	Cassie Hunt, track and field/cross-country
2007	Kevin Anderson, tennis
	Yvonne Mensah, track and field
2008	J Leman, football
	Angela Bizzarri, track and field/cross-country
2009	Paul Ruggeri, gymnastics
	Angela Bizzarri, track and field/cross-country
2010	Scott Langley, golf
	Angela Bizzari, track and field/cross-country
2011	Andrew Riley, track and field
	Melissa Fernandez, gymnastics
2012	Andrew Riley, track and field
	Colleen Ward, volleyball
2013	Justin Parr, baseball
	Ashley Spencer, track and field
2014	Jesse Delgado, wrestling
	Jannelle Flaws, soccer
2015	Tyler Jay, baseball
	Stephanie Richartz, track and field
2016	Isaiah Martinez, wrestling
	Jocelynn Birks, volleyball
2017	Isaiah Martinez, wrestling
	Nicole Evans, softball

BIG TEN CONFERENCE
MEDAL OF HONOR WINNERS

Since 1915, the Big Ten Conference Medal of Honor has been awarded annually at each conference school to a male (and, since 1982, a female) senior student-athlete who demonstrates proficiency in scholarship and athletics.

1915	Edward A. Williford, basketball
1916	Elmo P. Hohman, track and field
1917	Clyde G. Alwood, basketball
1918	J. Leo Klein, football and baseball
1919	G. C. Gucheit, football
1920	John B. Felmley, basketball
1921	John S. Prescott, track and field
1922	Clarence F. Crossley, baseball
1923	Otto H. Vogel, football and baseball
1924	Walter Roettger, basketball and baseball
1925	Gilbert J. Roberts, football

1926	John W. Mauer, basketball
1927	Doran T. Rue, track and field
1928	Richard G. Finn, baseball
1929	Robert B. Orlovich, track and field
1930	Richard C. Oeler, gymnastics
1931	Lee H. Sentman Jr., track and field
1932	Edward F. Gbur, baseball
1933	R. Dean Woolsey, cross-country/track and field
1934	Ralph J. Epstein, fencing
1935	Irving Seely, track and field
1936	Arthur E. Fisher, gymnastics
1937	Harry Combes, basketball
1938	Allen Sapora, wrestling
1939	Archie Deuschman, wrestling
1940	Frank E. Richart Jr., golf
1941	Park L. Brown, cross-country/track and field
1942	William Hocking, basketball
1943	Edwin S. Parker, basketball and baseball
1944	Warren F. Goodell Jr., track and field
1945	Donald Delaney, basketball
1946	Robert L. Phelps, track and field
1947	Robert E. Richards, track and field
1948	George Fischer, baseball
1949	T. Dwight "Dike" Eddleman, football, basketball, and track and field
1950	Russell W. Steger, football and baseball
1951	Donald R. Laz, football, and track and field
1952	Richard W. Calisch, track and field
1953	Clive Follmer, basketball and baseball
1954	Robert E. Lenzini, football, and track and field
1955	Edwin G. Jackson Jr., wrestling
1956	Daniel E. Dudas, baseball
1957	Robert H. Dintelmann, cross-country, and track and field
1958	Lee H. Sentman III, fencing
1959	Abraham Grossfeld, gymnastics
1960	Robert J. Madix, baseball
1961	Charles E. Campbell, fencing
1962	Stuart Cohn, fencing
1963	David Downey, basketball
1964	Richard Deller, football
1965	Bogie Redmon, basketball, and track and field
1966	James Grabowski, football
1967	Robert Bachman, swimming
1968	Paul Shapin, gymnastics
1969	Dennis Rott, wrestling
1970	Lawrence Schwartz, fencing
1971	Ernest Clements, tennis
1972	Robert Bucklin, football
1973	Robert Mango, track and field
1974	Howard Beck, gymnastics
1975	Howard Beck, gymnastics
1976	Glenn Hummel, tennis
1977	Craig Virgin, track and field, and cross-country
1978	Steve Yasukawa, gymnastics
1979	John Davis, gymnastics
1980	Dave Stoldt, gymnastics
1981	John Kakacek, wrestling
1982	Randy Conte, baseball
	Lisa Robinson, basketball
1983	Rich Baader, track and field
	Mary Ellen Murphy, golf
1984	Kerry Dickson, track and field
	Karen Brems, gymnastics
1985	Peter Bouton, tennis
	Sue Arildsen, tennis
1986	Jim Juriga, football
	Christy Flesvig, tennis
1987	Graeme McGufficke, swimming
	Jonelle Polk, basketball
1988	Tim Simon, track and field
	Disa Johnson, volleyball
1989	Peter Freund, football
	Chris Schwarz, volleyball
1990	John Murray, tennis
	Celena Mondie-Milner, track and field
1991	Aaron Mobarak, track and field
	Lynn Devers, gymnastics
1992	Mike Hopkins, football
	Kate Riley, basketball
1993	Brad Lawton, track and field
	Lindsey Nimmo, tennis
1994	Forry Wells, football/baseball
	Tonya Booker, basketball
1995	Steve Marianetti, wrestling
	Carmel Corbett, track and field
1996	Marko Koers, track and field
	Dawn Riley, track and field
1997	Seth Brady, wrestling
	Kelly Scherr, volleyball
1998	Eric Siebert, wrestling
	Ashley Berggren, basketball
1999	Bobby True, track and field
	Stacy Schapiro, tennis
2000	Travis Romagnoli, gymnastics
	Tara Mendozza, track and field
2001	Graydon Oliver, tennis
	Betsy Spicer, volleyball
2002	John Lockhart, wrestling
	Gia Lewis, track and field
2003	Andy Schutzenhoffer, baseball
	Michelle Webb, tennis

2004 Phil Stolt, tennis
Jennifer McGaffigan, tennis
2005 Jack Ingram, basketball
Cynthya Goulet, tennis
2006 Dee Brown, basketball
Christen Karniski, soccer
2007 Warren Carter, basketball
Yvonne Mensah, track and field
2008 J Leman, football
Mary Therese McDonnell, soccer
2009 Trent Meacham, basketball
Emily Zurrer, soccer
2010 Jon Asamoah, football
Angela Bizzarri, track and field/cross-country

2011 Scott Langley, golf
Hillary Haen, volleyball
2012 Luke Guthrie, golf
Jenna Carosio, soccer
2013 Brandon Paul, basketball
Alina Weinstein, gymnastics
2014 Nathan Scheelhaase, football
Vanessa DiBernardo, soccer
2015 Will Krug, baseball
Liz McMahon, volleyball
2016 Charlie Danielson, golf
Allie Bauch, softball
2017 Joe Spencer, football
Nicole Evans, softball

ILLINOIS NEWCOMERS OF THE YEAR

1990 Steve Bridges, track and field
Peggy Pullman, gymnastics
1991 Deon Thomas, basketball
Mandy Cunningham, basketball
1992 Marko Koers, track and field
Becky Biehl, golf
1993 Simeon Rice, football
Kirsten Gleis, volleyball
1994 Jerry Turek, tennis
Nicole Viernes, gymnastics
1995 Robert Holcombe, football
Erin Borske, volleyball
1996 Karl Roesler, wrestling
Kim Berres, gymnastics
1997 Chris Jones, track and field; Cary Franklin, tennis
Tisha Ponder, track and field
1998 Adam Tirapelle, wrestling
Aleisha Latimer, track and field
1999 Cory Bradford, basketball; Jason Van Swol,
    track and field
Allison Curtin, basketball

2000 Brandon Lloyd, football
Shavonna Hunter, basketball
2001 Amer Delic, tennis; Phil Stolt, tennis
Jennifer McGaffigan, tennis; Susanna Kallur,
    track and field
2002 Drew Davidson, baseball
Ashley Williams, gymnastics
2003 Alex Tirapelle, wrestling and Rajeev Ram, tennis
Rachelle Coriddi, softball
2004 E. B. Halsey, football
Cassie Hunt, track and field, and cross-country
2005 Kevin Anderson, tennis
Macall Harkins, tennis
2006 Kyle Hudson, football and baseball
Julie Crall, gymnastics
2007 Gakologelwang Masheto, track and field
Angela Bizzarri, track and field, and cross-country
2008 Arrelious Benn, football
Allison Buckley, gymnastics
2009 Andrew Riley, track and field
Michelle Bartsch, volleyball

2010	D.J. Richardson, basketball	2014	Chandler Eggleston, gymnastics
	Pepper Gay, softball		Kandie Bloch-Jones, track and field
2011	Nathan Scheelhaase, football	2015	Isaiah Martinez, wrestling
	Vanessa DiBernardo, soccer		Brandi Donnelly, volleyball
2012	C. J. Maestas, gymnastics	2016	Alex Diab, gymnastics
	Ashley Spencer, track and field		Jordyn Poulter, volleyball
2013	Fred Hartville, gymnastics	2017	Michael Feagles, golf
	Morolake Akinosun, track and field		Jacqueline Quade, volleyball

ILLINOIS SPIRIT AWARD WINNERS

1990	Darrick Brownlow, football	2004	Erik Garnett, gymnastics
	Heather Singalewitch, gymnastics		Kelly Walker, soccer
1991	Andy Kpedi, basketball	2005	Chris Martin, tennis
	Tonja Buford, track and field		Erin Virtue, volleyball
1992	Mike Hopkins, football	2006	Alex Tirapelle, wrestling
	Kate Riley, basketball		Rasa Virsilaite, volleyball
1993	Scott Turner, football and track and field; Pete Frew, baseball	2007	Shawn Roof, baseball
			Caroline Moore, swimming
	Tonya Booker, basketball	2008	J Leman, football
1994	Steve Bridges, track and field		Shannon McDonnell, soccer
	Merrill Mullis, volleyball	2009	Chester Frazier, basketball
1995	Ernest Benion, wrestling		Kayani Turner, volleyball
	Dina Slomski, gymnastics; Lissa Kimmel, tennis	2010	Isiah "Juice" Williams, football; Luke Stannard, gymnastics
1996	Jeremy Sutter, tennis		Megan Fudge, tennis
	Laura Mindock, track and field	2011	Chad Wiest, gymnastics
1997	Ernest Benion, wrestling		Krystin Miller, soccer
	Kelly Scherr, volleyball	2012	Nathan Scheelhaase, football
1998	Gavin Sontag, tennis		Amy Allin, tennis
	Missy Kann, soccer	2013	Corey Lewis, football
1999	Travis Romagnoli, gymnastics		Shayla Mutz, soccer
	Trisha Henry, swimming	2014	Ross Guignon, tennis
2000	Joe Sprengard, baseball		Jennifer Beltran, volleyball
	Melissa Beitz, volleyball	2015	Reilly O'Toole, football
2001	Babatunde Ridley, track and field		Melissa Kopinski, tennis
	Betsy Spicer, volleyball	2016	Joe Spencer, football
2002	Mike Kosta, tennis; Chad Hay, wrestling		Taylore Peterson, soccer
	Ade Oshinowo, track and field	2017	Tracy Abrams, basketball
2003	Jerrance Howard, basketball		Jill Nicklas, softball
	Sara Baumgarter, softball		

VARSITY "I" ACHIEVEMENT AWARD WINNERS

Year	Recipient	Graduation Date	Sport
1970	Claude H. "Buddy" Young	1946	Football - Track and Field
1971	Leland M. T. Stilwell	1924	Basketball
1972	Barton Cummings	1935	Football - Track and Field
1973	Ray Eliot	1932	Football - Baseball
1974	Robert C. Wright	1936	Football - Track and Field
1975	Willard G. "Bill" Franks	1949	Football - Track and Field
1976	Perry Graves Sr.	1915	Football - Baseball
1977	George S. Halas	1918	Football - Basketball - Baseball
1978	Charles W. Bennis	1935	Football
1979	Charles R. Carney	1922	Football - Basketball
1980	Duane A. Cullinan	1937	Track and Field
1981	Wayne D. Paulson	1966	Football
1982	Cirilo A. McSween	1954	Track and Field
1983	T. Dwight "Dike" Eddleman	1949	Football - Basketball - Track and Field
1984	Thomas C. Stewart	1950	Football
1985	Russell W. "Ruck" Steger	1948	Football - Baseball
1986	Willard P. Thomson	1955	Track and Field
1987	Louis Boudreau	1963	Basketball
1988	Dave Downey	1963	Basketball
1989	Tom Riggs	1941	Football
1990	Dick Butkus	1965	Football
1991	Tom Haller	1959	Baseball - Basketball - Football
1992	Bill Butkovich	1947	Baseball - Football
1993	Jerry Colangelo	1962	Basketball

Year	Recipient	Graduation Date	Sport
1994	Bob Mitchell	1958	Football - Track and Field
1995	Tal Brody	1965	Basketball
1996	Joe Tanner	1972	Swimming
1997	Eddie Johnson	1981	Basketball
1998	John Wright	1968	Football
1999	Doug Mills	1962	Football - Basketball - Baseball
2000	Joel Hirsch	1963	Golf
2001	Arthur Wyatt	1949	Golf
2003	Mark Hogan	1973	Manager
2004	James DeBord	1969	Swimming
2005	Charles Finn	1955	Football Manager
2006	Mannie Jackson	1960	Basketball
2007	Ron Bess	1968	Football
2008	Justin Dooley	1986	Gymnastics
2009	Roderick "Rick" Schmidt	1975	Basketball
2010	Steve Stricker	1989	Golf
2011	Bob Noelke	1980	Football
2012	Richard Erickson	1968	Football
2013	Ron Guenther	1967	Football
2014	Stu Levenick	1976	Football
2015	David Clapp	1982	Baseball
2016	Bob Bucklin	1972	Football
	Sheila Crump Johnson*	1970	Cheerleading

*first-ever female recipient

ALL-TIME FIGHTING ILLINI
LETTER-WINNER LIST

Approximately ten thousand men and women have earned varsity letters as athletes in intercollegiate athletics at the University of Illinois from 1878 through the fall of 2016. This list reflects the cumulative information contained within UI's sports summary books. Team managers, who often earned varsity letters, have not been included due to inconsistent information. Female athletes are listed by their maiden names. As with any list of this magnitude, there could be inadvertent errors or omissions. Please contact the UI Athletic Public Relations office should you discover a mistake.

BASEBALL

Adsit, Bertram W.	1899, 1900, '01
Agase, Herbert	1950, '51
Ahrens, Carl	1951, '52, '53
Alcock, Warren J.	1917
Alexander, Joe W.	1939
Allen, Aleck M.	1883
Allen, Art	1965
Alley, Mike	1972
Altobelli, Dominic	2006, '08, '09
Anderlik, Robert	1945, '47, '48
Anderson, Gary	1971, '72, '73
Anderson, Jason	1998, '99, 2000
Anderson, John	2009, '10, '11
Anderson, Jon	1996, '97, '98, '99
Anderssohn, Henry	1948, '49, '50
Andrews, Donald H.	1927, '28, '29
Andrews, William T.	1879, '80, '81
Antonacci, Bill	1995, '96
Arbuckle, Leon	1914, '15, '16
Arft, Kevin	2000
Argo, Willie	2009, '10, '11, '12
Arlis, Patrick	2001, '02
Arneson, Paul	1959, '60, '61
Arrandale, Matt	1992, '93
Arrasmith, William S.	1919
Ashmore, James N.	1902, '03
Astroth, Lavere L.	1939, '40, '42
Atherton, George H.	1891, '92
Backs, Jason	1988
Baker, Jerry	1964
Balestri, George	1943
Ballantine, Fred	1949
Ballard, Brady	2000, '01
Bane, Frank M.	1914, '15
Banker, Edward H.	1922
Baranski, Jerome	1951, '52

Barickman, Joel	2006
Barklage, Oliver F.	1918, '19
Barnes, Robert A.	1921, '22
Barnett, Scott	1980
Barrett, Bill	2007, '08, '11
Barszcx, Casey	1957, '58, '59
Barta, Joseph T.	1925
Bartley, Boyd O.	1941, '42, '43
Bartulis, Joe	1931
Basak, Chris	1998, '99, 2000
Baum, Harvey W.	1894, '95
Beadle, J. Grant	1885, '86, '87, '88
Beebe, Fred L.	1902, '03
Belden, Edgar S.	1888, '89, '90
Bellair, Cole	2016
Belsole, Bob	1963, '64
Bennett, Cleaves	1888
Bennett, Mike	1970
Bennett, Sean	1995
Bensko, Dusty	2002, '03, '04, '05
Berg, Howard M.	1935, '36
Berner, John R.	1938
Berry, Rex	1958
Bessone, Amo	1941
Beyer, George F.	1904, '06, '07
Bickhaus, Dick	1961
Bickhaus, Jim	1954, '55, '56
Biel, Joseph	1981
Bills, Victor	1982
Binder, Richard	1967, '68, '69
Bisbele, Fred B.	1933
Bishop, Emanuel	2005
Black, Marty	1990, '91
Blackaby, Ethan	1960
Blackburn, Nick	2013, '14, '15, '16
Blakaslee, James W.	1896
Blandy, D. C.	1883
Blomquist, Brian	2002, '03, '05, '06

Bock, Brian	1979, '80, '81, '82
Boehler, Michael	1977
Bogan, Raki	1995
Bolk, Bill	1956, '57, '58
Bonadonna, Joe	2006, '07, '08, '09
Bonk, Bill	1960
Borg, Gary	1982, '83, '84, '85
Borgialli, Dominic	1978, '79
Borre, Steven	1977, '78
Boudreau, Louis	1937
Bouton, Charles S.	1888, '89, '90, '91
Bowen, Herbert L.	1890
Bower, Lynn K.	1929
Boyd, C. N.	1879, '80, '81
Bozich, John	1956
Brackett, Jerry	1969, '70, '71
Bradley, John T.	1914, '15, '16
Braun, Wes	2008, '10, '11
Brenton, J. F.	1912
Brewer, Joseph	1951
Brewer, William R.	1939, '41, '42
Briggs, C. W.	1886, '87, '88
Brittin, John	1943, '47
Brooks, Richard A.	1905, '06
Brown, Donald	1929, '30
Brozek, Gary	1982
Bruin, W. W.	1931
Bunn, Charles M.	1910
Bunton, F. L.	1887
Burlage, Bob	1996, '97, '98, '99
Busche, Justin	1995, '97
Bushnell, Howard	1905, '06, '07
Butkovich, William	1944, '45
Butler, F. L.	1895, '96
Butzer, Glenn D.	1910, '11
Buzwick, John W.	1908, '10
Cahill, James	1977, '78, '79
Callaghan, Rich	1963, '64, '65

Callahan, John H. 1936, '37, '38
Calza, Tom 1968, '69
Campbell, Charles M. 1941, '42
Canan, Rich 1985
Cann, Fremont G. 1928
Capparelli, Rich 1986—89
Cappetta, Pete 2008, '09, '10, '11
Carlson, Clifford C. 1933, '34
Carnahan, David H. 1893, '95, '96
Carnahan, Franklin G. 1891, '92
Carpenter, Hubert V. 1896, '97
Carrithers, Ira T. 1906, '07
Cashman, Brandon 2002, '03
Cashmore, Richard 1948
Castellanos, Ryan 2013, '14
Catalano, Phil 1959, '60
Cavallo, Ernest S. 1938, '39
Cawley, Mitchell 1980
Champagne,
    Brannon "Boo" 1984, '85, '86
Charvat, Bill 2012
Chase, Morton E. 1879
Chervinko, Paul 1931, '32, '33
Chmielewski, Nick 2008, '09, '12
Christensen, Bob 1987, '88, '89, '90
Christiansen,
    Donald W. 1938
Christopher, Ron 1964
Ciaramelli, Robert 1943
Cimack, Jeffrey 1975
Clapp, David 1979
Clark, Arthur S. 1883
Clark, George 1915, '16
Clarkson, James F. 1888, '89, '90
Cochran, Phillip 1969
Coffey, Lawrence 1984, '85
Cogdal, Harry F. 1913, '14, '15
Cohick, Emmitt 1989, '90
Colangelo, Jerry 1960
Colby, Greg 1972, '73, '74
Colton, Seth W. 1880
Conley, Frank C. 1938
Conroy, Jimmy 2002, '03, '04, '05
Conte, Randy 1979, '80, '81, '82
Cook, Gary 1973
Cook, James F. 1900, '01, '02, '03
Cook, Louis P. 1903, '04
Cooper, Paul H. 1892, '94, '95, '96
Cordova, Randy 1971, '72, '73
Cortesi, Bob 1971, '72, '73
Cox, Henry R. 1917

Craan, David 2016
Crangle, Walter F. 1921
Crawford, Ken 1993, '94
Crews, Randy 1968, '69, '70
Cross, Charles W. 1889, '90, '91, '92
Crossley, Clarence F. 1920, '22
Crotser, Max 1959, 1960, '61
Crouse, Dave 1964, '65, '66
Cuchran, Don 1988, '89, '90
Cummins, Christian 2010
Cvik, James 1958, '59
Dahlhein, Bruce 1975, '76, '77
Dalbeck, Leon 1927
Dalesandro, Mark 1987, '88, '89, '90
Dancisak, Edward J. 1936
Daukus, Anthony 1936
Davidson, Drew 2002, '03, '04, '05
Davis, Adam 2010, '11
Davis, James O. 1883
Davis, John 1951, '52
Davis, John E. 1915, '16, '17
Davis, Lars 2006, '07
de la Torriente, Brian 2010, '12
Delveaux, Jack 1958, '59
Demmitt, Charles R. 1905, '06
DePaolis, Carl 1978, '80
DePew, Daren 1984
Depken, Gerhard C. 1933
DeVelde, H. S. 1900, '01, '02
Devermann, Zak 2016
Devero, James 1946
Dicke, Otto A. 1906, '07
Dickinson, Andy 2000, '01, '02
Diehl, Harold A. 1919
Dierkes, Alfred 1952
Diffenbaugh, Harry 1879, '80, '81
DiMaria, Vince 2001, '02, '03, '04
Disosway, Mark D. 1907, '08
Dittman, Matt 2009, '11
Dixon, Wesley 1970, '71, '72
Dobry, Tim 1994
Dorn, Ernest F. 1927, '28, '29
Doss, Paul C. 1918, '19
Doty, Dick 1971, '72
Dougherty, Floyd C. 1921, '22
Doyle, Russell 1938
Drago, Anthony 2016
Drechsler, Russell E. 1939, '40, '41
Dressen, Mark 1989, '90, '91, '92
Drish, John W. 1939, '40, '41
Duchene, Kevin 2013, '14, '15

Dudas, Daniel 1954, '55, '56
Duffner, John 1934, '35, '36
Durant, Phillip S. 1921, '23
Dystrup, Andrew 1967
Eads, Robert 1944
Ecklund, Arthur 1945
Edwards, James B. 1918, '19
Eichelberger, Tony 1960, '61, '62
Eilbracht, Lee P. 1943, '46, '47
Ellis, George H. 1883, '84, '85
Emerick, Bill 1971
Engle, David 1970, '71, '72
English, Frank J. 1917, '20
Engvall, Phillip W. 1929
Ericks, John 1986, '87, '88
Erickson, Carl V. 1925
Evans, Edwin R. 1907
Evers, Walter A. 1939
Eyer, Lawrence 1975, '76, '77
Eymann, Eric 2003, '04
Falkenburg, Fred P. 1900, '01, '02
Farr, Alvin I. 1909
Farrington, Charles E. 1938
Fazzini, Pat 1974, '75, '76, '77
Feigenbutz, Vince 1952, '53, '54
Feldman, Stanley 1948, '49
Felichio, Francis 1960, '61, '62
Fencl, G. S. 1930, '31, '32
Ferry, Josh 2012
Feuerbach, William J. 1892
Filippo, Richard 1980, '81, '82
Fillipan, John 1976
Finn, Richard G. 1926, '27, '28
Finn, Robert L. 1941, '42
Fischer, George 1947, '48
Fischer, Rob 1999, 2000, '01
Fitzgerald, Joseph 1954, '55
Fleager, Clarence E. 1898, '99
Fletcher, Casey 2014, '15
Fletcher, Charles H. 1912, '13
Fletcher, Darrin 1985, '86, '87
Fletcher, Tom 1962
Flock, Ward J. 1917
Flodin, Lloyd 1961, '62, '63
Flynn, James 1954, '57, '58
Flynn, Pat 2002
Follmer, Clive 1952, '53
Fort, Charles 1952, '53, '54
Foss, William 1967, '68, '69
Frangos, John 1992
Franklin, Murray 1935, '36, '37

Frazier, Bruce 1951, '52, '53
Frederickson,
 Daniel T. 1894
Frederickson, George 1891, '92, '93, '94
Frederickson, Trevor 2001, '02, '03, '04
Frederickson, William 1887, '88
Frees, Herman 1893, '94, '96
Frentz, William 1956
Frew, Pete 1994
Frighetto, Mark 1975, '76
Frillman, James 1955, '57
Frink, Frederick F. 1932, '33, '34
Fritz, Alan 1969, '70, '71
Frk, Chad 2001, '03, '04, '05
Fuller, James R. 1887, '88, '89
Fulton, G. T. 1892, '93
Fulton, Robert B. 1899, 1900, '02
Fulton, William J. 1895, '96, '97, '98
Funk, Brian 1997, '98
Funk, Clarence P. 1883
Furber, William A. 1891
Fuzak, William G. 1930, '31
Galla, George 1963
Gantt, Dave 1959
Gardenhire, Toby 2005
Gasparich, Timothy 1981
Gawron, William 1958
Gbur, Edward F. 1930, '31, '32
Gedvilas, Leo 1944, '45, '46
Gellinger, Terry 1958, '59, '60
Gerber, Joey 2016
Gertz, Jeff 1999, 2000, '01
Giller, Michael 2008, '10
Gillespie, Gordon 1944
Gilliland, William 1887, '89, '90
Glade, Henry A. 1928
Godeke, Frank B. 1925
Gold, Josh 2001, '02
Goldstein, Charles B. 1933
Goldstein, Jason 2013, '14, '15, '16
Gorski, Tim 2001, '02, '04
Goss, James 1975, '76
Gotfryd, Peter J. 1943
Grant, Alan S. 1939, '40, '41
Graves, Marvin 1953, '55
Graves, Perry H. 1914
Gregory, Flint 1968, '69, '70
Gregory, Gregg 1966, '67
Gribble, Paul A. 1927
Groth, Gene 1965
Gugala, John 1947, '48, '49

Gundlach, Norman J. 1926, '27, '28
Gunkel,
 Woodward W. 1914, '15, '16
Gunn, Charles A. 1891, '92
Gunn, Richard 1955, '56
Gunning, Delany T. 1905, '06, '07
Gussis, Lloyd 1967, '68, '69
Guth, Glenn 1971
Haake, Eric 1988
Haas, Raymond C. 1918, '20
Hadsall, H. H. 1896, '97
Haefler, Robert E. 1936, '37
Haff, Ryan 2016
Hahn, Casey 2003
Haig, Phil 2008, '09
Hainline, Chase 2014
Halas, George S. 1916, '17
Halas, Walter H. 1914, '15, '16
Hall, Albert R. 1899
Haller, Thomas 1957
Hammond, Trent 2016
Hamstra, Daniel 1980, '82, '83, '84
Hanson, Michael 1983
Hanssen, Gustav A. 1887, '88, '89, '90
Hapac, William J. 1939, '40
Happeny, J. Clifford 1923
Hargis, Douglas 1981, '82
Harold, Robert 1975, '76
Harper, Robert H. 1924
Harrington,
 Raymond B. 1928
Harris, Newton M. 1891
Harshbarger, John 1977, '78
Hart, Ralph W. 1892
Harvey, Donald 1958, '59
Harvey, Ted 1963
Haskell, Howard H. 1893, '94, '95, '96
Haskins, Richard 1952, '53
Hastings, Ryan 2004, '06, '07, '08
Hawkins, LeShawn 1992, '93, '94
Hayes, Doug 2016
Hazlitt, Albert M. 1897, '98
Hazzard, E. M. 1930, '31
Heberer, Ronald 1951, '52
Hecht, Brian 1995, '96, '97
Heikes, Samuel I. 1920
Heinrich, Tom 1971, '72
Heinz, Vince 1999, 2000
Hellstrom, Norton E. 1921, '22, '23
Hendrickson, Davis 2010, '11, '12, '13
Henry, Wilbur L. 1935, '36, '37

Herzog, Shawn 1994
Hess, G. R. 1913
Hester, Jack 1952
Hester, John 1953, '54
Higgins, Charles H. 1901, '02
Hill, Arthur H. 1901, '04
Hills, Stacy R. 1894
Hinrichsen, George C. 1907
Hinze, Victor H. 1936, '37
Hobbs, Glenn M. 1890
Hodges, Bill 1970, '71, '72, '73
Hoffenberg, Earl 1967
Hoffman, George O. 1925, '26, '27
Hoffman, Thomas 1949
Hoffman, William 1950, '51
Hohl, Brandon 2010, '11, '12, '13
Hohm, Harley D. 1916
Holland, Pat 1962, '63
Holtzman, Ken 1965
Hooper, Max 1952, '53, '54
Hotchkin, Robert 1935
Hotchkiss, Robert J. 1894, '95
Hrnyak, Nick 1983
Hudson, Kyle 2006, '07, '08
Huff, George A. 1889, '90, '91, '92
Huff, Roger G. 1910
Huff, Walter W. 1907
Huisinga, Trevor 2003, '04, '05, '06
Hull, James M. 1924
Hull, Thomas F. 1942
Humay, Dan 1965, '66, '67
Humphrey, Darryl 1986
Huntley, Converse R. 1879, '80, '81
Hurwitz, Michael 2012, '13, '14, '16
Hyde, Rich 1989, '90, '91
Iavarone, Greg 1982, '83, '84, '85
Ifft, Aaron 2005, '07
Ingle, Scott 1903
Ingram, Daniel 1974, '75, '76
Ingrum, Ronald 1967, '68, '69
Ingwersen, Burton A. 1918, '19, '20
Innis, Brian 1982
Innis, Jeffrey 1981, '82, '83
Ippolito, Vince 1998
Irwin, Doug 1992, '93
Jackson, Clifford L. 1921, '22, '23
Jackson, Matt 1995, '96
Jackson, T. J. 1997, '98, '99
Jackson, Trenton 1965
James, Matthew 2015, '16
Janicki, Nick 1970

Jasper, Thomas	1890, '91, '92, '93	
Jay, Tyler	2013, '14, '15	
Jestes, Edmiston R.	1924, '25	
Johansen, Bob	1965	
Johns, John	1944, '45	
Johnson, Aaron	2008, '09, '10	
Johnson, Dennis	1981, '83	
Johnson, Drasen	2012, '13, '14, '15	
Johnson, E. Thomas	1919, '20, '21	
Johnson, Kevin	2010, '11, '12, '13	
Johnson, Ron	1961, '62	
Johnson, Tony	1955	
Johnston, Arthur R.	1897, '98, '99, 1900	
Jonas, Joel	1964	
Jones, Carl	1984, 85, 87	
Jones, Douglas	1980, '82, '83	
Jordan, Jerome J.	1925, '26	
Journell, Jimmy	1998, '99	
Joy, Samuel S.	1898	
Joyce, Luke	2011, '12	
Judson, Howard	1944, '45	
Judson, Phil	1955, '56	
Jurack, Mike	1991, '92, '93	
Jurasevich, John	1958, '59, '60	
Juul, Herbert V.	1906	
Kadir, Omar	2007	
Kaires, Gerald	1945, '46, '48	
Kaiser, Paul W.	1919	
Kal, Harris	1974, '75, '76	
Kallis, Leonard	1938, '40	
Kandel, Bruce	1975, '76, '77	
Kane, Doug	1985, '86, '87	
Kasch, Fred W.	1933, '34	
Kasper, Ray	1964, '65, '66	
Kating, John	1956, '57, '58	
Kay, Charles J.	1913	
Kelso, E. L.	1879	
Kemman, Herbert F.	1911	
Kempf, George A.	1911	
Kerian, David	2013, '14, '15	
Kilbane, James	1946, '47, '48	
Kimball, Edwin R.	1883, '84	
Kimes, Corey	2009, '10, '11	
Kinderman, Fred W.	1924, '25, '26	
Kingman, Charles D.	1895, '96	
Kinkead, David R.	1887, '88, '89	
Kirby, Marty	1977	
Kissinger, Donald K.	1918, '20	
Klaus, Robert	1957, '58, '59	
Kleber, Doug	1974, '75, '76, '77	
Klein, J. Leo	1916, '17, '18	

Klemm, Frederick	1965, '66, '67	
Klimek, Josh	1993, '95, '96	
Kliment, Chase	2006	
Knebelkamp, Kent	1983, '84	
Knotts, Tom	1974, '75	
Koch, Paul	1965, '66	
Koestner, Elmer	1955	
Kolakowski, Zack	2016	
Kolb, Gary	1960	
Kopale, Robert	1979, '81, '82	
Kopatz, Jim	1974	
Kopka, John	1949	
Kopp, William K.	1918, '19, '20	
Koptik, Bohumil J.	1915, '16, '17	
Kortkamp, Andy	1993, '94, '95	
Kowalski, August J.	1935	
Kraft, Mike	1989, '90	
Krantz, Louis	1950, '51, '52	
Kravetz, John	2012, '13, '14, '15	
Krebs, Wilbur E.	1914, '15, '16	
Krug, Will	2012, '13, '14, '15	
Krupar, Charles F.	1918	
Kucera, Richard K.	1938, '40	
Kuehl, Edwin C.	1923	
Kuehn, Clyde	1968, '69, '70	
Kumerow, Ernie	1959, '60, '61	
Kusinski, John	1926, '27, '29	
Kvasnicka, Ryan	2000, '01	
Kyes, J. R.	2005	
Lachky, Joe	1972	
Laing, George D.	1912	
Lalor, Foster M.	1917, '18	
Lane, Josh	2002, '03	
Lanter, Wayne	1957	
Lapins, Ron	1973, '74, '75	
Larson, Lambert L.	1913	
Latham, E. B.	1883	
Laurvick, Brett	1994, '95, '96	
Lavery, Tim	1997, '98, '99	
Lawrence, Ryan	2000	
Lawrence, Sean	1991	
Lechowicz, Craig	2003	
Leonard, Berny	1966	
Leonardi, Anthony	1982, '83	
Lewis, Ben C.	1933, '34, '35	
Ligare, Edwardo	1886	
Light, Curtis R.	1911	
Lincoln, Alex	2012, '13	
Lindauer, Thomas	2011, '12, '13	
Lindbeck, Emerit	1955, '56	
Linden, Frank W.	1898	

Long, Brian	2006, '07	
Long, Frank B.	1884, '85, '86, '87	
Lorenz, Bob	1966	
Lotz, John R.	1898, '99, 1900, '01	
Lowes, Forrest M.	1894, '95	
Ludlam, John S.	1926	
Lukaszewski, Don	1955, '56, '57	
Lundgren, Carl L.	1899, 1900, '01, '02	
Lundine, Dan	1995	
Lundstedt, Dave	1972, '73, '74, '75	
Lutes, Craig	2008, '09, '10	
Lymperopoulous, J.	1928, '29, '30	
Mackay, John L.	1884 '85	
Madix, Bob	1958, '59, '60	
Maier, George	1951	
Majercik, Larry	1970	
Major, Charles F.	1925, '26	
Maksud, Mike	1954	
Malley, Robert	1946, '47	
Mamlic, Andrew	2015, '16	
Manson, Kevin	2007, '08, '10	
Margolis, Ralph	1924, '25, '26	
Marquie, Craig	1997, '98, '99, 2000	
Marsillo, Paul	1977, '78, '79, '80	
Martin, Aaron	2006, '07, '08, '09	
Martin, Jeff	1993, '94, '95, '96	
Martin, Russel	1958, '59, '60	
Masek, Albert	1934	
Mason, Lou	1908	
Massey, Keith	1984, '85, '86	
Matejzel, August	1968, '69, '70	
Mathews, Clyde	1899, 1900, '01, '02	
Mathis, Jake	2009	
Matt, John	1960, '61, '62	
Maurer, Ron	1963, '64, '65	
Maxwell, John R.	1893	
Mayville, Mike	1974, '76	
Mazeika, Anthony M.	1938, '39	
Mazurek, Dave	2002, '03	
McBride, Kevin	1977, '78, '79	
McCabe, Claude P.	1933	
McCann, Thomas E.	1921	
McClure, Brian	1993, '94, '95, '96	
McClure, Ora D.	1890	
McClure, Todd	1996, '97, '98, '99	
McCollum, Greg	1984, '85, '86, '87	
McCollum, Harvey	1897, '98, '99, 1900	
McConnell, Thomas M.	1937, '38, '39	
McCormick, Olin	1892	
McCully, Matt	1994, '95	

Name	Years	Name	Years	Name	Years
McCune, Henry L.	1880, '81, '83	Murray, Bill	1966, '67, '68	Parenti, Joe	2000, '02, '03
McCurdy, Henry H.	1920, '21, '22	Murray, James	1977, '78, '79	Parker, Edwin S.	1942, '43
McDonald, John J.	1936, '37	Myers, William	1946, '47	Parker, Roy S.	1902, '03, '04
McDonald, Robert	1980	Nagle, Ryan	2014, '15	Parks, Ryan	2002
McDonnell, Rob	2014, '15	Naprstek, Frank J.	1911	Parr, Jordan	2012, '13
McEathron, William J.	1883	Nash, Joseph	1977	Parr, Josh	2009, '10, '11
McGill, Ruel S.	1897, '98	Naso, Charlie	2014, '16	Parr, Justin	2011, '12, '13
McIlduff, Thomas E.	1879, '81	Neal, John	1949, '50	Parr, S. W.	1883
McInerney, Pat	2015, '16	Needham, James	1892	Parsons, Wil	1989, '90
McKinney, Jerry	1956	Nelligan, Ryan	1990, '91	Patrick, Sean	2002, '03
McMillan, Jalin	2016	Nelson, H. A.	1879, '80, '81	Paul, Earl A.	1927
McMullen, Rolla	1956, '57	Nelson, Robert	1969	Pawlow, Richard	1957
McMurray, Casey	2008, '09, '10, '11	Neufeldt, James	1945, '47	Paxton, Albert E.	1925
McRobie, Douglas	1914	Nevins, Arthur S.	1913	Payne, Donnie	1992, '93, '94
Meagher, T. F.	2001, '02, '03	New, Nash	1968	Payton, David	1984, '85, '86, '87
Mee, Julian E.	1920, '21	Newcom, Gregory	1980, '81	Peach, John	1976, '77, '78
Meissner, Brendan	2016	Nicholson, Garry	1970, '71	Pearson, W. W.	1889, '90
Melino, Castanzo	1936	Nieckula, Aaron	1995, '96, '97, '98	Peden, Don C.	1921, '22
Merrifield, Albert W.	1889, '90, '91, '92	Nielsen, J. D.	2013, '14, '15, '16	Peekel, Rick	1972, '73, '74
Mershon, Brian	1986, '87	Niezgoda, Joe	1962, '63	Peelman, Aaron	1998
Mershon, Mike	1988	Niezyniecki, Ted	1986, '87	Peirce, Fred D.	1883
Meyer, Irwin H.	1929	Niklewicz, F. T.	1934, '36, '37	Penn, Albert	1908
Meyers, William	1945	Noble, John	1884	Penn, Henry	1909, '10
Michalak, Tony	1984, '85, '86, '87	Norris-Jones, Kelly	2012, '13, '15	Perry, Lloyd W.	1943
Milazzo, Anthony	2012	Noth, Charles J.	1942	Pershell, Russell M.	1935
Miller, Fred C.	1900, '03	Nusspickel, R. E.		Peterson, Carl	1962, '63
Miller, Jerome	1952, '53	[Eliot]	1930	Peterson, Mike	1964, '66
Miller, Lester	1946, '47, '48	Nykeil, Theodore	1938	Peterson, Reuben W.	1917
Mills, Doug	1960, '61, '62	O'Connor, Forrest E.	1923, '24	Petreshene, Victor	1955, '56, '57
Mills, George A.	1930, '31, '32	O'Connor, Kevin	1989, '90	Pfeffer, Frank	1904
Milner, Ty	2008	Oestreich, John	1992, '93, '94, '95	Phelps, John C.	1912, '13, '14
Milosevich, Paul	1940, '41, '42	Offenbecher, Bill	1959	Philbrick, Alvah	1883, '84, '85, '86
Milroy, Matt	2010, '11, '12	O'Grady, John	1928	Philbrick, Solon	1883, '84
Mitter, Todd	1988, '89	Ohman, Tom	1966, '67	Phillip, Andres M.	1942, '43, '47
Mohr, Scott	1978	Oien, Charles	1979	Pierce, Charles I.	1889
Molaro, Steve	1959	O'Keefe, James A.	1926	Pike, Max N.	1932
Moler, Jason	1989, '90	Olker, Joseph	1982, '83, '84	Pillsbury, Arthur L.	1889
Montgomery, Chris	2008, '09	Olson, Justin	1999, 2000, '01, '02	Pitts, R. L.	1903, '04, '05
Moore, Barry	1966	O'Neill, Dan	1996, '97, '98, '99	Plain, Henry A.	1949, '50
Moore, Robert	1951, '52, '53	Oros, James	1977, '78, '79	Planert, Edward	1944, '45, '46
Morris, James	2004, '05	Orsag, James	1983, '84, '85	Plews, Herb	1948, '49, '50
Morrison, John E.	1907, '08	Ossola, Ken	1970, '71, '72, '73	Poat, Raymond W.	1937
Moyer, Carlisle E.	1933, '34, '35	Ovitz, Ernest G.	1906, '07, '08	Pogue, Bob	1966
Mroz, Wallie	1945	Paarlberg, Jeff	2004, '05	Pollak, Mike	1972
Muck, Ronnie	2012, '13, '14	Pack, Chris	2011	Polock, Bob	1971, '72, '73
Muirhead, William	1953	Pacotti, John B.	1938, '40	Ponting,	
Mulligan, Sean	1989, '90, '91	Palacio, Bob	1990	Theophilus C.	1925
Mundt, Craig	1964	Pall, Donn	1983, '84, '85	Possehl, Louis	1944
Munson, Mike	1985, '86, '87, '88	Palmer, Howard	1944	Possehl, Robert	1946
Murawski, Michael	1967, '68, '69	Panique, Ken	1973	Potter, Robert	1952
Murphy, Brandon	2004, '05	Parenti, George	1949, '51	Powers, Tim	1987, '88

Powers, Tom	1986, '87	Rotblatt, Marvin	1945, '46, '47, '48	Schwartz, Lloyd	1910
Prentiss, William	1943	Roth, Robert J.	1942	Schwarz, Jeff	1975
Prindiville, Frank J.	1912, '13	Rothgeb, Claude J.	1904, '05	Sconce, Harvey J.	1896
Provenzano, Tony	1961, '62, '63	Rounds, William P.	1886, '87	Scott, Donald G.	1893
Pullen, Robert	1981, '82, '83, '84	Rowbottom, Dan	2016	Scott, Steve	1974, '75, '76, '77
Pyrz, Anthony C.	1939, '40	Rowe, Enos M.	1912	Scott, Tom	1953, '54
Quarles, Samuel	1975, '76	Rowe, Ted	2002, '03, '04	Secrest, John	1964, '65
Quayle, Robert H.	1909, '10	Roysdon, William I.	1892, '93, '94, '95	Sedlock, Cody	2014, '15, '16
Quinn, E. J.	1890, '91	Rozmus, Jerry	1962	Sefcik, Quinten	2016
Radford, Norman H.	1927	Rucks, Jim	1972, '73	Seifert, Dave	1992, '93
Raklovits, Richard	1950, '51	Rudden, Kevin	1996, '97, '98, '99	Shannon, James S.	1887
Ray, Hugh L.	1905, '06	Rush, Ira L.	1913, '14, '15	Shapland, Robert	1969, '70, '71
Raymond, Brian	2001, '02, '03, '04	Russell, Chas. M.	1880, '81	Shaw, Joseph E.	1928
Rear, David	1981, '82	Russell, David	1966, '68	Shaw, Scott	2006, '07, '08
Reed, Jim	1965, '66, '67	Russell, Frank H.	1935	Sheean, Frank T.	1899
Reeser, Ben	2006, '07, '08, '09	Ruth, Mike	1992	Sheehan, Pat	2011
Rehrer, Travis	1996, '97, '98, '99	Ryan, Howard R.	1917, '19, '20	Shelton, Thomas	2010, '11, '12
Reichle, Richard W.	1920, '22	Rykovich, Julius	1943, '47	Shields, Raymond J.	1908
Reinhart, Freddie A.	1935, '36, '37	Ryniec, Al	1972, '73, '74	Shilling, Luke	2016
Rekitzke, Philip	1983	Ryniec, Dave	1963, '64, '65	Shlaudeman, Harry	1884, '85, '86
Renner, Jerry	1961, '62, '63	Ryniec, Lou	1959, '60, '61, '62	Shoptaw, Robert	1955, '56, '57
Rhodes, Danny	1995, '96, '97, '98	Ryniec, Tim	1987	Shuler, Hugh M.	1896, '97, '98
Rhodes, Dusty	1995, '96, '97, '98	Sabalaskey, John	1952, '53, '54	Shumway, Horatio G.	1884
Richards, Jeff	1988, '89	Sainati, Leo	1938	Siegel, Jeff	1974, '75, '76
Richards, Ronald	1957	Salter, Cody	1995, '96, '97, '98	Sigerich, Andy	2004
Richardson, Timothy	1980, '81, '82, '83	Samuels, Jonathan H.	1885, '86, '87, '88	Silkman, John M.	1913
Rickman, T.	1929	Sander, Matt	1992, '93	Simmons, Luke	1999, 2000, '01, '02
Righter, Edwin B.	1908, '10	Sanford, Derek	1967	Simonetti, Robert	1949
Rightnowar, Brad	1996	Saving, Aaron	2004, '05	Simonich, Louis J.	1924, '25
Rinaker, Lewis	1888	Schaefer, Paul V.	1908, '09	Sinak, Tom	1993, '94, '95
Rizzo, Kenneth	1967, '68	Scharf, Albert	1943, '46, '47	Sipes, Stanton	1976
Roark, Tanner	2006, '07	Scheidegger, Bruce	1979, '80	Siron, Jon	1973, '74, '75
Roberts, Brian	1989, '90, '91	Schierer, Charles	1967, '68, '69	Sisco, August C.	1937
Roberts, Bryan	2009, '10, '13	Schiller, Charles L.	1942	Skikas, Norm	1960
Roberts, Ralph O.	1903, '04	Schinker, Lee	1962, '63	Skizas, Gus	1949, '50
Robertson, Thomas	1976	Schlapprizzi, Lester B.	1923, '24	Skizas, Peter	1982
Robinson, Chris	2003, '04, '05	Schlichter, John	2008	Skonieczny, Mark	2016
Robinson, Mark	1984, '87	Schlueter, Bill	1965	Slocum, Karl R.	1905
Robinson, William B.	1924	Schmitke, Todd	1979, '80, '81, '82	Slusher, Carroll	1969, '70, '71
Rodgerson, Mike	1965, '66, '67	Schober, Max W.	1905	Small, Andy	1989, '90, '91, '92
Roettger, Walter H.	1922, '23, '24	Scholz, Mike	1973, '74	Smiley, Jack	1946
Rogers, Greg	1984	Schrader, Alfred C.	1883, '84, '85	Smiley, Jonathan	2007
Rogowski, Ryan	2004, '05	Schuckman, Meyers	1937	Smiser, Todd	1991, '92, '93
Rohde, Mike	2005, '06, '07	Schuldt, James	1953	Smith, Charles	
Rommelman,		Schullian, Brian	1992, '93, '94, '95	"Bubba"	1989, '90, '91
Douglas	1978, '79	Schultz, Dave	2006	Smith, Daniel N.	1933
Roof, Shawn	2004, '05, '06, '07	Schumacher, Greg	1962	Smith, Gerald	1953, '54
Roper, Reid	2012, '13, '14, '15	Schumaker, Jason	1991, '92, '94	Smith, Jerome	1952
Roper, Ryne	2014, '15	Schustek, Ivan D.	1932, '34	Smith, Maurice, Jr.	1967
Rosenfeldt, H.	1931	Schutzenhofer, Andy	2000, '01, '02, '03	Smith, Mick	1966
Rosenthal, Frank V.	1929, '31	Schwartz, Frank	1956, '57, '58	Smith, Reilly	2001, '02, '03

Snowden, Ryan 2006, '07
Snyder, Ira D. 1929
Snyder, James B. 1906, '07, '08
Sokol, Steven 1978
Sommer, Chuck 1972, '73
Spaulding, Tony 1991
Spencer, James E. 1884, '85, '86
Spiezio, Scott 1991, '92, '93
Sprengard, Joe 1997, 2000
Stahl, Floyd S. 1926
Stahl, Garland 1901, '02, '03
Stange, Harold 1946, '49
Stankiewicz, Mike 2007, '08, '09
Steele, Phil 1886, '87
Steger, Kurt 1976, '77, '78
Steger, Peter 1978
Steger, Russell "Ruck" 1947, '48, '49, '50
Steinwedell, Carl 1900, '01, '02, '03
Sterk, Mike 2008, '10
Steuernagel, Fred W. 1930, '31, '32
Stewart, Jake 2005, '06
Stewart, James R. 1926, '27, '28
Stewart, Paul J. 1921, '22, '23
Stewart, Thomas, Jr. 1974, '75, '76
Stierwalt, Mitch 1979, '80, '81
Stiles, Leroy C. 1915, '16
Stockwell, Nick 2007, '08, '09
Strack, Will 2009, '10, '11
Strainis, Frank 1961, '62, '63
Studebaker, Adam 1991, '94
Sullivan, Rob 2005
Suter, Earl R. 1913
Sutton, Larry 1989, '90, '91, '92
Svihlik, D. J. 1997, '98, '99, 2000
Swakon, Larry 1971, '72, '73, '75
Swanson, Harold A. 1935, '36, '37
Swasney, E. H. 1879, '80, '81
Sweeney, Ira J. 1926, '27, '28
Swikle, Charles G. 1934, '35, '36
Switzer, Robert M. 1900
Szukala, Jerry 1965, '66
Tangman, Horace J. 1949, '50
Tarajack, Bill 1996
Targgart, Shawn 1997, '99
Tarkoff, Daniel 1978, '79
Taylor, Joseph W. 1904, '05, '07
Tedesco, Robert 1957, '58
Theobald, William G. 1933
Thienpont, Greg 1984
Thomas, Glen H. 1916
Thomas, Raymond R. 1910, '11, '12

Thomas, Robert E. 1912, '13
Thomas, Tim 1988
Thompson, Andy 1991, '92, '93, '94
Thompson, Fred L. 1895, '86
Thonn, Ray 1956, '57, '58
Thornton, Robert I. 1897, '98
Throneburg, Derek 2001
Thurlby, Burdette 1948, '50
Tieken, Theo 1886, '87
Toncoff, John 1933, '34
Toohey, Jake 2005, '06, '07
Tookey, Bill 1964
Toriani, Keith 1990, '91, '92, '93
Travis, Terrence 1983
Trayser, Tom 1999
True, Bill 1992, '93
Trugillo, Glen 1949, '50
Tryban, Edward E. 1930, '31, '32
Turchin, Doran 2016
Twist, Clarence C. 1911
Ultes, Ronald 1952, '53, '54
Valente, John 1986, '87, '88
Vandagrift, Carl W. 1905, '06, '07
Van Gundy, Charles P. 1886, '87, '88
Van Gundy, Claude 1910, '11
VanHooreweghe, Joseph 1943
Vanselow, Harold 1968, '69
Vayda, John 1954, '55, '56
Venegoni, John 1978, '79
Vermette, Jim 1958, '59
Vincent, Randall 1974, '77
Vitacco, Alfred G. 1939
Vogel, Otto H. 1921, '22, '23
Vopicka, Jim 1964, '65
Vorreyer, Richard 1955, '56, '57
Vorwald, Matt 1999, 2000, '01
Wagers, Brad 1996
Wahl, Edward C. 1931, '32
Wahl, Robert T. 1941
Wakefield, James 1945
Walenga, Frank 1951, '52
Walewander, John 1986, '87, '88
Walk, Mitch 1999, 2000
Walker, Harold B. 1928, '29
Wallace, Edward 1911
Walton, Adam 2014, '15, '16
Warfield, Roy M. 1891
Warford, Dennis 1980
Warmbier, Kenneth 1982, '83, '84, '85
Warner, Earl A. 1904

Waters, Alan 1965, '66, '67
Watts, Claude H. 1911, '12, '13
Webb, Daniel 2007, '08
Weber, Brett 1996, '97, '98
Weber, Edward W. 1934, '35, '36
Weber, W. Henry 1910, '11, '12
Wedding, James 1968
Weisenborn, Harold 1963
Wells, Forry 1991, '92, '93, '94
Wells, Terry 1983, '84, '85
Wentz, Brad 1986, '87, '88
Wenzel, Rusty 1979
Wernham, James I. 1897, '98, '99
West, Ron 1954
Weygandt, Jerry 1962, '63, '64
Whitaker, Creston 1999, 2000
White, Brian 1980, '81, '82, '83
White, Frank 1879
Whitmore, Harold 1905
Whitmore, Matt 2005, '06
Wicker, Brett 2002
Wickersham, Don 1971, '72
Wickland, Albert 1947, '48
Widdersheim, John 1977, '78
Wiedow, Roy W. 1944, '45, '46
Wikoff, Brandon 2007, '08, '09
Wilder, Frank S. 1900
Williams, David 1955, '56, '57
Williams, Milton L. 1929, '30
Williams, Sean 1994, '95
Wiman, Robert 1954, '55
Windmiller, Robert 1969, '70, '71
Wing, Roger 1952, '53
Winston, Charles S. 1898
Witte, Theodore C. 1929, '30, '31
Wohlwend, Dave 1992, '93, '94
Wojs, Dennis 1966, '67, '68
Wollard, Jason 1993, '94, '95, '96
Wolters, Mike 1986, '87, '88
Worth, John C. 1925, '26
Wrobke, Dewey 1918, '19, '20
Wrobke, Floyd 1932, '33
Wuethrich, David 1981, '82
Yalowitz, Jack 2016
Yeaton, Frederick C. 1934
Young, Everett 1944
Yule, John S. 1929, '32, '33
Yurtis, Barry 1969, '70
Zangerle, Adolph A. 1903, '04
Zeller, Roger L. 1939
Zerrusen, Lee 2008, '09, '10, '11

Zidlicky, Tom	1997, '98
Ziemba, Chester J.	1939, '41
Ziemba, Joe	2000, '03, '04
Zinker, Edward	1950, '51

MEN'S BASKETBALL

Abdullah, Halim	1997
Abrams, Tracy	2012, '13, '14
Adams, Rich	1975, '76, '77, '78
Alexander, Rodney	2008
Altenberger, Bill	1955, '56, '57
Altenberger, Doug	1983, '84, '85, '87
Altenmeyer, Vern	1959, '60
Alwood, Clyde	1915, '16, '17
Anderson, Earl	1918
Anderson, Nick	1988, '89
Anderson, Van	1948, '49, '50
Applegran, Clarence	1916
Archibald, Robert	1999, 2000, '01, '02
Arnold, Marcus	2006, '07
Augustine, James	2003, '04, '05, '06
Austin, Alex	2016
Bane, Frank	1914, '15
Bardo, Stephen	1987, '88, '89, '90
Bartholomew, Robert	1930, '31, '32
Battle, Kenny	1988, '89
Bauer, Larry	1964
Baumgardner, Max	1951, '53
Beach, Ted	1950, '51
Bemoras, Irvin	1951, '52, '53
Benham, Harold	1935, '36
Bennett, Caslon	1931, '32, '33
Bennett, Robert	1992, '93, '94, '95
Berardini, Kevin	2013
Bergeson, Carl	1930
Bernstein, Louis	1909, '10
Bertrand, Joseph	2011, '12, '13, '14
Beyers, Rich	1998
Beynon, Jack	1934, '35
Black, Leron	2015
Blackwell, Glynn	1986, '87, '88
Blackwell, Mel	1964
Blout, Bryon	1936, '37
Boline, Jelani	1997, '98
BonSalle, George	1955, '56, '57
Bontemps, Kevin	1980, '81, '82, '83
Boudreau, Lou	1937, '38
Bowman, P. J.	1989, '90
Bradford, Cory	1999, 2000, '01, '02
Braun, Howard	1934, '35, '36
Bredar, James	1951, '52, '53

Bresnahan, Neil	1977, '78, '79, '80
Breyfogle, Larry	1958
Britton, Earl	1924
Brock, Calvin	2006, '07, '08, '09
Brody, Tal	1963, '64, '65
Brothers, Bruce	1954, '55, '56
Brown, Bob	1964, '66
Brown, Cleotis	1999, 2000
Brown, Daniel "Dee"	2003, '04, '05, '06
Brundage, Avery	1908
Bunkenberg, Bruce	1958, '59, '60
Burmaster, Jack	1945, '46, '47, '48
Burwell, Bill	1961, '62, '63
Busboom, Les	1967, '68, '69
Bushell, Tim	1974
Caiazza, Ted	1957
Caldwell, Herb	1996, '97
Cann, Fremont	1928
Carlwell, Brian	2007
Carmichael, Tom	1974, '75
Carney, Charles	1920, '21, '22
Carter, Warren	2004, '05, '06, '07
Cermack, Jerome	1907
Chisholm, Andrew "Bubba"	2009, '10
Chukwudebe, Victor	1997, '98, '99, 2000
Clarida, Doug	1992
Clark, Shelly	1994, '95
Clemons, Rennie	1991, '92, '93
Cobb, Levi	1977, '78, '79, '80
Cohen, Larry	1972
Colangelo, Jerry	1960, '61, '62
Colbert, Austin	2014, '15
Cole, Bill	2008, '09, '10, '11
Coleman-Lands, Jalen	2016
Collins, Walter	1921, '22
Combes, Harry	1935, '36, '37
Conner, Nick	1971, '72, '73
Cook, Brian	2000, '01, '02, '03
Cosby, Aaron	2015
Craig, Hal	1946
Crane, Dudley	1914
Crews, Randy	1968, '69, '70
Cronk, Howard	1940
Cross, Gene	1993, '94
Cross, Joe	2000, '01
Curless, Jerry	1961
Dadant, Maurice	1906, '07, '08
Dahringer, Homer	1912, '13
Daniels, Jay	1982, '83

Daugherity, Russell	1925, '26, '27
Davidson, Marc	1992, '93
Davies, Carl	1938
Davis, Arias	1998, '99
Davis, Mike	2008, '09, '10, '11
Dawson, Jeff	1973, '74
Dawson, Jim	1965, '66, '67
DeDecker, Jim	1971, '72
Dehner, Lewis "Pick"	1935, '38, '39
Deimling, Keaton	1926, '27, '28
Delaney, Donald	1944, '45
DeMoulin, Ray	1944
Deputy, Donn	1974
Dezort, Tom	1970
Dillon, David	1941
Djimde, Ibrahima "Ibby"	2012, '13
Doolen, Bryan	1926
Dorn, Ernest	1927, '28, '29
Doster, Robert	1946, '47
Douglas, Bruce	1983, '84, '85, '86
Downey, Dave	1961, '62, '63
Drew, Earl	1928, '29
Drish, John	1939, '40, '41
Duis, Mike	1992
Duner, Sven	1913, '14, '15
Dunlap, Ron	1966, '67
Dutcher, James	1954, '55
Eddleman, T. Dwight "Dike"	1947, '48, '49
Edwards, Bill	1962, '63, '64
Egwu, Nnanna	2012, '13, '14, '15
Ekey, Jon	2014
Elwell, Dan	1916
Erickson, William	1947, '48, '49, '50
Evers, Walter	1940
Farnham, Brad	1974, '75
Felmley, John	1917, '20
Fencl, Fred	1934
Fencl, George	1930, '31, '32
Ferdinand, Ken	1976, '77
Ferguson, Blandon	2002, '03
Ferguson, Jeff	1964
Finke, Michael	2016
Flessner, Deon	1966, '67
Fletcher, Ralph	1919
Fletcher, Rodney	1950, '51, '52
Foley, Richard	1947, '48, '49
Follmer, Clive	1951, '52, '53
Follmer, Mack	1950, '51
Foster, Jed	1971, '72, '73

Fowler, Charles	1942	
Frandsen, Lee	1959, '60	
Frank, Joseph	1938, '39, '40	
Frazier, Chester	2006, '07, '08, '09	
Freeman, David	1997, '98	
Freeman, Don	1964, '65, '66	
Fronczak, Stan	1948	
Froschauer, Frank	1933, '34, '35	
Fulton, Clifton	1943, '50	
Gandy, Chris	1994, '95, '96, '97	
Garris, Kiwane	1994, '95, '96, '97	
Gates, Ralph	1912	
Gates, William	1936	
Gatewood, Roy	1950	
Gedvilas, Leo	1945	
Gee, Jarrod	1995, '96, '97, '98	
Geers, Tim	1990, '91	
Gerecke, Herbert	1951, '52	
Gerhardt, Tom	1976, '77, '78	
Gibbs, Paul	1933	
Gibson, Ken	1990	
Gill, Kendall	1987, '88, '89, '90	
Gillespie, Gordon	1944	
Gosnell, Alan	1958, '59, '60	
Graff, Dennis	1974	
Gray, Reno	1978, '80	
Green, Fred	1946, '47, '48, '49	
Green, Jim	1987	
Greene, Rayner	1934, '35	
Griffey, Tyler	2010, '11, '12. '13	
Griffin, James	1979, '80, '81, '82	
Griffin, Marcus	2000, '01	
Guttschow, Roy	1934, '35	
Haffner, Scott	1985	
Haines, Leonard	1924, '25, '26	
Halas, George	1917, '18	
Hall, Albert	1910, '12	
Haller, Tom	1957	
Hamilton, Lowell	1986, '87, '88, '89	
Handlon, Colin	1938, '39, '40	
Hapac, William	1938, '39, '40	
Harper, Charles	1929, '30, '31	
Harper, Derek	1981, '82, '83	
Harrington, Sean	2000, '01, '02, '03	
Harris, Davin	1993	
Harrison, Jodie	1968, '69	
Hawkins, Fess	1999	
Head, Luther	2002, '03, '04, '05	
Heldman, Matt	1995, '96, '97, '98	
Hellmich, Hudson	1932, '33, '34	
Hellstrom, Norton	1921, '23	
Henry, Myke	2012, '13	
Henry, Wilber	1935, '36, '37	
Hester, Jerry	1994, '95, '96, '98	
Hicks, Chris	2006, '07, '08	
Hill, Herbert	1929	
Hill, Malcolm	2014, '15, '16	
Hinton, Larry	1964, '65, '66	
Hocking, William	1940, '41, '42	
Hoffmann, Robert	1913	
Holcomb, Derek	1979, '80, '81	
Holdren, Steve	2008	
Hollopeter, Cecil	1925	
Hooper, Max	1952, '53, '54	
Hortin, Gordon	1944	
How, John	1928, '29	
Howard, Jerrance	2001, '02, '03, '04	
Howat, Rick	1969, '70, '71	
Huge, Nick	2003	
Humphrey, Dwight	1946, '47	
Ingram, Jack	2004, '05	
Ingwersen, Burt	1918, '19, '20	
Jackson, Charles "C. J."	2007, '09	
Jackson, Greg	1969, '70, '71	
Jackson, Mannie	1958, '59, '60	
Johansen, Bob	1965, '66, '67	
Johnson, Brian	1995, '96, '97, '98	
Johnson, Eddie	1978, '79, '80, '81	
Johnson, Howard	1974, '75	
Johnson, Lucas	1999, 2000, '01, '02	
Jones, Mike	1978	
Jones, Rich	1966, '67	
Jones, Rodney	1990	
Jordan, Aaron	2016	
Jordan, Jeff	2008, '09, '10	
Judson, Howard	1944, '45	
Judson, Paul	1954, '55, '56	
Judson, Phil	1955, '56	
Judson, Rob	1977, '78, '79, '80	
Juul, Herbert	1906, '07	
Kamm, Albert	1933, '34	
Kamm, Alfred	1934	
Kamp, Elbert	1930, '31, '32	
Kamp, Robert	1930, '31, '32	
Karnes, T. D.	1924, '25	
Kassel, Charles	1925, '26	
Kaufmann, Andy	1990, '91, '93	
Kawal, Ed	1930	
Keene, Richard	1993, '94, '95, '96	
Keller, Charles	1986	
Keller, Dominique	2009, '10	
Kerr, John	1952, '53, '54	
Kersulis, Walt	1945, '48, '49, '50	
Kircher, Helmuth	1913, '14	
Kirk, Walt	1944, '45, '47	
Klusendorf, Don	1984	
Kopp, William	1919	
Kpedi, Andy	1990, '91	
Krelle, Jim	1970, '71, '72	
Krupalija, Damir	1999, 2000, '01, '02	
Kujawa, Jens	1986, '87, '88	
Kunz, Phil	1987, '88	
Landt, Louis	1959, '60	
Langford, Devin	2013	
Lanter, Steve	1977, '79	
Lasater, Harry	1938	
LaTulip, Mike	2013, '14, '15, '16	
Leddy, George	1946	
Leeper, Sam	1962	
Legion, Alex	2009	
Leighty, Rick	1976, '77	
Leo, Herbert	1911, '12	
Leonard, Bryan	1981, '82, '83	
Leonard, Meyers	2011, '12	
Lewis, Khalid	2016	
Liberty, Marcus	1989, '90	
Lindsay, Forrest	1926	
Lipe, Cordon	1923, '24, '25, '26	
Lipe, K. Jack	1925, '26	
Liss, Cameron	2015	
Louis, Benny	1966, '67, '68	
Love, John	1962, '64	
Lovelace, Jay	1962	
Lubin, Larry	1976, '77, '78, '79	
MacDonald, Mike	1989	
Makovsky, Ed	1953, '54	
Manzke, Edward	1989	
Marks, James	1948, '49	
Marks, John	1951	
Markworth, Martin	1936	
Martin, Hollie	1926	
Mast, Nate	1999, 2000, '01	
Mathisen, Arthur	1941, '42, '43	
Matthews, Audie	1975, '76, '77, '78	
Mauer, John	1924, '25, '26	
May, Elbridge	1929, '30, '31	
McBride, John	1973	
McBride, Rich	2004, '05, '06, '07	
McCamey, Demetri	2008, '09, '10, '11	
McClain, Sergio	1998, '99, 2000, '01	
McClure, Ray	1946	
McKay, Ernest	1917	

McKay, Robert	1927	Popken, Roland	1922, '23, '24	Shoaff, Oliver	1943
McKeown, Bill	1964, '65	Popperfuss, Henry	1908, '09, '10	Small, Bill	1961, '62, '63
McLaurin, Sam	2013	Poston, Emmett	1909, '11	Small, Ervin	1988, '89, '90
Meacham, Trent	2007, '08, '09	Potter, Glenn	1922, '23, '24	Smiley, Arthur	1942, '43, '46, '47
Mee, Julian	1920, '21	Powell, Roger	2002, '03, '04, '05	Smith, Dave	1974
Meents, Scott	1983, '84, '85, '86	Price, Mike	1968, '69, '70	Smith, Jamar	2006, '07
Melton, Brett	2001	Probst, J. S.	1918	Smith, Larry	1987, '88, '89, '91
Menke, Ken	1942, '43, '47	Pruitt, Shaun	2005, '06, '07, '08	Smith, Mark	1978, '79, '80, '81
Menke, Robert	1946	Randle, Brian	2004, '06, '07, '08	Smith, Nick	2002, '03, '04, '05
Mettile, Jerry	1967	Range, Perry	1979, '80, '81, '82	Solyom, Andrew	1928
Meyer, Matt	1979	Redmon, Bogie	1963, '64, '65	Spears, Aaron	2004
Michael, Tom	1991, '92, '93, '94	Reitsch, Henry	1921	Staab, Jake	1944, '45
Miller, Fred	1969, '70, '71	Rennacker, Roy	1909	Starks, Ahmad	2015
Mills, Coke	1935	Renner, Jerry	1961	Starnes, Bob	1961, '62, '63
Mills, Doug	1961, '62	Reynolds, Kenneth	1925, '26, '27	Sterneck, Morris	1954
Mills, Douglas	1928, '29, '30	Rice, Rayvonte	2014, '15	Stewart, Charles	1906, '07
Mittleman, Benjamin	1918, '19	Richardson, Dietrich		Stilwell, Leland	1922, '23, '24
Montgomery, George	1982, '83, '84, '85	"D. J."	2010, '11, '12, '13	Storey, Awvee	1998
Moore, Vernon	1932	Richardson, Quinn	1981, '82, '84	Stout, Hiles	1955, '56, '57
Morgan, Maverick	2014, '15, '16	Richmond, Jereme	2011	Sunderlage, Don	1949, '50, '51
Morris, Bill	1972	Richmond, Robert	1939, '41	Swanson, Harold	1936, '37
Morton, Robert	1944, '45	Ridley, William	1954, '55, '56	Tabor, Hubert	1922
Mroz, Wallie	1946	Riegel, Robert	1935, '36, '37	Tallmadge, Floyd	1906
Nisbet, Tom	1937, '38, '39	Riley, Roy	1906	Tarwain, John	1930
Nkemdi, Fred	2004, '05	Robisch, Brett	1995	Tate, Jaylon	2014, '15, '16
Norman, Ken	1985, '86, '87	Roberson, Garvin	1972, '73	Taylor, Brooks	1990, '91, '92, '93
Notree, Bryant	1995, '96, '97	Roberts, Dave	1973, '74, '75	Taylor, Curtis	1986
Nunn, Kendrick	2014, '15, 16	Roettger, Walter	1922, '23	Taylor, Paul	1918, '19, '20
O'Neal, Alvin	1971	Roth, Steve	1992, '93, '94, '95	Taylor, Roger	1957, '58, '59
O'Neal, Robert	1941	Rowe, Robert	1946	Theobald, William	1933
Ohl, Don	1956, '57, '58	Rucks, Bill	1974,75	Thomas, Clayton	2003
Olson, Everette	1927	Rucks, Jim	1972	Thomas, Deon	1991, '92, '93, '94
Orr, John	1945	Ryan, Edward	1906, '07	Thomas, Derrick	1995
Osterkorn, Walter	1948, '49, '50	Sabo, John	1921, '22	Thompson, Thomas	1908, '09, '10
Otto, Gordon	1916	Sachs, Henry	1939, '40, '41	Thoren, Duane "Skip"	1963, '64, '65
Owen, W. Boyd	1931, '32, '33	Schafer, Tom	1984	Thurlby, Burdette	1948, '49, '50
Pace, Dennis	1967, '68, '69	Schmidt, Harv	1955, '56, '57	Tisdale, Mike	2008, '09, '10, '11
Parker, Curtis	1924	Schmidt, Rick	1973, '74, '75	Tucker, Craig	1981, '82
Parker, Edwin	1942	Schmidt, Ryan	2015	Tucker, Otho	1973, '75, '76
Parker, Kenneth	1943	Scholz, Dave	1967, '68, '69	Turner, Kevin	1995, '96, '97, '98
Patrick, Stan	1944	Schroeder, C. J.	1972, '73, '74	Tuttle, Will	1992
Paul, Brandon	2010, '11, '12, '13	Schuldt, James	1951, '53	Vail, Charles	1918, '20, '21
Paul, John	1957, '58	Searcy, Ed	1960	Vance, Eugene	1942, '43, '47
Pearson, Preston	1966, '67	Selus, Jean	2012	Vaughn, Govoner	1958, '59, '60
Penn, Albert	1908	Semrau, Richard	2008, '09, '10	Vopicka, James	1936, '37
Perry, Edward	1958, '59, '60	Seyler, Jim	1944, '45, '46	Vopicka, Jim	1964, '65
Peterson, Robert	1951, '52, '53	Shapiro, Harold	1939, '40, '41	Walquist, Lawrence	1920, '21, '22
Phillip, Andrew	1942, '43, '47	Shapland, Bob	1970, '71	Wardley, George	1937, '38, '39
Phillips, Charles	1938	Shapland, Mark	1989	Washington, Mike	1975, '76
Pierce, Scott	1991, '92	Shaw, Mike	2012, '13	Watson, Carl	1909, '10
Plew, Elmer	1953, '54	Shirley, Alton	1943	Weatherspoon, Nick	1971, '72, '73

Welch, Anthony	1982, '83, '85, '86
Wente, Mike	1974
Wessels, John	1959, '60, '61
Westervelt, Kevin	1980
Westfall, Curtis	1907
Wheeler, Thomas "T. J."	1992, '93, '94
White, James	1911, '12, '13
Williams, Dennis "D. J."	2016
Williams, Deron	2003, '04, '05
Williams, Frank	2000, '01, '02
Williams, Nate	1975, '76
Williford, Edward	1913, '14, '15
Wilson, Kenneth	1919, '20
Wilson, Kyle	2003
Windmiller, Bob	1969, '70
Winters, Efrem	1983, '84, '85, '86
Woods, Ralf	1915, '16, '17
Woods, Ray	1915, '16, '17
Woodward, Reggie	1986
Woolston, William	1911, '12
Wright, James	1952, '53, '54
Wukovits, Victor	1940, '41, '42
Wysinger, Tony	1984, '85, '86, '87

WOMEN'S BASKETBALL

Acuna, Maggie	2003, '04, '05, '06
Albers, Sally	1996, '97, '98
Allen, Jae	1975
Anderson, Betty	1975, '76, '77
Beach, Becky	1976, '77, '78
Berggren, Ashley	1995, '96, '97, '98
Bjork, Lori	2006, '07, '08
Blackburn, Brenda	2001, '02, '03, '04
Blauser, Susan	1999, 2000
Blinn, Macie	2009, '10, '11, '12
Bond, Kris	1995, '96, '97, '98
Boner, Susan	1976, '77, '78
Booker, Tonya	1991, '92, '93, '94
Bradley, Lisa	1985, '86, '87, '88
Brauer, Liz	1979, '80, '81
Brombolich, Kim	1981, '82
Buher, Chelsea	2008
Burke, Alexis	2011, '12
Carie, Doris	1987, '88, '89, '90
Carlson, Jan	1975, '76
Carmichael, Carol	1977, '78, '79
Carter, Brittany	2015
Catchings, Tauja	1997, '98, '99, 2000
Cattenhead, Kennedy	2015

Chelleen, Stephanie	2005, '06, '07, '08
Clinton, Anita	1993, '94
Coleman, Amarah	2015
Coleman, Katie	1997, '98
Crawford, Ivory	2012, '13, '14, '15
Crutcher, Danyel	2005, '06, '07
Cundiff, Monica	1989, '90, '91, '92
Cunningham, Mandy	1991, '92, '93, '94
Curtin, Allison	1999, 2000, '01
Curtin, Suzanne	2000, '01
Dallas, Cindy	2001, '02, '03, '04
Daugherty, Brittney	2003, '04. '05, '06
Davis, Eriel	2013
Deeken, Dee Dee	1987, '88, '89
Dexter, Kelly	1996, '97, '98
Dial, Stephanie	1990
Dilger, Cindy	1992, '93
Dill, Marchoe	1994, '95, '96, '97
Dluzak, Marijo	1975, '76, '77
Dumoulin, Cassie	2013
Dupps, Kris	1992, '93, '94, '95
Eickholt, Diane	1981, '82, '83, '84
Estey, Jill	1990, '91, '92, '93
Faulkner, Kristi	2000
Flannigan, Kathy	1977, '78, '79, '80
Gallagher, Joyce	1979
Gantt, Kendra	1982, '83, '84, '85
Gleason, Taylor	2014, '15
GodBold, Adrienne	2010, '11, '12
Gordon, Chelsea	2006, '07, '08, '09
Grant, Jacqui	2014, '15
Gratton, Danielle	2006, '07
Guarneri, Lisa	1998, '99
Guth, Allison	2002, '03, '04
Guthrie, Tiffanie	2002, '03, '04, '05
Hagberg, Karen	2000, '01, '02, '03
Hanna, Cindi	1993, '94, '95, '96
Harris, Rebecca	2007, '08
Harris, Sandra	1988, '89
Hartwell, Sarah	2014, '15
Haynes, Kristen	1987, '88, '89, '90
Hemann, Jackie	1992
Henderson, Ann	1994, '95, '96, '97
Henderson, Carrie	1986
Hofer, Lori	1983
Horvath, Cheryl	1978, '79
Hudgins, Lesley	1986, '87, '88
Hughes, Janelle	2003, '04, '05, '06
Hunter, Shavonna	2000, '01, '02
Hutchinson, Martha	1978, '79, '80, '81
Inman, Bridget	1993

Issenmann, Jeré	2002, '03, '04, '05
Johnson, Jennifer	1985, '86, '87, '88
Jones, Brianna	2010
Josil, Fabiola	2009, '10
Kissinger, Brooke	2015
Klingler, Vicki	1991, '93, '94
Kordas, Judy	1978, '79
Lawrence, Cathy	1983
Leonard, Brett	2003, '04
Leonhardt, Casey	1997, '98
Lewis, Gia	1998
Limestall, Susan	1975, '76, '77
Livingston, Sarah	2014
Magas, Barbella	1975, '77, '78
Magrum, Kersten	2010, '12, '13
Marcauskaite, Iveta	2001, '02
Martin, Kylie	1999, 2000
McCarthy, Erin	2006, '07, '08
McClellan, Angie	1986, '87
McClelland, Kim	1989
McConnell, Ashley	2014, '15
McCully, Lydia	2009, '10, '11, '12
McGee, Centrese	2011
Means, Pam	1983, '84, '86
Middeler, Jenny	1983, '84, '85, '86
Mitchell, Eboni	2009, '10, '11, '12
Moore, Amber	2011, '12, '13, '14
Morency, Pat	1979, '80, '81, '82
Morris, Kierra	2012, '13
Mowen, Kira	2004
Nelson, Barbara	1975
Nyquist, Megan	2006
Oden, Nia	2012, '13, '14, '15
O'Neil, Anne	2001
Owens, Courtney	2011
Parker, Melissa	1997, '98, '99, 2000
Penn, Karisma	2010, '11, '12, '13
Pfeiffer, Stacey	1984
Piper, Mckenzie	2013
Platt, Lolita	1992, '93
Polk, Jonelle	1984, '85, '86, '87
Preacely, Robbyn	1993
Prina, Jodi	1977, '78
Reinking, Krista	1995, '96, '97, '98
Ricketts, Diane	1982
Riley, Kate	1989, '90, '91, '92
Roach, Arlena	1990, '91
Roberts, Linda	1975, '76
Robertson, Currie	1995
Robinson, Lisa	1979, '80, '81, '82
Robinson, Lynnette	1979, '80, '81, '82

Rodriguez, Sandra	1978	Achtien, Tom	1975	Dickenson, Roger	1925
Romic, Stephanie	1983, '84, '85, '86	Adams, Paul	1975	Dickison, Marc	1991, '92, '93
Roosevelt, Rita	1977	Alexander, Joe	1993, '94, '95, '96	Dickson, Kerry	1979, '80, '81, '83
Ruholl, Connie	1991, '93	Allen, Bill	1972, '73	Diettrich, Henry	1941
Rukavina, Lana	2009, '10,' 11, '12	Allman, John	1920	Dintleman, Bob	1955, '56
Sanderson, Lauren	1997	Aronson, Justin	2005, '06, '07	Domantay, Greg	1982
Shade, Susan	1975	Atchison, Jereme	2012, '15	Donahue, Mark	2012
Sharp, Sarah	1988, '89, '90, '91	Avery, Mark	1974, '75, '76, '77	Downs, Robert	1947, '48, '49
Sheeler, Alicia	1997, '98, '99	Babb, Dick	1970	Duffy, Walter	1979, '80, '81
Shellander, Nancy	1984	Barnett, Ian	2012, '13, '14, '15	Dufresne, Jacques	1932, '33, '34
Simmons, Kyley	2015	Basting, Bryce	2014	Dunn, Clarence	1941, '42, '46
Simpson, Lacey	2007, '08, '09, '10	Bauer, Craig	1981, '84	Durkin, Mike	1971, '72, '73, '74
Smith, Aimee	1994, '95, '96, '97	Baughman, Lynn	1934	Dusenberry, Paul	1921
Smith, Alexis	2012, '13, '14	Berckman, Chas	1998	Dykstra, Greg	1967, '68, '69
Smith, Jenna	2007, '08, '09, '10	Bill, Jason	2002, '03, '04, '06	Eason, Ryan	1997, '98, '99, 2000
Smith, Yolanda	2001, '02	Bilsbury, Norman	1988, '89	Eckburg, David	1990, '92, '93, '94
Stein, Cindy	1982, '83	Bissell, Lonnie	1979	Eicken, Jim	1975, '76, '77, '78
Steuby, Chrissy	1996	Bohne, Nathan	2009	Engelhorn, Rich	1966
Stevenson, Margot	1975	Bolander, Harold	1913	Engnell, Kyle	2009, '10, '11
Tabon, Audrey	2004, '05, '06, '08	Bowe, Christopher	1985	Evans, Paul	1929, '30
Taylor, Deb	1980, '81	Bowers, James	1957, '58, '59	Fairfield, David	1925, '27
Terrien, Molly	1984, '85	Brenneman, Bruce	1946	Fash, Dan	1997
Thomas, Kelly	1985	Brewster, Will	2013, '14	Ffitch, Pete	1980, '81
Todd, Josie	1988	Bridges, Jan	1963	Finney, Bruce	1971
Toone, Whitney	2009, '10	Bridges, Mike	1972, '73, '74	Fisher, Ralph	1933
Tortorelli, Jeanne	1983	Brooks, Dave	1971, '73	Flaherty, Matthew	2004, '05, '06
Travnik, Mary Pat	1976, '77, '78, '79	Brooks, Rich	1973, '74, '75	Flannery, Jim	1979
Tuck, Taylor	2012, '13, '14, '15	Brown, John	1958	Francissen, Vern	1980
Umbach, Dana	1975	Brown, Ken	1960	Frazier, Scott	1982
Vana, Dawn	1999, 2000, '01, '02	Brown, Park	1938, '40	Fritz, Bill	1974, '75, '77
Vandertop, Sara	1996, '97, '98	Burgoon, David	1915	Gaines, Harry	1935
VanHandel, Kerry	1987, '88, '89, '90	Calvario, Rich	2003	Galland, Michael	1933, '35
Vasey, Nicole	1995, '96, '97, '98	Campbell, Robert	1942	Gardner, Rob	1969
Vossen, Michele	1981, '82, '83, '84	Capelle, Mark	1981	Gassmann, Neal	1985, '86, '88, '89
Walker, Sharmella	1989, '91, '92	Carius, Allen	1962, '63	Gilbert, Dwight	1986, '87, '88
Washington, Acquanetta	1988	Cepulis, Wade	1983, '84, '85	Gladding, Donald	1942
Waters, Sonya	1989, '90, '91, '92	Cherot, Tony	1968	Gold, Alex	2016
White, Liz	1983, '84, '85, '86	Clausen, Ian	2005	Gould, William	1930
Whitehead, Chenise	1983, '85, '86	Cleveland, Clarence	1937	Gow, Nick	2000
Wigley, Erin	2004, '05, '06, '07	Cline, Dick	1954	Gray, Dan	1985
Williams, Angelina	2002, '03, '04, '05	Close, Tim	1977, '78	Grinter, Caleb	1999, 2000
Wilson, Holly	1999, 2000, '01, '02	Cobb, Larry	1969, '70, '71	Gross, Rick	1969, '70, '71
Wright, Carolyn	1980, '81	Cope, Walter	1912	Hall, Dick	1967, '68
Wright, Jessica	2003	Cowlin, Joe	2016	Hall, Melvin	1923
Wunder, Linda	1978, '79, '80, '81	Cox, Jeff	1975	Halle, Dave	1984, '85, '86, '87
Wustrack, Sarah	1999	Cullen, Joe	1980	Hamer, Paul	1944
Yanni, Aminata	2001, '02, '03, '04	Cunningham, Kris	2002, '03	Harris, Harold	1957, '58
Zurek, Elizabeth	1996, '97, '98	Dale, Zach	2016	Hartman, Bill	1963
		Davis, Jon	2016	Hebert, Jordan	2010, '11, '12
		deBeers, Jim	1990, '91	Hedgcock, Frank	1956, '57
		DeSilva, Christopher	2008, '09, '10, '11	Heming, Lance	1962

MEN'S CROSS-COUNTRY

Abbott, David	1927, '28

Name	Years
Henson, Eric	1992, '93, '94
Hill, Greg	1984
Hiserote, Kim	1971
Hobbs, Tim	2002, '03
Hoerr, Trent	2003, '04, '06, '07
Homoly, Andy	1988, '89, '91
Horyn, Dan	1997, '98, 2000
Houseworth, Jon	2002, '03, '04, '06
Howse, Ken	1968, '69, '70
Hughes, Eric	1945
Huston, Paul	1947, '48
Inch, Chris	1987, '88
Jacobs, Jeff	1982, '83, '84, '86
Jacobson, John	1986, '87
Janssen, Andrew	2001
Jellema, Paul	2002
Jewsbury, Walter	1948, '49
Jirele, Jeff	1975, '76
Johannigmeier, Eric	2007
Johnston, Charles	1925
Jonsson, Karl	1955, '56, '57
Karkow, Waldemar	1947
Kelley, Michael	2005, '06, '07
Kelly, John	1968, '69, '70
Kelly, Tim	2005
King, Tommy	2012, '13
Kivela, Paul	1982, '84, '85, '86
Koers, Marko	1991, '92, '95
Krause, Dennis	1965
Kremske, Daniel	2008, '09, '10, '11
Kronforst, John	1999, '01
Kurtz, Andrew	1998
LaBadie, Lee	1969, '70, '71
Lafond, Dylan	2016
Lally, Rick	1962
Lamb, Cortney	1995, '96, '97, '98
Lamb, Lawton	1949
Lamoreux, John	1966, '67, '68
Landmeier, Verne	1933
Lathrop, Dan	2016
Lee, Garrett	2014, '15, '16
Leuchtmann, Joe	1986, '87
Lin, Richard	2000, '01
Line, H. E.	1930, '31, '32
Lucchesi, Mike	1997, '98, '99, 2000
Luker, Tom	1954, '55, '56
Lynch, George	1950
Maddux, Scott	1989, '90, '91, '92
Maddux, Troy	1990
Magnesen, Billy	2016
Maier, Timothy	2005, '07
Makeever, Sam J.	1923, '24, '25, '26
Markham, Liam	2013, '16
Marzulo, Sam	1923
Mason, Arthur	1913
Mazur, Dan	1991, '92, '93
McClennan, Scott	1996, '97, '98, '99
McClowry, Sean	1996
McDonnell, Brendan	2013, '14
McElwee, Ermel	1925, '26, '27
McElwee, Jim	1960, '61
McGinnis, Gordon	1921
Meier, Mike	1972
Mickow, Colin	2008, '09, '10, '11
Mickow, Hunter	2008, '12
Mieher, Edward	1922, '23, '24
Miller, Harold	1924
Mitchell, Justin	1999, '01
Moran, Tim	1999, '01
Mumaw, Gary	1975, '76
Munnis, James	1931
Murray, Michael	2007, '08, '09
Myers, Les	1976
Nachel, Jacob	2006, '07
Nauta, Mike	1963
Nolan, Dan	1990, '93
Novack, Joseph	1926, '27
O'Connell, John	1935
Olszewski, John	1978, '79, '80
Painter, David	1979, '80
Palumbo, Adam	2001, '02, '03
Patterson, Bruce	1921
Patton, Mike	1981, '82, '83, '84
Pearman, Barry	1993, '94
Pengelly, Sean	2016
Petefish, William	1930
Peterson, Jim	1961
Pfeiffer, Brent	2000, '01, '03
Pompei, Phil	2008, '09, '10, '11
Ponsonby, Charles	1966
Ponzer, Howard	1927
Powers, John	1985, '87, '88, '89
Pykosz, Rob	2006
Reasoner, Melton	1930
Rehberg, Robert	1941
Reiser, Jesse	2016
Reynolds, Greg	1981, '86
Richardson, Jared	2007, '08, '09
Riddle, James	2008, '09, '10, '11
Rideout, Blaine	1935
Rideout, Wayne	1935
Ripskis, Stan	1962
Russell, Jon	1997, '98, '99
Saarima, Matt	1997
Saunders, Chris	1994
Scheirer, Mark	1988, '89, '90, '91
Schmidt, Jon	1979, '80, '81
Scott, Russell	1921, '22
Seib, Robert	1941, '42
Seiwert, Tim	2000, '01
Seldon, John	1928
Sheuring, Verland	1954, '55, '56
Siegel, Bill	1969
Siglin, Brett	1993, '94, '95, '96
Sitko, Len	1987, '88, '89, '90
Smaidris, Mike	1993, '94, '95
Smith, Zack	2016
Sneberger, James	1937
Sniegorski, Maciej	2004, '05, '06
Steinberg, Philip	1944
Stellner, Frank	1925
Stevens, Jeremy	2006, '07, '08
Stevens, Tom	1980, '81, '82
Stine, Francis	1927, '28
Stock, Dan	2004, '05, '06
Swanson, Reuben	1921
Talbot, Paul	1993
Teifer, Sam	2012
Thanos, Jon	1984, '85, '86, '87
Tietz, Eric	2003
Toepfer, Jannis	2012, '13, '14
Topper, Martin	1922
Troester, Nathan	2008, '09, '10, '11
Twomey, John	1946, '47
Twomey, Victor	1945, '47, '48, '49
Ummel, Kregg	1989, '90, '91
VanSwol, Jason	1998, '99
Virgin, Craig	1973, '74, '75, '76
Wahls, Aaron	1999, 2000, '01, '02
Walker, George	1966, '67
Wallor, Eric	2005
Walters, Dave	1974, '76, '77, '78
Weaver, Garrett	2008
Wells, Edwin	1922
Welsh, Roger	1912
Welyki, Joseph	1946
West, Jason	1991, '92
West, William	1931, '32, '33
Wharton, Russell	1921
White, Charlie	1975, '77, '78
White, Harold	1925
Whitlow, Jamey	1993
Wieneke, Mark	1985

Wilson, Richard 1978
Winfield, Robert 1995, '96, '97
Winship, Harold 1977
Wolf, Ty 1983, '84
Wood, Arthur 1940, '42
Woolsey, Robert 1930, '31, '32
Yarcho, Wayne 1938
Zeman, Paul 2013, '14, '15
Zieren, Jason 1994, '95, '96, '97
Zimner, David 1988

WOMEN'S CROSS-COUNTRY

Abrahamson, Kristen 1993
Anderson, Linda 1980
Aufmann, Madeline 2011, '12
Baliga, Stephanie 2006, '07, '08, '09
Balzer, Teresa 1980
Beaird, Christina 2008
Bethke, Breanne 1997
Bice, Marcy 2000, '01
Bizzarri, Angela 2006, '07, '08, '09
Blazek, Audrey 2014, '15, '16
Bobart, Valerie 2014, '15, '16
Boyle, Elizabeth 2008, '09
Branch, Denise 2014, '15, '16
Braun, Joy 2001
Brokaw, Theresa 2006, '07, '08, '09
Brooks, Adrienne 1985
Bruene, Carol 1985, '86
Brusa, Jamie 2009
Bullard, Becky 2000
Burke, Shannon 1998
Carlisle, Amy 1989
Carroll, Maggie 2004, '05, '06, '08
Choquette, Nicole 2016
Christopher, Amy 1997
Clark, Maureen 1997
Cole, Audrey 1986
Dickerson, Marianne 1979, '80, '81, '82
Dietzen, Cecilia 1999, 2000, '01
Donato, Michelle 1989, '90
Donohue, Kimberly 1994, '95, '96
Drewes, Elizabeth 1978
Dunnavan, Lyndsey 1999, 2000
Elsen, Virgina 1981
Engel, Katie 2005, '07, '08
Falsey, Colette 2001, '14
Fonzino, Danielle 1996, '97
Fox, Amanda 2012, '13, '14, '15, '16
Frakes, Erin 2000, '01

Frigo, Meghan 2010, '11
Garrett, Rebekah 1991, '94, '95, '96
Grabski, Erin 1998
Groenwoud, Chantelle 2007, '08, '09, '10
Gross, Samantha 1991, '92, '93
Guard, Amy 2001
Hackett, Colleen 1983, '84, '85
Hague, Stacy 2008, '10, '11
Harpell, Danielle 1988, '89, '90, '91
Hawkins, Leslie 1985, '86, '87
Hawkins, Michelle 1988, '89, '90, '91
Heise, Jennifer 1996
Hennessy, Katie 1999, 2000
Herberger, Lynn 1997
Hernandez, Rachel 2004, '05, '06, '07
Hoogheem, Aimee 1997
Hunt, Amber 1999, 2000, '01
Hunt, Cassie 2003, '04, '05, '06
Hynes, Meagan 2012
Irion, Rachel 2012, '13
Kelleher, Rachel 1992
Kenyon, Leigh Anne 2001
Knop, Nancy L. 1977, '78
Kraiss, Katherine 1994, '95
Kuhl, Jamie 2005
Lamantia, Michelle 2004
Lantis, Julie E. 1982, '83
LaSusa, Deanna 1981
Legue, Abby 2000
Lehnhoff, Michelle 1985
Lemersal, Megan 2014, '15, '16
Lipa, Diane 2016
Locascio, Sharon 1986, '88, '90
Madsen, Wendy 1993
Marianetti, Gina 1996
Marine, Jennifer S. 1993, '95, '96
Martin, Lindsay 1997, '98
Mastoris, Helen 1989
Mayback, Laurie 1980
McGlone, Catherine 1980
McKee, Kelly 1983, '84, '85
Mendozza, Tara 1996, '97, '98
Meneses, Sandra 1996
Mengyan, Elizabeth 2005, '06
Michal, Mary 1992
Miller, Casey 2012
Morgan, Stephanie 2010, '13
Morris, Karen J. 1990, '91, '92, '93, '94
Morris, Kathy A. 1991, '92, '93

Moyer, H. Anita 1977, '78, '79
Mulchrone, Margaret 2008, '09, '10
Murphy, Meghan 2009
Nicholson, Candace 1996, '97, '98
Oberle, Betty 1978, '79
Oberle, Elizabeth 1982
Paul, Renae 1993, '94
Petrey, Britten 2011, '13, '14, '15
Phelan, Shannon 2006, '07, '09
Phillips, Lisa 2003, '04
Pinzarrone, Ellie 2002
Porada, Katie 2011, '12, '13
Race, Carrie 1980
Rakosnik, Lindsey 2012
Reu, Lindsey 2004
Robbins, Laura 1998, '99
Russell, Donna 1986, '87, '88
Schmidt, Chloe 2012, '14
Schmidt, Melissa 2010
Schneider, Alyssa 2012, '13, '14, '15
Schultz, Julia 2016
Schwab, Jennifer 1992, '93, '94
Scigousky, Brooke 1995
Seger, Kim 2015, '16
Seiler, Kelsey 2015
Simmering, Laura 1988, '89, '90, '91
Simms, Stephanie 2003, '04, '05, '06
Simpson, Casie 2001, '02, '03
Speer, Lindsay 1996, '97, '98
Stack, Amber 2010
Sterneman, Ruth 1981, '83, '84, '85
Stetson, Deborah 1981, '82, '83, '85
Stevens, Lisa 1980, '81, '82, '83
Stoltz, Christina 1980
Stoltz, Teresa 1985, '86
Straza, Melissa 1986, '87, '88, '90
Sutherland, Kristin 2008, '09, '10
Tellin, Tracy 1990, '91, '93
Thompson, Ashley 2008, '09, '10
Tochihara, Tama 1993
Tomlinson, Amy 1990, '91, '92, '94
Turilli, Jaime 2001
Tweedy, Jennifer 1990
Tysse, Kate 2008
Villagrana, Lorena 1995
Vogel, Margaret 1983, '84, '85
Vogel, Michelle 1981, '83, '84, '85
Volling, Tabitha 2002, '03, '04
Wabick, Breanna 2000
Waldinger, Brenda 1979
Walter, Beth 1979

Walters, Kathy	1977, '78, '79
Ward, Cheryl	1981, '83, '84
Welch, Wendy	1990, '91, '93
Williams, Cecelia	1999, 2000
Winter, Hanna	2013, '14, '15, '16
Withrow, Loretta	1988, '89, '90
Wolf, Pamela	2003
Woods, Danelle	2007, '09
Worman, Hannah	2012
Wynn, Natalie	2013
Yaeger, Courtney	2009, '10, '11, '12
Zimmerman, Beth	1980
Zobel, Julie	1986, '88, '89, '90

MEN'S FENCING

Abel, Kevin J.	1989, '90, '91, '92
Abell, William A.	1958
Abraham, William	1967, '68, '69
Abraham, William J.	1947
Acker, Alan S.	1971, '72, '73, '74
Albers, Daniel P.	1981
Albrecht, A. J.	1912, '13
Aminzia, Norbert	1993
Anderson, Truman O.	1984
Armstrong, David T.	1975, '76, '77
Arneborn, Mikael	1992, '93
Atkin, Leonard	1951
Aufrecht, Ronald J.	1965, '66, '67
Ausich, William I.	1973, '74
Ballard, Albert D.	1970, '71
Barousse, Ignacio C.	1922
Bartga-Nagy, Rudolfo	1963, '64
Barth, Frederic C.	1981
Baumann, Erich S.	1991, '92, '93
Bebak, Arthur P.	1981, '82, '83
Becker, Robert H.	1958, '59, '60
Beebe, Kenneth J.	1911, '12
Beider, David	1978, '79
Bell, Craig	1963, '64, '65
Bell, James F.	1953, '54, '55
Bengard, E. Donald	1948, '49
Benham, Milford J.	1935
Bennett, Austin H.	1922
Bernstein, Lionel M.	1942
Bishop, J. Scott	1986, '87
Blahouse, Charles, Jr.	1955
Blazich, John L.	1947
Bluhm, Ronald	1970
Boland, Chester H.	1940, '41
Boland, John S.	1936
Boyles, John K.	1954

Brennan, Thomas M.	1961, '63
Brewer, Dave	1968
Brooks, Eron B.	1925
Brownlee, John J.	1926
Bunting, William L.	1923
Burke, Christopher J.	1989, '90, '91, '92
Bushche, Fred	1965
Bye, Gary L.	1975
Calderisi, Michael	1987, '88, '89, '90
Cameron, John K.	1952, '53
Camp, William F.	1958
Campbell, Charles E.	1959, '60, '61
Campoli, Douglas	1983, '84, '85
Carlson, Carl E.	1952
Carlson, David A.	1970, '71
Cawley, Kevin J.	1977, '78, '79, '80
Cha, Henry	1964
Chaio, Richard	1983, '84, '85
Chiprin, William	1935, '36, '42
Cho, David J.	1990, '91, '92, '93
Choi, Charles Y.	1982, '83
Clinton, Edgar T.	1928
Cohen, Tsafrir	1991, '92, '93
Cohn, Richard D.	1953, '54
Cohn, Stuart L.	1960, '61, '62
Cook, Eugene	1915
Craig, Herbert W.	1927
Crawford, David	1972
Dammann, James E.	1954, '55, '56
Dammers, Clifford R.	1962, '63, '64
Danzer, Warren	1958, '59, '60
Davis, Oral L.	1940
Delaet, Thomas E.	1975, '76
Delismon, Ronald J.	1957, '58
Diamond, Arthur S.	1976, '77, '78
D'Orazio, Vincent T.	1950, '51, '52
Epstein, Ralph J.	1932, '33, '34
Evans, David P.	1964, '65, '66
Fleischer, Kenneth	1970, '71, '73
Forhan, Richard M.	1962
Fornof, John	1963
Forsythe, Robert W.	1948, '49, '50
Franke, Steven C.	1980, '81
Franklin, Richard	1976, '77
Franks, Robert D.	1941
Frase, Robert C.	1964, '65
Fredericks, Brian	1972
Fretz, Karl	1967, '68, '69
Fricker, Donald P.	1957
Friduss, Janvis H.	1941, '42
Friedberg, J. Frank	1931

Frye, Richard N.	1939
Garret, Roger	1964, '65, '66
Garrett, T. C. Scott	1971
Gates, Markland T.	1964, '65
Gelman, Max M.	1938
Gerard, Gregory G.	1977
Gerard, Michael R.	1976, '77
Gerten, Nicholas	1916
Gillette, Steven M.	1986, '87, '88, '89
Gilman, Adam	1993
Ginsburg, Marvin	1956
Gladish, Ronald L.	1963, '64
Goddard, Robert F.	1928
Golden, Craig	1980, '81
Gorin, James C.	1932
Gorzowski, Jacek J.	1990, '91, '92
Grahl, Carl H.	1934
Green, Morris L.	1936, '37
Griffin, J. M.	1912, '14
Gross, Chalmer A.	1929, '30
Grossman, Thomas	1981, '82, '83, '84
Guthrie, Russell D.	1958
Guyton, Fred F., Jr.	1959
Haier, Otto C.	1929, '30
Hainsworth, Joseph	1980, '81, '82, '83
Handelman, Hyman	1938
Harris, David	1959
Harris, Harvey	1968, '69
Harter, Charles E.	1965, '66, '67
Hartz, Sylvester H.	1934, '35
Haslett, James M.	1978, '79, '80
Haslhuhn, Gerald	1956, '57
Haywood, Nate	1972, '73
Heald, Paul J.	1979, '80, '81
Hensley, Timothy T.	1985, '86, '87, '88
Hewitt, Ronald	1955, '56
Hochstrasser, Ronald	1981, '82, '83, '84
Howard, Joseph Omar	1969, '70, '71
Hum, Tyler R.	1956, '57
Ishu, Albert P.	1983, '84, '85, '86
Jackson, James L.	1937
Jankowsky, Alexandre	1961, '62
Jebe, Tod A.	1986, '87
Jobson, Robert F.	1942
Johnson, Karl E.	1989, '90, '91, '92
Johnson, Ken	1972
Johnson, Steve	1970
Johnston, Scott	1969, '70
Jones, Richard	1973
Kadota, Paul	1957
Kaihatsu, Edward J.	1981, '82, '83

Kamper, Reiner H.	1985, '86, '87	Neisz, W. Royce	1964	Schwartz, Larry	1969, '70
Kaplan, Hyman H.	1936	O'Brien, Kevin	1978, '79	Schwartz, Michael	1992, '93
Karnezis, Phillip P.	1989, '90, '91	Oberrotman, Alan	1971, '72	Schwartz, Steven H.	1972, '73, '74, '75
Katz, William B.	1937	O'Connell, James P.	1984	Sentman, Lee H., III	1957, '58
Kaufman, Larry L.	1954, '55, '56	Ofner, Clyde N.	1971, '72	Sheffield, Jay	1954, '56
Kemner, Carl A.	1973, '74, '75	Oliver, Alfonso L.	1970, '71, '72, '73	Shewchuk, William	1953, '54
Kennedy, Dan W	1963, '64	Olson, William E.	1962, '63	Shipka, Ronald B.	1958, '59
Kennedy, David R.	1959	Orr, Charles R.	1961, '62	Siebert, Fred W.	1929, '30, '31
Kim, Jin B.	1988, '89, '90, '91	Osinski, Henry S.	1948, '49	Silva, Hugo	1988, '89, '90, '91
Kim, Sukhoon	1978, '79, '80, '81	Osness, James	1982	Silverman, Lawrence	1952, '53
Knauff, Lawrence F.	1962, '63	Pacini, Michael S.	1978, '79, '80, '81	Silverman, Leslie	1936
Kniss, Steve E.	1967, '68	Palanca, Paul	1980, '81, '82	Silverstone, Abbey	1958, '59, '60
Knowles, Richard T.	1941	Pengilly, H. E.	1911, '12, '13	Smith, Ronald C.	1962, '63
Koshkarian, Kent A.	1983, '84, '85, '86	Perdue, Ralph P.	1926	Snow, Mark P.	1979, '80, '81, '82
Kraft, Gerald G.	1940	Perdue, Thomas W.	1931	Socolof, Joseph D.	1986, '87, '88, '89
Kramer, Martin	1958, '59, '60	Pereira, Leonard	1929	Song, Kenneth K.	1986, '87, '88, '89
Kriviskey, Bruce M.	1960, '61, '62	Perella, Edward	1933	Stahl, C. N.	1921
Kronenfeld, Phillip	1970, '71, '72	Perella, P. J.	1932	Stammer, Steven E.	1987, '88, '89
Kuhfuss, John D.	1970, '71	Perry, Michael	1976	Stephenson, Robert	1933
Larimer, Mark R.	1948	Perry, Russell A.	1929	Stern, Simon H.	1933, '34
Larkin, Erik	1990	Phillips, Miles D.	1985, '86, '87	Sternfeld, Robert	1937, '38
Laurence, Daniel L.	1969	Pianferri, Brian M.	1990, '91, '92, '93	Stevens, Terrence C.	1990, '91, '92, '93
Lavelle, Kenneth E.	1975, '76, '77, '78	Pilenyi, Janos A.	1990, '91, '92	Stoll, Steven G.	1964, '65
Laws, Joe W.	1975, '76, '77	Post, Warren M.	1970, '71	Streed, Jack A.	1942
Leever, Nicholas J.	1980, '81, '82, '83	Priest, Edwim N.	1976, '77	Stuebe, Louis F.	1921
Lehmann, J. Dan	1970, '72, '73, '74	Priest, Eric	1977, '78, '79, '80	Stuebe, Louis M.	1947, '48, '49
Leiken, Richard W.	1962, '63	Puccetti, Ronald P.	1947	Sublette, Bruce M.	1950, '51, '52
Lempke, Duane A.	1959	Quiros, Jorge L.	1950, '51, '52	Sullivan, Warren	1947
Lipson, Lee	1948, '49	Rachmeler, Dale	1970	Suqui, Zeyad	1984
Littell, David A.	1972, '73, '74	Ramirez, Robin	1991, '92, '93	Suritz, Charles S.	1967
Lucas, Anatole	1948, '49	Reamer, Owen J.	1935	Sutton, Michael G.	1977, '78, '79
Lynch, James R.	1965, '66	Reddish, Paul W.	1932	Swensen, Charles C.	1950, '51
Malik, Warren C.	1941, '42	Reed, Scott D.	1975, '76	Szluha, Nicholas	1960, '61, '62
Manaois, Arnold C.	1982, '83, '85	Reilly, Edward F.	1975	Taliaferro, Mike	1963
McDevitt, William	1962, '63	Roberts, Rodney	1967, '68, '69	Taylor, C. B.	1915
McDonald, John, Jr.	1941	Ross, James E.	1952, '53	Thompson, Paul W.	1976, '77, '78
McRae, Thomas	1993	Rush, Scott	1989, '90, '91, '92	Tibbetts, James D.	1962, '63, '64
Mench, Mark	1976	Sandstrom, James	1954, '55	Tingley, Loyal	1969
Menke, Wilbur	1929	Sawin, Frank L.	1941	Tish, Allen I.	1978, '79, '80, '81
Meyer, Ronald H.	1950, '51	Sayre, C. B.	1911, '12, '13	Titus, Rayburn L.	1942
Meyer, Werner	1950, '51	Scanlan, Robert W	1947, '48, '49	Tjaden, Dean A., Jr.	1969, '70, '71
Miller, Jeff A.	1980	Schankin, Arthur A.	1956, '57, '58	Tocks, John H.	1964, '65, '66
Mills, Allen	1950, '51, '52	Schicker, Blake R.	1986, '87	Todaro, Steven B.	1976
Milstein, Sidney M.	1971, '72, '73	Schicker, Eric	1984, '85, '86, '87	Tolman, Robert G.	1921
Mohan, Edgar H.	1921, '22	Schicker, Glenn R.	1988, '89	Tomars, Peter T.	1956
Moll, William D.	1956	Schiller, Arthur M.	1952, '53	Traynham, Floyd, Jr.	1937, '39
Moore, Ron	1970, '72	Schlicker, P. F.	1929, '31	Tripp, Robert S.	1959, '60
Moreno, David R.	1983, '84, '85, '86	Schrader, Henry C.	1939	Trobe, Pete	1968, '69, '70
Mosser, Keith M.	1984, '85, '86, '87	Schroeder, Michael	1966, '67, '68	Urbanik, Edward J.	1949
Munson, Keith E.	1983, '84, '85, '86	Schurecht, H. S.	1914	Urso, Philip J.	1952, '53
Murowitz, Herbert	1957	Schwartz, Daniel	1968, '69	Van Aken, Harry	1968

Van Matter, Francis	1914, '15, '16
Vasaune, Steve	1992, '93
Veatch, David S.	1977, '78, '79, '80
Veatch, Paul D.	1975
Velasco, Herman	1954, '55, '56
Vitoux, Michael E.	1968, '69
Walker, Michael L.	1968, '69
Ward, Bruce N.	1979
Warshaw, Lawrence	1979, '80, '81, '82
Weingartner, Harold	1937, '38, '39
Weisman, Jonathan	1982, '83
West, Donald J.	1942
Whalin, Brian G.	1973, '74, '75
Wheeler, Paul A., Jr.	1930, '31
White, David C.	1965, '66, '67
Williamson, James	1957, '58, '59
Wilmot, Ralph	1939, '40
Wolff, Leon V.	1939
Wolfson, Robert H.	1966, '67
Zimmerman, Kenneth	1962, '63
Zindell, Lee H.	1961
Zombolas, Anthony	1953, '54

FOOTBALL

Abdullah, Muhammad	1998, '99, 2000, '01
Abdullah, Sharriff	2003, '04, '05, '06
Abraham, George E.	1932
Acks, Ron	1963, '64, '65
Adams, Conrad	1995, '96
Adams, Earnest	1977, '78, '79, '80
Adams, Neil	2000
Adams, Paul	1956, '57
Adeyemo, Ade	2001, '03, '04
Adkins, Jason	1994
Adsit, Bertram W.	1898, '99, 19
Agase, Alex	1941, '42, '46
Agase, Louis	1944, '45, '46, '47
Agee, Mel	1987, '88, '89, '90
Agnew, Lester P.	1922
Agyeman, Nana	2000, '01
Aikens, Walt	2009
Aina, David F.	1984, '85
Allan, Chris	2001
Allegretti, Nick	2015, '16
Allen, Derek	1993, '94
Allen, Jeff	2008, '09, '10, '11
Allen, Larry	1970, '71, '72
Allen, Lawrence T.	1903
Allen, Robert	1956, '57, '58
Allen, Steve	1969

Allen, William M.	1965
Allie, Glen	1967
Allison, Geronimo	2014, '15
Amaya, Doug	1987, '88
Amundsen, Ben	2005
Anders, Alphonse	1939
Anderson, Harold B.	1909
Anderson, Kai	1965, '66
Anderson, Neal	1961, '62
Anderson, Paul T.	1921
Anderson, William W.	1915, '16
Antilla, Arvo A.	1933, '34, '35
Antonacci, Rich	1977
Applegate, Frank G.	1903
Applegran, Clarence O.	1915, '19
Archer, Arthur E.	1948
Argueta, Julio	1995
Armstead, Charles	1981, '82
Armstrong, James W.	1891, '92
Armstrong, Lennox F.	1913, '14
Arneson, Jeff	1991, '92, '93
Arvanitis, George	1984
Asamoah, Jon	2006, '07, '08, '09
Ash, David	1957, '58, '59
Ashley, Richard, Jr.	1892
Ashlock, Dennis	1976, '77
Astroth, Lavere L.	1939, '40, '41
Atherton, George H.	1891, '92, '93
Atkins, Kelvin	1979, '80, '81
Avery, Galen	1972
Avery, Todd D.	1984, '85
Ayoola, Dami	2012
Ayres, John	1983, '84
Babcock, Patrick	2001, '02, '03, '04
Babyar, Chris	1981, '82, '83, '84
Bachouros, Peter F.	1950, '51, '52
Badal, Herbert	1954
Baietto, Robert E.	1954, '55
Bailey, Aaron	2013, '14
Bailey, Charles	2004, '05
Bailey, Gordon R.	1931
Bain, Robert	2013, '14, '16
Baker, Clarence	1977
Bali, Alan	2003, '04, '05,' 06
Ballow, Daryle	2008, '09, '10
Bardwell, Roy	1999
Bareither, Charles	1967, '68, '69
Bargo, Ken	1967, '68, '69
Barker, John K.	1891
Barnes, Jeff	1978

Barr, Martize	2013, '14
Barter, Harold H.	1903
Barton, Taylor	2016
Baskin, Neil	1969
Bass, Mike	1980, '81, '82
Bassett, Denman J.	1947
Bassey, Ralph C.	1943
Batchelder, Robert "Bo"	1964, '65, '66
Bateman, James M.	1905
Bates, Melvin B.	1953, '54, '55
Bauer, John A.	1930
Bauer, John R.	1951, '52, '53
Baughman, James	1951
Baum, Benjamin F.	1907, '08, '09
Baum, Harry W.	1893, '94, '95
Bauman, Frank	1946
Baumgart, Tom	1970, '72
Beadle, Thomas B.	1895, '97
Beaman, Bruce	1972, '73, '74, '75
Beaver, Daniel	1973, '74, '75, '76
Becker, Zach	2008, '09, '11, '12
Beckmann, Bruce	1958, '59
Bedalow, John	1970, '71, '72
Beebe, Charles, D.	1894, '95, '96
Beers, Harley	1902, '03
Bell, Frank E.	1936, '37
Bell, Kameno	1989, '90, '91
Bellamy, Mike	1988, '89
Bellamy, Travon	2006, '08, '09, '10
Bellephant, Joe F.	1957
Belmont, Lou	1980, '81
Belting, Charles H.	1910, '11
Belting, Paul E.	1911
Benn, Arrelious	2007, '08, '09
Bennett, Caslon K.	1930
Bennett, James	1985
Bennett, Ralph E.	1937, '38, '39
Bennett, Theodore "Tab"	1970, '71, '72
Bennis, Charles W.	1932, '33, '34
Bennis, William	1937
Benson, Cam	1980, '81, '82, '83
Benson, Ivan	1996, '97, '98
Bentley, V'Angelo	2012, '13, '14, '15
Berg, Man	2016
Bergeson, C. H.	1928
Berner, John R.	1935, '36, '37
Bernhardt, George W.	1938, '39, '40
Bernstein, Louis S.	1909, '10

Berry, Gilbert I.	1930, '31, '32	
Berschet, Marvin	1951	
Bess, Bob	1968, '69	
Bess, Ronald W.	1965, '66, '67	
Beutjer, Jon	2002, '03, '04	
Beverly, Dwight	1982, '83	
Bevis, Joe	2000, '01, '02, '03	
Beynon, Jack T.	1932, '33, '34	
Bias, Moe	1982, '83	
Bierman, Randy	1992, '93	
Bieszczad, Bob	1968, '69	
Bingaman, Lester A.	1944, '45, '46, '47	
Birky, David A.	1984, '85	
Bishop, Dennis	1981, '82	
Bishop, Robert E.	1952, '53	
Black, Harry	2016	
Blackaby, Ethan	1959, '60	
Blackman, Ken	1992, '93, '94, '95	
Blakely, David A.	1977	
Block, Eric	2005, '07, '08, '09	
Blondell, Jim	1985, '86, '87	
Bloom, Robert J.	1932, '33	
Boatright, David	1983, '84, '85	
Bodman, Alfred E.	1930, '31, '32	
Bodman, Stanley L.	1930	
Boeke, Greg	1978, '80, '81	
Boeke, Leroy	1977, '78, '79, '80	
Boerio, Charles	1950, '51	
Bohm, Ron	1983, '84, '85, '86	
Bolen, Brock	2004	
Boles, Chris	2015	
Bonahoom, Peter	2013	
Bonner, Bonjiovanna	1978, '79	
Bonner, Lory T. "L. T."	1957, '58	
Booze, MacDonald C.	1912	
Borman, Herbert R.	1951, '52, '53	
Bosch, Jared	2008	
Boso, Cap	1984, '85	
Bostrom, Kirk	1979, '80	
Boughman, James A.	1951	
Bourke, Timothy E.	1984, '85, '86, '87	
Bowen, Herbert L.	1890	
Bower, Brad	2004	
Bowlay-Williams, Victor	1988, '89	
Boyd, Arthur	2003, '04, '05, '06	
Boyer, Darren	1990, '91, '92	
Boykin, Rod	1991, '92, '93, '94	
Boyle, Kenny	2000, '01, '02	
Boysaw, Greg	1986, '88, '89	
Boyter, Brett	2003	
Bradley, John J.	1905, '06	
Bradley, Kendall R.	1935	
Bradley, Theron A.	1943	
Brady, Edward	1980, '81, '82, '83	
Braid, Ken	1971, '72, '73	
Branch, James M.	1894, '95, '96	
Brasic, Tim	2005, '06	
Bray, Edward C.	1943, '44, '45	
Brazas, Steven E.	1984	
Bremer, Lawrence H.	1908	
Breneman, Amos L.	1915	
Brennan, Conner	2016	
Brennan, Rich	1969, '70	
Brent, Josh	2007, '08, '09	
Brewer, Melvin C.	1937, '38, '39	
Brewster, Tim	1982, '83	
Brice, Romero	1987, '88, '89, '90	
Briggs, Claude P.	1900	
Briley, Norman P.	1899	
Britton, Earl T.	1923, '24, '25	
Broerman, Richard	1952	
Brokemond, George R.	1958	
Bronson, George D.	1902	
Brookins, Mitchell	1980, '82, '83	
Brooks, Carson C.	1966, '67, '68	
Brooks, Richard A.	1906	
Brosky, Alfred E.	1950, '51, '52	
Brosnan, Brian	2002, '03, '04, '05	
Brown, Charles A.	1923, '24, '25	
Brown, Charles E.	1948, '49, '50	
Brown, Chico	1995	
Brown, Chris	1995, '96, '97	
Brown, Cyron	1995, '96	
Brown, Darrin I.	1984, '85, '86	
Brown, Gary W.	1959, '60, '61	
Brown, Horace T.	1909	
Brown, James	2000, '02	
Brown, James E.	1958, '59, '60	
Brown, Jerry	2007, '08	
Brown, Jonathan	2010, '11, '12, '13	
Brown, Joseph A.	1937	
Brown, Julyon	1988, '89, '90, '91	
Brown, William D.	1958, '59, '60	
Brownlow, Darrick	1987, '88, '89, '90	
Brundage, Martin D.	1901	
Bryant, Melvin	2003, '04, '05	
Brzuszkiewicz, Michael	1976	
Bubin, Sean	2000, '01, '02, '03	
Buchanan, Michael	2009, '10, '11, '12	
Bucheit, George C.	1918	
Bucklin, Robert	1969, '70, '71	
Bujan, George P.	1943, '44, '45	
Bulow, Dan	1977	
Bundy, Herman W.	1901, '02	
Burchfield, Brian	1986, '87	
Burdick, Lloyd S.	1927, '28, '29	
Burgard, Peter	1980, '81, '82	
Burk, Andrew	2005	
Burkland, Theodore L.	1896	
Burlingame, Keith	1978	
Burman, Jon	1988	
Burns, Bob	1968, '69, '70	
Burrell, William G.	1957, '58, '59	
Burris, Merlyn G.	1938	
Burroughs, Wilbur G.	1904, '05, '06	
Buscemi, Joseph A.	1946, '47	
Bush, Arthur W.	1891	
Bussey, Nate	2007, '08, '09, '10	
Butkovich, Anthony J.	1941, '42	
Butkovich, William	1943, '44, '45	
Butkus, Luke	1998, '99, 2000, '01	
Butkus, Mark	1980, '81, '82, '83	
Butkus, Richard M. "Dick"	1962, '63, '64	
Butler, Charles	1954, '56	
Button, Lyle A.	1947, '48, '49	
Butzer, Glenn D.	1908, '09, '10	
Byrd, Darryl	1981, '82	
Byrd, Rodney	1993, '94, '95, '96	
Cabell, Kevin	1976	
Cahill, Leo H.	1948, '49, '50	
Cain, Desmond	2015	
Cajuste, Abe	2014	
Caldwell, Darrius	2012	
Callaghan, Richard T.	1962, '63, '64	
Campbell, Robert A.	1939	
Campbell, Tracy	1973, '74	
Campos, Lou	1984, '85, '86, '87	
Cantwell, Francis R.	1934, '35	
Capel, Bruce	1962, '63, '64	
Capen, Bernard C.	1902	
Carbonari, Gerald M.	1965, '66	
Carlini, Perry	1983, '84	
Carlton, Matt	1998, '99	
Carmien, Tab	1978, '80	
Carney, Charles R.	1918, '19, '20, '21	
Caroline, J. C.	1953, '54	
Carpenter, Chris	1986	
Carr, Chris	1979	

Carr, H. Eugene, Jr. 1958
Carrington, Michael 1978, '79, '80, '81
Carrithers, Ira T. 1904
Carson, Paul H. 1931
Carson, Sam 2005, '06, '07, '08
Carson, W. Howard 1934, '37
Carter, Archie 1982, '83
Carter, Donald H. 1911
Carter, Vincent 1978
Cast, Dick L. 1961
Castelo, Robert E. 1936, '37, '38
Catlin, James M. 1952
Cazley, Dillan 2013, '14, '15, '16
Cerney, Bill 1974, '75, '76
Chalcraft, Kenneth G. 1961
Chamblin, Jack 1953, '54
Chapman, Ralph D. 1912, '13, '14
Charest, Jacob 2009
Charles, William W. 1936
Charpier, Leonard L. 1916, '17
Chattin, Ernest P. 1930
Cheeley, Kenneth D. 1940, '41
Cherney, Eugene K. 1957, '58
Cherry, Robert S. 1940, '41
Chester, Guy S. 1894
Christensen, Paul G. 1916
Christofilakos, Peter 2001, '02
Chronis, Tony 1973
Chrystal, Jeff 1973, '74, '75
Church, Devin 2013, '14
Cies, Jerry B. 1944, '45
Ciszek, Ray A. C. 1943, '44, '45, '46
Cklamovski, Mike 2007
Clark, Danny 1996, '97, '98, '99
Clark, George
   "Potsy" 1914, '15
Clark, Jamaal 2000, '01, '02
Clark, Robert 1922
Clark, Ronald 1949, '50
Clarke, Curtis 1983, '85
Clarke, Edwin B. 1890
Clarke, Frederick W. 1890
Clary, Tim 2013, '14, '15
Claussen, Tom 1996
Clayton, Clark M. 1898, '99
Clear, Brandon 2011
Clear, Samuel 1979, '80
Clements, Jarrod
   "Chunky" 2013, '14, '15, '16
Clements, John H. 1930
Clements, Tony 1968, '69

Clinton, Edgar M. 1896
Coady, Tom 1979, '80
Cobb, Glenn 1987, '88
Coffeen, Harry C. 1896, '97
Colby, Greg 1971, '72, '73
Cole, E. Joseph 1949, '50, '51
Cole, Jerry 1969, '70
Cole, Jewett 1935, '36
Cole, Mike 1992, '93
Cole, Terry 1980, '81, '82, '83
Coleman, DeJustice 1957, '58, '59
Coleman, James 1976, '77
Coleman, Norris 1969
Coleman, Roger 1973, '74
Collier, Glenn 1969, '70, '71
Collier, Steve 1982
Collins, Clark 2000
Collins, John J. 1962
Collins, Michael E. 1976
Collins, Tyrone 1993
Connor, Rameel 1996, '98, '99
Conover, Robert J. 1930
Conradt, Greg 1988
Conroy, John 1996
Cook, David F. 1931, '33
Cook, Jameel 1998, '99, 2000
Cook, James F. 1898, 1900, '01, '02
Cook, James W. 1891, '92
Cooledge,
   Marshall M. 1925
Cooper, James 2003, '04, '05
Cooper, Norm 1970
Cooper, Paul H., Jr. 1893, '94, '95
Cooper, Ralph 2011, '12, '13, '14
Cooper, Valdon 2011
Copher, Chad 1991, '92, '93, '94
Corbin, Reggie 2016
Cornell, Jack 2010, '11
Correll, Walter K. 1941, '42
Counts, John E. 1959
Coutchie, Stephen A. 1922, '23
Covington, Jim 1981
Cox, Fred 1990, '91, '92
Cozen, Douglas 1978, '79
Craciunoiu, Mike 1999
Craig, Ryan 1995, '96, '97
Cramer, Willard M. 1937, '38
Crane, Russell J. 1927, '28, '29
Crangle, Walter F. 1919, '20, '21
Craven, Forest, I. 1932
Cravens, Robert D. 1961

Crawford, James 2014, '15, '16
Crawford, Walter C. 1923
Crouch, Chayce 2015, '16
Crum, Tom 1968
Crumpton, Robert 1991, '92, '93, '94
Cruz, Ken 1983, '84
Cumberland, Jeff 2006, '07, '08, '09
Cummings, Barton A. 1932, '33, '34
Cunz, Robert W. 1945, '46, '47
Curran, John 1994
Curry, Jack C. 1943
Curtis, Joe 1980, '81, '82
Cushing, Matt 1994, '95, '96, '97
Custardo, Fred 1963, '64, '65
Cutter, Dan 1999, 2000, '01
D'Ambrosio, Arthur L. 1925, '26, '27
Dadant, Maurice G. 1907
Dahl, Andres W. 1934
Dallenbach, Karl M. 1909
Damos, Donn 1970
Damron, Tim 1981, '82
Daniel, Cullen 1980
Daniels, Drew 1990
Danosky, Anthony J. 1958
Dardano, Rusty 1981
Darlington, Dan 1969, '70, '71
Daugherity, Russell S. 1925, '26
Davenport, Sedrick 2001
Davis, Andrew 2015, '16
Davis, Carey 2000, '01, '02, '03
Davis, Chester W. 1910, '11
Davis, Jason 2002, '03, '04, '05
Davis, John 1966, '67
Davis, Jon 2011, '12, '13, '14
Davis, Larry 1998
Davis, London 2009
Davis, Scott 1983, '85, '86, '87
Davis, Tommy 2012
Davis, Vontae 2006, '07, '08
Davis, Will 2005, '06, '07, '08
Dawson, Bobby 1986, '87
Dawson, George 1922
Day, Caleb 2013, '14, '15
Day, Mark 1996
Dean, Michael 1996, '97, '98, '99
DeDecker, Darrel 1959, '60
DeFalco, Steven 1976
Deimling, Keston J. 1927, '28
dela Garza, Gabriel 1987
Delaney, Robert F. 1956, '57
Deller, Dick 1961, '62, '63

Delveaux, Jack 1956, '57, '58
DeMoss, Clarence W. 1952, '53
Denmark, Brandon 2010, '11
Dennis, Mark 1983, '84, '85, '86
Dentino, Greg 1980
DeOliver, Miguel 1981, '82
Depler, John C. 1918, '19, '20
Derby, Sylvester R. 1913, '14
DesEnfants, Robert E. 1954, '55
Dickerson,
    Charles F., Jr. 1961
Dickinson, Henry 2011
Diedrich, Brian 1974, '75, '76
Diehl, Dave 1999, 2000, '01, '02
Dieken, Doug 1968, '69, '70
Diener, Walter G. 1902, '03, '04
DiFeliciantonio, John 1974, '75, '76
DiLauro, Christian 2014, '15, '16
Dilger, Ken 1991, '92, '93, '94
Dillinger, Harry 1903, '04
Dillon, Chester C. 1910, '11, '12
Dillon, David 1939, '40
Dimit, George 1946
Dimke, Derek 2008, '09, '10, '11
Dismuke, Mark 1978
Dobrzeniecki, Mike 1971
Dobson, Bruce 1971, '72, '73
Doepel, Robert F. 1920
Dollahan, Bruce E. 1957, '58
Dombroski, Jack 1975, '76
Dombrowski,
    Robert J. 1984, '85
Doney, Scott 1979, '80
Donnelly, George 1962, '63, '64
Donnelly, Patrick 1988, '89, '90
Donnelly, Tyler 1993
Donoho, Louie W. 1946
Donovan, Dan 1988, '89
Doolittle, Areal 1986, '87
Dorr, Dick 1964
Doud, William O. 1901
Douglass, Paul W. 1949, '50
Douthard, Talib "Ty" 1993, '94, '95, '96
Doxey, Samuel 1891
Doxy, Cedric 2013, '14, '15
Drayer, Clarence T. 1921
Driscoll, Denny 1970
Dubrish, Bob 1973
Dudek, Mike 2014
Dufelmeier, Arthur J. 1942, '46, '47
Dufelmeier, Jamie 1969, '70

Dufrene, Daniel 2007, '08, '09
Duke, Austin L. 1952
Dulick, Jason 1993, '94, '95, '96
Dundy, Michael W 1961, '63
Duniec, Brian J. 1962, '63, '64
Dunlap, Jaylen 2013, '15, '16
Durant, Philip S. 1921
Durrell, Kenneth 1978, '79, '80
Dusenbury,
    Marshall V. 1951
Duvalt, Chris 2006, '07, '08, '09
DuVernois, Justin 2011, '12, '13, '14
Dwyer, Dave 1979, '80, '81
Dykstra, Eugene R. 1934, '35, '36
Dysert, Terry 1970
Eason, Charles C.
    "Tony", IV 1981, '82
Easter, Robert A. 1961, '62, '63
Easterbrook,
    James C. 1940
Easterbrook, John W. 1958, '59, '60
Eastman, Jack 2008
Eberhart, Jason 1997, '98, '99, 2000
Echard, Nathan 2014, '15, '16
Eddleman, T. Dwight
    "Dike" 1946, '47, '48
Edwards, Charles 1994
Edwards, David 1980, '82, '83, '84
Edwards, Garrett 2007, '08, '09
Edwards, Jason 1993, '94
Ehni, Ralph E. 1938, '39, '40
Eichorn, Greg 1988, '89, '90, '91
Eickman, Gary 1963, '64, '65
Eliot (Nusspickel),
    Raymond E. 1930, '31
Eller, Matt 2008, '09
Ellington, Russell 2008, '09
Elliott, John 1984, '85
Ellis, Donald C. 1949
Ellis, Jody 2005, '06
Ellsworth, Sam 1983, '84, '86, '87
Elsner, Bernard W. 1950, '52
Elting, Donald N. 1938, '39
Ems, Clarence E. 1917, '20
Engel, Elmer H. 1940, '41, '42
Engel, Greg 1990, '91, '92, '93
Engels, Donald J. 1949, '50, '51
Enochs, Claude D. 1897
Epps, Nick 1982
Erb, Bruce 1967, '68, '69

Erickson, Richard J. 1965, '66, '67
Erlandson, Jim 1981, '82
Ernst, Donald W. 1951, '52, '53
Evans, John C. 1930, '31
Fagan, Jordan 2015
Fairweather,
    Charles A. 1901, '02, '03, '04
Falkenstein, Elry G. 1952, '53
Falkenstein, Robert R. 1940
Fay, Richard B. 1936, '37
Fayson, Jarred 2009, '10
Feagin, Steve 1989, '90, '91, '92
Fearn, Ronald R. 1961, '62, '63
Feeheley, Tom 1974
Fejedelem, Clayton 2014, '15
Feldmeyer, Jacob 2012, '13
Ferguson, Josh 2012, '13, '14, '15
Ferrari, Ron 1980, '81
Fields, Kenneth E. 1928
Fields, Willis E., Jr. 1965, '66, '67
Finch, James 1985, '86
Finis, Jerry 1974, '75, '76
Finis, Marty 1980
Finke, Jeff 1987, '88, '89, '90
Finney, Eric 2013, '14, '15
Finzer, David 1977, '78
Fischer, John 1934
Fischer, Louis E. 1895, '96, '97
Fisher, Fred D. 1925
Fisher, Leon 1986
Fisher, Shane 1992, '93, '94, '95
Fisher, William 1975
Fit, Stan 1985, '86, '87, '88
Fitts, Steve 1998, '99, 2000, '01
Fitzgerald, Richard J. 1963
Flaar, Mike 1997
Flavin, Pat 2014, '15
Fletcher, Ralph E. 1918, '19, '20
Fletcher, Robert H. 1918, '19, '20
Flisakowski, Cory 2001
Florek, Ray 1946
Flowers, Clarence
    "Bo," Jr. 2007, '08
Flynn, Dennis 1977, '78, '81
Foggey, Erik 1989, '90, '91, '92
Follett, Dwight W. 1924
Forbes, Stuart F. 1897
Ford, Brian 1974, '75
Ford, Jason 2008, '09, '10, '11
Fordham, Mike 1997
Forseman, Eric 1981

Forst, Lawrence H. 1943, '45
Forte, Dominic J. 1976
Forzley, Nick 2013
Foster, Dale W. 1952
Foster, Glenn 2010, '11, '12
Foster, Greg 1978, '79, '80
Foster, Kendrick 2016
Fouts, L. H. 1893
Fox, Charles M. 1949, '50
Fox, Wylie B. 1962, '63, '64
Frain, Ryan 2015, '16
Francis, Frank D. 1899
Francis, Gary 1954, '55, '56
Francis, Tony 1996, '97, '98, '99
Franklin, Robert 1997, '98, '99, 2000
Franks, Willard G. 1946, '47
Frazier, Kieron 2006
Frederick, George R. 1935
French, A. Blair 1926, '27
Freund, Peter 1987, '88
Friel, Marty 1974, '75, '76
Frierson, Evan 2009
Frink, Frederick F. 1931, '33
Froschauer, Frank E. 1932, '33, '34
Fulk, Robert T. 1984, '85
Fullerton, Theron B. 1913
Fulton, Xavier 2004, '05, '07, '08
Fultz, Duane E. 1939
Furber, William A. 1890
Furimsky, Paul 1954
Gabbett, William T. 1961, '62
Gabrione, Pete 1992, '93, '94
Gal, Joe 2001
Galbreath, Charles S. 1933, '34, '35
Gallagher, Thomas B. 1946, '47, '48
Gallivan, Raymond P. 1924, '25, '26
Gamble, Brian 2007
Gann, John 1971, '72, '73
Gano, Clifton W. 1935
Gardiner, Lion 1906, '07, '08
Gardner, Morris
    "Moe" 1987, '88, '89, '90
Garner, Donald S. 1930
Garrett, Eric 1998, '99, 2000
Gartrell, Willie 1974, '75
Garza, Billy 2007
Gates, Andrew W. 1890, '91
Gatton, Joe 1996
Gaut, Robert E. 1892, '93, '94
Gawelek, Mike 2001, '02, '03, '04

Gedman, Stacy 1967
Genis, John E. 1941, '42, '46
George, Jeff 1988, '89
George, Jeff, Jr. 2016
George, Richard 1978, '79, '80, '81
Geraci, Joseph L. 1959
Gerometta, Arthur L. 1943
Gianacakos, Richard 1990
Gibbs, Robert 1940, '42
Gibson, Alec 1984, '85
Giddings, Mike W. 1984, '85
Gillen, Conor 2008
Gillen, John 1977, '78, '79, '80
Gillen, Ken 1979, '80, '82
Gilstrap, Charles 2000, '01, '02, '03
Glasson, Steve 1986, '87, '88, '89
Glauser, Glenn L. 1961
Glazer, Herbert 1935
Glielmi, Rob 1982, '83, '84, '85
Glosecki, Andy R. 1936
Gnidovic, Donald J. 1950, '51
Gockman, John 2001, '02, '03
Goelitz, Walter A. 1917
Golaszewski, Paul P. 1961
Goldberg, Jeff 1976
Golden, Bud 2010
Golden, Scott 1981, '82, '83
Gomez, Mike 2002, '03
Gongala, Robert B. 1952, '54
Good, Richard, J. 1940, '41, '42
Gordon, James 1986, '87
Gordon, Louis J. 1927, '28, '29
Gordon, Stephen M. 1976
Gorenstein, Sam 1931
Gosier, Harry 1983
Gottfried, Charles 1946, '47, '48, '49
Gould, Dennis C. 1961
Gould, Maurice 1941
Gow, Mike 1972, '73, '74
Grable, Leonard M. 1925, '26, '27
Grabowski, James S. 1963, '64, '65
Graeff, Robert E. 1955
Gragg, Elbert R. 1932, '33
Graham, Hubie 2008
Graham, John 1970, '71
Graham, Walter 1976
Grange, Garland A. 1927
Grange,
    Harold E. "Red" 1923, '24, '25
Grant, African 1985, '86, '87

Grant, Randy 1983, '84
Grant, Zach 2014, '15, '16
Graves, Perry H. 1913, '14
Gray, Zach 2003, '04
Greathouse,
    Forrest E. 1925
Greco, Dale 1964, '65
Green, Chris 1987, '88, '89, '90
Green, Gordon 1985
Green, Howard S. 1906, '07
Green, Justin 2009, '10, '11, '12
Green, Robert K. 1932
Green, Stanley 2016
Green, Stanley C. 1946
Green, Vivian J. 1922, '23
Green, William, J. 1924, '25
Greene, Earl B. 1921
Greene, Steve 1972, '73, '74, '75
Greenwood,
    Donald G. 1943, '44
Gregus, Dan 1980, '81, '82
Gregus, Kurt 1986, '87, '88, '89
Gremer, John A. 1955, '59
Gress, Aaron 2009, '10
Grierson, Ray G. 1941, '42, '46
Grieve, Robert S. 1935, '36
Griffin, Donald D. 1941, '42
Griffith, Howard 1987, '88, '89, '90
Grimes, Zepheniah 2012, '13, '14
Grimmett, Richard 1977
Grothe, Don 1953, '57, '58
Gryboski, Edward 1933, '34, '35
Grzelakowski, Brian 2004, '05
Guard, Jason 1986, '87, '88, '89
Guenther, Eric 1995, '96, '97, '99
Guenther, Ronald 1965, '66
Gumm, Percy E. 1908, '09
Gusich, Mike 1995, '96, '97, '98
Gustafsson, Jon 1991
Hadsall, Harry H. 1895
Hairston, Ray 1984, '85, '86
Halas, George S. 1917
Hall, Albert L. 1911
Hall, Arthur R. 1898, '99, 19
Hall, Charles V. 1928, '30
Hall, Harry A. 1923, '24, '25
Hall, Joseph W. 1950, '52
Hall, Michael 2001, '02
Hall, Orville E. 1944
Hall, Richard L. 1923, '24

Hallendorff, James 2012
Haller, Thomas F. 1956, '57
Halsey, E. B. 2003, '04, '05, '06
Halstrom, Bernhard C. 1915
Hamner, Jerry 1987, '88, '89, '90
Haney, Maurice 2007
Hannum, P. E. 1903
Hanschmann, Fred R. 1915, '18
Hansen, Don 1963, '64, '65
Hansen, Jake 2016
Hansen, Jarrett 1994
Hanson, Martin E. 1900
Hanson, Rodney 1955, '56, '57
Hanton, Jamie 2001, '02
Happenney, J. Clifford 1922
Harbour, Dave 1986, '87
Hardee, Justin 2012, '13, '14, '16
Hardeman, Donsay 2008, '09
Harding, Dele 2016
Hardy, Dale G. 1976, '77, '78
Hardy, Kevin 1992, '93, '94, '95
Harford, Doug 1965, '66
Harkey, Lance 1985, '86
Harmon, Ivan G. 1903
Harms, Frederick E. 1965, '66, '67
Harper, William 1965
Harris, Antoineo 1999, 2000, '01, '02
Harris, Spencer 2010, '11, '12, '13
Harris, Theron 1994
Harrison, Justin 2004, '05, '06, '07
Hart, R.W. 1890, '91, '92
Hartley, Frank 1988, '89, '90
Hartmann, Brad 1990
Harvey, Rausell
 "Rocky" 1998, '99, 2000, '01
Haselwood, John M. 1903, '04
Hasenstab, Jeff 1991, '92, '93
Hatfield, Joe 1972, '73, '74
Hathaway, Ralph W. 1938, '39
Hauser, Bob 1979
Havard, Steve 1995, '97, '98, '99
Hawthorne, Terry 2009, '10, '11, '12
Hayden, Kelvin 2003, '04
Hayer, Joseph C. 1949
Hayes, Ahmari 2016
Hayes, Bob 1972
Hayes, Erik 1992
Haynes, Clint 1982, '83
Haywood, Brad 2000, '01, '02, '03
Hazelett, John 1943

Heaven, Mike 1981, '82, '83, '84
Hedtke, William A. 1931
Heinrich, Frank M.
 "Mick" 1972, '73
Heiss, William C., Jr. 1944, '45, '46
Heitz, Michael 2011, '12, '13, '14
Helbling, James L. 1943
Helle, Mark 1980, '81, '82
Hellstrom, Norton E. 1920
Hembrough, Gary 1959, '60, '61
Henderson, William R. 1956, '57, '58
Hendrickson,
 Richard W. 1957
Henkel, Bill 1987, '88, '89, '90
Henry, Trulon 2010, '11
Henry, Wilbur, L.
 "Wib" 1934, '35, '36
Herr, Rich 1989
Hickey, Robert 1957, '58, '59
Hickman, Elmer 1997, '98, '99
Hickman, Robert Z. 1928
Hicks, Dere 2006, '07, '08,' 09
Hicks, Tom 1972, '73, '74
Higgins, Albert, G. 1890
Higgins, Doug 1987, '88, '89, '90
Higgins, Jason 1996
Hilderbrand, David 2001, '02, '03
Hill, Alexander 2011, '12, '13, '14
Hill, David 1990, '91
Hill, LeRon W. 1957, '58
Hill, Sam H. 1922
Hill, Stanley 1912
Hills, Otto R. 1928, '29, '30
Hinkhouse, Dallas 2014
Hinkle, Robert 1947
Hinsberger, Mike 1973
Hirth, Zach 2013, '14, '15
Hodel, Nathan 1997, '98, '99, 2000
Hodges, Aaron 2000, '01, '02, '03
Hodges, Brian 1998, '99, 2000, '01
Hodges, James D. 1937, '38
Hoeft, Julius 1932
Hoekstra, Mark 1996, '97, '98
Hofer, Lance 1980
Hoffman, Chris 1996, '97, '98, '99
Hoffman, James H. 1966
Hoffman, Robert W. 1912
Hogan, Mickey 1967, '68
Hogan, Richard 1982
Holcombe, Robert 1994, '95, '96, '97

Holden, Lamont 2001
Holecek, John 1991, '92, '93, '94
Hollenbach, Jeff 1973, '74
Holmes, Mike 1979, '80
Hood, Estus 2001, '02, '03
Hood, Marcus 2000
Hoomanawanui,
 Michael 2006, '07, '08, '09
Hopkins, Brad 1990, '91, '92
Hopkins, Michael 1988, '89, '90, '91
Horn, John 1993
Horsely, Robert E. 1931
Hotchkiss, R. J. 1894, '95
Howard, Dana 1991, '92, '93, '94
Howe, Jake 2011, '13, '14
Huber, William W. 1946
Huddleston,
 Thielen B. 1930
Hudelson, Clyde W. 1912
Hudson, Kyle 2005, '06, '07
Huebner, Dave 1976
Huff, George A. 1890, '92
Hughes, Henry L. 1920
Huisinga, Larry 1970, '71, '72
Hull, Steve 2010, '11, '12, '13
Hull, Walker F. 1908, '09
Humay, Daniel M. 1966
Humbert, Fred H. 1927, '28, '29
Hungate, Eddie 1985
Hunt, Randall 2008, '09, '10
Huntoon, Harry A. 1901, '02, '03, '04
Hurley, O. Landis 1940
Hurst, Lonnie 2003, '04
Hurtte, Frank 1944
Huston, William E. 1966, '67, '68
Hyinck, Clifton F. 1931
Hylton, Julian 2015, '16
Ijei, Justin 2007
Imeokparia, Mike 2003
Immekus, Nick 2012
Ingle, Walden M. 1938
Ingwersen, Burton A.
 "Burt" 1917, '18, '19
Iovino, Vito J. 1956
Ivy, Mario 2001
Jackson, Anterio 2010
Jackson, Bobby 1997, '98, 2000, '01
Jackson, Davis 1967, '68, '69
Jackson, Earl A. 1931
Jackson, Kenyon 2016

Jackson, Kevin	1992, '94	Jones, Julian	2015, '16	Kirk, Todd	1904, '05
Jackson, Marc	1999, 2000, '02, '03	Jones, Keith	1985, '86, '87, '88	Kirkpatrick, Jesse B.	1918
Jackson, Trenton	1962, '65	Jones, Kendrick	2002, '03, '04, '05	Kirschke, John W	1938, '39
Jacques, Virgus	1973	Jones, Mark	1981, '82	Kirwan, Jim	1975, '76
James, Antonio	2006, '07, '08, '09	Jones, Martin	1994, '95	Kisner, James W.	1984, '85
James, Brad	1987	Jones, Robert B.	1945	Kittler, Bud	1973
James, Chris	2006, '08, '09	Jones, Shawn	1986	Kittner, Kurt	1998, '99, 2000, '01
James, Chris	2016	Jones, Tom	1969, '70	Kleber, Doug	1973, '74, '75
James, David	1994, '95, '96, '97	Joop, Lester	1943, '44, '45	Kleckner, Bill	1972, '73, '74
James, Paul, III	2014	Jordan, Larry E.	1965, '66, '67	Kleckner, Kyle	2003, '04, '05
Janata, John	1981, '82	Jordan, Stephen	1987, '88	Klein J. Leo	1915, '16, '17
Janecek, Bill	1967, '68	Jordan, Taman	2001, '02, '03, '04	Klein, Jim	1992, '93, '94
Janicki, Nick	1969	Judson, Will	2008	Klemp, Joseph B.	1937
Janitz, Brad	2013	Julian, Anthony	2000	Klimek, Anthony F.	1948, '49, '50
Jansen, Earl	1935	Junghans, Brian	1986	Kmiec, Kenneth K.	1965, '66, '67
Janssen, Donald	1944	Jurczyk, Gary	1975, '76, '77	Kmiec, Tom	1968
Jefferson, Dustin	2008, '09, '10	Juriga, Jim	1982, '83, '84, '85	Knapp, Clyde G.	1926
Jefferson, Harry	1954, '55, '56	Jutton, Lee	1901	Knell, Phil D.	1965, '66
Jenkins, A. J.	2008, '09, '10, '11	Kaiser, John	1969, '70	Knezetic, Kyle	2004, '05, '06, '07
Jenkins, Eddie	1971, '72, '73	Kane, John F.	1943	Knight, Kenny	2014
Jenkins, Richard H.	1951	Kanosky, John P.	1935	Knop, Robert O.	1916
Jenkins, Terrence D.	1984, '85	Karras, John	1949, '50, '51	Knox, Carl W.	1937
Jenks, Charles N.	1925	Karras, Ted	2012, '13, '14, '15	Knox, Rodney	1974
Jenner, Kris	1983	Kasap, George	1951	Koch, Brian	2002, '03, '04
Jensen, Stanley C.	1930, '31	Kasap, Mike	1942, '46	Koch, George W.	1919
Jenson, Spencer	2004, '06	Kassel, Charles E.	1924, '25, '26	Koerwitz, Chris	1994, '95, '96
Jerzak, Edward	1957	Kasten, Frederick W.	1902, '03, '04	Koester, Kraig	1991, '92, '93
Jeske, Thomas	1971	Kautter, Brett	1999, 2000, '01, '02	Kogut, Chuck	1971, '72, '73
Johnson, Ainslie	2016	Kavathas, Sam	1974	Kogut, James K.	1976, '77
Johnson, Bob	1972	Kawai, E. J.	1929	Kohlhagen,	
Johnson, Carl	1956, '57, '58	Kearney, Herschel P.	1943	Richard M.	1952, '53
Johnson, Donald T.	1944	Kee, Dick	1963, '64, '65	Kolb, Gary A.	1959
Johnson, Filmel	1990, '91, '92, '93	Keely, Tad	2008, '09	Kolens, S. William	1940, '45
Johnson, Frank	1973, '74, '75, '76	Keely, Tyler	2006	Kolfenbach, Edwin J.	1931
Johnson, Garrett	1995, '96, '97, '98	Kehoe, Scott	1983, '84, '85, '86	Kolloff, Thomas	1977
Johnson,		Keith, Alvin	1970, '71, '72	Kopatz, Jim	1974, '75
Herschel E., Jr.	1966, '68	Kelly, Darwyn	2016	Kopp, William K.	1918, '19
Johnson, Jackie	1984, '85	Kelly, David J.	1976, '77, '78, '79	Kornfeld, Mark	2002, '03, '04
Johnson, Jay	1976	Kelly, Mark	1985, '86, '87, '88	Kowalski, August J.	1932
Johnson, Johnny	1993, '94, '95	Kelly, Moe	1969, '70, '71	Kraft, Don	1955
Johnson, Kirk	1998, '99	Kennedy, John H., Jr.	1931	Kraft, Reynold R.	1915, '16, '17
Johnson, Mike	1982, '83	Kent, David	1993	Krakoski, Joseph	1960
Johnson, Mikki	1993, '94, '95	Kerr, Jonathan	1991, '92, '93, '94	Krall, William E.	1945
Johnson, Nathan E.	1939, '40, '41	Kersulis, Walter T.	1944, '47, '48, '49	Kreitling, Richard A.	1957, '58
Johnson, Richard L.	1966, '67, '68	Khachaturian, John	1976	Krueger, Bernard E.	1946, '47, '48, '49
Johnson, William M.	1936	Kiler, William H.	1894, '95	Krueger, Kerry	1980, '82, '83
Johnston, Arthur R.	1897, '98, '99	Kimbell, Steve	1965	Krueger, Kurt	1981, '83
Jolley, Walter	1927, '28, '29	King, Harless W.	1891	Kruger, Jordan	2004
Jones, Amos I.	1949, '50	King, J.W.	1898	Kruze, John J.	1960, '61
Jones, Cliff	1977	Kingsbury, Brian G.	1976, '77	Kuchenbecker, Jay	1995, '96
Jones, Henry	1987, '88, '89, '90	Kinney, Jeff	1990, '91, '92	Kuhn, Clifford W.	1933, '35, '36

Name	Years
Kulaga, Jay	1998, '99, 2000, '01
Kustock, Al	1972, '73
Kwaaning, Davontay	2014, '15
Kwas (Kwasniewski), Eugene S.	1945, '46
Kynard, Tim	2011, '12, '13
LaBonte, James	2004, '05, '06
LaCosse, Matt	2011, '12, '13, '14
Lamb, Shane	1986
Lange, Gary	1969
Langhorst, Oliver M.	1928
Lankford, Ryan	2010, '11, '12, '13
Lansche, Oral A.	1913
Lantz, Simon E.	1894
Lanum, Franklin B.	1926, '29
Lanum, Harold B.	1910
Lanum, Ralph L.	1918
Larimer, Floyd C.	1917, '20
Larsen, Brett	1992, '93, '94, '95
Lasater, Harry A., Jr.	1936, '37
Laster, Tony	1989, '90, '91
Lattimore, Carlos	1999, 2000, '01
Lauzen, Joe	1997, '98
Lavery, Larry B.	1959, '60
Lavery, Tim	1997
Lawlor, Mike	1983
Lawlor, Sean T.	1984, '86
Laz, Donald R.	1950
Lazier, Murney	1947, '48
Leach, Todd	1991, '92, '93
Lee, Gary	1980, '81
Lee, Willie	1971
Leistner, Charles A.	1943
Leitch, Neal M.	1918
Leman, Jeremy "J"	2004, '05, '06, '07
Lenich, William	1937, '38, '39
Lennon, J. Patrick	1960
Lenti, Frank	2005, '06, '07
Lenzini, Robert E.	1951, '52, '53
Leonard, Marion R.	1924, '25
Lepic, Mike	1974
Leshoure, Mikel	2008, '09, '10
Lester, Wagner	1989, '90
Levanti, John	1971, '72, '73
Levanti, Louis	1947, '48, '49
Levenick, Stu	1974, '75
Levitt, Lloyd	1978, '79
Lewis, Corey	2008, '09, '13
Lewis, Greg	1999, 2000, '01, '02
Lewis, Ivery	1999
Lewis, James W.	1928
Lewis, Joe	1970, '71, '72
Lifvendahl, Richard A.	1919
Lindbeck, Emerit D. "Em"	1953, '54, '55
Lindberg, Lester L.	1933, '34, '35
Linden, Russell W.	1920
Lindgren, Justa M.	1898, '99, 1900, '01
Lindquist, David	2005, '06, '07, '08
Line, Jerry	1967
Lingner, Adam	1979, '80, '81, '82
Litt, Leon B.	1907
Little, Charles D.	1984, '85, '86, '87
Little, Jevaris	2013, '14, '15
Liuget, Corey	2008, '09, '10
Livas, Steve	1969
Lloyd, Brandon	1999, '01, '02
Logeman, Ron	1976
Lollino, Frank V.	1961, '62
Lonergan, Charles P. A.	1904
Long, Mon	1997, '98, '99, 2000
Long, Robby	1999, 2000, '01
Longe, Anthony	2002
Lopez, John	1979, '80, '81
Lovejoy, Charles E.	1917, '18, '19
Lovelace, Curtis	1987, '88, '89, '90
Lovellette, Lindell J.	1960
Lowe, Kevin	1974
Lowenthal, Fred	1898, '99, 1900, '01
Ludington, Lashon	1993, '94, '95
Lugo, Nelson	2015
Luhrsen, Paul H.	1952, '53
Lundberg, Albert J.	1937, '38, '39
Lundgren, Carl L.	1899, 1900
Lunn, Robert J.	1945
Lunt, Wes	2014, '15, '16
Lyle, Duane	1994, '95
Lynch, Clinton	1990, '91, '93
Lynch, James	1985, '86
Lynch, Lynn	1949, '50
Lyons, Thomas E.	1909, '10
MacArthur, John E.	1942
Macchione, Rudolph J.	1944
Machado, J. P.	1996, '97, '98
MacLean, Dan	1979, '80
Macomber, F. B.	1914, '15, '16
Maddox, Matt	2003, '04, '05, '06
Madsen, Olav	1914
Maechtle, Donald M.	1946, '47, '48
Maggioli, Archille F. "Chick"	1946, '47
Major, Fred, Jr.	1950
Majoy, Rob	1995, '96, '97, '98
Malczyk, Mike	2000, '01
Malinsky, Robert E.	1948
Maloney, Mike	2002, '03, '04
Marable, Terence	1995
March, Dean	1974, '76
Marinangel, Jim	1967
Markland, Jeff	1986, '87
Marlaire, Arthur G.	1940
Marriner, Lester M.	1925, '26, '27
Marriner, Scott T.	1931
Marshall, Paul	1993, '94, '95, '96
Martignago, Aldo A. "Al"	1947, '48, '49
Martin, Jeffery C.	1984, '85, '86
Martin, John	1992
Martin, Michael	2014, '15, '16
Martin, Mike	1980, '81, '82
Martin, Robert W.	1898
Martin, Russel	1958
Martin, Wesley P.	1938, '39
Masar, Terry	1969, '70, '71
Mason, Antonio	2002, '03
Mason, Marcus	2003, '04
Mason, Taylor	1978
Mastrangeli, Al A.	1946, '47, '48
Matha, Ryan	2002, '03, '04, '05
Mathews, C. M.	1900
Mathis, Ben	2011, '13
Mathis, Mark	1985, '86
Mattiazza, Dominic L.	1941
Mattison, Steve	1994
Mauck, Jeff	1985
Mauzey, John	1968, '69
May, Robert D.	1931, '32
Mays, Sam	2015, '16
Maze (Mazeika), Anthony	1936, '37
McAfee, Floyd H.	1954, '55
McAvoy, Tim	1979, '80, '81
McBain, Mike	1983, '84, '85
McBeth, Mike	1979
McCarren, Larry	1970, '71, '72
McCarthy, James P.	1941, '42
McCarthy, Tim	1969, '70
McCartney, Tom	1972, '73
McCaskill, Arthur	1964
McCleery, Ben H.	1909

<table>
<tr><td>McClellan, Anthony</td><td>2001, '02, '03, '04</td></tr>
<tr><td>McClellan, Lynn</td><td>1987, '88</td></tr>
<tr><td>McCloud, Tim</td><td>1992, '93, '94, '95</td></tr>
<tr><td>McClure, Robert T.</td><td>1978, '79</td></tr>
<tr><td>McClure, William E.</td><td>1927, '28</td></tr>
<tr><td>McCormick, Olin</td><td>1892, '93</td></tr>
<tr><td>McCormick, Roscoe C.</td><td>1898</td></tr>
<tr><td>McCracken, L. M. "Mac"</td><td>1975, '76</td></tr>
<tr><td>McCray, Michael P.</td><td>1976, '77</td></tr>
<tr><td>McCullough, Lawrence</td><td>1978, '79</td></tr>
<tr><td>McCullough, Thomas M.</td><td>1941</td></tr>
<tr><td>McCullum, Thomas</td><td>1961</td></tr>
<tr><td>McDade, Richard L.</td><td>1958, '61</td></tr>
<tr><td>McDonald, George</td><td>1995, '96, '97, '98</td></tr>
<tr><td>McDonald, James W</td><td>1937, '38</td></tr>
<tr><td>McDonald, Ken</td><td>1979</td></tr>
<tr><td>McDonald, Mark</td><td>1977</td></tr>
<tr><td>McDonald, Phil</td><td>1974, '75, '76</td></tr>
<tr><td>McDonald, Ryan</td><td>2005, '06, '07, '08</td></tr>
<tr><td>McDonough, Mike</td><td>1967, '68</td></tr>
<tr><td>McGann, David G.</td><td>1961</td></tr>
<tr><td>McGann, Mike</td><td>1983</td></tr>
<tr><td>McGarry, Shawn</td><td>1987, '88</td></tr>
<tr><td>McGee, Eddie</td><td>2007, '08, '09, '10</td></tr>
<tr><td>McGee, Michael</td><td>1996, '97, '98, '99</td></tr>
<tr><td>McGoey, Eric</td><td>2000, '02, '03</td></tr>
<tr><td>McGovern, Edward F.</td><td>1943</td></tr>
<tr><td>McGowan, Mark</td><td>1985, '86, '87, '88</td></tr>
<tr><td>McGrane, Bryan</td><td>1987</td></tr>
<tr><td>McGregor, John L.</td><td>1915, '17</td></tr>
<tr><td>McGrew, Henry</td><td>2015, '16</td></tr>
<tr><td>McGushin, Sean</td><td>2012</td></tr>
<tr><td>McIlwain, Wallace W.</td><td>1922, '23, '24</td></tr>
<tr><td>McIntosh, Hugh</td><td>1969</td></tr>
<tr><td>McKee, James H.</td><td>1895, '96</td></tr>
<tr><td>McKeon, Larry</td><td>1969</td></tr>
<tr><td>McKinley, George H.</td><td>1901, '02</td></tr>
<tr><td>McKissic, Dan</td><td>1967, '69</td></tr>
<tr><td>McKnight, William A.</td><td>1901, '02, '03</td></tr>
<tr><td>McLane, E. C.</td><td>1897, '98, '99</td></tr>
<tr><td>McLaughlin, Chase</td><td>2016</td></tr>
<tr><td>McLaurin, Carlos</td><td>1997</td></tr>
<tr><td>McMahon, Drew</td><td>2004, '06, '07</td></tr>
<tr><td>McMillan, Ernest</td><td>1958, '59, '60</td></tr>
<tr><td>McMillen, James W</td><td>1921, '22, '23</td></tr>
<tr><td>McMillin, Kirk</td><td>1969, '70</td></tr>
<tr><td>McMillin, Troy</td><td>1978, '79, '81</td></tr>
<tr><td>McMillin, Ty</td><td>1972, '73, '74</td></tr>
<tr><td>McMullen, Rolla</td><td>1955, '56</td></tr>
<tr><td>McPartlin, Chris</td><td>1994</td></tr>
<tr><td>McPhearson, Derrick</td><td>2005, '06</td></tr>
<tr><td>McQuinn, Mike</td><td>1980, '81, '82</td></tr>
<tr><td>Megginson, Gabe</td><td>2016</td></tr>
<tr><td>Mele, Joe</td><td>2004</td></tr>
<tr><td>Melsek, Daniel</td><td>1976</td></tr>
<tr><td>Mendenhall, Rashard</td><td>2005, '06, '07</td></tr>
<tr><td>Mendenhall, Walter</td><td>2005, '07</td></tr>
<tr><td>Menkhausen, Brian</td><td>1986, '87, '88, '89</td></tr>
<tr><td>Mercilus, Whitney</td><td>2009, '10, '11</td></tr>
<tr><td>Merker, Henry F.</td><td>1897</td></tr>
<tr><td>Merriman, John R.</td><td>1909, '10, '11</td></tr>
<tr><td>Meyer, John</td><td>1977</td></tr>
<tr><td>Meyers, Curtis</td><td>1980</td></tr>
<tr><td>Meyers, Melvin</td><td>1959, '60</td></tr>
<tr><td>Michel, Chris</td><td>1985, '86</td></tr>
<tr><td>Middleton, George E.</td><td>1920</td></tr>
<tr><td>Milan, Jamal</td><td>2016</td></tr>
<tr><td>Miles, Joe</td><td>1980, '81, '82, '83</td></tr>
<tr><td>Miller, Bob</td><td>1982, '83, '84</td></tr>
<tr><td>Miller, Brit</td><td>2005, '06, '07, '08</td></tr>
<tr><td>Miller, David H.</td><td>1939</td></tr>
<tr><td>Miller, Kenneth R.</td><td>1951, '52, '53</td></tr>
<tr><td>Miller, Richard R.</td><td>1952, '55, '56</td></tr>
<tr><td>Miller, Roy A.</td><td>1922, '23, '24</td></tr>
<tr><td>Miller, Terry</td><td>1965, '66, '67</td></tr>
<tr><td>Millines, Darius</td><td>2010, '11, '12</td></tr>
<tr><td>Millington, Akim</td><td>2006, '07</td></tr>
<tr><td>Mills, Douglas C.</td><td>1961</td></tr>
<tr><td>Mills, Douglas R.</td><td>1927, '28, '29</td></tr>
<tr><td>Milosevich, Paul</td><td>1939, '40, '41</td></tr>
<tr><td>Minnes, Mason</td><td>1970, '71, '72</td></tr>
<tr><td>Minnes, Matt</td><td>2002, '03, '04</td></tr>
<tr><td>Minor, James R.</td><td>1955, '56</td></tr>
<tr><td>Minor, William B.</td><td>1962, '63, '64</td></tr>
<tr><td>Minsker, Robert S.</td><td>1933</td></tr>
<tr><td>Mitchell, Bill</td><td>1967</td></tr>
<tr><td>Mitchell, Kaeman</td><td>2012</td></tr>
<tr><td>Mitchell, Kevin</td><td>2004, '05, '06, '07</td></tr>
<tr><td>Mitchell, Robert C.</td><td>1955, '56, '57</td></tr>
<tr><td>Mitchem, Rickie</td><td>1975, '76, '77</td></tr>
<tr><td>Mitterwallner, Merwin H.</td><td>1925, '27</td></tr>
<tr><td>Mohr, Albert W. T., Jr.</td><td>1918, '19, '20, '21</td></tr>
<tr><td>Mohr, Scott</td><td>1987, '88</td></tr>
<tr><td>Mongreig, Louis M.</td><td>1917</td></tr>
<tr><td>Monheim, Mason</td><td>2012, '13, '14, '15</td></tr>
<tr><td>Moore, Brandon</td><td>1998, '99, 2000, '01</td></tr>
<tr><td>Moore, Craig</td><td>1986, '87</td></tr>
<tr><td>Moore, Paul</td><td>1976</td></tr>
<tr><td>Moore, Ryan</td><td>1995, '96</td></tr>
<tr><td>Moorehead, Aaron</td><td>1999, 2000, '01, '02</td></tr>
<tr><td>Morgan, Joe</td><td>2006, '07</td></tr>
<tr><td>Morgan, Octavus</td><td>1971, '72, '73</td></tr>
<tr><td>Morris, Harold H.</td><td>1916</td></tr>
<tr><td>Morris, LaRue</td><td>1936</td></tr>
<tr><td>Morris, Max</td><td>1943</td></tr>
<tr><td>Morscheiser, Jack</td><td>1971</td></tr>
<tr><td>Morton, Christian</td><td>2000, '01, '02, '03</td></tr>
<tr><td>Mosely, Darius</td><td>2013, '14, '15, '16</td></tr>
<tr><td>Mosely, Marquis</td><td>1993, '94, '96</td></tr>
<tr><td>Mosley, Larry</td><td>1980, '81</td></tr>
<tr><td>Moss, Perry L.</td><td>1946, '47</td></tr>
<tr><td>Moss, Scott</td><td>2002, '03, '04, '05</td></tr>
<tr><td>Mota, Joseph L.</td><td>1961</td></tr>
<tr><td>Motuliak, Dan</td><td>2007</td></tr>
<tr><td>Mountjoy, Earl L.</td><td>1909</td></tr>
<tr><td>Mountz, Robert E., III</td><td>1960, '61</td></tr>
<tr><td>Mourans, Edgar</td><td>2006</td></tr>
<tr><td>Moynihan, Charles J.</td><td>1903, '04, '05, '06</td></tr>
<tr><td>Muegge, Louis W.</td><td>1925, '27</td></tr>
<tr><td>Mueller, Dave</td><td>1963, '64</td></tr>
<tr><td>Mueller, Richard A.</td><td>1948, '49, '50</td></tr>
<tr><td>Mueller, Steven</td><td>1988, '90, '91, '92</td></tr>
<tr><td>Muhl, Clarence A.</td><td>1923, '24, '25</td></tr>
<tr><td>Muhl, Fred L.</td><td>1903</td></tr>
<tr><td>Mulchrone, John</td><td>1979, '80</td></tr>
<tr><td>Mulchrone, Pete</td><td>1979, '81, '82</td></tr>
<tr><td>Mullin, Tom</td><td>1972, '73</td></tr>
<tr><td>Munch, Donald C.</td><td>1930</td></tr>
<tr><td>Murdock, Marchie</td><td>2014, '15</td></tr>
<tr><td>Murnick, Scott</td><td>1987</td></tr>
<tr><td>Murphy, Mike</td><td>1979, '80, '81, '82</td></tr>
<tr><td>Murphy, Patrick</td><td>1960, '61</td></tr>
<tr><td>Murphy, Ryan</td><td>1995, '96, '97, '98</td></tr>
<tr><td>Murphy, Thomas W.</td><td>1951, '52</td></tr>
<tr><td>Murray, Edward</td><td>1973, '74</td></tr>
<tr><td>Murray, Lindley P.</td><td>1931</td></tr>
<tr><td>Muti, Joe</td><td>1990, '91</td></tr>
<tr><td>Myers, Ty</td><td>2000, '01, '02, '03</td></tr>
<tr><td>Myles, Charles</td><td>2005, '06</td></tr>
<tr><td>Nabolotny, Michael</td><td>2006, '08</td></tr>
<tr><td>Naponic, Robert</td><td>1966, '67, '68</td></tr>
<tr><td>Navarro, Mike</td><td>1970, '71, '72</td></tr>
<tr><td>Nawrocki, Nolan</td><td>1998, '99</td></tr>
<tr><td>Neal, T. J.</td><td>2013, '14, '15</td></tr>
<tr><td>Neathery, Herbert</td><td>1950, '51, '52</td></tr>
<tr><td>Needham, James</td><td>1891, '92</td></tr>
<tr><td>Nelson, Evert F.</td><td>1927</td></tr>
</table>

Nelson, Jesse W.	1914, '15	Orr, John M.	1944	Pesek, James	1990, '91, '92
Nelson, Kenneth J.	1934, '35, '36	Osby, Vince	1982, '83	Peters, Forrest I.	
Nelson, Kenny	2013, '14, '15	Osei, Miles	2011, '12, '13	"Frosty"	1926, '28, '29
Nelson, Patrick	2016	Osley, Willie	1970, '71	Peterson, Clifford L.	1938, '40
Nelson, Ralph W.	1956	O'Toole, Reilly	2011, '12, '13, '14	Peterson, Daniel E.	1951
Nelson, Steve	1983, '84	Ovelman, John W	1930	Peterson, Mark	1972, '73, '74
Nelson, Steve	1989, '91	Owen, Boyd W	1930	Pethybridge, Frank H.	1914
Newell, Richard E	1960, '61	Owens, Isaiah H.	1941, '46, '47	Petkus, Bob	1965
Nicastro, Chip	1998, '99	Pacha, Tyler	2008	Petraitis, Luke	1989
Nichols, Sidney W.	1917	Pagakis, Chris N.	1949, '50	Pettigrew, James Q.	1906, '07, '08
Nickerson, Hardy, Jr.	2016	Palma, Gus	1990, '91	Petty, Harold O.	1932
Nickol, Edgar	1926, '28	Palmer, Harry M.	1933	Petty, Lawrence O.	1916, '19
Niedzelski, Clifford T.	1941	Palmer, Nathan	2009	Petty, Manley R.	1914, '15, '16
Nietupski, Ronald	1956, '57, '58	Palmer, Peter	1952, '53	Petty, Zane	2013, '14
Nitschke, Ray E.	1955, '56, '57	Palmer, Ralph W.	1943	Pezzoli, Phillip A.	1938
Nixon, Patrick	2009, '10, '11, '12	Palmer, Ryan	2007, '08, '09, '10	Pfeffer, John E.	1892, '93, '94, '95
Noelke, Robert	1978, '79	Pancratz, Kevin	1975, '76, '77	Pfeifer, Myron P.	1940, '41, '42
Nordmeyer, Richard J.	1955, '56, '57	Panique, Ken	1971	Phillips, Carroll	2014, '15, '16
Norman, Tim	1977, '78, '80	Parfitt, Alfred W., Jr.	1943	Phillips, James E.	1938, '39, '40
Norris, John	2004, '05, '06	Parker, Quintin	1986, '88, '89, '90	Phillips, Jim	
North, Nick	2014	Parker, Roy S.	1901, '02	"Chubby"	1973, '74, '75, '76
Norton, John	1977	Parker, Walter A.	1891, '93	Phipps, Thomas E.	1903
Norwell, Chris	2004, '05, '06, '07	Parola, Jerry F.	1961	Piatt, Charles L.	1931, '33
Nosek, Stephen A.	1951, '53, '54	Parola, Tony	1964	Piazza, Nick	2000, '01
Nowack, Albert J.		Parrilli, Anthony K.	1959, '60, '61	Piazza, Sam J.	1948, '49, '50
"Butch"	1926, '27, '28	Pashos, Tony	1999, 2000, '01, '02	Pickering, Mike	1969, '71
Nowak, Bill	1967, '68	Pasko, Larry	1956	Piel, Mike	1986, '87
Nudera, Jim	2014, '15	Pasko, William	1961, '62, '63	Pierce, Alfred	1992
Nurse, Clay	2008, '09, '10	Passmore, Don	1981, '82, '83, '84	Pierce, Jack B.	1945, '47, '48
Oakes, Bernard E	1922, '23	Pater, Matt	1987, '88	Pierce, Stephen	1985, '86
O'Bradovich, Edward	1959, '60	Patrick, Gerald J.	1958, '59	Piggott, Bert C.	1946
O'Brien, Mike	1999, '01, '02, '04	Patterson, John D.	1939	Pike, David R.	1962
O'Connell,		Patterson, Paul L.	1944, '46, '47, '48	Pilcher, Doug	2006, '07, '08, '09
Thomas B.	1951, '52	Patton, Antwoine	1992, '93, '94, '95	Pillath, Jerry	1968
O'Conner, Chris	2014, '15	Paulson, Wayne	1963, '64	Pillsbury, Arthur L.	1890
Odenigbo, Tito	2016	Pavesic, Ray	1977	Pinckney, Frank L.	1905, '06
O'Donnell, Martin	2004, '05, '06, '07	Pawlowski, Joseph G.	1940, '41, '42	Pinder, Cyril C.	1965, '66
Offenbecher, Bill	1956, '57	Payne, Franklin	2004, '05	Pittman Donald C.	1947
Ogata, B. J.	2000	Pazan, Chris	2003, '04, '05	Pittman, Rodney	2005, '06, '07, '08
O'Keefe, Arthur F.	1931	Peach, John W.	1976, '77	Pitts, R. L.	1902, '03
Olander, Milton M.	1918, '19, '20, '21	Pearlman, Gavin	1992	Pixley, Arthur H.	1893, '94, '95, '96
Oliver, Chauncey B.	1909, '10, '11	Peden, Don C.	1920, '21	Plankenhorn, James	1961, '62, '63
Oliver, Percy L., Jr.	1954, '55, '56	Pedersen, Zak	2010, '11, '12	Platt, Damien	1993, '94
Olson, David	1990, '91, '92, '93	Pepper, Cam	1989, '90	Pleas, Asim	1996, '97, '98, '99
Oman, Steve	1967, '68	Perez, Peter J.	1943	Pleviak, Anthony J.	1966, '67, '68
O'Neal, Ronald D.	1961	Perez, Richard B.	1956, '57	Plummer, Ashley	1980, '81
O'Neill, Dick A.	1931	Perkins, Bernon G.	1931	Pnazek, Karl	1969
O'Neill, Robert J.	1939	Perkins, Cecil	1926, '27	Pocic, Graham	2009, '10, '11, '12
Onyegbule, Wisdom	2011	Perkins, Clyde M.	1943, '45	Podmajersky, Paul	1943
Ormsbee, Terry	1974, '76	Perrin, Lonnie	1972, '73, '75	Pogue, Harold A.	1913, '14, '15
Ornatek, Tony	1968	Perry, Jemari	2000, '01	Pokorny, Ray	1976

Polaski, Clarence L.	1936	Reitsch, Robert	1925, '26, '27	Russell, Eddie L.	1963, '64, '65
Pollard, Troy	2008, '09, '10, '11	Renfro, Rick	1983	Russell, Mike	1992, '93
Pollock, Dino	1989	Renn, Donald D.	1954, '55	Russell, Tim	2011, '12, '13
Poloskey, Michael	1990, '91	Rettinger, George L.	1938, '39	Russell, W. Hunter	1930, '32
Poole, Leslie	2015	Rhodes, Ora M.	1896	Rutgens, Joseph C.	1958, '59, '60
Popa, Elie C.	1950, '51	Rice, Simeon	1992, '93, '94, '95	Ryan, Clement J., Jr.	1955
Pope, Jean A.	1904	Richards, Edward J.	1922, '23	Ryan, Corey	1995
Portman, Crain P.	1933, '34	Richards, James V.	1908, '09	Ryan, James	2004, '05, '06
Postmus, Dave	1987, '88	Richards, Lloyd	1992, '93, '94	Ryan, John "Rocky"	1951, '52, '53
Potter, Phil H.	1916	Richardson, Chris	1991, '92, '93, '94	Ryan, Mike	1968, '69
Powell, Larry D.	1978, '79	Richie, James K.	1908	Rykovich, Julius	1946
Powell, Marwan	1995	Richman, Harry E.	1927, '28	Ryles, Richard	1982
Powell, Teko	2013, '14	Riehle, John	1968	Rylowicz, Robert A.	1950, '51
Powless, Dave	1963, '64	Riggs, Thomas J., Jr.	1938, '39, '40	Saban, Joseph P.	1945
President, Gimel	2016	Ringquist, Clarence L.	1928	Sabino, Daniel, F.	1950, '51, '52
Preston, Duke	2002, '03, '04	Roberson, Garvin	1971, '72, '73	Sabo, John P.	1918, '20, '21
Price, Samuel L.	1963, '64, '65	Roberts, Chester C.	1909, '10, '11	Sajnaj, Chester B.	1943
Priebe, Michael	1978, '79	Roberts, Clifford	1958, '59, '60	Samojedny, George	1969, '71
Primous, Marlon	1988, '89, '90, '91	Roberts, Gilbert J.	1922, '23, '24	Samuels, Brian	1990, '91
Prince, David C.	1911	Roberts, Melvin	1992, '93, '94, '95	Sanders, Bobby	1993, '94, '95
Prokopis, Alexander	1944	Robertson, Robert	1966, '67	Sanders, Justin	2006, '07
Prosch, Jay	2010, '11	Robinson, Darrell	1969, '70, '71	Sands, Tyler	2011, '12
Pruett, Eugene F.	1913	Robinson, Lee	2003	Sanni, Supo	2008, '09, '11, '12
Prymuski, Robert M.	1946, '47, '48	Robinson, Olaf E.	1929, '30	Santella, Anthony	2007, '08, '09, '10
Pugh, Dwayne	1982, '83, '84, '85	Robinson, Roy	1972, '73, '74	Santini, Veto	1969
Purvis, Charles G.	1939	Robinson, Thomas	1998	Saunders, Don	1964
Quade, John C.	1893, '94	Robison, Morris W.	1922	Sayre, Elvin C.	1934, '35, '36
Qualls, Mark	1988, '90	Rodgers, Randy	1968	Scarcelli, Tony	1980, '81, '83
Quinn, Bob	1969, '71	Rogers, Johnny	1998, '99	Schacht, Frederick W.	1894, '95, '96
Quintana, Daniel	2013	Rokusek, Frank E.	1922, '23, '24	Schaefering, Brian	2001, '02, '04
Rackers, Neil	1996, '97, '98, '99	Romani, Melvin C.	1959, '60, '61	Schalk, Edward A.	1931
Raddatz, Russ	1968	Rooks, Thomas	1982, '83, '84, '85	Scharbert, Robert D.	1961, '62
Radell, Willard W., Jr.	1965	Root, Clark W.	1930	Schau, Ryan	1995, '96, '97, '98
Railsback, Fay D.	1906, '07, '08	Root, George H.	1893	Schau, Tom	1995, '96, '97, '98
Raklovits, Richard F.	1949, '50	Rose, Jerry	1968	Scheelhaase, Nathan	2010, '11, '12, '13
Ralph, Stanley	1975, '77, '78, '79	Ross, Steve	1970, '72	Schertz, Thomas	1986, '87
Ramein, Robert O.	1982	Rothgeb, Claude J.	1900, '02, '03, '04	Schertz, Todd	1986
Ramsey, Jack	2009, '10, '11, '12	Rotzoll, Dan	1970, '71	Scheuplein, Bret	1994, '95, '96
Ramshaw, Jerry	1977, '78	Rouse, Eric V.	1976, '77, '78	Schlosser, Merle J.	1947, '48, '49
Rathke, Phil	1993	Rouse, Patrick	1999, 2000, '01	Schmidt, Austin	2013, '14, '15, '16
Rebecca, Sammy J.	1950, '51	Rouse, Tyler	2004, '05, '06, '07	Schmidt, Burton J.	1947, '48, '49
Reda, Jason	2004, '05, '06, '07	Roush, D. William	1928, '29	Schmidt, Gerald, C.	1967
Redmann, Doug	1967, '68, '69	Rowe, Enos M.	1911, '12, '13	Schnack, Jason	1993
Redziniak, Ray	1997, '98, '99, 2000	Royer, Joseph W	1892	Schneider, Craig	1986, '87, '88, '89
Reeder, James W.	1937, '38, '39	Rucker, Derrick	1990, '91, '92	Schnettgoecke, Kyle	2005
Reese, Jerrold A.	1984, '86	Rucks, Jim	1970, '71, '72	Schobinger, Eugene	1912, '13, '14
Reeves, Harley E.	1892	Rue, Orlie	1913, '14	Schoeller, Julies E.	1905
Reichle, Richard W.	1919, '21	Ruffin, Jeff	2001, '02, '03	Schooley, Thomas	1977
Reinhart, Rick	1973	Rump, Charles A.	1905	Schrader, Charles	1956
Reisner, David	2014	Rundquist, Elmer T.	1915, '16, '17	Schulte, Rick	1981, '82, '83, '84
Reitsch, Henry O.	1920	Russ, Jerald B.	1945	Schultz, Arthur F.	1930

Schultz, Emil G. 1922, '23, '24
Schultz, Ernest W. 1925, '26, '27
Schulz, Larry 1974, '75, '76
Schumacher,
    Gregg H. 1962, '63, '64
Schumacher, Henry N. 1930
Schumacher, Jerry 1999, 2000, '01
Schustek, Ivan D. 1931, '32, '33
Schwarzentraub, Jeff 1993
Sconce, Harvey J. 1894, '95
Scott, Bob 1975, '76, '77
Scott, Brian 1999
Scott, John 1977, '78
Scott, Robert E. 1952
Scott, Tom 1968, '69, '70
Scully, Mike 1983, '84, '85, '87
Seamans, Frank L. 1932
Searcy, Todd M. 1984, '85
Sebring, Bob 1984, '85
Seiler, Otto E. 1909, '10, '11
Seliger, Vernon L.
    "Blinky" 1946, '47, '48
Senneff, George F. 1912, '13
Serpico, Ralph M. 1943, '44, '45, '46
Sewall, Luke 1980, '81, '82, '83
Shafer, Dominic 2005
Shaffer, Jim 1989, '90
Shapland, Earl P. 1912
Shattuck, Walt F. Sr. 1890
Shavers, Errol 1989
Shaw, Kenny 1979
Shea, Dan 1980
Shelby, Aaron 1990, '91, '92, '93
Sheppard,
    Lawrence D. 1904
Sherrod, Michael 1978, '79, '80
Shively, Bernie A. 1924, '25, '26
Shlaudeman, Harry R. 1916, '17, '19
Short, William E. 1927
Shuler, Hugh M. 1897
Siambekos, Chris 1986, '89
Sidari, John 1990, '91, '92, '93
Siebens, Arthur R. 1913
Siebold, Harry P. 1937, '40
Siegel, Kenneth C. 1944
Siegert, Herbert F. 1946, '47, '48
Siegert, Rudolph 1954, '55
Siegert, Wayne 1949, '50
Sigourney, Chris 1979, '81, '82, '83
Siler, Rich 1981
Siler, Roderick W. 1901

Silkman, John M. 1912, '13
Silva, Dave 1989
Simmons, J. J. 2003, '04, '05
Simpson, Tim 1988, '89, '90, '91
Sinclair, Matt 2001, '02, '03, '04
Singleton, Bobie 2000
Singman, Bruce 1962
Sinnock, Pomeroy 1906, '07, '08
Skarda, Edward J. 1936, '37
Skubisz, Joe 1987, '88
Slater, William F. 1890, '91, '92
Slimmer, Louis F. 1923, '24
Sliva, Oscar 1969
Slowinski, Art 1991
Small, Terrance 1998
Smalzer, Joe 1974, '75
Smerdel, Matthew T. 1942
Smid, Jan 1952, '53, '54
Smith, Bobby J. 1976
Smith, Charles J. 1944
Smith, Darrell 1981
Smith, Donald I. 1950
Smith, Dwayne 2000, '01
Smith, Eugene R. 1920
Smith, J. Dale 1956, '57
Smith, James A. 1939, '41, '42
Smith, Kevin 1975
Smith, M. Rex 1950, '51, '52
Smith, Marshall F. 1948
Smith, Mick 1965, '66
Smith, Rahkeem 2007, '08, '09
Smith, Stuyvesant C. 1919
Smith, Thomas D. 1965, '66
Smith, Wilbert 1995, '96
Smith, Willie 1969
Smock, Walter F. 1900
Smoot, Dawaune 2013, '14, '15, '16
Snavely, Edwin R. 1931
Snook, John K. 1932, '33
Soebbing, Mark H. 1976
Somlar, Scott 1980
Sorey, Revie 1972, '73, '74
Sowa, Nick 1979
Spence, Akeem 2010, '11, '12
Spence, Eaton 2012, '13, '14, '15
Spencer, Brad 1995
Spencer, Joe 2013, '14, '15, '16
Spiller, John 1969
Sprague, Stanley R. 1945
Springe, Otto 1909, '10, '11
Spurgeon, A. Lowell 1935, '36, '37

Squier, George K. 1914, '15
Squirek, Jack S. 1978, '79, '80, '81
Stahl, Garland
    "Jake" 1899, 1900, '01, '02
Stallings, Dennis 1994, '95, '96
Standring, Bob 1973
Stanley, Tim 1982, '85
Staples, Justin 2009, '10, '11, '12
Stapleton, John M. 1959
Starghill, Trevor 1994, '95, '96, '97
Starks, Marshall L. 1958, '59, '60
Stasica, Stanley J. 1945
Stauner, Jim 1974, '75, '76
Steele, Antonio 2006, '07
Steele, James 1890, '91
Stefanski, Steve 1993
Steger, Kurt 1975, '76, '77
Steger, Russell W.
    "Ruck" 1946, '47, '48, '49
Steinhaus, Steve 1994
Steinman, Henry J. 1929
Stellwagen, Joel 1966
Stelter, Chris 1994
Stephenson, Lewis A. 1901
Stern, Matt 1991
Sternaman,
    Edward C. 1916, '17, '19
Sternaman, Joseph T. 1921
Stevens, Don 1949, '50, '51
Stevens, Lawrence J. 1951, '52
Stevenson, Jeff 1985
Stewart, Baird E. 1952, '53, '54
Stewart, Charles A. 1905, '06
Stewart, David L. 1957, '58
Stewart, Frank 1914, '15, '16
Stewart, James R.
    "Bud" 1926, '27
Stewart, Lynn 1962, '63, '64
Stewart, Thomas C. 1946, '47, '48, '49
Stine, Mike 1983
Stone, Clyde E. 1902
Stone, Richard R. 1965
Stotz, Charles H. 1938
Stotz, James T. 1966
Stotz, Richard A. 1966
Stout, Hiles G. 1954, '55, '56
Stowe, Bob 1980, '81, '82, '83
Strader, Wayne 1977, '78, '79, '80
Strauch, Donald J. 1916
Straw, Thomas C. 1931, '32, '33
Streeter, Sean 1988, '89, '90, '91

Strong, David A.	1936
Strong, Derrick	2000, '01, '02, '03
Strong, Jasper	1992, '93, '94
Strong, Manuel	1996, '97
Studley, Charles B.	1949, '50, '51
Studwell, Scott	1973, '75, '76
Stuessy, Dwight T.	1926, '27, '28
Sturrock, Tom	1968
Suarez, Mike	1993, '94
Sullivan, Beau	2012
Sullivan, Bruce E.	1965, '66
Sullivan, Gerry	1971, '72, '73
Sullivan, John	1974, '75, '77, '78
Sullivan, Marques	1997, '98, '99, 2000
Sullivan, Mike	1974, '75
Sullivan, Tom	2008
Summers, W. Michael	1961, '62, '63
Sumpter, Frank	2016
Suppan, Mike	1974
Surdyk, Florian J.	1937
Sutter, Kenneth F.	1956
Sutton, Archie M.	1962, '63, '64
Svetina, Mike	2012, '13, '16
Swanson, Mark B.	1930
Sweney, Don	1893, '94, '95, '97
Swienton, Kenneth R.	1952, '53, '54
Swoope, Craig	1982, '83, '84, '85
Sykes, Fred	2008, '09, '10, '11
Tabloff, Ryan	1997
Tabor, Hubert B.	1921
Tackett, William C.	1892, '93
Tagart, Mark	1984, '85
Taliaferro, Mike	1962, '63
Tarnoski, Paul T.	1905
Tarwain, John	1928
Tate, Albert R.	1948, '49, '50
Tate, Donald E.	1951, '52, '53, '54
Tate, Kyle	1994
Tate, Richard A.	1965, '66, '67
Tate, William L.	1950, '51, '52
Taylor, Brent	1995, '96, '97
Taylor, Carooq	1977, '80
Taylor, Dionte	2013, '14, '15, '16
Taylor, Joseph W.	1904
Taylor, Keith	1983, '85, '86, '87
Taylor, Randall R.	1976, '77, '78
Taylor, Winston	2002, '03
Teafatiller, Guy	1984, '85
Tee, Darrin	1986, '87
Tee, David	1982
Teitsma, Jack	2011, '12, '13, '14
Tesdall, Seth	1997, '98, '99
Theodore, James J.	1934
Theodore, John A.	1935
Thiede, John	1977, '78
Thomas, Calvin	1978, '79, '80, '81
Thomas, Earnest, III	2011, '12, '13, '14
Thomas, Ian	2008, '09, '10, '11
Thomas, Karleton	1997, '98, '99
Thomas, Ken	1987, '89
Thomas, Marcus "Miami"	2007, '08
Thomas, Pierre	2003, '04, '05, '06
Thomas, Stephen K.	1961
Thomases, Robert	1938
Thompson, Darryl	1982, '83
Thompson, Herbert P.	1911
Thorby, Charles H. J.	1895
Thornhill, Anthony	2004, '05, '06, '07
Thornton, Bruce	1975, '76, '77, '78
Thornton, Hugh	2009, '10, '11, '12
Thorp, Don	1980, '81, '82, '83
Thrash, Joelil	2009
Tilton, Harry W	1894
Timko, Craig S.	1965, '66, '67
Timm, Judson A.	1927, '28, '29
Tischer, Josh	2002, '03, '04, '05
Tischler, Matthew	1935
Tohn, Clarence G.	1943
Tomanek, Emil	1944
Tomasula, David G.	1965, '66, '67
Tregoning, Wesley W.	1941, '45
Trigger, Jeff C.	1966, '67, '68
Trudeau, Jack	1983, '84, '85
Trumpy, Bob	1964
Tubbs, J. J.	2000, '01, '02, '03
Tucker, Cameron	2015
Tucker, Derwin	1975, '76, '77, '78
Tumilty, Richard J.	1941
Tupper, James O.	1913
Turek, Joseph J.	1939, '40
Turnbull, David	1937
Turner, E. Scott	1991, '92, '93, '94
Turner, Elbert	1988, '90, '91
Turner, Greg	1986, '87, '88
Turner, Malik	2014, '15
Turner, Shawn	1985, '86, '88
Twist, John F.	1908, '09, '10
Uecker, Bill	1972, '73, '74
Ulrich, Charles, Jr.	1949, '50, '51
Umnus, Leonard	1922, '23, '24
Uremovich, George	1971, '72, '73
Usher, Darryl	1983, '84, '85, '87
Utz, George J.	1956, '57
Valek, James J.	1945, '46, '47, '48
Valentino, R. Rudolph	1949, '51
Van Dyke, Jos. A.	1932
Van Hook, Forest C.	1906, '07, '08
Van Meter, Vincent J.	1932
VanMiegham, Brennan	2014
VanOrman, Ellsworth G.	1935
Vanosky, Brian	1995
Varrige, Tom	1980, '81, '82
Vaughn, Ke'Shawn	2015, '16
Venegoni, John	1978, '80, '81
Venegoni, Mark	2007
Verduzco, Jason	1989, '90, '91, '92
Vernasco, Joseph P.	1950, '51
Vernasco, Walter L.	1952, '53, '54
Veronesi, Don	1993
Versen, Walter G.	1944
Vierneisel, Phil	1973, '74, '75, '76
Villunas, Eddie	2010, '11, '12
Virgil, Morris	2002, '03, '04, '05
Voelker, Gary	1992, '93
Vogel, Otto H.	1921
Vogel, Rob	1993
Vohaska, William J.	1948, '49, '50
Volkman, Dean E.	1965, '66, '67
Von Oven, Fred W.	1896, '97
Vukelich, John J.	1949
Vyborny, Julian	1969, '70
Wachter, John	1986, '88, '90
Wadsworth, Albert M.	1899
Wagner, Alexander	1912, '13, '14
Wagner, Richard B.	1922
Wainwright, Jack	1964
Wakefield, Fred	1997, '98, '99, 2000
Waldbeser, Clifford H.	1951, '52, '53
Waldron, Ralph H.	1966, '68
Walker, David R.	1955, '56
Walker, Derek	2005, '06, '07, '08
Walker, Frank H.	1927, '28, '29
Walker, Mike	1970, '72
Walker, Thurman	1960, '61, '62
Wall, Joe	1991
Wallace, Douglas A.	1957, '58, '59
Wallace, Stanley H.	1951, '52, '53
Waller, Mike	1972, '74, '75
Waller, Trayvon	1999, 2000
Waller, William H.	1934

Wallin, Robert W.	1940, '42	
Wallner, Neil	1986, '87	
Walls, LaKeith	2013, '14, '15	
Walquist, Lawrence W.	1918, '19, '20, '21	
Walser, Herman J.	1931, '32, '33	
Walsh, George	1954, '55	
Walsh, L. Ed	1965	
Walters, Jay	1967	
Ward, Brian	1982, '83, '85	
Ward, Dustin	2000, '01, '02, '03	
Ward, Jihad	2014, '15	
Ward, Raymond C.	1943, '44	
Wardell, Roosevelt	1988	
Wardley, George P., Jr.	1936, '37, '38	
Ware, Michael	2007	
Warren, DaJuan	2004, '05, '06, '07	
Warren, James B.	1962, '63	
Washington, Edward W.	1962, '63, '64	
Washington, Keith	1997	
Washington, Quincy	1999	
Washington, Terrell	1999, 2000, '01	
Washington, Tyrone	1992, '93, '94, '95	
Waters, Alan J.	1964, '65, '66	
Watkins, Cameron	2016	
Watson, Carl P.	1908	
Watson, Chauncey B.	1911, '12	
Watson, John W.	1913, '14, '15	
Watson, Tre	2015, '16	
Wax, Shawn	1988, '89, '90	
Weatherford, Steve	2002, '03, '04, '05	
Weaver, Scott	1993, '94, '95, '96	
Weber, Charles	1977, '78	
Weddell, Robert W., Jr.	1951, '52	
Wehrli, Robert J.	1937, '38	
Weil, Ross	2004, '05, '06, '07	
Weingrad, Mike	1982, '83	
Weiss, Richard M.	1978	
Weisse, Jeff	1995, '96, '97, '98	
Wells, Forry	1990, '91, '92, '93	
Wells, John	1982	
Wells, Mike	1970, '71, '72	
Welsh, Jim	1970, '71	
Wendryhoski, Joseph S.	1959, '60	
Wendt, Pat	1991, '92	
Wenskunas, Mac P.	1942, '45, '46	
West, Kevin	1982	
Westerlind, Dan R.	1978	
Whalen, Bryson	2008	
Wham, Charles	1910	
Wham, Fred L.	1905, '07, '08	
Wheatland, John A.	1961, '63	
White, Chris	1983, '84, '85	
White, Earl A.	1906, '07	
White, Edward L.	1984, '85, '86	
White, Ron	1975, '76	
White, Sean "Taylor"	2015	
White, Tyler	2013, '14, '15, '16	
Whiteside, Jim	1967, '68	
Whitlow, Jeremy	2014	
Whitman, Doug	1967, '68	
Whitman, Josh	1997, '98, '99, 2000	
Wickhorst, George N.	1925	
Widner, Albert E.	1943	
Wietz, L. J.	1927, '28, '29	
Wile, Dan	1955	
Wiley, Francis R.	1903	
Wilk, Adam	2003, '06	
Wilkins, Marques	2006, '07	
Willett, Chris	2010	
Williams, Anthony	1984, '85, '86, '87	
Williams, Ashante	2009, '10, '11, '12	
Williams, Brian	1988, '89	
Williams, Christopher	1976	
Williams, David	1983, '84, '85	
Williams, Greg	1973, '74	
Williams, Isiah " Juice"	2006, '07, '08, '09	
Williams, James	1995, '96, '97	
Williams, Justice	2016	
Williams, Melvin R.	1984, '85	
Williams, Oliver	1981, '82	
Williams, Rick	1973, '75	
Williams, Scott	1890, '91	
Williams, Sirod	2005, '07, '09	
Williams, Steven	1985, '86, '88, '89	
Williams, Travis	2002, '03, '04, '05	
Willis, Jacob	2006, '07	
Willis, Lenny	1995, '97, '98, '99	
Willis, Norman L.	1960, '62	
Willis, Remond	2005	
Willis, Steve	1995, '96, '97	
Willis, William W.	1949	
Willmann, Dean E.	1954	
Wilmarth, George H.	1897, '98	
Wilmoth, Fred	1954	
Wilson, Brett	1983	
Wilson, Craig	2008, '09, '10, '11	
Wilson, Darryl	1979, '80, '81	
Wilson, David C.	1980	
Wilson, David D.	1921, '22	
Wilson, Eugene	1999, 2000, '01	
Wilson, Evan	2010, '11, '12, '13	
Wilson, John	1971	
Wilson, Joseph W.	1902	
Wilson, Kenneth L. "Tug"	1925	
Wilson, Kirby	1981, '82	
Wilson, Martez	2007, '08, '10	
Wilson, Norman K.	1912, '13	
Wilson, Ray	1983, '84, '85, '86	
Wilson, Robert A.	1941, '42	
Wilson, Tavon	2008, '09, '10, '11	
Wilson, Thomas P.	1930, '35, '36	
Wilson, Wendell S.	1925, '26	
Wiman, Robert L.	1953, '54	
Windy, Gary	1970	
Wineland, Harold S.	1962	
Winslow, Len	1967, '68	
Winsper, Edwin S.	1930	
Wintermute, Bob	1969, '70	
Witek, Roger	1987	
Wiza, John	1970, '71, '72	
Wodziak, Frank S.	1950, '51, '52	
Wolf, Fred	1967, '68	
Wolf, Roger E.	1952, '53, '54	
Wolgast, Arnold E.	1927, '29	
Wood, Gerald A.	1959, '60	
Woods, DeJazz	2013, '14	
Woods, Toriano	1993, '94, '95, '96	
Woodson, Abraham B.	1954, '55, '56	
Woodward, Harold C.	1921, '22	
Woody, Frederick W.	1892, '93, '94	
Woolston, William. H.	1910, '11, '12	
Worban, John C.	1940	
Worthy, Tyrone	1979, '80	
Wrenn, John M.	1946, '47	
Wright, Dave	1970, '71, '72	
Wright, John, Jr.	1990, '91	
Wright, John, Sr.	1965, '66, '67	
Wright, Richard	1969, '71	
Wright, Robert C.	1935	
Wright, Royal	1890, '91, '93	
Wright, Sidney B.	1908	
Wyatt, R. D.	1906	
Wycoff, Eric	1984, '85	
Yadron, Paul	1973, '74	
Yanuskus, P. J.	1929, '30, '32	

Name	Years
Yavorski, Mike	1962
Yeazel, Donald R.	1957, '58, '59
Yelton, Kyle	2006
Yochem, Ron	1955
Young, Al	1975
Young, Claude H. "Buddy"	1944, '46
Young, Donovonn	2011, '12, '13, '14
Young, Herbert T.	1938
Young, Michael	1997, '98, '99, 2000
Young, Roy M.	1904, '05
Young, W. Cecil	1961, '62
Young, Walter	1999, 2000, '01, '02
Young, Willie	1981
Yukevich, Stanley F., Jr.	1959, '60, '61
Zaborac, Thomas F.	1945, '46
Zalewski, Taylor	2012, '13, '14, '15
Zatkoff, Samuel	1944, '46, '47
Zeppetella, Anthony J.	1961
Zimmerman, Albert G.	1945
Zimmerman, Ken W., Jr.	1961, '62
Zimmerman, Kenneth W.	1936, '37, '38
Zimmerman, Walter H.	1895, '96
Zirbel, Craig	1980, '81, '82
Zitnik, Mark	1988, '89, '90, '91
Zochert, Dave	1969, '70, '71
Zuppke, Robert E.	1937

WOMEN'S GOLF

Name	Years
Ahem, Erin	2004
Arnholt, Cheryl	1984, '85, '86, '87
Beach, Becky	1976, '77, '78
Berro, Terrie	1981, '82, '83, '84
Biehl, Becky	1992, '93, '94, '95
Biehl, Lia	1988, '89, '90, '91
Borbeck, Connie	1985, '86, '87
Burden, Casey	1985, '86, '87
Calamaro, Jacqueline	2013
Campbell, Allison	1975
Campbell, Michelle	1984, '85, '87
Carroll, Michelle	2001, '02
Cheney, Stephanie	2000, '01, '02
Cook, Kristine	2005, '06, '07, '08
Cowell, Andrea	1996, '97
Cox, Marla	2001, '02, '03, '04

Name	Years
Dilger, Katelin	2009, '10, '11, '12
Eaton, Carol	1979
Eaton, Jane	1979
Eckols, Molly	1998
Evans, Wendy	1992, '93, '94
Featherstone, Nancy	2006, '07, '08, '09
Garrett, Christine	1992, '93, '94, '95
Grumish, Julie	1989, '90, '91
Gwillim, Linda	1976
Hannam, Gail	1975, 1976
Hayes, Jessica	1998
Heiken, Renee	1990, '91, '92, '93
Hopton, Raquel	2008, '09, '10, '11
Ittersagen, Jill	1981, '82, '83, '84
Joers, Emily	2014, '15
Johnson, Julie	1980
Johnston, Allison	1985, '86, '87, '88
Kallergis, Kristin	2007, '08
Kanda, Laurin	2000, '01, '02, '03
Karmazin, Karen	1995, '96, '98
Kelleher, Elizabeth	1988, '89, '90
Kim, Sarah	1999
Kimpel, Janice	1975, '76, '77
Klein, Kristen	1988, '90, '91
Koschmann, Hailey	2009, '10, '11, '12
Lang, Susan	1981, '82, '83, '84
Larson, Laurie	1976, '77, '78, '79
Leech, Rhonda	1975, '76
Leishman, Jane	1983
Lin, Michelle	1996, '97, '98
Lucas, Nora	2009, '10, '11, '12
Lynch, Jennifer	1992, '93, '94, '95
Lyttle, Lorette	1997, '98, '99, 2000
Macconnachie, Brenda	1985, '86, '87, '88
Macke, Nell	1997, '98, '99, 2000
Maxwell, Nancy	1977, '78, '79, '80
Mayer, Michelle	2013
McCloskey, Pam	1984, '85, '86
McKinzie, Laura	1976, '77
Miller, Diane	1975, '76, '77, '78
Miller, Justi Rae	1986, '87, '88, '89
Miller, Stephanie	2014, '15, '16
Milligan, Lyndsey	2004, '05
Mory, Stephanie	2005, '06, '07, '08
Mulcahy, Kourtney	1994, '96
Murphy, Jane	1980, '81, '82, '83
Murphy, Mary Ellen	1980, '81, '82, '83
O'Neal, Kelsey	2006
O'Neal, Megan	2004, '05, '06
Park, Grace	2015, '16

Name	Years
Park, Seul Ki	2005, '06, '07, '08
Pirk, Stacey	1991, '92
Pope, Sally	1979, '80
Postillion, Sam	2013, '14
Prapassarangkul, Chayanid "Jan"	2015, '16
Redington, Nancy	1980
Reynolds, Shelly	1985
Rogala, Alexis	1991
Rubin, Jacqueline	1994, '95, '96, '97
Schuldt, Ember	2011, '12, '13, '14
Scott, Christine	1999, 2000
Seyman, Sandy	1977, '78, '79
Sielicki, Carmel	2001, '02, '03
Singhsumalee, Bing	2016
Sitter, Jillian	1996, '97, '98, '99
Sloan, Samantha	2009, '10, '11, '12
Smith, Crystal	2013
Sutton, Christin	1997, '99
Sutton, Sandy	1982, '83, '84
Tate, Barb	1981
Tex, Cathy	1977
Thirati, Pimploy	2013
Treseler, Kristie	1994
Walters, Mari	2000, '02
Wampler, Kaitlyn	2010
Webb, Ashley	1995, '96, '97, '98
Webb, Leslie	1997
Winkelman, Susan	1987, '88, '89, '90
Wood, Shellie	1989, '90
Young, Renata	2000, '01, '02, '03
Zimmerman, Valerie	1993

MEN'S GOLF

Name	Years
Affrunti, Joe	2004
Alafoginis, Frank	2005, '06, '07
Alexander, Charles	1970, '71, '72
Allen, Mike	1990, '91, '92
Almquist, Robert	1959, '60
Alpert, S. G.	1930, '31, '32
Anderson, E. J.	1927
Anderson, W. J.	1926
Arendt, James W.	1968
Atkinson, Brian	1994, '95, '96, '98
Baker, Robert	1933, '34
Bakke, Niles	1970, '71, '72, '73
Barlow, Zach	2007, '08, '09, '10
Barr, John	1934
Bartelstein, Alan	1977, '78
Beard, Trevor	1990, '91, '92
Beck, Bruce	1970, '71, '72

Name	Years
Becker, William	1962
Beckman, Gary A.	1969
Billings, Albert F.	1938, '39
Bishop, Danny H.	1967, '68, '69
Blatt, Larry	2008
Bootz, Harold	1946
Bridenthal, C. F.	1908
Briggs, Randy	1991, '93
Brill, Tyson	2000
Bristol, R. S.	1921
Brown, James F.	1942
Brown, Lloyd	1946, '47
Bruce, Ben	1989, '90, '91, '92
Buenzli, James J.	1980, '81, '82, '83
Burden, Joe	1970, '71, '72, '73
Burge, Alex	2012, '13, '14
Buzick, John W.	1941
Cable, Dave	1991, '93, '94, '95
Campbell, Brian	2012, '13, '14, '15
Campbell, Robert S.	1938
Carlson, Ralph O.	1937, '38, '39
Carlson, Roger W.	1982
Carpenter, Jordan	2004, '05
Carter, W. E.	1928
Cashman, Dennis	1965, '66, '67
Cassady, Donald	1951, '52, '53
Castelo, Robert "Chip"	1972, '74
Chadwick, Michael	1979, '80, '81, '82
Chaussard, Garrett	2002, '03, '04, '05
Clark, Tom	1961
Cockrell, Paul F.	1927
Coghill, John R.	1938
Connell, Byron	1955, '56
Correll, Charles Richard	1956, '57, '58
Crawford, Heath	1987, '88, '89, '90
Crowe, R. H.	1930, '31, '32
Culp, George	1949
Culp, John D., Jr.	1947
Cwik, Ronald	1957, '58, '59
Cyboran, John V.	1982, '83
Cyboran, Steve	1990
Danielson, Charlie	2013, '14, '15
Davies, Richard	1955
Dawson, George	1924
Dayiantis, George	1948, '50
Dechert, Douglas	1981, '82
DeForest, Chris	2008, '09, '10, '11
Detry, Thomas	2013, '14, '15
Dilsaver, Carl	1953, '54
Dobrovolny, Chris	2000, '01
Dray, Don	1973, '74, '75, '76
Edwards, Don	1985, '86, '87, '88
Edwards, Richard	1978, '80
Ellerbeck, Ron	1960
Emery, Eugene	1944, '45
England, Joseph	1960, '61, '62
Evans, Terry L.	1966, '67
Fairbanks, Jamie	1991, '92, '93, '94
Fairfield, Kevin	1987, '88, '89, '90
Fassnacht, Bill	1950, '51
Fiser, Chuck	1985, '86, '87
Fish, C. M., Jr.	1927, '28
Fleming, John D.	1965, '66, '67
Fletcher, Pete	1950
Fletcher, Rodney	1950
Flood, Gerold	1950, '51
Foley, Henry J.	1955
Fornof, J. R.	1908
Foster, Douglas	1962, '63, '64
Frankenberg, Ross	2010, '11, '12
Frederickson, J. L.	1921, '22
Funkhouser, Mark R.	1982
Garvin, Steve	1971
Georlett, Clem	1958, '59
Gibala, Nick	1970, '71, '72
Gindler, Matt	1994, '95, '96, '97
Goldstein, Jake	1995, '97
Goldwater, R. W.	1929
Goulding, Bob	1963, '64, '65
Graff, Ryan	1992, '93, '94, '96
Green, Jim	1974
Guthrie, Luke	2009, '10, '11, '12
Haime, Kevin	1984, '85, '86
Hall, John	1961, '62, '63
Harder, Harold	1972, '73, '74, '75
Hardy, Nick	2015
Harkins, Blair	2005, '06
Hatch, Lemoine S.	1923
Haubold, Bill	1986
Hauter, Jonathan	2014
Hawkins, Burford Haynes	1952, '53, '54
Hayes, John C.	1941
Healy, Patrick	1979
Hedges, Elsum G.	1936
Henderson, Mark	1996, '97, '98, '99
Hill, Elton	1934, '35, '36
Hirsch, Joel	1963
Hobart, John A.	1936, '37, '38
Hoffman, Lyle	1933, '34
Hoffman, Matt	2007, '08, '09, '10
Holmes, John A., Jr.	1966, '67
Holmstrom, John T.	1940, '41, '42
Hosick, Kyle	2005, '06, '07
Hougham, Kym	1973, '74, '75, '76
Humphreys, John	1923, '24, '25
Hunt, L. D.	1924, '25
Hurst, Joe	1964, '65
Hutchinson, Edgar B.	1937, '38, '39
Iantorno, Tony	1974
Jacobs, Mason	2009, '11, '12, '13
Jaronik, Frank J.	1941, '42
Jaronik, Stanley	1945
Jemsek, Gregory	1947, '48
Keck, Frank	1954
Keen, J. Patrick	1969, '70, '71
Kehlor, J. M.	1912
Kellaney, Kenneth	1975, '76, '77, '78
Kennedy, Brian S.	1982, '83, '84
Kim, David	2013, '14
Kimpel, Raymond	1948, '49, '50
King, Andrew	1976, '77, '78
Kirchner, Peter A.	1968
Kisselburg, B. M.	1915
Kohr, Charles	1963, '64, '65
Kokes, Wilbert J.	1935, '36, '37
Krick, Jon	2007, '08
Kuntstadler, R. H.	1925, '26, '27
Kurz, W. C.	1928
Langley, Scott	2008, '09, '10, '11
LeBosquet, Maurice	1921, '22
Leighty, Brad	1986, '87
Lepp, James	2002, '03
Lewis, Randy R.	1981, '82, '83, '84
Logan, David	1948, '49, '50
Lound, Geoff	2000, '01, '02, '03
Lukasik, Fred, Jr.	1968
Lyon, F. S.	1929, '30, '31
MacDonald, J. M.	1917
Mack, Andy	2005, '06
Mahon, John	1985
Malstrom, Gordon	1960
Mann, Philip	1977, '78
Marquardt, Robert	1952
Martin, R. S.	1929, '30, '31
Mason, W. T.	1926
Mazzetta, Ozzie	1954
McCarthy, James P.	1942, '43
McCloskey, Bob	2000
McKinzie, James	1951, '52
Meier, Joseph	1979, '80

Metcalf, Robert L.	1939
Meyer, Dylan	2015
Mickelson, A. M.	1935
Miller, Stephen	1979, '80
Modjeska, Eugene F.	1940, '43
Moore, Ryan	2001, '03, '04
Mudrock, Mark	1979, '80
Mueller, Roger	1955, '56
Mulliken, John W.	1966, '67, '68
Murphy, Frank, Jr.	1947
Nagle, Patrick	2003, '04, '06, '07
Needler, L. Q.	1921
Newell, Lee	1964, '65
Niva, George	1957, '58
Novotny, A. L.	1921, '22, '23
Nuger, Larry	1998, '99, 2000
O'Neal, Mike	2002, '03, '04, '05
O'Neal, Roger D.	1934, '35
Ogren, Mark	2004, '06, '07, '08
Olsen, C. F.	1914, '15
Olson, Evan	2000, '01, '02
Orsi, Tom	1957, '58, '59
Parga, Ed	1996, '97, '98, '99
Parkhill, Clayton	2009, '10, '11
Parkhill, Thomas S.	1965, '66, '67
Patton, Herbert R.	1938, '39, '40
Pegoraro, Robert A.	1969, '70, '71
Pell, Robert	1957
Peressini, Tony	2001
Peressini, William	1975, '76, '77, '78
Persin, Scott	1996, '97
Petersen, Gregory A.	1981, '82, '84
Peterson, Eugene	1950
Peterson, James H.	1955
Pieters, Thomas	2011, '12, '13
Pittenger, Greg	1997, 2000
Points, D. A.	1998, '99
Pray, Lee	1933
Prince, Tom	1988, '89, '90
Prouty, E. C.	1912, '14
Quackenbush, Justin	1949
Ramey, F. W.	1917
Ramsey, R. W.	1915
Rascher, Vernon	1951, '52
Rasmussen, Rich	1974, '75
Reed, Ross C.	1940, '41, '42
Reif, John P.	1947, '48
Reitsch, Robert	1954, '55, '56
Renwick, F. W.	1932
Reston, James B. "Scotty"	1931, '32
Richart, Frank E., Jr.	1939, '40, '46
Riley, Tim	1998, '99, 2000, '01
Ring, Wayne	1945, '46, '47
Ripley, C. T.	1908
Rolfe, Rial E.	1922, '23, '24
Rowader, Thomas	1952, '53, '54
Rugg, Robert F.	1976, '77, '78, '79
Russo, Tony	1989
Schiene, Martin	1977, '78, '79, '80
Schroder, Robert	1944, '45
Scott, Jay	1992, '93, '94, '95
Shiels, Andrew	2007
Simon, Donald	1963, '64
Simpson, J. M.	1915, '16, '17
Slattery, Edward T.	1983, '84
Slothower, James B.	1956, '57
Small, Mike	1985, '86, '87, '88
Smith, Dale J.	1956, '57
Smith, Gerald	1961, '62, '63
Smith, Harold R.	1949, '50
Sparks, Frank	1960
Stasica, Stanley	1946
Stricker, Steve	1986, '87, '88, '89
Suitor, Rick	1970, '71, '72, '73
Sutin, L. R.	1928, '29
Tanous, Jerry	1961
Tapscott, Robert	1943, '48
Tendall, Ryan	2001, '02, '03, '04
Tewksbury, W. J.	1925, '26, '27
Thompson, John	74
Toliuszis, Mike	1960, '61, '62
Triebel, Albert	1936
Turnbow, Charles R.	1943
Turner, T. R.	1985
Usinger, William A.	1940, '41
Voyda, John F.	1956, '57, '58
Walch, Leo	1952
Walduck, C. L.	1912
Walker, John	1969
Wallace, Robert R.	1967, '68, '69
Walton, H. R.	1915
Weems, C. L.	1915
Weise, Robert W.	1942
Welsh, Alex 1940,	1941
West, Byron Kenneth	1952, '53, '54, '55
Wheatland, Alan	1962
Whitacre, Andrew	1984, '85
White, F. H.	1914, '15
White, H. H.	1917
Whitelaw, J. C.	1914, '15
Whyte, G. K.	1928
Wiley, D. F.	1928, '29
Williams, R. C.	1912
Winters, C. P.	1915
Wolfley, Richard F.	1941
Woodcock, Scott	1994
Wyatt, Arthur R.	1946, '47, '48, '49
Zahn, Dene W.	1936
Zambole, Nicholas	1979, '80, '81, '82
Zimmerman, Danny	2005, '06

MEN'S GYMNASTICS

Adamson, Steve	1981, '83, '84, '85
Adkins, John D.	1941, '42
Adler, Leon	1917
Adler, Maurice A.	1922, '23
Albuquerque, Gilberto	1981, '82, '84, '85
Almy, W. H.	1905
Antoniolli, Carl	1978
Aufrecht, Michael	1960, '61, '62
Austin, Jeffrey	1952, '53, '54, '55
Ayalon, Yuval	1995, '96, '97, '98
Baker, Bobby	2015, '16
Baker, Nicholas	1990, '91, '92, '93
Baley, James A.	1941
Ballou, Donald	1963, '64
Barasch, Alvin	1960
Bare, Frank	1952, '53, '54
Barmes, William	1950
Barr, Ken	1970, '71, '72
Barrett, Brad	1972
Bauer, Ronald	1966
Beck, Howard W.	1972, '73, '74, '75
Bedard, Irvin	1950, '51
Bennett, Austin H.	1922
Bird, Patrick	1958, '59, '60
Black, William	1905
Blair, Gavin	1956, '63
Blazek, Frank	1956
Blazek, James	1957, '58, '59
Bohaty, Zdenek A.	1942
Boyer, Michael	2006, '07, '08
Bradley, Logan	2013, '14, '15, '16
Bradley, Ross	2005, '06, '08, '09
Bralower, Leonard	1948
Bredfeldt, Charles	1920
Brinkmeyer, Gilbert	1952, '53
Brockman, Robert A.	1975
Broome, Robert	1967, '68
Brown, Harold J.	1941
Brown, Malcolm	2010, '11, '12. '13
Brown, Randall	1966, '67

Name	Years		Name	Years		Name	Years
Brown, Ted	2004, '05, '06		Eggleston, Chandler	2014, '16		Ham, Jonathan	1998, '99, 2000, '01
Browning, Richard	1953, '54		Eliason, John	1964, '65, '66		Hamman, James	1981
Bucher, E. G.	1913, '14		Elkin, David	1993, '94, '95		Hand, Nick	2002, '03, '04, '05
Buck, P. E.	1913, '14		Ensalaco, Robert	1964		Harrington, Peter J.	1947, '48
Buck, Steve	1977		Erwin, Frank K.	1973, '74, '75, '76		Hartville, Fred	2013, '14, '15, '16
Bull, Tyson	2015, '16		Feinstein, Victor	1976, '77, '78, '79		Harvey, Allan F.	1957, '58, '59
Burgeson, Lennart B.	1937		Fenske, Greg	1971, '72, '73		Hayasaki, Casey	2003, '04
Butler, Paul L.	1939		Field, David A.	1939, '40		Heil, Robert	1957
Butts, Larry	1968, '69, '70		Filla, Michael	2001, '02, '03, '04		Heimovics, I.	1922
Cadle, Robert W.	1932, '33		Fina, John	1948, '49		Henderson, Sean	1990, '91, '92
Calhoun, Dean	1966, '67		Fina, Joseph	1947, '48, '49, '50		Hettinger, Kurt	1996, '97, '98, '99
Calvetti, Joseph A.	1942, '48, '49		Fina, Louis R.	1940, '41, '42		Highsmith, Charles	1955
Cannon, James	1951		Fina, Paul	1939, '40, '41		Hirsch, Alan	1990, '91
Cason, Robert	1961		Fina, Paul, Jr.	1981		Hlinka, Anthony	1955
Chance, Watts W.	1931		Fisher, Arthur E.	1935, '36		Hlinka, Charles	1950
Chapple, Steve	1967, '68, '69		Flodin, Forest	2001		Hoang, Linh	1998, '99, 2000, '01
Cheriel, Ricardo	1990, '91, '92, '93		Flood, William	1962, '63		Hochhauser, Daniel	1970, '71, '72
Cherry, William L.	1930, '31		Forman, Marvin N.	1939		Hois, William	1977
Chhay, Vuthik	1991, '92, '93		Foster, Matt	2014, '15, '16		Hollman, Edward E.	1912
Christian, William A.	1929, '31		Fulton, William J.	1927, '28, '29		Holmes, Harold	1961, '62, '63
Claycomb, Gordon	1959		Gardner, Thomas	1953, '54, '55		Holveck, Gary	1967
Cleary, James	1951		Garnett, Erik	2002		Horimura, Hirosh	1916, '17
Clow, Robert J.	1940		Geissler, Burkhard	1963, '64		Hosfield, Mark	1976, '77, '78
Coats, Wayne	1968, '69		Geist, Harry F.	1912		Hoskins, Robert N.	1926
Cobb, C. Caton	1941, '42		Giallombardo, Joseph J.	1938, '39, '40		Houser, Edwin	1951
Cook, Greg	1998, '99, 2000		Gibbs, Thomas	2014, '15, '16		Howorth, Ronald	1961
Corbitt, Jon	1998, '99, 2000		Gill, Matt	1998, '99, 2000		Hudachek, Lawrence	1941
Crawford, Sean-Paul	1999, 2000, '01, '02		Glasser, Julian	1931, '32, '33		Hughes, Edgar O.	1936, '38
Cress, John M., Jr.	1939, '40		Glomb, Robert	1961, '62		Hughes, Gaylord	1948, '49, '50
Cryer, Walter	1950, '52		Goldstein, William J. "Bill Goldie"	1938, '39, '40		Hunt, Paul	1971, '72, '73
Culbertson, Jon	1954, '55, '56		Gombos, Edward	1957, '58, '59		Hutchings, Steven	1990
Dallenbach, John W.	1939		Goodrich, John	1960		Iffland, Llewellyn	1963, '64, '65
Danner, Richard M.	1958		Goone, David	1981, '82, '83		Illingworth, Michael	1978
Danzer, John	1929		Goren, Zach	2005		Im, Oscar	1985, '86
Davis, John	1956, '57, '58		Gossett, William P.	1922		Jacobson, Johnny	2016
Davis, John	1968, '69		Grace, Dale	1961, '62		Jenkinson, Hugh R.	1928, '29, '30
Davis, John	1977, '78, '79		Grace, Sterling	1963		Jennings, Alpha M.	1935
Deutschman, F. J.	1902		Grant, Kimp	1991, '92, '93		Jirus, Richard	1954, '55, '56
Dewey, Carter	1928		Gray, James N.	1931, '32, '33		Joudakin, Al	1961
Diab, Alex	2016		Grieb, Donald L.	1972, '75		Juengert, Steve	1983, '84, '86, '87
Diamond, Robert N.	1958		Grimes, Michael	1971, '72, '73, '74		Kalin, Gene	1970, '71, '72
Diamond, Scott	1988		Grossfeld, Abie	1957, '58, '59, '60		Kamm, Rufus M.	1914
Dillon, Andrew	1987, '88, '89		Grossi, George	1964		Kaplan, Mark	1967, '68, '69
Dixon, Arthur G.	1924		Haagensen, Wes	2005, '06, '07, '08		Karon, Michael	1956, '57
Dolan, Francis "Frank"	1949, '50, '51		Hackleman, Michael	1963		Karpen, William E.	1972, '73, '74, '75
Dooley, Justin	1985, '86		Hadley, Raymond	1960, '61, '62		Katzman, Jesse	1994
Draper, E. L.	1902		Hailand, Frank	1956, '57, '58		Ketchen, John G.	1999, 2000, '01, '02
Drollinger, Jon	2005, '06, '07, '08		Hale, Clarence	1937		Kimball, Jason	1995
Echols, Holly	1949		Halkin, Daniel	1979		Kingsbury, Franklin L.	1924
Edwards, Robert W.	1937, '38					Kirby, Eugene	1960, '61
						Klausman, Henry	1960, '61, '62

Name	Years	Name	Years	Name	Years
Kobylinski, Brian	1992, '93, '94, '95	McMurchie, Kevin	1980, '81, '82, '83	Posey, Douglas	1962
Koehnemann, Harry E.	1939, '40, '41	Michalek, Matt	2004	Potter, Richard N.	1936, '37
Komm, Joseph	1927	Mierzwa, Fred	1967, '68	Prather, Paul	1935, '37
Komm, Rudolph	1932	Mingle, David	1984, '85, '87, '88	Prochaska, Brad	1971, '72
Koperski, Kevin	1995, '97	Mingle, Michael	1989	Pummer, Adam	2003, '04, '05, '06
Kostick, Andrew	1957	Minicucci, Dominick	1988, '89	Quade, Charles "Chip"	1979, '80
Kowalski, Charles	1992, '93, '94	Minton, Dennis	2015, '16	Rafaloski, Dennis	1971
Kraft, Michael	1980, '81	Mitchell, Jeffrey	1979, '80, '81, '82	Raymond, Edward	1968, '69, '70
Kratz, A. P.	1905	Mizoguchi, Tyler	2009, '10, '11	Reali, Craig	1977, '78, '79, '80
Kring, Charles W.	1931, '32	Mkchyan, Tigran	1985, '86, '87, '88	Redman, Matthew	1994, '95, '96, '97
Kushner, Terry	1969	Moe, Kyle	2010, '11, '12	Redmond, John	1991
Lakes, Charles	1983, '84, '85	Monk, Marvin E.	1937	Reed, Robert	1965, '66
Landon, R. H.	1927, '28	Morf, F. P.	1925	Rehor, Joseph, Jr.	1932, '35
Landry, Jeremiah	1992, '93, '94, '95	Mori, Yoshi	2010, '11, '12, '13	Reiter, E. L.	1928, '29, '30
Lane, Randy	1986, '87, '88	Murchison, R. R.	1905	Ribeiro, Daniel	2008, '09, '10, '11
Lat, Paul	1975, '76, '77, '78	Murray, Robert	1951	Rodriguez, Paul	1980, '81, '82, '83
Lawler, William	1960, '61, '62	Murray, William	1975	Roemer, John	1970, '71, '72
Lechner, Steven	1978, '79, '80, '81	Nagel, Richard	1971, '72	Rogers, Bob	2001, '02
Ledvora, Joseph	1983, '84, '86	Newman, Ben	2002, '03, '04, '05	Rogers, Cameron	2011, '12, '13, '14
Lenke, E. H.	1902	Ngai, Brandon	2015, '16	Rollo, Cook	1966, '67, '68
Levitt, David	1973	Nilsen, P. J.	1914, '15	Romagnoli, Travis	1997, '98, '99, 2000
Lifvendahl, Richard A.	1920	Nishimoto, Eric	1998, '99, 2000, '01	Romero, David	1986, '87, '89, '90
Linder, Raymond	1947, '48, '50	Norwood, E. E.	1923, '24, '25	Rosch, Frank	1980, '81, '82, '83
Lindner, Paul	1987, '88	Oeler, R. C.	1928, '29, '30	Ross, H. A.	1917
Linhart, George	1990, '91	O'Hare, John	1966	Ruggeri, Paul	2008, '09, '10, '12
Linnenburger, Paul	1999, 2000	O'Heron, John	1947	Ruppert, Thomas	1959
Lirot, Daniel	1954, '55, '56	Oka, Leo	1998, '99, 2000	Russo, Anthony	2003,' 04, '05, '06
Liscovitz, Brian	2007, '08, '09, '10	Olson, Carlton	1976, '78, '79, '80	Saavedra, Andres	2007, '08, '09, '10
Luketin, Nate	2009	Oltendorf, Kevin	1981, '82, '83	Sacramento, Anthony	2009, '10, '11, '12
Lundien, Edwin	1950	Orr, R. V.	1914	Sader, Melvin	1935
Lung, Chris	2006, '07, '08, '09	Padera, C. I.	2009, '10, '11, '12	Salemo, Charles	1981
Luyando, David	1984	Padera, Kyle	2009, '10	Salemo, Lloyd	1980
Macedo, Goncalo	1993, '94, '95, '96	Palmer, Richard	1950, '51	Salter, John	1960, '62
Maestas, C. J.	2012, '14, '15	Palmer, William	1964	Samsten, Kari	1981, '82, '83, '84
Maher, Steve	1984, '85	Pangrle, Brian	1981, '82, '83	Sanches, Gilmarcio	1981, '82, '83, '84
Mann, A. S.	1913	Panozzo, Brad	1995, '96, '97, '98	Sanchez, Victor	1964, '65, '66
Margolis, Andrew	2011, '12, '13, '14	Pasek, Roger	2008, '09	Scanlan, John	1983, '84
Marrero, Emilio	1988, '89, '92	Pearlstein, David	1990, '91, '92, '93	Schmeissing, Roy	1961
Marshall, Douglas G.	1937	Peltzer, A.	1927, '30	Schmidt, Michael	1976, '78, '79
Martin, Blake	2016	Perlman, S. L.	1923, '24	Schreier, Marc	1995
Mason, Chad	2011, '12, '13, '14	Peters, Joey	2013, '14, '15	Schroeder, John R.	1967
Matson, George A.	1942	Peterson, David	1981, '82	Schutt, Steve	1973, '74
Mayr, Max	2013, '14, '15, '16	Petritis, Daniel	1990, '91	Schwitzer, G. B.	1922, '23
McCarthy, John	1967, '68, '69	Phillips, Austin	2009, '11, '12, '13	Sepke, Arnold	1968, '69
McDonald, B. A.	1925, '26	Phillips, Oliver J.	1942	Seward, Ed	2002
McFarland, P. E.	1924	Phillips, R. J.	1925	Shapin, Paul	1966, '67, '68
McGlaun, Gregory	1994, '95, '96, '97	Plante, Jonathan	2002	Sharp, John	1949
McGlone, Chris	1996, '97	Pletta, D. H.	1925, '26, '27	Shaw, Harold	1966, '67, '68
McKee, Christopher	1986, '87, '88, '89	Polaski, Kenneth	1964	Shostchuk, Peter	2002
McLellan, Harry	2015, '16	Portocarrero, Maxwell	2011	Sidlinger, Bruce	1951

404

Silcox, Chris	2005, '06, '07, '08
Silhan, William	1964, '66, '67
Silverman, David	1969
Sims, C. E.	1915
Singer, R. B.	1923, '24
Smidl, E.	1917
Smith, Cole	2011, '12, '13, '14
Smith, Taylor	2014, '15, '16
Smurro, Vince	2012, '13
Spelic, Bob	2000,' 01, '02, '03
Sperry, L. B.	1925
Spring, Justin	2003, '04, '05, '06
Spurney, Robert	1975, '76, '77, '78
Stahl, Archie	1922, '23
Stahl, Cecil	1922
Stango, Nick	2006, '07, '09
Stannard, Luke	2007, '08, '09, '10
Stoldt, David	1977, '78, '79, '80
Stone, Kenneth	1954, '55, '56
Stuebe, Louis F.	1921
Stuermer, Raymond J.	1937
Styles, Edward B.	1910, '11, '12
Su, Kenneth	1994, '95
Sullivan, Robert	1951, '52, '53
Swonick, Robert	1970, '71
Taylor, Jonathan	2002
Temple, Harry	1934
Thompson, M.	1928
Thompson, Ross	2016
Ticknor, Anthony	1985, '86
Tilsley, Jake	2013, '14, '15
Tolmie, T. W.	1917
Tonry, Donald	1956, '57, '59
Torres, Nathan	2000, '01, '02
Torres, Ricardo	1933, '34
Trabert, M. L.	1935
Trujillo, Oscar	1994
Tucker, Brandon	1996, '97, '98
Tucker, Joel	1986, '87, '88, '89
Turnbull, Jeffrey	1993
Uster, Eric	2015
Valdez, Jordan	2011, '12, '14, '15
Valentino, John	1974
VanEtten, Gary	1971
Varga, Alex	2011, '12, '13, '14
Vernon, Marion	2016
Von Ebers, Donald	1947, '48, '49
Wagner, Wayne	1963, '64, '65
Wagstaff, C. D.	1917
Wakerlin, Warren	1961, '62, '63
Walters, Michael W.	1956, '57, '58

Warga, F. J.	1928, '29, '30
Wasik, Jon	1994, '95
Wayman, Leonard	1934, '35
Weber, Charles	1965, '66, '67
Weintraub, Edward	1964
Weirsema, H. A.	1913
Weiss, Raymond	1938, '39, '40
Wetterling, Scott	2001, '02, '03, '04
Whipple, G. B.	1928
White, Matthew	1992, '93, '94
Whitney, E. M.	1935
Wiest, Chad	2007, '08, '09, '10
Williamson, Tyler	2007, '08, '09, '10
Wills, Eric	1998, '99, 2000
Wilner, Mike	2012, '13, '14, '15
Wilson, Josh	2012, '13
Wolochuk, Lee	1988, '90, '91
Wolochuk, Mark	1990, '91
Yahiro, Mark	1978
Yamauchi, Tyler	2005, '06, '07, '08
Yasukawa, Steven	1974, '76, '77, '78
Yeaton, F. D.	1905
Yi, Theodore	1977, '78
Zak, Kyle	1996, '97, '98, '99
Zander, Anthony	1975, '76, '77
Zavell, Howard	1986, '88, '89
Zeddies, David	1986, '87, '88, '89
Ziegler, A. W.	1920, '21
Zinzi, Vito	1947, '48
Zitzewitz, A. F.	1924
Zitzler, Earl	1931, '32
Zopf, William	1992
Zunich, Andreja "Butch"	1977, '78, '79, '80

WOMEN'S GYMNASTICS

Adams, Susan	1988, '89, '90, '91
Althans, Tracey	1993, '94, '95, '96
Amico, Mary	1981
Ashton, Becky	1996, '97, '98, '99
Baffes, Kathy	1978, '79, '80
Bagel, Jean	1976
Barrett, Jennifer	2000
Barrow, Christine	1984
Bathke, Kimberly	1991, '92, '93, '94
Bedrosian, Tammy	1977
Berg, Allison	2000, '01, '02
Berres, Kim	1996, '97, '98, '99
Botterman, Danye	2004, '05, '06, '07
Botterman, Marijka	2006, '07, '08, '09
Brems, Karen	1981, '82, '83, '84

Buchanan, Erin	2014, '15, '16
Buckley, Allison	2008, '09, '10, '11
Buranich, Michelle	2000, '01, '02, '03
Carmicheal, Patty	1977
Carr, Bridget	1980, '81, '82
Castle, Jennifer	1978
Charpentier, Mary	1978, '79, '80, '81
Ciccarelli, Nicki	1994, '95, '96, '97
Ciccarelli, Tracey	1996, '97
Clisham, Mary Beth	1991, '92, '93, '94
Cole, Jessica	2003, '04, '05
Collias, Emily	1984, '85, '86
Corso, Kara	1990, '91, '92, '93
Cowart, Nicole	2007, '08, '09, '10
Crall, Julie	2006, '07, '08, '09
Cuppy, Becca	2016
Danke, Cheryl	1985
Dann, Margaret	2002, '03, '04, '05
Delact, Joan	1977
Devers, Lynn	1988, '89, '90, '91
Dixon, Phaedra	1998, '99, 2000, '01
Donovan, Rachael	2016
Dorwart, Melanie	1996, '97, '98, '99
Drummond, Becky	1994
Dumich, Sara	2003, '04, '05
Durdil, Jennifer	1989, '90, '92
Earle, Emily	2003, '04, '05, '06
Eberle, Mimi	1980
Eberly, Kelsi	2012, '13, '14, '15
Ericson, Carissa	1998, '99, 2000, '01
Farrar, Kelli	1995, '96, '97, '98
Fernandez, Carmella	1997, '98, '99, 2000
Fernandez, Melissa	2008, '09, '10, '11
Fiedler, Sarah	2011, '12, '13, '14
Fleischmann, Gayle	1977, '78, '79, '80
Foley, Heather	2013, '14, '15, '16
Forsthoefel, Natalie	1993, '94, '95, '96
Fujinami, Tori	2013
Gaa, Becky	1990, '91, '92, '93
Gallagher, Jana	2000, '01, '02, '03
Gardner, Laura	1978
Garrity, Allison	1984, '85, '86, '87
Gill, Elise	2011, '12
Givens, Jordyn	2015, '16
Greathouse, Teresa	1975, '76
Gruss, Gena	1997, '98, '99, 2000
Hamilton, Gail	1989
Hawley, Karen	2000, '01, '02, '03
Helmke, Heidi	1981, '82, '83, '84
Hicks, Laura	1985, '86
Hogan, Kelly	1994, '95, '96, '97

Horth, Mary Jane	2014, '15, '16
Howell, Lisa	1979
Hutcherson, Julia	2016
Hyatt, Macy	2010, '11, '12
Joannides, Kelsey	2009, '10, '11, '12
Johnson, Gaye	1978, '79, '80
Kalal, Randy	1975
Kanchanavaleerat, Suren	2015
Kantecki, Jaclyn	2010, '11, '12, '13
Kapernekas, Kara	2002, '03, '04, '05
Karubas, Kari	1994, '95, '96, '97
Kato, Sunny	2013, '14, '15, '16
Kaufman, Amanda	2000, '01, '02, '03
Kirzow, Kim	2004
Knutson, Laura	1987, '88, '89, '90
Kontur, Tracy	1987, '88, '89, '90
Kruk, Kim	2006, '07, '08, '09
Lacki, Michelle	1998
Lamborn, Denise	1987, '88, '90
LaPlante, Liz	1978
LeDuc, Lizzy	2016
Lennon, Emily	2014
Lunquist, Debra	1977
Lyons, Sarah	2015, '16
Maart, Michelle	1985, '86, '87, '88
MacAdams, Maggie	1976, '77, '78
Matiya, Joellyn	1980, '81, '82
McGee, Cindy	1983
McGrady, Michelle	2005, '06, '07, '08
McNabb, Elizabeth	2012, '13, '14
Melcarek, Krystal	2005, '06, '07, '08
Mesik, Michelle	2000, '01, '02
Montero, Kristin	1995, '97, '98
Montgomery, Lisa	1982
Moore, Cindy	1982, '83
Moradi, Mina	1999, '01, '02
Morris, Lashlee	2008, '09, '10
Murin, Laura	1981
Naleway, Jordan	2012, '13, '14, '15
Neilson, Dotty	1983
Newcomb, Lauren	2002, '03, '04, '05
Nguyen, Brielle	2016
Numrych, Charlene	1981, '82, '83, '84
O'Connor, Giana	2013, '14, '15, '16
Orozco, Ursula	2007
Osowski, Jan	1979, '80, '81
Pedregal, Marianne	1984, '85, '86, '87
Pellegrinetti, Lisa	1998, '99, 2000, '01
Perino, Samantha	2008, '10, '11
Peterson, Anne	1978, '79, '80

Peterson, Karla	1992, '93, '95
Pollack, Allyson	1981, '82
Polz, Laura	1990, '91, '92
Pomeroy, Cara	2004, '05, '06, '07
Pontious, Joyce	1978, '79, '80, '81
Powers, Terri	1978, '79, '80
Pullman, Peggy	1990, '92
Rechenmacher, Jayne	1978, '79, '80, '81
Rechenmacher, Jill	1986
Redmond, Stacy	1995, '96
Reid, Connie	1983
Roberts, Luann	1983, '84, '85, '86
Robinson, Deborah	1975
Roe, Haylee	2016
Rosenwinkel, Pam	1975
Roska, Sarah	1976
Rossetto, Karen	1989, '90, '91
Rudnicki, Patsy	1982, '83, '84, '85
Ruf, Michelle	1985, '86, '87, '88
Ruffolo, Laura	2002
Salinas, Maria	1975, '76
Schmidt, Sarah	2007, '08, '09, '10
See, Amber	2011, '12, '13, '14
Segers, Alicia	1976
Semeniuk, Tanya	1993
Sheppard, Sarah	1978, '79, '80
Shively, Debbie	1987, '88
Simpson, Faith	1991
Singalewitch, Heather	1987, '88, '89, '90
Singer, Melissa	2004, '05, '06, '07
Slomski, Dina	1992, '94, '95
Smith, Karen	1975
Smith, Lindsey	2006, '07, '08, '09
Smith, Shari	1988, '89
Sullivan, Kelcey	1991
Tex, Cathy	1975
Thies, Nancy	1976, '77
Travis, Lee	1975, '77
Viernes, Nicole	1994, '95, '96, '97
Ward, Nicole	1992, '93, '94, '95
Wasserman, Sarah	1991, '92
Weber, Cynthia	1975, '76, '77, '78
Webster, Julie	1980
Weinstein, Alina	2010, '11, '12, '13
Welker, Hannah	2010, '12
Wiechmann, Gina	1998, '99, 2000, '01
Wild, Katie	2003, '04, '05, '06
Williams, Ashley	2002, '03, '04, '05
Woolf, Laura	2008, '09
Wurtzel, Melissa	1997
Yonezuka, Natacha	1984, '85

ICE HOCKEY

Austin, Roswell M., Jr.	1943
Babbitt, Richard K.	1939
Balestri, George L.	1942, '43
Beaumont, James D.	1939
Benson, Herschel G.	1942, '43
Bessone, Amo	1941, '42, '43
Carlson, Edward H.	1939
Coupe, Henry J., Jr.	1943
Fee, Richard M.	1939
Ferranti, Louis	1942
Fieldhouse, George, Jr.	1939, '40
Gannon, Joseph F.	1941
Gillan, John H.	1940, '41, '42
Jaworek, Thomas E.	1939, '40, '41
Karakas, Thomas J.	1943
Kaufmann, Eugene H.	1939
Killen, Ray T.	1941, '42
Kopel, Howard F.	1940, '41
Lotzer, Joseph J.	1940, '41, '42
McCune, Clinton C.	1941, '42
McKibbin, Wayne J.	1940, '41
Mettler, Charles W.	1940
Miller, Robert F.	1942
Owen, Starr H.	1941
Palazzari, Aldo	1941, '42
Prentiss, William L.	1943
Priestley, Gilbert P.	1941
Priestley, Russell T.	1942
Rolle, Glenn L.	1943
Sigerson, Charles W.	1939
Slater, C. Paul	1940
Sterle, Norbert J.	1941
Stewart, Charles M.	1940
Thompson, Maurice P.	1939, '40
Twitchell, Thomas H.	1942, '43
Welsh, Alex	1939
White, John M.	1939, '40
Ziemba, Chester J.	1939, '40, '41

POLO

Alyea, Lou	1934
Anger, Edward	1934
Bauer, Gene	1936, '37, '38
Croninger, Carl	1939
Cunningham, Thomas	1941
Douglas, Art	1935
Durfee, Ted	1934
Ely, Graham	1941

Garrett, Frank	1938, '39
Gordon, Michael J.	1935, '36
Harris, Bryan	1941
Jaeger, Robert O.	1939, '40, '41
Johnson, Robert	1936, '37, '38
Kovacic, Ivan	1934, '35
Lord, Chester	1941
Martin, James	1939, '40
McCrackin, Robert	1941
Mercer, Frank	1934, '35
Peritz, Ray	1940, '41
Rodgers, Lee	1936, '38
Schaefer, Frank J.	1937, '38, '39, '40
Teeman, Hall	1934, '35
Walker, John	1939
Wood, Harlington	1941
Wright, Frederick W.	1935, '36, '37, '38

MEN'S SOCCER

Ader, Richard F.	1930, '31, '32
Anderson, Wilbur H.	1932, '33
Arkema, Edward L. S.	1927
Bert, Vernon J., Jr.	1931
Borri, Robert P.	1934
Byman, Ellis	1928
Cassell, Charles W.	1927
Chamy, Luis F.	1927, '28
Chen, Yu Hwa	1927
Cohn, P. E.	1933
Contratto, James	1930
Ehnborn, Gustave B.	1927, '28, '29
Fearey, Hiram D.	1928
Fencl, George S.	1929, '30, '31
Floreth, John	1928, '29
Florio, A. E.	1933
Forsberg, Vernon A.	1932
Gasparich, Stephen J.	1928
Granata, William J.	1927
Hagen, Jack L.	1927
Hastings, Douglas A., Jr.	1929, '30, '31
Hayes, Edwin R.	1931, '32, '33
Higgins, John Norris	1927
Hodge, John R.	1932
Hult, Bernard E.	1930, '31
Hult, Richard E.	1930, '31
Jackson, Robert V., Jr.	1933
Kamin, Burt	1929
Kautt, Elmer C.	1927
Keys, John J.	1927
Kott, John H.	1930, '31, '32

Krakower, Irving	1929
Kwint, Joseph A.	1931
Levine, Julius	1932
Lewin, Maxwell M.	1928, '29
Lindall, Fred H.	1932
Locke, Seward C.	1932
MacLean, William P.	1934
McFadzean, John	1927, '28, '29
McMahon, John E.	1933, '34
Mink, Ely H.	1930, '31, '32
Morse, Roger W.	1931, '33
Patterson, James A.	1927, '28
Pflager, Miller S.	1933, '34
Piano, Louis J.	1930, '31, '32
Pinsley, H. H.	1929
Priddle, George H.	1932, '33
Radebaugh, Gus H.	1934
Reston, James B. "Scotty", Jr.	1929, '30, '31
Reynolds, Thomas E.	1928, '29
Rumana, Henry	1932, '33
Schachtman, Milton R.	1932, '33, '34
Siegal, Irving J.	1927
Simon, Frank	1928
Smith, Warren H.	1934
Strzepek, Alfred W.	1933
Vlach, William P.	1934
Walter, George	1929, '30
Willig, Joseph H.	1932
Wilson, A. Gordon	1931
Wright, Noel N.	1927
Young, Aitken F.	1928, '29, '30
Zbornik, Joseph J.	1932

WOMEN'S SOCCER

Aberle, Sarah	1997, '98, 2000
Abu-Douleh, Alia	2014
Alcia, Leisha	2001, '02, '03, '04
Alvis, Jamie	2005, '07, '08
Anderson, Sarah	2000
Baldwin, Lisa	1998, '99
Bayne, Jessica	2003, '04, '05, '06
Bell, Courtney	2006, '07, '08, '09
Bergschneider, Kristin	1997
Bessette, Amy	1997, '98, '99
Breece, Nicole	2012, '13, '14
Brown, Emily	1998, '99, 2000
Brown, Kassidy	2010, '11, '12, '13
Brown, Molly	1998
Brown, Sarah	2003, '04

Buszkiewicz, Kelly	1997, '98, '99
Campbell, Kelly	2002, '03, '04, '05
Carosio, Jenna	2008, '09, '10, '11
Carstens, Lindsey	2005, '06, '07
Conine, Casey	2013, '14
Cooke, Charlotte	2005, '07, '08
D'Addario, Hope	2013, '14
Denenberg, Nicole	2010, '11, '12
Desjarlais, Marti	2005, '06, '07, '08
DiBernardo, Vanessa	2010, '11, '12, '13
Doetzel, Kim	1998, '99
Dombart, Caitlin	2009, '10, '11
Elinsky, Abby	2014
Ewing, Julie	2008, '09, '10, '11
Faherty, Paula	2002, '03, '04, '06
Farrell, Christina	2010, '11, '12, '13
Feher, Amy	2012, '13, '14
Flaws, Jannelle	2011, '13, '14
Frank, Rachel	2005
Freeman, Laura	1999, 2000, '01
Fogelson, Kim	1997
Garrett, Brittany	2006, '07, '08, '09
Gierman, Kristen	2012, '13
Gordon, Ashley	1997
Gostisha, Kara	2004, '05, '06, '07
Green, Julie	1997
Green, Megan	2013, '14
Guerra, Jackie	2011
Gunville, Alaree	2001, '02, '04
Heggen, Sarah	1998, '99
Hennes, Annemarie	2000
Hilbrands, Jordan	2007, '08, '09, '10
Hodson, Sue	1999, 2000
Holden, Marissa	2010, '11, '12
Holman, Kristen	1998, '99, 2000
Holtzman, Heidi	1998, '99, 2000, '01
Hurless, Tara	2001, '02, '03, '04
Johnson, Lindsay	1998, '99, 2000, '01
Johnson, Rebecca (Patrick)	1998, 2000, '01, '02
Johnston, Meegan	2013
Joyce, Colleen	2000, '01
Kann, Missy	1997
Kapicka, Alexandra	2007, '08, '09, '10
Karniski, Christen	2002, '03, '04, '05
Karniski, Natasha	2002, '03, '04, '05
Keeler. Missy	1998
Kellett, Maggie	2000, '01
Kenney, Robyn	1998
Knutson, Laura	2007, '08, '09, '10
Kolze, Meghan	1999, 2000, '02, '03

Kot, Danielle	2007, '08, '09, '10
Lantz, Laura	1997, '98, '99
Leary, Noelle	2013, '14
Levitt, Jessica	2006, '07, '08
Liang, Debbie	1998
Loechl, Erica	1997
Marbury, Kara	2014
Masar, Ella	2004, '05, '06, '07
McDonnell, Mary Therese	2004, '05, '06, '07
McDonnell, Shannon	2006, '07
Medellin, Anastasia	2013
Miller, Jenna	2014
Miller, Krystin	2008, '09, '10
Mitchell, Sarah	1997
Mutz, Shayla	2009, '10, '11, '12
Mykines, Marissa	2008, '09, '10, '11
Nadeau, Heather	1999
Nitsche, Mary	2002
Nweke, Chichi	2006, '07, '08, '09
Osoba, Allie	2012, '13
Osoba, Emily	2014
Panozzo, Steph	2011, '12
Parkin, Lauren	2013
Pawloski, Megan	2010, '11, '12, '13
Peterson, Taylore	2012, '13
Pouse, Stephanie	2011
Pyter, Leah	1997
Ratz, Katherine	2014
Read, Niki	2009, '10, '11, '12
Redmond, Laura	2002, '03, '04, '05
Reynolds, Quinn	2003, '06
Ridgeway, Andrea	2001, '02, '03, '04
Robishaw, Reagan	2012, '13, '14
Rowland, Sarah	1999, 2000, '01
Sahly, Christina	2008, '09
Santacaterina, Jackie	2006, '07, '08, '09
Schueller, Julie	1997, '98, '99, 2000
Schuling, Tara	1999, 2000, '01, '02
Schurr, Hollie	1999, 2000, '01, '02
Sinak, Christine	2001, '02, '03, '04
Sinisalo, Elina	1997
Smith, Jennifer	2000, '01, '03
Smith, Rachel	1997
Smith, Tailor	2012
Steigerwald, Cory	2007, '08, '09
Steinhoff, Stephanne	1997, '98, '99
Strickland, Eva	2003, '04, '05, '06
Stucky, Allison	2013, '14
Taccona, Leanne	1997
Twyning, Kris	1997, '98
Tyler, Erin	2002
Tyler, Katie	1997
Walker, Kelly	2000, '01, '02, '03
Walker, Tiffani	2000, '01, '02, '03
Ward, Brittany	2003, '04
Ward, Emily	2001
Warren, Sarah	2014
Weeks, Kristy	2005, '06, '07
Weykamp, Aliina	2012, '13, '14
Wheatley, Claire	2013, '14
Zurrer, Emily	2005, '06, '07, '08

SOFTBALL

Abello, Stephanie	2016
Acosta, Sam	2015, '16
Adishian, Jamie	2009
Almanza, Pam	2000
Armstrong, Lana	2006, '07, '08, '09
Arnold, Shelese	2012, '13, '14, '15
Balicki, Julie	2002, '03, '04, '05
Bauch, Allie	2013, '14, '15, '16
Baumgartner, Sarah	2001, '02, '03, '04
Behrens, Bailey	2007, '08, '09, '10
Bird, Karyn	2001
Black, Heather	2000
Booker, Alex	2011, '12, '13, '14
Bradarich, Erin	2010, '11
Bradley, Jami	2002, '03, '04
Bradley, Katie	2003
Brocker, Mari Anne	2000
Brodner, Emily	2015, '16
Brown, Vicky	2007, '08
Bryers, Sarah	2006, '07, '08
Burchill, Christine	2002
Butcher, LeeAnn	2002, '03, '04, '05
Buzard, Brooke	2007, '08, '09
Call, Taylor	2008, '09
Cannizzo, Laura	2000
Carrillo, Alexis	2016
Castellanos, Vivi	2011
Ceisel, Jessica	2000
Christensen, Kelly	2000
Christopoulos, Christine	2007, '08, '09
Colantuono, Kim	2000
Conrad, Ashley	2008, '09, '10, '11
Coonce, Kacey	2006
Coriddi, Rachelle	2003, '04, '05, '06
Creydt, Lindsey	2000
Cuevas, Stephanie	2010, '11, '12, '13
Davis, Jessica	2010, '11, '12, '13
Davis, Nickie	2000
Detrick, Linnea	2009, '10, '13
DeVreese, Claire	2005, '06, '07, '08
Diekemper, Jackelyn	2003, '04, '05
Diller, Shanna	2005, '06, '07, '08
Edwards, Taylor	2016
Estill, Sami	2013
Evans, Nicole	2014, '15, '16
Evans, Reed	2000
Farina, Leigh	2005
Farina, Leigh	2015, '16
Fleming, Annie	2015, '16
Floyd, Jenny	2000
Fortune, Amanda	2001, '02, '03, '04
Gaitros, Katie	2005, '06, '07, '08
Gallagher, Katie	2015, '16
Gallien, Audrey	2008, '09, '10, '11
Gardner, Angie	2000
Gavoni, Gabe	2009, '10
Gay, Pepper	2010, '11, '12, '13
Giddens, Kate	2015, '16
Gronski, Lauren	2001, '02, '03, '04
Gunther, Alyssa	2014, '15, '16
Guy, Jackie	2010, '11, '12, '13
Hackett, Meredith	2009, '10, '11, '12
Hall, Jenna	2003, '04, '05, '06
Hamma, Lindsey	2001, '02, '03, '04
Hammel, Alicia	2001, '02
Hardwick, Abby	2000
Hofert, Kim	2000
Hooegeveen, Courtney	2006
Howell, Hope	2007, '08, '09, '10
Hubbard, Kim	2000
Huitink, Megan	2004
Johnson, Kylie	2013, '14, '15, '16
Jones, Erin	2001, '02, '03, '04
Jones, Jean	2000
Koester, Brittany	2004, '05, '06
Lawhead, Molly	2004, '05, '06
Lesemann, Kelly	2003
Linares, Nicole	2010
Lindgren, Shannon	2001
Lisy, Sydney	2006
Lockett, Keri	2002
Loies, Lauren	2012
Lovejoy, Abby	2002
Lowry, Chris	2000
Lutes, Katie	2009, '10
Manley, Betty	2000
Martin, Kisten	2004, '05, '06

Mexicano, Angelena	2005, '06, '07, '08	Williams, Taylor	2012	Borman, Michael	1974
Miller, Mary	2004, '05	Wonderly, Breanna	2015, '16	Borst, G. E.	1925
Montgomery, Erin	2001, '02, '03, '04	Wright, Ashley	2007, '08, '09, '10	Boston, Bill	1962
Most, Amanda	2004	Zobrist, Laura	2003, '04, '05, '06	Bouchard, Mike	1956, '59, '60
Mychko, Jenna	2011, '12, '13, '14	Zymkowitz, Danielle	2008, '09, '10, '11	Bowen, C. L.	1922, '23
Needham, Brandi	2014			Boyce, Chuck	1965, '67
Nevard, Kathryn	2001	**MEN'S SWIMMING**		Branca, Tom	1963, '64, '65
Nicklas, Jill	2015, '16	Ackerman, Owen	1957, '58, '59	Branch, Robert	1948, '49, '50
O'Connell, Katie	2001, '02, '03, '04	Ahlem, Ted	1975, '76	Brandt, Todd	1982, '83, '84
Pasquesi, Gina	2000	Albecker, Walter	1980	Brekke, William C.	1941, '42, '43
Perez, Remeny	2013, '14, '15, '16	Alcorn, Stanley W.	1937, '39	Brennan, William	1975
Perkins, Jess	2012, '13, '14, '15	Alderson, E. W.	1920	Brinck, Per Ake	1983
Perry, Monica	2009, '10	Allen, Robert	1987, '88, '89	Brock, J.	1931, '32, '33
Pieruccini, Hailey	2015, '16	Anderson, Bob	1968, '69, '70	Brooks, H. M.	1908
Pinchback, Hollie	2008, '09, '10, '11	Anderson, Daniel C.	1941, '42	Brouk, John J.	1937
Planinsek, Elene	2002, '03, '04, '05	Anderson, Darryl	1966	Brown, James M.	1941, '42, '43
Pluta, Bridget	2002, '03	Anderson, H. B.	1910	Bulaw, Adolph	1935
Powaga, Jenny	2000	Anderson, John V.	1938	Burton, Gary	1961, '62, '63
Prather, Denise	2006	Anderson, Richard	1966, '67, '68	Cady, G. H.	1930
Ramey, Becca	2008	Anderson, Richard F.	1941	Cajet, Arnold	1954, '55, '56
Repole, Katie	2013, '14	Anderson, Tom	1972	Carey, Robert	1955, '56
Rivera, Ruby	2014, '15, '16	Andrew, Philip	1989	Carnes, Brian	1978
Ross, Katrina	2006, '07, '08, '09	Andrews, L. E.	1917	Carpenter, Lee	1968, '69, '70
Roytek, Paige	2015	Arrison, Kevin	1985	Carpenter, Tom	1972, '73, '74
Ruelius, Veronica	2016	Ash, Homer	1950, '51	Carstensen, Bob	1988, '89, '90, '91
Rymer, Annie	2000	Bachman, Bob	1965, '66, '67	Cary, M. C.	1920
Sanchez, Brittany	2012, '13, '14, '15	Banks, Daniel	1982, '83, '85	Castator, Alan	1965, '66, '67
Sartini, Janna	2001, '02, '03	Barber, Thomas	1946	Castles, Bryan	1980, '83
Sauter, Kristie	2001, '02	Barnes, David	1974, '75, '76, '77	Chadsey, C. P.	1923, '24, '25
Schaeffer, Lori	2000	Barnett, James	1983, '84, '85, '86	Chaney, Dennis	1971
Schkade, Jamie	2012, '13	Barry, G. W.	1929	Chapman, E. N.	1915
Schnake, Kristin	2006	Bartholomew, F. G.	1930, '31, '32	Chapman, John	1963, '64
Simpson, Nikki	2009, '10, '11, '12	Bates, Pete	1965, '66, '67	Chase, Dean	1912
Smith, Jade	2013	Bates, Rob	1991	Chiappe, David	1982, '83, '84
Smith, Makenzie	2005, '06, '07, '08	Baughter, George	1947	Christ, G. P.	1920
Starinieri, Amy	2007, '08	Beaumont, G. S.	1912, '13, '14	Christensen, Gary	1970
Sullivan, Dana	2013, '14	Beebe, H. K.	1923	Clemons, Robert	1952, '53, '54
Tanner, Lindsey	2001, '02	Beebe, W. E.	1920, '22	Clooney, Donald	1949, '50, '51
Tarnawa, Laura	2011	Bell, Brian	1992	Collora, N. A.	1928
Taylor, Sherri	2001, '02, '03, '04	Benner, Jeffery	1981	Colwell, Gary	1978
Thomas, Carly	2015, '16	Berry, Mark	1981, '82	Condon, V. H.	1922, '23
Tobon, Nicole	2013, '14, '15, '16	Bezella, Bruce	1990, '91	Congreve, George	1973, '74, '75, '76
Trezzo, Danielle	2013, '14, '15, '16	Bigger, Hamilton	1946	Conrad, Joseph A.	1941
Vaji, Danielle	2008, '09, '10, '11, '12	Bihl, Pete	1977	Cook, Ed	1964
		Bishop, David	1978, '79	Copeland, J. R.	1925
Vecvanags, Jade	2014, '15, '16	Blackman, E. O.	1926	Cortis, R. P.	1923
Watson, Megan	2001	Blankley, W. H.	1926, '27	Cramer, Curt	1968, '69, '70
Wedel, Kelley	2009, '10, '11, '12	Block, F. L.	1930	Crane, D. W.	1916
Wheeler, Paige	2000	Bockman, Ted	1950	Crosby, F. H.	1934
White, Anitra	2000	Boedicker, Charles	1978, '79, '80, '81	Cryer, Walter	1951, '52
Williams, DeAnna	2000	Boor, Alden K.	1941, '42	Cutter, Robert L.	1937

410

Cutter, W. C.	1910	
Davey, Tim	1992	
DeBord, Jim	1967, '68, '69	
Dennett, Kenneth	1920, '21	
Denzler, Mike	1988	
Deuss, E.	1927, '28	
Diamantos, Tony	1974, '75	
Dillman, Greg	1988, '89	
Dixon, Terence	1983, '84, '85, '86	
Dollins, Matthew	1989	
Donohue, John	1958, '59, '60	
Dooley, Dick	1961, '62, '63	
Dowd, Donald	1955, '56	
Drake, Greg	1988, '89, '90, '91	
Driemeyer, Dan	1971	
Driscoll, John	1944	
Druz, Dave	1972, '74, '75	
Dupon, Norm	1962	
Dvorak, R. F.	1921	
Eberhardy, Richard	1957, '58, '59, '60	
Ekstrom, Lee	1969	
Eldredge, L. E.	1924, '25	
Ellis, Elias L.	1937, '38	
Engstrom, DeWayne	1980	
Enochs, C. H.	1928, '29	
Erickson, Keith	1984, '85	
Erwin, John R.	1936	
Essick, Raymond	1955	
Essick, Raymond	1978, '79, '80, '81	
Etzbach, W. H.	1930	
Faircloth, S. E.	1917, '20	
Falkenberg, G. V.	1920	
Fieldhouse, Jim	1970, '71, '72, '73	
Fifield, C. W.	1916	
Fisher, F. L.	1925, '26, '27	
Fix, John	1957, '58, '59	
Flachmann, Charles O.	1933, '34, '35	
Flachmann, John M.	1941	
Flanders, J. A.	1909	
Fletemeyer, Richard	1957, '59, '60	
Florio, Dave	1965, '66, '67	
Folts, Thomas	1980, '81, '82, '83	
Fornof, John	1961	
Forsythe, William	1957	
Foster, Bruce	1969	
Fox, A. L.	1922, '23	
Franks, Mark	1992	
Frazier, Ernest	1945	
Fulling, B. C.	1927	
Funk, Mark	1981, '82	
Gale, E. O.	1922	
Garland, John	1955, '56, '57	
Gaynor, Allen	1974, '75	
Gaynor, Duffy	1972, '73	
Gelwicks, Greg	1988, '89	
Gerometta, Robert	1947, '48	
Gfroerer, George	1952, '53, '54, '55	
Gill, Richard J.	1942	
Givot, Michael	1985, '86, '87, '88	
Gordon, N.	1931	
Gore, Stanley A.	1944	
Gossett, J. E.	1910, '11	
Gould, P. N.	1917	
Gray, J. M.	1917	
Green, Lonsdale	1910, '11, '12	
Green, Ralph	1913, '14	
Grey, N. E.	1916	
Grider, Chris	1987	
Griffin, J. M.	1913, '14, '15	
Grimmer, Mike	1974, '75, '76, '77	
Groh, Harold	1927, '28, '29	
Grossman, Jake	1954, '55, '56	
Gruben, Peter	1987, '89, '90, '91	
Gruenberg, A. A.	1924	
Gruenfeld, Julius J.	1943	
Guerrera, Chris	1987, '88, '89	
Gwin, Greg	1962, '63, '64	
Haig, Thomas	1981, '82	
Hallden, John T.	1937	
Hallerud, Dean	1959	
Hammel, Jeff	1975, '76	
Hansen, David	1955, '56	
Hansen, Henry F.	1935, '36	
Hanson, Eric	1983	
Hardacre, G. K.	1922	
Harmeson, Terry	1969	
Harrold, Norman M.	1942	
Hartman, Leo P.	1940, '41, '42	
Hatfield, Doug	1969	
Haulenbeck, John	1945, '46	
Haymaker, Chris	1989	
Hays, Bill	1964	
Hegeler, Edward	1944	
Helwig, Kent	1981, '82, '83, '84	
Henry, C. D.	1911	
Hewitt, F. E.	1932, '33, '34	
Hickey, James J.	1935	
Hill, Arthur	1982, '84, '85, '86	
Hines, N. W.	1932, '33	
Hoffman, Dennis	1960, '61	
Holbrook, F. W.	1928, '29, '30	
Holbrook, Jim	1962, '63, '64	
Holquist, Henry J.	1939, '40, '41	
Hopwood, Milton T.	1937, '38, '39	
Houcek, Richard	1946, '47	
Huebner, Louis H.	1944	
Hunsaker, Joe	1957, '58, '59	
Hunt, Robert	1956, '57, '58	
Huyler, Joe	1959, '60, '61, '62	
Jager, William	1979, '80, '81	
Janota, Neil	1972, '73, '74, '75	
Jansen, Earl	1934	
Jensen, George	1947	
Johns, D. C.	1916, '17	
Johnson, H. M.	1925	
Johnson, Harlan	1946	
Johnson, Roy	1946	
Jones, Benton	1950, '51, '52	
Jones, Billy M.	1938, '39, '40	
Jones, John C.	1934	
Jones, Reese	1989, '90, '91	
Jones, Steven	1982, '83, '84	
Jurgens, Carl	1971	
Karafotas, Phil	1962, '63, '64	
Karpinchik, Nick	1954, '57	
Keenan, Donald	1955, '56	
Keinlen, Tom	1963, '64	
Kelley, Bill	1991, '92	
Kennesey, George	1992	
Kerr, John K.	1943	
Kesler, Robert	1948, '49	
Keswick, Bruce	1970, '71, '72, '73	
Kieding, Ray	1928, '29, '30	
Kienlen, Donald L.	1939, '40, '41	
Kireilis, Raymond W.	1939, '41	
Kirkland, Alfred Y.	1939, '40, '41	
Kjellstrom, Theodore	1952	
Klapperich, Andrew	1979, '80, '81, '82	
Klingel, Martin	1961, '63	
Kneesi, C. W.	1927	
Konstant, Anthony	1945, '46	
Kosakiewicz, Anthony	1945	
Kostick, Eugene	1958	
Kozlowski, Aaron	1990, '91	
Kracen, Scott	1968, '69	
Kral, Ed	1961, '62, '63	
Kramp, Robert	1952, '53, '54	
Kratz, Paul	1950	
Kuhlman, Erich	1991, '92	
Kunde, Mark	1988	
Kurlak, Peter	1939, '40, '41	

Name	Years
Kuypers, Bob	1974, '75
Lakin, J. C.	1931
Lamb, F. W.	1925, '26
Lane, Thomas	1948
Larsen, Eric M.	1934, '35
Larson, Donald	1955, '56, '57
Lary, Brad	1947
Layne, Allen	1991, '92
Lehman, Fred	1951, '52
Lehmkuhl, Richard	1981
Lentz, Jac	1938
Levin, M.	1924
Levine, Bob	1968, '69, '70
Lewis, Norman B.	1936, '37
Lewis, Tom I.	1942
Lichter, J. P.	1913
Linden, O. W.	1921
Lively, Thomas G.	1938
Loar, Ned	1955, '56, '57
Lockwood, W. W.	1930
Lopater, Dave	1971
Lovin, Christopher	1983, '84, '85, '86
Lowe, George A.	1937, '38, '39
Lubeck, Chris	1988, '89, '90, '91
MacDonald, Rod	1972, '73, '74, '75
Mackie, Chris	1986, '87
Mackin, James	1987, '88, '89
Madsen, Harry	1950, '51
Maier, John	1977, '78
Makielski, Ward	1988
Malmberg, Kenneth	1985, '86, '87, '88
Maloney, Russ	1990, '91, '92
Mann, William E.	1944, '45, '46
Marine, Gar	1966
Marshall, John	1930
Marten, Brad	1968, '69, '70
Mathieu, Bud	1976, '77, '78
Matthei, L. P.	1931
Mauck, Eugene H.	1936
Mautner, Henry	1947
Mayer, S. R.	1924
McCarthy, Terence	1983, '84, '85
McConnell, Douglas	1976, '77, '78, '79
McDonald, A. P	1914, '16
McDyer, Dale	1958, '59
McFarland, P. E.	1924
McGufficke, Graeme	1983, '85, '86, '87
McKinley, Robert O.	1940, '41
McLarty, Brandon	1992
McNally, Andrew	1920, '21
McNamara, Brian	1991, '92
McPheron, Ron	1984
McVey, Andrew	1987, '88, '89
Meeland, Tor	1942, '43
Melnicove, Gary	1962, '63
Mersbach, David	1953, '54
Metcalf, Doug	1975
Meyer, Russ	1973, '74, '75, '76
Michelson, Larry	1960
Middleton, James R.	1942
Milani, Anthony	1980
Miller, Robert	1955, '56, '57
Mix, M. I.	1912
Moench, R. G.	1931
Moore, Christopher	1982
Moore, Henry H.	1944, '45
Moore, Merrill D.	1945
Moore, Tom	1991, '92
Morley, George	1964
Moskiewicz, John	1954
Mottern, H. M.	1913
Mueller, William	1983, '84, '85, '86
Mullins, George	1947, '48, '49
Mulloy, Chris	1991, '92
Munro, Dan	1983, '84, '85
Musch, Tom	1969, '70
Nedrud, Brad	1973, '74, '75
Nelson, John	1988, '89
Nevels, Charles	1944
Newell, Bruce	1964, '65
Neylon, Brian	1985, '86, '87, '88
Nichols, Pete	1960
Nielsen, Kurt	1979
Niziolek, Frank	1990, '91, '92
Novosel, Brett	1991
Novosel, Scott	1988, '89, '90, '91
Nowack, Carl	1978, '79
Nowack, Steven	1980
O'Brien, W. C.	1925, '26
Olcott, G. W.	1924
Olin, Jon	1964, '65
Olsen, Hugh H.	1945
Olsen, R. S.	1921, '22
Orr, George	1923
Ott, J. E.	1916
Overman, Warren C.	1935, '36, '37
Padgett, Christopher	1983, '84, '85
Pala, Steve	1990, '91
Pashby, R. W.	1930
Paul, Jim	1974, '75, '76
Pauly, Patrick	1982, '83, '84, '85
Pearson, Jack	1950
Pendleton, James	1951, '52
Peragine, Tom	1989, '90, '91, '92
Perrle, J. L.	1927
Peters, Scot	1984
Petersen, Neal	1971, '72
Pierce, Steve	1985, '86
Piggott, A.	1923
Pihera, Otto	1947
Pillinger, R. A.	1908
Piper, John	1928, '29
Pope, Kip	1967, '68, '69
Postle, D. E.	1921, '22
Potter, Keith	1976, '77, '78, '79
Powers, Robert	1983
Pribil, Martin	1976
Puchalski, Don	1959
Quackenbush, B. H.	1924
Quigley, Phillip	1976, '77, '78, '79
Read, Phil	1969
Reitsch, Charles	1949, '50, '51
Rempert, John	1982
Rezab, Ray	1983
Richter, Gary	1986, '87, '88, '89
Rick, Dickson	1926
Roach, James W.	1941, '42, '43
Roddick, Lawrence	1986
Roos, E. G.	1916
Rosenbaum, Lee	1980
Ross, Roy	1950
Rotkis, Walter A.	1937
Rotteld, Herb	1971
Royal, T. E.	1921, '22, '23
Ruben, Benjamin	1953
Rubenstein, Allan	1956, '57, '58
Rucker, Douglas	1948, '49
Rusackus, Charles J.	1936
Sammons, Donald	1954
Sandor, Bela	1960
Sarussi, Marty	1984, '86, '87
Sawicki, Tom	1965, '66, '67
Schanel, James	1976, '77, '78, '79
Scherrer, Steve	1983, '84, '86
Scherwat, Don	1947, '48, '49
Schick, A. I.	1932
Schindehette, Russell	1980, '81, '82, '83
Scholz, Robert	1953
Schroeder, F. R.	1928, '29, '30
Schwartz, Terry	1973, '74
Scott, Greg	1973, '74, '75, '76
Scotty, Brian	1980, '84
Scotty, Matthew	1985, '86, '87, '88

412

Scotty, Thomas	1983, '85, '86
Seaman, Glen	1977, '78
Seaman, Richard	1986, '87
Seidler, Burton A.	1943
Seiwert, Herb	1948, '49
Seybold, Harvey	1974, '75, '76
Sharer, Rock	1959, '60, '61
Shattuck, W. F.	1926, '27, '28
Shea, Jeft	1963
Shoemaker, Kenn	1975
Shriner, William	1961, '62, '63
Siegert, Philip	1960, '61
Simmons, G. E.	1924
Simpson, Ken	1967, '68
Sims, Robert	1992
Sinnock, Pommery	1932
Skunberg, Craig	1982
Smiley, Larry	1967, '68, '69
Smith, Andrew	1983
Solbert, Michael	1983
Sommer, Joseph	1961, '62, '63
Spasott, Tom	1962
Spreitzer, Fred	1963
Spreitzer, James	1961, '62, '63
Staples, Paul	1988, '89
Stapleton, Christopher	1986, '87, '88
Stark, Art	1966, '67, '68
Stelton, Peter	1960, '61, '62
Sterba, Tony	1970, '71, '72, '73
Sterrett, David	1955, '56, '57
Stettensen, Jim	1970, '71, '72, '73
Stluka, Gary	1970, '71, '72
Stout, W. H.	1928, '29
Straker, Steven	1979, '80, '81
Strange, Rob	1978, '79
Sullivan, Robert	1953
Sutton, M.	1924
Swatek, E. T.	1907
Sweetman, Frank	1929
Taber, B. F.	1911, '12, '13
Tack, Joseph	1979, '80
Tague, Chris	1977, '78, '79, '80
Tait, Fred	1952, '53
Tanner, Jim	1968
Tanner, John	1972, '73, '74, '75
Tanner, Joseph R.	1970, '71, '72
Tanner, Tom	1977, '78, '79
Taylor, F. M.	1925
Taylor, W. H.	1921, '22, '23

Thompson, H. P.	1912
Thompson, Jett	1992
Thompson, O. H.	1914
Thompson, T. H.	1912
Tiedemann, Lance	1988, '89, '90, '91
Tothero, Steve	1989, '90, '91, '92
Trigger, Tom	1966, '67
Turek, Marry	1992
Van Gunter, M. B.	1933
Van Heltebrake, Jerry	1971
Van Rossen, Donald	1953
Van Tuin, J. W.	1933, '35
Vial, H. C.	1917
Vinke, Bob	1973, '74, '75
Voelkner, Alvin	1960
Vokac, Frank G.	1935, '36
Vosburgh, William R.	1911, '12, '13
Wagner, E. H.	1929
Wahlstrom, Marvin	1946
Waldo, J. H.	1917, '20
Walker, Rick	1979
Walker, Thomas	1957, '58, '59
Walker, Wesley	1980, '81, '82
Wannemanker, Bob	1970, '72
Ward, Richard	1980, '81
Warren, Kent	1990, '91
Watson, James	1953
Weathertord, Harold	1976
Weber, Glenn	1946
Webster, G. A.	1928, '29, '30
Weiss, G. S.	1925
Werner, James	1978, '79, '80
Werner, Robert	1979, '80, '81, '82
Werremeyer, Kit	1966, '67, '68
Wessberg, Tom	1986, '87
Wheeler, R. L.	1922
White, Scott	1972
Whittaker, Dick	1959
Whittaker, Lorin, Jr.	1957, '58
Wich, Fred	1975, '76, '77, '78
Williams, John	1974, '75, '76
Williamson, Esby	1932
Williamson, J. C.	1930, '31
Willingham, Thomas	1983
Wilson, Anthony	1985, '86, '87
Wilson, Paul	1991, '92
Wine, John	1984, '85, '86, '87
Wollrab, James C.	1939, '40, '41
Wolters, Brett	1992
Woodbury, Ed	1973, '74, '75, '76

Younger, Charles	1961, '62
Zimmerman, Wessel	1984
Zitz, John	1990, '91

WOMEN'S SWIMMING

Ackermann, Mary	1991, '92, '93, '94
Adair, Lorrie	1978, '79, '80
Adams, Tessa	2010, '11, '12
Adler, Darcy	1998, '99, 2000, '01
Adrian, Laura	2009
Aegerter, Ashley	2015, '16
Ahlsund, Annukka	1984, '85
Apel, Patti	1977, '78
Armstrong, Sue	1979, '80, '81, '82
Arnoff, Alison	1983, '84
Auclair, Renee-Claude	1988, '89
Aveyard, Jessica	1999, 2000, '01, '02
Bachell, Kyla	2007, '08
Bain, Jackie	2004, '05, '06, '07
Beavis, Ann-Marie	1987, '88, '89, '90
Beinke, Luann	1975
Bell, Elizabeth	2011
Benedict, Katie	2003, '04
Benz, Adrienne	1997
Berg, Kristi	1993
Bergsma, Bonnie	1982, '83, '84, '85
Bernardo, Abbey	2005, '06, '07, '08
Bethke, Gabrielle	2015, '16
Bieryzchudek, Anne	1989, '90
Billish, Teresa	1986, '87
Binneboese, Kim	1998
Black, Marcie	1997, '98, '99, 2000
Blackwell, Amanda	1990
Bogle, Stacy	2001
Bollinger, Traci	1997, '98, '99, 2000
Booth, Hailey	2012, '13, '14, '15
Bordwell, Amanda	2002, '03
Bower, Allison	1997
Boyd, Casey	2001, '02, '03, '04
Bradley, Meghan	2005, '06, '07
Braun, Ashley	1999, 2000, '01, '02
Brecik, Deann	1984, '85, '86, '87
Brown, Christy	1995, '96, '97, '98
Brown, Michelle	1985, '86, '87, '88
Brunka, Christina	2003, '04, '05, '06
Burke, Brigid	1994
Burke, Rachel	2014
Busch, Molly	1998, '99, 2000, '01
Byars, Mary	1978
Canino, Toni	1983, '84

Name	Years
Caraker, Lori	1995
Casas, Nelly	2015, '16
Chavez, Alexa	2012, '13
Chiappe, Carole	1978, '79
Christiansen, Anna	1998, '99, 2000, '01
Chuang, Cara	2011, '12, '13, '14
Ciucci, Michelle	1990
Clapp, Marissa	2006, '07, '08, '09
Clifford, Jessica	2013, '14, '15, '16
Coady, Jennifer	2013, '14, '15, '16
Coady, Sarah	2010, '11, '12, '13
Conner, Meghan	2006
Conroy, Caitlin	2009, '10, '11
Cordero, Jackie	1996
Corniuk, Raquel	2015
Costello, Sonya	1984, '85, '86, '87
Craft, Mallory	2005, '06, '07, '08
Cronin, Rosanne	1980, '81, '82, '83
Cronin, Sheila	1981
Curry, Adelaide	2015, '16
Czmarko, Alison	2000, '01, '02, '03
Daill, Kris	1976, '77, '78
David, Amy	1991, '92
DeAngelis, Alison	2014, '15
DeAngelis, Andrea	2012, '13
de Camp, Veronica	1997
Dempsey, Terry	1979, '80, '81, '82
DeSalle, Rebecca	2008
DesEnfants, Kate	1986, '87
Didde, Erin	1996, '97, '98, '99
Dietrich, Cathy	1991, '92, '93, '94
Dikmen, Ilkay	2001, '02, '03, '04
Dittmann, Martha	1977
Dixon, Michele	1988, '89, '90
Dlugopolski, Kayla	2012, '13, '14, '15
Doll, Jill	1989, '90, '91, '92
Domitrz, Cheri	1985, '86, '87, '88
Dowdeswell, Marla	1992, '93
Downing, Amy	2002, '03, '04, '05
Dudley, Sue	1975, '76, '77
Duffy, Robin	1979, '80, '81, '82
Durbin, Cathy	1976
Easey, Kathryn	2004, '05, '06
Eaton, Jessica	2000, '01, '02, '03
Eberhardt, Keri	2010, '11, '12, '13
Eckblad, Rebecca	2016
Eckenroad, Susanne	1981
Eckert, Toni	1999, '01, '02
Eichmeier, Katy	1976
Everaert, Christine	1992, '93
Farrell, Colleen	1999, 2000, '01
Farrell, Meghan	2004, '06, '07, '08
Feldman, Marla	1975, '76
Fish, Lisa	2001, '02, '03, '04
Fisher, Britni	2009, '10, '11
Flynn, Katy	1979, '80, '81, '82
Fontaine, Simone	1990, '91, '93
Forsberg, Amy	2007, '08, '09, '10
Franck, Lindsey	2003
Fransene, Sarah	1995, '97
Fung, Emily	2012, '13, '14, '15
Funk, Kelly	2005, '06
Galan, Anna	1988, '89
Gamboa, Renee	1995, '96
Gardiner, Allison	1986, '87, '88, '89
Garrison, Emily	2001, '02
Gatlin, Anne	1979
Gibson, Sabrinne	2012, '13, '14, '15
Gilman, Morgan	2007, '08, '09, '10
Gnade, Gail	1977
Goering, Anne	2011, '12, '13, '14
Gomery, Shannon	1996, '97, '98
Gorman, Colleen	2002, '03, '04, '05
Gowdy, Sam	2016
Grandcolas, Andrea	2007
Grandcolas, Michelle	2004, '05, '06, '07
Grandcolas, Sarah	1985, '86, '87, '88
Grant, Liz	1985, '86, '87, '88
Gregory, Melissa	1978, '79, '80
Grenier, Adrienne	1996
Guinn, Deb	1975
Gullickson, Jennifer	1987, '88, '89
Gutterridge, Theresa	1985, '86, '87, '88
Haag, Eileen	1980
Hackett, Kady	1993, '94, '95
Hackler, Sarah	1995, '96, '97, '98
Hamann, Carolyn	1983, '84, '85, '86
Hamann, Suzi	1981, '82, '83
Handel, Kelly	1997, '98, '99, 2000
Hansmann, Katie	1995
Harmon, Alyssa	2010
Hartman, Sarah	2001, '02, '03, '04
Hatch, Bailey	2007
Heck, Kirsten	1995, '96
Heckert, Monica	1990
Hein, Stephanie	2013, '14, '15, '16
Hejnicki, Jennifer	1992, '93
Henry, Trisha	1995, '96, '97, '99
Hess, Jennifer	1992, '93
Hichhalter, Cheri	1983
Hill, Barb	1984
Holquist, Sue	1975, '76
Holz, Jessica	2011, '12, '13, '14
Homenock, Nicola	1996, '97, '98, '99
Hooper, Jill	1981, '83
Hopkins, Kristine	1984, '85, '86
Howard, Mary Beth	2012, '13, '14
Huttenlocher, Gail	1985, '86, '87, '88
Ivarson, Jen	2007, '08, '09, '10
Jansson, Britta	2003, '04, '05, '06
Japp Joyce, Rachel	2009, '10, '11, '12
Joesten, Holly	1982, '83
Johnson, Amy	2007, '08, '09, '10
Johnson, Anna	2007, '08, '09, '10
Joyce, Kaitlyn	2015, '16
Jutton, Jerry	1977, '78
Kalafut, Christine	1999
Kalenda, Kimberly	2010, '11, '12, '13
Karich, Sarah	1987
Kassouni, Olivia	2014, '15, '16
Kasten, Corey	2008, '09, '10, '11
Kats, Judith	1988
Keehn, Ali	2006, '07, '08, '09
Keeley, Bridget	2009, '10
Kelley, Melissa	2001
Kelly, Jennifer	1987
Kelly, Sue	1980, '81
Kerr, Marsha	1975
Kielty, Kathy	2000, '01, '02
Kloeckener, Kristen	2007, '08, '09, '10
Knight, Kathleen	2010, '11, '12, '13
Koepcke, Kristen	2002, '03, '04, '05
Kuhn, Madeline	2016
Kunkel, Kelly	2009, '10, '11, '12
Lakatos, Trisha	2002, '03, '04, '05
Lamb, Erin	2010, '11, '12, '13
LaMere, Dorothy	1977
Landers, Kathleen	1987
Lawson, Kris	1999, 2000, '01
Lazear, Jessica	1999, 2000
Ledgin, Autumn	2016
Lee, Joyce Lynn	1989, '90, '91, '92
Leibold, Samantha	2004, '05, '06
Loper, Torrey	2009, '10, '11, '12
Lubeck, Kim	1992
Lynn, Erica	2011, '12, '13, '14
Lynn, Lori	2013, '14, '15, '16
Lyons, Kristin	2000, '01
Macari, Molly	2000
MacGregor, Ellen	1985, '86, '87, '88

414

Name	Years	Name	Years	Name	Years
Mackin, Beth	1987, '88	Olson, Aby	2016	Schilling, Amelia	2014, '15, '16
Madej, Diane (Tina)	1976, '77	Oostendorp, Heather	1989, '90	Schillmoeller, Renatta	1983
Mainville, Tanya	1997	Oostendorp, Kristen	1988, '89, '90	Schofield, Jane	1987, '88, '89, '90
Mamakos, Lisa	2000, '01	Palekas, Audrey	1979, '80, '81	Schomer, Susan	1980
Manias, Kristen	2009, '10, '11, '12	Palton, Mary	1978	Schwartz, Debbie	1994, '95, '96
Marchuk, Megan	2012, '13, '14, '15	Pasztor, Janna	1999	Scoville, Kristen	2002
Marizu, CeCe	2007, '08, '09, '10	Patterson, Mary	1975, '76, '77, '78	See, Tracy	1990, '91, '92, '93
Mason, Meghan	2008, '09, '10, '11	Patton, Jenny	1999, 2000, '01, '02	Serniute, Gabriele	2016
Matthews, Joyce	1985	Patton, Mary Andrea	1978	Shirley, Lindsey	2006, '07, '08
Matthias, Astrid	2000, '01, '02, '03	Paulson, Kirsten	1991, '92	Simmons, Jill	1979, '80
McAdam, Chrystal	2001, '02, '03, '04	Payette, Rebecca	1986, '87	Skrna, Mary	1980
McCarthy, Kathleen	1987, '88	Pederson, Laurie	1981, '82, '83, '84	Smith, Hollie	2013, '14, '15, '16
McClain, Amy	1985, '86, '87	Peters, Jennifer	1999, 2000, '01, '02	Smith, Jodi	1996, '97, '98, '99
McDermott, Callan	2012, '13, '14, '15	Petruzzello	2010, '11, '12, '13	Smithwick, Kelly	2007, '08, '09, '10
McDermott, Darragh	2010, '11, '12, '13	Plattner, Sharon	1992, '93, '94, '95	Snook, Erin	2001
McDermott, Sloane	2013, '14, '15, '16	Poetz, Rebecca	2004, '05, '06, '07	Sommerville, Jessica	1993
McGauvran, Kelly	2001, '02, '03	Pogofsky, Marcy	1997, '98	Soucheck, Elizabeth	1995, '96
McGowan, Brittany	2009, '10, '11, '12	Polanek, Eileen	1980	Spillone, Nikki	2007, '08, '09, '10
McKee, April	2009, '10, '11, '12	Pope, Courtney	2011, '12, '13, '14	Spivak, Courtney	2007, '08, '09, '10
McSwine, Becky	1977, '78	Pottgen, Jennifer	1994, '95, '96	Staples, Stephanie	1998, '99
Mehnert, Michelle	2009, '10, '11, '12	Povey, Jeannine	1996	Stephens, Sarah	1995, '96, '97, '98
Mendoza, Marina	2006	Powelski, Andrea	1999, 2000, '01, '02	Stevens, Kellie	2005, '06, '07, '08
Meng, Alison	2012, '13, '14, '15	Prasse, Erin	1999	Sticha, Cherie	1995, '96, '97, '98
Mercer, Lindy	1995	Prather, Allison	2002, '03	Stillwell, Jennifer	1996
Meriweather, Michele	1987, '88	Quigley, Stephanie	1980	Stimpfle, Lisa	1990, '91, '92, '93
Merklein, Katie	2003	Rakoski, Kristen	1992, '93, '94, '95	Stoneburg, Sara	2008, '09, '10, '11
Messmer, Natasha	1997, '98, '99, 2000	Rakoski, Lisa	1990, '91, '92	Stratford, Samantha	2015, '16
Meyer, Mallory	2006, '07	Randell, Jillian	1995	Suess, Frederica	1986, '87
Meyers, Sascha	2015, '16	Reber, Dawn	1995, '96	Sullivan, Patricia	1989, '90
Miller, Ann	2008, '09, '10, '11	Richards, Debby	1989, '90	Sundahl, Karen	1987
Moody, Krista	2003	Richart, Jane	1986, '87	Swann, Leeda	1994
Moore, Caroline	2004, '05, '06, '07	Richter, Lori	1990	Sykstus, Sarah	2013, '14, '15, '16
Mowrer, Jessica	2000	Richter, Padra	1989, '90	Taaffe, Sabine	1989, '90, '92, '93
Mueller, Kristie	1993, '94, '95	Richter, Sandra	1989, '90	Takata, Chris	1981
Murphy, Erika	2012, '13, '14, '15	Richter, Susan	1986	Taylor, Kelli	1989, '90, '91, '92
Murphy, Jacqueline	2006	Rodawig, Audrey	2016	Theil, Linda	1976, '77, '78, '79
Musiek, Annette	1979	Rodriquez, Erin	2010, '11, '12, '13	Theissen, Katie	2006, '07, '08, '09
Nagel, Betsy	1997, '98, '99, 2000	Roeing, Katie	2012, '13	Theobald, Nan	1978, '79, '80
Netzel, Denise	1979	Roscetti, Erin	1988	Thompson, Marin	2011, '12, '13
Nichols, Talyna	1997	Roth, Barb	1983, '84, '85	Tobin, Marni	1994, '95
Noonan, Peggy	1976	Rothenberg, Jessica	2004, '05, '06, '07	Toland, Alyssa	2011, '12, '13, '14
Nosal, Paula	2001, '02, '03, '04	Ryan, Amy	1994	Torchia, Meta Rose	1985, '86, '87, '88
Novotny, Meg	1992, '94	Ryan, Kate	1995	Toth, Anne	1995
Nowak, Ann	2007	Ryan, Kristi	1994	Toth, Magdalena	1983, '84, '85, '86
Nowak, Mary	2002, '03	Sadler, Jenny	1990, '94	Tracy, Leigh Ann	2004, '05, '06, '07
Ochab, Jennifer	2000, '01, '02, '03	Salmon, Kalli	1989, '90, '91, '92	Tratt, Kerrie	1990
O'Connor, Laura	2001	Sampey, Eileen	1989, '90	Treado, Kristine	1987, '88, '89
O'Fallon, Sara	2000, '01, '02, '03	Sands, Jennifer	1995, '96, '97, '98	Trenda, Pamela	1989, '90, '91, '92
Ohr, Jessica	1998, '99, 2000, '01	Schamber, Isabella	2013, '14, '15, '16	Veerman, Beth	1990
Olech, Allison	1998, '99, 2000, '01	Scheurich, Katie	1999, 2000, '01		

Viney, Barbie	2004, '05, '06, '07
Vrieze, Ashley	2003
Vuong, Megan	2016
Wachholz, Paige	2010
Wailing, Karen	1983, '84, '85, '86
Wang, Emily	1997, '98, '99, 2000
Ward, Lindsey	1995, '96, '97, '98
Weber, Amanda	1995
Weidner, Karla	1986, '87
Werder, Beth	1979
Westhoff, Sue	1980, '81, '82, '83
Westohoff, Karen	1981
Whitaker, Kim	1976
Wike, Charli	2016
Wilhite, Noelle	1998, '99, '01
Wilkinson, Elaine	2009
Wilkinson, Emily	2011, '12, '13
Williams, Emma	2011, '12, '13
Williams, Janet	1976
Wilson, Jenny	2005
Wismer, Lauren	2010, '11
Witte, Christy	2000
Wopat, Paula	1977
Worth, Carolyn	1984, '85, '86, '87
Wylie, Mary	1982, '83, '84, '85
York, Pam	1980, '81, '82, '83
Yount, Amy	1975, 76
Zborek, Kristen	2013, '14, '15, '16
Zyga, Kiki	2004, '05

MEN'S TENNIS

Abdelnour, Bruno	2010, '11, '12, '13
Abrams, Jack	1952
Adams, Neil	1981, '82, '83, '84
Alcock, Warren	1948
Alden, Brian	2011
Amaya, Manuel	1973, '74
Ambielli, Adam	1982
Anderson, Kevin	2005, '06, '07
Appleman, Jim	1975
Archer, Corbin	1995, '97, '98
Bailie, Clyde	Unknown
Basson, Michau	1993, '94, '95
Bauer, Tom	1964, '65, '66
Bazarnik, Blake	2014, '15
Beck, Walt	Unknown
Becker, Robert	1934
Bennorth, Robert	1950, '51, '52
Besant, Wilson	1949, '50
Bielefeld, Roger	1954, '55, '58

Bishop, Lee	1951
Black, Todd	1979, '80, '81, '82
Blain, Brady	1995, '96, '97, '98
Boatman, Tom	1960, '61, '62
Bouton, Peter	1982, '83, '84, '85
Bradley, Ed	1950, '51
Brandt, Harry	1954, '55, '56
Braun, Cyril	1938
Breckenridge, Robert	1957, '58, '59
Brooke, Shawn	2000
Brown, David	1947, '48, '49
Brown, Neil	1988, '89, '90
Brown, Thurston	1962
Burkholder, Robert	1967
Bush, Roger	1940
Buwick, Eugene	1949, '50, '51
Calkins, Michael	2001, '02, '03, '04
Chambers, Franklin	1961
Chanowitz, Harry	1938, '39, '40
Chaudhuri, Mickey	1991, '92
Childers, Julian	2013, '14, '16
Chin, Waylon	2008, '09
Chiricosta, Anthony	1976, '77, '78, '79
Clapper, Kenneth	1942, '43
Clark, Keith	1945
Clark, Ryan	1991, '92, '93
Clatfelter, Jack	1943
Clements, Chip	1969, '70, '71
Confer, Warren	1938
Conlan, Jack	1981, '82, '83
Cook, Jeff	1968, '69, '70
Cookman, Aubrey	Unknown
Cordes, Rob	1993
Cossette, Bryan	1993
Crain, Delmar	1939, '40
Crawford, Arden	Unknown
Crawmer, Charly	1993, '94
Czerwinski, Marek	2009, '10
Dabir, Pramod	2003, '04, '05, '06
Dankert, William	1952, '53
Davis, Brandon	2005, '06, '07, '08
Davis, Jared	1944, '45
Davitz, Joel	1944
Daw, Joe	1981, '82
Dawson, Jim	1965
Dean, Paul	1939
DeHeart, Ryler	2003, '04, '05, '06
Delic, Amer	2001, '02, '03
DeVore, Adrian	1991, '92
DeVore, Chris	1994, '95, '96

Dillman, Brian	1988, '89, '90
Downs, Roger	1946, '47
Dunlap, Tom	1968, '69, '70
Earl, Robert	1976, '77, '78, '79
Eberly, Mike	1991, '92
Edidin, Norman	1941
Edwards, Jeffrey	1977, '78, '79, '80
Elbl, Michael	1967, '68
El Tabakh, Meedo	2009, '10
Epkins, Joe	1958, '59, '60
Farmer, Alan	1952
Fisher, Ben	1948
Franklin, Cary	1997, '98, '99, 2000
Franks, Bruce	1974, '75, '76, '77
Freelove, Oliver	1996, '97, '98, '99
Frei, Tom	1984, '85, '86
Garfield, Marvin	1949
Gates, James	1942, '43, '46
Geist, Harvey	1934
Gilmore, George	1957, '58, '59
Glass, Doyle	1954
Gonzales, Ruben	2005, '06, '07, '08
Goodman, David	1983, '84
Gorham, Sidney	1956
Gosea, Farris	2012, '13, '14, '15
Gottman, Jay	1986
Greenberg, Scott	1984, '86, '87
Greenleaf, John	1954, '55
Groppel, Jack	1973
Gudeman, Gene	1958
Gueche, Sadri	1990, '92
Guignon, Ross	2012, '13, '14, '15
Hamui, Johnny	2010, '11
Harris, Miles	1970, '71, '72, '73
Hartenstein, Harvey	1952
Hawthorne, Jamison	1993, '94
Hayne, Webb	1973, '74, '75
Hedden, Dan	1963
Heiser, Billy	2007, '08, '09
Heller, Steve	1961, '62
Henderson, Tom	1980, '81, '82
Hertz, Jed	1968, '71
Hicks, Bruce	1935, '36
Hill, Stephen	1953, '54
Hiltzik, Aron	2015, '16
Hiltzik, Jared	2013, '14, '15, '16
Hirsch, Asher	2016
Hobson, Alex	2000, '01, '02, '03
Hoffman, Robert	1951, '52
Hoh, Stephen	2010, '11, '12, '13

Holden, David	1966, '67, '68	Maxwell, Barry	1970, '71, '72	Rowe, Ryan	2005, '06, '07, '08
Holtmann, Al	1957, '58, '59	McCollum, Tom	1963, '64	Saikley, Frank	1941, '42, '43
Hoppenjans, Mark	1991	McCoy, William	1937, '38	Sarkary, Xerxes	1991
Howie, Bill	1986, '87	McCraven, Steve	1988, '89	Schalin, Guy	1981
Hulvey, Walter	1953	McDonald, Richard	1956, '57	Schantz, Eric	1985, '86
Hummel, Glenn	1973, '74, '75, '76	McInich, Nelson	1935	Schreiber, Ben	2000, '01
Isenburg, Orville	1940	McKenzie, Nick	1986	Schroeder, Rod	1970, '71, '72
Jesse, Alex	2013, '14, '16	Mesch, Dan	1959, '60	Schuder, John	1938
Jiang, Pengxuan	2016	Meurisse, Charles	1975, '76, '77, '78	Schunk, Charles	1947, '48
Johnson, Howard	1939	Meyer, Mike	1983, '84, '86	Schwartz, Kevin	1995, '96, '97
Johnson, Jerry	1965, '66	Migdow, Ben	1946, '47	Schwarz, Robert	1939, '40, '41
Johnson, Kenneth	1939, '40	Minkus, Marc	1974	Shapiro, Richard	1974, '75, '77
Jones, Arthur	1941	Mioduski, Moseph	1939	Shineflug, Bob	1963, '64
Jones, Ebon	1938, '39, '40	Moll, Joe	1934, '35, '36	Simons, Steve	1965, '66
Jones, G. D.	2004, '05, '06, '07	Morrey, Kevin	1971, '72, '73, '74	Singh, K. U.	2011
Kalmanovich, Roy	2008, '09, '11, '12	Morrison, Wayne	1975	Sisson, John	1963, '64, '65
Karacan, Ercument	1945	Moses, James	1949, '50, '51	Snyder, Matthew	1997, '98, '99, 2000
Kell, Dick	1961	Moss, Larry	1962, '63	Sommers, Scott	1979, '80, '81, '82
Kelso, Kevin	1972, '73, '74, '75	Most, Fred	1952, '55	Sontag, Gavin	1996, '97, '98
Kennett, Greg	1988, '89	Muresan, Alex	2001, '02	Souza, Abe	2009, 2010, '11
Knowlton, Brett	1988	Murnighan, Conner	2003, '04, '05	Spicijaric, Marc	2006, '07, '08, '09
Knue, Jordan	2007	Murray, John	1988, '89, '90	Staake, Donal	1944
Kopinski, Tim	2012, '13, '14, '15	Nair, Madhu	1985, '86	Stafford, Bruce	1960, '61, '62
Kosta, Mike	1999, 2000, '01, '02	Nasser, David	1989, '90, '91, '92	Stafford, Harold	1952, '53
Krajewski, Mark	1989, '90, '91, '92	Nasser, Mark	1993, '94	Steers, Fred	1946, '47, '48
Kramer, Mike	1978, '79, '80, '81	Nevolo, Dennis	2009, '10, '11, '12	Stewart, Dave	1953
Lambert, Andre	1983, '84	Noble, Carl	1956, '57, '58	Stolt, Phil	2001, '02, '03, '04
Landa, Pablo	2016	Noble, Frank	1962, '63, '64	Sutter, Jeremy	1994, '95, '96
Lansford, Bob	1959, '60	O'Connell, Tim	1925, 26, 27, 28	Teply, Jakub	1996, '97, '98
Lantin, Arnaud	1998, '99	O'Neal, George	1945	Thatcher, Chris	1993
Lapriore, Chris	1985	Olefsky, Jerry	1962, '63	Thompson, Edwin	1967, '68, '69
Laski, Jeff	1997, '98, '99, 2000	Oliver, Graydon	2000, '01	Tucker, Monte	2005
Leininger, Joseph	1980	Ortiz, Hector	1987, '88, '89, '90	Turek, Jerry	1994, '95, '96, '97
Lejeck, Edward	1932	Page, Brian	2013, '14, '16	Van Tine, James	1955, '56, '57
Levenson, Steve	1966, '67, '68	Parker, Drew	1995	Velasco, Manny	1986, '88, '89
Levy, Bertram	1944	Parker, Jamal	1999, 2000, '01, '02	Von Spreckelsen, Ray	1942, '46
Lewers, Richard	1935, '36	Pearne, Gary	1987, '88, '89, '90	Voss, George	1969
Lewke, Bob	1965, '66	Pechous, Ed	1954	Vukic, Aleks	2015, '16
Littell, Dave	1972	Philiotis, Greg	1985	Wack, Rick	1970, '71, '72
Little, Roger	1945, '48, '49, '50	Pilz, Clifford	1942	Waddell, Barry	1981, '83
Livingston, Brian	2009	Puentes, Rey	1992	Wagner, Mark	1977
Lobb, Andrew	1986, '87	Ram, Rajeev	2003	Weaver, Robert	1943
Lombardi, Vince	1993	Ramey, Royce	1999, 2000	Weinstein, David	1978
Long, Mark	1985, '86, '87, '88	Randoll, Melvin	1946, '47, '48	Weiss, Joe	1947, '48
Losito, John	1984, '85	Rich, William	1936, '38	Weiss, Jon	1956
Lothrop, James	1942, '43	Riepma, Paul	1944, '45	Westberg, Carey	1979
MacDonald, Don	1953	Riley, James	1960, '61	Wilson, Brian	2002, '03, '04
Manpearl, David	1994, '95, '96	Roelofse, Ruan	2009	Woods, Conrad	1954, '55
Martin, Chris	2002, '03, '04, '05	Rosborough, Terrill	1968, '69	Wright, Jack	1935
Matsuya, Toshiki	2015	Roth, Connor	2010, '11	Wurtzel, Frederic	1965, '66, '67

Yeaton, Edward	1937
Zeder, Evan	2003, '04, '05
Zeder, Nathan	1999, 2000, '01, '02
Zych, Jon	1991, '93, '94

WOMEN'S TENNIS

Abajian, Chelcie	2009, '10, '11, '12
Adsuar, Natalie	1995, '96
Aguero, Liana	1997
Akritas, Pavlina	2004, '05, '06
Allin, Amy	2009, '10, '11, '12
Arildsen, Susan	1982, '83, '84, '85
Baillon, Madie	2015,' 16
Baldrich, Camille	1992, '93, '94, '95
Bareis, Barbara	1982, '84, '85
Barki, Jessica	2003
Barretta, Emily	2013, '14, '15, '16
Basolo, Margaret	1977, '78, '79
Batt, Jaclyn	1994, '96
Bjerknes, Lisa	1980
Boomershine, Kate	2002
Boone, Jerricka	2014, '15, '16
Brouder, Cynthia	1978, '79
Bruce, Lindsey	1997
Buchanan, Lisa	1980, '81
Burgess, Sandra	1980, '81
Burgess, Sharon	1978, '79, '80
Burns, Sheila	1984, '85, '86, '87
Buwick, Cynthia	1977, '78, '79
Casati, Alexis	2014, '15, '16
Cathrall, Jodi	1989
Cehajic, Leila	2002, '03, '04, '05
Chambers, Cynthia	1988, '89, '90, '91
Choe, Eva	2001, '02, '03, '04
Clery, Colleen	1976, '77
Corcoran, Maura	1988
Costigan, Carrie	1986, '87, '88, '89
Crane, Donna	1980
Cuadra, Alejandra Meza	2005, '06, '07, '08
Cunningham, Nancy	1978
Davé, Shivani	2006, '07, '08, '09
Davis, Barbara	1975, '76,
Daw, Jessie	1984, '85, '87, '88
DeSilva, Gayathri	1980, '81, '82, '83
Eichner, Astrid	1987, '88, '90
Eklov, Tiffany	2001, '02, '03, '04
Ensslin, Sabine	1989, '90, '91
Faford, Ann	1976, '77, '78
Falkin, Allison	2011, '12, '13, '14

Fazlic, Eldina	2000, '01, '02, '03
Ferney, Brooke	1999, 2000
Finnegan, Leigh	2008, '09, '10, '11
Flesvig, Christine	1983, '84, '85, '86
Fraker, Elizabeth	2002
Fudge, Megan	2007, '08, '09, '10
Gates, Linda	1989, '90, '92
Goecke, Michelle	1992
Goern, Sandra	1985, '86, '87, '88
Gottlieb, Allison	1996, '97, '98, '99
Goulet, Cynthia	2002, '04, '05
Harkins, Macall	2005, '06
Harris, Jean	1975
Haubold, Lois	1977, '78, '79, '80
Hilton, Jade	2015, '16
Hogan, Dorothy	1980
Holmes, Kam	1976, '77
Hoppmann, Rita	1981, '82, '83, '84
Hutchinson, Susan	1981, '82, '83, '84
Jackson, Nicole	1996
Jamieson, Julia	2012, '13, '14, '15
Jarosz, Isabel	2004
Johnson, Amy	1991
Johnson, Cathryn	1976, '77
Jones, Kristen	1992, '93, '94, '95
Kane, Laurie	1990, '91
Kazarian, Stacey	1985, '86
Kedzierski, Misia	2011, '12, '13, '14
Kestly, Christie	1991
Kewney, Kathryn	1982
Kimmel, Lissa	1992, '93, '94, '95
Klapper, Jessica	1994, '95, '96, '97
Knowles, Stacey	1986, '87, '89
Knue, Brianna	2003, '04, '05, '06
Kole, Kathy	1975, '76, '77, '78
Kopinski, Melissa	2012, '13, '14, '15
Kung, Simone	1998, '99, 2000, '01
Kwong, Louise	2014, '15, '16
Lambropoulos, Marisa	2008, '09, '10, '11
Land, Susanne	1994, '95, '96, '97
Loebnitz, Natascha	2000
Loffelmacher, Kara	1996, '97, '98
Manasova, Natalia	1999, 2000
Marshak, Sara	1993, '94, '95
Matz, Jenny	1982
McCarthy, Annie	2008, '09, '10, '11
McGaffigan, Jennifer	2001, '02, '03, '04
McNamara, Colleen	1975, '76, '77
McNamara, Maura	1981, '82, '83, '84

Mehlman, Romy	1996
Meola, Kristi	1992, '93, '94
Minor, Kristina	2007, '08, '09, '10
Neil, Kathy M.	1985, '86, '87, '88
Nelson, Maureen	1976, '77, '78, '79
Nimmo, Lindsey	1991, '92, '93
O'Connor, Audrey	2013
Olson, Sara	1981
Panique, Lisa	1998
Pedraza Novak, Daniela	2016
Pratt, Margaret	1975
Pullman, Cheri	1993, '95
Qu, Momei	2005, '06, '07, '08
Rickard, Kelley	1982
Roberts, Jennifer	1982
Rosenberg, Carla	1998, '99, 2000, '01
Rydberg, Laura	1994, '95, '96, '97
Salamone, Kristina	1975, '76, '77, '78
Schapiro, Stacey	1996, '97, '98, '99
Scherschligt, Barbra	1985, '86
Smolensky, Loren	1987, '88, '90
Smutko, Breanne	2010, '11, '12, '13
Sokolova, Anastasia	2005, '06
Strauss, Deborah	1978
Stromberg, Christine	2008, '09, '10
Strout, Susan	1985, '86, '87, '88
Switkes, Jaclyn	2016
Tapak, Grace	2015, '16
Vias, Ines	2016
Wang, Emily	2004, '05, '06, '07
Webb, Michelle	2000, '01, '02, '03
Welsh, Barb	1978
Wentink, Nancy	1975
White, Rachel	2010, '11, '12, '13
Wickiser, Jo	1983
Willey, Kristin	1990, '91
Williams, Mary Beth	1990, '91, '92
Wise, Megan	1998, '99, 2000
Wujek, Kathy	1975
Young, Amy	1978, '79, '80

MEN'S TRACK

Abbott, David	1928, '29
Abbot, Richard R.	1943
Achtien, Tom	2010
Ackerman, Jade	2012, '13
Adamczyk, John E.	2005, '06, '07, '08
Adams, Alfred O.	1933, '34
Adkins, Kenneth	2014, '15, '16

Agase, Louis	1945	Barrett, Jesse L.	1905, '06, '07	Bolander, Harold B.	1912, '13, '14
Aihara, Henry K.	1945	Barron, James L.	1911	Booker, Harry G.	1970, '71, '72
Ainsworth, Walter W.	1912	Barron, Oliver D.	1931	Borden, W. T.	1899
Akers, Todd A.	1989	Barth, George B.	1978	Boswell,	
Alberts, Dewey V.	1921	Basting, Bryce	2015, '16	Thomas E., Jr.	1947
Alexander, Joe	1996	Bates, Charles R.	1903	Bowe, Christopher L.	1986, '87, '88
Allen, James C.	1893	Bauer, Craig	1985	Bowers, James S.	1958, '59, '60
Allen, William	1974	Bauer, John R.	1953, '54	Boyd, Edward P.	1899, '00, '01
Allman, John C.	1920, '21	Baughman, V. Lynn	1934, '35	Boyd, George E.	1896
Allman, Omar L.	1933	Beaird, Brian	2007, '08, '09, '10	Bradley, James C.	1897, '98, '99
Ames, Waldo B.	1915, '16, '17	Bear, Ernest R.	1900, '02, '03	Brede, Erwin C.	1921
Andersen, Harry E.	1947, '48, '49	Beary, Matt	1992, '93, '94, '95	Brenneman, G. Bruce	1946
Anderson, Samuel	1952	Beastall,		Bridges, Dave	1968
Angel, Wendell W.	1981	Theodore W.	1959, '60	Bridges, Jan M.	1964, '65
Angelo, Louis	1991, '93	Beck, H. Clint	1909	Bridges, Lee A.	1986, '87, '88, '89
Angier, Milton S.	1922, '23, '24	Becker, David L.	1963, '64, '65	Bridges, Michael R.	1975
App, Benjamin R.	1973, '74, '75	Bedell, David T.	1946, '47, '48	Bridges, Steve	1990, '92, '93, '94
Applequist, J. G.	1899	Beebe, Charles D.	1894	Briggs, Thomas	1949
Aranda, Ezequlel	1891	Behan, Paul F.	1948	Brode, Luther D.	1893, '94
Armstrong, Edward	1988	Behrensmeyer,		Brookins, Mitchell	1981, '83
Armstrong, James W.	1893	George	1891, '92	Brooks, Arvella	1990, '91
Armstrong, Jay L.	1898	Beile, Charles W.	1943, '47	Brooks, David	1974
Armstrong, Sherman	1998, '99, '00, '01	Bekermeier,		Brooks, Kevin U.	1984, '85, '86, '87
Arning, Louis H.	1932	Herbert W.	1943	Brooks, Richard	1974, '75, '76
Arnold, Mark D.	1982, '83, '84, '85	Bell, Oscar C.	1901	Brown, David E.	1919, '20, '21
Aronson, Justin A.	2008	Bell, Richard	1973	Brown, Edward W.	1908, '10
Ascher, Vernon W.	1922	Belnap, Nuel D.	1912, '13	Brown, Hamilton A.	1989, '90
Ashley, Robert L.	1937, '38, '39	Belting, Charles H.	1911, '12	Brown, Joseph A.	1937
Asper, Orville W.	1930	Benberry, Hershel	1969, '70, '71	Brown, Kenneth	1942
Atchison, Jereme	2016	Bennett, Basil	1916, '17, '20	Brown, Kenneth	1959, '60
Avery, Mark E.	1975, '77, '78	Benso, Bryan M.	1987, '88	Brown, Lewis	1899, '00
Axelrod, David J.	1974, '75	Benson, Shujaa	2011	Brown, Nicholas M.	2005, '06, '07, '08
Ayoub, David M.	1978, '79, '80, '81	Bergstrom, Hugo E.	1927	Brown, Park L.	1939, '40, '41
Ayres, Robert B.	1922, '23, '24	Berschet, Marvin W.	1950, '51, '52	Brown, Wallace W.	1919
Azie, Stanley	2009, '10, '11, '12	Bertelsman,		Brown, William D.	1959, '60, '61
Baader, Richard P.	1982, '83	George A.	1929, '31	Brownell, Dean G.	1923, '24, '25
Baietto, Michael E.	1972, '73, '74, '75	Best, David H.	1944, '45	Brubaker, James C.	1967, '68, '69
Bailey, Donald	1940, '41	Beyers, Ben	1993, '94, '95	Bruder, Henry L.	1937
Baird, William	1901	Biebinger, Isaac N.	1896, '97	Brundage, Avery	1908, '09
Baldwin, Alex	2009, '10, '11, '12	Bila, Michael S.	1984, '86, '87	Brundage, M. D.	1899, '00
Bales, Edwards J.	1926	Bill, Jason	2003, '04, '05, '06	Brunton, Richard W.	1936, '37, '38
Bane, Matthew	2011, '12, '13, '14	Birks, John M.	1919	Buchanan,	
Banschbach,		Bissell, Lonnie	1980	Gordon, Jr.	1920
Edward A.	1893, '94, '95	Blanchard, John	1968, '69	Buchheit, George C.	1919
Bareither, Charles	1968	Blanheim, Melvin L.	1962, '63, '64	Bullard, Edward W.	1911, '13
Barmes, Andy	1982, '83	Blankley, Alfred R.	1905	Bullard, Robert I.	1895, '96
Barnes, George H.	1925, '26, '27	Blom, G. Peter	1945	Bunning, Walter F.	1928, '29
Barnett, Ian	2012, '13, '14, '15	Blomfeldt, Allen A.	1907	Burch, Clarence	1967, '68, '69
Barnum, Robert V.	1948, '50, '51	Blount, Walter P.	1919	Burgener, David B.	1979, '71, '72
Baron, Dan	1974	Bobert, Dave	1968, '69, '70	Burgess, Oscar W.	1916

Burghardt, Charles A.	1945	
Burgoon, David W.	1916	
Burke, Ralph	1912, '14	
Burke, William H.	1894, '95	
Burkhart, George H.	1929	
Burleigh, C. H.	1898	
Burns, Joseph K.	1910, '11	
Burns, Matt	2015, '16	
Burroughs, Wilbur G.	1905, '06, '07	
Burton, Charles	1999, '00, '01, '02	
Burwash, Arthur E.	1911	
Bush, Alexander T.	1916	
Bush, Pierre D.	2005, '06, '07, '08	
Buster, William E.	1945, '46, '48, '49	
Butt, Harley M.	1912, '13, '14	
Byrne, Lee	1896, '97, '98	
Byrnes, Nick	2004, '05	
Cabeen, Joshua	1897	
Cadwallader, Douglas P.	1904	
Caiazza, Theodore	1957, '58	
Caldwell, Randolph	1917	
Calisch, Richard W.	1950, '51, '52	
Campbell, Alvin C.	1988, '89	
Campbell, Laverne C.	1944	
Cannon, Ward C.	1921, '22	
Capelle, Mark	1982	
Carius, Allen B.	1962, '63, '64	
Carlson, Herbert N. R.	1922	
Carper, Robert J.	1977, '78, '79	
Carr, Robert J.	1928, '29, '30	
Carrel, Brandon	2014	
Carrison, Henry C.	1931	
Carrithers, Ira T.	1905, '07	
Carroll, Charles	1918, '19	
Carroll, Luke	2013, '14	
Carroll, Robert C.	1932, '33, '34	
Carson, Paul H.	1932	
Carter, Dale	1923, '24	
Carter, William S.	1915, '16	
Case, John R., Jr.	1912, '13	
Caskey, George R.	1919	
Casner, Sidney	1913	
Cave, James A.	1929, '30, '31	
Cayou, F. M.	1900, '01, '02	
Celaya, Robert	1931	
Chambers, Alan R.	1928	
Chambers, Robert L.	1929, '30	
Chandler, George A.	1922	
Chatten, Melville C.	1893, '94	
Cheney, Howard L.	1912	
Cherco, Clint	2003, '04	
Cherot, Anthony	1969, '70	
Christiansen, Harold A.	1932, '33	
Christiansen, Jared	2016	
Claar, Elmer A.	1913, '14	
Clancy, Timothy	1987, '88, '89, '90	
Clarida, T. W.	1915	
Clark, A. C.	1892, '93, '94, '95	
Clark, Howard	1894, '95, '96, '97	
Clarke, Edwin B.	1890	
Clarke, Frederick W.	1890	
Claypool, Mark J.	1978, '79, '80, '81	
Clayton, C. M.	1899	
Clinton, Edgar M.	1896, '97	
Cobb, Laurence J.	1970, '71, '72	
Coffeen, Harry C.	1895, '96	
Colbrese, William L.	1969	
Coleman, Delbert L.	1959, '60	
Coleman, Richard A.	1950, '51, '52	
Collins, John H.	1922, '23	
Cook, David F.	1932, '33, '34	
Cook, James W.	1892	
Cook, William D.	1947, '48	
Cooley, William M.	1945, '46	
Cope, Walter A.	1911, '12, '13	
Corley, Joseph W.	1952, '53, '54	
Cornelius, William	1970	
Correll, Walter K.	1942	
Cortis, Frederic B.	1911, '12, '13	
Costar, Lloyd	1912	
Coughlin, John A.	1923	
Courter, Anson O.	1927	
Cowell, Joe	2016	
Coxworth, James L.	1974, '75, '76	
Crane, Robert L.	1942, '43	
Crumpton, Robert	1994	
Cryer, Henry	1951, '52, '55	
Cullinan, Duane A.	1935, '36, '37	
Culp, John D.	1914, '15, '16	
Cummings, Barton A.	1933	
Cunningham, Kris	2005	
Currier, Donald E.	1914, '15	
Cutter, Scott C.	1893	
Dadant, Louis C.	1899, '00	
Dailey, Bo	1993, '96	
Daniel, Shane	2010, '11	
Davies, Richard O.	1965	
Davis, George F.	1893	
Davis, James T.	1960	
deBeers, James	1989, '90, '91, '92	
Decker, Gene W.	1950, '51	
DeLong, Edward	1956, '57	
Deloye, Parker	2015, '16	
DeMoss, Clarence	1953	
DePuy, Orval C.	1905, '06	
DeSilva, Chris	2010, '11, '12	
Deuchler, Gustave H.	1918	
Dickinson, Charles F., Jr.	1930, '31	
Dickinson, Richard J.	1893	
Dickinson, Roger F.	1926	
Dickison, Marc	1994	
Dickson, Kerry	1980, '81, '82, '84	
Diefenthaler, Robert J.	1937, '38, '39	
Diettrich, Henry J.	1942	
Dill, Arthur W.	1893	
Dillavou, Lanny D.	1986	
Dillon, Roy H.	1897	
Dintelmann, Robert H.	1955, '56, '57	
DiSilvestro, Eric	2004, '05, '06, '07	
Dlesk, David C.	1979, '80	
Dodds, Ben	2013, '14, '15, '16	
Domantay, Gregory	1983	
Donoghue, R. C.	1894, '99	
Donohoe, Philip H.	1920, '21	
Dossey, Doug	1992, '93, '94, '95	
Dowling, Ralph	1944	
Downey, William H.	1948, '49	
Downs, H. Burton	1938, '39, '40	
Downs, Robert B.	1947, '48, '49, '50	
Dozier, Benjamin A.	1970, '71, '72	
Drake, Elmo S.	1911	
Drake, Waldo H.	1911	
Dufresne, Jacques A.	1933, '34, '35	
Dunbar, Harry B.	1903	
Duncan, Earl J.	1931	
Duncan, James F.	1926	
Dundy, Michael W.	1962, '63	
Dunham, N. C.	1906, '07	
Dunn, Clarence L.	1942, '43, '47	
Dunning, Frank W.	1905, '07	
Durham, Thea	1995, '96	
Durkin, John F.	1969, '70, '71	
Durkin, Michael K.	1972, '73, '74, '75	
Durland, Clyde E.	1903, '04	
Dusenberry, Paul B.	1920, '21	

Dykstra, Greg — 1968, '69, '70
Dykstra, Larry R. — 1970, '71, '72
Dziedzic, Matsen — 2015, '16
Eader, Matt — 2009
Eason, Ryan — 1999, '2001
East, Warren E. — 1910
Eastin, Edward M. — 1966
Eckburg, David — 1994, '95
Eckert, Vernon M. — 1934, '35
Eddleman, T. Dwight "Dike" — 1943, '46, '47, '48, '49
Edwards, Charles F. — 1940, '42
Edwards, James F. — 1967, '68, '69
Edwards, Steve — 1973
Ehizuelen, Charlton O. — 1974, '75, '76, '77
Ehlers, Norman F. — 1958
Eicken, James H. — 1976, '77, '78, '79
Einbecker, Brett — 2010, '11, '12, '13
Eiring, Konrad — 2016
Elder, R. M. — 1903
Elders, Gerald W. — 1940, '41
Elliott, John A. — 1984, '85, '86, '87
Ellis, Eugene D. — 2008
Ely, Warren G. — 1947, '48
Emery, Robert S. — 1918, '19, '20
Emrich, Jon B. — 1982
Enck, James A. — 1964, '65, '66
English, E. C. — 1899, '00
Engnell, Kyle — 2009, '10, '11, '12
Enochs, Claude D. — 1896, '97, '98
Enochs, Delbert R. — 1898
Estes, Raymond A. — 1975, '76, '77, '78
Etnyre, Roy E. — 1930, '32
Evans, Harry, Jr. — 1923, '24, '25
Evans, Paul B. — 1930, '31
Evans, Robert H. — 1893, '94, '95
Evers, Walter A. — 1940
Fairfield, David — 1927, '28
Fairweather, Charles — 1903
Fasules, James W. — 1971, '72, '73, '74
Feldman, Ed — 1968
Fell, Milan T. — 1925, '26
Fessenden, Douglas A. — 1922, '24
Fessenden, Ralph J. — 1952, '53, '54, '55
Ffitch, Peter B. — 1982
Field, David E. — 1917
Fields, David W. — 1921
Finney, Bruce — 1972

Finney, Damon W. — 1975
Fiore, Phillip J. — 1977
Fish, Julian L. — 1914
Fisher, Ralph M. — 1933
Fitch, Horatio M. — 1922, '23
Flannery, James M. — 1977, '79
Floto, E. C. — 1903
Floyd, Thomas — 1951, '52, '53
Flynn, Thomas F. — 1893
Folks, Jamaal — 2003
Fonnesbeck, Casey — 2007, '08, '09, '10
Ford, Gary — 2012, '13
Foreman, Paul L. — 1959, '60, '61
Forman, Hamilton M. — 1908
Foskett, Roy M. — 1903, '04, '05
Foster, Alfred B. — 1893
Foster, Dale W. — 1952, '53, '54, '55
Foster, Duane — 1958
Fournier, Josh — 2002, '03, '04, '05
Fouts, L. H. — 1892, '94, '95
Fraker, Davis — 2011, '12, '13, '14
Frandsen, Lee R. — 1959
Franks, Willard G. — 1946
Franz, Frederick W. — 1977, '78, '79, '80
Frary, C. Deane — 1936, '37, '38
Frazier, Leotis K., Jr. — 1956
Freeland, Chesley B. — 1909
Freese, John A. — 1902
Frey, Hugh W. — 1935
Fritz, Timothy — 1984
Froom, Albert N. — 1906
Fruin, Leon T. — 1930
Fuller, Michael K. — 1971, '72
Fullerton, Thomas C. — 1943, '44
Fultz, Duane — 1940
Furness, Carl N. — 1921
Gage, John C. — 1930, '31
Gaines, Harry E. — 1936, '37, '38
Gajos, Bernard M. — 2008
Galardy, Blaze — 2014, '15, '16
Gale, Eli P. — 1901
Gallo, Michael P. — 1964
Gantz, Howard S. — 1915, '17
Gardiner, Lion — 1907, '08
Gardiner, Robert P. — 1918, '19
Gardner, Robert — 1970
Garrett, Richard P. — 1897, '99, '00
Gassmann, Neal M. — 1990
Gault, Ben — 1999
Gaumer, Tim — 2010, '11
Gay, Pharaoh — 1994, '95, '96

Gentry, Derrick L. — 1981, '82, '83, '84
Gerard, Kenneth C. — 1928
Gerrish, William G. — 1965, '66
Gibson, Charles — 1994, '95, '96, '97
Gibson, Robert L. — 1978, '79, '80
Gilbert, Dwight A. — 1988, '89
Gilbertson, Hunter — 1950, '51
Gilkerson, Thomas J. — 1904, '05
Gill, John S. — 1936
Gillon, Randy — 1997, '98, '99
Gist, Joshua L. — 2008
Gladding, Donald K. — 1942, '43
Glass, Rufus C. — 1928
Glavash, Zach — 2004, '05
Glesne, Kurt — 2004, '05
Glosecki, Andy R. — 1936, '38
Goelitz, William H. — 1913, '14, '15
Gold, Alex — 2016
Gonzalez, Joseph A. — 1951, '52
Gonzalez, Marcelino — 1943, '44, '45, '46
Goodell, Warren F., Jr. — 1943
Goodspeed, A. C. — 1903
Goodspeed, Wilbur F. — 1901
Goretzke, Fritz A. — 1964, '65, '66
Gould, Maurice S. — 1942
Gould, William C. — 1931
Gow, Nick — 1999, '00, '01, '02
Grady, Bernard — 2000, '01, '02, '03
Gragg, George L. — 1938, '39
Graham, Paul J. — 1909, '10, '11
Grant, Wendell E. — 1962, '63, '64
Gray, Brandon — 2008
Greanias, Evon C. — 1943
Grear, Sidney E. — 1905, '06
Greathouse, Forrest G. — 1926
Green, Dorian — 1994, '95, '96, '97
Green, Earnest — 2009
Green, Juan Paul — 2013
Gridley, Chad M. — 2006, '07, '08
Grieve, Robert S. — 1935, '36, '37
Gross, Richard G., II — 1970, '71, '72
Groves, James C. — 1904
Guercio, Anthony M. — 1983, '84
Gunn, Charles A. — 1890, '91, '92
Haab, Nic — 2009, '10, '11, '12
Haas, Brian L. — 1988, '89, '90, '91
Hackett, Theodore N. — 1936, '37
Haight, Joe — 2016
Haisley, Ernie — 1958, '59

Name	Years
Hale, Clyde S.	1940, '41
Hale, Hugh K.	1926, '28
Haley, Arthur E.	1893
Halik, Edwin J., Jr.	1968, '69
Halik, Kevin C.	2003
Hall, Melvin E.	1923, '24
Hall, Raymond T.	1927
Hall, Richard	1968
Hall, Seymour E.	1895
Halle, David A.	1985, '86, '87, '88
Hamer, Charlton P.	1985, '86, '87, '88
Hamer, Paul E.	1944, '45
Hamlett, Robert T.	1927, '28
Hammitt, Andrew B.	1913, '14, '15
Hammon, Corey	2012, '13, '14, '15
Hammond, James	1960, '61, '62
Hampton, Keith	1930, '31, '32
Hanley, James T.	1908, '09, '10
Hanlon, James A.	1973, '74, '75, '76
Hanssen, G. A.	1889
Harford, Douglas	1965, '66, '67
Harford, Josh	2002
Harney, J. M.	1901
Harper, Bueford R.	1929, '30
Harper, Gordon K.	1929
Harris, Harold E.	1958, '59, '60
Harris, Mark	1976
Harshbarger, Terry L.	1962, '63
Hart, William W.	1914
Hartman, William H.	1965, '66
Harts, D. H.	1899
Haviland, William D.	1939
Hayes, Bannon D.	1986, '87, '88, '89
Hayes, Joseph C.	1945
Hebert, Jordan	2011, '12, '13, '14
Hedgcock, Frank M.	1956, '57, '58
Heinsen, Norman K.	1928
Heitmeyer, Troy A.	1988
Hellmich, Hudson A.	1932, '33, '34
Henderson, Cole	2015, '16
Henderson, Fred	1912, '13, '14
Henry, Smith T.	1901, '02
Henson, Eric	1993, '94, '95, '96
Herrick, G. Wirt	1909, '10, '11
Herrick, Lyle G.	1899, '02, '03
Hill, Aaron	1932
Hill, Cliff	1977, '81
Hill, Gregory H.	1982, '83, '84, '85
Hill, Sam H.	1921, '22, '23
Hiller, William C.	1952, '53
Hills, Otto R.	19931
Hinkle, Robert S.	1944, '48, '49, '50
Hinman, Lawrence D.	1908
Hinton, Larry	1964
Hoagland, John C.	1897
Hoagland, John K.	1895, '97, '98, '99
Hobble, Arthur C.	1899, '00
Hobbs, Glenn M.	1889, '90, '91, '92
Hobbs, Tim	2002, '03, '04, '05
Hodges, Joey	2007
Hodur, Josh	2010, '11, '12, '13
Hoerr, Trent J.	2005, '06, '07, '08
Hohman, Elmo P.	1914, '15, '16
Holbrook, Michael	1963, '64
Hollingsworth, Elbert R.	1931, '32
Homoly, Andy	1992
Hoover, H. Harold	1899
Houseworth, Jon	2004, '05, '07
Houston, Edward N.	1960
Howard, Daniel O.	1920
Howard, Glen	1992, '95
Howland, Dennis R.	1969, '70, '71
Howse, Kenneth R.	1969, '70, '71
Hughes, Eric L.	1946
Hughes, Seth M.	1923, '24, '25
Hugill, William	1939
Hull, W. H.	1912
Hunsley, Lorne E.	1924, '25
Hunter, James A.	1911, '12, '13
Huntley, Osman H.	1936
Husted, Guy H.	1913
Husted, Merle R.	1916, '17
Huston, Paul E.	1948
Hutchinson, Scott R.	1987
Hutchinson, Thomas W.	1978
Hye, Michael	2015, '16
Imrie, Earl D.	1958
Inch, Christopher A.	1988
Irons, Louis M.	1947, '48, '49, '50
Jackson, Frederick L.	2007, '08
Jackson, Trenton	1963, '64, '65
Jacobs, Jeffrey P.	1983, '84, '85, '86
Jacobson, John D.	1986, '87, '88
Jarboe, Marcus	1993, '95
Jenkins, Earl A.	1990, '91, '92, '93
Jenkins, Edwin M.	1906, '07, '08
Jenkins, Jerome J.	1986, '87, '88, '89
Jenner, Kyle W.	1982
Jennings, Scott A.	1981, '83
Jewsbury, Walter M.	1949, '50, '53
Jirele, Jeffrey S.	1976, '77
Johnson, A. M.	1900
Johnson, Clarence E.	1898
Johnson, Franklin P.	1922, '23, '24
Johnson, Gerald P.	1950
Johnson, Joseph	1944, '45
Johnson, Paul E.	2005, '06, '07, '08
Jones, Abe	2004, '05, '06
Jones, Anthony M.	1991, '93, '94
Jones, Bruce L.	1975
Jones, Chris	1997, '98
Jones, Daniel P.	2008, '10, '11
Jones, Gordon E.	1934
Jones, Joshua	2012, '13, '14
Jones, Roger	2009, '10
Jones, Tyrone	1997, '98, '99, '00
Jones, W. Ray	1908, '09, '10
Jones, William N.	1976
Jonsson, Karl	1955, '56, '57
Jordan, Arthur I.	1910
Jordan, Vanier	2013, '14
Jumper, T. J.	1998, '99, '00
Kabba, Bai	2010
Kabel, Robert L.	1953
Kaczkowski, Thomas H.	1974, '75
Kaemerer, David W.	1972, '73, '74
Kamin, Mike	1994, '95
Kamm, Albert C.	1933, '34
Kaplan, Bruce S.	1972
Kariher, Harry C.	1898, '99
Karkow, Waldemar	1947, '48
Karnopp, E. B.	1903
Kats, Jerry H.	1951
Kay, Michael	1970
Kearney, Thomas	1974, '75
Keator, Edward O.	1898, '99, '00, '02
Keifer, Martin	2001, '02, '03
Keller, Charles I.	1938
Keller, James	2006, '07
Keller, Thomas O.	1974, '75
Kelley, Jon	1990
Kelley, Michael L.	2008
Kelley, Robert A.	1942
Kelley, Robert L.	1943, '44, '45
Kendziera, David	2014, '15, '16
Kenney, Wendell L.	1920
Kennicott, Robert M.	1933
Kerr, George E.	1958, '59, '60
Ketzle, Henry B.	1901, '02
Keys, Melvin	1983, '84, '85

Kienlen, Donald L. 1940, '41
Kimball, C. B. 1891
Kimmel, Lyman B. 1925, '28
Kincaid, Brian V. 1990, '91, '92
Kinda, Yawusa 2008, '09
King, Aaron 2003, '04, '05
King, James 2003
King, Tommy 2013
Kinsey, Daniel C. 1924, '25
Kirkpatrick, John W. 1906
Kivela, Paul 1984, '86
Klein, Cody 2011, '12, '13, '14
Klein, Kenneth J. 2008
Klima, Matt 1995, '96, '97, '98
Kline, William G. 1903, '05, '06
Kloepper, Victor F. H. 1922
Knaus, Pete 2004
Knight, E. J. 1905
Knight, William A. 1933
Knox, J. H. 1905
Knuffman, Joe 1997, '98
Kocian, Frederick M. 1981, '82
Koenig, Thomas E. 1964, '65
Koers, Marko 1992, '93, '94, '95
Kolasa, Richard J. 1987, '89, '90, '91
Koonz, John C. 1924
Kopf, Frank A. 1912
Koster, Mark R. 1969, '70, '71
Krainik, Anthony 1978, '79, '80, '81
Kratz, J. P. 1899, '00
Krause, Dennis W. 1966
Kreidler, Chester J. 1917, '18
Kremske, Dan 2010, '11, '12
Kriegsmann, Michael 1990, '93, '94
Krivec, John J. 1939, '40
Kronforst, John 2000, '01, '02, '03
Kruidenier, Jeremy 2004, '05, '06, '07
Kubala, Tom 1973
Kuehr, Trevor 2015, '16
Kueker, Brian A. 1975, '76, '77, '78
Kurlinkus, Charley 2004, '05, '06
Kusz, William 1937
LaBadie, Lee D. 1970, '71, '72
Lafond, Dylan 2015, '16
La Frank, Samuel E. 1971, '72, '73
Lally, J. Richard 1963, '64
Lamb, Courtney 1996, '97, '98, '99
Lamb, Lawton B., Jr. 1950, '51, '52
Lamoreax, John R. 1967, '68
Landmeier, Vernon O. 1934
Lang, Alvin L. 1917, '18

Langston, Donnell 1972
Lankford, Ryan 2012
Lansche, Oral A. 1915
Larson, Lyman B. 1963
LasCasas, Vince A. 1952
Lasley, Matt 2000
Lathrop, Dan 2016
Lattimore, John A. 1958, '59, '60
Lawrence, C. G. 1897, '98, '99
Lawton, Brad 1992, '93
Laz, Donald R. 1949, '50, '51
Laz, Douglas L. 1976, '77
Lazear, Weston B. 1907
Leach, William F. 1963
LeCrone, Armand J. 1959, '60, '61
LeCrone, Charles M. 1958, '59, '60
Ledbetter, Shawn 2009, '10
Lee, Garrett 2014, '15, '16
Lee, Malik 2014, '15
Lee, Omar C. 1928
Leek, Walter C. 1932
Lehmann, Jeffery G. 1983, '84, '85
Lehmann, Michael H. 1979, '80, '81, '82
Lehmann, William 1936, '38
Leigh, William L. 1979, '80
Lenington, Ernest 1931, '32, '33
Lenzini, James R. 1978, '79, '80, '81
Lenzini, Robert E. 1952
Leo, Herbert T. 1910, '11, '12
Leonard, Travis 2007, '09
Leuchtmann,
   Joseph W. 1986, '87
Leuthold, Donald W. 1947, '48, '49, '50
Levanti, Louis 1946
Lewis, Charles M. 1892, '93, '94,
   '95, '96
Lewis, Kenneth S. 1918
Lewis, William M. 1940, '41, '42
Lifshitz, Oz 2010, '11
Lifvendahl, Richard A. 1919
Lindall, Fred H. 1931, '32
Lindberg,
   Edward F. J. 1906, '07, '08, '09
Linde, Gerald H. 1924
Lindley, Jake 1999, '2001
Line, Harold E. 1932
Lloyd, Brandon 2000
Lloyd, R. C. 1901
Lockett, Boyea 2010
Lohr, Lane 1984, '85, '86, '87
Long, Harold D. 1932

Long, Troy L. 1901, '05
Loughman, Philip G. 1971
Louis, Benjamin E. 1966
Lowe, Marquis 2003
Luker, Thomas P. 1956, '57
Lundeen, Jeffery 1964, '65
Lynn, Ryan 2011, '12, '13
Lyon, Daniel R. 1926, '27, '28
Maartens, Hendrik 2009
Maat, Molefi 2015, '16
Macintyre, James 196
Mackay, J. J. 1904, '03, '06
Maddux, Scott 1992
Magnesen, Billy 2016
Mail, Isaac P. 1941, '42, '43
Makeever, Samuel J. 1924, '25, '30
Malz, Peter J. 1951
Mammoser, Mitch 2013, '14, '15, '16
Mango, Robert J. 1970, '71, '72, '73
Mann, Arthur R. 1895
Marchese, Thomas 2001
Marcum, Jay 2006
Marczewski, Jeff 1981, '82
Maris, Ronald W. 1957
Markham, Liam 2013, '14, '15, '16
Marley, James A. 1903, '05
Martin, John D. 1946
Martin, Lorenzo E. 1956
Martin, Robert W. 1899, '00, '01
Marzulo, Sam C. 1923, '24
Masheto,
   Gakologelwang 2007, '08, '09
Mason, Arthur H. 1914, '15, '16
Mason, Richard W. 1958, '59
Masterson, Daniel 1966
Masterson, Donald J. 1966
Mastney, Edward 2006, '07
Mathers, Manley B. 1913
Mathis, William 1946, '47
Matter, Herbert J., Jr. 1942, '43, '47
Maxwell, John R. 1893
May, William W. 1906, '07, '08, '09
Maynard, Eugene E. 1952, '53, '54
Mazur, Dan 1994, '95
McAsey, Joseph 2012, '14, '15, '16
McBride, Willis B. 1893
McCaskrin, Henry M. 1892, '93, '94
McClennan, Scott 1999, '00, '01
McClure, L. Milton 1936
McCord, Ralph N. 1908, '09, '10
McCown, Wilbur M. 1938, '39, '40

McCroy, Kendall 1999, '00, '01, '02
McCulley, C. T. 1903, '04
McCulley, Daniel M. 1980, '81
McDermont, Verne A. 1929, '30, '31
McDonald-Ashford,
    George 1999
McDonnell, Brendan 2014, '15
McDonough, Daren 1993, '94, '95
McElfresh, Fred M. 1893, '94
McElwee, Ermel J., Jr. 1961, '62
McElwee, Ermel J., Sr. 1926, '27, '28
McGinnis, Gordon F. 1921, '22
McGraw, Arthur C. 1936
McHose, Joseph C. 1924
McHugh, Matthew C. 2008, '10, '11
McKeever, Donald 1927
McKenley, Herbert H. 1946, '47
McKeown, John L. 1913, '14, '15
McKinney, Norman 1917
McKown, Robert W. 1956, '57, '58
McLellan, Jeffery C. 1967, '68, '69
McNabb, Lou 1970
McNulty, Joel M. 1951, '52, '53
McSween, Cirilo A. 1951, '52, '54
Meharry, J. E. 1899
Mehock, Harry E. 1925, '26
Meislahn, Arthur C. 1925, '26, '27
Melin, Carl A. 1903, '04
Melton, Albert, Jr. 1974, '75, '76
Merigold, Julian S. 1925
Merrifield, Albert W. 1889, '90, '91, '92
Merrill, Stillwell F. 1900
Merriman, John R. 1911
Michel, Ryan 2010, '11, '12, '13
Michl, Isaiah 2016
Mickow, Hunter 2009, '10, '11, '12
Mieher, Edward C., Jr. 1924, '25
Mies, Harold H. 1938
Mikolay, Mikel 1997
Miles, Rutherford T. 1899, '1901
Miller, C. Marshall 1934
Miller, Clarence B. 1907, '08
Miller, Gary E. 2008, '09
Miller, Harold R. 1925
Miller, Terry 1966, '67
Miller, Thomas S. 1928, '30
Miller, V. Ward, Jr. 1959
Miller, William G. 1892
Mills, Morton J. 1919
Mills, Ralph 1897, '99
Milne, Edward L. 1895, '96, '97

Missev, Matt 1993
Mitchell, George W. 1892
Mitchell, Justin 2003
Mitchell, Robert 1957, '58
Mitchell, Ronald L. 1952, '54, '58, '59
Mitizia, Albert M. 1935, '36
Mkwezalamba,
    Maxwell M. 2008
Mobarak, Aaron A. 1990, '91
Mongreig, Louis M. 1917
Monte, Steve 2010, '11, '12, '13
Moore, Terrance D. 1985
Moorman, Anthony 2001, '02
Moran, Mark A. 1898, '99
Morehouse, Merritt J. 1889
Morrill, Guy L. 1910, '11, '12
Morris, George 1967, '68, '69
Morris, Graham 2013, '14
Morris, R. Jeffery 1976
Morrison, Heraldo E. 1986
Mors, Robert J., Jr. 1960
Muldoon, Sean 2006, '07
Mullen, R. Patrick 1964, '65, '66
Murphy, Frank D. 1910, '11, '12
Murray, Michael B. 2007, '08, '09, '10
Murray, Oscar J. 1914
Muschler, George 1974
Myers, Carl 1993, '94, '95, '96
Nachel, Jacob R. 2007, '08, '09
Nagle, James 1954
Nagle, Perry I. 1921
Nast, Wayne A. 1951
Naughton,
    Frank U., Jr. 1920, '21
Nauta, Michael 1965
Nelle, Richard S. 1932
Nevins, Arthur S. 1911, '12, '13
Nichols, David C. 1944, '45
Nickol, Edgar 1927, '28
Nipinak, Michael 1974
Noe, Brandon 2012, '13, '14, '15
Nolan, Dan 1992
Norberg, Justin 1998, 2000
Norris, Ralph V. 1905, '06, '07
Norton, James M. 1965, '66, '67
Novak, Joseph C. 1928
O'Connell, John J. 1936
O'Meara, Allan R. 1916
Oakes, Bernard F. 1924
Ockert, Carl 1946
Olesen, Robert J. 1986, '87, '89, '90

Olsen, Donald E. 1940, '41, '42
Olson, Gail 1979, '80, '81, '82
Olszewski, John M. 1978, '80
Orlovich, Michael G. 1937
Orlovich, Robert B. 1927, '28, '29
Orr, E. E. 1893, '95
Osborn, Harold M. 1920, '21, '22
Osley, Willie 1970
Ostaszewski,
    Walter R. 1932
Ottoson, Eric R. 1987, '88, '89
Overbee, William B. 1917
Paden, J. C. 1905
Paetau, Gary 1970
Paetau, Holger 1972, '74
Pamilton, Stephon 2013, '14
Panzer, Ernest D. 1924, '25
Panzer, Howard S. 1927, '28
Parham, Earl R. 1988, '89
Parker, George T. 1915
Parola, J. Tony 1964
Paterson, James A 1928, '29, '30
Patrick, Stanley A. 1944
Patterson, Asa E. 1991, '93, '94
Patterson, Bruce 1921, '22
Patterson, Paul L. 1944
Pattison, Richard H. 1923
Patton, Michael K. 1982, '83, '84, '85
Pearman, Barry 1995, '96, '97
Peck, Ken E. 1969, '70, '71
Peebles, Thomas A. 1904, '05, '06
Pellant, F. Robert 1956, '57, '58
Pendarvis, Harry R. 1916, '17
Pengelly, Sean 2016
Peoples, Stephen 1982
Perryman, Alvin 1977, '78, '79, '80
Petefish, William M. 1931
Peters, Forrest I.
    "Frosty" 1927
Peterson, James M. 1961, '62
Peterson, Michael 1984
Peterson, Ralph 1954
Pettigrew, James Q. 1908, '09
Pettinger, R. G. 1899, '00
Phelps, John C. 1912, '13
Phelps, Robert L. 1943, '44, '45, '46
Phelps, Scott L. 2007, '08, '09, '10
Phillips, Donald J. 1982, '83
Phillips, Ronnie E. 1970, '71, '72
Pierce, Jack B. 1946
Pierre-Louis, Gandy 1995

Pierson, Adam 2003, '04
Pierzynski, Thaddens 1945, '47
Pike, Albert M. 1918
Pinder, Cyril C. 1966
Pivovar, Greg M. 1971, '72, '73
Plant, Francis B. 1899, '00
Pogue, Harold A. 1914, '15, '16
Polakow, A. H. 1914
Pollard, Ray A. 1941
Pollensky, Charles 1935
Pompei, Phil 2011, '12
Porter, Horace C. 1896, '97
Portman, Crain P. 1934
Post, Clarence F. 1903
Powers, John P. 1988, '89
Pratt, Bryan 2004, '05, '06, '07
Prescott, John S. 1919, '20, '21
Prickett, F. W. 1897
Prince, Eric W. 1990
Puhse, Scott W. 2006, '07, '08
Purma, Frank L. 1931, '32
Putnam, Edmund D. 1966
Pykosz, Robert J. 2006, '08
Quinn, Devin 2016
Radloff, Ronald L. 1979
Ragusa, Matthew T. 2007, '08
Railsback, Fay D. 1908, '09
Ramirez, Brett 2011, '12, '13
Rapp, J. H. 1914
Rayburn, Cecil C. 1894, '95
Read, E. N. 1899
Reavis, Rudolf W., Jr. 1976, '77, '78, '79
Redhed, William S. 1909, '10
Redmon, G. Bogie 1963, '64, '65
Reeder, James W. 1938
Rehberg, Robert 1942, '46, '47
Rehm, Arthur C. 1923, '25
Reiser, Jesse 2016
Reising, Richard K. 1939, '40
Replogle, Vernon L. 1929
Reynolds, Greg 1982, '87
Reynolds, Richard W. 1951, '52
Rice, James E. 1967
Richards, James V. 1908, '09, '10
Richards, Robert E. 1946, '47
Richardson, Brad J. 1969
Richardson, Jared A. 2007, '08
Richardson,
   William H. 1905, '06, '07
Richie, James K. 1908, '09, '10
Ricketts, C. Alan 1950

Riddle, Jim 2011, '12, '13
Ridley, Babatunde 1997, '98, '99, '01
Riegel, Robert W. 1935, '36
Riley, Andrew 2009, '10, '11, '12
Ringquist, Mauritz E. 1935
Ripskis, Stanley 1962, '63
Ritter, Michael G. 1989
Robbins, Isaiah T. 2007, '08
Robinson, Herman 1931, '32
Robinson, J. T. 1936, '37, '38
Robinson, James O. 1939, '40
Rodgers, Robert A. 1928, '29, '30
Rodman, Charles S. 1901, '02, '03, '04
Rodriguez, Matt 1997
Rogers, Aaron M. 1989, '90, '91
Rohrer, Carl J. 1909, '10, '11
Romein, Daniel C. 1977
Root, George H. 1894
Ropp, Franklin N. 1907
Ross, Alister 2007
Rothgeb, Claude J. 1902, '03, '04, '05
Rothlisberger, Curt 1984, '86
Rothwell,
   William F., Jr. 1966
Rowland, E.M. 1900
Royer, James M. 1927
Rudolph, David L. 1961
Rudolph, Leonard 1937
Rue, Doran T. 1925, '26, '27
Ruff, Robert 1976
Ruleau, John G. 1985
Runkle, Willard C. 1926
Ruscin, Mark J. 1989
Russell, Brian 1983
Russell, James T. 1985, '86
Russell, Jon 1999, '00
Russell, W. Hunter 1934
Ruther, Robert E. 1944, '49
Saarima, Matt 1998
Salyers, R. 1905
Sandeen, John D. 1966, '67, '68
Sanders, Floyd W. 1929
Sanders, Ralph L. 1912, '13, '14
Sanner, J. David 1968, '69
Sarros, James J. 1978
Saunders, Chris 1995, '96
Sawtelle, Stephen E. 1978
Schaeffer, William J. 2008, '09, '10, '11
Schellenberg, Steven 1977, '78
Schildhauer, Fred J. 1923, '24
Schilke, Renold E. 1962, '63

Schlansker, D. Lynn 1932, '33
Schlapprizzi, Fred H. 1921, '22
Schleizer, Shawn M. 1990, '93, '94
Schmeig, David 2016
Schmidt, Edward S. 1961
Schmidt, Jon 1979, '80, '81, '82
Schmidt, Mark S. 1978, '79
Schneck, Sereno W. 1894
Schnittgrund, Gary D. 1968, '69
Schobinger, Eugene 1913, '14, '15
Schoch, Philip F. 1924, '25, '26
Schoeninger,
   Joseph F. 1934
Schubert,
   Wolfgang M. 1939
Schuh, Charles R. 1918, '19, '20
Schultz, Greg 1999, '00
Scott, J. Russell 1922, '23
Scott, Lawson 1892
Seely, Irving R. 1933, '34, '35
Seely, Ralph W. 1933
Seib, Robert C. 1942, '43
Seiler, Otto E. 1910, '11
Seldon, John M. 1929
Self, Bruce 1967, '68, '69
Sentman, Lee H., Jr. 1929, '30, '31
Shank, Robert 1988, '89, '90, '91
Shepherd, John W. 1903
Sherline, Charles H. 1986, '88
Sherry, H. Raymond 1968, '69, '70
Shively, Bernie A. 1925, '26, '27
Shockey, Victor E. 1980, '81, '82, '83
Shogbuyi, Azeez O. 2009, '10, '11
Shroka, Gregory C. 2007, '08, '09, '10
Shuman, Donald L. 1946, '47, '49
Sibbitt, J. P. 1928
Siders, Stacey A. 1951, '52, '53
Siegel, William 1970
Siglin, Brett 1995, '96
Sikich, John 1939, '40, '41
Siler, R. W. 1900
Simon, Frank 1928, '29
Simon, Joseph V. 1926, '27, '28
Simon, Timothy 1985, '86, '87, '88
Sitko, Leonard J. 1988, '89, '90, '91
Sittig, John F. 1925, '26, '27
Slack, Jerry, Jr. 1950, '51
Slogan, John C. 1975, '76, '77, '78
Smith, Al 1971
Smith, C. F. 1899
Smith, Claire H. W. 1905, '06, '07

Name	Years	Name	Years	Name	Years
Smith, Dave P.	1988	Sullivan, Harold F.	1926	Upton, Richard A.	1949, '50
Smith, Dewitt	1893	Sullivan, James	2011, '12, '13	Urbanckas, Alfred	1956, '57
Smith, Ed	1983, '84	Sutter, J. H.	1899	Useman, Ernest M.	1930
Smith, Fred D.	1903, '05	Swank, Roger L.	1950, '51, '52	Usher, Darryl C.	1985, '86
Smith, Harvey H.	1932	Swanson, Reuben E.	1922	Usrey, Vergil R.	1924
Smith, Julian	2013, '14	Swartzendruber,		Utt, Arthur H.	1918
Smith, Leonard A.	1969	Frederick	1945	Vadeboncoeur,	
Smith, Russell W.	1923	Sweeney, Marshall J.	1923, '24, '25	Nathan	2004, '05, '06
Smith, Timothy C.	1975, '76, '77, '78	Sweet, Gayln L.	1971, '74	Van Inwagen, F.	1905, '06, '07
Smith, Tramell	2003, '04, '05, '06	Sweet, Paul C.	1921, '22, '23	Van Kirk, William K.	1979, '82
Smith, Zack	2016	Sweney, Don	1893, '94, '95, '98	Van Meter, Vincent J.	1934, '35
Sniegorski, Maciej	2005, '06, '07	Swift, A. Dean	1938	Van Oven,	
Snyder, Ray E.	1945	Tackett, William C.	1893	Frederick W.	1896, '97, '98
Somers, Aloysius J.	1917	Talbot, Paul	1994	Van Swol, Jason	1999, '00, '01, '02
Spakowski, Scott	1988, '89	Tanthavong, Branden	2012, '14, '15	Veirs, David C.	1899, '00, '01
Spangler, Scott	1983	Tapping, Charles H.	1914, '15	Vieth, Wayne	1951
Speer, Kenneth R.	1935, '36, '37	Taylor, Deryck L.	1961, '62, '63	Viney, Cam	2013, '14, '15, '16
Spink, Phillip M.	1916, '17, '20	Taylor, Kyle	1993, '94, '95, '96	Virgin, Craig	1974, '75, '76
Sprague, Stanley R.	1945	Taylor, Malcolm	2010, '11, '12, '13	Vitalleto, Nick	1997, '98
Springe, Otto	1910	Teach, Jeffrey D.	1991, '93, '94, '95	Voris, Alvin C.	1893
Spurgeon, Lowell	1936, '37	Telfer, Sam	2013	Vranek, Lee R.	1943, '47, '49
Spurlock, Albert C.	1936	Thanos, Jon D.	1986, '87, '88	Waarich, Herman	1949, '50, '51
St. Clair, Tim	1984	Thomas, Ranis	1944	Wachowski,	
Staff, Lawrence M.	1955, '56, '57	Thompson, Frank L.	1900, '01	Theodore J.	1927, '28
Stanners, Jerry K.	1955, '56, '57	Thompson, Fred B.	1898	Wagner, Bertram E.	1950, '51
Starck, Robert W.	1940, '41, '42	Thompson, Harwell C.	1912, '13	Wagner, David A.	1978
Starkey, Dean E.	1986, '87, '88, '89	Thomson, Willard P.	1952, '53, '54, '55	Wahls, Aaron	2001, '02, '03
Stead, Charles B.	1917	Tilton, Leon D.	1913	Walker, Adrian	2003, '04, '05, '06
Steinberg, Philip	1945	Timm, Judson A.	1928, '29	Walker, George	1966, '67, '68
Stellner, Frank L.	1926	Timmerhaus, Klaus	1948	Walker, George	1945, '46, '47, '48
Stephenson, Roger A.	1909	Tjarksen, Donald E.	1958, '59	Walker, John A.	1949, '50
Sterrenberg,		Tockstein, L. A.	1929	Wallace, Henry S.	1921, '22
Ronald K.	1977, '78	Toepfer, Jannis	2013, '14, '15	Wallace, Oscar	1973
Stevens, Jeremy	2007	Toerring, Christian J.	1891	Wallace, Samuel H.	1920, '21, '22
Stevens, Thomas	1980, '81, '82, '83	Tolbert, Roderick L.	1986, '87, '88, '89	Wallace, William H.	1924, '25, '26
Stevenson, Amos M.	1899, '00	Topol, Bradley	2006	Walters, David B.	1975, '76, '78, '79
Stewart, D. Larry	1957, '58, '59	Townsend, Rolla E.	1903	Walters, Thorn D.	1963
Stillwell, Al	1974	Trandel, Eugene J.	1946	Wanger, David E., Jr.	1930
Stine, Francis B.	1927, '28, '29	Trapp, Harold F.	1896	Ward, Russell "Andy"	2007, '08
Stirton, James C.	1914, '15, '16	Travis, Foster L., Jr.	1964, '65, '66	Ware, J. W.	1905
Stitzel, Clarence M.	1911, '12	Trimble, Leon	1929	Ware, Paul R.	1952
Stoddard, David	1973, '74	Trimble, Ocie	1951, '52, '53	Warner, E. A.	1903
Stone, Richard R.	1965, '66	Troester, Nathan	2011	Warner, Gale A.	1925
Stone, W. W.	1899	True, Bobby	1996, '97, '98, '99	Washburn, Ludlow J.	1908, '09, '10
Stotlar, Samuel D.	1948, '49	Turner, E. Scott	1991, '92, '93, '94	Washington, Lester	1983, '84, '85
Stout, Lorence S.	1939, '40, '41	Turner, Elbert L., III	1989, '90, '91	Washington, Quincy	1999
Stovall, David	1994	Turner, John H.	1940, '41	Wasser, Norman	1947, '48, '49
Stringfellow, Efrem Z.	1978, '79, '80, '81	Twardock, A. Robert	1951, '52, '53	Wasson, Roy A.	1941
Stryganek, Brandon	2012, '13, '14, '15	Twomey, John E.	1946, '47	Watkins, Maurice	2013, '14, '15
Studzinski, James D.	1950	Twomey, Vic L.	1946, '48, '49, '50	Watson, Carl P.	1908
Stuttle, Fred L.	1925, '26, '27	Tyson, Steven M.	1984, '85, '86, '87	Watson, William A.	1966, '67

Wayda, George	2014, '15, '16
Weatherford, Steve	2003, '04, '05
Webb, Terrence	1969, '70, '71
Webster, Frederick F.	1916, '17
Wedding, C. Nugent	1938
Weedman, Frederick J.	1892, '93, '94
Wehling, Fred J.	1935, '36
Weiler, W. Richard	1946
Weiss, John N.	1918, '20, '21
Welker, Douglas J.	1977, '78
Wells, Edwin S., Jr.	1921, '22, '23
Wells, Jonathan	2015, '16
Welter, Cullen J.	1989, '90, '91
Welty, William R.	1936
Werner, Charles D.	1925, '26
West, Jason D.	1991, '92, '93
West, William O.	1932, '33
Wham, James B.	1940
Wham, Richard A.	1952, '53, '54
Wharton, Russell F.	1920, '21, '22
Wheeler, H. H.	1904
White, Charles V.	1975, '76, '77, '78
White, Donald R.	1978, '79
White, Earl C.	1926, '27, '28
White, Harold R.	1926, '28, '29
White, James E., Jr.	1991
White, Sylvester, Jr.	1989
Whitehead, Donell	1984
Wieneke, Mark J.	1986
Wiley, Raymond S.	1899
Wilkerson, Michael R.	1985
Wilks, Aaron	2014, '15, '16
Will, Larry D.	1977, '78, '79, '80
Williams, Durrell L.	2007, '08
Williams, Gil	1964, '65
Williams, Tyrone	1995
Williams, Willie J.	1952, '53, '54
Willis, Stephen I.	1972
Wilson, Kenneth L.	1918, '19, '20
Wilson, Norman K.	1912
Winfield, Rob	1997, '98
Winship, Harold L.	1977
Wisslead, Cody J.	2008, '09, '10, '11
Wolf, Ty	1984, '85
Wolff, Gary L.	1962, '63
Womick, John P.	1966
Wood, Arthur	1941
Wood, Charles H.	1904, '08
Woodin, D. E.	1904, '05, '06

Woods, John T.	1978
Woods, Stanley W.	1957
Woodson, Abraham B.	1954, '55, '56
Woolsey, Robert D.	1931, '32, '33
Worsley, Dominique L.	2006, '08
Wright, James W., Jr.	1953, '54
Wright, John W., Sr.	1966, '67
Wright, Laurence S.	1923, '24, '25
Wright, Newton A.	1914, '15
Wright, Robert	1936
Wright, Royal	1889
Wright, Wesley E.	1974, '75, '76
Wyatt, Nathaniel C.	1977, '78, '79
Yarcho, Wayne B.	1938, '39
Yarnall, Thomas C.	1925, '26
Yates, Howard N.	1920, '21, '22
Yates, Robert W.	1926
Yavorski, Michael T.	1962, '64
Yesko, Matt	1997, '99
Young, Anthony, Jr.	2004, '05, '06, '07
Young, Claude H. "Buddy"	1944
Young, Maurice	1995
Young, Richard	1944
Zahn, D. J.	2012, '13, '14, '15
Zea, Tony	2015, '16
Zebe, Zebo	2011, '12, '13, '14
Zeman, Paul	2013, '14, '15, '16
Zieren, Jason	1995, '96, '97, '98
Zimmerman, Al	1945
Zimmerman, John H.	1919
Zinzer, Josh	2010, '11, '12, '13
Zollner, Andrew T.	2006, '07, '08, '09

WOMEN'S TRACK

Ackerman, Courtney	2015
Adeokun, Mobolaji	2014
Akinosun, Moriyike	2013, '14
Anderson, Linda	1980, '81
Angel, Katherine	1979, '80, '81, '82
Ania, Emma	2000
Armstrong, Tiara	2005, '06, '07, '08
Aschoff, Laura	1999
Aufmann, Madeline	2010, '12, '13
Austin, Analisa	2008
Baine, Shayla	1988, '89, '90
Baker, Yolanda	1991, '92, '93
Balagtas, Lisa	1987, '88, '89

Bass, Rachel	1983
Bates, Melissa	2008, '09, '10, '11
Bayne, Jessica	2002, '03
Bearfield, Chequetta	1999, 2000, '01, '02
Beckford-Stewart, Alecia	2007, '08, '09, '10
Bennent, Taylor	2007
Benson, Lisa	1980
Berry, Jasmine	2015, '16
Beverly, Leticia	1986, '87, '88, '89
Bizzarri, Angela	2007, '08, '09, '10
Blazek, Audrey	2016
Bloch-Jones, Kandie	2014, '15, '16
Bobart, Valerie	2016
Bodden, Shirley	1986, '87, '88
Bodey, Kimberly	1987, '89
Boyd, Ryisha	2009, '10, '11, '12
Boyle, Elizabeth	2009, '10, '11
Branch, Denise	2016
Brooks, Kawanna	2010, '11, '12, '13
Brown, Deserea	2009
Brown, Jana	1980
Brown, Mekelayaie	1991, '92
Bruene, Carol	1986, '87
Buciarska, Joanna	1999
Buford, Tonja	1990, '91, '92, '93
Bullard, Becky	2002
Burkett, Aspen	1995, '96, '98
Carr, Renee	1986, '87, '88, '90
Carroll, Maggie	2005
Carver, Dorothy	1979, '80
Choquette, Nicole	2014, '15, '16
Christopher, Amy	1998
Coleman, Breeana	2012, '13, '15
Conda, Rolanda	1985, '86
Cooper, Alondra	2005, '07, '08
Coppin, Katie	2005
Corbett, Carmel	1992, '93, '94, '95
Crutchfield-Tyus, Terra	1993, '94, '95, '96
Cunningham, Briana	2006, '07, '08
Dale, Charlene	1980, '81, '82
Davis, Emone	2016
DeBellis, Jennifer	2013, '14, '15, '16
Des Enfants, Laura	1979
Dickerson, Marianne	1981, '82
Dietzen, Cecelia	2000, '01, '02
Drewes, Elizabeth	1979
Driver, Briana	2016

Dunlap, Kim — 1983, '84, '85, '86
Dunnavan, Lyndsey — 2000, '01
Duvenedack, Amanda — 2011, '12, '13, '14
Eitzen, Elizabeth — 2011, '12, '13
Ejesieme, Jesica — 2012, '13, '14
Elsen, Virginia G. — 1982
Engel, Katie — 2007, '08
Estes, Carolyn — 1999, '01, '02
Evans, Aja — 2008, '09, '10
Falsey, Colette — 2012, '13, '14, '15
Felicien, Perdita — 2000, '01, '02, '03
Fernandez, Juana — 1985, '86
Fonzino, Danielle — 1996, '98
Ford, Mary — 1981, '82, '83
Fox, Amanda — 2014, '15
Frakes, Erin — 2002
Frigo, Meghan — 2011, '12, '13
Fulcher, Victoria — 1987, '88
Garrett, Rebekah — 1992, '94, '95, '96
Gentry, Gretchen — 1984
Gerke, Laura — 2002, '03, '04, '05
Gilliean, Allisa — 1995, '96
Glade, Jayne — 1981, '82, '83, '84
Gliottoni, Rachael — 2005
Golliday, Marissa — 2010, '11, '12, '13
Grant, Stacy Ann — 1996, '97, '98, '99
Greene, Mariesa — 2005, '06, '07
Greiner, Sue — 1983
Grier, Gretchen Y. — 1982, '83
Griffith, LaToya — 2009, '10, '11, '12
Grimes, Emma — 2015
Groenewoud, Chantelle — 2008, '10, '11
Gross, Samantha — 1992, '93
Gulick, Catherine — 1979
Hackett, Colleen — 1983, '84, '85
Hall, Pamela — 1982, '83, '84
Hansen, Michelle — 1991
Hargrove, Sade — 2016
Harpell, Danielle — 1989, '90, '91, '92
Harrison, Yvonne — 1996, '97, '98
Hawkins, Leslie L. — 1987
Heise, Jennifer — 1995
Heitz, Angie — 1984, '85
Helfer, Cheryl — 1979
Henry, Ann — 1985, '86
Henson, Nina — 2003, '04, '05, '06
Hernandez, Rachel — 2008
Hilmersson, Marie — 2002

Hogan, Mollie — 2003
Holder, Nikkita — 2007, '08, '09
Holingsworth, Lauren — 2013
Howard, Gillian — 1991
Huffman, Shannon — 1994, '95, '96
Hunt, Amber — 2000, '01
Hunt, Cassie — 2004, '05, '06
Hunziker, Janae — 1979, '81
Johnson, Janelle — 1993, '94
Jones, Bernette — 1991, '92
Jones, Kristina — 2004, '05, '06, '07
Kaiser, Becky — 1979, '80, '81, '82
Kallur, Jenny — 2001, '02
Kallur, Susanna — 2001, '02
Kelley, Benita — 1995, '96, '97, '98
Kelly, Ashley — 2009, '10, '11, '12
Kieger, Claire — 2014
Kladar, Kristina — 2016
Knop, Nancy — 1979
Kopko, Amy — 1980, '81, '82, '83
Koster, Bridget — 1985
Kraiss, Katherine — 1995
Kuenne, Jill — 1979, '80, '81
Lantis, Julie — 1983, '84
Latimer, Aleisha — 1998, '99, 2000, '01
Lawrence, Cynthia — 1987, '88, '89, '90
Lemersal, Megan — 2016
Levanti, Katie — 2003
Levanti, Kristie — 2003
Lewis, Gia — 2000, '01, '02
Lickhart, Audrey — 2003, '04
Locascio, Sharon — 1987, '88, '89
Long, Kelly — 1980
Lottes, Jan — 1983
Madsen, Wendy — 1991, '92, '93
Marine, Jenny — 1996, '97
Marry, Miranda — 2015, '16
Martin, Lindsay — 1998, '99
Martin, Lyria — 1997, '98, '99, 2000
Mason, Melissa — 1982
Mastoris, Helen — 1988, '89, '90
Mayer, Patricia — 1979
Mazikowski, Carol — 1980, '81, '82, '83
McArthur, Jayla — 2010, '12
McCaugherty, Kendall — 2011
McClatchey, Angela — 1986, '87, '88, '89
McGlone, Cathy — 1981
McKeeman, Sara — 2015, '16
McNee, Kelly — 1983, '84, '85, '86

Mendozza, Tara — 1997, '98, '99, '01
Mengyan, Liz — 2008
Mensah, Yvonne — 2004, '05, '06, '07
Meyer, Jordana — 2000, '01, '02
Meyle, Wendy J. — 1981, '82, '83, '84
Miles, Donna — 1982, '85
Miles, Kathy — 1980
Miller, Christine — 1991, '92
Mindcock, Laura — 1994, '95, '96
Mondie-Milner, Celena — 1987, '88, '89, '90
Morgan, Cheria — 2011
Morgan, Stephanie — 2011, '14
Morris, Karen Jo — 1992, '94
Morris, Kathy Ann — 1992, '94
Morrison, Kristin — 2012, '13
Moss, Tracy — 2000, '01, '02
Moyer, Anita — 1979
Murphy, Samantha — 2011, '13
Nesfield, Tiffany — 2005, '06
Neverstitch, Lisa — 1979, '80
Newsome, Collinus — 1995, '96, '97, '98
Nicholson, Candace — 1998, '99
Nuhsbaum, Tanja — 1991, '92
O'Brien, Kelly — 1989, '90, '92
Oldham, Yvonne — 1983, '84, '85, '86
Oshinowo, Adeoti — 1999, 2000, '01, '02
Palm, Stacy — 1987
Pannier, Kathy — 1980, '81, '82
Penney, Jessica — 2008, '09
Petrey, Britten — 2014, '15, '16
Phelan, Shannon — 2008, '09, '10
Pickett, Shanna — 2002, '03, '04, '05
Pintaro, Amanda — 2006, '07
Piotrowski, Mary — 1992
Plummer, Lisa — 1980, '81, '82
Ponder, Tisha — 1997, '98, '99, 2000
Porada, Katie — 2011, '12, '13
Powell, Shontel — 1998, '99
Pulcher, Victoria J. — 1987
Rakosnik, Lindsey — 2014, '15, '16
Reu, Lindsey — 2002, '04, '05
Richards, Kerry Ann — 1996, '98, '99, 2000
Richartz, Stephanie — 2011, '12, '13, '15
Riggins, Pat — 1980
Riley, Crystal — 2000, '01, '02, '03
Riley, Dawn — 1993, '94, '95, '96
Rimar, Jeanne C. — 1993
Robinson, Camile — 2004, '05, '06, '07
Robinson, Carlene — 2004, '05, '06, '07

428

Robinson, Tamika — 2008, '10, '11
Rogers, Janile — 2015, '16
Rogers, Rhea A. — 1981
Russell, Donna — 1987, '88, '89, '90
Sabin, Beth — 1980
Sanders, Hope — 1992, '93, '94, '95
Scheideggar, Samantha — 2006
Schmidt, Chloe — 2012, '13, '14, '15
Schneider, Alyssa — 2013, '14, '15
Schwab, Jennifer — 1992, '93
Scigousky, Brooke — 1995
Seger, Kim — 2016
Seymour, Pedrya — 2015, '16
Shimmon, Lauren — 2002, '03, '05
Simmering, Laura — 1989, '91, '92, '93
Simms, Stephanie — 2005, '06, '07
Simpson, Casie — 2002, '03
Smith, Alexandria — 2009
Smith, Deborah — 1988, '89
Smith, Kayla — 2010, '11, '12
Smith, Mariah — 2013, '14, '15
Smith, Suzanne — 1977, '79
Smith, Terika — 1991, '92
Smyers-Jones, Kortni — 2016
Speer, Lindsay — 1997, '98
Spencer, Ahlivia — 2013, '14
Spencer, Ashley — 2012, '13
Stack, Amber — 2011, '12
Stecyk, Amy — 1979
Sterneman, Ruth — 1985, '86
Stetson, Deborah — 1984, '85
Stewart, Jayla — 2016
Stoltz, Terry — 1987
Stone, Melissa — 1989
Straza, Melissa — 1987, '88
Streeter, Paris — 2008, '09
Sutherland, Kristin — 2009, '10
Taylor, Kymbriona — 2013, '14, '15, '16
Thomas, Althea — 1989, '90
Thomas, Asia — 2012, '13, '14
Thompson, Samone — 2014, '15
Thurmon, Kimberly — 1991, '92
Tiffin, Donna — 1977
Tochihara, Tama — 1991, '92, '93, '94
Tomlinson, Amy — 1992, '93, '94
Turilli, Jaime — 2004, '05, '06
Tweedy, Jennifer — 1990, '91, '92, '93
Ugiagba, Omoye — 2006, '07, '08, '09
Vogel, Margaret — 1982, '84, '85
Volling, Tabitha — 2003, '04, '05

Wacaser, Jan — 1980, '82
Waldinger, Beth — 1982
Wall, Audrea — 2003
Wallace-Sipp, Jazjuan — 2013, '14, '15
Waller, LaNeisha — 2005, '06, '07, '08
Walling, Rochelle — 1996
Walters, Kathy — 1979
Walters, Vicki — 1983
Ward, Cheryl — 1982, '83, '84, '85
Washington, Bev — 1976, '77, '78
Washington, Kelly — 2010, '11
Weber, Nora — 1994, '95, '96, '98
Welch, Wendy — 1992
Werkowski, Amy — 1987, '88, '89
Weygand, Tricia — 1994, '95
Whitman, Nicole — 2002, '03
Whittaker, Ashley — 2005, '06, '07
Williams, Allison — 2001, '02, '03
Williams, Camee — 1999, 2000, '01, '02
Williams, Katherine — 1991, '92, '93, '94
Williams, Kimetha — 2003, '04
Williams, Tonya — 1993, '94, '95, '96
Wilson, Kristen — 2013, '14
Winter, Hanna — 2015, '16
Withrow, Loretta — 1989, '90
Wolf, Pam — 2006
Woods, Danelle — 2008
Yaeger, Courtney — 2010, '11, '12, '13
Yonke, Martha — 1979
Young, Natalie — 2003, '04, '05, '06
Ziegler, Jackie — 2007
Zimmerman, Beth — 1982

VOLLEYBALL

Abrahamovich, Courtney — 2010, '11, '12, '13
Alde, Stefanie — 2006, '07
Anderson, Kristine — 2007, '08
Anderson, Lori — 1984, '85, '86, '87
Argabright, Lisa — 2000, '01, '02, '03
Bailey, Ellen — 1980
Bangert, Johannah — 2007, '08, '09, '10
Bartsch, Michelle — 2008, '09, '10, '11
Bastianelli, Ali — 2015, '16
Bazzetta, Kathleen — 2001, '02 '03, '04
Bazzetta, Lizzie — 2005, '06, '07, '08
Beitz, Melissa — 1996, '97, '98, '99
Belter, Jessica — 2001, '02, '03, '04
Beltran, Jennifer — 2010, '11, '12, '13
Bielfedt, Matti — 2014
Binkley, Elizabeth — 1984, '85, '86, '87

Birks, Jocelynn — 2012, '13, '14, '15
Bochte, Sue — 1974, '75, '76
Borske, Erin — 1994, '95
Bourne, Keelin — 2009
Bowers, Stephanie — 1988, '89, '90
Boyle, Bridget — 1986, '87, '88, '89
Breen, Melissa — 1975, '76, '77, '78
Brickley, Amy — 1991, '92, '93, '94
Brookhart, Nancy — 1986, '87, '88, '89
Brown, Vicki — 2004, '05, '06, '07
Bukenas, Dale R. — 1974
Bush, Laura — 1987, '88, '89, '90
Calabrese, Vanessa — 1974
Carver, Dorothy — 1974, '75, '76
Cavato, Carrie — 1995, '96, '97, '98
Chapman, Cristy — 1997, '98
Chatterton, Amy — 1995
Clasey, Jody — 1979, '80, '81, '82
Coleman, Mary — 1995, '96, '97, '98
Collymore, Karen — 1979, '80, '81, '82
Conard, Julie — 2012, '13, '14, '15
Conway, Anne — 1989, '90, '91
Cook, Jennie — 1994, '95
Coulter, Heidi — 1994, '95, '96, '97
Criswell, Morganne — 2011, '12, '13, '14
Crittenden, Naya — 2015, '16
Culligan, Catherine — 2008
Davis, Danielle — 2013, '14, '15, '16
Dayton, Devin — 1975
DeBruler, Laura — 2007, '08, '09, '10
Dikhoff, Carolien — 1995
Dillman, Lisa — 1987, '88, '89, '90
Dippel, Kathy — 1982, '83
Dluzak, Marijo — 1974
Donnelly, Brandi — 2014, '15, '16
Dorn, Anna — 2011, '12, '13, '14
Douglass, Paula — 1984, '85, '86, '87
Dowdy, Chris — 1979, '80, '81, '82
Dvorak, Gerry — 1982
Edinger, Ashley — 2006, '07, '08, '09
Edwards, Julie — 1991, '92, '93, '94
Eggers, Mary — 1985, '86, '87, '88
Eiserman, Betsy — 1999, 2000, '01
Falcon, Dee Dee — 1981
Feldman, Rachel — 2008, '09, '10, '11
Fracaro, Denise — 1982, '83, '84, '85
Gard, Lydia — 1998, '99, 2000, '01
Gartland, Eileen — 1975, '76, '77
Gartland, Kathleen — 1976, '77, '78
Gereau, Annika — 2016
Gleis, Kirsten — 1992

Glynn, Kathy	1977, '78, '79
Greenwood, Brittney	1995
Griffin, Meg	2003, '04
Haddad, Shadia	1998, '99, 2000, '01
Haen, Hillary	2007, '08, '09, '10
Harkins, Eileen	1991
Harks, Lauren	2001, '02, '03, '04
Haselhorst, Laura	1995, '96, '97, '98
Hebeisen, Kellie	1990, '91, '92, '93
Helfrich, Kim	1974
Henderson, Lorna	1989, '90, '91, '92
Henderson, Rachel	2005, '06, '07
Henriksen, Kristin	1990, '91, '92, '93
Hill, Kate	2000
Holtz, Carla	1974
Hranicka, Blayke	2016
Hrischuk, Amy	1994
Hynds, Jen	2004
Jendryk, Jessica	2010, '11, '12
Johnson, Disa	1984, '85, '86, '87
Johnson, Erin	2009, '10, '11, '12
Jones, Amy	1990, '91, '92, '93
Kavanaugh, Kendal	2016
Kelsay, McKenna	2013, '14, '15, '16
King, Nancy	1974
Kissinger, Molly	1983
Koester, Anne	1999, 2000
Korte, Kaylin	2016
Krolik, Ann	1976, '77
Kump, Nicole	2007, '08, '09, 10
Laverman, Petra	1988, '89, '90
Lee, Jessica	1994
Lenti, Kim	1978, '79, '80, '81
Lindner, Amber	1998, '99, 2000, '01
Livingston, Mary	1974
Lottes, Jan	1979, '83
Lourcey, Linnea	1974, '75
Luhrsen, Annie	2010, '11, '12
Macdonald, Meghan	2003, '04, '05, '06
Marshall, Tracey	1996, '97, '98, '99
Mayers, Maddie	2013, '14, '15
McArthur, Joan	1974
McCulley, Kylie	2006, '07, '08, '09
McMahon, Liz	2011, '12, '13, '14
Meyer, Cari	2004
Moeck, Peggy	1974, '75, '76
Moskovitz, Bonnie	1983
Mullis, Merrill	1990, '91, '92, '93
Neal, Melissa	1994
Nelson, Abby	2007, '08, '09
Nemec, Carrie	1978, '79, '80

Norris, Joan	1984
Nucci, Sue	1991, '92, '93, '94
Obermeier, Stephanie	2004, '05, '06
O'Bryan, Shelly	2000, '01, '02, '03
Onion, Tayler	2009, '10, '11, '12
Orozco, Jazmine	2010, '11
Owen, Holly	1977, '78, '79
Palash, Amy	2006, '07
Palmer, Allison	2014, '15, '16
Parrish, Melissa	1989
Pedelty, Amy	1984
Pjrnhaber, Martha	1988
Podlecki, Karen	1977
Polkoff, Kathryn	2012, '13, '14, '15
Pomeroy, Sarah	2000
Poulter, Jordyn	2015, '16
Pratapas, Katy	2003, '04, '05
Prentice, Paula	1995, '96, '97, '98
Prince, Beth	2015, '16
Quade, Jacqueline	2106
Rea, Sally	1985, '86
Rimzdius, Nancy	1975, '76, '77, '78
Roberts, Janet	1975, '76, '77, '78
Rogers, Tina	1990, '91, '92, '93
Roustio, Katie	2013, '14, '15, '16
Rumpel, Carol	1985
Samuelson, Jill	1983, '84, '85
Sanchez, Gina	1993
Scherr, Kelly	1993, '94, '95, '96
Schlinkman, Jean	1975, '76, '77
Scholtens, Sandy	1985, '86, '87, '88
Schorn, Dena	1999
Schwarz, Chris	1985, '86, '87, '88
Schwarz, Liz	1979, '80, '81
Schwarz, Margie	1978, '79, '80, '81
Schwarz, Rita	1982, '83, '84, '85
See, Kelly	1981, '82, '83
Shannon, Kathleen	1991, '92, '93
Shipman, Tracy	1988
Skorus, Nina	1980, '81
Skudlarek, Mary	1980, '81
Smith, Joyce	1988
Sorrell, Sara	1996, '97, '98, '99
Spicer, Betsy	1997, '98, '99, 2000
Stadick, Katie	2013, '14, '15, '16
Stark, Ali	2012, '13, '14, '15
Stecyk, Amy	1977, '78, '79
Stettin, Megan	1992, '93, '94, '95
Stoessel, Annie	1996, '97, '99
Strizak, Michelle	2013, '14, '15, '16

Sullivan, Jeanne	1978, '79, '80, '81
Ternelli, Esra	1982
Turner, Kayani	2005, '06, '07, '08
Vandrey, Melissa	2000, '01, '02, '03
VanMeter, Rachel	2002, '03, '04, '05
Venkus, Laura	1978, '79
Viliunas, Alexis	2012, '13, '14, '15
Virsilaite, Rasa	2002, '03, '04, '05
Virtue, Erin	2001, '02, '03, '04
Vrdsky, Beth	2003, '04, '05, '06
Wacaser, Jan	1979
Ward, Colleen	2010, '11
Watters, Laurie	1981, '82, '83
Webber, Sue	1999, 2000, '01, '02
Welsh, Caroline	2016
Wheeler, Missy	1984
Wilson, Heather	1997, '98, '99, 2000
Wilson, Mary Ellen	1975, '76, '77
Winsett, Barb	1987, '88, '89, '90
Wolfe, Jackie	2009, '10, '11, '12
Yario, Sue	1980, '81, '82, '83
Yoss, Jeanne	1984, '85
Zarytsky, Lea	2007
Zenarosa, Rena	1992, '93

WRESTLING

Abromovich, Phil	1951
Acheson, Adam	2012, '13, '14, '15
Adams, William	1934, '35
Agase, Alex	1942, '43
Agase, Louis	1945
Alexander, Jeff	1993
Alexander, Robert	1955, '56
Allen, Earl	1981, '82
Allen, Guy	1981
Aloia, Alex	1941, '42
Ambler, Basil	1931
Anastasia, Dana	1985
Anderson, Darin	1989
Anderson, Kerry	1967, '68
Anderson, Rob	1996
Andrew, Arthur	1954
Andrews, Charles	1934, '35
Anthonisen, Norman	1942, '46, '47
Aprati, Fred	1964, '65, '66
Archer, Arthur	1948
Arlis, Clint	2007, '08, '09, '10
Armstrong, Tucker	2012
Azinger, Kirk	1985, '86, '87, '88
Baird, Dave	1984, '85, '86, '87
Barbour, Dave	1987, '88

Barczak, Joe	2008, '09, '10	
Barnes, Harvey	1925	
Bartley, John	1943	
Battaglia, Frank	1937, '38	
Bauerle, Louis	1929, '30	
Beam, Bruce	1973, '74, '75	
Beattie, Clayton	1963, '64, '65	
Beck, Denver	1970, '71, '72	
Beechy, Jake	2009, '10	
Behnke, Mike	2004, '05	
Benion, Ernest	1994, '95, '96, '97	
Benson, Scott	1994, '95, '96, '97	
Berger, Matt	1985, '86	
Berger, Ryan	2000, '01, '02	
Bergren, Mark	1973, '74, '75	
Bernardoni, Edwin	1943	
Bernstein, Matt	1989, '92	
Berry, Kenneth	1940, '41, '42	
Birkhiner, D. James	1941	
Black, Brooks	2015, '16	
Blanton, Jordan	2009, '10, '12, '13	
Blount, Al	1981	
Blum, Bill	2001	
Blum, Daniel	1936, '37	
Bohannon, Edward	1945	
Bollman, Keith	1991, '92	
Bond, Patrick	2007, '08, '09, '10	
Borland, Harold	1922	
Bower, Ed	1944, '45	
Bowman, John	1980	
Boyd, Jesse	1939, '40	
Boyd, Mike	2004, '05	
Brady, Seth	1994, '95, '96, '97	
Brannan, Jon	1961	
Brennan, James	1939	
Brenne, Gary	1968	
Briggs, John	1980	
Briggs, Steve	1977, '78, '79	
Brittain, Alpheus	1929	
Brown, C. Addison	1925	
Brownridge, Enis	1970, '71, '72	
Brownson, Pat	2006, '07, '08	
Brownstein, Harold	1956, '57, '59	
Brunkow, N. F.	1912, '13	
Brunson, Zac	2014, '15, '16	
Burdick, Lloyd	1930	
Burns, Bruce	1965, '66	
Burwell, Robert	1945	
Bussey, Charles	1926	
Butler, Jason	1999, 2000	
Byrd, Tyrone	2002, '03, '05, '06	

Callaghan, Rich	1963, '64, '65
Callahan, Phil	1982, '84, '85, '86
Campbell, Albert	1928
Carek, Frank	1934
Carpenter, Kenneth	1934, '35, '36
Carso, L.	1931
Castillo, Anthony	2001, '02, '03, '04
Castillo, Mike	1998, '99, 2000, '01
Catarello, Dan	1998, '99
Catlett, Stan	1965
Causey, Juan	1978, '79
Chamberlain, Jess	1937
Chandler, Kyle	2006
Check, Robert	1974, '75, '76, '77
Chirico, Doug	1975, '76
Chirico, Phillip	1975, '76
Chirico, Randy	1973
Cianciarulo, Howard	1962
Citron, Abraham	1935
Claypool, Austin	1928, '29
Close, Greg	1981, '82
Cochran, R. Bruce	1978, '81, '82
Collum, Paul	2001
Columbo, J. B.	1911, '13
Comfort, Jim	2004, '05, '06, '07
Compton, Norton	1952, '53
Cook, Shane	2000
Cope, Lorin	1915, '16, '17
Cortez, Ralph	1978, '80, '81
Cosneck, Barney	1932, '33, '34
Crane, Russell	1928, '29
Cravens, Brian	2000, '01, '02
Crenshaw, Derrick	1990
Crum, Edward	1933
Cummins, J. R.	1914
Curby, Nick	2000, '01, '02, '03
Cutler, John	1912, '13, '14
Dahl, Andrew	1934, '35
Dallago, Tony	2011, '12, '13, '14
Daugherty, Troy	1983
Davis, Chris	1981, '82, '83, '84
DeAno, Jon	1962, '63
Delgado, Jesse	2012, '13, '14, '15
DeLong, George	1944
DeMarco, Vic	1964
Deneen, John	2008, '09, '10
Dergo, John	2007, '08, '09, '10
Deutschman, Archie	1937, '38, '39
Devor, Forest	1958, '59, '64
Dick, C. D.	1915
Dietzen, Anton	2001, '02, '03, '04

Diewald, Emil	1955
Dillon, Edward	1941
Doerrer, Steve	1997, '98, '99
Domko, Joe	1964
Dooley, Kyle	2012, '13
Dooley, Wilbur	1929, '30, '31
Dowell, Wilbur	1932
Drury, Ian	1987, '88
Ducato, Phil	1987
Dunn, Merle	1952
Durlacher, Dave	1988, '89
Durlacher, Lindsey	1994, '95, '96, '97
Dwyer, Robert	1949, '50
Dziedzic, Dave	1993
Eagermann, Aaron	1995, '96, '97
Echternacht, T. J.	1930
Edelen, Francis	2016
Edgren, Thomas	1974, '75
Edison, Markwood	1933
Emmons, Bob	1931, '32, '33
Emmons, David	1939
Emmons, James	1940
Ervin, Brock	2016
Ervin, Caleb	2013, '14, '15
Escobar, Ryan	2000, '01
Esslinger, Paul	1922
Esterl, Jason	1996, '97, '98
Ferrari, Patrick	1977, '78
Ferreira, Al	1983
Ferrill, Dent	1911
Ferry, Cal	2003, '04, '05
Fetherston, J. M.	1913
Fiorini, Tim	1978
Fitz, Eugene	1928
Fletcher, Matt	2003, '04, 05, '06
Flood, Paul	1929
Flores, Gabe	2005, '06, '07, '08
Flostrom, Victor	1922
Fonzino, Joe	2000, '01
Foor, Doug	1988
Ford, Jay	1993
Fotos, Lambros	2005
Fotos, Paris	2000, '01
Frederick, E. M.	1915
Fredericks, W. M.	1933, '34
Fregeau, John	1968, '69, '70, '71
Fricker, David	1956
Friedl, Ben	2008, '09, '10
Friedl, Pete	2003, '04, '05, '06
Froehlich, Peter	1976, '78, '79, '80
Fullerton, Willard	1930

Furlong, Mark	1976, '77, '78	Helman, David	1938, '39	Kerestes, Tim	1969
Futrell, B. J.	2009	Helmick, Dave	1981, '83	Keuhl, Doug	1973
Gabbard, Thomas	1957, '58, '59	Herman, Jevon	1995, '96, '97, '98	Kimberlin, Jake	2009, '10
Gabbard, William	1956, '58	Hesmer, Theodore	1927, '28	Kimberlin, Ryan	2005
Garcia, Joe	1946, '47, '48, '49	Hestrup, Joel	1976, '77	King, Andrew	1976
Gary, Charles	1992, '93, '94, '95	Hewitt, Wilfred	1931	King, Ben	1999, 2000, '01
Gaumer, Gilbert	1948, '49, '50	Hicks, Danny	2015	Kinger, Ryan	2005, '06
Gaumer, Wayne	1949, '50	Hill, Kimbrell	1940	Kirby, Guy	2012
Geis, Clarence	1925, '26	Hill, Robert	1916	Kirkpatrick, Bruce	1968, '69, '70
Gerdes, Ken	1991, '93	Hoerr, Blake	1999, 2000	Klaas, Palmer	1972, '73, '74
Gibson, James	1974, '75, '77	Hoffman, Harold	1920	Klass, Craig	1973
Gillespie, Conor	2001, '02	Holzer, Werner	1957, '58, '59	Koenig, Tom	1963
Ginay, John	1936, '37, '38	Houghton, Eldon	1932, '33, '34	Koepke, Jeff	2013, '14, '15, '16
Gingerich, Jacob	2014	Howell, Edward	1936	Korfist, Matt	1990, '92
Glassgen, Al	1944	Huddleson, Clyde	1912	Kotowski, Joe	2008
Glick, Sanford	1932	Hughes, John	1940	Kraml, Ken	1959
Glynn, Brian	2002, '03, '04, '05	Hughes, Robert	1943, '44	Kranz, Richard	1945
Gomez, Joe	2006, '07	Hull, Wendell	1957	Krom, Dave	1965
Gonzalez, Mario	2011, '12, '13, '14	Humphreys, Albert	1926	Kummerow, Walter	1966
Gottfried, Charles	1947, '48, '49	Hurry, Tyler	1997	Kusmanoff, Tony	1963
Goverdare, Paul	1940, '41	Huth, William	1939	Laase, F. H.	1924
Gradman, Harold	1930, '31	Inman, Dave	1970	Lackey, Matt	2000, '01, '02, '03
Graham, James	1978	Irle, Joseph	1974	Langdon, Bill	1963
Green, Richard	1928	Irussi, Bruce	1979, '80	Langenderfer, Kyle	2015, '16
Greenawalt, Andy	2007	Jackson, Edwin, Jr.	1951, '54, '55	Lanning, John	2000, '01
Greene, Joe	1995	Jacob, Paul	1970, '71	Lansche, Oral	1915
Grieshaber, Gary	1973	Jacobson, Ken	1962, '63, '64	Law, Glenn	1926
Grunwald, Carl	1946	Jayne, Mark	2002, '03, '04, '05	Layer, Bruce	1968
Gudeman, Will	1998	Jeffery, Dan	1964, '66	Leasure, Scott	1983
Guida, Nick	2007	Jeffery, John	1964	Ledbetter, George	1934, '35
Gunlock, Virgil	1926, '27	Jimenez, Nico	2012	Lee, Andre	2016
Haas, Dan	1969	Jodeh, Mousa	2016	Lee, Jamie	1994, '95
Hale, LaDaryl	1999, 2000, '01	Johnson, Rick	1976, '77, '78, '79	Lee, Matt	2008
Hankenson, Lew	1960, '61, '62	Johnson, Scott	1978	Lee, Stanley	1943, '48
Hankenson, Steve	1986, '87, '88, '89	Johnston, Jeff	1983	Lee, Thomas	1996, '97
Hansen, Jay	1993	Jurinek, George	1961, '62	Lehnerer, Jim	1964, '65
Hanson, Tim	1983, '85	Jurtzrock, E. V.	1917	Leischaruring, M. F.	1913
Harding, Matt	2004, '05, '06, '07	Kachiroubas, Lou	1946, '47, '52	Lembeck, Tom	1983
Harkness, Roland	1945	Kagen, Irving	1941, '42	LePretre, Tyler	2012
Harp, Jeff	1985, '86	Kahon, Don	1966	Levanti, Mike	1970, '71, '72
Harris, Andre	1999	Kakacek, John	1979, '81	Levanti, Mike	2000, '01, '02
Harris, Robert	1941	Kanke, Tim	1994, '95	Leverich, Wesley	1939
Harshbarger, Thad	1959	Karr, Joel	2004, '05, '06, '07	Lewis, Chester	1973
Hart, Brett	1994, '95, '96	Kastor, Frank	1954, '55	Lindy, Donald	1940
Hatton, Troy	1995, '96, '97, '98	Kays, William	1977	Little, Chris	2003, '04, '05
Hay, Ben	2001, '02, '03, '04	Kelly, John	1979	Llewellyn, Chris	1982, '84
Hay, Chad	1999, 2000, '01, '02	Kelly, Pat	1962	Llewellyn, Jon	1988, '89, '90, '91
Hayes, John	1942	Kennedy, Jimmy	2007, '09, '10	Locascio, Victor	1952
Healy, Keith	1985, '86, '87, '88	Kenney, Gene	1950	Lockhart, John	1999, 2000, '01, '02
Heffernan, Brendan	2001, '02	Kenney, Harold		Loewe, Richard	1948 '50
Heffernan, Patrick	2001, '02, '03, '04	"Hek"	1924, '25, '26	Loffredo, Bob	1966, '67, '68

Lopez, Brandon	2013, '14	Morse, Jackson	2012, '13, '14, '15	Pillath, Jerry	1967, '79
Lopez, Chris	2013, '14, '15	Mota, Dan	1983, '84, '85	Pineda, Ron	1960
Lorenz, Ed	1969	Mottlowitz, Kevin	1987, '88, '89	Player, John	1923, '24
Lukas, Peter	1942	Muegge, Louis	1928	Poeta, Mike	2006, '07, '08, '09
Luthringer, Marshall	1924, '25	Mueller, Erik	1987, '88	Polkwalski, H.	1912
Lutz, Charles	1940	Muther, William	1956, '57, '58	Polz, Chris	1990
Lutz, Robert	1952, '53	Mutter, Charles	1936, '37, '38	Polz, Clinton	2008, '09, '10
Macomber, Bart	1966, '67, '68	Nalls, Alonzo	1987	Polz, Conrad	2010, '11, '12, '13
Madden, Kelly	2000, '01, '02, '03	Nelson, Dale	1949	Polz, Jeff	1963, '65
Mahaney, Brendan	2011, '12, '13, '14	Nelson, Steve	1984, '85	Polz, John	1960, '61, '62
Major, John	1983, '84	Nichols, Mike	1991, '92, '93	Ponder, Max	1952
Maniar, Anuj	1996, '97, '98	Nicoll, Shawn	1980	Porter, Tom	1961
Mann, William	1947, '48 '50	Nora, Matt	2013, '14, '15	Potter, Jason	2001, '02, '03, '04
Manning, Joel	2001, '02	Nordquist, Ken	1953	Powell, Griff	1999, 2000, '01, '02
Manzella, Dan	2004, '05, '06, '07	Norman, Bob	1957, '58	Powers, John	1983
Marianetti, Steve	1992, '93, '94, '95	Norman, Jake	2007, '08, '09, '10	Prater, Ryan	2008, '09, '10, '11
Marlin, Ken	1946, '47, '49	Novak, Eric	2002, '03	Preissner, Paul	1994, '95
Marshall, Chuck	1968, '69	Novak, Mike	1990, '91, '92, '93	Price, Dale	1940
Martin, Michael	2004, '05	Oaks, John	1972, '73	Price, Henry	1951
Martinez, Isaiah	2015, '16	O'Brien, Dan	1989, '90, '92	Prout, Charles	1936
Mathers, Manley	1911, '12	O'Brien, Mike	1985, '86, '87, '88	Provinse, Jason	1994, '95, '96
Mathis, Archie	1924, '25	O'Laughlin, Mike	1959, '61	Puebla, Kevin	1976, '77, '78, '79
Matlock, Gary	1974, '75, '76, '78	Olivieri, Dominic	2013, '14, '15	Puerta, Joe	1931, '32, '33
Matsumoto, Yukio	1953, '54	Ontiveros, John	1953, '54, '55	Puracchio, Lou	2004, '06
May, Roger	1966, '67, '68	Opiola, Anthony	2000, '01	Purvin, Theodore	1940, '41
Mayer, Bob	1970, '71, '72, '73	Orth, Glen	1932, '33	Pusey, Frank	1911, '12
McBride, Corey	2001	Ott, Kyle	2003, '04, '05, '06	Quirk, Pat	1998, '99, 2000, '01
McCabe, Dennis	1972	Pakutinsky, Frank	1936	Radell, Will	1965
McCarron, Dennis	1955, '56	Pakutinsky, Pete	1934, '35, '36	Rallo, Charlie	1999, 2000, '01
McCarter, Matt	2010, '12	Paloucek, Keith	1980, '81, '82, '83	Rasmussen, Chuck	1959
McCracken, Brian	1985, '86, '87	Pancratz, Kevin	1974, '75, '76, '77	Ray, Andy	2001
McCullum, Al	1964, '65, '66	Parke, Glenn	1969	Rayburn, Roland	1942, '43
McDermith, Harry	1933	Parker, Emery	2016	Read, Richard	1951, '52
McDonald, Mark	1978	Passaglia, Andy	1971, '72, '73, '74	Redman, Louis	1933
McIlvoy, Jack	1935, '37	Paswall, Grant	2008	Rehling, C. H.	1915
McMillen, James	1923, '24	Patrick, Nate	1999, 2000, '01	Reinemann, Isaac	2016
Mechling, Paul	1953, '54	Paul, Victor	1958	Resner, Peter	1977
Medley, Earl	1970, '71	Paun, Joe	2000, '01, '02	Reyes, Nikko	2014, '15
Meeks, Richard	1952, '53, '55	Pearson, Roland	1961, '62	Reynolds, Donny	2004, '05, '06
Mellen, William	1953, '55, '56	Pedrosa, Tony	2003	Richards, Zane	2014, '15, '16
Merzian, Chuck	1951	Pelton, Lance	1991, '92, '93, '94	Riggins, Paul	1950, '51
Meyer, Wayne	1953	Pero, Jason	1996, '98	Ritz, John	1926, '27
Miller, Phil	1972, '73, '74, '75	Perry, Carl	1997, '98, '99, 2000	Robinson, Darrell	1970
Minot, George	1926, '29	Perry, Joe	1967	Robinson, Frank	1956
Minsker, Bob	1934	Perry, Thomas	1942, '43	Rodrigues, Steven	2013, '14, '15, '16
Mizue, Evan	1997	Petry, Jack	1946	Roesler, Karl	1996, '97, '98, '99
Monson, Jeff	1993	Petry, Paul	1939, '40, '41	Rome, Wade	1990
Moore, David	1956, '57, '58	Pham, Twan	2002, '03	Romersberger, Richard	1942
Morrison, Allie	1929, '30	Picard, Richard	1949, '50, '51	Romine, Wesley	1999
Morrison, R. C.	1928	Pierre, Don	1956, '58	Roth, Michael	1973, '75, '76
Morrissey, Don	1959, '60	Pigozzi, Ray	1950, '51		

Rott, Dennis	1967, '68, '69	
Rotter, G. E.	1915	
Rowan, Zeke	2009	
Roy, Willie	1963	
Rubiner, John	1987	
Rudin, Greg	1989, '90, '91	
Rundquist, Elmer	1916	
Runneberg, Elton	1915	
Rusk, Steve	1994, '95	
Russell, Dave	1963, '64	
Ryan, Dean	1947, '48	
Ryan, Eric	1995, '96, '97, '98	
Salata, Bob	1959	
Salomente, D.	1931	
Sapora, Allen	1936, '37, '38	
Sapora, Joe	1928, '29, '30	
Sargent, Norbert	1955, '56, '57	
Saric, Robert	1978	
Sauer, Andrew	1943	
Scamen, Warren	1976	
Schram, Bill	1959	
Schrieder, G. W.	1912	
Schroeder, Bill	1971	
Schroeder, G. W.	1913, '14	
Schulrz, Arthur	1931	
Schultz, Alfred	1925	
Schwartz, Martin	1950, '51	
Schwartz, Richard	1952	
Seabrooke, Theodore	1940, '41, '42	
Seamen, Warren	1976	
Sears, John	1999, 2000, '01	
Shapiro, David	1946, '47, '48	
Shatiko, Basil	1924	
Shaub, Mike	2008	
Shaw, Ward	1925	
Sheahan, Pat	1998	
Sheahan, Tim	1995, '96, '97	
Shively, Bernie	1926, '27	
Shively, Bob	1965	
Siebert, Eric	1995, '96, '97, '98	
Siebert, Tony	1997, '98, '99, 2000	
Sikich, John	1939, '40, '41	
Sikora, Brad	1997, '98, '99	
Silverstein, Ralph	1935, '36, '37	
Simi, Art	1961	
Sizer, Richard	1941	
Skisak, Chris	1973, '74	
Slomski, Dennis	1995	
Smerdel, Matthew	1943	
Smith, George	1970	
Smith, Martin	2009, '10, '11, '12	
Smith-Bergsrud, Roger	2006, '07, '08, '09	
Snyder, Ray	1945	
Soga, Susumu	1926, '27	
Stangle, Solomon	1926	
Stelter, Dan	2010, '11, '12	
Stelzer, Robert	1960	
Stewart, Brian	1991, '93, '94, '95	
Stitzel, Stan	1966	
Stoltz, David	1999, 2000, '01	
Stonitsch, Mike	1991, '92, '93, '94	
Strange, Robert	1949	
Strong, H. D.	1914	
Struznik, Mark	1993	
Sulaver, Randy	1972, '73, '74, '75	
Sullivan, Albert	1977, '78	
Sullivan, Dave	1992, '93, '94	
Sullivan, Paul	1990, '91	
Sullivan, Raben	1976	
Swartz, Joel	1960	
Szabo, Steve	1955, '56, '57	
Taylor, Trent	1979, '80, '81, '82	
Temmler, Bernard	1961	
TenPas, Larry	1954, '55, '56	
Terrazas, Eric	2009, '10, '12	
Thacker, Edgar	1926, '27	
Thomas, Daryl	2010, '13	
Thomas, Harry	1916	
Thompson, Earl	1942	
Tiernan, Terry	1962	
Tirapelle, Adam	1998, '99, 2000, '01	
Tirapelle, Alex	2003, '04, '05, '06	
Tirapelle, Troy	2006, '07, '08, '09	
Tofft, Leonard	1935	
Tomala, Andy	1978	
Tomaras, William	1941, '42, '46	
Toncoff, Jean	1929, '30	
Tosetti, Arthur	1924, '25	
Townsell, William	1988	
Treadman, Jack	1944	
Trenkle, Howard	1922	
Trousil, Tom	1959, '60	
Trowbridge, Sam	1931	
Turner, Bill	1954, '55	
Unruh, Dan	1979, '80, '81	
Valvano, Dominic	2000, '01, '02, '03	
Vandersteeg, Jeff	1969, '70	
Vaughn, Jon	1994, '95, '96, '97	
Veercruysee, Bob	1973	
Vercelli, Vince	2009, '10	
Vestuto, Paul	1977, '78, '79	
Vincens, Jason	2002, '03	
Vogt, Gary	1962, '63	
Vohaska, William	1949 '50	
Voorhees, George	1944, '45	
Wagemann, Matt	2005, '06	
Walker, Carl	1961, '62	
Walker, Pat	2010, '12, '13	
Walsh, Kevin	1989	
Watts, James	1945	
Watts, Larry	1966, '67	
Weber, Joe	2001, '02	
Weber, Ron	1994, '95, '96	
Webster, Ralph	1926, '28	
Wedel, John	1952	
Wedell, Mark	1975	
Weight, Matt	2001, '04, '05, '06	
Weitz, L. J.	1929	
Welsh, Roger	1915	
Werner, Franklin	1938	
White, Harold	2009	
Whitelatch, Rex	1958, '59	
Whitson, Herman	1920	
Wiesenborn, Kurt	1977	
Williams, Derrick	1984, '85, '86	
Williams, Elvie	1976, '77	
Williams, Marty	1978	
Willman, Dean	1952, '53	
Wilson, Bob	1946	
Winterhalter, Matt	2004, '05, '06, '07	
Wise, John	2006, '07, '08, '09	
Witt, Terry	1966	
Wolff, Quentin	1969, '70, '71	
Woodcock, Geoff	1990, '92	
Woodcock, Gregg	1989, '90	
Wright, Ernie	1967	
Wyller, Tim	1998, '99	
Yates, Michael	1982, '83, '84	
Zander, Andy	1965, '67	
Zander, John	1960, '61, '62	
Zanetakos, William	1952	
Zeman, Bill	1997, '98, '99, 2000	
Zeman, Dan	2005, '06, '07, '08	
Zuidema, Greg	1970, '71, '72	
Zulauf, Ben	2006, '07	

YEAR-BY-YEAR SUMMARIES

The following is a year-by-year summary of University of Illinois athletic teams through the 2015–16 season. History has been documented more completely for some sports than others, but an attempt has been made to chart each of the twenty-four sports that have attained varsity status. Big Ten championship teams are denoted in boldface.

BASEBALL

Year	Overall Record	Big Ten Record	Big Ten Finish/ Tournament W-L	Year	Overall Record	Big Ten Record	Big Ten Finish/ Tournament W-L
1879	1-0			1909	11-3	9-3	2nd
1880	1-0			**1910**	**14-0**	**11-0**	**1st**
1881	0-1			**1911**	**18-2**	**14-1**	**1st**
1882	no team			1912	13-3-1	10-2-1	2nd
1883	3-0			1913	11-5-1	8-4	3rd
1884	1-1			**1914**	**11-7-1**	**7-3**	**1st**
1885	1-0			**1915**	**18-1-1**	**9-1-1**	**1st**
1886	4-2			**1916**	**13-1**	**8-1**	**1st**
1887	4-4			1917	13-7	8-3	2nd
1888	3-4			1918	13-6	7-3	2nd
1889	1-2-1			1919	13-5	7-4	2nd
1890	5-3			1920	16-8	6-4	3rd
1891	8-2			**1921**	**17-3**	**10-1**	**1st**
1892	8-3			**1922**	**17-2-1**	**8-2**	**1st**
1893	14-8			1923	14-6-1	7-4	2nd
1894	8-6			1924	10-6-1	4-3-1	5th
1895	10-4			1925	11-8-0	6-5	5th
1896	15-4			1926	16-7-1	7-4	3rd
1897	8-9-1			**1927**	**10-7-3**	**7-3-1**	**1st-T**
1898	12-9			1928	32-12-5	6-6	NA
1899	13-11	10-4	2nd	1929	13-7-2	6-5	4th
1900	12-2-1	11-2	1st	1930	15-5-0	8-2	2nd
1901	12-7	9-5	2nd	**1931**	**15-4**	**8-2**	**1st**
1902	12-4	8-3	2nd	1932	10-5	7-3	2nd
1903	**17-1**	**13-1**	**1st**	1933	13-3	8-2	2nd
1904	**23-4**	**11-<?>**	**1st**	**1934**	**15-3**	**9-1**	**1st**
1905	14-5	11-5	2nd	1935	12-4	7-3	2nd
1906	**13-3**	**8-3**	**1st**	1936	13-4	10-2	2nd
1907	**10-1**	**7-0**	**1st**	**1937**	**14-3**	**9-1**	**1st**
1908	**11-3**	**11-3**	**1st**	1938	8-8	4-4	6th

Year	Overall Record	Big Ten Record	Big Ten Finish/ Tournament W-L	Year	Overall Record	Big Ten Record	Big Ten Finish/ Tournament W-L
1939	7-7-2	4-5	8th	1978	25-22-1	6-12	9th
1940	**16-5**	**9-3**	**1st-T**	1979	14-30-1	3-15	10th
1941	13-7	7-4	3rd	1980	18-33	6-10	6th
1942	9-9	5-7	5th	1981*	35-26	11-3	4th/0-2
1943	8-6	5-3	3rd	1982*	49-23	14-2	4th/0-2
1944	9-3-2	5-2-2	3rd	1983*	23-24-2	6-9	4th West/DNP
1945	10-10-1	6-5-1	3rd	1984*	46-21	3-10	5th West/DNP
1946	13-8-0	6-3	3rd	1985*	46-21	12-4	1st West/0-2
1947	**22-6**	**9-3**	**1st**	1986*	34-19-2	8-8	4th West/DNP
1948	**20-7-1**	**10-2**	**lst-T**	1987*	32-24	9-7	2nd-T West/DNP
1949	9-8-1	6-5-1	5th	1988*	26-20	12-16	7th/DNP
1950	13-6	6-5	4th	1989*	42-16	17-11	2nd-T/3-0
1951	16-9	8-3	2nd	1990*	43-21	19-9	2nd-T/3-0
1952	**20-11-1**	**10-5**	**1st**	1991*	26-30	13-15	7th/DNP
1953	**17-6**	**10-3**	**1st-T**	1992*	36-20	16-12	4th/l-2
1954	16-15	4-11	9th	1993	32-23	12-16	8th-T/DNP
1955	14-10	7-6	4th	1994	26-26	12-16	7th/DNP
1956	15-18-1	4-11	10th	1995	25-31	14-14	5th-T/DNP
1957	17-9	7-4	2nd	1996	37-22	17-10	2nd/3-2
1958	18-10	8-6	4th	1997	32-27	17-11	3rd/1-2
1959	22-9	9-6	2nd	1998	42-21	19-5	1st/2-2
1960	21-10	6-8	7th	1999	34-22	15-12	3rd/l-2
1961	22-8	9-4	4th	**2000**	**41-23**	**17-11**	**1st-T/4-1**
1962	**25-6**	**13-2**	**1st**	2001	29-28	13-14	5th/1-2
1963	**18-13**	**10-5**	**1st**	2002	32-19	14-15	6th-T/DNP
1964	9-22	1-14	10th	2003	27-26	12-19	8th/DNP
1965	14-9	8-6	5th	2004	22-23	11-21	9th/DNP
1966	14-14	5-7	6th	2005	33-23-1	20-12	1st/0-2
1967	17-21	5-11	9th	2006	29-29	15-17	5th-T/0-2
1968	18-19	7-10	6th	2007	31-27	16-14	5th/1-2
1969	22-20	11-7	2nd	2008	31-25	16-15	4th/1-2
1970	19-16-1	8-10	6th	2009	34-20	16-8	4th/1-2
1971	20-16-1	10-7-1	4th	2010	26-26	10-14	9th/DNP
1972	16-21	5-9	8th	2011	30-27	15-9	1st/3-0
1973	21-13	8-10	7th	2012	28-25	11-13	6th-T/DNP
1974	27-11	9-7	4th	2013	35-20	14-10	5th-T/1-2
1975	25-17-1	4-11-1	9th	2014	32-21	17-7	3rd/1-2
1976	20-22	3-12	10th	**2015**	**50-10-1**	**21-1**	**1st/2-2**
1977	23-25	8-10	6th	2016	28-23	12-12	8th-T/DNP

* Conference divided into East and West Divisions, with top two teams from each division competing in playoffs and divisional system eliminated, top four teams advancing to playoffs.

MEN'S BASKETBALL

Year	Overall Record	Big Ten Record	Big Ten Finish/ Tournament W-L	Year	Overall Record	Big Ten Record	Big Ten Finish/ Tournament W-L
1906	6-8	3-6	4th	**1949**	**21-4**	**10-2**	**1st**
1907	1-10	0-8	5th	1950	14-8	7-5	3rd-T
1908	20-6	6-5	3rd	**1951**	**22-5**	**13-1**	**1st**
1909	7-6	5-6	4th	**1952**	**22-4**	**12-2**	**1st**
1910	5-4	5-4	4th	1953	18-4	14-4	2nd
1911	6-6	6-5	4th	1954	17-5	10-4	3rd-T
1912	8-8	4-8	5th	1955	17-5	10-4	2nd-T
1913	10-6	7-6	5th	1956	18-4	11-3	2nd
1914	9-4	7-3	3rd	1957	14-8	7-7	7th
1915	**16-0**	**12-0**	**1st**	1958	11-11	5-9	8th-T
1916	13-3	9-3	2nd-T	1959	12-10	7-7	5th-T
1917	**13-3**	**10-2**	**1st-T**	1960	16-7	8-6	3rd-T
1918	9-6	6-6	4th-T	1961	9-15	5-9	7th
1919	6-8	5-7	5th	1962	15-8	7-7	4th-T
1920	9-4	8-4	3rd	**1963**	**20-6**	**11-3**	**1st-T**
1921	11-7	7-5	4th-T	1964	13-11	6-8	6th-T
1922	14-5	7-5	4th-T	1965	18-6	10-4	3rd
1923	9-6	7-5	4th-T	1966	12-12	8-6	3rd-T
1924	**11-6**	**8-4**	**1st-T**	1967	12-12	6-8	7th-T
1925	11-6	8-4	3rd-T	1968	11-13	6-8	7th-T
1926	9-8	6-6	5th-T	1969	19-5	9-5	2nd-T
1927	10-7	7-5	4th-T	1970	15-9	8-6	3rd-T
1928	5-17	2-10	9th-T	1971	11-12	5-9	5th-T
1929	10-7	6-6	5th-T	1972	14-10	5-9	8th-T
1930	8-8	7-5	4th-T	1973	14-10	8-6	3rd-T
1931	12-5	7-5	5th	1974	5-18	2-12	10th
1932	11-6	7-5	5th	1975	8-18	4-14	9th-T
1933	11-7	6-6	5th-T	1976	14-13	7-11	7th-T
1934	13-6	7-5	4th	1977	16-14	8-10	6th
1935	**15-5**	**9-3**	**1st-T**	1978	13-14	7-11	7th
1936	13-6	7-5	3rd-T	1979	19-11	7-11	7th
1937	**14-4**	**10-2**	**1st-T**	1980	22-13	8-10	6th-T
1938	9-9	4-8	8th-T	1981	21-8	12-6	3rd
1939	14-5	8-4	3rd	1982	18-11	10-8	6th
1940	14-6	7-5	4th-T	1983	21-11	11-7	2nd-T
1941	13-7	7-5	3rd-T	**1984**	**26-5**	**15-3**	**1st-T**
1942	**18-5**	**13-2**	**1st**	1985	26-9	12-6	2nd
1943	**17-1**	**12-0**	**1st**	1986	22-10	11-7	4th-T
1944	11-9	5-7	6th	1987	23-8	13-5	4th
1945	13-7	7-5	3rd	1988	23-10	12-6	3rd-T
1946	14-7	7-5	5th-T	1989	31-5	14-4	2nd
1947	14-6	8-4	2nd-T	1990	21-8	11-7	4th-T
1948	15-5	7-5	3rd-T	1991	21-10	11-7	3rd-T

Year	Overall Record	Big Ten Record	Big Ten Finish/ Tournament W-L
1992	13-15	7-11	8th
1993	19-13	11-7	3rd-T
1994	17-11	10-8	4th-T
1995	19-12	10-8	5th-T
1996	18-13	7-11	9th
1997	22-10	11-7	4th-T
1998	**23-10**	**13-3**	**1st-T/1-1**
1999	14-18	3-13	11th/3-1
2000	22-10	11-5	4th/2-1
2001	**27-8**	**13-3**	**1st-T/1-1**
2002	**26-9**	**11-5**	**1st-T/1-1**
2003	25-7	11-5	2nd/3-0
2004	**26-7**	**13-3**	**1st/2-1**

Year	Overall Record	Big Ten Record	Big Ten Finish/ Tournament W-L
2005	**37-2**	**15-1**	**1st/3-0**
2006	26-7	11-5	2nd-T/0-1
2007	23-12	9-7	4th-T/2-1
2008	16-19	5-13	9th-T/3-1
2009	24-10	11-7	2nd-T/1-1
2010	21-15	10-8	5th/1-1
2011	20-14	9-9	4th-T/0-1
2012	17-15	6-12	9th-T/0-1
2013	23-13	8-10	7th-T/1-1
2014	20-15	7-11	8th-T/1-1
2015	19-14	9-9	7th-T/0-1
2016	15-19	5-13	12th/2-1

WOMEN'S BASKETBALL

Year	Overall Record	Big Ten Record	Big Ten Finish/ Tournament W-L
1975	10-11		
1976	15-10	5th*	
1977	15-9	5th*	
1978	9-9	5th-T*	
1979	9-12	DNP*	
1980	6-21	5th*	
1981	20-11	DNP*	
1982	21-9	2nd*	
1983	14-14	9-9	6th
1984	12-16	6-12	8th
1985	13-15	7-11	6th
1986	20-10	12-6	3rd
1987	19-10	11-7	4th
1988	9-19	3-15	6th-T
1999	11-18	6-12	8th
1990	11-17	5-13	8th
1991	9-19	6-12	8th
1992	9-19	6-12	8th
1993	12-15	7-11	7th
1994	10-17	5-13	10th
1995	10-17	3-13	10th-T/0-1

Year	Overall Record	Big Ten Record	Big Ten Finish/ Tournament W-L
1996	13-15	6-10	8th/1-1
1997	**24-8**	**12-4**	**1st-T/2-1**
1998	20-10	12-4	2nd/0-1
1999	19-12	10-6	3rd/2-1
2000	23-11	11-5	4th/1-1
2001	17-16	9-7	6th/2-1
2002	15-14	7-9	8th/0-1
2003	17-12	9-7	6th/0-1
2004	10-18	4-12	8th-T/0-1
2005	17-13	7-9	7th/1-1
2006	16-15	6-10	7th-T/1-1
2007	19-12	8-8	4th/0-1
2008	20-15	8-10	9th/3-1
2009	10-21	5-13	9th/1-1
2010	19-15	7-11	8th-T/1-1
2011	9-23	2-14	11th/2-1
2012	11-19	5-11	9th-T/0-1
2013	19-14	9-7	5th-T/0-1
2014	9-21	2-14	12th/0-1
2015	15-16	6-12	10th/0-1
2016	9-21	2-16	14th/0-1

*Tournaments from 1976 to 1982 were not sanctioned by the Big Ten Conference.

MEN'S CROSS-COUNTRY

Year	Dual Meet Record	Big Ten Finish	NCAA Finish	Year	Dual Meet Record	Big Ten Finish	NCAA Finish
1905	——	2nd		1948	2-0-1	2nd	
1906	no team			1949	1-2	2nd	8th
1907	no team			1950	0-2	6th	
1908	no team			1951	——	UI did not enter.	
1909	no team			1952	——	UI did not enter.	
1910	no team			1953	——	UI did not enter.	
1911	no team			1954	1-1	3rd	
1912	——	7th		1955	1-1	2nd	
1913	1-1	2nd		1956	3-1	2nd	4th
1914	——	3rd		1957	3-1	3rd	
1915	——	5th		1958	0-2	4th	
1916	0-1	UI did not enter.		1959	1-0	UI did not enter complete team.	
1917	World War I						
1918	World War I			1960	0-2	UI did not enter complete team.	
1919	1-1	7th					
1920	1-1	2nd		1961	0-2	UI did not enter complete team.	
1921	**1-0**	**1st**					
1922	1-0	4th		1962	2-2	4th	
1923	1-0	2nd		1963	4-1	5th	
1924	0-0-1	5th		1964	no team		
1925	0-1	3rd		1965	0-4	7th	
1926	0-1	4th		1966	3-4	8th	
1927	2-0	2nd		1967	4-7	10th	
1928	0-2	7th		1968	4-5	6th	
1929	0-1	9th		1969	9-1	2nd	5th
1930	1-0	3rd		1970	6-1-1	4th	25th
1931	——	4th		1971	3-3	5th	
1932	——	2nd		1972	5-5	8th	
1933	4-0	no meet held		1973	4-1-1	4th	
1934	1-2-1	no meet held		1974	6-3	3rd	
1935	4-0	no meet held		1975	5-1	4th	10th
1936	0-5	no meet held		1976	3-1	2nd	5th
1937	1-2	no meet held		1977	5-0	2nd-T	22nd
1938	1-2	no meet held		1978	4-1	5th	
1939	no team			1979	2-3	4th	
1940	1-1	UI did not place.		1980	1-0	3rd	21st
1941	2-2	4th	10th	1981	1-0	2nd	
1942	0-3	2nd	5th	1982	1-1	4th	9th
1943	World War II			1983	0-2	4th	14th
1944	0-1	5th		**1984**	**1-0**	**1st**	
1945	0-1	4th		1985	1-0	5th	
1946	——	3rd		1986	1-0	2nd	7th
1947	**2-0**	**1st**		1987	——	2nd	

Year	Dual Meet Record	Big Ten Finish	NCAA Finish
1988	——	4th	
1989	——	2nd	
1990	——	4th	
1991	——	5th	
1992	——	4th	
1993	0-1	8th	
1994	0-1	4th	
1995	——	4th	
1996	1-0	4th	
1997	3-0	9th	
1998	——	8th	
1999	——	8th	
2000	——	10th	
2001	——	10th	
2002	——	8th	
2003	——	9th	
2004	——	8th	
2005	——	10th	
2006	——	8th	
2007	——	6th	
2008	——	9th	
2009	——	7th	
2010	——	6th	
2011	——	7th	
2012	——	4th	
2013	——	5th	
2014	——	6th	
2015	——	2nd	
2016	——	6th	

WOMEN'S CROSS-COUNTRY

Year	Dual Meet Record	Big Ten Finish	NCAA Finish
1978	5-0	4th*	
1979	5-1	9th*	
1980	2-1	9th*	
1981	not available	9th	
1982	1-1	6th	
1983	1-0	6th	
1984	1-0	2nd	
1985	1-0	3rd-T	
1986	——	7th	
1987	——	8th	
1988	——	8th-T	
1989	——	7th	
1990	——	6th	
1991	——	7th	
1992	——	7th	
1993	——	6th	
1994	1-0	4th	
1995	——	9th	
1996	——	6th	
1997	——	6th	
1998	——	8th	
1999	——	10th	
2000	——	4th	
2001	——	7th-T	
2002	——	9th	
2003	——	7th	
2004	——	2nd-T	20th
2005	——	2nd	5th
2006	——	5th	8th
2007	——	4th	6th
2008	——	4th	10th
2009	——	2nd	12th
2010	——	9th	
2011	——	12th	
2012	——	9th	
2013	——	9th	
2014	——	9th	
2015	——	2nd	
2016	——	10th	

*Championships from 1978 to 1980 were not sanctioned by the Big Ten Conference.

FENCING

Year	Dual Meet Record	Big Ten Finish	NCAA Finish
1910–11	**2-4**	**1st**	
1911–12	**2-2**	**1st**	
1912–13	**0-2**	**1st-T**	
1913–14	0-1		
1914–15	1-0		
1915–16	1-1		
1916–17	2-0		
1917–18	World War I		
1918–19	World War I		
1919–20	**1-0**	**1st**	
1920–21	1-0		
1921–22	**1-1**	**1st**	
1922–23	1-0	3rd	
1923–24	2-0		
1924–25	2-1	2nd	
1925–26	2-0-1	4th	
1926–27	4-0	3rd-T	
1927–28	1-3	2nd	
1928–29	**5-0**	**1st**	
1929–30	**3-2**	**1st**	
1930–31	**4-0**	**1st**	
1931–32	**4-0-1**	**1st**	
1932–33	**4-0-1**	**1st**	
1933–34	4-3	2nd	
1934–35	**5-2**	**1st**	
1935–36	5-4	2nd	
1936–37	6-1	2nd	
1937–38	4-4	2nd	
1938–39	8-2	2nd	
1939–40	4-5-1	4th	
1940–41	8-2	3rd	2nd
1941–42	**7-3**	**1st**	**3rd**
1942–43	**0-0**	**1st**	
1943–44	World War II		
1944–45	World War II		
1945–46	World War II		
1946–47	4-3	2nd	6th
1947–48	3-6	2nd	15th
1948–49	7-2	2nd	10th
1949–50	**6-3-1**	**1st**	**17th**
1950–51	**9-0**	**1st**	**5th**
1951–52	**8-0**	**1st**	**5th**
1952–53	**9-0**	**1st**	**6th**
1953–54	**8-2**	**1st**	**8th**
1954–55	9-2	2nd	5th
1955–56	**10-0**	**1st**	**1st**
1956–57	8-3	2nd	6th
1957–58	**8-4**	**1st**	**1st**
1958–59	8-4	2nd	4th
1959–60	**10-1**	**1st**	**8th**
1960–61	**6-5**	**1st**	**9th**
1961–62	**11-1**	**1st**	**4th**
1962–63	10-2	2nd	8th
1963–64	**12-0**	**1st**	**7th**
1964–65	**13-1**	**1st**	**6th**
1965–66	**7-7**	**1st**	**15th**
1966–67	12-3	2nd	12th
1967–68	**11-6**	**1st**	**12th**
1968–69	13-4	2nd	14th
1969–70	18-5	2nd	15th
1970–71	14-4	4th	
1971–72	**15-3**	**1st**	**6th**
1972–73	**17-2**	**1st**	**8th**
1973–74	**11-3**	**1st**	**13th**
1974–75	**8-4**	**1st**	
1975–76	14-5	4th	
1976–77	15-4	2nd	16th
1977–78	13-2	3rd	
1978–79	17-2	2nd-T	23rd
1979–80	**20-4**	**1st**	**11th**
1980–81	**25-2**	**1st**	**15th**
1981–82	15-3	2nd	13th
1982–83	**17-2**	**1st**	**11th**
1983–84	24-4	3rd-T	20th
1984–85	20-3	2nd	17th
1985–86	**15-1**	**1st**	**13th**
1986–87	22-1	8th	
1987–88	25-0	7th	
1988–89	23-1	11th	
1989–90	27-2	14th	
1990–91	24-2	13th	
1991–92	17-1	10th	
1992–93	22-3	10th	

FOOTBALL

Year	Overall Record	Big Ten Record	Big Ten Finish	Bowl
1890	1-2-0			
1891	6-0-0			
1892	9-3-2			
1893	3-2-3			
1894	5-3-0			
1895	4-2-1			
1896	4-2-1	0-2-1	6th-T	
1897	6-2-0	1-1-0	4th	
1898	4-5-0	1-1-0	4th	
1899	3-5-1	0-3-0	6th-T	
1900	7-3-2	1-3-2	8th	
1901	8-2-0	4-2-0	4th	
1902	10-2-1	4-2-0	4th	
1903	8-6-0	1-5-0	7th	
1904	9-2-1	3-1-1	4th	
1905	5-4-0	0-3-0	6th-T	
1906	1-3-1	1-3-0	5th	
1907	3-2-0	3-2-0	3rd	
1908	5-1-1	4-1-0	2nd	
1909	5-2-0	3-1-0	3rd	
1910	**7-0-0**	**4-0-0**	**1st-T**	
1911	4-2-1	2-2-1	4th-T	
1912	3-3-1	1-3-1	6th-T	
1913	4-2-1	2-2-1	5th	
1914	**7-0-0**	**6-0-0**	**1st**	
1915	**5-0-2**	**3-0-2**	**1st-T**	
1916	3-3-1	2-2-1	4th-T	
1917	5-2-1	2-2-1	5th-T	
1918	**5-2-0**	**4-0-0**	**1st**	
1919	**6-1-0**	**6-1-0**	**1st**	
1920	5-2-0	4-2-0	4th	
1921	3-4-0	1-4-0	8th-T	
1922	2-5-0	2-4-0	6th	
1923	**8-0-0**	**5-0-0**	**1st**	
1924	6-1-1	3-1-1	2nd-T	
1925	5-3-0	2-2-0	4th-T	
1926	6-2-0	2-2-0	6th-T	
1927	**7-0-1**	**5-0-0**	**1st-T**	
1928	**7-1-0**	**4-1-0**	**1st**	
1929	6-1-1	3-1-1	2nd	
1930	3-5-0	1-4-0	8th	
1931	2-6-1	0-6-1	9th-T	
1932	5-4-0	2-4-0	7th	
1933	5-3-0	3-2-0	5th	
1934	7-1-0	4-1-0	3rd	
1935	3-5-0	1-4-0	9th-T	
1936	4-3-1	2-2-1	6th	
1937	3-3-2	2-3-0	8th	
1938	3-5-0	2-3-0	7th	
1939	3-4-1	3-3-0	6th	
1940	1-7-0	0-5-0	9th	
1941	2-6-0	0-5-0	9th	
1942	6-4-0	3-2-0	3rd-T	
1943	3-7-0	2-4-0	6th	
1944	5-4-1	3-3-0	6th	
1945	2-6-1	1-4-1	7th	
1946	**8-2-0**	**6-1-0**	**1st**	**Rose Bowl**
1947	5-3-1	3-3-0	3rd-T	
1948	3-6-0	2-5-0	8th	
1949	3-4-2	3-3-1	5th-T	
1950	7-2-0	4-2-0	4th	
1951	**9-0-1**	**5-0-1**	**1st**	**Rose Bowl**
1952	4-5-0	2-5-0	6th-T	
1953	**7-1-1**	**5-1-0**	**1st-T**	
1954	1-8-0	0-6-0	10th	
1955	5-3-1	3-3-1	5th	
1956	2-5-2	1-4-2	7th-T	
1957	4-5-0	3-4-0	7th	
1958	4-5-0	4-3-0	6th	
1959	5-3-1	4-2-1	3rd-T	
1960	5-4-0	2-4-0	5th-T	
1961	0-9-0	0-7-0	9th-T	
1962	2-7-0	2-5-0	8th	
1963	**8-1-1**	**5-1-1**	**1st**	**Rose Bowl**
1964	6-3-0	4-3-0	4th-T	
1965	6-4-0	4-3-0	5th	
1966	4-6-0	4-3-0	3rd-T	
1967	4-6-0	3-4-0	5th-T	
1968	1-9-0	1-6-0	8th-T	
1969	0-10-0	0-7-0	10th	
1970	3-7-0	1-6-0	9th-T	
1971	5-6-0	5-3-0	3rd-T	
1972	3-8-0	3-5-0	6th-T	
1973	5-6-0	4-4-0	4th-T	
1974	6-4-1	4-3-1	5th	
1975	5-6-0	4-4-0	3rd-T	

FOOTBALL

Year	Overall Record	Big Ten Record	Big Ten Finish	Bowl
1976	5-6-0	4-4-0	3rd-T	
1977	3-8-0	2-6-0	8th-T	
1978	1-8-2	0-6-2	9th	
1979	2-8-1	1-6-1	9th	
1980	3-7-1	3-5-0	6th-T	
1981	7-4-0	6-3-0	3rd-T	
1982	7-5-0	6-3-0	4th	Liberty Bowl
1983	**10-2-0**	**9-0-0**	**1st**	**Rose Bowl**
1984	7-4-0	6-3-0	2nd-T	
1985	6-5-1	5-2-1	3rd	Peach Bowl
1986	4-7-0	3-5-0	6th-T	
1987	3-7-1	2-5-1	8th	
1988	6-5-1	5-2-1	3rd-T	All-American Bowl
1989	10-2-0	7-1-0	2nd	Citrus Bowl
1990	**8-4-0**	**6-2-0**	**1st-T**	**Hall of Fame Bowl**
1991	6-6-0	4-4-0	5th	John Hancock Bowl
1992	6-5-1	4-3-1	4th	Holiday Bowl
1993	5-6-0	5-3-0	4th-T	
1994	7-5-0	4-4-0	5th-T	Liberty Bowl
1995	5-5-1	3-4-1	7th-T	
1996	2-9-0	1-7-0	9th-T	

Year	Overall Record	Big Ten Record	Big Ten Finish	Bowl
1997	0-11-0	0-8-0	11th	
1998	3-8-0	2-6-0	7th	
1999	8-4-0	4-4-0	6th-T	Micron PC Bowl
2000	5-6-0	2-6-0	9th-T	
2001	**10-1-0**	**7-1-0**	**1st**	**Sugar Bowl**
2002	5-7	4-4	5th_T	
2003	1-11	0-8	11th	
2004	3-8	1-7	10th-T	
2005	2-9	0-8	11th	
2006	2-10	1-7	10th-T	
2007	9-4	6-2	2nd-T	Rose Bowl
2008	5-7	3-5	6th-T	
2009	3-9	2-6	9th	
2010	7-6	4-4	4th-T	Texas Bowl
2011	7-6	2-6	5th (Div.)	Kraft Bowl
2012	2-10	0-8	6th (Div.)	
2013	4-8	1-7	5th (Div.)	
2014	6-7	3-5	5th (Div.)	Zaxby's Heart of Dallas Bowl
2015	5-7	2-6	5th-T (Div.)	
2016	3-9	2-7	6th (Div.)	

MEN'S GOLF

Year	Dual Meet Record	Big Ten Finish	NCAA Finish
1908	1-0		
1909	no team		
1910	no team		
1911	no team		
1912	1-0		
1913	——		
1914	1-0		
1915	1-0		
1916	2-0		
1917	1-0		
1918	World War I		
1919	World War I		
1920	——	3rd-T	

Year	Dual Meet Record	Big Ten Finish	NCAA Finish
1921	1-2	3rd-T	
1922	0-3	4th	
1923	**5-0**	**1st**	
1924	5-0	3rd	
1925	2-2	4th	
1926	2-2	2nd	
1927	**3-2**	**1st**	
1928	3-2	3rd	
1929	4-2	*	
1930	**6-0**	**1st**	
1931	**6-0**	**1st**	**5th**
1932	2-1	4th	
1933	1-3-1	6th	

Year	Dual Meet Record	Big Ten Finish	NCAA Finish
1934	2-3-1	4th	
1935	3-1	6th	
1936	3-3	3rd	
1937	3-3-1	3rd	
1938	4-2	4th	
1939	5-2	6th	
1940	**5-2**	**1st**	**4th**
1941	**7-1**	**1st**	**4th**
1942	3-3-1	5th	
1943	5-2	5th	
1944	1-5	7th	
1945	1-1	5th	
1946	3-5	9th	
1947	3-4	5th	
1948	5-6	6th	
1949	0-9	8th	
1950	4-7	6th	7th
1951	3-9	9th	
1952	1-9	9th	
1953	4-5	8th	
1954	3-8	5th	
1955	5-6-1	8th	
1956	5-6-1	6th-T	
1957	8-3	8th	
1958	7-6-2	7th	
1959	4-8	10th	
1960	2-5-1	10th	
1961	3-6	10th	
1962	1-11	6th	
1963	4-5	7th-T	
1964	5-3	9th	
1965	1-1	10th	
1966	2-2	9th	
1967	0-1	8th	
1968	4-4	8th	
1969	1-1	8th	
1970	2-1-1	7th	
1971	4-2	4th-T	
1972	——	6th	
1973	——	3rd	
1974	——	8th	
1975	——	5th-T	

Year	Dual Meet Record	Big Ten Finish	NCAA Finish
1976	——	7th	
1977	——	6th	
1978	——	7th	
1979	——	5th	
1980	——	8th	
1981	——	8th	
1982	1-0	3rd-T	
1983	1-1	7th	
1984	1-1	5th	28th
1985	2-1	10th	
1986	1-0	2nd	
1987	2-0	4th	
1988	——	**1st**	**23rd-T**
1989	——	2nd	
1990	——	2nd	
1991	——	4th	
1992	——	9th	
1993	——	6th	
1994	——	8th	
1995	——	5th	
1996	——	10th	
1997	——	9th	
1998	——	7th	
1999	——	3th	
2000	——	11th	
2001	——	10th	
2002	——	2nd	18th
2003	——	2nd	21st
2004	——	2nd	
2005	——	11th	
2006	——	5th	
2007	——	9th-T	
2008	——	3rd	17th
2009	——	**1st**	**21st**
2010	——	**1st**	**19th**
2011	——	**1st**	**5th-T**
2012	——	**1st**	**21st**
2013	——	**1st**	**2nd**
2014	——	2nd	5th-T
2015	——	**1st**	**3rd-T**
2016	——	**1st**	**4th**

WOMEN'S GOLF

Year	Dual Meet Record	Big Ten Finish	NCAA Finish	Year	Dual Meet Record	Big Ten Finish	NCAA Finish
1975	——	4th*		1996	——	11th	
1976	——	2nd*		1997	——	11th	
1977	——	4th*		1998	——	10th	
1978	——	8th*		1999	——	11th	
1979	——	8th*		2000	——	11th	
1980	——	9th*		2001	——	11th	
1981	——	7th*		2002	——	5th	
1982	——	4th		2003	——	7th	
1983	——	5th		2004	——	9th-T	
1984	——	6th		2005	——	9th	
1985	——	5th		2006	——	10th	
1986	——	5th		2007	——	6th	
1987	——	6th		2008	——	11th	
1988	——	5th		2009	——	9th	
1989	——	5th		2010	——	9th	
1990	——	6th		2011	——	9th	
1991	——	6th		2012	——	5th	
1992	——	3rd		2013	——	12th	
1993	——	3rd-T		2014	——	5th	
1994	——	3rd-T		2015	——	9th	
1995	——	3rd		2016	——	4th-T	

*Championships from 1975 to 1981 were not sanctioned by the Big Ten Conference.

MEN'S GYMNASTICS

Year	Dual Meet Record	Big Ten Finish	NCAA Finish	Year	Dual Meet Record	Big Ten Finish	NCAA Finish
1898	——			1918	World War I		
1902	——			1919	World War I		
1905	——	3rd		1920	0-1	3rd	
1910	0-1	2nd		1921	0-1	4th	
1911	**1-0**	**1st**		1922	0-1	4th	
1912	**1-0**	**1st**		1923	0-2	5th	
1913	0-1	4th		1924	0-2	5th	
1914	0-1	3rd		1925	0-3	7th	
1915	1-1			1926	0-3	7th	
1916	0-2	4th		1927	3-1	3rd	
1917	0-2	4th		1928	2-1	3rd	

Year	Dual Meet Record	Big Ten Finish	NCAA Finish	Year	Dual Meet Record	Big Ten Finish	NCAA Finish
1929	**4-0**	**1st**		1973	2-12	6th	
1930	3-1	2nd		1974	8-9	4th	
1931	3-0	3rd		1975	10-8	4th	
1932	5-0	3rd		1976	5-8	3rd	
1933	4-2	3rd		1977	5-3	2nd	
1934	5-3	3rd		1978	6-3	2nd	
1935	**9-0**	**1st**		1979	7-3	4th	
1936	6-1	3rd		1980	12-3	4th	
1937	7-3	3rd		**1981**	**7-3**	**1st**	**8th**
1938	8-3	2nd		1982	8-5	2nd	11th
1939	**6-0**	**1st**	**1st**	**1983**	**9-1**	**1st-T**	**6th**
1940	**8-1**	**2nd**	**1st**	1984	8-3	4th	9th
1941	**6-0**	**1st**	**1st**	1985	5-5	4th	11th
1942	**8-2**	**1st**	**1st**	1986	11-4	3rd	12th
1943	World War II			1987	8-3	4th	12th
1944	World War II			**1988**	**11-0**	**1st**	**2nd**
1945	World War II			**1989**	**7-1**	**1st**	**1st**
1946	World War II			1990	1-3	4th	
1947	3-2	2nd		1991	4-4	5th	
1948	2-3	2nd	3rd	1992	7-3	3rd	13th
1949	7-1	2nd	3rd	1993	9-1	4th	6th
1950	**7-1**	**1st**	**1st**	1994	3-4	6th	
1951	**7-0**	**1st**	**2nd-T**	1995	4-5	5th	
1952	**4-1**	**1st**	**3rd**	1996	4-6	6th	
1953	**5-2**	**1st**	**2nd**	1997	2-4	5th	8th
1954	**6-0**	**1st**	**2nd**	1998	4-3	5th	3rd
1955	**9-1**	**1st**	**1st**	1999	6-5	6th	7th
1956	**4-3**	**1st**	**1st**	2000	4-5	3rd	8th
1957	**11-0**	**1st**	**2nd**	2001	7-2	4th	8th
1958	**10-1**	**1st**	**1st**	2002	6-1	5th	9th
1959	**10-1**	**1st**	**2nd**	2003	3-5	6th	5th
1960	**8-3**	**1st**	**3rd**	**2004**	**4-3**	**1st**	**3rd**
1961	7-2	2nd	5th	2005	5-0-1	2nd	3rd
1962	7-0	3rd	4th	2006	7-1	2nd	2nd
1963	1-8	6th	11th-T	2007	2-4	5th	5th
1964	3-6	5th		2008	6-2	2nd	3rd
1965	1-8-1	6th		**2009**	**6-0**	**1st-T**	**5th**
1966	5-3	3rd	4th	**2010**	**6-1**	**1st**	**4th**
1967	9-2	4th	4th	**2011**	**2-2**	**1st**	**3rd**
1968	8-4	4th		**2012**	**4-1**	**1st**	**1st**
1969	4-6	3rd		2013	3-4	5th	6th
1970	6-3	3rd		2014	8-3	4th	4th
1971	7-3	3rd		2015	6-3	2nd	8th
1972	2-7	6th		2016	3-2	2nd	4th

WOMEN'S GYMNASTICS

Year	Dual Meet Record	Big Ten Finish	NCAA Finish	Year	Dual Meet Record	Big Ten Finish	NCAA Finish
1974–75	Incomplete	4th*		1995–96	13-5	5th	
1975–76	**6-2**	**1st***		1996–97	8-10	6th	
1976–77	**5-3**	**1st***		1997–98	12-5	6th	
1977–78	3-5	3rd*		1998–99	10-7-1	5th	
1978–79	6-5	2nd*		1999–2000	7-10	6th	
1979–80	14-4	2nd*		2000–01	3-10	7th	
1980–81	7-12	4rh		2001–02	5-11	6th	
1981–82	8-8	6th		2002–03	7-12	6th	
1982–83	8-7	3rd		2003–04	10-7	6th	
1983–84	12-11	4th-T		2004–05	17-5	5th	
1984–85	7-8	5th		2005–06	11-4	7th	
1985–86	11-7	5th		2006–07	9-8	3rd	
1986–87	11-6	4th		2007–08	6-10	2nd	
1987–88	9-3	3rd		2008–09	17-7	2nd	12th
1988–89	9-5	4th		2009–10	12-7	6th	
1989–90	**7-2**	**1st**		2010–11	13-4-1	3rd	11th
1990–91	3-8	4th-T		2011–12	7-6-2	5th	
1991–92	2-14	6th		2012–13	12-7	4th	11th
1992–93	2-14	7th		2013–14	12-5	4th	11th
1993–94	4-14	7th		2014–15	14-3	2nd	
1994–95	6-12	5th		2015–16	23-10	8th	

*Championships from 1975 to 1981 were not sanctioned by the Big Ten Conference.

ICE HOCKEY

Year	Overall Record	Big Ten Record
1938	0-4	0-3
1939	3-7	0-6
1940	3-11	1-7
1941	17-3-1	6-1-1
1942	10-4-2	4-0
1943	10-2	5-1

POLO

Year	Overall Record
1934	0-7
1935	4-5
1936	2-2
1937	3-2
1938	7-4-1
1939	9-5
1940	8-6
1941	5-7

MEN'S SOCCER

Year	Overall Record
1927	1-1
1928	3-0
1929	3-0
1930	4-0-1
1931	7-0-1
1932	4-2-3
1933	5-2-1
1934	5-2
1935	2-3-1

WOMEN'S SOCCER

Year	Overall Record	Big Ten Record	Big Ten Finish/ Tournament W-L	Year	Overall Record	Big Ten Record	Big Ten Finish/ Tournament W-L
1997	7-10	1-8	10th	2003	16-4-2	7-1-2	2nd/3-0*
1998	12-8	3-6	8th/0-1	2004	16-6-2	5-3-2	4th/1-1
1999	12-8-2	3-5-2	6th/1-1	2005	12-7-3	6-3-1	4th/1-1
2000	14-8	6-4	4th/1-1	2006	16-8	8-2	2nd/2-1
2001	12-8-1	6-3-1	3rd/2-1	2007	12-7-2	6-3-1	3rd/0-1-1
2002	9-11-1	4-6	8th/0-1	2008	12-9-2	5-5	5th/0-0-1

WOMEN'S SOCCER

Year	Overall Record	Big Ten Record	Big Ten Finish/ Tournament W-L
2009	7-9-3	2-6-2	8th-T
2010	13-5-1	6-3-1	4th
2011	17-5-2	8-2-1	2nd/2-0-1*
2012	10-9-4	6-4-1	4th-T/1-1-1
2013	11-9-3	5-5-1	5th-T/1-1
2014	10-8-2	5-6-2	7th/0-1
2015	10-6-3	4-4-3	8th/0-1
2016	6-11-2	3-6-2	11th

*Big Ten Tournament champions

MEN'S SWIMMING

Year	Dual Meet Record	Big Ten Finish	Year	Dual Meet Record	Big Ten Finish
1910–11	**2-1**	**1st**	1935–36	2-3	4th
1911–12	**2-2**	**1st**	1936–37	2-3-1	5th
1912–13	**3-2**	**1st**	1937–38	1-5	6th
1913–14	1-3	2nd	1938–39	5-0	4th
1914–15	2-2	3rd	1939–40	2-4	6th
1915–16	2-2	3rd	1940–41	3-4	6th
1916–17	0-3	3rd	1941–42	3-5	8th
1917–18	World War I		1942–43	3-2	8th
1918–19	World War I		1943–44	2-1	8th
1919–20	2-2	3rd	1944–45	3-3-1	7th
1920–21	2-2	3rd	1945–46	4-4	6th
1921–22	2-2	4th	1946–47	0-6-1	8th
1922–23	4-2	4th	1947–48	1-6	8th
1923–24	1-4	8th	1948–49	2-4	9th
1924–25	2-1	5th	1949–50	4-2	9th
1925–26	3-2	6th	1950–51	2-7	9th
1926–27	3-3	5th	1951–52	1-5	10th
1927–28	6-0	4th	1952–53	1-6	8th
1928–29	5-0	3rd	1953–54	8-2	4th
1929–30	6-0	4th	1954–55	7-3	8th
1930–31	2-2	6th	1955–56	6-4	7th
1931–32	2-1	5th	1956–57	8-1	5th
1932–33	5-1	3rd	1957–58	10-2	5th
1933–34	3-2	4th	1958–59	7-2	6th
1934–35	3-2	2nd	1959–60	6-2	6th

Year	Dual Meet Record	Big Ten Finish
1960–61	5-4	7th
1961–62	4-5	8th
1962–63	7-4	10th
1963–64	1-7	10th
1964–65	1-8	9th
1965–66	10-5	9th
1966–67	5-3	7th
1967–68	4-4-1	7th
1968–69	3-6	8th
1969–70	5-6	7th
1970–71	2-5	7th
1971–72	3-5	8th
1972–73	7-3	8th
1973–74	7-3	5th
1974–75	6-5	6th
1975–76	5-5	5th
1976–77	3-4	6th

Year	Dual Meet Record	Big Ten Finish
1977–78	3-1	8th
1978–79	4-5	7th
1979–80	4-2	8th
1980–81	4-4	8th
1981–82	4-5	9th
1982–83	4-2	7th
1983–84	6-2	5th
1984–85	7-4	5th
1985–86	8-3	5th
1986–87	1-7	7th
1987–88	2-5	9th
1988–89	2-4	9th
1989–90	4-7	8th
1990–91	1-8	10th
1991–92	1-9	11th
1992–93	4-8	11th

WOMEN'S SWIMMING

Year	Dual Meet Record	Big Ten Finish	NCAA Finish
1974–75	not available	6th*	
1975–76	7-4	6th*	
1976–77	3-9	7th*	
1977–78	3-5	10th*	
1978–79	3-2	9th*	
1979–80	6-3	10th*	
1980–81	7-5	10th*	
1981–82	3-3	7th	
1982–83	3-3	6th	
1983–84	2-4	9th	
1984–85	5-7	8th	
1985–86	5-4	8th	
1986–87	4-3	5th	
1987–88	1-5	9th	
1988–89	2-5	9th	
1989–90	2-7	9th	
1990–91	1-7	9th	
1991–92	2-6	11th	
1992–93	0-9	10th	
1993–94	3-9	10th	
1994–95	9-3	8th	

Year	Dual Meet Record	Big Ten Finish	NCAA Finish
1995–96	8-7	8th	
1996–97	13-4	6th	
1997–98	9-3	6th	
1998–99	9-6	6th	
1999–2000	8-5	7th	
2000–01	4-7	9th	
2001–02	4-6-1	8th	
2002-03	5-8	10th	
2003–04	6-5	11th	39th-T
2004–05	4-8	9th	39th-T
2005–06	5-9	9th	
2006–07	4-1	9th	
2007–08	1-3	11th	
2008–09	5-4	11th	
2009–10	7-6	11th	
2010–11	7-3	11th	
2011–12	5-7	10th	
2012–13	2-8	11th-T	
2013–14	8-6-1	12th	
2014–15	6-4	12th	
2015–16	8-4	12th	

*Championships from 1975 to 1981 were not sanctioned by the Big Ten Conference.

MEN'S TENNIS

Year	Dual Meet Record	Big Ten Finish	NCAA Finish	Year	Dual Meet Record	Big Ten Finish	NCAA Finish
1904	0-1			1947	9-1	2nd	
1905	1-2-1			1948	9-2	4th	
1906	1-0-1			1949	3-2	5th-T	
1907	——			1950	8-1	2nd	
1908	0-3			1951	9-1	4th-T	
1909	2-1			1952	3-5	6th	
1910	——			1953	1-5	7th	
1911	——			1954	7-3	5th	
1912	——			1955	12-2	3rd	
1913	1-0			1956	5-4	5th	
1914	2-2	2nd		1957	14-2	4th	
1915	3-3			1958	6-1	2nd	
1916	3-2			1959	12-3	2nd	
1917	**2-0**	**1st**		1960	8-4	4th	
1918	World War I			1961	7-4	5th	
1919	World War I			1962	5-5	4th	
1920	4-1-1			1963	4-8	7th	
1921	3-4			1964	9-10	7th	
1922	**6-2**	**1st**		1965	9-4	5th	
1923	4-4			1966	15-5	4th	
1924	4-0-3	2nd		1967	9-12	6th	
1925	3-1-1			1968	15-6	8th	
1926	**5-0**	**1st**		1969	4-12	5th	
1927	**4-1**	**1st**		1970	7-7	5th	
1928	**4-1**	**1st**		1971	12-6	5th	
1929	3-1			1972	17-5	4th	
1930	4-1			1973	13-4	5th	
1931	5-3			1974	19-5	6th-T	
1932	**8-3**	**1st**		1975	16-11-1	5th	
1933	9-1-2			1976	13-5-1	5th	
1934	4-5-2	5th		1977	7-7	5th	
1935	4-1-1	3rd		1978	8-10	10th	
1936	4-3	5th-T		1979	5-16	9th	
1937	2-8	8th		1980	21-17	10th	
1938	5-5	5th-T		1981	18-12	7th	
1939	9-2	4th		1982	18-12	5th	
1940	8-2	5th-T		1983	16-16	5th	
1941	3-8	did not enter		1984	23-9	2nd	
1942	7-4	4th		1985	20-16	3rd	
1943	4-0	2nd		1986	12-20	6th	
1944	3-3	7th-T		1987	16-13	3rd	
1945	4-2-1	7th		1988	11-13	10th	
1946	**10-0**	**1st**		1989	11-16	8th	

Year	Dual Meet Record	Big Ten Finish	NCAA Finish
1990	8-17	7th	
1991	10-13	10th	
1992	11-11	6th	
1993	4-23	11th	
1994	13-15	5th	
1995	18-10	7th	
1996	14-10	2nd	First Round
1997	**18-10**	**1st**	**First Round**
1998	**21-6**	**1st**	**First Round**
1999	**28-4**	**1st**	**Semifinals**
2000	**25-4**	**1st**	**Quarterfinals**
2001	**22-7**	**1st**	**Round of 32**
2002	**26-5**	**1st**	**Quarterfinals**
2003	**32-0**	**1st**	**National Champions**
2004	**32-1**	**1st**	**Semifinals**
2005	**25-4**	**1st**	**Round of 16**
2006	24-7	2nd	Round of 16
2007	23-9	2nd	National Runner-Up
2008	20-9	2nd	Round of 16
2009	23-9	2nd	Round of 16
2010	20-11	2nd	Second Round
2011	18-11	4th	Round of 16
2012	**19-8**	**1st**	**Round of 16**
2013	17-11	2nd	Second Round
2014	25-8	2nd	Round of 16
2015	**27-5**	**1st**	**Round of 16**
2016	20-11	2nd	Second Round

WOMEN'S TENNIS

Year	Dual Meet Record	Big Ten Finish	NCAA Finish
1975	6-0	5th*	
1976	5-3-1	9th*	
1977	5-7	9th*	
1978	6-6	10th*	
1979	5-11	10th*	
1980	18-9	10th*	
1981	21-21	10th*	
1982	22-16	8th	
1983	16-21	8th	
1984	15-18	7th	
1985	17-20	5th	
1986	16-16	7th	
1987	12-18	7th	
1988	10-17	10th	
1989	6-22	7th	
1990	15-14	8th	
1991	19-9	5th	
1992	16-8	4th	
1993	14-6	2nd	
1994	13-9	5th	
1995	14-10	6th	
1996	12-14	7th	
1997	11-14	5th	
1998	8-13	8th	
1999	13-11	4th	
2000	12-13	4th	
2001	18-8	2nd	
2002	11-12	4th	
2003	17-8	3rd	Second Round
2004	17-6	3rd	First Round
2005	12-11	5th	
2006	8-15	8th	
2007	5-17	10th	
2008	12-11	4th	First Round
2009	19-8	3rd	Second Round
2010	15-10	3rd	First Round
2011	11-13	5th-T	
2012	18-8	3rd-T	First Round
2013	14-11	5th-T	
2014	14-10	5th-T	
2015	14-10	6th-T	
2016	15-9	8th	

*Championships from 1975 to 1981 were not sanctioned by the Big Ten Conference.

452

WOMEN'S TRACK AND FIELD

Year	Big Ten Indoors	Big Ten Outdoors	NCAA Indoors	NCAA Outdoors	Year	Big Ten Indoors	Big Ten Outdoors	NCAA Indoors	NCAA Outdoors
1975	—	—			**1996**	**1st**	**2nd**	**6th**	**4th**
1976	—	4th*			1997	4th	7th-T	18th	
1977	—	3rd*			1998	3rd	3rd	31st	15th
1978	4th*	6th*			1999	6th	5th	19th	
1979	9th*	6th*			2000	7th	8th	42nd	34th
1980	8th*	8th*			2001	8th	7th	27th	18th
1981	6th*	7th*			2002	3rd	3rd	13th	10th-T
1982	7th	6th	7th		2003	6th	7th	27th-T	21st
1983	8th	4th			2004	8th	3rd	65th	
1984	8th	10th			**2005**	**2nd**	**1st**	**57th-T**	**29th-T**
1985	8th	9th			2006	2nd	4th	22nd-T	23rd
1986	4th	3rd			**2007**	**3rd**	**1st-T**	**56th-T**	**67th-T**
1987	5th	2nd	46th		2008	6th	4th	53rd-T	31st-T
1988	**3rd**	**1st**	**14th**	**17th**	2009	5th	4th	27th-T	12th-T
1989	**1st**	**1st**	**13th**	**7th**	2010	7th	5th	21st-T	
1990	2nd-T	2nd	40th-T		2011	7th	4th	50th-T	66th-T
1991	2nd	2nd	—	27th	2012	4th	2nd-T	48th-T	17th-T
1992	**1st**	**1st**	—	**13th-T**	2013	1st	2nd	14th	14th
1993	**1st**	**2nd**	**16th-T**	**21st-T**	2014	9th	11th		
1994	2nd	2nd	12th-T	29th-T	2015	10th	11th	32nd	35th-T
1995	**1st**	**1st**	**24th**	**4th**	2016	13th	12th		

*Championships from 1975 to 1981 were not sanctioned by the Big Ten Conference.

MEN'S TRACK AND FIELD

Year	Big Ten Indoors	Big Ten Outdoors	NCAA Indoors	NCAA Outdoors	Year	Big Ten Indoors	Big Ten Outdoors	NCAA Indoors	NCAA Outdoors
1901	5th				1911	2nd	2nd		
1902	5th				**1912**	**1st**	**1st**		
1903	5th-T				**1913**	**1st**	**1st**		
1904	5th				**1914**	**1st**	**1st**		
1905	5th-T				1915	2nd	3rd		
1906	4th				**1916**	**1st**	**2nd**		
1907	**1st**				1917	2nd	2nd		
1908	3rd				1918	4th	2nd		
1909	**1st**				1919	3rd	3rd		
1910	**1st**				**1920**	**1st**	**1st**		

Year	Big Ten Indoors	Big Ten Outdoors	NCAA Indoors	NCAA Outdoors
1921	1st	1st	1st	
1922	1st	1st	4th	
1923	2nd	2nd	6th	
1924	1st	1st	10th	
1925	4th	5th	10th	
1926	4th	2nd	8th	
1927	5th	1st	1st	
1928	1st	1st	3rd	
1929	2nd	1st	3rd	
1930	2nd	2nd	6th	
1931	2nd	2nd	3rd	
1932	4th	4th	7th	
1933	3rd	3rd	18th	
1934	3rd	1st	19th	
1935	5th	7th	32nd	
1936	4th	5th	32nd	
1937	5th	4th	32nd	
1938	6th	6th		
1939	9th	7th	17th	
1940	5th	5th		
1941	4th	6th	44th	
1942	2nd	2nd	15th	
1943	3rd	2nd	7th	
1944	2nd	2nd	1st	
1945	2nd	1st	2nd	
1946	1st	1st	1st	
1947	1st	1st	1st	
1948	2nd	3rd	4th	
1949	3rd	4th	36th	
1950	3rd	2nd-T		
1951	1st	1st	14th	
1952	1st	1st	6th-T	
1953	1st	1st	2nd	
1954	1st	1st	2nd	
1955	4th	2nd	29th	
1956	5th	7th		
1957	10th	4th	18th-T	
1958	1st	1st	6th	
1959	2nd	1st	9th	
1960	2nd	1st	10th	
1961	4th	3rd	24th-T	
1962	5th	7th		
1963	6th	5th		
1964	6th	3rd	9th	
1965	5th	7th	25th-T	
1966	7th	7th	39th-T	
1967	9th	8th		
1968	9th	5th		
1969	5th	6th		
1970	7th	4th		
1971	7th	3rd	44th-T	33rd-T
1972	2nd	2nd	7th-T	20th
1973	5th	7th	24th-T	25th-T
1974	2nd-T	5th	6th	18th-T
1975	2nd	1st	20th	11th
1976	3rd	4th	4th	25th
1977	1st	1st	4th	7th
1978	5th-T	4th		
1979	6th	5th	40th	
1980	3rd	3rd	46th-T	
1981	1st	3rd	27th-T	24th-T
1982	4th	4th	14th-T	38th-T
1983	6th	3rd	58th-T	
1984	5th	5th	56th-T	
1985	2nd	3rd	27th-T	58th-T
1986	2nd	2nd	21st-T	51st
1987	1st	1st	17th-T	8th
1988	1st	1st	2nd	7th
1989	1st	1st	14th	51st-T
1990	3rd	3rd		
1991	2nd	2nd	51st	71st
1992	6th	5th	30th-T	43rd
1993	2nd	2nd	15th-T	21st-T
1994	3rd	1st	17th-T	17th-T
1995	2nd	2nd	4th	41st
1996	4th	4th	18th	16th
1997	2nd	4th	43rd-T	
1998	4th	8th	17th	56th-T
1999	2nd	4th	40th	30th
2000	2nd	5th	47th	36th
2001	6th	10th	55th	
2002	Cancelled	10th		
2003	8th	8th		
2004	4th	5th	34th-T	
2005	3rd	4th		
2006	3rd	5th-T	23rd	62nd
2007	10th	6th	47th-T	45th-T
2008	7th	9th		
2009	7th	9th	47th-T	37th-T
2010	10th	6th	40th-T	27th-T
2011	7th	7th	22nd-T	12th-T
2012	7th	8th	13th	11th-T
2013	2nd	4th	49th-T	49th-T
2014	4th	2nd	45th-T	
2015	2nd	1st	23rd	10th-T
2016	10th	12th	64th-T	

VOLLEYBALL

Year	Overall Record	Big Ten Record	Big Ten Finish	NCAA Finish
1974	19-9			
1975	15-14-1	2nd*		
1976	25-14	5th*		
1977	18-17-6	5th-T*		
1978	28-14	3rd*		
1979	18-20	5th-T*		
1980	22-32	5th*		
1981	17-27	9th*		
1982	17-20	8-5	3rd-T	
1983	5-25	2-11	10th	
1984	18-15	6-7	6th	
1985	39-3	16-2	2nd	9th
1986	**36-3**	**18-0**	**1st**	**5th-T**
1987	**31-7**	**17-1**	**1st**	**3rd-T**
1988	**30-4**	**18-0**	**1st**	**3rd-T**
1989	27-8	13-5	2nd	5th-T
1990	21-12	11-7	4th	
1991	19-10	14-6	4th	
1992	**32-4**	**19-1**	**1st-T**	**5th-T**
1993	18-13	14-6	3rd-T	1-1 Second Round
1994	23-14	12-8	4th	0-1 First Round
1995	24-9	12-8	4th-T	1-1 Reg. Semifinal

Year	Overall Record	Big Ten Record	Big Ten Finish	NCAA Finish
1996	13-15	8-12	7th	
1997	17-13	8-12	7th	
1998	22-11	13-7	4th	2-1 Reg. Semifinal
1999	17-11	12-8	4th	1-1 Second Round
2000	13-18	4-16	10th	
2001	21-9	13-7	4th-T	1-1 Round of 32
2002	13-16	7-13	9th	
2003	26-7	15-5	2nd-T	2-1 Round of 16
2004	19-11	11-9	5th	0-1 First Round
2005	16-15	7-13	7th	
2006	15-15	6-14	9th	
2007	16-14	8-12	8th	
2008	26-8	15-5	3rd	2-1 Round of 16
2009	26-6	16-4	2nd	2-1 Round of 16
2010	24-9	14-6	2nd	2-1 Round of 16
2011	32-5	16-4	2nd	5-1 Nat'l Runner-Up
2012	14-16	8-12	8th	
2013	18-15	12-8	4th-T	2-1 Round of 16
2014	26-8	16-4	3rd	2-1 Round of 16
2015	21-13	10-10	7th-T	2-1 Round of 16
2016	17-14	10-10	7th-T	

*Championships from 1975 to 1981 were not sanctioned by the Big Ten Conference.

WRESTLING

Year	Dual Meet Record	Big Ten Finish	NCAA Finish
1911	0-1		
1912	0-2		
1913	**2-0**	**T-1st***	
1914	1-0		
1915	2-0-1	4th	
1916	1-2-1	4th	
1917	**4-0**	**1st**	
1918	Did not compete in intercollegiate wrestling.		
1919	Did not compete in intercollegiate wrestling.		
1920	**3-0**	**1st**	

Year	Dual Meet Record	Big Ten Finish	NCAA Finish
1921	2-1	5th	
1922	**6-0**	**1st**	
1923	4-2		
1924	**5-0**	**1st-T**	
1925	**5-0**	**1st-T**	
1926	**4-2**	**1st**	
1927	**6-0**	**1st**	
1928	**7-0**	**1st**	
1929	6-1	2nd	
1930	**6-0**	**1st**	

Year	Dual Meet Record	Big Ten Finish	NCAA Finish
1931	6-1		
1932	**5-0**	**1st-T**	
1933	5-3-1		
1934	7-2-1	2nd	
1935	**5-1**	**1st**	**3rd-T**
1936	5-2	3rd	
1937	**6-2**	**1st**	
1938	7-2	3rd	2nd
1939	6-3	2nd-T	4th-T
1940	6-4	4th-T	
1941	6-6	2nd-T	
1942	8-0	2nd-T	8th
1943	4-1	3rd-T	
1944	4-3	4th-T	
1945	4-1	3rd	
1946	**4-4**	**1st**	**3rd**
1947	**6-2-1**	**1st**	**6th**
1948	4-4	2nd-T	3rd
1949	6-1-2	5th	10th-T
1950	8-2	9th	10th
1951	5-4-1	4th	
1952	**5-5-2**	**1st**	
1953	7-5-2	4th	
1954	7-5	6th	12th-T
1955	11-2	3rd	9th
1956	6-6-1	8th	8th-T
1957	6-3-1	4th	6th-T
1958	8-3-1	2nd	6th
1959	4-7-1	5th	25th-T
1960	3-11	9th	
1961	10-1	5th	21st-T
1962	6-6	8th	19th-T
1963	6-6-2	10th	40th-T
1964	7-6-1	7th	46th-T
1965	3-11	4th	22nd-T
1966	2-11	10th	
1967	2-10	9th	
1968	1-9	8th	
1969	9-11-1	7th	
1970	6-8	9th	
1971	2-13	10th	
1972	3-9	10th	
1973	8-8	10th	

Year	Dual Meet Record	Big Ten Finish	NCAA Finish
1974	7-13	7th	
1975	10-9-1	7th	
1976	10-8-1	9th	
1977	3-11	9th	
1978	8-8	9th	
1979	12-10	6th	24th-T
1980	8-12	8th	
1981	7-9-1	10th	
1982	9-8	9th	
1983	1-13-1	8th	
1984	4-8	9th	
1985	11-10	6th	
1986	5-8	8th	38
1987	13-7	4th	40th-T
1988	3-9	7th	33rd
1989	3-10	10th	28th
1990	3-9	10th	19th
1991	3-11	10th	19th
1992	2-11	8th	54th-T
1993	9-4	8th	23rd-T
1994	7-5-1	9th	37th-T
1995	13-2	4th	9th
1996	11-6	4th	12th
1997	14-1	3rd	9th
1998	11-3	6th	7th
1999	13-2	4th	12th
2000	14-1	3rd	6th
2001	12-2	2nd	5th
2002	12-4	5th	10th
2003	11-3	5th	9th
2004	13-1	3rd	7th
2005	**16-1-1**	**1st**	**6th**
2006	10-2-1	2nd	25th
2007	11-1	7th	19th
2008	13-4	4th	14th
2009	13-2	2nd	8th
2010	8-8	8th	23rd
2011	6-5-1	5th	22nd
2012	16-4	4th	7th
2013	7-6-1	5th	9th
2014	11-8	6th	13th
2015	13-5	6th	12th
2016	13-5	8th	9th-T

MEN AND WOMEN WHO HAVE PORTRAYED CHIEF ILLINIWEK

1926–1928	Lester G. Leutwiler	1968–1969	Gary Simpson
1929–1930	A. Webber Borchers	1970–1973	John Bitzer
1931–1934	William A. Newton	1974–1976	Mike Gonzalez
1935–1938	Edward C. Kalb	1977–1979	Matt Gawne
1939–1940	John Grable	1980	Pete Marzek
1941–1942	Glenn Holthaus	1981–1983	Scott Christensen
1943	Idelle Stith Brooks	1984–1985	William Forsyth
1944	Kenneth Hanks	1986–1987	Michael Rose
1945–1946	Robert Bitzer	1988–1989	Tom Livingston
1947	Robert Bischoff	1990–1991	Kurt Gruben
1948–1950	James A. Down	1992	Steve Raquel
1951–1952	William G. Hug	1993	Jeff Beckham
1953–1955	Gaylord "Dean" Spotts	1994–1995	John Creech
1956	Ronald S. Kaiser	1996–1997	Scott Brakenridge
1957–1959	John W. Forsyth	1998–2000	John Madigan
1960–1963	Ben Forsyth	2001–2004	Matt Veronie
1964–1965	Fred Cash	2004–2006	Kyle Cline
1966–1967	Rick Legue	2006–2007	Dan Maloney

PERSONNEL HISTORY OF THE UNIVERSITY OF ILLINOIS DIVISION OF INTERCOLLEGIATE ATHLETICS (ATHLETIC ASSOCIATION)

This personnel history was compiled through research of University of Illinois souvenir athletic programs, its athletic summary books, UI staff directories, and the Big Ten Conference record book. Some of the lists are incomplete due to insufficient information. Please contact the UI Athletics Communications office should you discover errors.

FACULTY REPRESENTATIVES

1896–1898	Henry H. Everett
1898–1899	Jacob K. Shell
1899–1906	Herbert J. Barton
1906–1929	George A. Goodenough
1929–1936	Alfred C. Callen
1936–1949	Frank E. Richart
1950–1959	Robert B. Browne
1959–1968	Leslie A. Bryan
1968–1976	Henry S. Stillwell
1976–1981	William A. Ferguson
1981–1989	John Nowak
1981–1987	Alyce T. Cheska
1988	Mildred B. Griggs
1989–2000	David L. Chicoine
1999–2001	Fred Delcomyn
2000–2002	Rose Mary CordovaWentling
2002–present	Matthew Wheeler
2003–2011	Nancy Sottos
2012–present	Chris Span

DIRECTORS OF ATHLETICS

1892–1894	Edward K. Hall
1894–1895	Fred H. Dodge
1895–1898	Henry H. Everett
1898–1901	Jacob K. Shell
1901–1936	George A. Huff
1936–1941	Wendell S. Wilson
1941–1966	Douglas R. Mills
1966–1967	Leslie Bryan (interim)
1967–1972	E. E. (Gene) Vance
1972	Charles E. Flynn (interim)
1972–1979	Cecil N. Coleman
1979	Ray Eliot (interim)
1980–1988	Neale R. Stoner
1988	Ronald E. Guenther (interim)
1988	Dr. Karol A. Kahrs (interim)
1988–1991	John Mackovic
1991–1992	Robert Todd (interim)
1992–2011	Ronald E. Guenther
2011–2015	Mike Thomas
2015–2016	Paul Kowalczyk (interim)
2016–present	Josh Whitman

ASSOCIATE/ASSISTANT ATHLETIC DIRECTORS

1958–1967	Melvin Brewer
1960–1978	Raymond Eliot
1973–1978	Richard R. Tamburo
1973–1979	Lynn J. Snyder
1974–1999	Dr. Karol A. Kahrs
1978–1999	Tom Porter
1984–2011	Dana Brenner
1987–1997	Rick Allen
1989–1992	Robert Todd
1993–2011	Terry Cole
1994–present	Warren Hood
1994–1996	Debbie Richardson
1994–1999	William Yonan
1996–1997	Lou Henson
1998–2003	Kelly Landry
1998–2012	Vince Ille

1999–2005	Harriet Weatherford
2000–2006	David Johnson
2000–2002	Sally Ross
2000–present	Chris Byron
2002–2014	Tom Michael
2002–present	Howard Milton
2002	Mary Ann McChesney
2003–present	Nick Rogers
2004–2006	Debbie Case
2004–2014	Chris Peacock
2005–present	Marty Kaufmann
2006–2011	Chris Hanna
2006–present	Kathy Hug
2006–2010	James Morton
2007–present	Susan Young
2010–present	Kevin Ullestad
2011–present	Ryan Squire
2011–present	Jason Lener
2011–present	Maria Ochoa Woods
2011–present	Holly Stalcup
2012–present	John Chipman
2012–2016	Rick Darnell
2012–2014	Jenny Larson
2013–2014	Loren Israel
2013–present	Jason Heggemeyer
2013–present	Zach Goins
2013–present	Derrick Burson
2013–present	Keiko Price
2014–present	Paul Kowalczyk
2014–present	Brad Wurthman
2014–present	Derryl Myles
2014–2016	Mike Waddell
2016–present	Corey Ansfield
2016–present	Carrie Ummel
2016–present	Bobbi Busboom
2016–present	Randy Ballard

SPORTS INFORMATION DIRECTORS

1922–1943	L. M. "Mike" Tobin
1943–1956	Charles E. Flynn
1956–1970	Charles M. Bellatti
1970–1974	Norman S. Sheya
1974–1989	Theodore A. "Tab" Bennett
1980–1985	Lani Jacobsen (women's SID)
1985–1987	Thomas Boeh (women's SID)
1987–1989	Mary Fowler (women's SID)
1989–1996	Michael G. Pearson
1996–1999	David Johnson (Asst. AD)
1999	Barbara Butler
2000–present	Kent Brown (Assoc. AD)

ATHLETIC TRAINERS

Pre-1913	William "Willie" McGill
1913–1916	Dr. Samuel Bilik
1916–1947	David M. "Matt" Bullock
1947–1951	Elmer "Ike" Hill
1951–1957	Richard Klein
1957–1969	Robert Nicollette
1969–1973	Robert Behnke
1973–1983	John "Skip" Pickering
1975–1978	Dana Gerhardt (women's)
1978–1980	Ellen Murray (women's)
1980–2008	Karen Iehl-Morse (women's)
1983–2013	Al Martindale
2013–2016	Paul Schmidt
2016–present	Randy Ballard

BUSINESS MANAGERS

1922–1927	Frank D. Murphy
1927–1930	Carl Lundgren
1930–1942	Charles E. "Chilly" Bowen
1943–1950	Clyde W. "Bud" Lyon*
1950–1969	Henry Thornes
1969–1974	R. William Sticklen
1975–1976	Carl W. Freeman
1977–1984	Thomas Johnson
1984–1986	Terry Hearne
1986–1987	Julie Frichtl
1987–1999	Tim Tracy
1999–2005	Harriett Weatherford
2006–present	Susan Young

*On leave of absence for war service from 1944 to 1946

EQUIPMENT MANAGERS

1913–1946	David M. "Matt" Bullock
1946–1972	Paul Schaede
1973–1981	Carl V. Rose
1981–1985	Marion Brownfield
1985–2010	Andy Dixon
2010–present	Rick Raven

FACILITIES DIRECTOR

1923–1938	Ben Crackel
1938–1947	Fred Brunner
1948–1966	Fred J. Stipe
1966	William Hagerman
1966–1973	Russell Mace
1973–1987	Robert L. Wright
1987–1994	John O'Donnell
1994–2001	Allan Heinze
2001–present	Lenny Willis

FIGHTING ILLINI SCHOLARSHIP FUND DIRECTORS

1969–1992	T. Dwight "Dike" Eddleman
1981–1983	Carl Meyer (Chicago Operation)
1981–1989	Wayne Williams (St. Louis Operation)
1983–1989	Ronald E. Guenther (Chicago Operation)
1989–1993	John Southwood (Chicago Operation)
1991–2007	Steven Greene (Chicago Operation)
1993–2004	Ken Zimmerman Jr. (Champaign Operation)
1999–2007	Shawn Wax (Director of Development)
2008–2011	Steve Greene (Director of Development)
2013–2016	Rick Darnell (Director of Development)
2013–present	Zach Goines (Chicago Operation)

TEAM PHYSICIANS

1933–1971	Dr. Leland M. T. Stilwell, MD*
1942–1945	Dr. Irwin W. Bach, MD (acting)
1971–1974	Dr. David Hamilton, MD
1973–1984	Dr. James Nauman, MD
1975–1978	Dr. L. M. Hursh, MD
1978–1983	Dr. David Hamilton, MD
1983–present	Dr. Robert Gurtler, MD
1983–2003	Dr. Stephen H. Soboroff, MD
1993–1996	Dr. Michael Gernant, MD
2001–2011	Dr. Jeff Kyrouac, MD
2004–present	Dr. Robert Bane, MD
2005–present	Dr. Jerrad Zimmerman, MD
2011–present	Dr. Amy MacDougall, MD
2013–present	Dr. Jeremy Henrichs, MD

*On leave of absence for war service from 1942 to 1945

TICKET MANAGERS

1924–1927	L. M. "Mike" Stohrer
1927–1942	Charles E. "Chilly" Bowen
1942–1947	Clyde W. "Bud" Lyon*
1944–1946	Jane Geiler (acting)
1947–1975	George A. Legg
1976	Paul J. Foil
1977–1989	Paul Bunting
1989–1998	Mike Hatfield
1999–2005	Cheryl Cain
2005–present	Jason Heggemeyer

*On leave of absence for war service from 1944 to 1946

VIDEO DIRECTOR

2004–2014	Andrew Young
2014–present	Derryl Myles

VARSITY I DIRECTOR

2006–present	Chris Tuttle

CONCESSIONS DIRECTOR

1994–present	Terry Conlon

BASEBALL COACHES

1878–1891	Student coaches appointed
1892–1894	Edward K. Hall
1895	Student coach appointed
1896–1919	George A. Huff
1920	George "Potsy" Clark
1921–1934	Carl L. Lundgren
1935–1951	Walter H. Roettger
1952–1978	Lee P. Eilbracht
1979–1987	Thomas Dedin
1988–1990	Augie Garrido
1991–2005	Richard "Itch" Jones
2006–present	Dan Hartleb

BASKETBALL COACHES-WOMEN'S

1974–1976	Steven Douglas
1976–1979	Carla Thompson
1979–1984	Jane Schroeder
1984–1990	Laura Golden
1990–1995	Kathy Lindsey
1995–2007	Theresa Grentz
2007–2012	Jolette Law
2012–2017	Matt Bollant
2017–present	Nancy Fahey

BASKETBALL COACHES-MEN'S

1906	Elwood Brown
1907	F. L. Pinckney
1908	Fletcher Lane
1909–1910	Herbert V. Juul
1911–1912	T. E. Thompson
1913–1920	Ralph R. Jones
1921–1922	Frank J. Winters
1923–1936	J. Craig Ruby
1937–1947	Douglas R. Mills
1948–1967	Harry Combes
1967–1974	Harv Schmidt
1974–1975	Gene Bartow
1975–1996	Lou Henson
1996–2000	Lon Kruger
2000–2003	Bill Self
2003–2012	Bruce Weber
2012–2017	John Groce
2017–present	Brad Underwood

CROSS-COUNTRY COACHES-MEN'S

1938–1960	Leo T. Johnson
1961	Edward Bernauer
1962–1963	Phillip Coleman
1965–1966	Robert C. Wright
1967–2002	Gary Wieneke
2003–2004	Paul Pilkington
2005–2010	Wendel McRaven
2011	Gavin Kennedy
2012–present	Jake Stewart

CROSS-COUNTRY COACHES-WOMEN'S

1977–1981	Jessica Dragicevic
1981–1983	Mary Beth Spencer
1984–1985	Patty Bradley
1985–1991	Gary Winckler
1992–1993	Mary Beth Spencer-Dyson
1994–2001	Gary Winckler
2002–2006	Karen Harvey
2007–2012	Jeremy Rasmussen
2013–present	Scott Jones

DIVING COACHES

1975–1993	Fred Newport
1993–1994	Teresa Fightmaster
1994–1996	Rhonda Kaletz
1996–97	Michelle Madden
1997–2000	Camie Kornely
2000–2003	Josh Seykora
2003–2006	Billy McGowan
2007–present	Chris Waters

FENCING COACHES

1911	R. N. Fargo
1912	K. J. Beebe
1913–1916	H. E. Pengilly
1917–1921*	A. J. Schuettner
1922–1923	R. G. Tolman
1924–1928	Waldo Shurnway
1929–1938	Herbert W. Craig
1939–1940	James L. Jackson
1941–1972**	Maxwell R. Garret
1973–1993	Arthur Schankin

*Intercollegiate Fencing suspended from 1918 to 1919 due to World War I

**Suspended from 1944 to 1946 due to World War II

FOOTBALL COACHES

1890	Scott Williams
1891	Robert Lackey
1892–1893	Edward K. Hall
1894	Louis D. Vail
1895–1896	George Huff
1897–1898	Fred L. Smith
1899	Neilson Poe
1900	Fred L. Smith
1901–1902	Edgar G. Holt
1903	George Woodruff
1904	Arthur R. Hall, Justa M. Lindgren, Fred Lowenthal, Clyde Mathews
1905	Fred Lowenthal
1906	Justa M. Lindgren
1907–1912	Arthur R. Hall
1913–1941	Robert C. Zuppke
1942–1959	Raymond Eliot
1960–1966	Peter Elliott
1967–1970	James Valek
1971–1976	Robert Blackman
1977–1979	Gary Moeller
1980–1987	Mike White
1988–1991	John Mackovic
1991–1996	Lou Tepper
1997–2004	Ron Turner
2005–2011	Ron Zook
2012–2014	Tim Beckman
2015	Bill Cubit
2016–present	Lovie Smith

GOLF COACHES-MEN'S

1922–1923	George Davis
1924	Ernest E. Bearg
1925–1928	D. L. Swank
1929–1932	J. H. Utley
1933	Robert Martin
1934	F. H. Renwick
1935–1938	J. H. Utley
1939–1943	W. W. Brown
1944–1966	Ralph Fletcher
1967–1971	Richard Youngberg
1972–1980	Ladd Pash
1981–2000	Ed Beard
2001–present	Mike Small

GOLF COACHES-WOMEN'S

1974–1978	Betsy Kimpel
1978–2006	Paula Smith
2006–present	Renee Slone

GYMNASTICS COACHES-MEN'S

1898	Adolph Kreikenbaum
1902	Adolph Kreikenbaum

1905	Leo G. Hana
1910–1913	Leo G. Hana
1914–1917*	R. N. Fargo
1921	A. J. Schuettner
1922	S. C. Staley
1924–1925	J. C. Wagner
1926–1929	R. C. Heidloff
1930–1942**	Hartley D. Price
1947–1948	Hartley D. Price
1949–1961	Charles Pond
1961–1962	Pat Bird (acting)
1962–1973	Charles Pond
1973–1993	Yoshi Hayasaki
1994–1996	Don Osborn
1997–2009	Yoshi Hayasaki
2010–present	Justin Spring

*Intercollegiate gymnastics suspended from 1918 to 1919 due to World War I

**Suspended from 1944 to 1946 due to World War II

GYMNASTICS COACHES-WOMEN'S

1974–1975	Kim Musgrave
1975–1977	Allison Milburn
1977–1993	Beverly Mackes
1993	Lynn Crane
1994–1999	Lynn Brueckman
2000–2010	Bob Starkell
2011–present	Kim Landrus

ICE HOCKEY COACHES

1938–1939	Raymond Eliot
1940–1943	Victor Heyliger

POLO COACHES

1934	Pepper Clay
1935–1939	Clifford B. Cole
1940	Alfred J. DeLorimer
1941	Philip R. Danley

SOCCER COACHES-MEN'S

1910	W. S. Strode
1927–1933	Hartley D. Price
1934–1935	King J. McCristal

SOCCER COACHES-WOMEN'S

1996–1998	Jillian Ellis
1999–2001	Trish Taliaferro
2002–present	Janet Rayfield

SOFTBALL COACHES

2000–2015	Terri Sullivan
2016–present	Tyra Perry

STRENGTH & CONDITIONING COACHES

1980–1988	William Kroll
1988–1996	Leo Ward
1996	Greg Scanlan
1997–1998	Pat Moorer
1999–present	Jim Zielinski

SWIMMING COACHES-WOMEN'S

1974–1975	Jeanne Hultzen
1975–1980	Ann Pollock
1980–1993	Donald Sammons
1993–1999	Jim Lutz
2000–present	Sue Novitsky

SWIMMING COACHES-MEN'S

1906–1909	W. H. Hockmeister
1910–1911	George B. Norris
1912–1917*	Edward J. Manley
1920–1952	Edward J. Manley
1953–1970	Allen B. Klingel
1971–1993	Donald Sammons

*Intercollegiate swimming suspended from 1918–19 due to World War I

TENNIS COACHES-MEN'S

1908–1913	P. B. Hawk
1914	W. A. Oldfather
1915–1917*	Student coaches appointed
1920–1924	E. E. Bearg
1925	B. P. Hoover
1926–1929	A. R. Cohn
1930	E. A. Shoaff
1931–1934	C. W. Gelwick
1935	Gerald Huff
1936–1937	Casper H. Nannes
1938–1942	Howard J. Braun
1943–1946	Ralph Johnson
1946–1964	Howard J. Braun
1965	Bob Lansford (acting)
1966–1972	Dan Olson
1972–1973	William Wright
1973–1977	Bruce Shuman
1977	John Avallone Jr. (acting)

1978–1981	Jack Groppel
1981–1985	Brad Louderback
1986–1992	Neil Adams
1992–2005	Craig Tiley
2005–present	Brad Dancer

*Intercollegiate tennis suspended from 1918 to 1919 due to World War I

TENNIS COACHES-WOMEN'S

1974–1975	Peggy Pruitt
1975–1978	Carla Thompson
1978–1981	Linda Pecore
1981–1987	Mary Tredennick
1987–1998	Jennifer Roberts
1999–2006	Sujay Lama
2006–1915	Michelle Dasso
2016–present	Evan Clark

TRACK AND FIELD COACHES-MEN'S

1895	Harvey Cornish
1896–1898	Henry H. Everett
1899–1900	Jacob K. Shell
1901–1903	H. B. Conibear
1904–1929	Harry L. Gill
1930	C. D. Werner
1931–1933	Harry L. Gill
1934–1937	Don C. Seaton
1938–1965	Leo T. Johnson
1965–1974	Robert C. Wright
1974–2003	Gary Wieneke
2003–2009	Wayne Angel
2009–present	Mike Turk

TRACK AND FIELD COACHES-WOMEN'S

1974–1975	Jerry Mayhew
1975–1981	Jessica Dragicevic
1981–1984	Mike Shine
1984–1985	Patty Bradley

1985–2008	Gary Winckler
2008–2013	Tonja Buford-Bailey
2013–present	Ron Garner

VOLLEYBALL COACHES

1974–1975	Kathleen Haywood
1975–1977	Terry Hite
1977–1980	Chris Accornero
1980–1983	John Blair
1983–1995	Mike Hebert
1996–2008	Don Hardin
2009–2016	Kevin Hambly
2017–present	Chris Tamas

WRESTLING COACHES

1911	R. N. Fargo
1912–1913	Alexander Elston
1914	Theodore Paulsen
1915–1917*	Walter Evans
1921–1928	Paul Prehn
1929–1943	Harold E. (Hek) Kenney
1944–1946	Glenn C. Law
1946–1947	Harold E. (Hek) Kenney
1948–1950	Glenn C. Law
1950–1968	B. R. Patterson
1968–1973	Jack Robinson
1973–1978	Thomas Porter
1978–1983	Greg Johnson
1983–1992	Ron Clinton
1992–2009	Mark Johnson
2009–present	Jim Heffernan

PHOTO CREDITS

THE EARLY DAYS

Jonathan Stoughton	UI Archives
Abraham Lincoln	UI Archives
Gov. Richard Oglesby	UI Archives
John Milton Gregory	UI Illio
1875 UI aerial	UI Illio
Learning & Labor button	UI Archives
University membership receipt	UI Illio
Dedication program	UI Illio
1890 football team	UI Athletics Communication
Football from first game	UI Athletics Communication
Selim Peabody	UI Illio
Athletic Park	UI Athletics Communication
Pres. James Smart	Purdue University
George Huff	UI Athletics Communication

1895–96

Moment:	The Palmer House Hilton
"I" on	UI Illio
Item:	UI Athletics Communication
List:	UI Athletics Communication
Legend:	UI Athletics Communication
Lore:	UI Illio

1896–97

Moment:	UI Athletics Communication
"I" on	UI Athletics Communication
Item:	UI Illio
List:	UI Archives
Legend:	UI Athletics Communication
Lore:	UI Archives

1897–98

Moment:	UI Athletics Communication
"I" on	UI Illio
Item:	UI Athletics Communication
List:	UI Illio
Legend:	UI Athletics Communication
Lore:	UI Archives

1898–99

Moment:	UI Illio
"I" on	UI Athletics Communication
Item:	UI Archives
List:	UI Archives
Legend:	UI Athletics Communication
Lore:	UI Archives

1899–1900

Moment:	UI Athletics Communication
"I" on	University of Iowa
Item:	UI Athletics Communication
List:	UI Archives
Legend:	UI Athletics Communication
Lore:	UI Archives

1900–01

Moment:	UI Athletics Communication
"I" on	UI Archives
Item:	UI Athletics Communication
List:	UI Illio
Legend:	UI Athletics Communication
Lore:	UI Archives

1901–02

Moment:	UI Athletics Communication
"I" on	UI Illio
Item:	UI Illio
List:	UI Athletics Communication
Legend:	UI Archives
Lore:	UI Illio

1902–03
Moment: UI Athletics Communication
"I" on: UI Athletics Communication
Item: Mrs. Margaret Grange
List: UI Illio
Legend: UI Athletics Communication
Lore: UI Archives

1903–04
Moment: UI Athletics Communication
"I" on: UI Illio
Item: UI Athletics Communication
List: UI Illio
Legend: UI Athletics Communication
Lore: UI Archives

1904–05
Moment: UI Illio
"I" on: UI Illio
Item: UI Illio
List: UI Illio
Legend: UI Athletics Communication
Lore: UI Archives

1905–06
Moment: UI Illio
"I" on: UI Illio
Item: UI Athletics Communication
List: UI Archives
Legend: UI Illio and author's collection
Lore: UI Archives

1906–07
Moment: UI Athletics Communication
"I" on: UI Athletics Communication
Item: UI Athletics Communication
List: UI Illio
Legend: UI Illio
Lore: UI Archives

1907–08
Moment: UI Illio
"I" on: University of Michigan
Item: UI Athletics Communication
List: Author's collection
Legend: UI Athletics Communication
Lore: UI Archives

1908–09
Moment: UI Athletics Communication
"I" on: UI Illio

Item: UI Athletics Communication
Lists: UI Athletics Communication
Legend: UI Athletics Communication
Lore: Urbana Library

1909–10
Moment: UI Athletics Communication
"I" on: UI Illio
Item: UI Athletics Communication
List: UI Illio
Legend: UI Illio
Lore: UI Archives

1910–11
Moment: UI Athletics Communication
"I" on: UI Illio
Item: UI Athletics Communication
List: UI Athletics Communication
Legend: UI Athletics Communication
Lore: UI Archives

1911–12
Moment: UI Athletics Communication
"I" on: UI Athletics Communication
Item: UI Athletics Communication
List: UI Athletics Communication
Legend: UI Athletics Communication
Lore: UI Illio

1912–13
Moment: UI Athletics Communication
"I" on: UI Illio
Item: UI Athletics Communication
List: UI Athletics Communication
Legend: UI Athletics Communication
Lore: UI Illio

1913–14
Moment: UI Athletics Communication
"I" on: UI Illio
Item: UI Athletics Communication
List: UI Athletics Communication
Lore: UI Archives

1914–15
Moment: UI Athletics Communication
"I" on: UI Illio
Item: UI Illio
List: UI Athletics Communication
Legend: UI Athletics Communication
Lore: UI Illio

1915–16
Moment: UI Illio
"I" on: UI Illio
Item: UI Illio
List: UI Athletics Communication
Legend: UI Archives
Lore: UI Illio

1916–17
Moment: UI Illio
"I" on: UI Athletics Communication
Item: UI Athletics Communication
List: Chicago Bears
Legend: UI Athletics Communication
Lore: UI Athletics Communication

1917–18
Moment: UI Illio
"I" on: UI Illio
Item: UI Illio
List: UI Illio
Legend: UI Athletics Communication
Lore: UI Illio

1918–19
Moment: UI Athletics Communication
"I" on: UI Illio
Item: UI Athletics Communication
List: UI Athletics Communication
Legend: Bing Ten Conference
Lore: UI Illio

1919–20
Moment: UI Athletics Communication
"I" on: UI Illio
Item: UI Archives
List: UI Athletics Communication
Legend: UI Athletics Communication
Lore: UI Illio

1920–21
Moment: UI Illio
"I" on: UI Athletics Communication
Item: UI Illio
List: UI Athletics Communication
Legend: UI Athletics Communication
Lore: UI Illio

1921–22
Moment: UI Illio
"I" on: UI Illio

Item: UI Athletics Communication
List: UI Illio
Legend: UI Athletics Communication
Lore: WILL Radio

1922–23
Moment: UI Athletics Communication
"I" on: UI Athletics Communication
Item: UI Athletics Communication
List: UI Illio
Legend: UI Athletics Communication
Lore: UI Archives

1923–24
Moment: UI Athletics Communication
"I" on: UI Athletics Communication
Item: UI Illio
Legend: UI Athletics Communication
List: UI Athletics Communication
Lore: UI Archives

1924–25
Moment: UI Athletics Communication
"I" on: UI Athletics Communication
Item: UI Athletics Communication
List: UI Athletics Communication
Legend: UI Athletics Communication
Lore: UI Archives

1925–26
Moment: UI Athletics Communication
"I" on: UI Athletics Communication
Item: UI Athletics Communication
Legend: UI Athletics Communication
Lore: UI Athletics Communication
Red Grange: UI Athletics Communication

1926–27
Moment: UI Athletics Communication
"I" on: UI Athletics Communication
Item: UI Athletics Communication
List: Mark Jones
Legend: UI Illio
Lore: UI Illio

1927–28
Moment: Author's collection
"I" on: UI Illio
Item: UI Athletics Communication
List: UI Athletics Communication

Legend: UI Athletics Communication
Lore: St. John's Church

1928–29
Moment: UI Athletics Communication
"I" on: UI Illio
Item: UI Athletics Communication
List: UI Athletics Communication
Legend: UI Athletics Communication
Lore: UI Archives

1929–30
Moment: UI Athletics Communication
"I" on: UI Athletics Communication
Item: Author's collection
List: UI Athletics Communication
Legend: UI Athletics Communication
Lore: UI Archives

1930–31
Moment: UI Athletics Communication
"I" on: UI Athletics Communication
Item: UI Illio
List: UI Athletics Communication
Legend: UI Athletics Communication
Lore: UI Archives

1931–32
Moment: UI Athletics Communication
"I" on: UI Illio
Item: UI Athletics Communication
List: UI Athletics Communication
Legend: UI Athletics Communication
Lore: UI Illio

1932–33
Moment: Author's collection and UI Athletics Communication
"I" on: UI Illio
Item: UI Athletics Communication
List: UI Illio
Legend: UI Illio
Lore: UI Archives

1933–34
Moment: UI Athletics Communication
"I" on: UI Athletics Communication
Item: UI Athletics Communication
Legend: UI Athletics Communication
List: UI Athletics Communication
Lore: UI Archives

1934–35
Moment: UI Athletics Communication
"I" on: UI Illio
Item: University of Michigan
List: UI Athletics Communication
Legend: UI Athletics Communication
Lore: Author's photo

1935–36
Moment: UI Athletics Communication
"I" on: UI Athletics Communication
Item: UI Athletics Communication
List: University of Chicago
Legend: UI Athletics Communication
Lore: UI Archives

1936–37
Moment: UI Athletics Communication
"I" on: UI Athletics Communication
Item: UI Athletics Communication
List: Sagamore Publishing
Legend: UI Athletics Communication
Lore: UI Illio

1937–38
Moment: Author's collection
"I" on: UI Athletics Communication
Item: UI Athletics Communication
List: UI Archives
Legend: UI Athletics Communication
Lore: UI Archives

1938–39
Moment: UI Athletics Communication
"I" on: UI Athletics Communication
Item: UI Athletics Communication
List: Baseball Hall of Fame
Legend: UI Athletics Communication
Lore: UI Archives

1939–40
Moment: UI Athletics Communication
"I" on: UI Illio
Item: UI Athletics Communication
List: UI Athletics Communication
Legend: UI Athletics Communication
Lore: UI Archives

1940–41
Moment: UI Illio
"I" on: UI Athletics Communication

466

Item: UI Athletics Communication
List: UI Illio
Legend: UI Athletics Communication
Lore: UI Archives

1941–42
Moment: UI Athletics Communication
"I" on: UI Illio
Item: UI Athletics Communication
List: UI Athletics Communication
Legend: Sport Magazine
Lore: UI Archives

1942–43
Moment: UI Athletics Communication
"I" on: UI Athletics Communication
Item: UI Athletics Communication
List: UI Athletics Communication
Legend: UI Athletics Communication
Lore: UI Archives

1943–44
Moment: UI Athletics Communication
"I" on: UI Athletics Communication
Item: UI Athletics Communication
Legend: UI Athletics Communication
List: UI Athletics Communication
Lore: UI Archives

1944–45
Moment: UI Athletics Communication
"I" on: UI Athletics Communication
Item: UI Athletics Communication
List: UI Athletics Communication
Legend: UI Athletics Communication
Lore: UI Archives

1945–46
Moment: UI Athletics Communication
"I" on: UI Athletics Communication
Item: UI Athletics Communication
List: UI Athletics Communication
Legend: UI Athletics Communication
Lore: UI Archives

1946–47
Moment: UI Athletics Communication
"I" on: UI Athletics Communication
Item: UI Athletics Communication
List: UI Athletics Communication

Legend: UI Athletics Communication
Lore: UI Archives

1947–48
Moment: UI Athletics Communication
"I" on: UI Athletics Communication
Item: UI Athletics Communication
List: UI Athletics Communication
Legend: UI Athletics Communication
Lore: UI Archives

1948–49
Moment: UI Athletics Communication
"I" on: UI Athletics Communication
Item: UI Athletics Communication
List: UI Athletics Communication
Legend: UI Athletics Communication
Lore: UI Archives

1949–50
Moment: UI Athletics Communication
"I" on: UI Athletics Communication
Item: UI Athletics Communication
List: UI Athletics Communication
Legend: UI Athletics Communication
Lore: UI Athletics Communication

1950–51
Moment: UI Athletics Communication
"I" on: UI Athletics Communication
Item: UI Athletics Communication
List: UI Athletics Communication
Legend: UI Athletics Communication
Lore: UI Illio

1951–52
Moment: UI Athletics Communication
"I" on: Chicago Bears
Item: UI Athletics Communication
List: UI Athletics Communication
Legend: UI Athletics Communication
Lore: UI Illio

1952–53
Moment: UI Athletics Communication
"I" on: UI Athletics Communication
Item: UI Athletics Communication
List: Philadelphia 76ers
Legend: UI Athletics Communication
Lore: WILL-TV

1953–54
Moment: UI Athletics Communication
"I" on: UI Athletics Communication
Item: UI Athletics Communication
List: UI Athletics Communication
Legend: UI Athletics Communication
Lore: UI Archives

1954–55
Moment: UI Athletics Communication
"I" on: UI Athletics Communication
Item: UI Athletics Communication
List: UI Athletics Communication
Legend: UI Athletics Communication
Lore: UI Archives

1955–56
Moment: UI Archives
"I" on: UI Athletics Communication
Item: UI Athletics Communication
List: UI Athletics Communication
Legend: UI Athletics Communication
Lore: UI Archives

1956–57
Moment: UI Athletics Communication
"I" on: UI Athletics Communication
Item: UI Athletics Communication
List: UI Athletics Communication
Legend: UI Athletics Communication
Lore: UI Archives

1957–58
Moment: UI Athletics Communication
"I" on: UI Athletics Communication
Item: Pro Football Hall of Fame
List: UI Athletics Communication
Legend: UI Athletics Communication
Lore: UI Illio

1958–59
Moment: UI Athletics Communication
"I" on: Topps Cards
Item: UI Athletics Communication
List: UI Athletics Communication
Legend: UI Athletics Communication
Lore: UI Athletics Communication

1959–60
Moment: UI Athletics Communication
"I" on: UI Athletics Communication

Item: UI Athletics Communication
List: UI Athletics Communication
Legend: UI Athletics Communication
Lore: UI Illio

1960–61
Moment: UI Athletics Communication
"I" on: UI Athletics Communication
Item: Mark Jones
List: Chicago Bears
Legend: UI Athletics Communication
Lore: UI Archives

1961–62
Moment: UI Athletics Communication
"I" on: UI Athletics Communication
Item: UI Athletics Communication
List: Purdue University
Legend: UI Athletics Communication
Lore: UI Archives

1962–63
Moment: UI Athletics Communication
"I" on: UI Illio
Item: UI Athletics Communication
List: Pro Football Hall of Fame
Legend: Mark Jones
Lore: UI Archives

1963–64
Moment: Michigan State University
"I" on: UI Athletics Communication
Item: UI Athletics Communication
List: UI Athletics Communication
Legend: UI Athletics Communication
Lore: UI Illio

1964–65
Moment: UI Athletics Communication
"I" on: Topps Cards
Item: UI Athletics Communication
List: UI Athletics Communication
Legend: UI Athletics Communication
Lore: UI Archives

1965–66
Moment: UI Athletics Communication
"I" on: UI Athletics Communication
Item: UI Athletics Communication
List: UI Athletics Communication

Legend: Mark Jones
Lore: UI Illio

1966–67
Moment: Champaign News-Gazette
"I" on: National Football League
Item: UI Athletics Communication
List: Green Bay Packers
Legend: Mark Jones
Lore: UI Archives

1967–68
Moment: UI Athletics Communication
"I" on: UI Illio
Item: UI Athletics Communication
List: Green Bay Packers
Legend: UI Athletics Communication
Lore: UI Archives

1968–69
Moment: UI Athletics Communication
"I" on: UI Illio
Item: UI Athletics Communication
List: UI Athletics Communication
Legend: UI Athletics Communication
Lore: UI Archives

1969–70
Moment: UI Athletics Communication
"I" on: UI Athletics Communication
Item: Baseball Hall of Fame
List: UI Athletics Communication
Legend: UI Athletics Communication
Lore: UI Archives

1970–71
Moment: UI Athletics Communication
"I" on: UI Athletics Communication
Item: UI Athletics Communication
List: Naismith Hall of Fame
Legend: UI Athletics Communication
Lore: UI Archives

1971–72
Moment: UI Athletics Communication
"I" on: UI Athletics Communication
Item: UI Athletics Communication
List: UI Athletics Communication
Legend: UI Athletics Communication s
Lore: UI Illio

1972–73
Moment: UI Athletics Communication
"I" on: UI Athletics Communication
Item: UI Athletics Communication
List: UI Athletics Communication
Legend: UI Athletics Communication
Lore: Author's photo

1973–74
Moment: UI Athletics Communication
Milestone: UI Athletics Communication
Item: UI Athletics Communication
List: UI Athletics Communication
Legend: UI Athletics Communication
Lore: UI Athletics Communication

1974–75
MEN
Moment: UI Athletics Communication
List: UI Athletics Communication
Item: UI Athletics Communication
Legend: UI Athletics Communication

WOMEN
Moment: UI Illio
List: UI Athletics Communication
Item: UI Athletics Communication
Legend: Mark Jones
Lore: UI Illio

1975–76
MEN
Moment: UI Athletics Communication
List: Michigan State University
Legend: UI Athletics Communication

WOMEN
Moment: UI Illio
List: UI Athletics Communication
Item: UI Athletics Communication
Legend: UI Athletics Communication
Lore: UI Archives

1976–77
MEN
Moment: UI Athletics Communication
List: UI Athletics Communication
Item: UI Athletics Communication
Legend: UI Athletics Communication

WOMEN
Moment: UI Illio
List: UI Athletics Communication
Item: UI Athletics Communication
Legend: NBC-TV
Lore: UI Illio

1977–78
MEN
Moment: UI Athletics Communication
List: UI Illio
Item: UI Athletics Communication
Legend: UI Athletics Communication

WOMEN
Moment: UI Athletics Communication
List: UI Athletics Communication
Item: UI Illio
Legend: Beverly Washington
Lore: UI Illio

1978–79
MEN
Moment: UI Illio
List: UI Athletics Communication
Item: UI Athletics Communication
Legend: UI Athletics Communication

WOMEN
Moment: UI Athletics Communication
List: UI Athletics Communication
Item: UI Athletics Communication
Legend: UI Athletics Communication
Lore: UI Illio

1979–80
MEN
Moment: UI Athletics Communication
List: UI Athletics Communication
Item: UI Athletics Communication
Legend: UI Athletics Communication

WOMEN
Moment: UI Illio
List: UI Illio
Item: UI Illio
Legend: UI Athletics Communication
Lore: UI Illio

1980–81
MEN
Moment: UI Athletics Communication
List: UI Athletics Communication
Item: UI Athletics Communication
Legend: UI Athletics Communication

WOMEN
Moment: NCAA
List: UI Athletics Communication
Item: UI Athletics Communication
Legend: UI Athletics Communication
Lore: UI Archives

1981–82
MEN
Moment: UI Athletics Communication
List: UI Athletics Communication
Item: UI Athletics Communication
Legend: UI Athletics Communication

WOMEN
Moment: Big Ten Conference
List: UI Athletics Communication
Item: UI Athletics Communication
Legend: UI Athletics Communication
Lore: UI Archives

1982–83
MEN
Moment: UI Athletics Communication
List: UI Athletics Communication
Item: UI Athletics Communication
Legend: UI Athletics Communication

WOMEN
Moment: UI Athletics Communication
List: UI Athletics Communication
Item: UI Athletics Communication
Legend: UI Athletics Communication
Lore: UI Archives

1983–84
MEN
Moment: UI Athletics Communication
List: UI Athletics Communication
Item: UI Athletics Communication
Legend: UI Athletics Communication

WOMEN
Moment: UI Athletics Communication
List: UI Athletics Communication
Item: UI Athletics Communication
Legend: UI Athletics Communication
Lore: UI Archives

1984–85
MEN
Moment: UI Athletics Communication
List: UI Athletics Communication
Item: UI Athletics Communication
Legend: UI Athletics Communication

WOMEN
Moment: UI Athletics Communication
List: UI Athletics Communication
Item: UI Athletics Communication
Legend: UI Athletics Communication
Lore: UI Archives

1985–86
MEN
Moment: UI Athletics Communication
List: UI Athletics Communication
Item: UI Athletics Communication
Legend: UI Athletics Communication

WOMEN
Moment: UI Athletics Communication
List: UI Athletics Communication
Item: UI Athletics Communication
Legend: UI Athletics Communication
Lore: UI Illio

1986–87
MEN
Moment: UI Athletics Communication
List: UI Athletics Communication
Item: UI Athletics Communication
Legend: UI Athletics Communication

WOMEN
Moment: UI Athletics Communication
List: UI Athletics Communication
Item: UI Athletics Communication
Legend: UI Athletics Communication
Lore: UI Archives

1987–88
MEN
Moment: UI Athletics Communication
List: UI Athletics Communication
Item: UI Athletics Communication
Legend: Athletic Journal

WOMEN
Moment: UI Athletics Communication
List: UI Athletics Communication
Item: UI Athletics Communication
Legend: UI Athletics Communication
Lore: UI Archives

1988–89
MEN
Moment: UI Athletics Communication
List: UI Athletics Communication
Item: UI Athletics Communication
Legend: UI Athletics Communication

WOMEN
Moment: UI Athletics Communication
List: UI Athletics Communication
Item: UI Athletics Communication
Legend: UI Athletics Communication
Lore: UI Archives

1989–90
MEN
Moment: Mark Jones
List: Mark Jones
Item: Mark Jones
Legend: Mark Jones

WOMEN
Moment: Mark Jones
List: Mark Jones
Item: Mark Jones
Legend: Mark Jones
Lore: Author's photo

1990–91
MEN
Moment: Mark Jones and UI
         Athletics Communication
List: Mark Jones
Item: Mark Jones
Legend: Mark Jones

WOMEN
Moment: Mark Jones
List: Mark Jones
Item: Mark Jones
Legend: Mark Jones
Lore: UI Athletics Communication

1991–92
MEN
Moment: Mark Jones
List: UI Athletics Communication
Item: Mark Jones
Legend: Mark Jones

WOMEN
Moment: Mark Jones
List: Mark Jones
Item: Mark Jones
Legend: Mark Jones
Lore: Mark Jones

1992–93
MEN
Moment: Mark Jones
List: Mark Jones
Item: Mark Jones
Legend: Mark Jones

WOMEN
Moment: Mark Jones
List: Mark Jones
Item: Mark Jones
Legend: Mark Jones
Lore: UI Archives

1993–94
MEN
Moment: Mark Jones
List: Mark Jones
Item: Mark Jones
Legend: Mark Jones

WOMEN
Moment: Mark Jones
List: Mark Jones
Item: Mark Jones
Legend: Mark Jones
Lore: Mark Jones

1994–95
MEN
Moment: Mark Jones
List: Mark Jones
Item: Mark Jones
Legend: Mark Jones

WOMEN
Moment: Mark Jones
List: Mark Jones
Item: Mark Jones
Legend: Mark Jones
Lore: UI Archives

1995–96
MEN
Moment: Orlando Downtown
         Athletic Club
List: Mark Jones
Item: Mark Jones
Legend: UI Athletics Communication

WOMEN
Moment: Mark Jones
List: Mark Jones
Item: Mark Jones
Legend: Mark Jones
Lore: UI Archives

1996–97
MEN
Moment: Mark Jones
List: Mark Jones
Item: Mark Jones
Legend: Mark Jones

WOMEN
Moment: Mark Jones
List: Mark Jones
Item: Mark Jones
Legend: Mark Jones
Lore: Author's photo

1997–98
MEN
Moment: Mark Jones
List: Mark Jones
Item: Mark Jones
Legend: Mark Jones

WOMEN
Moment: Mark Jones
List: Mark Jones
Item: Mark Jones
Legend: Mark Jones
Lore: Bill Wiegand, UI News Bureau

1998–99
MEN
Moment: Mark Jones
List: Mark Jones
Item: Mark Jones
Legend: Mark Jones

WOMEN
Moment: Mark Jones
List: Mark Jones
Item: Mark Jones
Legend: Mark Jones
Lore: Author's photo

1999–2000
MEN
Moment: Mark Jones
List: Mark Jones
Item: Mark Jones
Legend: Mark Jones

WOMEN
Moment: Mark Jones
List: Mark Jones
Item: Mark Jones
Legend: Mark Jones
Lore: UI Illio

2000–2001
MEN
Moment: Mark Jones
List: Mark Jones
Item: Mark Jones
Legend: Mark Jones

WOMEN
Moment: Drake University
List: Mark Jones
Item: Mark Jones
Legend: Mark Jones
Lore: Mark Jones

2001–02
MEN
Moment: Mark Jones
List: Mark Jones
Item: Mark Jones
Legend: Mark Jones

WOMEN
Moment: Mark Jones
List: Mark Jones
Item: Mark Jones
Legend: Mark Jones
Lore: Mark Jones

2002–03
MEN
Moment: University of Georgia
List: Mark Jones
Item: Mark Jones
Legend: Mark Jones

WOMEN
Moment: Mark Jones
List: Mark Jones
Item: Mark Jones
Legend: Mark Jones
Lore: Author's photo

2003–04
MEN
Moment: Mark Jones
List: Mark Jones
Item: Mark Jones
Legend: Mark Jones

WOMEN
Moment: Mark Jones
List: Mark Jones
Item: Mark Jones
Legend: Mark Jones
Lore: UI Illio

2004–05
MEN
Moment: Mark Jones
List: Mark Jones
Item: Mark Jones
Legend: Mark Jones

WOMEN
Moment: Mark Jones
List: Mark Jones
Item: Mark Jones
Legend: Mark Jones
Lore: University Archives

2005–06
MEN
Moment: Mark Jones
List: Mark Jones
Item: Mark Jones
Legend: Sports Illustrated

WOMEN
Moment: Mark Jones
List: Mark Jones
Item: Mark Jones
Legend: Mark Jones

2006–07
MEN
Moment: Mark Jones
List: Mark Jones
Item: Mark Jones
Legend: Mark Jones

WOMEN
Moment: Mark Jones
List: Mark Jones
Item: Mark Jones
Legend: Mark Jones
Lore: Author's photo

2007–08
MEN
Moment: Mark Jones
List: Mark Jones
Item: Mark Jones
Legend: Mark Jones

WOMEN
Moment: Mark Jones
List: Mark Jones
Item: Mark Jones
Legend: Mark Jones

2008–09
MEN
Moment: Mark Jones
List: Mark Jones
Item: UI Athletics Communication
Legend: Mark Jones

WOMEN
Moment: Mark Jones
List: Mark Jones
Item: Mark Jones
Legend: Mark Jones
Lore: Author's photo

2009–10
MEN
Moment: Mark Jones
List: Mark Jones
Item: Mark Jones
Legend: Mark Jones

WOMEN
Moment: Mark Jones
List: Mark Jones
Item: Mark Jones
Legend: Mark Jones
Lore: UI Archives

2010–11
MEN
Moment: Mark Jones
List: Mark Jones
Item: Mark Jones
Legend: Mark Jones

WOMEN
Moment: Mark Jones
List: Mark Jones
Item: Mark Jones
Legend: Mark Jones
Lore: UI DRES

2011–12
MEN
Moment: Mark Jones
List: Mark Jones
Item: Mark Jones
Legend: Mark Jones

WOMEN
Moment: Mark Jones
List: Mark Jones
Item: Mark Jones
Legend: Mark Jones
Lore: UI Archives

2012–13
MEN
Moment: Mark Jones
List: Mark Jones
Item: UI Athletics Communications
Legend: Mark Jones

WOMEN
Moment: Mark Jones
List: Mark Jones
Item: Mark Jones
Legend: Mark Jones
Lore: Author's photo

2013–14
MEN
Moment: NASA
List: Mark Jones
Item: Mark Jones
Legend: Mark Jones

WOMEN
Moment: Mark Jones
List: Mark Jones
Item: Mark Jones
Legend: Mark Jones
Lore: UI Archives

2014–15
MEN
Moment: Mark Jones
List: Mark Jones
Item: UI Athletics Communications
Legend: Mark Jones

WOMEN
Moment: Mark Jones
List: Mark Jones
Item: Mark Jones
Legend: Mark Jones

2015–16
MEN
Moment: Mark Jones
List: Mark Jones
Item: Mark Jones
Legend: Mark Jones

WOMEN
Moment: Mark Jones
List: Mark Jones
Item: Mark Jones
Legend: Mark Jones
Lore: Author's photo

Mike Pearson is a freelance writer and video producer. He was Sports Information Director at the University of Illinois from 1989 to 1996 and has written the "Illini Legends, Lists, & Lore" column for the *News Gazette* since 1996.

The University of Illinois Press
is a founding member of the
Association of American University Presses.

Text designed by Jim Proefrock and Dustin J. Hubbart
Composed in 10/12 Avenir Standard Book
with ITC Machine display
by Jim Proefrock
at the University of Illinois Press
Cover designed by Dustin J. Hubbart
Cover photos: Tatyana McFadden (Courtesy of
University of Illinois Disability Resources and
Educational Services); State Farm Center, Thomas
Pieters, Dick Butkus, Perdita Felicien, Dee Brown,
and Kevin Anderson (Courtesy of University of Illinois
Division of Intercollegiate Athletics)
Manufactured by Bang Printing

University of Illinois Press
1325 South Oak Street
Champaign, IL 61820-6903
www.press.uillinois.edu